D1368686

EVIDENCE AND THE ADVOCATE: A CONTEXTUAL APPROACH TO LEARNING EVIDENCE

EVIDENCE AND THE ADVOCATE: A CONTEXTUAL APPROACH TO LEARNING EVIDENCE

CHRISTOPHER W. BEHAN
Southern Illinois University School of Law

ISBN: 978-1-4224-8193-6

Library of Congress Cataloging-in-Publication Data

Behan, Christopher W.
   Evidence and the advocate : a contextual approach to learning evidence / Christopher W. Behan.
      p. cm.
   Includes index.
   ISBN 978-1-4224-8193-6
   1. Evidence (Law)--United States. I. Title.
      KF8935.B38 2012
      347.73'6--dc23

2012001090

NOTE TO USERS

To ensure that you are using the latest materials available in this area, please be sure to periodically check the LexisNexis Law School web site for downloadable updates and supplements at www.lexisnexis.com/lawschool.

Editorial Offices
121 Chanlon Rd., New Providence, NJ 07974 (908) 464-6800
201 Mission St., San Francisco, CA 94105-1831 (415) 908-3200
www.lexisnexis.com

MATTHEW◆BENDER

(2012–Pub.3314)

To my parents, R. Wayne and Sharla K. Behan. Thank you for always believing in me.

Acknowledgements

I would like to thank the following individuals and institutions: My research assistants, Steve Boling, Andrew Flynn, David Aubrey and Stephanie Black. My secretary, Carol Manis. My evidence students at the Southern Illinois University School of Law, who endured multiple drafts of this book as I was writing it. My good friends and evidence colleagues Peter Alexander, Hugh Selby, Charlie Rose and Bill Schroeder. Southern Illinois University School of Law, for providing the institutional support and encouragement to write this book. The United States Army Judge Advocate General's Legal Center and School — and in particular, the Criminal Law Department — where I got my start in evidence teaching and scholarship. I will always be a Criminal at heart. Professor Edward Kimball, my evidence professor at Brigham Young University's J. Reuben Clark Law School, who inspired me with a love for the law of evidence. The Honorable Patrick J. Robb, Missouri 5th Judicial Circuit Court, for teaching me the importance of combining practice and theory in the courtroom. And last but not least, for their patience and unwavering support, my wife Valery and our children: Cara, Jake, Joe, Megan, Bonnie, Sam and James.

Preface

Nowhere is the gulf between law school theory and practice wider than in the law of evidence. I have taught evidence and trial advocacy for several years, for a variety of audiences and in divers environments: law students at Southern Illinois University, newly licensed attorneys, supervisory attorneys and military judges at the United States Army Judge Advocate General's Legal Center and School, trial advocacy students at several law schools, experienced lawyers in advocacy training courses, and judges at the National Judicial College.

In all of those environments, I have been struck by the extent to which law students and new attorneys struggle to apply what they learned about evidence in the classroom to the much different environment of the courtroom. Judges and supervisory attorneys lament the extra time they must spend to walk new counsel through relatively simple evidentiary applications in the courtroom.

I wrote *Evidence and the Advocate* with a specific outcome in mind: a student who knows black-letter evidence law well enough to pass a bar exam, understands evidence theory sufficiently to make creative evidentiary arguments at trial and on appeal, and possesses a sound practical ability to apply the rules in the courtroom. The text also has the secondary goal of developing in students an appreciation for the rich tapestry of evidence law formed by the interweaving of social policy, scholarship and case law.

To accomplish these goals, *Evidence and the Advocate* teaches each rule of evidence using a three pronged approach: (1) a treatise-like explanation of the rule, its purposes, exceptions and foundations; (2) cases, discussion questions and hypothetical problems related to the rule; and (3) an application section in which the students must prepare a courtroom exercise putting the rule into action. This approach forms a teaching template for each rule of evidence.

Each application exercise stands alone and has been designed to illuminate the rule being taught. The application exercises range from simple form-of-question drills to full-fledged evidentiary hearings. Some require minimal preparation, and others require significant out-of-class research and preparation. In the exercises, students serve as attorneys, witnesses, judges, and, in the more involved exercises, as a court of appeals. The exercises build on each other. The initial exercises focus on fundamental advocacy skills such as conducting a direct examination or laying the foundation for an exhibit. Later exercises incorporate these foundational skills for more complicated tasks such as writing a motion, impeaching a witness, or conducting a *Daubert* hearing on the reliability of expert testimony.

The law of evidence is a rich, fascinating and rewarding field of study. But it is more than that: it represents centuries of experience in solving practical problems of proof. This book is designed to help students bring theory and practice together and prepare them for a lifetime of solving real problems of proof in the demanding environment of the courtroom.

— *Chris Behan*
Carbondale, Illinois

Using This Book

All incidents in *Evidence and the Advocate* take place in the State of Calamity. The State of Calamity has adopted the Federal Rules of Evidence in their entirety. Other than Supreme Court case law, there is no binding precedential case law in Calamity.

Each chapter contains the following basic elements:

1. A list of chapter objectives.

2. Background and explanatory material. This includes the rule itself, as well as a treatise-like explanation of the rule, its historical development, and how it is used and interpreted in the courtroom.

3. Cases pertaining to the rule.

4. Discussion questions.

5. Hypothetical problems.

6. A "Quick Hits" summary of the rule.

7. References to major treatises that discuss the rule.

8. The application exercise.

Each chapter contains two versions of the rule of evidence under discussion: the version in place until Dec. 1, 2011; and the re-styled version that will take effect on Dec. 1, 2011. I have included both versions because it will likely be some time before all the states that have adopted versions of the Federal Rules of Evidence switch to the re-styled rules.

Finally, the appendix contains the rules of evidence (both versions) in their entirety.

TABLE OF CONTENTS

TABLE OF CONTENTS

TABLE OF CONTENTS

TABLE OF CONTENTS

TABLE OF CONTENTS

TABLE OF CONTENTS

TABLE OF CONTENTS

TABLE OF CONTENTS

TABLE OF CONTENTS

TABLE OF CONTENTS

TABLE OF CONTENTS

TABLE OF CONTENTS

TABLE OF CONTENTS

TABLE OF CONTENTS

TABLE OF CONTENTS

TABLE OF CONTENTS

TABLE OF CONTENTS

PART ONE

INTRODUCTION TO THE ADVERSARIAL TRIAL AND THE PROCEDURAL RULES OF EVIDENCE

Chapter 1

INTRODUCTION

> **Chapter Objectives:**
>
> - Explain the purposes of evidence law at trial
> - Trace the development of evidentiary rules from the common law to modern evidence codes such as the Federal Rules of Evidence
> - Introduce the setting, players and basic rules of the modern adversarial trial

I. THE PURPOSES OF EVIDENCE LAW

Human beings are a contentious species, prone to committing crimes against each other or engaging in disputes over property rights, commercial transactions, family relations, broken promises, real or imagined injuries to person or reputation, and so on. Frequently, the parties to a dispute are unable even to agree with each other about the basic facts involved, such as whether or when an event occurred, what was promised, the existence or extent of harm or damage, who did what (and to whom), or why an event occurred.

Given the historical prevalence of crime, disagreements and conflicts, there has always been a need for someone other than the disputants to decide what happened, fix responsibility, and remedy the problem. The rule of law evolved over time to fulfill this need, and along with it, specialized tribunals with fact-finding, adjudicative and appellate responsibilities.

Fact-finding is one of the most important functions of a trial court. Once facts become fixed as part of a trial record, they can only be changed under extraordinary circumstances, such as the discovery of new evidence or the revelation that evidence at trial was improperly altered, suppressed or destroyed. Thus, the decisions that are made at the trial level by a fact-finder — whether judge or jury — are matters of considerable import. The type, quality and permissible uses of the evidence presented to the fact-finder play a powerful role in influencing these decisions.

The law of evidence regulates, restricts and assigns weight to the information that a decision-maker can consider when determining what happened and how to resolve it. To this end, evidentiary rules must balance a number of factors: relevance, fairness to the parties, the strengths and limitations of juries, efficiency,

3

external social policies, and even the preservation of historically anomalous doctrines that have always been part of the common-law adversary trial system.[1]

The over-arching goals of modern evidentiary law are succinctly summarized by Federal Rule of Evidence 102.

Through Dec. 1, 2011	After Dec. 1, 2011
Rule 102. Purpose and Construction	**Rule 102. Purpose**
These rules shall be construed to secure fairness in administration, elimination of unjustifiable expense and delay, and promotion of growth and development of the law of evidence to the end that the truth may be ascertained and proceedings justly determined.	These rules should be construed so as to administer every proceeding fairly, eliminate unjustifiable expense and delay, and promote the development of evidence law, to the end of ascertaining the truth and securing a just determination.

One of the purposes of this course is to help you critically analyze the rules of evidence and determine whether they meet the aspirations of Rule 102.

II. THE HISTORICAL DEVELOPMENT OF EVIDENCE LAW

Ancient Methods of Discerning Truth

Modern evidentiary doctrines are a long way removed, both in time and philosophy, from ancient methods of discerning truth such as trial by ordeal or battle. These ancient methods used survival as proof of whether an individual was innocent or guilty. Professor J. Alexander Tanford describes the trial by ordeal as follows:

> In an ordeal, a defendant's guilt was tested by his or her susceptibility to injury. A defendant was required to walk nine yards holding a pound of hot iron, retrieve a number of stones from a pot of boiling water, or walk barefoot across burning wood. If the defendant was burned and blistered from the ordeal, he or she was deemed guilty, because God would have intervened to protect the innocent from harm. A more lenient ordeal was the test of cold water, in which the defendant was bound and lowered into a pond that had been blessed with holy water. If the accused sank, the water had received the defendant with God's blessing (if they accidentally drowned, at least they went to heaven). However, if the accused floated, he

---

[1] Evidence scholars Christopher Mueller and Laird Kirkpatrick have identified five functions served by modern rules of evidence: (1) to protect the jury from receiving information it might improperly use at trial; (2) to promote substantive policies, such as the burden of persuasion and standard of proof, at trial; (3) to further extrinsic social policies that are considered to outweigh the importance of some types of relevant evidence at trial; (4) to ensure accurate fact-finding; (5) to control the scope and duration of trials. *See* CHRISTOPHER B. MUELLER & LAIRD C. KIRKPATRICK, EVIDENCE § 1.1, at 2–3 (4th ed. 2009).

or she was found guilty because pure water would not receive the body of an impure person.[2]

An older variation of the water ordeal (but with opposite presumptions pertaining to guilt and innocence) was employed in ancient Mesopotamia, where temple personnel administered the Divine River Ordeal, in which parties to a dispute were dropped into the river. An individual who sank was considered guilty, but one who floated was considered innocent.[3]

In time, trial by jury replaced the older and more violent forms of trial in England. Early jury trials differed considerably from modern trials in today's courtrooms. For example, jurors were drawn from the neighborhood in which the dispute arose and were expected either to already know the facts themselves or to inform themselves of the facts independently.[4] In essence, the earliest jurors served as witnesses, jurors, and, to an extent, even as judges; they could follow or ignore a judge's advice on the law at their whim. Attorneys and judges played a much smaller role than in modern trials. Since everyone involved in the trial knew what had happened, there was little need for rules of evidence or procedure.

Common Law Evidentiary Doctrines

As the concept of trial by jury continued to evolve, however, jurors gradually became increasingly removed from the facts and circumstances of the cases before them. Causes of actions and pleadings became more technical and complex. The common law developed a mistrust of lay jurors and their ability to understand or properly apply certain types of evidence, such as hearsay or character evidence. This mistrust, along with other factors such as the need to regulate the flow of information at trial, resulted in a complex set of evidentiary doctrines that required considerable expertise by lawyers and judges in the courtroom.

The British brought the common law trial system with them to the American colonies. The Constitution was written in light of the adversarial common law jury trial, with its rules of pleading, procedure and evidence. The Constitution guarantees trial by jury in three places. Article III, Section 2, Clause 3 states that "The Trial of Crimes, except in cases of Impeachment, shall be by Jury." The Sixth Amendment grants the accused "the right to a speedy and public trial, by an impartial jury of the State and district wherein the crime shall have been committed." The Seventh Amendment provides for trial by jury "in Suits at common law, where the value in controversy shall exceed twenty dollars."

The Constitution also contains three rules of evidence. Article II, Section 3, Clause 1 requires the testimony in a treason case of two witnesses or a confession by the accused in open court to the overt acts of levying war against the United States or "in adhering to their Enemies, giving them Aid and Comfort." The Fifth

---

[2] J. ALEXANDER TANFORD, THE TRIAL PROCESS: LAW, TACTICS, AND ETHICS 3 (4th ed. 2009). For a much more thorough discussion of the ordeal, see Trisha Olson, *Of Enchantment: The Passing of the Ordeals and the Rise of the Jury Trial*, 50 SYRACUSE L. REV. 109, 110–28 (2000).

[3] RUSS VERSTEEG, EARLY MESOPOTAMIAN LAW 60–61 (2000).

[4] TANFORD at 3–5.

Amendment guarantees that no one "shall be compelled in any criminal case to be a witness against himself." The Sixth Amendment guarantees the accused the right to be "confronted with the witnesses against him."

Since the Constitution's ratification in 1789, common law trials in the United States evolved on a different path than common law trials in Great Britain and the Commonwealth countries. Each state developed its own doctrines, as did federal courts. From an evidentiary standpoint, most common law evidence doctrines were fundamentally similar, but differed in application and interpretation from one jurisdiction to another.

Codification of the Federal Rules of Evidence

The disparity in evidentiary rules in different American jurisdictions led to calls for a standard code of evidence that would provide uniformity in application and ease of ascertaining the rules. This process began after the enactment of the Federal Rules of Civil Procedure in 1937. A variety of proposed codes were written over the years, some more influential than others, but the goal of codification remained unrealized until the Judicial Conference of the United States appointed a special committee to inquire into the feasibility and advisability of creating federal rules of evidence.[5] After the committee determined that the project was feasible and desirable, the Chief Justice appointed an Advisory Committee in 1965 to draft the Rules; this Committee consisted of practitioners, judges and law professors. Over a period of eight years, the Committee produced two drafts and a putative final version that the Supreme Court approved.

Under normal circumstances, the version approved by the Supreme Court would have become effective at the end of 90 days, absent Congressional action. The Rules were considered controversial, however, and Congress held extensive hearings and committee meetings on the form and substance of the Rules. Finally, after extensive revisions, Congress enacted the Rules in statutory form in 1975.

The Rules have had a tremendous impact since their inception. Not only are they used throughout the federal system, but more than 80% of the states have adopted evidentiary codes that closely track the Rules. The Rules are also influential in states that have not adopted them; practitioners and appellate courts cite them, they are used as the organizing principle for treatises,[6] and their underlying principles influence the development of evidentiary law in non-Rules jurisdictions.

Although the overall success and influence of the Rules is undeniable, students of evidence should recognize that the Rules are not perfect. Read the following excerpt from the Federal Rules of Evidence Manual to identify some of the problems and issues that remain with the Rules:

---

[5] STEPHEN A. SALTZBURG, MICHAEL M. MARTIN & DANIEL J. CAPRA, 1 FEDERAL RULES OF EVIDENCE MANUAL 1 (Matthew Bender 9th ed. 2006).

[6] *See, e.g.*, William A. Schroeder, West's Missouri Practice Series; and William A. Schroeder, West's Illinois Practice Series. In each of these practitioner treatises, Professor Schroeder organizes the evidentiary law of common law jurisdictions on the framework provided by the Federal Rules of Evidence.

After more than thirty years under the Rules, it is fair to state that the goals of codification — increased certainty as to what the rules are, predictability, efficiency, and uniformity of result — have been met in large part, but not completely. There is still some disuniformity and unpredictability. Part of the reason for disparate results is that several of the most important Rules (such as Rule 403 and the residual exception to the hearsay rule) call for an ad hoc judgment on the part of the Trial Judge that will necessarily vary from case to case. As to other Rules, the disuniformity is largely due to vague or misguided statutory language. . . .

Also, there is no question that some of the Rules are poorly drafted, and this has often led the Courts to reach results that they believe to be correct and just, even though such results are not mandated (and are even arguably prohibited) by the Rule. In a world of perfect codification, the rule itself would always lead to fair and just results. . . . Case law has often diverged from the text of the Federal Rules.[7]

Finally, some commentators have complained that under the Rules, Judges have lost the common-law power to promulgate new exclusionary rules of evidence, and that Judges are forced to admit evidence in certain circumstances even where they have legitimate doubts about its reliability or where exclusion would serve public policy. . . .

Still, on balance, the Federal Rules of Evidence have been a success. . . . Litigators and Judges undoubtedly have found it easier to master the Rules rather than a morass of common-law precedent; and many of the Rules have been uncontroversial and have led to uniform and just results in the Federal Courts.

One important question that has arisen is whether the codification of rules of evidence has totally supplanted the common law previously developed in the Federal Courts. The Supreme Court has visited this question on several occasions, and a unifying principle can be derived from these cases. In United States v. Abel, 469 U.S. 45 (1984), the Court quoted with approval the statement that as a matter of principle, "under the Federal Rules no common law of evidence remains." Yet the Court in Abel analyzed and applied the common-law rule permitting impeachment for bias, even though there is nothing specifically concerning impeachment for bias in the Federal Rules. Given the widespread use of impeachment for bias at the time the Federal Rules were being drafted and adopted, the Abel Court found it unlikely that the drafters "intended to scuttle entirely the evidentiary availability of cross-examination for bias."

This would suggest that widespread common-law practice would still be relevant in the absence of a Federal Rule on the point or put another way, that common-law concepts have been subsumed within the parameters of

---

[7] [n.1] Part Four of this Manual contains an article from one of the authors highlighting the case law that diverges from the Federal Rules. *See* Capra, *Case Law Divergence from the Federal Rules of Evidence* in Part Four, *infra.*

Rule 402 (providing that relevant evidence is admissible) and Rule 403 (giving the judge discretion to exclude relevant evidence under certain circumstances).

Any common-law rule will be supplanted, however, if there is an Evidence Rule that is in conflict with the common law. Thus, in Bourjaily v. United States, 483 U.S. 171 (1987), the Court rejected the applicability of a widespread practice under the common law, finding that it had been supplanted by an explicit Federal Rule. Under common law, the prosecution was required to establish independent evidence of conspiracy by a preponderance of the evidence before a coconspirator's hearsay statement could be admitted. The Bourjaily Court found no support for this practice in the language of the Federal Rules, and stated that under the explicit terms of Rule 104, the coconspirator's hearsay statement itself could be used by the Judge in determining whether a conspiracy existed.

More recently, in Daubert v. Merrell Dow Pharmaceuticals, 509 U.S. 579 (1993), the Court rejected the well-known common-law Frye test for assessing scientific expert testimony, and held that it was superseded by Federal Rule 702. The Daubert Court explained that common-law principles could serve as an "aid" to the application of the Federal Rules, but that they are superseded insofar as they are inconsistent with "a specific Rule that speaks to the contested issue."

As the authors of the Federal Rules of Evidence Manual point out, codification of the Federal Rules of Evidence was not a panacea that solved all evidentiary issues that existed under the common law. For example, the Rules do not contain a comprehensive scheme for privileges; for reasons that will be discussed more thoroughly later in this book, Congressional sponsors of the Rules deleted the privilege rules as a legislative compromise to ensure passage of the rest of the Rules, thereby leaving privilege rules to be defined either by federal common law in criminal cases or state law in civil cases under the *Erie* doctrine. Furthermore, the Rules inexplicably failed to include venerable common-law evidentiary doctrines such as impeachment for bias and impeachment by specific contradiction; doctrines that appellate courts have since declared are still binding and valid in federal courtrooms. Nevertheless, the codified Federal Rules of Evidence continue to exert tremendous practical and normative influence, even in jurisdictions that have not adopted them.

III. SETTING AND PLAYERS IN THE ADVERSARIAL SYSTEM

Trials in American courtrooms are based on the adversary system, also known as the adversarial system. In this system, partisan advocates present their cases to a neutral fact-finder, either a judge or a jury. The fact-finder, using only the information presented in the courtroom, must decide which party should prevail. The theory is that the truth will emerge from a vigorous contest between opposing viewpoints and theories. The goal of the adversarial system is a legally and factually sound verdict that is based on the truth.

In practice, this goal is not always achieved; the metaphysical search for truth often takes a back seat to the quest for victory. It is possible in an adversarial system to be right, tell the truth, and lose; and it is also possible to be wrong, say nothing, and win. Factors such as the skill or experience level of counsel, juror bias and judicial competence can affect a verdict.

This section introduces the setting and discusses the role of the players in the adversarial system.

Setting

Trials take place in the formal setting of a courtroom. Hearkening back to the original links between earthly and divine justice, the courtroom, like a place of worship, is set apart from the rest of society. Although open to the public, the courtroom is a place of ritual with its own unique rules and conventions. Even the physical design of the courtroom bespeaks its ritualistic purposes in the search for truth and justice. For example, the well of the courtroom, where disputes are decided, is generally separated from the audience gallery by a physical bar. The judge wears a black robe and sits elevated above the attorneys and the parties. The jury is physically separated from the well of the courtroom and often elevated above it, although not to the same extent as the judge. Courtroom personnel, like the lesser priests in ancient temples, attend to the auxiliary functions of the court, ensuring its smooth operation.

Federal Rules of Evidence 101 and 1101 speak to the setting in which the Rules operate.

Through Dec. 1, 2011	After Dec. 1, 2011
Rule 101. Scope These rules govern proceedings in the courts of the United States and before the United States bankruptcy judges and United States magistrate judges, to the extent and with the exceptions stated in rule 1101.	**Rule 101. Scope; Definitions** **(a) Scope**. These rules apply to proceedings in United States courts. The specific courts and proceedings to which the rules apply, along with exceptions, are set out in Rule 1101. **(b) Definitions**. In these rules: (1) "civil case" means a civil action or proceeding; (2) "criminal case" includes a criminal proceeding; (3) "public office" includes a public agency; (4) "record" includes a memorandum, report, or data compilation; (5) a "rule prescribed by the Supreme Court" means a rule adopted by the Supreme Court under statutory authority; and (6) a reference to any kind of written material or any other medium includes electronically stored information.

Through Dec. 1, 2011	After Dec. 1, 2011
Rule 1101. Applicability of Rules	**Rule 1101. Applicability of the Rules**
(a) Courts and judges. These rules apply to the United States district courts, the District Court of Guam, the District Court of the Virgin Islands, the District Court for the Northern Mariana Islands, the United States courts of appeals, the United States Claims Court, and to United States bankruptcy judges and United States magistrate judges, in the actions, cases, and proceedings and to the extent hereinafter set forth. The terms ''judge'' and ''court'' in these rules include United States bankruptcy judges and United States magistrate judges.	**(a) To Courts and Judges.** These rules apply to proceedings before: • United States district courts; • United States bankruptcy and magistrate judges; • United States courts of appeals; • the United States Court of Federal Claims; and • the district courts of Guam, the Virgin Islands, and the Northern Mariana Islands.
(b) Proceedings generally. These rules apply generally to civil actions and proceedings, including admiralty and maritime cases, to criminal cases and proceedings, to contempt proceedings except those in which the court may act summarily, and to proceedings and cases under title 11, United States Code.	**(b) To Cases and Proceedings.** These rules apply in: • civil cases and proceedings, including bankruptcy, admiralty, and maritime cases; • criminal cases and proceedings; and • contempt proceedings, except those in which the court may act summarily.
(c) Rule of privilege. The rule with respect to privileges applies at all stages of all actions, cases, and proceedings.	**(c) Rules on Privilege.** The rules on privilege apply to all stages of a case or proceeding.
(d) Rules inapplicable. The rules (other than with respect to privileges) do not apply in the following situations:	**(d) Exceptions.** These rules — except for those on privilege — do not apply to the following:
(1) Preliminary questions of fact. The determination of questions of fact preliminary to admissibility of evidence when the issue is to be determined by the court under rule 104.	(1) the court's determination, under Rule 104(a), on a preliminary question of fact governing admissibility;
(2) Grand jury. Proceedings before grand juries.	(2) grand-jury proceedings; and
(3) Miscellaneous proceedings. Proceedings for extradition or rendition; preliminary examinations in criminal cases; sentencing, or granting or revoking probation; issuance of warrants for arrest, criminal summonses, and search warrants; and proceedings with respect to release on bail or otherwise.	(3) miscellaneous proceedings such as: • extradition or rendition; • issuing an arrest warrant, criminal summons, or search warrant; • a preliminary examination in a criminal case; • sentencing;
(e) Rules applicable in part. In the following proceedings these rules apply to the extent that matters of evidence are not provided for in the statutes which govern procedure therein or in other rules prescribed by the Supreme Court pursuant to statutory	

The Federal Rules apply to most proceedings in federal courtrooms, with some exceptions. Rule 1101(d) provides exceptions for preliminary hearings under Rule 104, grand jury proceedings, and miscellaneous courtroom proceedings that do not involve the finality of a verdict. We will study hearings under Rule 104 in the next chapter. Rule 1101(e), omitted above, has provisions for the partial applicability of the Rules, depending on language found in other statutes that also have evidentiary provisions.

For the purposes of this class, you should always assume that proceedings are occurring in a courtroom governed by the Federal Rules of Evidence. Unless the situation involves a hearing under Rule 104, the Federal Rules of Evidence apply in full, as per Rules 101 and 1101.

The Judge

In the common-law adversarial trial, the judge presides over the trial but generally does not play an active role in questioning witnesses. This is in contrast to the inquisitorial system used in civil-law countries, in which judges play the central role at trial.

The judge in an adversarial trial performs the following basic functions: (1) presides over the trial, maintaining order and decorum, setting trial dates and trial times, calling the proceedings to order, and holding all other parties accountable for compliance; (2) rules on substantive, procedural and evidentiary matters; (3) determines the applicable law and, where applicable, instructs the jury thereon; (4) sentences defendants in criminal cases. To use a metaphor from the world of sports, the judge is more of a referee or umpire than a contestant.

Rule 611(a) discusses the judge's duty to control the presentation in the courtroom.

Through Dec. 1, 2011	After Dec. 1, 2011
Rule 611. Mode and Order of Interrogation and Presentation	**Rule 611. Mode and Order of Examining Witnesses and Presenting Evidence**
(a) Control by court. The court shall exercise reasonable control over the mode and order of interrogating witnesses and presenting evidence so as to (1) make the interrogation and presentation effective for the ascertainment of the truth, (2) avoid needless consumption of time, and (3) protect witnesses from harassment or undue embarrassment.	**(a) Control by the Court; Purposes.** The court should exercise reasonable control over the mode and order of examining witnesses and presenting evidence so as to: (1) make those procedures effective for determining the truth; (2) avoid wasting time; and (3) protect witnesses from harassment or undue embarrassment.

This rule permits the judge to interrupt the normal flow of trial to accommodate other concerns, such as the schedules of witnesses. For example, if a necessary defense witness would only be available in the middle of the plaintiff's case-in-chief, the judge could permit the defense to present one of its witnesses out-of-turn. The rule also provides authority for the judge to limit the time available for the presentation of witnesses and evidence. In appropriate cases, the rule also gives the judge authority to stop an examination whose purpose or effect is primarily the humiliation of a witness.

Although the trial judge's role is normally limited to supervising the proceedings, there are occasions when the judge may want to call witnesses of her own, or question witnesses the parties have called. Rule 614 recognizes that such functions are appropriate and within the inherent supervisory authority of the judge.

Through Dec. 1, 2011	After Dec. 1, 2011
Rule 614. Calling and Interrogation of Witnesses by Court	**Rule 614. Court's Calling or Examining a Witness**
(a) Calling by court. The court may, on its own motion or at the suggestion of a party, call witnesses, and all parties are entitled to cross-examine witnesses thus called.	**(a) Calling**. The court may call a witness on its own or at a party's request. Each party is entitled to cross-examine the witness.
(b) Interrogation by court. The court may interrogate witnesses, whether called by itself or by a party.	**(b) Examining**. The court may examine a witness regardless of who calls the witness.
(c) Objections. Objections to the calling of witnesses by the court or to interrogation by it may be made at the time or at the next available opportunity when the jury is not present.	**(c) Objections**. A party may object to the court's calling or examining a witness either at that time or at the next opportunity when the jury is not present.

Advocates

Advocates play the central role in an adversarial trial. Advocates are responsible to identify causes of action and defenses, brief the judge on applicable laws, object to inadmissible evidence, present the case to the jury, and make arguments. The adversarial trial system is only as good as the advocates who appear in court. All the rules of evidence apply to advocates, who are responsible to know them well enough to effectively and zealously represent their clients in court.

As you consider the role of advocates in the adversarial trial system, read the following excerpt from an American Bar Association report on professional responsibility written by Lon Fuller:[8]

> In a very real sense, it may be said that integrity of the adjudicative process itself depends upon the participation of the advocate. . . . The arguments

---

[8] Lon L. Fuller & John D. Randall, *Professional Responsibility: Report of the Joint Conference*, 44 A.B.A. J. 1159, 1160–61 (1958).

of counsel hold the case, as it were, in suspension between two opposing interpretations of it. While the proper classification of the case is thus kept unresolved, there is time to explore all its peculiarities and nuances.

These are the contributions made by partisan advocacy during the public hearing of the case. When we take into account the preparation that must precede the hearing, the essential quality of the advocate's contribution becomes even more apparent. . . . Each advocate comes to the hearing prepared to present his proofs and arguments, knowing at the same time that his arguments may fail to persuade and that his proofs may be rejected. It is part of his role to absorb these possible disappointments. The deciding tribunal, on the other hand, comes to the hearing uncommitted. It has not represented to the public that any fact can be proved, that any argument is sound, or that any particular way of stating a litigant's case is the most effective representation of its merits. . . .

The institution of advocacy is not a concession to the frailties of human nature, but an expression of human insight in the design of a social framework within which man's capacity for impartial judgment can attain its fullest realization.

When advocacy is thus viewed, it becomes clear by what principle limits must be set to partisanship. The advocate plays his role well when zeal for his client's cause promotes a wise and informed decision of the case. He plays his role badly, and trespasses against the obligations of professional responsibility, when his desire to win leads him to muddy the headwaters of decision, when, instead of lending a needed perspective to the controversy, he distorts and obfuscates its true nature.

As Fuller points out, advocates make or break the adversarial system. In the following excerpt, Professor Bruce Green goes a bit further than Fuller and suggests that the rules of evidence actually encourage deceit in an adversary trial system:[9]

In theory the law of evidence, like the adversary process in general, is intended to promote the discovery of the truth. In practice, however, the evidentiary rules sometimes foster either the misperception that lawyers and their witnesses are deceitful or the accurate perception of actual deceit on the part of lawyers and their witnesses, thereby undermining the search for truth at trial. The evidentiary rules promote the appearance of deceit by restricting the introduction of evidence that jurors expect to receive; they promote actual deceit by legitimizing prevailing methods of witness preparation that make testimony less truthful, rather than more truthful.

In the public's mind, the manner in which the truth is ascertained at trial is perhaps best symbolized by the oath that witnesses are required to take before testifying — in the most familiar formulation, an oath "to tell the

---

[9] Bruce A. Green, *"The Whole Truth?": How Rules of Evidence Make Lawyers Deceitful, in* SYMPOSIUM: DOES EVIDENCE LAW MATTER? THE CONNECTIONS BETWEEN EVIDENCE RULES, SOCIAL VALUES AND POLITICAL REALITIES, 25 LOY. L.A. L. REV. 699 (1992).

truth, the whole truth, and nothing but the truth." Although designed to send a message to the witnesses themselves, the oath also sends a message to jurors and to the public about the witnesses' undertaking at trial. It connotes that the witnesses are required to represent events accurately, not to dissemble, and to represent events completely, not to withhold. More broadly, the oath conveys that the trial is dedicated to eliciting accurate and complete accounts of all the events that bear on the parties' contentions.

The popular conception, that the truth is ascertained at trial, is reinforced and refined by other aspects of adversary proceedings which — like the requirement of the oath — are encapsulated in the evidentiary rules. For example, witnesses on direct examination provide their accounts in response to the nonleading questions of the lawyers who call them to the stand. This mode of presentation gives the impression that the witnesses are answering spontaneously, drawing on their own recollection, and speaking in their own words, so that it is fair for jurors to evaluate the truthfulness of the testimony in light of their own experience in assessing the credibility of those with whom they deal on a day-to-day basis. Similarly, cross-examination underscores the traditional notion that the truth will make itself known through the clash of adversaries. The lawyers, each dedicated single-mindedly to his or her client's cause, skillfully challenge the opposing witnesses in an effort to reveal lies, misstatements and omissions.

When viewing the conduct of lawyers in the context of the expectations reinforced in the course of a trial, jurors are sometimes led to conclude that trial lawyers are being deceitful when in fact the lawyers are simply abiding by the rules of evidence. [Green uses an example in which the hearsay rules might prevent the jury from hearing why a police officer acted in a certain way during an investigation.] . . .

Lawyers also engage in conduct that is in fact deceitful, albeit entirely lawful. Unbeknownst to the jury, and contrary to the jury's expectations, in many cases lawyers carefully craft and rehearse the testimony of witnesses before calling them to the stand. Professor Applegate's recent analysis of the professional literature on how to prepare witnesses for trial reviews the various ways in which lawyers shape both the content and style of witnesses' testimony. For example, by apprising their witnesses of the law relevant to the case and of the statements made by others, as well as by asking questions in a suggestive manner, lawyers cause witnesses to recall things differently from how they originally perceived them; by rehearsing their witnesses' testimony, lawyers make witnesses inordinately certain of the quality of their recollections; by molding the personality of their witnesses, lawyers make them more believable than they would ordinarily appear.

Witnesses

With limited exceptions, nothing is brought to the fact-finder's attention without the testimony of a witness. The law of witnesses and their role at trial will be discussed more thoroughly later in this course.

For now, however, you should be aware that the law of evidence limits the manner in which a witness may participate in telling her story at trial. No witness is allowed simply to walk into a courtroom and deliver a narrative about what happened. Instead, witness testimony is carefully channeled through rules that control both the form of testimony and its substance.

The party who calls a witness conducts a direct examination of the witness. The purpose of the direct examination is to elicit information required to support of the party's claim or defense. Questions on direct examination are generally limited in form to non-leading questions. A non-leading question is an open question that does not suggest its own answer. Examples include the following:

"What is your name?"

"Where do you live?"

"On the 15th of July, did you witness an automobile accident?"

"What did you see?"

The opposing party conducts a cross-examination of the witness. A purpose of cross-examination is to discredit or call into question the witness's testimony on direct examination. The use of leading questions — closed questions that suggest their own answers — is permitted and encouraged on cross-examination. Examples include the following:

"Your name is Bob Smith, isn't it?"

"Isn't it true that you live in Carterville, Illinois?"

"You witnessed an automobile accident in July, didn't you?"

"You saw the red car hit the blue car?"

Rule 611 establishes the form for questions on direct and cross examination.

Through Dec. 1, 2011	After Dec. 1, 2011
Rule 611. Mode and Order of Interrogation and Presentation	**Rule 611. Mode and Order of Examining Witnesses and Presenting Evidence**
(b) Scope of cross-examination. Cross-examination should be limited to the subject matter of the direct examination and matters affecting the credibility of the witness. The court may, in the exercise of discretion, permit inquiry into additional matters as if on direct examination.	**(b) Scope of Cross-Examination**. Cross-examination should not go beyond the subject matter of the direct examination and matters affecting the witness's credibility. The court may allow inquiry into additional matters as if on direct examination.
(c) Leading questions. Leading questions should not be used on the direct examination of a witness except as may be necessary to develop the witness' testimony. Ordinarily leading questions should be permitted on cross-examination. When a party calls a hostile witness, an adverse party, or a witness identified with an adverse party, interrogation may be by leading questions.	**(c) Leading Questions**. Leading questions should not be used on direct examination except as necessary to develop the witness's testimony. Ordinarily, the court should allow leading questions: (1) on cross-examination; and (2) when a party calls a hostile witness, an adverse party, or a witness identified with an adverse party.

The Jury

A jury consisting of lay citizens is one of the unique features of the Anglo-American trial. The collective wisdom and judgment of ordinary people is used to resolve thorny factual issues and to decide complex legal problems. The jury's factual findings are binding at trial and on appeal. In criminal cases, the jury has the extraordinary and unreviewable power to acquit — even in the face of overwhelming evidence of guilt and contrary to the legal instructions given to them by the judge — for any reason or no reason at all; this power is referred to as jury nullification.

The jury is simultaneously the great strength and weakness of the adversarial trial system. From an evidentiary standpoint, the jury is a source of tension. On one hand, the virtues of the jury are enshrined in the Constitution, and the jury is generally recognized as one of the great bulwarks of freedom in the Western world. On the other hand, many of the rules of evidence are predicated on mistrust of the juror's ability to understand or properly apply certain types of information. This tension is a constant presence in evidentiary law, and we will frequently discuss throughout the course.

Introduction to Evidence: Quick Hits

- In the adversarial trial system, the rules of evidence strike a balance between fairness and efficiency, with an overall goal of assisting the jury to determine the truth in a just manner.

  - The advocates offer an object to evidence and bear the primary responsibility to prove their cases in a persuasive manner.

  - The judge presides over the trial, rules on matters of law, and instructs the jury on substantive and evidentiary law issues.

  - The jury applies the facts to the law in determining a verdict.

- The rules of evidence control the manner and substance of evidence that can be presented to the jury.

- The Federal Rules of Evidence are used in most Federal courts and have exerted enormous influence on the development of evidentiary law in state jurisdictions.

Chapter References

CHRISTOPHER B. MUELLER & LAIRD C. KIRKPATRICK, EVIDENCE §§ 1.1, 1.2, 6.54–6.57, 6.70, 10.2–10.5 (4th ed. 2009).

GLEN WEISSENBERGER & JAMES J. DUANE, FEDERAL RULES OF EVIDENCE: RULES, LEGISLATIVE HISTORY, COMMENTARY AND AUTHORITY §§ 101–02, 611, 614, 1101 (6th ed. 2009).

JACK B. WEINSTEIN & MARGARET A. BERGER, WEINSTEIN'S FEDERAL EVIDENCE §§ 101–02, 611, 614, 1101 (Joseph M. McLaughlin ed., Matthew Bender 2d ed. 1997).

KENNETH S. BROUN, MCCORMICK ON EVIDENCE §§ 5–6, 8, 21, 52, 56, 212–243.1 (6th ed. 2006).

STEVEN J. GOODE & OLIN GUY WELLBORN III, COURTROOM HANDBOOK ON FEDERAL EVIDENCE Ch. 5 (West 2010).

IV. DISCUSSION QUESTIONS AND APPLICATION EXERCISES

DISCUSSION QUESTIONS

Consider the following questions in preparation for your classroom discussion.

1. Is the adversarial system the best mechanism for the discovery of the truth? Why or why not?

2. What other mechanisms or forums can you think of for discovering the truth and resolving disputes?

3. Do codified rules reduce the importance of the judge at trial? Why or why not?

4. In the interests of uniformity and predictability, should the rules reduce the independence and discretion of the judge even more than they already do? Why or why not? Should they increase the independence and discretion of the judge?

5. Compare Fuller's article on the salutary aspects of the adversarial system with Green's article on the deceptions created by the rules of evidence in this system. Who is right? Is there a way to reconcile the viewpoints of Green and Fuller?

6. Do the technical requirements related to the mode and format of witness testimony advance or degrade the search for truth at trial? Why or why not?

Application Exercises

There are two application exercises for this chapter. Bring hard copies of each of these exercises to the first class.

1. Rule of Evidence Drafting Exercise

Imagine that you have been tasked with creating a completely new evidentiary code for an adversarial court system. But there are a few constraints with which you must comply. First, your entire code can consist of only one rule, which can be no longer than a paragraph in length. Second, your rule must satisfy the aspirational language of FRE 102 and the purposes and values of the adversarial trial system. Third, your rule must be easy to understand and apply. Fourth, your rule cannot discriminate against one side or another. Draft a rule complying with these four requirements and bring a hard copy of it to the first session of class.

2. Form of Question Exercise

Pick a story about yourself that you are comfortable telling to others, on one of the following topics: (1) a time when you were famous; (2) your decision to attend this law school; (3) a challenge you have overcome in your life. The story should take no longer than 3-5 minutes to tell, but it should be complete.

Write a direct examination, using single-fact, non-leading questions, that tells your story. Use a question-and-answer format, as follows:

Q: *Let's talk about a time when you were famous.*

A: *Okay.*

Q: *How old were you?*

A: *Fifteen.*

Q: *Where were you living at the time?*

A: *Brandon, South Dakota.*

Write the same story a second time, this time using single-fact, leading questions.

Q.   *Let's talk about a time when you were famous.*

A: *Okay.*

Q: *You were fifteen years old, weren't you?*

A: *Yes.*

Q: *And you lived in Brandon, South Dakota?*

A: *Yes.*

Q: *Brandon is a small town, isn't it?*

A: *Yes.*

Chapter 2

PROCEDURAL BASICS: OBJECTIONS & RULINGS, ERROR & APPEAL AND THE RULE OF COMPLETENESS

> **Chapter Objectives:**
>
> - Introduce and explain the following concepts: (1) evidentiary error; (2) the basic procedural tools used at trial to identify, correct, and preserve evidentiary errors for appeal; (3) appellate standards for reviewing evidentiary error; and (4) the rule of completeness
> - Analyze and discuss evidentiary errors and the rule of completeness
> - Apply the concepts from this chapter in courtroom application exercises.

I. BACKGROUND AND EXPLANATORY MATERIAL

Evidentiary Error and the Role of Counsel

Evidentiary rules and doctrines exist to ensure legally and factually sound verdicts based on admissible evidence. Litigants do not, however, have an absolute right to a trial in which all the evidence fully complies with the rules. Instead, the procedural rules of evidence place most of the responsibility for evidentiary compliance on the advocates. Subject to very narrow exceptions, if an advocate believes her opponent's evidence violates the rules, she must object, or the issue is forfeited on appeal. Furthermore, the objection must be timely and specific; if the objection comes too late or is vague, the issue is forfeited on appeal. If an advocate believes a judge has improperly excluded her evidence from trial, she must make an offer of proof (essentially, putting on the record what evidence she would have offered absent the judge's ruling) to preserve the issue for appeal.

In most instances, the judge has no *sua sponte* (on his or her own motion or initiative) duty to correct evidentiary errors at trial; instead, the judge rules on the evidentiary objections and motions made by the advocates. The judge must also properly instruct the jury about the permissible uses of evidence at trial. Rather than combing the record in search of evidentiary errors made by the parties during the trial, appellate courts focus on motions, objections, offers of proof and judicial rulings, examining the record to determine whether evidentiary issues were properly raised at trial and preserved for appeal. Only under the most limited circumstances will an appellate court give relief for evidentiary errors in the absence of an objection by the aggrieved party.

There are sound reasons for placing the burden of evidentiary compliance on the parties. First, it is consistent with the philosophical basis of the adversarial trial, which puts the advocates at center stage in the search for truth. Second, it reinforces the importance of the trial itself. Parties cannot "sandbag" at trial, hoping to leave the record littered with unaddressed errors they can later exploit on appeal. Parties have a powerful incentive to get the trial right the first time. Third, it gives deference to the tactical choices made by parties at trial. In reality, nearly every trial features the admission of evidence that technically violates the governing rules of evidence for the jurisdiction, but whose introduction actually helps both parties by moving the case along. Finally, the policy gives considerable deference to the trial judge, who is in the best position to observe the demeanor of witnesses, the actions of counsel, and the impact of the evidence on the jury.

Evaluating Error on Appeal

Even if a party has properly objected to an evidentiary error and preserved the issue for appeal on the record, there is no guarantee of appellate relief. There are three primary appellate doctrines that apply in evaluating evidentiary errors.

The first doctrine is the abuse of discretion standard of review.[1] Under this standard of review, an appellate court might disagree with the decision a trial judge made, but will not grant relief unless the judge's decision was "based on a clearly erroneous finding of fact or an erroneous conclusion of law or manifest[ed] a clear error in judgment."[2] This deferential standard of review makes it extremely difficult for a party to obtain relief on appeal for evidentiary errors that occurred at trial and emphasizes the importance of the trial itself in resolving evidentiary issues.

The second doctrine is the harmless error rule, under which appellate courts grant relief only for evidentiary errors that affect the substantial rights of the parties. The harmless error doctrine requires the appellate court to examine errors in light of the record as a whole. This policy helps ensure the finality of verdicts and recognizes that some items of evidence are more important than others at trial.

The third doctrine is the plain error rule, which provides a narrow window for relief where the parties have failed to bring an evidentiary error to the attention of the trial court. The error must, of course, affect a substantial right of a party. In addition, the error has to be clearly obvious from the record, and one that would

---

[1] The Supreme Court has recognized the abuse of discretion standard of review as the appropriate standard for evaluating the evidentiary rulings of federal district court judges. *See* Old Chief v. United States, 519 U.S. 172, 174 n.1 (1997) ("The standard of review applicable to the evidentiary rulings of the district court is abuse of discretion.").

[2] 1-103 Weinstein's Federal Evidence § 103.40 (quoting United States v. Jenkins, 313 F.3d 549, 559 (10th Cir. 2002)).

affect the fairness, integrity or public reputation of judicial proceedings if left uncorrected. As one might imagine from its stringent requirements, obtaining relief under the plain error doctrine is a rare event.

Basics of Evidentiary Procedure

The previous subsection has discussed several aspects of evidentiary procedure and introduced new terms and concepts. This section introduces Rules 103 and 105, the basic rules for evidentiary procedure; further defines and explains the terms used in those rules; and outlines the basic mechanisms of evidentiary procedure.

The text of Rules 103 and 105 follow:

Through Dec. 1, 2011	After Dec. 1, 2011
Rule 103. Rulings on Evidence	**Rule 103. Rulings on Evidence**
(a) Effect of erroneous ruling. Error may not be predicated upon a ruling which admits or excludes evidence unless a substantial right of the party is affected, and	**(a) Preserving a Claim of Error**. A party may claim error in a ruling to admit or exclude evidence only if the error affects a substantial right of the party and:
(1) Objection. In case the ruling is one admitting evidence, a timely objection or motion to strike appears of record, stating the specific ground of objection, if the specific ground was not apparent from the context; or	(1) if the ruling admits evidence, a party, on the record:

(A) timely objects or moves to strike; and
(B) states the specific ground, unless it was apparent from the context; or |
(2) Offer of proof. In case the ruling is one excluding evidence, the substance of the evidence was made known to the court by offer or was apparent from the context within which questions were asked.	(2) if the ruling excludes evidence, a party informs the court of its substance by an offer of proof, unless the substance was apparent from the context.
Once the court makes a definitive ruling on the record admitting or excluding evidence, either at or before trial, a party need not renew an objection or offer of proof to preserve a claim of error for appeal.	**(b) Not Needing to Renew an Objection or Offer of Proof**. Once the court rules definitively on the record — either before or at trial — a party need not renew an objection or offer of proof to preserve a claim of error for appeal.
(b) Record of offer and ruling. The court may add any other or further statement which shows the character of the evidence, the form in which it was offered, the objection made, and the ruling thereon. It may direct the making of an offer in question and answer form.	**(c) Court's Statement About the Ruling; Directing an Offer of Proof**. The court may make any statement about the character or form of the evidence, the objection made, and the ruling. The court may direct that an offer of proof be made in question-and-answer form.
(c) Hearing of jury. In jury cases, proceedings shall be conducted, to the extent practicable, so as to prevent inadmissible evidence from being suggested to the jury by any means, such as making statements or offers of proof or asking questions in the hearing of the jury.	**(d) Preventing the Jury from Hearing Inadmissible Evidence**. To the extent practicable, the court must conduct a jury trial so that inadmissible evidence is not suggested to the jury by any means.
(d) Plain error. Nothing in this rule precludes taking notice of plain errors affecting substantial rights although they were not brought to the attention of the court.	**(e) Taking Notice of Plain Error**. A court may take notice of a plain error affecting a substantial right, even if the claim of error was not properly preserved.

Through Dec. 1, 2011	After Dec. 1, 2011
Rule 105. Limited Admissibility	**Rule 105. Limiting Evidence That Is Not Admissible Against Other Parties or for Other Purposes**
When evidence which is admissible as to one party or for one purpose but not admissible as to another party or for another purpose is admitted, the court, upon request, shall restrict the evidence to its proper scope and instruct the jury accordingly.	If the court admits evidence that is admissible against a party or for a purpose — but not against another party or for another purpose — the court, on timely request, must restrict the evidence to its proper scope and instruct the jury accordingly.a substantial right, even if the claim of error was not properly preserved.

The following terms and concepts are critical to understanding evidentiary procedure and Rules 103 and 105.

Objection. An objection occurs when an advocate makes known to the court her opposition to the introduction of an opponent's evidence. An objection should be timely, precise, and specific. The objection should occur as soon as a question is asked, but before the witness answers. For example, if a question calls for hearsay, the opposing counsel should stand up and say, "Objection. Hearsay." Vague or overbroad objections, such as "irrelevant, incompetent and immaterial," generally do not preserve issues for appeal.

Motion to Strike. When objectionable material has already been introduced to the jury, an attorney may object and ask the judge to strike from the record the objectionable material. Motions to strike are appropriate where the objectionable nature of a witness's response is not readily apparent from the question, as in the following example.

Q: What color was the van that hit your car?

A: My wife told me the van was green.

           Opposing Counsel: Objection, your honor, and move to strike the witness's response. This is hearsay.

In this example, the witness's response includes information that might be precluded under the hearsay rule. It would have been impossible for opposing counsel to have objected prior to the answer, because the question did not call for hearsay. The only remedy is an after-the-fact objection, coupled with a motion to strike the testimony from the record. A motion to strike is almost always accompanied by an instruction from the judge to the jury admonishing them to disregard the objectionable evidence.

Response. Following an objection at trial, the opposing party generally gets the opportunity to briefly respond. The response should be directed to the judge, not opposing counsel, and should be concise, precise and specific. For example, a typical response to a hearsay objection might be, "Your honor, this is not hearsay. It is not being offered for the truth of the matter asserted."

Offer of Proof. When an advocate's evidence is excluded, an offer of proof makes a record of the substance of the excluded evidence. This is done for two purposes: (1) to persuade the trial court to reconsider its ruling; and (2) to preserve the issue for appeal. An offer of proof can be as simple as a statement to the judge regarding the substance of the excluded testimony, or as elaborate as a hearing outside the presence of the jury with the witness present. We will revisit the offer of proof in the application exercises for this chapter.

Motion in limine. "In limine" means "at the outset." A motion in limine is a pretrial motion to admit or exclude evidence. Advocates file these motions to shape the evidentiary landscape of the upcoming trial and assist them in planning their case presentations. If necessary, a hearing under Rule 104 may be held to develop evidence for the motion in limine.

Ruling. The judge's decision, usually phrased in answer to objections as "sustained" or "overruled." For more complicated issues, such as those raised in motions in limine, the ruling should contain sufficient facts and information for the appellate court to understand the factual context of the ruling and the judge's legal analysis of the issue.

Definitive Ruling. Parties have the duty to object to and identify evidentiary errors whenever they are made at trial. However, if a judge has definitively ruled on an evidentiary issue, the losing party is not required to renew its objection if the evidence is later introduced. Suppose, for example, that the plaintiff wants to introduce at trial an incriminating out-of-court statement the defendant made to a friend. The defendant raises the issue in a pretrial motion in limine, seeking to preclude the evidence at trial. If the judge gives a definitive ruling admitting the evidence, the defendant does not have to object again at trial to preserve the issue on appeal. If, however, the judge defers ruling on the issue, and the defendant fails to object to its introduction during the trial, the issue will be waived on appeal.

Stipulation. An agreement between the parties that evidence or testimony is admissible. A stipulation avoids the necessity of complying with evidentiary rules and can be a window through which otherwise inadmissible evidence enters the courtroom.

Limiting Instruction. Pursuant to Rule 105, a judge should give an evidentiary instruction to the jury when evidence is admitted for a permissible purpose but not for an impermissible purpose. One of the peculiarities of evidence law is that a fact in evidence can be absolutely inadmissible for if used for one purpose, but present no obstacles to admission if used for another purpose. For instance, in a civil tort case, a statement about the subsequent repair of a hazard could be properly used by the jury to show ownership or control of the property by the defendant, but could not be used to prove that the defendant was responsible for the plaintiff's injury. The judge would have to give a limiting instruction to ensure that the jury considered the evidence for its proper purpose.

The Rule of Completeness

In the adversarial system, the advocates determine the substance and timing of the evidence presented at trial. As we have seen in this chapter, it is also up to the advocate to decide whether and when to object to the other party's evidence. In addition, the opponent is permitted to test the other party's witnesses in the crucible of cross-examination. The party with the burden of proof presents its case first, followed by the other party. The procedures for introducing evidence at trial are well-established and orderly: direct examination (with possible objections by any opponent); cross-examination (with possible objections by the direct examiner); and, perhaps, re-direct or re-cross examination.

One of the values of the adversarial trial system, as represented by the requirement to make specific and timely objections, is that the judge should have the opportunity to correct errors during the trial itself in order to provide certainty and finality to the proceedings. The rule of completeness allows a party to prevent an opponent from unfairly presenting portions of writing or recordings out of context. The rule provides for the substantially contemporaneous admission of the rest of the writing or recording, or any other writings or recordings that should in fairness be considered as well. The rule of completeness is codified in Rule 106:

Through Dec. 1, 2011	After Dec. 1, 2011
Rule 106. Remainder of or Related Writings or Recorded Statements	**Rule 106. Remainder of or Related Writings or Recorded Statements**
When a writing or recorded statement or part thereof is introduced by a party, an adverse party may require the introduction at that time of any other part or any other writing or recorded statement which ought in fairness to be considered contemporaneously with it.	If a party introduces all or part of a writing or recorded statement, an adverse party may require the introduction, at that time, of any other part — or any other writing or recorded statement — that in fairness ought to be considered at the same time.

According to the Advisory Committee, the rule of completeness is "based on two considerations. The first is the misleading impression created by taking matters out of context. The second is the inadequacy of repair work when delayed to a point later in the trial."[3] Thus, consistent with the adversarial trial system's general philosophy of correcting evidentiary error at the earliest opportunity, this rule gives the judge discretion to require a party to halt its chosen case presentation so that the remainder of a document or recording — or other related documents or recordings — can be entered into evidence at substantially the same time. On its face, the rule applies only to writings or recorded statements, but there is case law authority that a judge can use Rule 611 to require the introduction of oral statements under Rule 106 if fairness requires it.[4]

---

[3]   FED. R. EVID. 106, advisory committee notes.

[4]   *See* GLEN WEISSENBERGER AND JAMES J. DUANE, FEDERAL RULES OF EVIDENCE: RULES, LEGISLATIVE HISTORY, COMMENTARY AND AUTHORITY § 106.1, notes 10–11 and accompanying text (6th ed. 2009).

Rule 106 does not operate automatically to admit the remainder of a document or recording. In most cases, cross-examination and the party's own presentation of evidence on its case in chief is sufficient to protect the party's interests. But in the relatively rare case that the normal procedures and protections of the adversarial system are not enough to ensure fairness, Rule 106 gives the trial judge a mechanism to make sure the jury is not misled.

II. CASES, QUESTIONS AND PROBLEMS

REAGAN v. BROCK
United States Court of Appeals, First Circuit

628 F.2d 721 (1st Cir. 1980) Plaintiff brought an action in the United States District Court for the District of Massachusetts alleging that defendant's restaurant negligently and in breach of the warranty of merchantability served her unfit food and thereby caused her to become seriously ill. At the close of the evidence, the court directed a verdict for defendant on the negligence court. The jury found that defendant did not breach any warranty by serving plaintiff contaminated food. Plaintiff attempts here to revive her claim by arguing that the district court committed several erroneous evidentiary rulings. We affirm.

We begin with what we perceive to be plaintiff's most substantial argument. At one point, the defendant was testifying about how she came to know of plaintiff's illness, and the following ensued under questioning from her counsel:

[Preliminary questions established that the defendant received a telephone call from someone named Allen.]

Q: *And what did he say to you with reference to this incident?*

A: *He said that Deborah had eaten there the other night and she had gotten ill and he thought it was from the food.*

Q: *And what did you say?*

A: *I asked what she had eaten and where she was.*

Q: *And did you find out where she was?*

A: *Yes, she was in the Pittsfield Hospital and I*

Q: *What did you do?*

A: *I got the name of the doctor and I called him and spoke to him.*

Q: *What was the result of your conversation?*

A: *Well, he said that from the tests they had done that there was no reason to believe that her problem had anything to do with the food.*

(Plaintiff's counsel): I object and move that be stricken.

THE COURT: I will let it stand. Could have been objected to before the question was answered.

(Plaintiff's counsel): Note my exception."

Plaintiff now argues that the district court erred in ruling that her counsel should have objected to the question rather than to the answer because the question does not strictly call for a hearsay response. Although we agree with plaintiff that the question is susceptible of an interpretation that does not call for an inadmissible answer, we do not think that the court committed reversible error.

If defendant's lawyer had asked her, "What did the doctor say to you?", the question would clearly have called for a hearsay response and plaintiff would have waived any objection to the answer if her counsel had not objected to the question. "(C)ounsel is not allowed to gamble upon the possibility of a favorable answer, but must object to the admission of evidence as soon as the ground becomes apparent. Usually this will be as soon as the question is asked, assuming that the question shows that it calls for inadmissible evidence." McCormick, Evidence s 52 at 115 (1954). The question we must address here is whether the court clearly erred in finding that the question in controversy called for an inadmissible answer. We hold that it did not.

(1) Reviewing the cold transcript of the hearing, one must admit that the question in controversy is ambiguous: "What was the result of the conversation?" Nonetheless, our ability to comprehend how this question was understood in the courtroom is vastly inferior to the district judge's. He hears the question with counsel's inflection, perceives the length and character of the pause between question and answer, and rules on the party's objection within the context of prior questioning and strategies. A district court's ruling on whether an ambiguous question calls for an inadmissible answer should not be reversed as clear error when its ruling has a reasonable basis.

(2) Here, the transcript demonstrates that the witness had been offering hearsay testimony just before the question in controversy was asked. Plaintiff objected to none of the previous questions or answers and the court could have well thought that plaintiff withheld objection because the testimony given was favorable to her claim. The inquiry about the result of the conversation between defendant and plaintiff's doctor seems more likely to have called for a hearsay response since the defendant's immediately prior testimony had been hearsay. Moreover, the court had seen plaintiff remain silent during the admission of favorable hearsay and could have perceived him as gambling that the hearsay responses would continue to be favorable. Thus, the context within which the question was asked gives substance to the court's determination that the question called for a hearsay response. Plaintiff offered no reason to the court for her failure to object to the question and thereby failed to develop any basis in the record for negating our perception that the court's ruling was properly based on the context in which the question was asked. Cf. Fed.R.Evid. 103(a) (specific objections must be made to rulings on evidence so court may correct errors). The ruling was not clearly erroneous.

Affirmed.

UNITED STATES v. GOMEZ-NORENA
United States Court of Appeals, Ninth Circuit
908 F.2d 497 (9th Cir. 1990)

[Using drug courier profiles, U.S. government agents became suspicious that the defendant was a drug courier. The defendant was traveling from Colombia to Australia with a single bag, had paid for his ticket with cash, was aimlessly wandering the terminal in the Los Angeles airport while waiting his connecting flight, and was traveling internationally for the first time. Agents put his bag through and X-ray machine and discovered a double compartment. Upon opening the compartment, they discovered 2kg of cocaine.]

A jury convicted Gomez for possessing cocaine with intent to distribute, in violation of 21 U.S.C. § 841(a)(1). Gomez argues on appeal that the district court improperly admitted testimony regarding the drug courier profile. . . .

II

Gomez first challenges the admissibility of Inspector Espinoza's testimony concerning his statements to the other Customs inspectors that Gomez fit the drug courier profile. Because the objections raised at trial are relevant to our standard of review, we reproduce the testimony in full:

Prosecutor: What did you tell Inspector Zito or Inspector Little or any of the others about-

Defense: Objection. Calling for hearsay.

Prosecutor: Your Honor.

The Court: Ladies and gentlemen. I permit this, which the law says I can, but only on the question of what was in the inspector's-those ones he told whatever he told to-mind at the time they carried on their activities. Now it is hearsay, the defendant wasn't there, but we do permit hearsay to be passed from one law enforcement officer to another, and this is appropriate, so the objection is overruled. With that instruction that you can consider only as to what the inspectors had in their mind when, and if, anything further happened in the presence of the defendant. With that instruction, objection overruled.

Prosecutor: Inspect[or] Espinoza, what did you say to the other inspectors about the defendant?

Espinoza: I instructed the inspectors to watch out for Mr. Gomez.

Prosecutor: Did you give them any particulars?

Espinoza: Yes, I did. I told them that in the past that we've intercepted cocaine couriers with the same-

Defense: Objection, your Honor. Move to strike. Rule 4[0]4(b) objection.

The Court: Same ruling. Overruled. Let's have a continuing objection. Continue. Overruled.

Prosecutor: Thank you, your Honor. I would appreciate it.

The Court: My instruction to the Jury, which I gave you, is to only determine what the inspectors who may have had further contact with the defendant, and we'll see about that. Otherwise, I'll strike it. But only with respect to what they had in their mind when they had further contact with the defendant. I'm talking about the people [Espinoza] talked to. All right? Got it? With that instruction, objection overruled.

Prosecutor: What did you tell them, Inspector?

Espinoza: I told them to look out after Mr. Gomez, because in the past we've had the same type of narcotics couriers with the same MO that Mr. Gomez had: Cash ticket, in transit, in transit without a [United States] Visa, to Australia, with one or more pieces of checked luggage.

Prosecutor: You said 'MO'; what did you mean by that?

Espinoza: The same-his profile, same cash ticket.

The Court: MO, Modus Operandi?

Espinoza: Yes.

The Court: That's what he asked you.

Prosecutor: What did you mean when you said with the same MO?"

Espinoza: Well, in the past we've had the same type of narcotics carriers coming from Colombia.

Prosecutor: Going in transit to Australia?

Espinoza: Yeah.

Reporter's Transcript at 40-42.

A.

Gomez's central claim on appeal is that Espinoza's testimony regarding the drug courier profile was unfairly prejudicial and thus inadmissible under Federal Rule of Evidence 403. However, he has not properly preserved that claim for review. As the transcript indicates, Gomez objected on two grounds: (1) inadmissible hearsay, see Fed.R.Evid. 802, and (2) improper character evidence, see Fed.R.Evid. 404(b).

A party challenging the admission of evidence must timely object and state the specific grounds for his objection. Fed.R.Evid. 103(a)(1). This rule serves to ensure that "the nature of the error [is] called to the attention of the judge, so as to alert him to the proper course of action and enable opposing counsel to take corrective measures." Advisory Committee's Note to Rule 103(a), 56 F.R.D. 183, 195 (1972). See generally McCormick on Evidence, § 52, at 126 (E.W. Cleary ed. 1984) [hereinafter McCormick] ("If the administration of the exclusionary rules of evidence is to be fair and workable the judge must be informed promptly of contentions that evidence should be rejected, and the reasons therefor.").

Thus, a party fails to preserve an evidentiary issue for appeal not only by failing to make a specific objection, but also by making the wrong specific objection; see generally 1 Wigmore Evidence § 18, at 828 (Tillers rev. 1983) ("A specific objection overruled will be effective to the extent of the grounds specified, and no further. An objection overruled, therefore, naming a ground which is untenable, cannot be availed of because there was another and tenable ground which might have been named but was not."); 1 J. Weinstein & M. Berger, Weinstein's Evidence ¶ 103[02], at 103-24-25 (1989) ("Rule 103 adopts Wigmore's position that a specific objection made on the wrong grounds and overruled precludes a party from raising a specific objection on other, tenable grounds on appeal.").

Because Gomez failed to make a Rule 403 objection below, we review the admission of the drug courier profile testimony for plain error. See Fed.R.Evid. 103(d). . . .

B.

. . .

[4] Courts are keenly aware of the dangers of admitting testimony concerning the drug courier profile. For example, the Eighth Circuit has held that such testimony may never be introduced as substantive evidence of guilt. The Eleventh and Ninth Circuits have stated in dictum that they also would condemn such use of the drug courier profile.

However, this case does not implicate those concerns. Here the government introduced Inspector Espinoza's testimony not to prove that Gomez was guilty, but to provide the jury with a full and accurate portrayal of the events as they unfolded on that Friday afternoon. Indeed, the district judge twice cautioned the jury that it could consider Espinoza's testimony only as background material. We agree with the Eleventh Circuit that admitting drug courier profile testimony for this limited purpose greatly reduces the potential for unfair prejudice and thus cannot amount to plain error.

For these reasons, the judgment of the district court is AFFIRMED.

DISCUSSION QUESTIONS

1. What lessons does *Reagan v. Brock* teach about the importance of listening carefully and reacting quickly at trial?

2. Of what significance is the phrase, "the cold transcript of the hearing," in understanding the thought process of an appellate court in examining an evidentiary issue? What differences exist between live testimony and a transcript?

3. In the *Gomez* case, assuming that Gomez could have excluded the evidence under some grounds, what purposes are served by requiring him to object on those precise grounds? As a corollary to the above question, shouldn't any kind of objection alert the judge to the existence of a problem?

4. Identify and examine the limiting instructions given by the judge in *Gomez.* How likely is it that the jury was actually able to follow them? What do you think of the presumption that a jury hears, understands and follows limiting instructions? Is this beyond the capacity of human beings?

PROBLEMS

Problem 2-1. At Dan Defendant's criminal trial for cocaine trafficking, the prosecution offered into evidence Dan's .44 magnum handgun. Dan's counsel timely objected, stating, "Your honor, the evidence is irrelevant and should be excluded under FRE 402." The prosecutor argued that the evidence was relevant because guns are "tools of the trade" in cocaine trafficking. The judge overruled the objection and admitted the evidence. Dan was convicted of cocaine trafficking. On appeal, he concedes that the gun was relevant but that its admission was unfairly prejudicial under FRE 403. How should the appellate court evaluate this issue under FRE 103?

Problem 2-2. While on vacation in Calamity State Park, Paula Plaintiff and her husband, Rick, rented bicycles from the Caveat Emptorium Outdoor Equipment Rental Shop. At the time they rented the bicycles, they received a hand-drawn map of bicycle routes from a Shop employee. They followed Route Red on the map because the employee said it offered the best view in the park. One portion of Route Red took them down a steep descent. Rick lost control of his bicycle, hurtled into a tree, and died. Paula Plaintiff sued the Shop, alleging breach of an express warranty that Route Red was safe for bicycle travel. At trial, Paula offered into evidence the Calamity State Park Service Bicycle Trail Standards, an official publication establishing the requirements for bicycle trails within Calamity State parks. The defense objected without stating any grounds. Paula's attorney responded, "Your honor, I really need this publication to prove my case. The jury ought to see it." The judge sustained the objection, and Paula went on to lose her case at trial. On appeal, Paula argues that the judge erred in granting the defendant's objection. She explains that the publication would show that Route Red was not actually a certified bicycle trail. How should the appellate court evaluate this issue under FRE 103?

Evidentiary Procedure: Quick Hits

- Advocates are responsible to identify evidentiary issues and bring them to the court's attention.

- If an advocate fails to object in a timely and specific manner, the issue is almost always forfeited on appeal.

- If an advocate objects on improper grounds, the issue is almost always forfeited on appeal.

- An advocate whose evidence is ruled inadmissible must make an offer of proof to preserve the issue for appeal.

- Advocates should seek definitive rulings on evidentiary issues to ensure that they do not forfeit the issue on appeal.

- In the absence of objection, even technically inadmissible evidence may be introduced at trial.

- A judge should give appropriate limiting instructions to help the jury consider evidence for its proper purpose. The jury is presumed

> to hear, understand and follow these instructions.
>
> • Under the rule of completeness, the judge can require a party to introduce the remainder of a document or recording, or other documents and recordings, in order to avoid unfairness to the opposing party and misleading the jury.

Chapter References

CHRISTOPHER B. MUELLER & LAIRD C. KIRKPATRICK, EVIDENCE §§ 1.3–1.9, 1.14–1.18 (4th ed. 2009).

GLEN WEISSENBERGER & JAMES J. DUANE, FEDERAL RULES OF EVIDENCE: RULES, LEGISLATIVE HISTORY, COMMENTARY AND AUTHORITY §§ 103, 105–06 (6th ed. 2009).

JACK B. WEINSTEIN & MARGARET A. BERGER, WEINSTEIN'S FEDERAL EVIDENCE, §§ 103, 105–06 (Joseph M. McLaughlin ed., Matthew Bender 2d ed. 1997).

KENNETH S. BROUN, MCCORMICK ON EVIDENCE §§ 56, 59 (6th ed. 2006).

STEVEN J. GOODE & OLIN GUY WELLBORN III, COURTROOM HANDBOOK ON FEDERAL EVIDENCE Ch. 5 (West 2010).

III. APPLICATION EXERCISES

Objections Exercise

Objective: To practice identifying errors and making objections to live testimony.

Factual Scenario: This will be provided to you in class. Your professor will identify objectionable words and concepts to you just before the exercise begins. During the examination of a witness, you must timely object if you hear the objectionable words or concepts.

Offer of Proof Exercise

An offer of proof is simply a description or explanation of what the excluded evidence would be. In many ways, it is similar to the endless debates conducted by sports fans about the effect of an injury or a bad call on a game, a season, or a championship.

Objective: To prepare different forms of an offer of proof and practice making arguments about the effect of excluded evidence at trial.

Factual Scenario: By statute, the Calamity Court of Sports and Justice (CCSJ) has jurisdiction to correct officiating mistakes during sporting events and provide "appropriate relief." There is no statute of limitations. Select a team from any sport, level and season that lost a meaningful game because of a bad call on the field by officials. You represent this team before the CCSJ. During trial, as you attempted to offer evidence of the bad call, the opposing party objected on grounds of speculation. You now need to preserve the record for appeal.

Advance Preparation: Prepare a written offer of proof, no more than 200 words, of the bad call and how the game of your selection would have turned out differently had the call not been made.

In-Class Exercise: Students will be selected at random to make offers of proof in a variety of formats: (1) oral assertion of counsel; (2) direct examination of a witness; (3) affidavit (for purposes of this exercise, your written product will satisfy the requirements of an affidavit.)

Chapter 3

PROCEDURES FOR PRELIMINARY HEARINGS

> **Chapter Objectives:**
>
> - Introduce Rule 104 and explain the types of preliminary evidentiary hearings, burdens and standards of proof in preliminary hearings, and the applicability of other rules of evidence in Rule 104 hearings
> - Analyze and discuss issues arising in FRE 104 hearings
> - Apply the concepts from this chapter in a courtroom application exercise.

I. BACKGROUND AND EXPLANATORY MATERIAL

Federal Rule of Evidence 104 provides a mechanism for judges to decide preliminary questions pertaining to the admissibility of evidence. It is one of the most important and often-used evidentiary rules at trial. The text of the rule follows:

Through Dec. 1, 2011	After Dec. 1, 2011
Rule 104. Preliminary Questions	**Rule 104. Preliminary Questions**
(a) Questions of admissibility generally. Preliminary questions concerning the qualification of a person to be a witness, the existence of a privilege, or the admissibility of evidence shall be determined by the court, subject to the provisions of subdivision (b). In making its determination it is not bound by the rules of evidence except those with respect to privileges.	**(a) In General**. The court must decide any preliminary question about whether a witness is qualified, a privilege exists, or evidence is admissible. In so deciding, the court is not bound by evidence rules, except those on privilege.
(b) Relevancy conditioned on fact. When the relevancy of evidence depends upon the fulfillment of a condition of fact, the court shall admit it upon, or subject to, the introduction of evidence sufficient to support a finding of the fulfillment of the condition.	**(b) Relevance That Depends on a Fact**. When the relevance of evidence depends on whether a fact exists, proof must be introduced sufficient to support a finding that the fact does exist. The court may admit the proposed evidence on the condition that the proof be introduced later.

Through Dec. 1, 2011	After Dec. 1, 2011
Rule 104. Preliminary Questions	**Rule 104. Preliminary Questions**
(c) Hearing of jury. Hearings on the admissibility of confessions shall in all cases be conducted out of the hearing of the jury. Hearings on other preliminary matters shall be so conducted when the interests of justice require, or when an accused is a witness and so requests.	**(c) Conducting a Hearing So That the Jury Cannot Hear It**. The court must conduct any hearing on a preliminary question so that the jury cannot hear it if:

(1) the hearing involves the admissibility of a confession; |
| **(d) Testimony by accused**. The accused does not, by testifying upon a preliminary matter, become subject to cross-examination as to other issues in the case. | (2) a defendant in a criminal case is a witness and so requests; or

(3) justice so requires. |
| **(e) Weight and credibility**. This rule does not limit the right of a party to introduce before the jury evidence relevant to weight or credibility. | **(d) Cross-Examining a Defendant in a Criminal Case**. By testifying on a preliminary question, a defendant in a criminal case does not become subject to cross-examination on other issues in the case. |
| | **(e) Evidence Relevant to Weight and Credibility**. This rule does not limit a party's right to introduce before the jury evidence that is relevant to the weight or credibility of other evidence. |

Rule 104 is a simple rule that does a great deal to further efficiency in the courtroom. The rule permits a judge to hold a hearing to decide preliminary questions of legal admissibility or determine whether a jury could find that the factual predicates exist to make an item of evidence relevant. The rule is extremely flexible. For example, the information a judge considers during a Rule 104 hearing does not itself have to be admissible in evidence. The hearing can be as formal or informal as the judge deems necessary. For matters other than the admissibility of confessions, a judge can conduct the hearing either in or outside the jury's presence.

Rule 104 applies to two aspects of evidence: legal admissibility and conditional relevance. Technically, whenever a judge makes a decision about either of these aspects of evidence, and regardless of the level of formality involved in the decision, Rule 104 comes into play.

Preliminary Questions of Legal Admissibility

One of the issues a judge must address for every challenged fact or item of evidence is whether it is legally admissible under the rules of evidence and binding interpretative case law. Legal rulings are the sole province of the judge. An example of a legal issue is whether scientific evidence meets the standards of Rule 702 and the *Daubert* line of cases that interpret Rule 702. Another example is whether an out-of-court statement offered for its truth is hearsay, and if so, whether it satisfies a recognized hearsay exception.

Judges often make simple and routine decisions of legal admissibility, such as whether evidence meets a hearsay exception, in the presence of a jury. More complex issues, such as those involving scientific evidence or the qualifications of expert witnesses, are decided outside the jury's presence. This can occur before trial in a hearing, or during trial, such as when a mid-trial hearing is held outside the presence of the jury.

In most cases, the proponent of the evidence has the burden of proof under FRE 104(a) for preliminary questions of legal admissibility. Although not specifically stated in FRE 104(a), the Supreme Court has held that the standard of proof is preponderance of the evidence.[1] It should be noted that the burdens and standards to satisfy the technical requirements to admit evidence may be different than those required to win at trial.

Conditional Relevance

The second key concept of Rule 104 is conditional relevance, codified in Rule 104(b). To be admissible, all evidence at trial must be relevant under Rule 401. Some evidence does not become relevant unless a preliminary factual condition is met. To illustrate: suppose the issue in a case is whether a landlord had notice that there was a broken step leading to his apartment building. The plaintiff has a witness who will claim she mentioned the broken step to the landlord while he was collecting rent. The alleged conversation may well be relevant at trial, *if it actually occurred.* Thus, whether the conversation occurred is an issue of conditional relevance.

The standard for conditional relevance is sufficient evidence for a reasonable jury to find the existence of the fact. This does not mean that a party has to prove the existence of the fact by a certain standard of proof (such as preponderance of the evidence or clear and convincing evidence), or that the judge has to make a finding of the fact's actual existence. The rule does not require the judge to believe that the preliminary fact actually occurred, but rather only that there is sufficient evidence for a reasonable jury to find that it did, thus satisfying the conditional relevance requirement of Rule 104. This is a subtle distinction that is the subject of the *Huddleston* case, *infra.*

---

[1] Bourjaily v. United States, 483 U.S. 171, 175 (1987). ("The preponderance standard ensures that before admitting evidence, the court will have found it more likely than not that the technical issues and policy concerns addressed by the Federal Rules of Evidence have been afforded due consideration.")

Criminal Law and Rule 104

Rule 104 contains two subsections that apply only in criminal cases. The first is contained in Rule 104(c), which states that hearings on the admissibility of confessions must take place outside the hearing of the jury. In addition, this subsection permits a criminal accused who is a witness to request that hearings on preliminary matters of admissibility occur outside the jury's presence.

Subsection (d) of Rule 104 provides that a criminal defendant can testify for limited purposes at a Rule 104 hearing. For example, to establish standing on a motion to suppress illegally seized evidence, an accused could testify to ownership of the property at a Rule 104 hearing. By so testifying, the accused does not open himself to cross-examination regarding other aspects of the case.

II. CASES, QUESTIONS AND PROBLEMS

HUDDLESTON v. UNITED STATES
Supreme Court of the United States
485 U.S. 681 (1988)

Chief Justice REHNQUIST delivered the opinion of the Court.

[Among other things, the petitioner was charged with receiving shipments of stolen Memorex videocassette tapes, knowing they were stolen. Evidence at trial established that the petitioner was trying to sell tapes with a manufacturing cost of $4.53 per tape in lots of 500 at a price of $2.75 to $3.00 per tape.]

There was no dispute that the tapes which petitioner sold were stolen; the only material issue at trial was whether petitioner knew they were stolen. The District Court allowed the Government to introduce evidence of "similar acts" under Rule 404(b), concluding that such evidence had "clear relevance as to [petitioner's knowledge]." App. 11. The first piece of similar act evidence offered by the Government was the testimony of Paul Toney, a record store owner. He testified that in February 1985, petitioner offered to sell new 12" black and white televisions for $28 apiece. According to Toney, petitioner indicated that he could obtain several thousand of these televisions. Petitioner and Toney eventually traveled to the Magic Rent-to-Own, where Toney purchased 20 of the televisions. Several days later, Toney purchased 18 more televisions.

[The second piece of evidence involved the petitioner attempting to sell $20,000 worth of stolen Amana appliances for $8,000 to an undercover FBI agent posing as a buyer for an appliance store.]

Petitioner testified that the Memorex tapes, the televisions, and the appliances had all been provided by Leroy Wesby, who had represented that all of the merchandise was obtained legitimately. Petitioner stated that he had sold 6,500 Memorex tapes for Wesby on a commission basis. Petitioner maintained that all of the sales for Wesby had been on a commission basis and that he had no knowledge that any of the goods were stolen.

In closing, the prosecution explained that petitioner was not on trial for his dealings with the appliances or the televisions. [The District Court gave a limiting instruction on the use of the evidence.] The jury convicted petitioner on the possession count only.

A divided panel of the United States Court of Appeals for the Sixth Circuit initially reversed the conviction, concluding that because the Government had failed to prove by clear and convincing evidence that the televisions were stolen, the District Court erred in admitting the testimony concerning the televisions. 802 F.2d 874 (1986). The panel subsequently granted rehearing [based on another case in the circuit that lowered the standard of proof to preponderance of the evidence] . . . On rehearing, the court affirmed the conviction. . . .

We granted certiorari to resolve a conflict among the Courts of Appeals as to whether the trial court must make a preliminary finding before "similar act" and other Rule 404(b) evidence is submitted to the jury. We conclude that such evidence should be admitted if there is sufficient evidence to support a finding by the jury that the defendant committed the similar act. . . .

Before this Court, petitioner argues that the District Court erred in admitting Toney's testimony as to petitioner's sale of the televisions. The threshold inquiry a court must make before admitting similar acts evidence under Rule 404(b) is whether that evidence is probative of a material issue other than character. The Government's theory of relevance was that the televisions were stolen, and proof that petitioner had engaged in a series of sales of stolen merchandise from the same suspicious source would be strong evidence that he was aware that each of these items, including the Memorex tapes, was stolen. As such, the sale of the televisions was a "similar act" only if the televisions were stolen. Petitioner acknowledges that this evidence was admitted for the proper purpose of showing his knowledge that the Memorex tapes were stolen. He asserts, however, that the evidence should not have been admitted because the Government failed to prove to the District Court that the televisions were in fact stolen.

Petitioner argues from the premise that evidence of similar acts has a grave potential for causing improper prejudice. For instance, the jury may choose to punish the defendant for the similar rather than the charged act, or the jury may infer that the defendant is an evil person inclined to violate the law. Because of this danger, petitioner maintains, the jury ought not to be exposed to similar act evidence until the trial court has heard the evidence and made a determination under Federal Rule of Evidence 104(a) that the defendant committed the similar act. Rule 104(a) provides that "[p]reliminary questions concerning the qualification of a person to be a witness, the existence of a privilege, or the admissibility of evidence shall be determined by the court, subject to the provisions of subdivision (b)." According to petitioner, the trial court must make this preliminary finding by at least a preponderance of the evidence.

We reject petitioner's position, for it is inconsistent with the structure of the Rules of Evidence and with the plain language of Rule 404(b). Article IV of the Rules of Evidence deals with the relevancy of evidence. Rules 401 and 402 establish the broad principle that relevant evidence-evidence that makes the existence of any fact at issue more or less probable-is admissible unless the Rules provide otherwise. Rule 403 allows the trial judge to exclude relevant evidence if, among other things, "its probative value is substantially outweighed by the danger of unfair prejudice." Rules 404 through 412 address specific types of evidence that have generated problems. Generally, these latter Rules do not flatly prohibit the introduction of such evidence but instead limit the purpose for which it may be introduced. Rule 404(b), for example, protects against the introduction of extrinsic act evidence when that evidence is offered solely to prove character. The text contains no intimation, however, that any preliminary showing is necessary before such evidence may be introduced for a proper purpose. If offered for such a proper purpose, the evidence is subject only to general strictures limiting admissibility such as Rules 402 and 403.

Petitioner's reading of Rule 404(b) as mandating a preliminary finding by the trial court that the act in question occurred not only superimposes a level of judicial oversight that is nowhere apparent from the language of that provision, but it is simply inconsistent with the legislative history behind Rule 404(b). [Court summarizes the legislative history.]

We conclude that a preliminary finding by the court that the Government has proved the act by a preponderance of the evidence is not called for under Rule 104(a). This is not to say, however, that the Government may parade past the jury a litany of potentially prejudicial similar acts that have been established or connected to the defendant only by unsubstantiated innuendo. Evidence is admissible under Rule 404(b) only if it is relevant. "Relevancy is not an inherent characteristic of any item of evidence but exists only as a relation between an item of evidence and a matter properly provable in the case." Advisory Committee's Notes on Fed.Rule Evid. 401, 28 U.S.C. App., p. 688. In the Rule 404(b) context, similar act evidence is relevant only if the jury can reasonably conclude that the act occurred and that the defendant was the actor. In the instant case, the evidence that petitioner was selling the televisions was relevant under the Government's theory only if the jury could reasonably find that the televisions were stolen.

Such questions of relevance conditioned on a fact are dealt with under Federal Rule of Evidence 104(b). Rule 104(b) provides: "When the relevancy of evidence depends upon the fulfillment of a condition of fact, the court shall admit it upon, or subject to, the introduction of evidence sufficient to support a finding of the fulfillment of the condition."

In determining whether the Government has introduced sufficient evidence to meet Rule 104(b), the trial court neither weighs credibility nor makes a finding that the Government has proved the conditional fact by a preponderance of the evidence. The court simply examines all the evidence in the case and decides whether the jury could reasonably find the conditional fact-here, that the televisions were stolen-by a preponderance of the evidence. See 21 C. Wright & K. Graham, Federal Practice and Procedure § 5054, p. 269 (1977). The trial court has traditionally exercised the broadest sort of discretion in controlling the order of proof at trial, and we see nothing in the Rules of Evidence that would change this practice. Often the trial court may decide to allow the proponent to introduce evidence concerning a similar act, and at a later point in the trial assess whether sufficient evidence has been offered to permit the jury to make the requisite finding.[2] If the proponent has failed to meet this minimal standard of proof, the trial court must instruct the jury to disregard the evidence.

We emphasize that in assessing the sufficiency of the evidence under Rule 104(b), the trial court must consider all evidence presented to the jury. "[I]ndividual pieces of evidence, insufficient in themselves to prove a point, may in cumulation prove it. The sum of an evidentiary presentation may well be greater than its constituent parts." Bourjaily v. United States, 483 U.S. 171, 179-180, 107 S.Ct. 2775, 2781, 97 L.Ed.2d 144 (1987). In assessing whether the evidence was sufficient to support a finding that the televisions were stolen, the court here was required to consider not only the direct evidence on that point-the low price of the televisions, the large quantity offered for sale, and petitioner's inability to produce a bill of sale-but also the evidence concerning petitioner's involvement in the sales of other stolen merchandise obtained from Wesby, such as the Memorex tapes and the Amana appliances. Given this evidence, the jury reasonably could have concluded that the televisions were stolen, and the trial court therefore properly allowed the evidence to go to the jury. . . .

Affirmed.

UNITED STATES v. GOMEZ-DIAZ
United States Court of Appeals, Fifth Circuit
712 F.2d 949 (5th Cir. 1983)

[The defendant arrived in New Orleans on an international flight from Cali, Columbia through Mexico City, Mexico. A customs inspector observed him exhibiting suspicious behavior and questioned him. A Chief Inspector Vaughn was brought in for additional questioning.] Vaughan, speaking in Spanish, informed Gomez-Diaz that he wished to have a hospital conduct an x-ray examination to determine if Gomez-Diaz was carrying drugs within his body. Gomez-Diaz verbally agreed to the x-ray procedures, but refused to sign a written consent form, explaining that he wanted to reserve his right to sue the government in case he became ill from the examination.

After Vaughan consulted the regional counsel of the Customs Office, the inspectors took Gomez-Diaz to East Jefferson Hospital. While Gomez-Diaz offered no physical resistance to planned procedures, he again refused to sign a consent form offered by hospital personnel. He stated as before that he wished to retain his right to sue the government in case of injury. Vaughan signed the authorization forms. After hospital personnel questioned Gomez-Diaz about allergies, previous illnesses and past x-rays, they took approximately nine x-rays. The record contains no indication that Gomez-Diaz did not physically cooperate in the procedures. The examination

---

[2] [n.7] "When an item of evidence is conditionally relevant, it is often not possible for the offeror to prove the fact upon which relevance is conditioned at the time the evidence is offered. In such cases it is customary to permit him to introduce the evidence and 'connect it up' later. Rule 104(b) continues this practice, specifically authorizing the judge to admit the evidence 'subject to' proof of the preliminary fact. It is, of course, not the responsibility of the judge sua sponte to insure that the foundation evidence is offered; the objector must move to strike the evidence if at the close of the trial the offeror has failed to satisfy the condition." 21 C. WRIGHT & K. GRAHAM, FEDERAL PRACTICE AND PROCEDURE § 5054, pp. 269-270 (1977) (footnotes omitted).

disclosed foreign objects in Gomez-Diaz's abdomen. He was arrested and taken to the Orleans Parish Prison Medical Unit where he naturally passed sixty-nine balloons. Each balloon contained cocaine. The amount retrieved totaled 445 grams.

Gomez-Diaz moved to suppress the cocaine alleging that the government lacked sufficient cause to conduct the x-ray examination. During the hearing on the motion, Vaughan testified that Gomez-Diaz verbally consented to the x-ray examination. Gomez-Diaz's attorney attempted to have his client testify at the suppression hearing. However, the magistrate refused to limit examination to the yes/no question of whether Gomez-Diaz gave his consent. The magistrate explained that should Gomez-Diaz take the stand during the hearing, the government would be allowed to cross-examine him about any matters relating to his alleged consent that occurred during the time he was detained for examination. As a result, Gomez-Diaz declined to testify at the hearing. The motion to suppress was denied and Gomez-Diaz was convicted on both charges. . . .

Consent is an exception to the warrant requirement. When consent is the justification for the search, the government bears the burden of demonstrating that it was freely and voluntarily given and was not simply an acquiescence to a claim of lawful authority. Whether consent was given is a determination to be made from the totality of the circumstances. The determination by the district court that consent was given is a factual finding and it will not be disturbed unless it is found to be clearly erroneous.

The magistrate found that Gomez-Diaz had verbally consented to the x-ray. The district court adopted the finding. Our review of the record convinces us that the finding was not clearly erroneous. Indeed, the sole, uncontradicted evidence before the district court was the testimony of Chief Inspector Vaughan who stated that Gomez-Diaz gave full oral consent. He testified that Gomez-Diaz refused to sign consent forms only because he wished to reserve his right to sue the government should any injury result. The circumstances also point to a finding of consent. . . . The record is replete with indications, both verbal and non-verbal, that Gomez-Diaz consented to the x-ray.

Gomez-Diaz now complains that the record would not be uncontradicted if the magistrate would have allowed him to testify. Gomez-Diaz sought to take the stand during the suppression hearing to answer the single question of whether he verbally agreed to the x-ray.[3] He maintains that he would have answered no. The magistrate, however, stated that if Gomez-Diaz took the stand, he would be open to cross-examination on any matter that occurred during his detention by customs officials which related to the issue of consent. Given that ruling, Gomez-Diaz chose not to testify. The magistrate ruled correctly. There is no federal right to limit the testimony of a witness on a preliminary matter to one single phase of an issue. The Federal Rules of Evidence provide that "the accused does not, by testifying upon a preliminary matter, subject himself to cross-examination as to other issues in the case." Fed.R.Evid. 104(d). The issue at this point in the case was whether Gomez-

---

[3] [n.1] A defendant at a suppression hearing may testify without fear that that testimony will be used against him at trial except for impeachment. Simmons v. United States, 390 U.S. 377, 88 S. Ct. 967, 19 L. Ed. 2d 1247 (1968).

Diaz consented to the x-ray. The issue of consent goes beyond a single yes or no answer to the question of whether he verbally agreed to the x-ray.

The magistrate correctly interpreted Rule 104(d) to permit full cross-examination on the "preliminary matter" of consent if Gomez-Diaz chose to take the stand on that matter at the suppression hearing.

Gomez-Diaz argues that Louisiana law allows the type of limited testimony that he sought in this case. This appeal of a federal criminal conviction is not controlled by Louisiana law.

The convictions are AFFIRMED.

DISCUSSION QUESTIONS

1. The appellant in *Huddleston* argued that the government should have been required to prove and the judge to find that the television sets had actually been stolen in order for the evidence to be relevant under FRE 404(b). Based on your reading of *Huddleston* and FRE 104, why did the drafters of the Federal Rules decline to adopt such a requirement for conditional relevance? What problems are created if parties do not have to actually prove the existence of a preliminary fact by a preponderance of the evidence? What issues would arise if parties were required to prove the existence of preliminary facts by either a preponderance of the evidence or clear and convincing evidence?

2. What is involved in the practice of "linking up" evidence at trial? What happens if an attorney fails to link up evidence? Is the remedy suggested in footnote 7 of *Huddleston* sufficient? Why or why not?

3. In *Gomez-Diaz*, the defendant wanted to take the stand in the courtroom and give a one-word answer — "no" — to the question of whether he consented to the X-ray of his abdomen. He declined to take the stand when the court informed him that if he testified at all on the issue of consent, he could be fully cross-examined on all circumstances and statements pertaining to the issue of consent. He claimed that Louisiana law would have permitted him to testify as he desired without opening the door to cross-examination. Evaluate the merits of the alleged Louisiana law and compare them to the decision reached by the 5th Circuit in *Gomez-Diaz*. From a policy standpoint, which rule is better, and why? Would the government's case have been harmed if the magistrate judge had permitted *Gomez-Diaz* to testify without cross-examination in the limited manner he suggested? What does *Gomez-Diaz* tell you about some of the considerations criminal defendants must make when deciding to take the stand?

PROBLEMS

Problem 3-1. Plaintiff, a handyman, has sued Defendant, a homeowner, for refusing to pay for certain repairs Plaintiff made to the exterior of Defendant's home. The parties had a written contract for the repairs. Defendant claims at trial that he verbally cancelled the contract and told Plaintiff not to make the repair, but Plaintiff did it anyway one weekend when Defendant was out of town. Plaintiff denies that such a conversation ever took place. In support of his defense,

Defendant seeks to call his next door neighbor, Val Voyeur, to testify that he overheard Defendant telling Plaintiff not to do the work, and that Plaintiff agreed not to do it. Plaintiff objects to Voyeur's testimony, arguing that because the conversation never took place, testimony about it is irrelevant. The judge decides to hold a hearing under FRE 104. During that hearing, Voyeur testifies about the alleged conversation and gives the time, date and circumstances of the alleged conversation. On cross-examination, Plaintiff's attorney points out several inconsistencies in Voyeur's testimony and brings up Voyeur's past perjury conviction in federal court for lying in a criminal trial. Plaintiff's attorney argues to the judge that Voyeur is not credible as a witness, and therefore, the conversation did not take place. The judge believes Voyeur is not credible and may not be telling the truth. Under Rule 104, how should the judge rule, and why?

Problem 3-2. In the case of *State v. Slayer*, the accused is charged with murdering a college student at Calamity State University. The state's main witness is the student's roommate, who identified Slayer in a police lineup. There is no other evidence linking Slayer to the crime. Slayer's attorney provides notice of his intent to call Dr. Iris Ocularia, a psychologist who lives in Australia, as an expert in eyewitness identification and its shortcomings. The judge schedules an FRE 104 pretrial hearing to determine whether Dr. Ocularia is qualified as a witness under FRE 702. Slayer's attorney offers into evidence Dr. Ocularia's curriculum vitae and hard copies of five articles Dr. Ocularia authored on eyewitness identification. Slayer's attorney also proposes to have Dr. Ocularia testify via Skype from Australia to answer any questions the judge might have. The prosecuting attorney objects that neither the documents nor the Skype testimony would be admissible at trial and therefore should not be considered by the judge in the hearing. Before the judge can rule, the prosecutor offers an affidavit from the director of the Calamity State Crime Lab which states, "Ocularia's reputation as a quack is well-known within the forensic science community. I fired Ocularia from the Calamity State Crime Lab after discovering that Ocularia was never actually awarded his Ph.D from Calamity State University." Slayer's attorney objects to the affidavit and adds that "Ocularia's credibility is an issue for the jury, not the court." How should the judge rule, and why?

Preliminary Admissibility: Quick Hits

- Rule 104 requires the judge to decide issues of preliminary admissibility.

- The judge decides purely legal questions under Rule 104(a)-such as the existence of a privilege, the qualifications of an expert witness, whether evidence should be excluded as hearsay, etc.

- The judge decides issues of conditional relevance under Rule 104(b), determining whether a juror could reasonably believe that a predicate fact existed.

- The rules of evidence, except for privileges, do not apply in a Rule 104 hearing or decision, thereby giving the judge maximum flexibility to decide important issues at trial.

Chapter References

CHRISTOPHER B. MUELLER & LAIRD C. KIRKPATRICK, EVIDENCE §§ 1.10–1.13 (4th ed. 2009).

GLEN WEISSENBERGER & JAMES J. DUANE, FEDERAL RULES OF EVIDENCE: RULES, LEGISLATIVE HISTORY, COMMENTARY AND AUTHORITY § 104 (6th ed. 2009).

JACK B. WEINSTEIN & MARGARET A. BERGER, WEINSTEIN'S FEDERAL EVIDENCE § 104 (Joseph M. McLaughlin ed., Matthew Bender 2d ed. 1997).

KENNETH S. BROUN, MCCORMICK ON EVIDENCE §§ 53, 58, 145 (6th ed. 2006).

STEVEN J. GOODE & OLIN GUY WELLBORN III, COURTROOM HANDBOOK ON FEDERAL EVIDENCE Ch. 5 (West 2010).

III. APPLICATION EXERCISE: CONDITIONAL RELEVANCE AND LIMITING INSTRUCTIONS

Using Limiting Instructions at Trial

In an adversarial trial system, the judge presides over the trial and acts as the lawgiver, instructing the jury on the legal and evidentiary principles they must follow in deciding the case. The common law trial is predicated on the useful legal fiction that the jury hears, comprehends and follows all the instructions of the judge. As discussed in the previous chapter, judges often instruct juries that they can consider evidence for one purpose, but not another.

Evidentiary instructions do not simply appear from thin air. Someone must draft them or adapt already-existing instructions to reflect the unique factual circumstances of a case. Many jurisdictions use standardized instructions that can be modified by the parties or the judge as needed. An advocate who anticipates evidentiary issues and drafts her own limiting instructions for submission to the judge gains an important tactical and advocacy advantage at trial.

The Exercise

Objective: To synthesize FREs 104 and 105 by preparing a limiting instruction on a factual issue of conditional relevance.

Factual Scenario: Use the facts given in the *Huddleston* case, above. Assume that you are the district court judge in the case and that you have decided to let the jury hear the evidence about the stolen television sets to help prove the defendant knew the videotapes were stolen.

Advance Preparation: Prepare a written limiting instruction that reflects the holding of *Huddleston* and properly instructs the jury on the appropriate use of the television set evidence. Use the form instructions in effect for your local federal district court.

In-Class Exercise:

Students will hand in their limiting instructions to the professor, who will select a few of them for discussion and evaluation by the class.

Chapter 4

ESTABLISHING FACTS AT TRIAL

Chapter Objectives:

- Introduce and explain the categories of evidence, burdens of proof and the procedures for establishing facts at trial by judicial notice or presumptions
- Analyze and discuss issues pertaining to judicial notice and presumptions
- Apply the concepts from this chapter in a courtroom application exercise

I. BACKGROUND AND EXPLANATORY MATERIAL

Direct and Circumstantial Evidence

The rules of evidence allow parties to introduce admissible evidence in support of their cases at trial. We have already learned that the vast majority of evidence at trial is introduced through the testimony of live witnesses who are qualified to testify based on their personal knowledge of the facts in a case. In addition to live witness testimony, evidence can also consist of documents, photographs, recordings, real evidence (such as guns or drugs), demonstrative evidence (such as models, mock-ups and diagrams), and electronic evidence. Finally, the rules permit substitutes for evidence, such as judicial notice and presumptions, both of which will be explained later in this chapter.

Evidence is relevant if it has "any tendency to make the existence of any fact that is of consequence to the proceedings more probable or less probable than it would be without the evidence."[1] Parties offer evidence at trial in order to help prove or disprove material facts that will help the fact-finder reach a decision about the issues in the case. Broadly speaking, all evidence can be divided into two main categories, direct evidence and circumstantial evidence.

---

[1] FED. R. EVID. 401.

Direct evidence, as its name suggests, provides direct proof of a factual proposition. For example, suppose Dan Defendant was charged with aggravated battery after stabbing another person with a knife during a bar fight. Direct evidence of the stabbing could come from a variety of sources: eyewitnesses who actually saw Dan stab the victim, surveillance video of the incident, or Dan's own admissions. Direct evidence is a strong form of proof, but given the vagaries of human nature and the variety of incidents that give rise to litigation, not all factual propositions lend themselves to easy proof by direct evidence.

The law also provides for proof by circumstantial evidence. Circumstantial evidence is indirect proof: the proponent offers evidence that requires the jury to draw inferences — to "connect the dots" — in order to find the existence of a material fact. Suppose, for example, that Dan Defendant was charged with aggravated battery for stabbing another person in a dark alleyway. The victim did not see an assailant, and there were no other witnesses to the incident. The prosecutor could offer circumstantial evidence to prove the stabbing: the presence of the victim's blood on Dan's clothing, Dan's ownership of a knife, and witness testimony that Dan had threatened the victim. None of these items constitutes direct proof, but each of them permits the fact-finder to apply common sense and human experience in concluding that Dan committed the stabbing. The presence of the victim's blood on Dan's clothing suggests that Dan was present when the victim was bleeding. Dan's ownership of a knife proves that Dan possessed the type of instrument that was used to stab the victim. Dan's threat shows a motive to commit the stabbing.

The rules of evidence do not differentiate between the admissibility of direct and circumstantial evidence at trial. A party may offer either or both in proving or disproving the material facts of a case. The following model jury instruction does an excellent job of explaining the differences between direct and circumstantial evidence and the way a jury should use them at trial:

> There are two types of evidence which you may properly use in reaching your verdict.
>
> One type of evidence is direct evidence. Direct evidence is when a witness testifies about something he knows by virtue of his own senses — something he has seen, felt, touched, or heard. Direct evidence may also be in the form of an exhibit where the fact to be proved is its present existence or condition.
>
> Circumstantial evidence is evidence which tends to prove a disputed fact by proof of other facts. There is a simple example of circumstantial evidence which is often used in this courthouse.
>
> Assume that when you came into the courthouse this morning the sun was shining and it was a nice day. Assume that the courtroom blinds were drawn and you could not look outside. As you were sitting here, someone walked in with an umbrella which was dripping wet. Then a few minutes later another person also entered with a wet umbrella. Now, you cannot look outside of the courtroom and you cannot see whether or not it is raining. So you have no direct evidence of that fact. But on the combina-

tion of facts which I have asked you to assume, it would be reasonable and logical for you to conclude that it had been raining.

That is all there is to circumstantial evidence. You infer on the basis of reason and experience and common sense from one established fact the existence or non-existence of some other fact.

Circumstantial evidence is of no less value than direct evidence; for, it is a general rule that the law makes no distinction between direct evidence and circumstantial evidence but simply requires that your verdict must be based on (e.g., a preponderance of) all the evidence presented.[2]

Judicial Notice

Judicial notice is a procedural mechanism for introducing facts into evidence. The judge "takes notice" of a fact and instructs the jury that it either may (in a criminal case) or must (in a civil case) consider the fact to be conclusively established. Judicial notice serves as a substitute for proof and promotes efficiency at trial. The text of Rule 201 follows:

Through Dec. 1, 2011	After Dec. 1, 2011
Rule 201. Judicial Notice of Adjudicative Facts	**Rule 201. Judicial Notice of Adjudicative Facts**
(a) Scope of rule. This rule governs only judicial notice of adjudicative facts.	**(a) Scope**. This rule governs judicial notice of an adjudicative fact only, not a legislative fact.
(b) Kinds of facts. A judicially noticed fact must be one not subject to reasonable dispute in that it is either (1) generally known within the territorial jurisdiction of the trial court or (2) capable of accurate and ready determination by resort to sources whose accuracy cannot reasonably be questioned.	**(b) Kinds of Facts That May Be Judicially Noticed**. The court may judicially notice a fact that is not subject to reasonable dispute because it:
	(1) is generally known within the trial court's territorial jurisdiction; or
	(2) can be accurately and readily determined from sources whose accuracy cannot reasonably be questioned.

---

[2] 4-74 Modern Federal Jury Instructions — Civil P 74.01, at 74-2 (Matthew Bender).

Through Dec. 1, 2011	After Dec. 1, 2011
Rule 201, cont'd. Judicial Notice of Adjudicative Facts	**Rule 201, cont'd. Judicial Notice of Adjudicative Facts**
(c) When discretionary. A court may take judicial notice, whether requested or not.	**(c) Taking Notice.** The court:
	(1) may take judicial notice on its own; or
(d) When mandatory. A court shall take judicial notice if requested by a party and supplied with the necessary information.	(2) must take judicial notice if a party requests it and the court is supplied with the necessary information.
(e) Opportunity to be heard. A party is entitled upon timely request to an opportunity to be heard as to the propriety of taking judicial notice and the tenor of the matter noticed. In the absence of prior notification, the request may be made after judicial notice has been taken.	**(d) Timing.** The court may take judicial notice at any stage of the proceeding.
	(e) Opportunity to Be Heard. On timely request, a party is entitled to be heard on the propriety of taking judicial notice and the nature of the fact to be noticed. If the court takes judicial notice before notifying a party, the party, on request, is still entitled to be heard.
(f) Time of taking notice. Judicial notice may be taken at any stage of the proceeding.	
(g) Instructing jury. In a civil action or proceeding, the court shall instruct the jury to accept as conclusive any fact judicially noticed. In a criminal case, the court shall instruct the jury that it may, but is not required to, accept as conclusive any fact judicially noticed.	**(f) Instructing the Jury.** In a civil case, the court must instruct the jury to accept the noticed fact as conclusive. In a criminal case, the court must instruct the jury that it may or may not accept the noticed fact as conclusive.

With respect to judicial notice, cases and treatises mention two types of facts: adjudicative facts and legislative facts. The Advisory Committee notes define them both as follows:

> Adjudicative facts are simply the facts of the particular case. Legislative facts, on the other hand, are those which have relevance to legal reasoning and the lawmaking process, whether in the formulation of a legal principle or ruling by a judge or court or in the enactment of a legislative body.[3]

Judges use legislative facts when interpreting the law, as opposed to finding the facts that are relevant to the direct dispute between the parties. Mueller and Kirkpatrick have identified several categories of facts that might be appropriately used in interpreting a statute, regulation, or constitutional provision: "legislative history, empirical research, medical literature, current social conditions, the

---

[3] FED. R. EVID. 201, advisory committee notes.

dangerousness of certain activities, aspects of human nature, factors affecting the maintenance of marital harmony, language and word usage, and miscellaneous other matters."[4] Legislative facts are not included within the coverage of Rule 201, although judges often take notice of them when interpreting the law.

Rule 201's coverage is limited to adjudicative facts, the specific facts a party must prove in order to prevail at trial. The rule recognizes two kinds of adjudicative facts: (1) those that are generally known within the territorial jurisdiction of the trial court; and (2) those that are capable of accurate and ready determination by resort to sources whose accuracy cannot reasonably be questioned.

For an example of the first type, suppose that an automobile accident occurred on Old Highway 13 between Carbondale and Murphysboro, Illinois. It is generally known in Carbondale and the surrounding environs that there are two roads named Highway 13 in Southern Illinois. The original road, Old Highway 13, is a secondary road that runs, interrupted by man-made lakes and other obstacles, through parts of Southern Illinois; it is commonly referred to, cleverly enough, as "Old 13." The other road, State Highway 13, runs generally parallel to Old Highway 13 but is a major state highway with four to six lanes that connects several communities across Southern Illinois; it is often called "New 13." A judge in Jackson County, which contains the cities of Carbondale and Murphysboro, could take judicial notice of the existence and route of Old Highway 13 because it is generally known within the jurisdiction of the trial court.

The phrase "generally known" means just that: the fact must be something that a typical member of the public would know. If the fact is generally known within a small subset of the community, then it is not appropriate for judicial notice on the grounds of general knowledge. For instance, if the coefficient of expansion for concrete is a fact generally known by all civil engineers in a particular county, it does not follow that the fact is generally known within the jurisdiction of the trial court. Similarly, the mere happenstance that a judge knows a fact does not qualify it as "generally known" within the meaning of Rule 201.

The second type of adjudicative fact has two elements: (1) the fact is capable of accurate and ready determination, (2) by sources whose accuracy cannot reasonably be questioned. Suppose, for instance, that the above-referenced accident occurred at 9 pm on an August evening. The judge could take judicial notice of the time the sun set that day, using an almanac or official government record, thereby sparing the parties the burden to call witnesses to testify about the time the sun set. This evidence would be valuable at trial in helping the jury to decide what visibility conditions were like at the time of the accident.

Judicial notice under Rule 201 is flexible. Parties may request the judge to take judicial notice, or the judge may take it on her own. Judicial notice may be taken at any time, including during post-trial matters. If a party requests judicial notice and provides the judge with sufficient information, the rule requires the judge to take notice. A party who objects to the taking of judicial notice is entitled to be heard on the matter, even if judicial notice has already been taken.

---

[4] Christopher B. Mueller & Laird C. Kirkpatrick, Evidence § 2.3, notes 5–14 and accompanying text (4th ed. 2009).

When a judge takes judicial notice of a fact in a civil case, the jury is instructed that it must take the judicial notice as conclusive on the matter. In this situation, judicial notice serves as a substitute for proof. In a criminal case, the jury may, but is not required to, take the judicial notice as conclusive on the matter.

Burdens of Pleading, Production and Persuasion

Most people are familiar with the term "burden of proof," which is often used loosely to describe the responsibility a party has to prove its case at trial. Prosecutors are said to have the burden of proving guilt beyond a reasonable doubt in criminal cases. Plaintiffs have the burden of proving their cases either by a preponderance of the evidence or by clear and convincing evidence in civil cases. Defendants have a burden of proof with respect to affirmative defenses or counterclaims. As a term of general use and understanding, "burden of proof" conveys what a party must do at trial to prevail.

But the term "burden of proof" is an imprecise phrase. More precision is needed to describe the different tasks a party must perform in order to prevail at trial. At every step of the way, a party must accomplish different proof-related tasks or risk dismissal of the case, a directed verdict by the judge, or an adverse verdict by the fact-finder.

The first burden in a case is the burden of pleading. This refers to the responsibility a party has to bring a cause of action or defense to the attention of the court. A party that fails to meet the burden of pleading a proper cause of action or defense may have its suit dismissed or may be prevented from presenting evidence relating to the matter at trial. A party that satisfies the burden of pleading earns the right to proceed to trial, there to present its evidence to the fact-finder.

At trial, there are two burdens pertaining to evidence and proof: the burden of production and the burden of persuasion. The burden of production is also known as the burden of "coming forward" with sufficient evidence to enable a rational fact finder to find in the party's favor. A party that satisfies the burden of production avoids a directed verdict at trial, keeping the issue alive for the fact-finder's ultimate decision.

To meet its burden of persuasion on a factual proposition, the party with the burden must convince the fact-finder of the fact's existence. If the party fails to meet its burden of persuasion, it loses the case; thus, the party with the burden of persuasion bears the risk of non-persuasion at trial. The quantum of evidence needed to meet the burden of persuasion is determined by the nature of the case (civil or criminal), the pleadings and the substantive law involved. In general, the burden may be characterized as preponderance of the evidence, clear and convincing evidence, or proof beyond a reasonable doubt.

In the majority of cases, the burdens of pleading, production and persuasion are tied together. In other words, the party that is trying to change the status quo pleads an issue, then has the burden to produce at trial sufficient evidence to persuade a reasonable juror of its position (burden of production) and also has the burden of persuasion (the risk of non-persuasion at trial). It is important to understand, however, that these burdens do not always fall on the same party. A party that does not have the burden of persuasion may have a burden of production with respect to an issue such as an affirmative defense, and if it fails to meet that burden of production it will suffer a directed verdict on the matter.

Presumptions

Introduction to Presumptions

As used in the law of evidence, the term "presumption" is not to be confused with the rhetorical label used to describe a criminal defendant's legal status at the beginning of trial — the "presumption of innocence." As McCormick notes, it would probably be better to refer to the presumption of innocence as the "assumption of innocence."[5] The presumption of innocence is nothing more than "a convenient introduction to the statement of the burdens upon the prosecution, first of producing evidence of the guilt of the accused and, second, of finally persuading the jury or judge of his guilt beyond a reasonable doubt."[6]

The evidentiary term "presumption" describes the relationship between two facts, the basic fact and the presumed fact. If a party proves the basic fact, then the existence of the second fact is presumed to be true. Depending on the effect given by law to the presumption at trial, the party against whom the presumption is directed may have the opportunity to rebut the presumption.

Presumptions are useful substitutes for proof when there is a disparity in access to the facts, when it would be virtually impossible for the party with the burden of production to prove a particular fact, or when other considerations of social policy or substantive law apply. Suppose, for example, that in a suit for non-payment of a bill, the debtor claims that he did in fact pay the bill by mailing payment to the creditor. The debtor is at an informational disadvantage in the case. If the item was sent by regular mail, he usually cannot prove that the creditor received it, or properly handled it upon receipt, because he will not have evidence of delivery from the postal service. The most he can prove is that he wrote the check and placed the payment, properly addressed, and with proper postage, into the postal system. If the debtor had to prove that the creditor actually received the letter containing the payment, he could rarely win the point.

In reality, most properly addressed letters reach their destinations. This fact is reflected in the presumption that a properly mailed letter was actually delivered. The basic fact in this case would be the debtor's placement of the properly addressed payment in the postal system. If the debtor meets his burden of production by introducing information sufficient for a reasonable juror to believe he properly mailed the payment, he is entitled to the benefit of the presumption. In this case, the presumed fact would be that the letter, and thus the payment, was actually delivered to the creditor.

---

[5] 2 McCormick on Evidence § 342, notes 20–25 and accompanying text (6th ed. 2006).

[6] *Id.*

In our example above, several questions arise. First, what is the effect of the presumption on the party against whom the presumption is directed? Second, what happens to the presumption when counterproof is offered? Third, how can the fact-finder use the presumption? Each of these questions will be addressed in turn.[7]

Effect on the Party Against Whom the Presumption is Directed

The first question to address is what obligations and effects a presumption imposes on the party against whom it is offered (the opposing party). Legislatures and courts often use imprecise terminology regarding presumptions. Accordingly, it is important to look past labels and examine the functional role of the so-called presumption at trial. In terms of effect on the opposing party, so-called presumptions fall into three main categories, which can be conceptualized as a continuum from the most compelling effect to the least compelling effect: mandatory, rebuttable and permissive.

(1) *The Mandatory or Conclusive Presumption.* At one end of the continuum is the so-called conclusive presumption, which treats the matter as conclusively established and not subject to question; the opposing party is not permitted to contest the "presumed fact." In reality, this is not a presumption at all, but rather is a rule of substantive law. An example of a conclusive presumption is that a child under the age of seven years is incapable of committing a felony. This is a rule of substantive law, and if it is applicable at trial, the opposing party is not entitled to prove that *this* seven year old was actually capable of committing a felony.

(2) *The Rebuttable Presumption.* Most presumptions at trial are rebuttable. This means that once the beneficiary of the presumption meets its burden of production by offering proof of the basic fact, the presumption comes into being. At this point, the burden of production shifts to the party against whom the presumption is directed (the opponent), who now has the burden to introduce evidence sufficient to meet or rebut the presumption. If the opponent fails to satisfy the burden of production, then the presumption remains alive in the case, but only if it has some evidentiary value in its own right. If the opponent fulfills its burden of production, the presumption no longer exists. The judge may treat it as a permissive inference and instruct the jury accordingly. American jurisdictions have adopted two primary approaches to rebutting presumptions, the "bursting bubble" rule and the Morgan rule. These two rules will be discussed in greater detail later in this chapter.

(3) *The Permissive Inference.* At the other end of the continuum is the permissive inference. Like the so-called conclusive presumption, an inference is not a presumption at all. Instead, it is a factual conclusion that the jury may, but is not required to, draw from the proof of a basic fact or facts. Thus, if the debtor offered proof that that he had properly mailed the payment, the jury would be instructed

---

[7] I am indebted to Professor Bill Schroeder for his assistance with this section of the book. I am also indebted to his analysis of presumptions in his treatise of Illinois Evidence. *See generally* WILLIAM A. SCHROEDER, 11 ILLINOIS PRACTICE SERIES: COURTROOM HANDBOOK ON ILLINOIS EVIDENCE Ch. 3 (West 2011 edition).

that they could find — but would not be required to do so — that the creditor had received the payment in the mail. A permissive inference imposes no burden of production on the opposing party.

Counterproof and Its Effect on the Presumption

The most vexing questions related to presumptions concern how the party against whom the presumption is offered can meet or rebut the presumption at trial. There are several options for attacking a presumption.

(1) *Attacking the Basic Fact.* In this approach, the opponent attacks the basic fact from which the presumption arises. In the letter example, the opponent would not question the presumption itself (that the letter, if properly mailed, was received), but rather the debtor's claim that he had mailed the letter. The opponent could, for example, call the debtor's roommate to testify that the debtor admitted to him that he had never actually mailed the payment. When an opponent attacks the basic fact, the jury must decide what evidence to credit. If they find the debtor's story credible, then the debtor is entitled to the presumption. If they find the creditor's version credible, then the debtor is no longer entitled to the presumption because of a failure to prove the basic fact to the jury's satisfaction.

(2) *Rebutting, or Meeting, the Presumption.* In this approach, the opponent attacks the presumed fact itself. For example, in the letter case, the creditor could accept the debtor's proof of the basic fact of sending the letter, but rebut the presumption of receipt by either calling a witness to say that no payment was received or by introducing records showing an absence of payment by the debtor. Jurisdictions vary in the methods and quantum of proof that are required to rebut a presumption, and in what happens to the presumption when the opponent rebuts it. The two main approaches are the "bursting bubble" rule and the Morgan rule.

(a) Bursting the Bubble. In jurisdictions that use this approach, the opponent has a burden of production to introduce evidence to rebut or meet the presumption. The opponent can introduce evidence that either attacks the basic fact, disproves the presumed fact, or both. Jurisdictions may vary in the quantum of evidence necessary to burst a bubble: they could require a mere claim, a scintilla of evidence, evidence sufficient for a reasonable person to find the nonexistence of the fact, proof by a preponderance of the evidence, or a greater quantum of proof depending on the case. The effect of bursting the bubble is that the presumption disappears. It is replaced, in effect, by a permissive inference: if the jury believes the basic fact, it may, but is not required, to infer the existence of the formerly presumed fact. Under the bubble-bursting approach to presumptions, the burden of persuasion on the issue never shifts; it remains on the party that originally had it.

Returning to the letter example, assume that the debtor in the case has the burden of persuasion on the issue of payment; to win the case and counter the creditor's claim of non-payment, he is required to prove that he tendered payment for his debt. If the debtor proves proper mailing of the payment, he will be entitled to the presumption that the creditor received the payment. If this presumption goes unrebutted, it will likely be enough to satisfy the debtor's burden of persuasion on the issue of mailing payment.

If, however, the creditor attacks the presumption and offers sufficient evidence under that jurisdiction's law to burst the bubble, the presumption disappears. The debtor will no longer be entitled to the jury instruction on the presumption but will instead receive an instruction on permissible inferences. In addition, the debtor retains the burden of persuasion and with it the risk of non-persuasion. If the debtor offers no additional evidence of payment, the jury is likely not to adopt the permissive inference and will find against the debtor on the issue.

(b) The Morgan Rule. Jurisdictions that use this approach to presumptions impose both a burden of production *and* a burden of persuasion on the party opposing the presumption. In other words, the opposing party is required to actually prove by some quantum of evidence that the presumed fact does not exist. The quantum of proof required could be any of the standard burdens of persuasion (preponderance, clear and convincing, beyond a reasonable doubt) depending on the governing law in the jurisdiction).

Returning to the non-payment case, assume the jurisdiction uses the Morgan rule and requires opponents of a presumption to prove by a preponderance of the evidence that the presumed fact is not true. If the debtor proved the basic fact of properly mailing the payment, the debtor would be entitled to the presumption that the creditor received the payment. The burden of production *and* persuasion on the issue would then switch to the creditor to prove that the presumption was not true.

How the Fact-Finder Uses the Presumption

(1) *Evidentiary Weight of a Presumption.* There is some question about the evidentiary weight that should be given to a presumption at trial. This is a matter of substantive law in any given jurisdiction.

One approach is to treat a presumption as having some evidentiary value, to be considered along with the other evidence in the case. As noted in the legislative history of Federal Rule of Evidence 301, this approach was popular at one time because it avoided the danger that the jury would view the presumption as being conclusive.[8] On the other hand, as was also observed in the legislative hearings on Rule 301, treating a presumption as evidence was viewed as confusing to juries, because of its requirement for the jury "to perform the task of considering 'as evidence' facts upon which they have no direct evidence."[9]

Another approach, ultimately adopted by Rule 301, is to treat the presumption simply as a procedural device to shift the burden of production on the issue to the party against whom the presumption is offered.

(2) *Instructions.* A party that proves the basic facts necessary to establish a presumption is also entitled to a jury instruction on the proper use of the information at trial. As we have previously discussed, the fact-finder is presumed to follow the judge's instructions at trial. The type of instruction given by the judge

---

[8] S. Rep. No. 93-1277, at 9 (1974).

[9] S. Rep. No. 93-1277, at 9 (1974).

depends on whether the opponent has met the burden of production imposed by the presumption.

(a) The Opponent Fails to Meet Its Burden of Production. If the opponent fails to meet its burden of production, the party benefiting from the presumption is entitled to a jury instruction on the effect of the presumption. There are two viewpoints on the substance of the instruction. The first, derived from the legislative history of Rule 301, is that the judge should instruct the jury that if it believes the basic fact was proved, it may infer (or may presume, depending on the selected language) that the presumed fact was also proved. The second, reflected in the model jury instruction below, is more conclusive: the judge should instruct the jury that if it believes the basic fact was proved, it must also find that the presumed fact was proved. It should be noted that in a "bursting bubble" jurisdiction, the likelihood of receiving this instruction is extremely low because an opponent can easily meet its burden of production to rebut the presumption. It should further be noted that this instruction could not be used against a defendant in a criminal case because it would relieve the prosecution of the burden to prove every element of the case beyond a reasonable doubt. A model jury instruction on presumptions is reproduced here:

> *Instruction 75-8: Presumptions — Rebuttable Presumption Defined*
>
> *You have heard arguments by counsel which call on you to make certain presumptions.*
>
> *What is a presumption? A presumption requires you to find one fact from the existence of another fact. (If applicable: In this case, for example, the law presumes that if one party has proved to your satisfaction that a letter was placed in an envelope which was properly addressed, stamped, sealed and deposited in the mails that the letter was actually delivered to the person to whom it was addressed.)*
>
> *Before you may find the presumed fact to exist, you must, therefore, determine whether the underlying or basic fact (e.g., the mailing) has been proved. Only if you find the basic fact to exist will the presumption operate to require you to find that the presumed fact (e.g., the delivery) also was proved.*
>
> *One word of caution. The mere existence of a presumption never shifts the burden of proof. In this case, even if you find the basic fact that compels you to find the presumed fact, the burden of proof still remains on the plaintiff (or defendant) to prove all the elements of his claim. The presumptive fact, therefore, would only be a circumstance to be considered along with all of the other circumstances in this case in deciding the issue of liability.*[10]

(b) The Opponent Meets its Burden of Production. If the opponent meets its burden of production, the presumption no longer exists; it becomes, in most cases, a permissive inference. If the jury believes the basic fact it may, but is not required to, believe the secondary fact. A judge might choose either to instruct the jury on inferences, or to leave the matter unaddressed in jury instructions. A model

---

[10] 4-75 MODERN FEDERAL JURY INSTRUCTIONS — Civil P 75.02 (Matthew Bender).

instruction on inferences is reproduced here:

Instruction 75-1: Inference Defined

During the trial you have heard the attorneys use the term "inference," and in their arguments they have asked you to infer, on the basis of your reason, experience, and common sense, from one or more established facts, the existence of some other fact.

An inference is not a suspicion or a guess. It is a reasoned, logical conclusion that a disputed fact exists on the basis of another fact which has been shown to exist.

There are times when different inferences may be drawn from facts, whether proved by direct or circumstantial evidence. The plaintiff asks you to draw one set of inferences, while the defense asks you to draw another. It is for you, and you alone, to decide what inferences you will draw.

The process of drawing inferences from facts in evidence is not a matter of guesswork or speculation. An inference is a deduction or conclusion which you, the jury, are permitted to draw — but not required to draw — from the facts which have been established by either direct or circumstantial evidence. In drawing inferences, you should exercise your common sense.

So, while you are considering the evidence presented to you, you are permitted to draw, from the facts which you find to be proven, such reasonable inferences as would be justified in light of your experience.[11]

---

[11] 4-75 Modern Federal Jury Instructions — Civil P 75.01 (Matthew Bender).

Presumptions and the Federal Rules of Evidence

The Federal Rules of Evidence contain two rules pertaining to presumptions, Rules 301 and 302.

Through Dec. 1, 2011	After Dec. 1, 2011
Rule 301. Presumptions in General in Civil Actions and Proceedings	**Rule 301. Presumptions in Civil Cases Generally**
In all civil actions and proceedings not otherwise provided for by Act of Congress or by these rules, a presumption imposes on the party against whom it is directed the burden of going forward with evidence to rebut or meet the presumption, but does not shift to such party the burden of proof in the sense of the risk of nonpersuasion, which remains throughout the trial upon the party on whom it was originally cast.	In a civil case, unless a federal statute or these rules provide otherwise, the party against whom a presumption is directed has the burden of producing evidence to rebut the presumption. But this rule does not shift the burden of persuasion, which remains on the party who had it originally.

Through Dec. 1, 2011	After Dec. 1, 2011
Rule 302. Applicability of State Law in Civil Actions and Proceedings	**Rule 302. Applying State Law to Presumptions in Civil Cases**
In all civil actions and proceedings not otherwise provided for by Act of Congress or by these rules, a presumption imposes on the party against whom it is directed the burden of going forward with evidence to rebut or meet the presumption, but does not shift to such party the burden of proof in the sense of the risk of nonpersuasion, which remains throughout the trial upon the party on whom it was originally cast.	In a civil case, state law governs the effect of a presumption regarding a claim or defense for which state law supplies the rule of decision.

Unless another rule applies, a presumption under Rule 301 has very little effect. If the party opposing the presumption meets its burden of production to oppose the presumption, the presumption disappears. The burden of persuasion on the issue never shifts.

In civil cases where state law provides the rule of decision, Rule 302 requires the application of state law pertaining to presumptions. The different approaches discussed in the previous subsection come into play, depending on the substantive law of the jurisdiction.

There is no rule in the Federal Rules of Evidence pertaining to presumptions in criminal cases. Instead, the issue is governed by Supreme Court jurisprudence on the Due Process Clause of the 5th and 14th Amendments, in which the Court has disapproved the prosecutorial use of presumptions that serve either to relieve the prosecution of its burden to prove each element of the offense beyond a reasonable doubt or shift the burden to the defense.[12] Jurisdictions are still permitted to use permissive inferences in criminal cases, if the inferred fact is rationally connected to the basic fact and more likely than not flows from that fact. An example is the inference that possession of a large amount of a controlled substance indicates intent to distribute the substance.

II. CASES, DISCUSSION QUESTIONS AND PROBLEMS

DIPPIN' DOTS, INC. v. FROSTY BITES DISTRIBUTION, LLC
United States Court of Appeals, Eleventh Circuit
369 F.3d 1197 (11th Cir. 2004)

Plaintiff-Appellant Dippin' Dots, Inc. ("DDI") brought suit against Defendant-Appellee Frosty Bites Distribution, LLC ("FBD") alleging trade dress infringement of DDI's product design and logo design, both in violation of the Lanham Act, 15 U.S.C. § 1125. The district court granted summary judgment in favor of FBD on both claims. For the reasons that follow, we affirm the judgment of the district court. . . .

DDI primarily sells its dippin' dots from colorful kiosks or stands at amusement parks, sporting venues, and shopping malls. To identify itself at these locations, DDI has a distinctive logo made up of an oval of blue, yellow, and pink spheres surrounding the product name, "dippin' dots," in blue letters. Below this oval of spheres is a tag line touting dippin' dots as the "Ice Cream of the Future."

Defendant FBD makes and sells a competing brightly-colored flash-frozen ice cream product, called "frosty bites," consisting of mostly small popcorn-shaped, along with some spherical-shaped, ice cream bites. FBD creates its product by streaming and dripping an ice cream solution into liquid nitrogen where it freezes and forms beads and clusters of frozen ice cream. The frozen product then passes through a "cluster buster," where the clusters are broken down into smaller pieces. The product then moves through a system of conveyor belts, further breaking the ice cream into small beads and popcorn-like clusters.

FBD principally sells its frosty bites from booths and kiosks. To identify itself, FBD has a distinctive logo consisting of an ice-like background upon which the words "Frosty Bites" are written in blue letters shadowed in pink. The "o" in the word "Frosty" is the torso of a cartoon caricature of a portly penguin holding a cup of yellow, green, blue, and red nuggets of ice cream. Below the words is a tag line touting frosty bites as "The Ultimate Ice Cream Sensation!".

In the Fall of 1999, several of DDI's retail dealers secretly started the FBD business while still under contract with DDI to sell dippin' dots at various locations. On March 16, 2000, eight of these dealers terminated their contracts with DDI. The following day, without changing locations, they began selling their frosty bites under the "Frosty Bites" logo.

---

[12] For a further discussion of this issue, see GLEN A. WEISSENBERGER & JAMES J. DUANE, FEDERAL RULES OF EVIDENCE: RULES, LEGISLATIVE HISTORY, COMMENTARY AND AUTHORITY § 301.5, notes 27–40 and accompanying text (6th ed. 2009).

DDI filed suit against FBD alleging infringement of DDI's trade dress (1) in the form of its unique, flash-frozen ice cream product, and (2) in the form of its unique logo design, both in violation of the Lanham Act, 15 U.S.C. § 1125. 4 FBD moved for summary judgment.

The district court granted FBD's motion for summary judgment finding that (1) DDI's product design - small, predominantly separated colored beads or pieces of ice cream - is functional and therefore not subject to trade dress protection, and (2) DDI's and FBD's logos are so dissimilar that, as a matter of law, DDI cannot prove any likelihood of consumer confusion as to the source of the products. In re Dippin' Dots Patent Litig., 249 F. Supp. 2d 1346, 1373-74 (N.D. Ga. 2003). DDI timely filed this appeal. . . .

Furthermore, the product design of dippin' dots in its individual elements and as a whole is functional under the traditional test. The color is functional because it indicates the flavor of the ice cream, for example, pink signifies strawberry, white signifies vanilla, brown signifies chocolate, etc. See, e.g., Qualitex, 514 U.S. at 163, 115 S. Ct. at 1303 (explaining that "the words 'Suntost Marmalade,' on a jar of orange jam immediately . . . signal a brand or a product 'source'; the jam's orange color does not do so"); Inwood Labs., Inc. v. Ives Labs., Inc., 456 U.S. 844, 853, 856, 102 S. Ct. 2182, 2188-89, 72 L. Ed. 2d 606 (1982) (concluding that district court did not err in finding that colors of certain prescription drugs were functional because, inter alia, many patients associated color with therapeutic effect); Warner Lambert Co. v. McCrory's Corp., 718 F. Supp. 389, 396 (D.N.J. 1989) (finding that in the mouthwash field, an amber colored liquid signifies a medicinal-tasting product, red signifies a cinnamon flavor, blue signifies peppermint, and green signifies mint). The district court took judicial notice of the fact that color indicates flavor of ice cream. DDI argues that such judicial notice was improper. We disagree.

Judicial notice is a means by which adjudicative facts not seriously open to dispute are established as true without the normal requirement of proof by evidence. Fed. R. Evid. 201(a) and (b); see also Fed. R. Evid. 201(a) advisory commit-tee's note (explaining that it is proper to take judicial notice of facts with a "high degree of indisputability" that are "outside the area of reasonable controversy"). Adjudicative facts are facts that are relevant to a determination of the claims presented in a case. Id.

One category of adjudicative facts subject to judicial notice (and the only category relevant in this case) is facts that are "generally known within the territorial jurisdiction of the trial court." Fed. R. Evid. 201(b). Such judicially-noticed facts are of breathtaking variety. See, e.g., Friend v. Burnham & Morrill Co., 55 F.2d 150, 151-52 (1st Cir. 1932) (noting the method for canning baked beans in New England); Seminole Tribe of Fla. v. Butterworth, 491 F. Supp. 1015, 1019 (S.D. Fla. 1980), aff'd, 658 F.2d 310 (5th Cir. 1981) (noting that bingo is largely a senior citizen pastime); First Nat'l Bank of South Carolina v. United States, 413 F. Supp. 1107, 1110 (D.S.C. 1976), aff'd, 558 F.2d 721 (4th Cir. 1977) (noting that credit cards play vital role in modern American society); Carling Brewing Co. v. Philip Morris, Inc., 277 F. Supp. 326, 330 (N.D. Ga. 1967) (noting that most establishments that sell beer also sell tobacco products); Colourpicture Publishers, Inc. v. Mike Roberts Color Prods., Inc., 272 F. Supp. 280, 281 (D. Mass. 1967), vacated on other grounds,

394 F.2d 431 (1st Cir. 1968) (noting that calendars have long been affixed to walls by means of a punched hole at the top of the calendar).

A court may take judicial notice of appropriate adjudicative facts at any stage in a proceeding, including at the summary judgment stage. See Fed. R. Evid. 201(f). While a court has wide discretion to take judicial notice of facts, see Fed. R. Evid. 201(c), the "taking of judicial notice of facts is, as a matter of evidence law, a highly limited process. " Shahar v. Bowers, 120 F.3d 211, 214 (11th Cir. 1997). "The reason for this caution is that the taking of judicial notice bypasses the safeguards which are involved with the usual process of proving facts by competent evidence in district court." Id. In order to fulfill these safeguards, a "party is entitled . . . to an opportunity to be heard as to the propriety of taking judicial notice." Fed. R. Evid. 201(e).

In this case, the district court took judicial notice of the fact that color is indicative of flavor in ice cream. This fact is adjudicative in nature and is generally known among consumers.[13] In addition, the district court specifically questioned DDI's counsel regarding the propriety of taking judicial notice of the fact:

> THE COURT: - would you agree that I could take judicial notice that chocolate ice cream is, generally speaking, brown, vanilla is white, strawberry is pink?

> [COUNSEL]: I think you could do that, I think you could, sir, but I think it would be appropriate to acknowledge that sometimes it's not. Chocolate can be white. I mean, that's not an uncommon occurrence. Certainly with M&M's, chocolate comes sometimes in a blue color.

> THE COURT: I'm just talking about ice cream.

> [COUNSEL]: Yes, sir.

> THE COURT: Ice cream is, generally speaking, chocolate is brown, vanilla is white, and strawberry is pink.

> [COUNSEL]: That's correct, sir, but it's not necessarily so. [R. Vol. 326 at 43.]

Therefore, the district court properly took judicial notice of the fact that the color of ice cream is indicative of its flavor. Likewise, we, who also questioned DDI's counsel at oral argument regarding the propriety of taking judicial notice, take judicial notice of the fact that color of ice cream is indicative of flavor. Accordingly, we conclude that color is functional in this case because it is essential to the purpose of the product and affects its quality.

---

[13] [n.8] DDI argued at oral argument that because a color does not necessarily indicate one particular flavor, such fact is not "generally known" and therefore cannot be judicially noticed. DDI's argument is misguided. In order to judicially notice that color is indicative of flavor, it is not necessary that consumers generally know that, for example, pink coloring denotes strawberry ice cream. Rather, it is necessary that consumers generally know that pink coloring denotes some flavor of ice cream, for example, strawberry, bubble gum, or cherry.

ST. MARY'S HONOR CENTER v. HICKS
Supreme Court of the United States
509 U.S. 502 (1993)

JUSTICE SCALIA delivered the opinion of the Court.

We granted certiorari to determine whether, in a suit against an employer alleging intentional racial discrimination in violation of § 703(a)(1) of Title VII of the Civil Rights Act of 1964, 78 Stat. 255, 42 U.S.C. § 2000e-2(a)(1), the trier of fact's rejection of the employer's asserted reasons for its actions mandates a finding for the plaintiff.

Petitioner St. Mary's Honor Center (St. Mary's) is a halfway house operated by the Missouri Department of Corrections and Human Resources (MDCHR). Respondent Melvin Hicks, a black man, was hired as a correctional officer at St. Mary's in August 1978 and was promoted to shift commander, one of six supervisory positions, in February 1980.

[Following a change of supervisors, Hicks became the subject of a number of disciplinary actions, including suspension, a letter of reprimand, demotion, and eventually discharge.]

Respondent brought this suit in the United States District Court for the Eastern District of Missouri, alleging that petitioner St. Mary's violated § 703(a)(1) of Title VII of the Civil Rights Act of 1964, 42 U.S.C. § 2000e-2(a)(1), and that petitioner Long violated Rev. Stat. § 1979, 42 U.S.C. § 1983, by demoting and then discharging him because of his race. After a full bench trial, the District Court found for petitioners. 756 F. Supp. 1244 (ED Mo. 1991). The United States Court of Appeals for the Eighth Circuit reversed and remanded, 970 F.2d 487 (1992), and we granted certiorari, 506 U.S. 1042 (1993).

II

Section 703(a)(1) of Title VII of the Civil Rights Act of 1964 provides in relevant part:

> "It shall be an unlawful employment practice for an employer —

> "(1) . . . to discharge any individual, or otherwise to discriminate against any individual with respect to his compensation, terms, conditions, or privileges of employment, because of such individual's race. . . . " 42 U.S.C. § 2000e-2(a).

With the goal of "progressively . . . sharpening the inquiry into the elusive factual question of intentional discrimination," Texas Dept. of Community Affairs v. Burdine, 450 U.S. 248, 255, n. 8, 67 L. Ed. 2d 207, 101 S. Ct. 1089 (1981), our opinion in McDonnell Douglas Corp. v. Green, 411 U.S. 792, 93 S. Ct. 1817, 36 L. Ed. 2d 668 (1973), established an allocation of the burden of production and an order for the presentation of proof in Title VII discriminatory-treatment cases. The plaintiff in such a case, we said, must first establish, by a preponderance of the evidence, a "prima facie" case of racial discrimination. Burdine, supra, at 252-253. Petitioners do not challenge the District Court's finding that respondent satisfied the minimal requirements of such a prima facie case (set out in McDonnell Douglas, supra, at 802) by proving (1) that he is black, (2) that he was qualified for the position of shift commander, (3) that he was demoted from that position and ultimately discharged, and (4) that the position remained open and was ultimately filled by a white man. 756 F. Supp. at 1249-1250.

Under the McDonnell Douglas scheme, "establishment of the prima facie case in effect creates a presumption that the employer unlawfully discriminated against the employee." Burdine, supra, at 254. To establish a "presumption" is to say that a finding of the predicate fact (here, the prima facie case) produces "a required conclusion in the absence of explanation" (here, the finding of unlawful discrimination). 1 D. Louisell & C. Mueller, Federal Evidence § 67, p. 536 (1977). Thus, the *McDonnell Douglas* presumption places upon the defendant the burden of producing an explanation to rebut the prima facie case — i.e., the burden of "producing evidence" that the adverse employment actions were taken "for a legitimate, nondiscriminatory reason." Burdine, 450 U.S. at 254. "The defendant must clearly set forth, through the introduction of admissible evidence," reasons for its actions which, if believed by the trier of fact, would support a finding that unlawful discrimination was not the cause of the employment action. Id., at 254-255, and n. 8. It is important to note, however, that although the *McDonnell Douglas* presumption shifts the burden of production to the defendant, "the ultimate burden of persuading the trier of fact that the defendant intentionally discriminated against the plaintiff remains at all times with the plaintiff." 450 U.S. at 253. In this regard it operates like all presumptions, as described in Federal Rule of Evidence 301:

> "In all civil actions and proceedings not otherwise provided for by Act of Congress or by these rules, a presumption imposes on the party against whom it is directed the burden of going forward with evidence to rebut or meet the presumption, but does not shift to such party the burden of proof in the sense of the risk of nonpersuasion, which remains throughout the trial upon the party on whom it was originally cast."

Respondent does not challenge the District Court's finding that petitioners sustained their burden of production by introducing evidence of two legitimate, nondiscriminatory reasons for their actions: the severity and the accumulation of rules violations committed by respondent. 756 F. Supp. at 1250. Our cases make clear that at that point the shifted burden of production became irrelevant: "If the defendant carries this burden of production, the presumption raised by the prima facie case is rebutted," Burdine, 450 U.S. at 255, and "drops from the case," id., at 255, n. 10. The plaintiff then has "the full and fair opportunity to demonstrate," through presentation of his own case and through cross-examination of the defendant's witnesses, "that the proffered reason was not the true reason for the employment decision," id., at 256, and that race was. He retains that "ultimate burden of persuading the [trier of fact] that [he] has been the victim of intentional discrimination." Ibid.

The District Court, acting as trier of fact in this bench trial, found that the reasons petitioners gave were not the real reasons for respondent's demotion and discharge. It found that respondent was the only supervisor disciplined for violations committed by his subordinates; that similar and even more serious violations committed by respondent's co-workers were either disregarded or treated more leniently; and that Powell manufactured the final verbal confrontation in order to provoke respondent into threatening him. 756 F. Supp. at 1250-1251. It nonetheless held that respondent had failed to carry his ultimate burden of proving that his race was the determining factor in petitioners' decision first to demote and then to dismiss him. In short, the District Court concluded that "although [respondent] has proven the existence of a crusade to terminate him, he has not proven that the crusade was racially rather than personally motivated." Id., at 1252.

The Court of Appeals set this determination aside on the ground that "once [respondent] proved all of [petitioners'] proffered reasons for the adverse employment actions to be pretextual, [respondent] was entitled to judgment as a matter of law." 970 F.2d at 492. The Court of Appeals reasoned:

> "Because all of defendants' proffered reasons were discredited, defendants were in a position of having offered no legitimate reason for their actions. In other words, defendants were in no better position than if they had remained silent, offering no rebuttal to an established inference that they had unlawfully discriminated against plaintiff on the basis of his race." Ibid.

That is not so. By producing evidence (whether ultimately persuasive or not) of nondiscriminatory reasons, petitioners sustained their burden of production, and thus placed themselves in a "better position than if they had remained silent."

In the nature of things, the determination that a defendant has met its burden of production (and has thus rebutted any legal presumption of intentional discrimination) can involve no credibility assessment. For the burden-of-production determination necessarily precedes the credibility-assessment stage. At the close of the defendant's case, the court is asked to decide whether an issue of fact remains for the trier of fact to determine. None does if, on the evidence presented, (1) any rational person would have to find the existence of facts constituting a prima facie case, and (2) the defendant has failed to meet its burden of production — i. e., has failed to introduce evidence which, taken as true, would permit the conclusion that there was a nondiscriminatory reason for the adverse action. In that event, the court must award judgment to the plaintiff as a matter of law under Federal Rule of Civil Procedure 50(a)(1) (in the case of jury trials) or Federal Rule of Civil Procedure 52(c) (in the case of bench trials). See F. James & G. Hazard, Civil Procedure § 7.9, p. 327 (3d ed. 1985); 1 Louisell & Mueller, Federal Evidence § 70, at 568. If the defendant has failed to sustain its burden but reasonable minds could differ as to whether a preponderance of the evidence establishes the facts of a prima facie case, then a question of fact does remain, which the trier of fact will be called upon to answer.[14]

---

[14] [n.3] If the finder of fact answers affirmatively — if it finds that the prima facie case is supported by a preponderance of the evidence — it must find the existence of the presumed fact of unlawful discrimination and must, therefore, render a verdict for the plaintiff. See Texas Dept. of Community Affairs v. Burdine, 450 U.S. 248, 254, 67 L. Ed. 2d 207, 101 S. Ct. 1089, and n. 7 (1981); F. James & G. Hazard, Civil Procedure § 7.9, p. 327 (3d ed. 1985); 1 D. Louisell & C. Mueller, Federal Evidence § 70, pp. 568-569 (1977). Thus, the effect of failing to produce evidence to rebut the McDonnell Douglas Corp. v. Green, 411 U.S. 792, 93 S. Ct. 1817, 36 L. Ed. 2d 668 (1973), presumption is not felt until the prima facie

If, on the other hand, the defendant has succeeded in carrying its burden of production, the McDonnell Douglas framework — with its presumptions and burdens — is no longer relevant. To resurrect it later, after the trier of fact has determined that what was "produced" to meet the burden of production is not credible, flies in the face of our holding in Burdine that to rebut the presumption "the defendant need not persuade the court that it was actually motivated by the proffered reasons." 450 U.S. at 254. The presumption, having fulfilled its role of forcing the defendant to come forward with some response, simply drops out of the picture. Id., at 255. The defendant's "production" (whatever its persuasive effect) having been made, the trier of fact proceeds to decide the ultimate question: whether plaintiff has proved "that the defendant intentionally discriminated against [him]" because of his race, id., at 253. The factfinder's disbelief of the reasons put forward by the defendant (particularly if disbelief is accompanied by a suspicion of mendacity) may, together with the elements of the prima facie case, suffice to show intentional discrimination. Thus, rejection of the defendant's proffered reasons will permit the trier of fact to infer the ultimate fact of intentional discrimination, and the Court of Appeals was correct when it noted that, upon such rejection, "no additional proof of discrimination is required," 970 F.2d at 493 (emphasis added). But the Court of Appeals' holding that rejection of the defendant's proffered reasons compels judgment for the plaintiff disregards the fundamental principle of Rule 301 that a presumption does not shift the burden of proof, and ignores our repeated admonition that the Title VII plaintiff at all times bears the "ultimate burden of persuasion" [citations omitted].

III . . .

We have no authority to impose liability upon an employer for alleged discriminatory employment practices unless an appropriate factfinder determines, according to proper procedures, that the employer has unlawfully discriminated. We may, according to traditional practice, establish certain modes and orders of proof, including an initial rebuttable presumption of the sort we described earlier in this opinion, which we believe McDonnell Douglas represents. But nothing in law would permit us to substitute for the required finding that the employer's action was the product of un-lawful discrimination, the much different (and much lesser) finding that the employer's explanation of its action was not believable. . . .

The judgment of the Court of Appeals is reversed, and the case is remanded for

---

case has been established, either as a matter of law (because the plaintiff's facts are uncontested) or by the factfinder's determination that the plaintiff's facts are supported by a preponderance of the evidence. It is thus technically accurate to describe the sequence as we did in Burdine: "First, the plaintiff has the burden of proving by the preponderance of the evidence a prima facie case of discrimination. Second, if the plaintiff succeeds in proving the prima facie case, the burden shifts to the defendant to articulate some legitimate, nondiscriminatory reason for the employee's rejection." 450 U.S. at 252-253 (internal quotation marks omitted). As a practical matter, however, and in the real-life sequence of a trial, the defendant feels the "burden" not when the plaintiff's prima facie case is proved, but as soon as evidence of it is introduced. The defendant then knows that its failure to introduce evidence of a nondiscriminatory reason will cause judgment to go against it unless the plaintiff's prima facie case is held to be inadequate in law or fails to convince the factfinder. It is this practical coercion which causes the McDonnell Douglas presumption to function as a means of "arranging the presentation of evidence," Watson v. Fort Worth Bank & Trust, 487 U.S. 977, 986, 108 S. Ct. 2777, 101 L. Ed. 2d 827 (1988).

further proceedings consistent with this opinion.

It is so ordered.

DISCUSSION QUESTIONS

1. Why was it appropriate for the district court in the *Dippin' Dots* case to take judicial notice of the relationship between color and flavor in food products such as ice cream? Is this a fact generally known, or is it verifiable by sources whose accuracy cannot reasonably be questioned?

2. Suppose the court had taken judicial notice of the fact that the color pink is indicative of the flavor strawberry, rather than the more general proposition that color is indicative of flavor, as it suggested it might do in its hypothetical discussion with the DDI counsel. Would this have presented a problem? Why or why not?

3. In the *St. Mary's Honor Center* case, the Supreme Court evaluated a presumption created by Title VII and its own interpretive case law. In order to qualify for the presumption, what burden of production and persuasion would the plaintiff have to meet at trial, and what is the quantum of required proof? What would the defendant have to do to burst the bubble of the presumption, and what is the quantum of required proof? Describe the defendant's burden of production.

4. According to *St. Mary's Honor Center*, what happens to presumptions at trial when the opposing party rebuts them? What effect does this have on the burden of persuasion at trial? In the absence of the presumption, does the plaintiff lose its ability to prove its case?

PROBLEMS

Problem 4-1. From his prison cell in the Calamity Federal Prison, where is serving a life sentence without possibility of parole, Darryl Dimebag is a prolific and serial pro-se litigator. Recently, he filed a voluminous lawsuit against personnel from the United States District Court for the District of Calamity. Among other things, he alleged that law clerks working for the court regularly wrote decisions and opinions which the judges signed without having read. In dismissing the lawsuit, the district court judge took judicial notice that it was the practice of judges in the court to read, edit and revise all decisions and opinions prepared by their clerks before signing them. On appeal, Dimebag argues that this was an improper exercise of judicial notice under Rule 201. Evaluate the judge's use of judicial notice.

Problem 4-2. Return to the basic facts of the *St. Mary's Honor Center* case. Assume that the defendant "burst the bubble" of the plaintiff's presumption. Would it be appropriate for the judge to instruct the jury that it could, nevertheless, infer discrimination on the facts presented? Draft a permissive inference instruction that would properly instruct the jury on this issue.

Judicial Notice, Burdens of Proof and Presumptions: Quick Hits

- Rule 201 provides for the judicial notice of adjudicative facts — i.e., the facts of the case — at trial.

- Judicial notice may be taken at any stage of the proceedings, either at the request of a party, or sua sponte by the judge, for facts that are either generally known in the jurisdiction of the court or that are easily verifiable by resort to sources whose accuracy cannot readily be questioned.

- Judicial notice conclusively establishes the noticed fact in a civil case, but is not conclusive in a criminal case.

- The party which has the burden of production at trial must produce sufficient evidence to avoid a directed verdict on the issue at trial.

- The burden of persuasion, often known as the burden of proof, requires the burdened party to produce evidence of a sufficient quantum of proof or bear the risk of non-persuasion.

- A presumption permits proof of a basic fact to be used to establish a presumed fact.

- A presumption imposes a burden on the party against whom it is directed to produce evidence to rebut, or meet, the presumption.

- In federal cases under Rule 301, the "bursting bubble" theory of presumptions applies.

- In cases using state law for the rule of decision under Rule 301, state rules for presumptions — which may include Morgan presumptions — apply.

- When the opposing party meets or rebuts a presumption under Rule 301, the presumption disappears but may be replaced by a permissive inference.

Chapter References

CHRISTOPHER B. MUELLER & LAIRD C. KIRKPATRICK, EVIDENCE §§ 2.1–2.13, 3.4–3.10 (4th ed. 2009).

GLEN WEISSENBERGER & JAMES J. DUANE, FEDERAL RULES OF EVIDENCE: RULES, LEGISLATIVE HISTORY, COMMENTARY AND AUTHORITY §§ 201, 301–02 (6th ed. 2009).

JACK B. WEINSTEIN & MARGARET A. BERGER, WEINSTEIN'S FEDERAL EVIDENCE §§ 201, 301–02 (Joseph M. McLaughlin ed., Matthew Bender 2d ed. 1997).

KENNETH S. BROUN, MCCORMICK ON EVIDENCE §§ 328–49 (6th ed. 2006).

STEVEN J. GOODE & OLIN GUY WELLBORN III, COURTROOM HANDBOOK ON FEDERAL EVIDENCE Ch. 5 (West 2010).

III.   APPLICATION EXERCISE

Presumptions at Trial

According to McCormick's influential treatise on evidence, there are literally hundreds of recognized presumptions.[15] Presumptions exist for a variety of reasons. Among other things, presumptions support substantive policies, help compensate for disparities in access to information or evidence, promote efficiency at trial. Parties to a lawsuit should be aware of the presumptions that may apply at trial, regardless of whether they would benefit from a presumption or be harmed by its operation against them at trial.

Sources of information pertaining to presumptions include evidence treatises, CLE guides such as those produced by state or local bar associations, statutes, case law, and pattern jury instruction books.

The Exercise

Objective: To demonstrate the ability to research and prepare to rely on or contest a presumption at trial.

Advance Preparation: As assigned by your professor, research a civil presumption in either your state or federal jurisdiction. Prepare a brief (1 page) memorandum containing the following information:

1. The name of the presumption.

2. Source of the presumption (statute, case law, etc.).

3. The burden of production and persuasion for the presumption. In other words, what basic fact must the proponent prove, and by what quantum of proof.

4. Effect on trial of the presumption (i.e., mandatory, conclusive, rebuttable).

5. The opponent's burden to meet the presumption. Describe the burden of production and its effect on the presumption. Describe whether the presumption is a bursting-bubble presumption or a Morgan presumption.

6. A sample jury instruction that tells the jury what the presumption is and how to use it at trial. This jury instruction should comply with the form or pattern jury instructions in your jurisdiction.

In-Class Exercise. The professor will select several memoranda for presentation and discussion in class.

---

[15] McCORMICK ON EVIDENCE § 343, note 10 (6th ed. 2006).

PART TWO

RELEVANCE

Chapter 5

AN INTRODUCTION TO RELEVANCE

Chapter Objectives:

- Introduce and explain Rules 401 and 402, the concept of relevance and the standards used for determining whether evidence is relevant at trial
- Analyze and discuss issues pertaining to relevance through case law and hypothetical problems
- Apply the concepts from this chapter in a courtroom application exercise

I.   BACKGROUND AND EXPLANATORY MATERIAL

The Concept of Relevance

Relevance forms the philosophical core of the Federal Rules of Evidence. Simply put, evidence that is related to and helpful in establishing a cause of action, defense, or theory of the case is relevant under the rules. In turn, the Rules provide that relevant evidence is generally admissible at trial, unless evidentiary exceptions, other laws, or constitutional doctrines mandate its exclusion. Rules 401 and 402 codify the foundational relevance concepts of the Federal Rules:

Through Dec. 1, 2011	After Dec. 1, 2011
Rule 401. Definition of "Relevant Evidence" "Relevant evidence" means evidence having any tendency to make the existence of any fact that is of consequence to the determination of the action more probable or less probable than it would be without the evidence.	**Rule 401. Test for Relevant Evidence** Evidence is relevant if: (a) it has any tendency to make a fact more or less probable than it would be without the evidence; and (b) the fact is of consequence in determining the action.

Theoretically, any evidence that can be connected to a case, no matter how attenuated the logical chain, is relevant under Rule 401. All that is required of the advocate is an explanation of how the evidence fits into the overall theory of her case. As the Advisory Committee observed,

> Relevancy is not an inherent characteristic of any item of evidence but exists only as a relation between an item of evidence and a matter properly provable in the case. Does the item of evidence tend to prove the matter sought to be proved? Whether the relationship exists depends upon principles evolved by experience or science, applied logically to the situation at hand.[1]

Technically, Rule 401 erects only the lowest of barriers in defining relevance; evidence is relevant even if it is relatively insignificant, so long as there is a plausible logical connection to the theory of the case.

Through Dec. 1, 2011	After Dec. 1, 2011
Rule 402. Relevant Evidence Generally Admissible; Irrelevant Evidence Inadmissible	**Rule 402. General Admissibility of Relevant Evidence**
All relevant evidence is admissible, except as otherwise provided by the Constitution of the United States, by Act of Congress, by these rules, or by other rules prescribed by the Supreme Court pursuant to statutory authority. Evidence which is not relevant is not admissible.	Relevant evidence is admissible unless any of the following provides otherwise: • the United States Constitution; • a federal statute; • these rules; or • other rules prescribed by the Supreme Court. Irrelevant evidence is not admissible.

Rule 402 states a rule of presumptive admissibility for relevant evidence. The rule also mandates the exclusion of evidence that is not relevant. Given the broad language of Rule 401, in which almost anything logically connected to the case could be considered relevant, attorneys and judges apply practical standards in determining issues of relevance. In practice, the relevance of evidence depends on a number of factors: the cause of action, the procedural posture of the case, the theory of the case, and who bears the burden of persuasion.

Frequently, attorneys and judges evaluate the probative value of evidence when determining its relevance at trial. The term "probative value" describes the *effect* of evidence at trial: its "plus value" to the finder of fact. Evidence has probative value when its introduction has a persuasive impact on the judge or jury. All evidence that has probative value is relevant, but not all relevant evidence has probative value. Strictly speaking, the concepts of relevance and probative value should be separated at trial, however, as Professor Crump points out in the article excerpt below, attorneys and judges often use the terms interchangeably in a trial setting.

---

[1] FED. R. EVID. 401 advisory committee's note (citing James, *Relevancy, Probability and the Law*, 29 CAL. L. REV. 689, 696 n.15 (1941), *in* SELECTED WRITINGS ON EVIDENCE AND TRIAL 610, 615 n.15 (Fryer ed. 1957)).

David Crump, *On the Uses of Irrelevant Evidence*
34 Hous. L. Rev. 1 (1997)

[Rule 401] requires only that the evidence make a legally significant fact "more . . . probable than it would be without the evidence," thus allowing information to be admitted based on the slightest increment in likelihood. This language is a helpful communication to the court of Professor McCormick's aphorism that "[a] brick is not a wall," or as Professor McBaine put it, "It is not to be supposed that every witness can make a home run."

But it is in the words "any tendency," which form the leading phrase in Rule 401's definition, that the liberality of the standard is most apparent. . . . "Any" is a word that connotes the broadest possible universality, including the minute or infinitesimal. The dictionary offers such alternate definitions as "in whatever quantity or number, great or small; some" or "in whatever degree; to some extent; at all." Taken literally, the word "any" thus signifies that the definition includes evidence with the slightest degree of probative value, even that which is infinitesimally small.

This definition of relevancy has a venerable pedigree. It reflects a choice between competing concepts advanced by the two greatest evidence scholars in history. Specifically, the drafters selected the Thayerian view that a lesser standard of "logical" relevance should be required, so that "evidence having only the slightest probative force" is admissible. In so doing, they rejected the Wigmorean preference for a test of "legal" relevance, which would have demanded "more than a minimum of probative value," alternatively stated as a "plus value" over such a minimum.

This description undoubtedly reflects the drafting and explanation of the Rule. It may not, however, perfectly reflect the actual application of the Rule. When two monumental thinkers disagree, it often is impossible to bury either of them. The drafters rejected Wigmore's proposal, but it may be that Wigmore's view has triumphed in the courts. The concept of minimum probative value, or at least of greater-than-insignificant probative value, is a useful way of understanding some judges' actual interpretations of Rule 401.

B. The Impossibility of "Literally Irrelevant" Evidence

Given Rule 401, it takes real ingenuity to come up with an example of evidence that seems truly irrelevant. One of my favorites comes from Dean Newell H. Blakely, who was a great classroom teacher. Imagine that the defendant is on trial in Chicago for theft. The indictment charges that he stole a television from the owner's home. The prosecutor offers testimony of an eyewitness, along with other evidence, including fingerprints, that is "of consequence" to the elements of the crime. This evidence sounds relevant, and under the Federal Rules it undoubtedly is.

But after the prosecution rests, the defense lawyer - with great fanfare, let us suppose - calls a witness to offer testimony that it was raining in Utah on the day in question. He then proposes, just as importantly, to call another witness who will read all of the names in the Los Angeles telephone book for the edification of the jury. Isn't this evidence "irrelevant"?

The paradoxical answer is, not by the definition in the Federal Rules. One can construct chains of experiential and logical propositions - long chains, admittedly - that connect each of these two items of evidence to the issues in the case. Rainfall in Utah has at least some statistical correlation to weather in Chicago, the site of the alleged crime. We can prove this proposition, if it is doubted, by producing an expert who will testify that precipitation in the Rockies correlates with weather systems elsewhere so that, ever so slightly, it is more probable that the weather was bad in Chicago given this fact than if we did not know it. And this inference, in turn, affects the credibility of eyewitness testimony identifying the defendant, thereby influencing the probability of existence of a fact that is of consequence. As for the names in the Los Angeles telephone book, they include several that are identical to the defendant's. To some degree - admittedly infinitesimally, but still to some degree - this dubious inference advances the proposition that the defendant is misidentified.

Professor McCormick told us that "[a] brick is not a wall." The Federal Rules stand for the analogous proposition that a single atom within a brick is not a wall either, but if the test is "any" substance no matter how small, then the atom qualifies just as the brick does. A structure of bricks can make a wall, and by the same token, so can a conglomeration of atoms. The Federal Rules, if taken literally, say that if the wall is what is at issue, the proponent need not offer a chunk as big as a brick. An atom - in fact, "any" atom that would, or could, or even might combine with others to build the wall - is admissible. In fact, the complete picture is even more universally inclusive than the rainfall-in-Utah example suggests. The definition of relevant evidence, I submit, is perfectly indiscriminate. It literally admits any arguable factual proposition in any case. First, at some statistical level, observed instances of any given fact will show some degree of positive or negative correlation with any other fact. Second, in a limited universe, exhaustion of all facts distinct from the fact at issue may be "relevant.". . .

C. The Rule 402 Exclusion of Evidence that Is "Not Relevant": An Elusive Nondefinition

At least three different concepts can be invoked to avoid the catastrophe that would result from admittance of rainfall-in-Utah evidence. . . . The first (although less desirable) solution is to declare that the evidence actually is not relevant, regardless of the implications of Rule 401. In this regard, the courts often interpret the definition of relevance as though it included a threshold requirement of more-than-minimal significance, a requirement at variance with the precise terms of the Rule. Occasionally, the courts are explicit in recognizing this interpretation as a judicial gloss upon the Rule, construing it to imply the exclusion of evidence that is "remote" or "speculative." More often, judges characterize the information as "not relevant" without focusing on the Rule, a characterization that probably is based on the same inferences as those that explicitly import a requirement of threshold significance. Either way, this methodology is an inferior solution, I submit, because

Rule 401 does not contain a threshold, and because the implication of a threshold by construction does not provide a test by which we can measure remoteness or speculativeness to determine when the threshold is not met.

The pragmatic solution of equating remoteness with irrelevance does obtain some arguable support from Rule 402, which contains the following elliptical sentence: "Evidence which is not relevant is not admissible." This provision implies that, notwithstanding the effect of Rule 401, there must be some kinds of evidentiary inferences that are so weak that they are "not relevant," otherwise Rule 402 would not make sense. The exclusionary directive in Rule 402 is cryptic, however, because the concept of irrelevance based on forensic weakness collides with both the text of Rule 401 and the drafters' intent. By rejecting Wigmore's view and embracing Thayer, the drafters apparently rejected any concept of a threshold or a test based on logical strength or remoteness alone. Furthermore, through their use of the "any tendency" formulation, the drafters embodied in the Rules a textual standard by which the slightest inference suffices. As we have seen, remoteness alone cannot make an item of evidence irrelevant if the definition in Rule 401 is applied according to its terms. Therefore, although Rule 402 excludes irrelevant evidence, its logical effect is to exclude nothing on grounds of forensic weakness, because Rule 401 defines relevance so that no inference is irrelevant merely because it is weak.

Perhaps this explication seems too literal; perhaps the tension between Rules 401 and 402, described here, seems too ethereal to be a real concern. One is tempted to conclude that trial judges have the capacity to recognize irrelevancy, in spite of language in the Rules that might confuse the issue. The trouble, however, is that the internal contradiction in the Rules does affect real-world arguments about circumstantial evidence, if only because lawyers and judges have firmly internalized the permissive standard of Rule 401. Against that standard, it is difficult to characterize marginal items of evidence as irrelevant even when they are as remote as rainfall-in-Utah evidence, because the standard eliminates remoteness as a barrier.

In other words, the text of the Rules does matter. The proponent of a piece of far-fetched evidence need only remind the judge of the terms of Rule 401 and then articulate a chain of reasoning tying his testimony to the case. The proponent can support the argument by emphasizing the policy favoring circumstantial inferences, by relying on the drafters' intent to leave the evaluation of such inferences to jurors who use their own experiences, and by pointing out that the evidence is not required to be the best possible in order to qualify for admissibility. In summary, although Rule 402 calls for the exclusion of evidence that is "not relevant," Rule 401 destroys the prospect of any pragmatic understanding of this term.

Regardless of whether judges apply a purist approach to Rule 401 by using only logic to determine relevance or a pragmatic approach that incorporates probative value, advocates must be prepared to persuasively argue for or against the admission of evidence on grounds of relevance. The tools for doing that are the subject of the following subsection.

Relevance in a Trial Setting

Ultimately, relevance is all about context. In an adversarial trial system, the advocate strives to persuade the fact-finder by presenting the strongest possible case, using the best available evidence in the light of the law and the facts. An effective advocate cannot afford to weaken her case through the introduction of evidence that is irrelevant, marginally relevant or lacking in probative value.

The process of case analysis is critical to determining the relevance of evidence at trial. Case analysis includes the following elements: factual investigation, discovery, legal analysis, witness preparation, and the development of case theories and themes. The methods used in achieving each of the elements of case analysis vary with the type of case, the personality of the advocate, the resources (including support staff, investigators and other attorneys) available, and what is at stake in the trial. An attorney who is prosecuting traffic court cases may have no more time available for case analysis than it takes to open a file and read an arrest report. Conversely, a team of advocates involved in "bet the company" litigation on behalf of a major corporation may spend a considerable amount of time in case analysis, constantly refining their approach to a case through years of discovery and motions practice.

All case analysis has a core function: to bring order out of chaos. The advocate must sift through disparate facts — sometimes, mountains of them — to determine which ones will best persuade a fact-finder. In accomplishing this task, the advocate uses the law, including jury instructions, as a framework for the case. Every cause of action, counterclaim, affirmative defense or criminal charge contains legal elements that the party with the burden of persuasion must prove in order to prevail. Once the framework is established, the advocate can decide which facts, witnesses, exhibits and other forms of evidence are useful in completing the structure of the case. Evidence that fits on the framework is relevant; evidence that does not fit is most likely not relevant and can be discarded or set aside.

The advocate must also examine facts and evidence from the opponent's point of view. In the memorable words of a military training axiom, the enemy gets a vote. In other words, the advocate who conducts a one-sided case analysis without accounting for weaknesses or anticipating defenses and counterattacks cannot hope to be successful at trial.

After conducting a thorough case analysis, the advocate knows what is and is not relevant in a case. This knowledge assists the advocate to do the following: (1) present a persuasive case unencumbered by evidence that is irrelevant, marginally relevant, or lacking in probative value; (2) object when an opponent attempts to introduce irrelevant evidence at trial; and (3) respond to relevance objections made by an opponent.

One of the products of case analysis is the theory of the case. This is a partisan statement that combines the relevant law with the specific facts of the case. A useful way to conceptualize the theory of the case is a statement beginning with the phrase, "We win because. . . . " For example, in a simple criminal battery case arising from a bar fight, the prosecution's theory of the case might be, "We win because the defendant intentionally struck the victim's torso with his hand in order to punish the victim for being a Green Bay Packers fan." In the same case, the defense theory might be, "We win because the defendant was acting in self defense after the alleged victim attempted to hit him with a closed fist during an argument about the merits of domestic v. imported beer."

The theory of the case helps crystallize responses to relevance objections. In other words, if an opponent objects to the relevance of evidence, the proponent of the evidence can respond by explaining how the evidence ties in to the theory of the case.

To illustrate, return to the example of the simple battery case above. Assume that the state criminal code defines battery as "intentionally or knowingly without legal justification and by any means (1) causing bodily harm to an individual or (2) making physical contact of an insulting or provoking nature with an individual." Assume further that the alleged battery took place at a sports bar during football season. The prosecution is questioning an eyewitness:

Q.   *What was the defendant wearing?*

A.   *A Chicago Bears jersey.*

Q.   *What was the victim wearing?*

            Defense counsel: Objection, your honor. This is irrelevant.

            Prosecution response: Your honor, the evidence is relevant because we intend to show that the defendant intentionally struck the victim and was motivated to do so because the victim was a Green Bay Packers fan. This would go directly to the mens rea for this offense."

            Judge: Objection overruled.

In this example, the prosecutor knows his theory of the case and is able to explain why the evidence is relevant.

To summarize, case analysis helps the advocate determine the relevance of available evidence at trial. The development of a case theory — a necessary product of case analysis — is essential to effectively respond to relevance objections.

II.   CASES, QUESTIONS AND PROBLEMS

BLINZLER v. MARRIOTT INT'L, INC.
United States Court of Appeals, First Circuit
81 F.3d 1148 (1st Cir. 1996)

[In this diversity action in the United States District Court for the District of Rhode Island, the plaintiff sued the defendant for the wrongful death of her husband. Plaintiff and her husband were staying at defendant's hotel in Somerset, New Jersey. Plaintiff's husband suffered a heart attack. Plaintiff called the hotel PBX (phone system) operator to request an ambulance. Although the operator promised to call immediately, she delayed calling by approximately 14 minutes, despite the fact that plaintiff called two more times to ensure that help was on the way. It took an ambulance 13 minutes to reach the hotel. Emergency personnel were able to revive plaintiff's husband and restore normal heartbeat, but he died three days later because of oxygen deprivation suffered during the incident. An expert witness testified that had emergency personnel arrived ten minutes earlier, he would have been able to recover.]

The defendant argues that it is entitled to a new trial because the district court erred in certain evidentiary rulings. Its chief complaint concerns the admission of evidence relating to the destruction of the so-called Xeta report (a printout that catalogues all outgoing calls from the hotel's PBX operator) for November 13, 1992. The defendant destroyed this telephone log approximately thirty days after the incident. Had the report been preserved, it would have pinpointed the very moment that the operator first placed the call for emergency assistance.

During the trial, the plaintiff sought to show that the defendant had destroyed this evidence. The defendant objected, contending that it discarded the Xeta report in the ordinary course of business, pursuant to established practice, and not as part of an effort to inter unfavorable evidence. The district court overruled the objection and permitted the plaintiff to introduce evidence at trial of the existence and subsequent destruction of the Xeta report, leaving the defendant's explanation to the jury. We review the district court's rulings admitting or excluding evidence for abuse of discretion. We see none in this instance.

When a document relevant to an issue in a case is destroyed, the trier of fact sometimes may infer that the party who obliterated it did so out of a realization that the contents were unfavorable. See Nation-Wide Check Corp. v. Forest Hills Distributors, Inc., 692 F.2d 214, 217 (1st Cir. 1982); see also 2 Wigmore on Evidence § 285, at 192 (James H. Chadbourn rev. ed. 1979). Before such an inference may be drawn, there must be a sufficient foundational showing that the party who destroyed the document had notice both of the potential claim and of the document's potential relevance. Even then, the adverse inference is permissive, not mandatory. If, for example, the factfinder believes that the documents were destroyed accidentally or for an innocent reason, then the factfinder is free to reject the inference.

In this case, the defendant contends that there was no direct evidence to show that it discarded the Xeta report for any ulterior reason. This is true as far as it goes — but it does not go very far. The proponent of a "missing document" inference need not offer direct evidence of a coverup to set the stage for the adverse inference. Circumstantial evidence will suffice.

We do not believe that the district court abused its considerable discretion in deciding that the totality of the circumstances here rendered such an inference plausible. A reasonable factfinder could easily conclude that Marriott was on notice all along that the Xeta report for November 13, 1992 was relevant to likely litigation. Although no suit had yet been begun when the defendant destroyed the document, it knew of both James Blinzler's death and the plaintiff's persistent attempts — including at least one attempt after Blinzler died — to discover when the call for emergency aid had been placed. This knowledge gave the defendant ample reason to preserve the report in anticipation of a legal action. When the evidence indicates that a party is aware of circumstances that are likely to give rise to future litigation and yet destroys potentially relevant records without particularized inquiry, a factfinder may reasonably infer that the party probably did so because the records would harm its case. In the circumstances at bar, the trial court acted within its discretion in admitting the Xeta report.

The defendant also chastises the court for admitting evidence of another missing record. The security officer's log for November 13, 1992 could not be located, and the judge permitted evidence of that fact to go to the jury. Once again, the ruling cannot be faulted. The defendant had no good explanation for the missing log, and the jury was entitled to infer that the defendant destroyed it in bad faith.

To cinch matters, these two pieces of evidence had a synergistic effect. We think it would be proper for a reasonable factfinder to conclude that the unavailability of two important documents, both of which bore upon the timing of the call for emergency assistance, was something more than a coincidence. The veteran district judge, after hearing all the evidence limning these mysterious disappearances, put it bluntly in the course of ruling on post-trial motions:

> I will tell you now that the Xeta Report raises a compelling inference in my mind that personnel at the Marriott Hotel did destroy that record willfully, along with the security officer's daily log of that date. The inference is compelling that the Marriott Hotel was hiding the delay of the telephone operator in making this telephone call.

This is a harsh assessment — but it is based on a firsthand appraisal of the testimony and it is one that a rational jury easily could draw on the record.

KELLY v. BOEING PETROLEUM SERVICES, INC.
United States Court of Appeals, Fifth Circuit
61 F.3d 350 (5th Cir. 1995)

[Kelly worked for BPS as a maintenance manager at St. James, Louisiana. He had back and neck problems resulting from injuries he suffered in the Marine Corps several years earlier. He and his immediate supervisor, Lemoine, had a toxic relationship. Over the years, Kelly made several requests for accommodations to BPS, none of which were granted. In some of those requests, he also referenced Lemoine's management style at work. In 1992, BPS transferred Kelly to New Orleans to put distance between him and Lemoine. Among other things, Kelly sued BPS for intentional handicap discrimination, alleging that this was a motivating factor in BPS's employment decisions regarding Kelly. At trial, he attempted to introduce evidence of Lemoine's allegedly discriminatory remarks to and about other BPS employees, but the district court refused to permit the evidence.]

II

ANALYSIS

A. Evidentiary Rulings

1. Standard of Review

We review the evidentiary rulings of the district court under the deferential abuse-of-discretion standard. When, as here, the district court has conducted, on the record, a carefully detailed analysis of the evidentiary issues and the court's own ruling, appellate courts are chary about finding an abuse of discretion. . . .

2. The Evidence Excluded

Kelly proposed to adduce testimony concerning Lemoine's insensitive actions and unsympathetic attitudes towards other employees who were members of several disadvantaged minority groups, including persons with medical, health and handicap problems, and Lemoine's "Bunker-esque" remarks, jokes and disparaging statements about these persons and groups. The district court, in response to BPS's pre-trial Motion in Limine, ruled inadmissible testimony regarding Lemoine's acts and statements that implicated matters other than handicap or disability discrimination. The court did so based on its findings that:

> (1) such evidence of other acts of discrimination not directed at plaintiff and unrelated to the type of discrimination at issue (i.e., disability discrimination) is irrelevant; [findings (2) and (3) are deleted here.]

In response to that part of Kelly's reply to the Motion in Limine in which he identified several individuals who would purportedly testify about Lemoine's acts and comments indicative of handicap discrimination or bias, however, the court agreed to "hear such witness' [sic] testimony in camera prior to their taking the witness stand to determine what portion, if any, of their testimony, this Court will permit at trial." The court thus denied BPS's Motion in Limine to the extent it sought to exclude testimony regarding other instances in which Lemoine's acts or utterances would directly demonstrate handicap or disability discrimination on his part.

The evidence excluded following the in camera hearing comprised testimony that Lemoine (1) disparaged one employee because he wore a hearing aid; (2) treated another employee in a "less friendly" and more businesslike manner when he returned to work following heart surgery; (3) treated another insensitively regarding her health concerns; and (4) was generally "insensitive and unsympathetic to the medical needs" of BPS employees.

Kelly advocated the admissibility of testimony regarding Lemoine's handicap-related discriminatory remarks towards other BPS employees as circumstantial evidence of intentional discrimination, but the court — after conducting its in camera review — determined that this testimony, like that excluded in limine, was irrelevant to the particular claims proffered by Kelly and that any probative value would be outweighed by its potential for unfair prejudice, confusion and delay. In addition, the court expressed the opinion that to allow such testimony would open the door to a series of separate "mini-trials" on each anecdotal incident, implying that such would further delay the proceedings and confuse the jury.

Kelly nevertheless insists on appeal that in excluding such testimony the district court abused its discretion by keeping from the jury evidence of Lemoine's "mind-set and biases towards those in his employ who were handicapped or infirm." As Kelly makes a facially plausible case both for the relevance of the testimony proffered in connection with his discrimination claim and for the probative value of that evidence not being outweighed by unfair prejudice, we proceed to scrutinize closely the evidence proffered in camera and the district court's alternative reasons for excluding such evidence.

3. Relevance

Kelly does not dispute that, to prevail on his discrimination claim under the Act, he had to show that BPS intentionally discriminated against him. In support of the district court's exclusion of the subject testimony, BPS argues that Kelly's proffered proof of Lemoine's alleged conduct regarding other employees is not relevant because it does not sufficiently resemble the treatment of which Kelly complained: job transfer and denial of pay raise resulting from handicap discrimination.

We have previously observed that "the standard for relevance is a liberal one." "Relevant evidence means evidence having any tendency to make the existence of any fact that is of consequence to the determination of the action more probable or less probable than it would be without the evidence." [FRE 401.]

Any comments that Lemoine might have directed at Kelly regarding his particular disability would be clearly relevant and thus admissible, for that would tend to show discriminatory animus. Less direct evidence of discriminatory intent — testimony of anecdotal instances of Lemoine's conduct towards other BPS employees-is a different matter and one that we must consider. We therefore turn to an examination of the testimony excluded in the court's ruling on the Motion in Limine and the testimony excluded after the court's in camera examination to decide whether the court abused its discretion in determining relevance.

a. Evidence of Acts Other Than Handicap or Disability

Discrimination

The court in its ruling on BPS's Motion in Limine prohibited Kelly from presenting testimony about Lemoine's alleged discriminatory or bigoted acts or statements regarding race, sex and other categories besides handicap or disability. We agree with other circuits that have cautioned that an appellate court should carefully examine blanket pre-trial evidentiary rulings. In this instance, our thorough consideration of the district court's pre-trial evidentiary ruling leads us to the conclusion that it was correct.

We do not believe that testimony about Lemoine's random acts and remarks concerning matters unrelated to handicaps or disabilities has any tendency to prove that Lemoine discriminated against Kelly on the basis of his handicap. In *Rauh v. Coyne*, the district court excluded evidence of racial animus in a case alleging discrimination based on sex and marital status because the court found that there existed only a "weak correlation" between sex and race discrimination. Similarly, we find a tenuous relationship here between discrimination that could be reflected in Lemoine's derogatory remarks about race, sex, and national origin and discrimination based on handicap, which is the focus of Kelly's complaint.

We therefore agree with the district court that Lemoine's acts of unrelated discrimination are irrelevant, particularly given that Lemoine was not one of the BPS executives who made or participated in the ultimate determinations (1) to transfer Kelly to the New Orleans site and deny him a designated parking space there, (2) to withhold Kelly's 1992 merit raise, and (3) to refuse to reduce the number and frequency of Kelly's inspections at the St. James site.

b. Evidence of Handicap or Disability Discrimination

When a plaintiff must prove intentional discrimination, a district court can abuse its discretion by limiting a plaintiff's ability "to show the 'atmosphere' in which the plaintiff[] 'operated.' " In seeking to demonstrate that the district court here thus abused its discretion, Kelly turns for support to a body of jurisprudence typified by the Eighth Circuit's opinion in *Estes v. Dick Smith Ford, Inc.* [856 F. 2d 1097 (8th Cir. 1988).

The Estes court held that a trial court abused its discretion by excluding evidence that tended to show a climate of race and age bias in a suit alleging discrimination on those grounds. Specifically, the Estes trial court had refused to admit evidence that the employer (1) excluded blacks from its work force, (2) fired two other employees because of their ages, (3) offered free rides to white customers, but not to black customers, and (4) referred pejoratively to blacks. The Eighth Circuit found, inter alia, that evidence of the employer's prior acts of race discrimination against customers was relevant to allegations of race discrimination against one employee, as the same persons were responsible for the same types of discrimination. The Estes court noted:

> It defies common sense to say, as [the employer] implies, that evidence of an employer's discriminatory treatment of black customers might not have some bearing on the question of the same employer's motive in discharging a black employee.

The Estes court also found that the district court abused its discretion in excluding evidence that one of the employees who participated in the decision to fire the plaintiff told racist jokes. Although the court noted that isolated racist comments do not themselves constitute a violation of Title VII, it reasoned that such evidence is probative whether an employee was discharged because of discriminatory animus.

[The Court also discussed at length another Eighth Circuit case, *Hawkins v. Hennepin Technical Center*, 900 F.2d 153 (8th Cir.), cert. denied, 498 U.S. 854 (1990) (sexual harassment), and a Third Circuit case, *Glass v. Philadelphia Electric Co.*, 34

F.3d 188 (3d Cir. 1994) (racial discrimination).]

Kelly urges that the logic of *Estes* and *Hawkins* applies here because Lemoine's allegedly discriminatory acts regarding the disabilities of other BPS employees — for example, his making fun of an employee's use of a hearing aid and his jokes about the disabled — could be probative of the question whether Lemoine had an invidious, discriminatory motive in recommending that Kelly, a handicapped employee, be transferred to the New Orleans site. Both *Este* s and *Hawkins* can be distinguished from the instant case, however, because in both of those cases the trial courts had excluded the evidence in question before the trials commenced, making blanket exclusions in response to motions in limine. . . .

In contrast, the evidentiary rulings to which Kelly most vociferously objects on appeal were made individually during the trial, and not under a blanket exclusion. The district court's careful, subjective consideration of the relevance of each proffered witness' testimony is a factor that we find significant in our analysis. Despite the distinguishing features of the *Estes*, *Hawkins*, and *Glass* cases, however, we too must examine the specific testimony proffered by Kelly to determine whether the trial court abused its discretion in finding the excluded evidence irrelevant to Kelly's claims.

In ruling on the admissibility of testimony by those remaining Kelly witnesses who purportedly would speak to Lemoine's acts or remarks implicating handicap or disability, the court conducted an in camera examination during the course of the trial. Our close reading of the transcript of the court's questioning of some of these witnesses and of Kelly's counsel, out of the hearing of the jury, convinces us that the court's ruling cannot be tarred with the brush of abuse of discretion. When the court analyzed the true nature of the proffered testimony, relevance essentially evaporated. In fact, the most telling revelation of the in camera proceeding may well have been the testimony of one of Kelly's proposed witnesses expressing his opinion that the reason Kelly and Lemoine "couldn't get along" was that each of them was a "strong manager" and simply had a "personality conflict." The proffered testimony reflected in the in camera transcript revealed, at most, that Lemoine engaged in typical, blue-collar (as distinguished from executive suite) workplace kidding, well short of cruel disparagement or mockery. For example, as characterized by counsel for BPS at oral argument to this court, Lemoine's remarks about an employee's use of a hearing aid were made in the same vein as the self-deprecating remarks that the wearer of the hearing aid himself made on occasion.

In sum, we are satisfied that the court's relevance rulings, both in limine and in camera, while admittedly close, did not rise to the level of abuse of discretion.

DISCUSSION QUESTIONS

1. Consider Crump's rainfall-in-Utah example in the article excerpt above. Does he make the case that the evidence is actually relevant under FRE 401? Why or why not?

2. What role should probative value play in determining the relevance of evidence at trial? If judges consistently require a showing of probative value in order to find

relevance, has the drafters' intent for defining relevance in Rule 401 been undermined?

3. In reading the *Blintzler* and *Kelly* cases above, what have you learned about the abuse of discretion standard of review? Suppose each trial judge had ruled opposite to their actual rulings in these cases. Do you think the appellate courts would still have affirmed their rulings? Why or why not?

4. Examine the *Kelly* case in light of Crump's article on irrelevant evidence. Setting aside the holding of the appellate court in this case, did the trial judge correctly decide the excluded evidence was not relevant? Be prepared to justify your answer.

PROBLEMS

Problem 5-1. Captain Carl Commando is the leader of an elite counterterrorism unit. On September 30, he received orders to deploy with his unit on October 5 to Central Asia to find and execute the leader of a notorious terrorist organization. On October 1, Commando informed his superior officers that he would not deploy with his unit because he no longer believed in extrajudicial killings. The unit deployed on October 5 without him. The military decided to court-martial Commando for failing to obey a lawful order under Article 92 of the Calamity Code of Military Justice. Article 92 contains the following elements: (1) that a member of the armed forces issued a certain lawful order; (2) that the accused had knowledge of the order; (3) that the accused had a duty to obey the order; and (4) that the accused failed to obey the order. Assume that all of these elements were met in Commando's case. During Commando's court-martial, the prosecution was permitted to introduce evidence that Commando's college fraternity — of which he was the alumni president — was hosting a reunion on October 7, and that Commando planned to attend the reunion and give a speech at the dinner. The prosecution was also permitted to introduce evidence that Commando e-mailed the fraternity listserv on October 1, telling them, "Come hell or high water, I'll be there on October 7." The defense objected that both items of evidence were irrelevant and inadmissible. During Commando's case in chief, he attempted to introduce evidence of his beliefs concerning extrajudicial killings, but the military judge excluded the evidence, ruling that it was irrelevant and inadmissible. Commando made a proper offer of proof to preserve the issue for appeal. Commando was convicted at trial, and his case is now pending before the Calamity Court of Military Appeals. On appeal, Commando argues that it was an abuse of discretion for the judge to admit the prosecution's evidence about the fraternity reunion and the e-mail, and a further abuse of discretion to exclude the evidence about his feelings regarding extrajudicial killings. How should the court rule on the prosecution's evidence? On Commando's excluded evidence?

Problem 5-2. On July 5, Pat Plaintiff suffered serious injuries in a one-car accident that occurred when her Foreign Motors Funcar abruptly accelerated and hit a telephone pole. The accident occurred at noon on a hot day. Plaintiff, a middle-aged librarian with a perfect driving record, was driving 5 mph under the speed limit and paying careful attention to road conditions. Plaintiff had complied with all maintenance requirements in the owner's manual and had kept complete maintenance records. Plaintiff sued Foreign Motors, alleging that the Funcar was defective and the Foreign Motors knew it. While investigating the case, her attorney discovered two other instances involving abrupt acceleration by Funcars that resulted in accidents and injuries. Both incidents had been reported to Foreign Motors through company maintenance channels. In the first incident, a newly-licensed teenage driver, while speeding through a concrete barrier and singing aloud to a popular radio song, experienced abrupt acceleration and hit a concrete barrier. The accident occurred at five pm on a hot day. No maintenance records were available for the vehicle, which the teenager's parents had purchased from the classified ads as a birthday gift for their child. In the second incident, a young married couple was having an argument about family finances when their Funcar abruptly accelerated and hit a pickup truck that was lawfully stopped at an intersection. The couple had never complied with any maintenance requirements and had kept no records since purchasing the car new two years earlier. The accident occurred at 10 am on a mild day. At trial, plaintiff's attorney attempts to offer evidence of the other two instances of abrupt acceleration to prove that the Funcar was defective and that Foreign Motors had notice of the defect. The defense objects on relevance grounds. What arguments should the plaintiff make in favor of the evidence? What arguments should the defense make against the evidence? How should the judge rule, and why?

Relevance: Quick Hits

- The standard for relevance under Rule 401 is low: any evidence that can logically be used to help prove a fact of consequence at trial is relevant under the Rule.

- In practice, many judges and attorneys apply the "plus value" test to relevance: evidence must not only be logically relevant to the case, but must have probative value to the fact-finder.

- Relevant evidence is admissible under Rule 402 unless other rules declare it to be inadmissible.

Chapter References

CHRISTOPHER B. MUELLER & LAIRD C. KIRKPATRICK, EVIDENCE §§ 4.2–4.8 (4th ed. 2009).

GLEN WEISSENBERGER & JAMES J. DUANE, FEDERAL RULES OF EVIDENCE: RULES, LEGISLATIVE HISTORY, COMMENTARY AND AUTHORITY §§ 401–02 (6th ed. 2009).

JACK B. WEINSTEIN & MARGARET A. BERGER, WEINSTEIN'S FEDERAL EVIDENCE §§ 401–02 (Joseph M. McLaughlin ed., Matthew Bender 2d ed. 1997).

KENNETH S. BROUN, MCCORMICK ON EVIDENCE §§ 184–85 (6th ed. 2006).

STEVEN J. GOODE & OLIN GUY WELLBORN III, COURTROOM HANDBOOK ON FEDERAL EVIDENCE Ch. 5 (West 2010).

III. APPLICATION EXERCISE

Making and Responding to Relevance Objections at Trial

Under Rule 401, the bar for admitting relevant evidence at trial is low. This does not mean that counsel should stand idly by while their opponents introduce evidence of marginal utility and questionable probative value. Objecting to an opponent's questions on grounds of relevance can help focus the proceedings and force opposing counsel to how the evidence fits its theory of the case. Responding to relevance objections should be viewed as an opportunity to explain to the judge, in the presence of the fact-finder, why the evidence matters and should be admitted at trial.

Case analysis and advance preparation can help counsel prepare to make and respond to relevance objections at trial. Relevance objections can be made either on direct or cross examination.

The Exercise

Objective: To demonstrate proficiency in making and responding to relevance objections in a trial setting.

Factual Scenario: Paula Plaintiff is suing Dan Defendant for injuries she suffered when Dan's car T-boned her car at the intersection of Garth and Brooks Avenues in Countryville, Calamity, a small town of about 3,500 people. The intersection was a four-way stop, with functional and visible stop signs at each corner. The incident occurred at 11:30 pm on Friday the 13th. There was a full moon, with no cloud cover and excellent visibility. There were no witnesses to the accident other than Paula and Dan. Each claims to have had the right of way at the time of the collision. Neither of them had been drinking, and both cars were in good operating condition and had been properly maintained:

Advance Preparation: Prepare a direct and cross examination of Dan Defendant on the above factual scenario. Be prepared to make appropriate objections, responses and offers of proof on the issue of relevance.

When preparing the direct examination of Dan, include the following additional facts:

Dan grew up in a poor working-class family in Newark, New Jersey. He is a third-year law student at Calamity State University School of Law and is ranked number 5 in his class. He earned his Eagle Scout Award at the age of 13. He graduated second in his high school class and third in his college class at Rutgers-Camden. His father died of a heart attack three years ago during a Philadelphia Eagles-New York Giants Game. Dan is an Eagles fan, but the rest of his family likes the Giants. Although he has always been a Democrat, Dan did not vote for John Kerry in the 2004 Presidential Election after hearing that John Kerry tried to order a Philly cheese steak sandwich with Swiss cheese. During college, Dan drove a bread delivery truck in the cities of Philadelphia, PA and Camden, NJ.

Include the following additional facts in your cross-examination of Dan:

At the age of seven, Dan tortured a gerbil to death during recess at school and was suspended for three weeks. Dan has averaged one speeding ticket every six months since he got his driver's license. He likes the Eagles because he and his father had a bad relationship, and he knew it would make his father angry. Dan regularly drinks Pabst Blue Ribbon beer because he is cheap. Three weeks ago, Dan bought a new smartphone. Dan plans to be a personal injury lawyer when he graduates and has already designed a billboard and telephone book advertisement.

In-Class Exercise: Four students will participate in this exercise: Plaintiff's attorney, Defendant, Defendant's attorney, and a judge. The Defendant's attorney will conduct a direct examination of Defendant, during which Plaintiff's attorney will make objections and the judge will rule. Plaintiff's attorney will then cross-examine Defendant as Defendant's attorney objects.

Chapter 6

RULE 403: EXCLUSION OF RELEVANT EVIDENCE DETRIMENTAL TO INTEGRITY OF FACT-FINDING PROCESS

> **Chapter Objectives:**
>
> - Introduce and explain Rule 403 and the concept of excluding relevant evidence that is unfairly prejudicial or detrimental to the integrity of the fact-finding process
> - Analyze and discuss issues pertaining to Rule 403 balancing through case law and hypothetical problems
> - Apply the concepts from this chapter in a courtroom application exercise

I. BACKGROUND AND EXPLANATORY MATERIAL

Rule 403 is the third part of the relevance triad at the heart of the Federal Rules. Rule 401 broadly defines relevance, and Rule 402 provides for the presumptive admissibility of relevant evidence. Rule 403 recognizes that even relevant evidence with high probative value can sometimes disrupt the integrity of the fact-finding process and should therefore be excluded. Because weighing the impact of evidence in a given trial requires the exercise of considerable judgment and discretion, Rule 403 also serves as a philosophical bridge between the almost unfettered discretion traditionally accorded to common law judges and the constraints imposed on judicial decision-making by a codified system of evidentiary rules.

Through Dec. 1, 2011	After Dec. 1, 2011
Rule 403. Exclusion of Relevant Evidence on Grounds of Prejudice, Confusion, or Waste of Time	**Rule 403. Excluding Relevant Evidence for Prejudice, Confusion, Waste of Time, or Other Reasons**
Although relevant, evidence may be excluded if its probative value is substantially outweighed by the danger of unfair prejudice, confusion of the issues, or misleading the jury, or by considerations of undue delay, waste of time, or needless presentation of cumulative evidence.	The court may exclude relevant evidence if its probative value is substantially outweighed by a danger of one or more of the following: unfair prejudice, confusing the issues, misleading the jury, undue delay, wasting time, or needlessly presenting cumulative evidence.

The Conceptual Underpinnings of Rule 403

Rule 403 is concerned with the integrity and efficiency of the fact-finding process. The rule's primary purpose is to ensure that the jury makes decisions for the right reasons. A secondary purpose is to help maintain judicial efficiency and economy during trial.

With respect to the rule's primary purpose, evidence can be excluded if its probative value is substantially outweighed by the danger of unfair prejudice, confusion of the issues, or misleading the jury. With respect to its secondary purpose, a judge can exclude evidence that might unduly delay the trial, waste time, or result in the needless presentation of cumulative evidence. These concepts are explained below.

Primary Purpose: To Avoid Unfair Prejudice and/or Decisions Made for Improper Reasons

The term "unfair prejudice" is essential in understanding how Rule 403 works. The deliberate choice of the adjective "unfair" suggests that in a trial, it is to be expected that the parties will introduce evidence that is prejudicial to their opponents. This is, in fact, the essence of the adversarial trial process. There is little point in introducing evidence at trial that does not in some way prejudice the opponent's case. On the other hand, unfairly prejudicial evidence undermines the integrity of the trial process and encourages juries to make decisions for the wrong reasons. To borrow a pugilistic metaphor, advocates in an adversarial system should be able to strike hard blows, but not unfair or foul ones.[1]

Attorneys frequently leave out the adjective "unfair" when objecting to evidence under Rule 403. A proper application of the rule, however, begins with the

---

[1] Berger v. United States, 295 U.S. 78, 88 (1935) (referring specifically to a prosecutor's responsibilities during the closing argument of a criminal trial).

knowledge that whereas prejudicial evidence is expected, *unfairly* prejudicial evidence cannot be tolerated.

There are two types of unfair prejudice that are of concern in the courtroom. The first is evidence that encourages the jury to make its decision based on emotions rather than facts. These emotions can include anger, hostility, revulsion, fear, or other similar reactionary thoughts and feelings. Evidentiary triggers for these emotions can include graphic photographs or testimony, such as particularly gruesome photographs of murder victims; testimony that links a defendant with hate groups or organizations on the fringes of society; or testimony about past crimes or offenses that might have been committed by the individual on trial. Under Rule 403, judges have to carefully balance each party's legitimate need to effectively prove its case, with the danger of inflaming the jurors' passions and prejudices to the point where emotion clouds their judgment. The *Old Chief* case that we will read later in this chapter is an example of this type of balancing.

The second type of unfair prejudice is evidence that is introduced for one purpose being used for an improper purpose by the jury. A common example of this is evidence of prior acts of misconduct under Rule 404(b). In the *Huddleston* case that we read in Chapter Two, the defendant was charged with attempting to sell stolen videotapes at a price below the tapes' cost of production. To prove the defendant's knowledge that the tapes were most likely stolen, the prosecution introduced evidence that the defendant had been involved in fencing stolen television sets and appliances in the past. The proper use of this evidence was to show knowledge, but the potential danger of the evidence was that the jury could use it to circumvent the prosecution's burden of proof, concluding that if the defendant had fenced stolen goods in the past, he had probably done so on this occasion as well. Judges must evaluate the potential misuse of evidence for an improper purpose and decide whether the jury is capable of compartmentalizing the evidence if properly instructed.

Similar to the dangers posed by unfairly prejudicial evidence, evidence that would confuse the issues or mislead the jury poses a serious threat to the integrity of the fact-finding process. Although some advocates may actually want to sow confusion in the courtroom or introduce facts that could influence a jury to decide a different issue than the one actually before them, Rule 403 bars such evidence at trial. The result is better verdicts.

Secondary Purpose: Promote Efficiency and Judicial Economy

The secondary purpose of Rule 403 is to promote efficiency and judicial economy. The rule states that evidence may be excluded "by considerations of undue delay, waste of time, or needless presentation of cumulative evidence." Given the broad limits of relevance under Rule 401, even the simplest case could last an eternity if attorneys were permitted such indulgences as reading the Los Angeles telephone directory into the record at trial. Rule 403 gives the judge a mechanism for excluding evidence when its probative value is marginal and its introduction would interfere with the values of efficiency and judicial economy. An advocate who understands the concepts of probative value and efficiency can effectively use Rule

403 objections to help streamline the trial process.

Rule 403 in Application

Like Rule 402, Rule 403 is a rule of presumptive admissibility for relevant evidence. If the evidence is relevant, the proponent is entitled to introduce it in the absence of an objection by the opponent. If the opponent believes the evidence will affect the integrity of the fact-finding process for any of the reasons listed in the rule, the burden of persuasion is on the opponent.

The balancing test of Rule 403 is frequently misunderstood. Some advocates believe that the rule keeps out prejudicial evidence unless the probative value of that evidence greatly outweighs its prejudicial impact. In reality, Rule 403, like Rule 402, is a rule of presumptive admissibility: relevant evidence comes in under Rule 403 unless its negative impact on the integrity of the fact-finding process substantially outweighs its probative value.

Rule 403 applies to nearly all evidentiary decisions made at trial. Even if an item of evidence is relevant and meets the admissibility standards of another rule — for example, a relevant document that is properly authenticated under Rule 902 and satisfies the business records exception to the hearsay rule under Rule 803(6) — it is still subject to exclusion under Rule 403.

The objecting party must make the case as to why the evidence should be excluded. For this reason, Rule 403 objections are often made during pretrial motions *in limine*, where the opponent has the opportunity to explain in detail the unfair prejudice or other detrimental effects at trial posed by the evidence. Of course, opportunities to object on Rule 403 grounds also occur spontaneously at trial, as illustrated by the following two examples.

In the first example, assume that the prosecution in a murder case wants to offer a particularly gruesome autopsy photograph of the victim's body. The defense has not moved *in limine* to exclude the photograph, so the objection must be made during the authentication process and before the photograph is published to the jury.

> *Defense Attorney: Objection, your honor. This photograph's prejudicial effect substantially outweighs its probative value under Rule 403.*
>
> *Judge (to Prosecutor): Your response?*
>
> *Prosecutor: This photograph is relevant to show the brain injuries suffered by the victim in this case.*
>
> *Judge (to both attorneys): Let's have the two of you approach for a sidebar so we can discuss the photograph. Defense counsel, what's the problem with the photograph?*
>
> *Defense Attorney: Your honor, this photograph shows the victim's skull opened up, with the skin peeled back from the face and the brain pan exposed, in a gruesome fashion. It will have a tendency to inflame the passions of the jury because of its shocking nature. Furthermore, the autopsy photograph is much more graphic and revealing than the actual*

crime-scene photographs of the victim. In addition, your honor, there are photographs available that are focused on the brain itself and not the face and skull of the victim. The prosecution could certainly show one of those photographs to show the brain injuries. The only conceivable purpose for introducing this photograph is to make the jury feel disgusted and to become angry with the defendant. For these reasons, the photograph is unfairly prejudicial.

Judge: I'm inclined to agree with you. The objection is sustained.

In the second example, assume that in a child custody case, the defendant mother has called several witnesses to testify that she is a good parent who provides a safe home for her family: her mother, a clergy member, two neighbors, and a school teacher. She now calls her best friend to the stand for the same purpose.

Plaintiff: Objection, your honor. Cumulative under Rule 403.

Defense: Your honor, the evidence is relevant and necessary to prove that the defendant is a good mother. It goes to the heart of our case.

Plaintiff: At this point, your honor, the defense has called five witnesses to say essentially the same thing. Unless this witness has something different to offer, her testimony is cumulative and will waste the court's time.

Judge: Defense counsel, is there any other reason for calling this witness?

Defense: No, your honor.

Judge: Then the objection is sustained. Let's move on.

As illustrated in the examples above, judges must apply considerable discretion in weighing evidentiary decisions under Rule 403. The next section discusses in more detail the discretionary nature of Rule 403.

The Judge's Discretion Under Rule 403

Rule 403 is different from the rest of the Federal Rules of Evidence because it grants judges a considerable degree of discretionary power. Furthermore, the rule uses terms such as "unfair," "prejudice," "confusion," and "misleading" — all of which are ambiguous, value-laden words that defy objective definitions. Finally, the appellate standard of review for decisions made under Rule 403 is whether the judge abused (or in some jurisdictions, clearly abused) her discretion in deciding whether to admit or exclude evidence under the Rule. A facial reading of the rule suggests that a judge could bring her own biases and prejudices into play in making decisions under Rule 403.

Given these factors, the question naturally exists as to whether Rule 403 essentially revives the common law role of the judge. Even if the rule does not revive the common law, its broad grant of power and discretion makes it one of the most important and influential rules in the Federal Rules of Evidence. Consider these issues as you read the following excerpt from an article by Professor Edward J. Imwinkelreid.

Edward J. Imwinkelreid, *The Meaning of Probative Value and Prejudice in Federal Rule of Evidence 403: Can Rule 403 Be Used to Resurrect the Common Law of Evidence?*
41 VAND. L. REV. 879 (1988)

Courts and commentators agree that the concept of probative value allows the trial judge to consider at least three elements in balancing under rule 403. First, a judge may consider the facial vagueness or uncertainty of the proposed testimony. When the weakness of testimony is evident on its face, a judge certainly should be permitted to consider that weakness. Second, a judge may consider the number of intermediate propositions between the item of evidence and the ultimate consequential fact that the item is offered to prove. The larger the number of intermediate inferences the jury must draw, the greater the probability that the jury will commit some inferential error. . . .

The common denominator of these elements is that a judge can evaluate them by considering the evidence on its face. Assume, for example, that a witness testifies, "I had a conversation with Duncan five years ago, and I've got a vague recollection that during the conversation he said that he'd fallen in love with a woman named Willet or Wilson or some name like that." The uncertainty of the testimony, the length of the chain of intermediate inferences, and the remoteness in time are obvious on the face of the testimony. A consensus exists that a judge may consider these elements in assessing probative value under rule 403.

The consensus ends, however, when a trial judge attempts to go beyond the face of the evidence to consider the credibility of the source of the evidence. [Imwinkelreid discusses at length the split of scholarly authority on whether a judge can consider credibility in making 403 decisions and notes that the weight of authority holds that a judge cannot do this.]

III. THE PREJUDICE SIDE OF THE RULE 403 BALANCE: MAY A TRIAL JUDGE EXCLUDE LOGICALLY RELEVANT EVIDENCE TO FURTHER AN EXTRINSIC SOCIAL POLICY?

It is relatively easy to demonstrate that rule 403 does not allow the trial judge to consider the credibility of the source of the item of evidence. The next issue is more troublesome, however. Rule 403 expressly authorizes a judge to exclude evidence on the ground that the admission of the evidence might cause "prejudice." Like "probative value," "prejudice" is ambiguous. The issue presented is whether "prejudice" should be construed as empowering a judge to bar relevant evidence in order to further some extrinsic social policy.

The common-law "legal relevancy" doctrine was the forerunner of Rule 403. Dean Wigmore popularized the doctrine and attempted to rationalize it. The early advocates of the doctrine argued that legal relevancy required that each item of evidence have "plus value" — probative worth exceeding bare logical relevance. Wigmore rejected that argument. He argued that the core concept of legal relevancy was balancing, weighing probative value against certain "auxiliary rules of probative policy." . . .

As previously stated, modern commentators concur that under both the common-law legal relevancy doctrine and rule 403, a judge must balance the probative value of an item of evidence against the impact of the item's admission on certain policies. The pivotal question is what policies may the judge consider under rule 403. There is agreement that a judge may consider judicial administration policies. For example, in the hypothetical involving the evidence of Duncan's earlier assault on Mr. Grimes, all the policies discussed relate to the way in which a trier of fact should decide a case — the trier of fact should concentrate on the central issues, avoid distractions, and ultimately decide the case on a proper basis. The focus, therefore, is on the cognitive behavior of the jury during the trial.

Although commentators concur that rule 403 allows a judge to consider intrinsic judicial administration policies, a major controversy persists over whether a judge also may consider extrinsic social policies. May a judge bar relevant evidence on the ground that the admission of the evidence might deter socially desirable conduct? To illustrate, assume that the police questioned Duncan about Mr. Wilson's killing. Assume further that during the questioning Duncan formed the impression that he was engaged in plea bargaining with the police. Duncan consequently made an incriminating statement; he believed that the statement was a quid pro quo for charge concessions. Could a judge exclude the statement under rule 403 on the theory that the admission of the statement would prejudice the extrinsic policy of encouraging plea bargaining? . . .

[R]ule 403 does not authorize a judge to exclude relevant evidence because he either doubts the credibility of the source of the evidence or wishes to promote an extrinsic social policy. The expression "probative value" in rule 403 empowers a judge to consider the facial definiteness of the evidence, the length of the chain of inferences, and the strength of those inferences. A judge can evaluate all those factors without usurping the jury's power to assess credibility. In the same vein, the term "prejudice" in the rule should be read narrowly. The concept of prejudice permits a judge to safeguard the integrity of the fact-finding process. A judge does so by shielding the jury from technically relevant evidence that threatens to prompt inferential error by the trier of fact. Expanding the notion of prejudice to include damage to extrinsic social policies would distort the concept, because that broad interpretation would deny the jury evidence that it is likely to value correctly and use properly. Depriving the jury of that type of evidence would undermine rather than enhance the accuracy of fact-finding.

The stakes involved in the dispute over the scope of rule 403 are critical. One of the stakes is the future of rule 403. Rule 403 has been called a cornerstone of the Federal Rules. After reviewing the legislative history of the rule, courts have concluded almost uniformly that Congress viewed exclusion of relevant evidence under the rule as an exceptional, extraordinary remedy. Congress intended that judges would invoke this drastic remedy sparingly and infrequently. An expansive reading of rule 403 would violate that intent. If "probative value" is interpreted to include credibility, or if "prejudice" is construed to include injury to an extrinsic social policy, rule 403 will lead to the exclusion of relevant evidence in far more cases than Congress contemplated. The frequent exclusion of evidence under rule 403 would be a misuse of the rule and an affront to the legislative intent underlying the rule.

Furthermore, a broad interpretation of rule 403 would imperil the future of the Federal Rules as a comprehensive evidence code. . . .

Finally, and most importantly, a broad reading of rule 403 would expand undesirably judicial power at the expense of both the jury and the legislature. One of the leading modern commentators on procedure, Professor Stephen Saltzburg, has documented convincingly the dangerous trend toward the unnecessary expansion of the trial judge's authority. A broad interpretation of rule 403 would exacerbate that trend and give the judiciary a potent license with which to justify its authority. When a judge bars probative evidence because of the judge's own doubt about the credibility of the source of the evidence, the judge arrogates the jury's authority. Likewise, when a judge excludes relevant evidence to promote an extrinsic social policy other than the policies inspiring an evidentiary privilege, the judge encroaches on the legislative function of formulating extrinsic policy. Under our democratic philosophy, the legislator is directly accountable to the community, and jurors serve at trials in part because they bring community values to bear on the process of dispute resolution. We may not share Lord Camden's pessimistic view of judicial discretion, but apologists for Jacksonian democracy have forced us to realize that to expand the judge's power at the expense of either the juror or the legislator has profound political implications. These implications, the legislative history of rule 403, and the comprehensive statutory scheme of the Federal Rules all point to the same conclusion: Congress never intended rule 403 to be construed as a panacea for all evidentiary ills. The common law of evidence is dead, and rule 403 cannot be used to resurrect it.

II.   CASES, DISCUSSION QUESTIONS AND PROBLEMS

OLD CHIEF v. UNITED STATES
Supreme Court of the United States
519 U.S. 172 (1997)

In 1993, petitioner, Old Chief, was arrested after a fracas involving at least one gunshot. The ensuing federal charges included not only assault with a dangerous weapon and using a firearm in relation to a crime of violence but violation of 18 U.S.C. § 922(g)(1). This statute makes it unlawful for anyone "who has been convicted in any court of, a crime punishable by imprisonment for a term exceeding one year" to "possess in or affecting commerce, any firearm. . . ." . . .

The earlier crime charged in the indictment against Old Chief was assault causing serious bodily injury. Before trial, he moved for an order requiring the Government [not to mention the name of the prior offense or any details about it], except to state that the Defendant has been convicted of a crime punishable by imprisonment exceeding one (1) year." App. 6. He said that revealing the name and nature of his prior assault conviction would unfairly tax the jury's capacity to hold the Government to its burden of proof beyond a reasonable doubt on current charges of assault, possession, and violence with a firearm, and he offered to [stipulate] "that he has been convicted of a crime punishable by imprisonment exceeding one (1) yea[r]." Id., at 7. He argued that the offer to stipulate to the fact of the prior conviction rendered evidence of the name and nature of the offense inadmissible under Rule 403 of the Federal Rules of Evidence, the danger being that unfair prejudice from that evidence would substantially outweigh its probative value.

[The Assistant U.S. Attorney refused to join the stipulation, arguing that he had the right to prove the case his own way. The District Court and the 9th Circuit affirmed. The Supreme Court granted certiorari.]

We now reverse the judgment of the Ninth Circuit.

[The Court rejected Old Chief's argument that the name of the prior offense was irrelevant under Rule 401, and that the issue of relevance was affected by the availability of alternative forms of proof such as a stipulation.]

If, then, relevant evidence is inadmissible in the presence of other evidence related to it, its exclusion must rest not on the ground that the other evidence has rendered it "irrelevant," but on its character as unfairly prejudicial, cumulative or the like, its relevance notwithstanding.

The principal issue is the scope of a trial judge's discretion under Rule 403 [Court quotes Rule 403]. Old Chief relies on the danger of unfair prejudice.

Such improper grounds certainly include the one that Old Chief points to here: generalizing a defendant's earlier bad act into bad character and taking that as raising the odds that he did the later bad act now charged (or, worse, as calling for preventive conviction even if he should happen to be innocent momentarily). As then-Judge Breyer put it, "Although . . . 'propensity evidence' is relevant, the risk that a jury will convict for crimes other than those charged-or that, uncertain of guilt, it will convict anyway because a bad person deserves punishment-creates a prejudicial effect that outweighs ordinary relevance." United States v. Moccia, 681 F.2d 61, 63 (C.A.1 1982). . . .

As for the analytical method to be used in Rule 403 balancing, two basic possibilities present themselves. An item of evidence might be viewed as an island, with estimates of its own probative value and unfairly prejudicial risk the sole reference points in deciding whether the danger substantially outweighs the value and whether the evidence ought to be excluded. Or the question of admissibility might be seen as inviting further comparisons to take account of the full evidentiary context of the case as the court understands it when the ruling must be made. This second approach would start out like the first but be ready to go further. On objection, the court would decide whether a particular item of evidence raised a danger of unfair prejudice. If it did, the judge would go on to evaluate the degrees of probative value and unfair prejudice not only for the item in question but for any actually available substitutes as well. If an alternative were found to have substantially the same or greater probative value but a lower danger of unfair prejudice, sound judicial discretion would discount the value of the item first offered and exclude it if its discounted probative value were substantially outweighed by unfairly prejudicial risk. As we will explain later on, the judge would have to make these calculations with an appreciation of the offering party's need for evidentiary richness and narrative integrity in presenting a case, and the mere fact that two pieces of evidence might go to the same point would not, of course, necessarily mean that only one of them might come in. It would only mean that a judge applying Rule 403 could reasonably apply some discount to the probative value of an item of evidence when faced with less risky alternative proof going to the same point. Even under this second approach, as we explain below, a defendant's Rule 403 objection offering to concede a point generally cannot prevail over the Government's choice to offer evidence showing guilt and all the circumstances surrounding the offense.

The first understanding of the Rule is open to a very telling objection. That reading would leave the party offering evidence with the option to structure a trial in whatever way would produce the maximum unfair prejudice consistent with relevance. He could choose the available alternative carrying the greatest threat of improper influence, despite the availability of less prejudicial but equally probative evidence. The worst he would have to fear would be a ruling sustaining a Rule 403 objection, and if that occurred, he could simply fall back to offering substitute evidence. This would be a strange rule. It would be very odd for the law of evidence to recognize the danger of unfair prejudice only to confer such a degree of autonomy on the party subject to temptation, and the Rules of Evidence are not so odd.

Rather, a reading of the companions to Rule 403, and of the commentaries that went with them to Congress, makes it clear that what counts as the Rule 403 "probative value" of an item of evidence, as distinct from its Rule 401 "relevance," may be calculated by comparing evidentiary alternatives. [The Court reviews the Advisory Committee Notes to Rules 401, 403 and 404(b).] Thus the notes leave no question that when Rule 403 confers discretion by providing that evidence "may" be excluded, the discretionary judgment may be informed not only by assessing an evidentiary item's twin tendencies, but by placing the result of that assessment alongside similar assessments of evidentiary alternatives. See 1 McCormick 782, and n. 41 (suggesting that Rule 403' s "probative value" signifies the "marginal probative value" of the evidence relative to the other evidence in the case); 22 C. Wright & K. Graham, Federal Practice and Procedure § 5250, pp. 546-547 (1978) ("The probative worth of any particular bit of evidence is obviously affected by the scarcity or abundance of other evidence on the same point").

2. In dealing with the specific problem raised by § 922(g)(1) and its prior-conviction element, there can be no question that evidence of the name or nature of the prior offense generally carries a risk of unfair prejudice to the defendant. That risk will vary from case to case, for the reasons already given, but will be substantial whenever the official record offered by the Government would be arresting enough to lure a juror into a sequence of bad character reasoning. Where a prior conviction was for a gun crime or one similar to other charges in a pending case the risk of unfair prejudice would be especially obvious, and Old Chief sensibly worried that the prejudicial effect of his prior assault conviction, significant enough with respect to the current gun charges alone, would take on added weight from the related assault charge against him.

The District Court was also presented with alternative, relevant, admissible evidence of the prior conviction by Old Chief's offer to stipulate, evidence necessarily subject to the District Court's consideration on the motion to exclude the record offered by the Government. Although Old Chief's formal offer to stipulate was, strictly, to enter a formal agreement with the Government to be given to the jury, even without the Government's acceptance his proposal amounted to an offer to admit that the prior-conviction element was satisfied, and a defendant's admission is, of course, good evidence. See Fed. Rule Evid. 801(d)(2)(A).

[Old Chief's admission would have been relevant and even conclusive on the element of the offense.]

3. There is, however, one more question to be considered before deciding whether Old Chief's offer was to supply evidentiary value at least equivalent to what the Government's own evidence carried. . . . [T]he Government invokes the familiar, standard rule that the prosecution is entitled to prove its case by evidence of its own choice, or, more exactly, that a criminal defendant may not stipulate or admit his way out of the full evidentiary force of the case as the Government chooses to present it. The authority usually cited for this rule is Parr v. United States, 255 F.2d 86 (CA5), cert. denied, 358 U.S. 824, 79 S.Ct. 40, 3 L.Ed.2d 64 (1958), in which the Fifth Circuit explained that the "reason for the rule is to permit a party 'to present to the jury a picture of the events relied upon. To substitute for such a picture a naked admission might have the effect to rob the evidence of much of its fair and legitimate weight.'" 255 F.2d, at 88 (quoting Dunning v. Maine Central R. Co., 91 Me. 87, 39 A. 352, 356 (1897)).

This is unquestionably true as a general matter. The "fair and legitimate weight" of conventional evidence showing individual thoughts and acts amounting to a crime reflects the fact that making a case with testimony and tangible things not only satisfies the formal definition of an offense, but tells a colorful story with descriptive richness. Unlike an abstract premise, whose force depends on going precisely to a particular step in a course of reasoning, a piece of evidence may address any number of separate elements, striking hard just because it shows so much at once; the account of a shooting that establishes capacity and causation may tell just as much about the triggerman's motive and intent. Evidence thus has force beyond any linear scheme of reasoning, and as its pieces come together a narrative gains momentum, with power not only to support conclusions but to sustain the willingness of jurors to draw the inferences, whatever they may be, necessary to reach an honest verdict. This persuasive power of the concrete and particular is often essential to the capacity of jurors to satisfy the obligations that the law places on them. Jury duty is usually unsought and sometimes resisted, and it may be as difficult for one juror suddenly to face the findings that can send another human being to prison, as it is for another to hold out conscientiously for acquittal. When a juror's duty does seem hard, the evidentiary account of what a defendant has thought and done can accomplish what no set of abstract statements ever could, not just to prove a fact but to establish its human significance, and so to implicate the law's moral underpinnings and a juror's obligation to sit in judgment. Thus, the prosecution may fairly seek to place its evidence before the jurors, as much to tell a story of guiltiness as to support an inference of guilt, to convince the jurors that a guilty verdict would be morally reasonable as much as to point to the discrete elements of a defendant's legal fault.

But there is something even more to the prosecution's interest in resisting efforts to replace the evidence of its choice with admissions and stipulations, for beyond the power of conventional evidence to support allegations and give life to the moral underpinnings of law's claims, there lies the need for evidence in all its particularity to satisfy the jurors' expectations about what proper proof should be. Some such demands they bring with them to the courthouse, assuming, for example, that a charge of using a firearm to commit an offense will be proven by introducing a gun in evidence. A prosecutor who fails to produce one, or some good reason for his failure, has something to be concerned about. . . . Expectations may also arise in jurors' minds simply from the experience of a trial itself. The use of witnesses to describe a train of events naturally related can raise the prospect of learning about every ingredient of that natural sequence the same way. If suddenly the prosecution presents some occurrence in the series differently, as by announcing a stipulation or admission, the effect may be like saying, "never mind what's behind the door," and jurors may well wonder what they are being kept from knowing. A party seemingly responsible for cloaking something has reason for apprehension, and the prosecution with its burden of proof may prudently demur at a defense request to interrupt the flow of evidence telling the story in the usual way.

In sum, the accepted rule that the prosecution is entitled to prove its case free from any defendant's option to stipulate the evidence away rests on good sense . . .

This recognition that the prosecution with its burden of persuasion needs evidentiary depth to tell a continuous story has, however, virtually no application when the point at issue is a defendant's legal status, dependent on some judgment rendered wholly independently of the concrete events of later criminal behavior charged against him. . . . The issue of substituting one statement for the other normally arises only when the record of conviction would not be admissible for any purpose beyond proving status, so that excluding it would not deprive the prosecution of evidence with multiple utility; if, indeed, there were a justification for receiving evidence of the nature of prior acts on some issue other than status (i.e., to prove "motive, opportunity, intent, preparation, plan, knowledge, identity, or absence of mistake or accident," Fed. Rule Evid. 404(b)), Rule 404(b) guarantees the opportunity to seek its admission. Nor can it be argued that the events behind the prior conviction are proper nourishment for the jurors' sense of obligation to vindicate the public interest. The issue is not whether concrete details of the prior crime should come to the jurors' attention but whether the name or general character of that crime is to be disclosed. Congress, however, has made it plain that distinctions among generic felonies do not count for this purpose; the fact of the qualifying conviction is alone what matters under the statute. "A defendant falls within the category simply by virtue of past conviction for any [qualifying] crime ranging from possession of short lobsters, see 16 U.S.C. § 3372, to the most aggravated murder." Tavares, 21 F.3d, at 4. The most the jury needs to know is that the conviction admitted by the defendant falls within the class of crimes that Congress thought should bar a convict from possessing a gun, and this point may be made readily in a defendant's admission and underscored in the court's jury instructions. [Furthermore, there would be no detriment to the prosecution because the stipulation would not interfere with the prosecution's ability to tell the story, in its natural sequence, of the defendant's current charges.] . . .

For purposes of the Rule 403 weighing of the probative against the prejudicial, the functions of the competing evidence are distinguishable only by the risk inherent in the one and wholly absent from the other. In this case, as in any other in which the prior conviction is for an offense likely to support conviction on some improper ground, the only reasonable conclusion was that the risk of unfair prejudice did substantially outweigh the discounted probative value of the record of conviction, and it was an abuse of discretion to admit the record when an admission was available. What we have said shows why this will be the general rule when proof of convict status is at issue, just as the prosecutor's choice will generally survive a Rule 403 analysis when a defendant seeks to force the substitution of an admission for evidence creating a coherent narrative of his thoughts and actions in perpetrating the offense for which he is being tried.

DISCUSSION QUESTIONS

1. Refer back to the article excerpt by Professor Imwinkelreid. The standard of review for Rule 403 decisions is abuse of discretion. When a rule uses amorphous terms such as "unfair," "prejudice" and "probative value," what can be done to guide or channel the discretion of judges at trial? Is the rule sufficient as written, or is something more needed?

2. Is it possible for a judge to avoid applying extrinsic policies and considerations when evaluating evidence under Rule 403? Should the judge even try?

3. From the *Old Chief* case, what is the general rule concerning a party's choice of the evidence it uses to prove its case? Does the ability to choose evidence for its persuasive effect matter? Why or why not?

4. Extract from *Old Chief* the Supreme Court's formula for deciding when to use evidentiary substitutes under Rule 403. Is this a realistically workable framework?

PROBLEMS

Problem 6-1. Calamity City Police brought Dirk Dirtbag — one of the "usual suspects"— to the police station to interview him about the theft of a tractor trailer containing consumer electronics from a local truck stop. Dirtbag had a long list of prior arrests and convictions for a wide variety of criminal activities, including thefts and burglaries. At the station, Dirtbag claimed that he knew nothing about the theft of the tractor trailer. He then ended the interrogation by invoking his 5th Amendment right to counsel. Other witnesses, however, identified Dirtbag as being involved in the theft, and local informants provided information that Dirtbag had spent unusually large amounts of cash the week after the trailer disappeared. Dirtbag was arrested, charged with larceny, and arraigned, but was released on bond pending trial. Freddie Fingers, another local ne'er-do-well, was also arrested in conjunction with the theft, pled guilty, and agreed to testify against Dirtbag at trial. While awaiting trial, Dirtbag paid for and took a polygraph test from a private investigator who had once worked for the Calamity State Police as a polygrapher. The polygrapher's report stated that Dirtbag was being truthful when he claimed no knowledge of the theft. At Dirtbag's larceny trial, his attorney attempts to introduce into evidence an exculpatory polygraph, claiming the polygraph is evidence of Dirtbag's innocence. What objection should the prosecution make to this evidence? How should the judge respond?

Problem 6-2. Alex was charged with providing material support to the Anarchist Army, a known terrorist group. The material support came in the form of bundled donations that Alex collected from sympathizers and provided to various front organizations of the Anarchist Army. In interviews with the police, Alex never denied knowing that the Anarchist Army was a terrorist organization, although he did deny collecting and bundling donations for the Army. Instead, he said that he was collecting money to be used for charitable purposes, such as building schools and bakeries. At trial, to prove Alex's knowledge of the Anarchist Army and its activities (an element of the "material support to a terrorist organization" offense), the prosecution showed a videotape of a speech in which an Army leader announced that the Anarchist Army would carry out a suicide bombing in London in a few hours. The prosecution was able to prove that Alex was in attendance at the speech. The bombing occurred as predicted in the speech. The prosecution then called Vernon Victim, who was visiting in London and present when his cousin was killed in the bombing, to testify about the bombing. The defense objected on 403 grounds, arguing that since Alex was not charged with the bombing, Victim's evidence was substantially more prejudicial than probative, as well as misleading. The defense also offered to stipulate that Alex knew the Anarchist Army was a terrorist organization; this would satisfy one of the elements of the statute. The judge overruled the objection, stating, "With respect to the speech in the video, the defendant was present when an Anarchist Army official announced a terrorist bombing. Testimony about this event is very probative and I weighed this against the prejudicial effect and I conclude that it did not substantially outweigh the probative value. I'm going to allow the testimony with the proviso that I will not have the witness testify about his cousin bleeding to death in his arms." After Victim's testimony, the defense asked the court to instruct the jury that there was no evidence or allegation that Alex had been involved in the bombing, but the judge refused. Alex's attorney appealed the judge's ruling, arguing that the judge abused his discretion under Rule 403 and *Old Chief.* How should the appellate court rule, and why?

Exclusion of Evidence under Rule 403: Quick Hits.

- Rule 403 is a rule of presumptive admissibility for relevant evidence. This means the opponent of the evidence must demonstrate that it somehow violates Rule 403 in order for it to be excluded.

- Rule 403 permits the exclusion of evidence that either causes the jury to make decisions for the wrong reasons or interferes with the efficiency of the trial process.

- Evidence will not be excluded under Rule 403 unless its detrimental impact on the trial substantially outweighs its probative value.

Chapter References

Christopher B. Mueller & Laird C. Kirkpatrick, Evidence §§ 4.9–4.10 (4th ed. 2009).

Glen Weissenberger & James J. Duane, Federal Rules of Evidence: Rules, Legislative History, Commentary and Authority § 403 (6th ed. 2009).

Jack B. Weinstein & Margaret A. Berger, Weinstein's Federal Evidence § 403 (Joseph M. McLaughlin ed., Matthew Bender 2d ed. 1997).

Kenneth S. Broun, McCormick On Evidence § 185 (6th ed. 2006).

Steven J. Goode & Olin Guy Wellborn III, Courtroom Handbook on Federal Evidence Ch. 5 (West 2010).

III. APPLICATION EXERCISE

Objecting and Responding to Evidence on 403 Grounds

Rule 403 is the basis for many objections before and during trial. Oftentimes, as part of the pretrial discovery and case analysis process, advocates learn what evidence their opponents intend to offer at trial. They can evaluate the evidence and decide whether to object to it. If they believe the evidence is unfairly prejudicial, they can file a pretrial motion *in limine* to have it excluded under Rule 403. This is the procedure the defense attorney in *Old Chief* used.

A motion is nothing more than a request for a particular type of action from the court, based on legal grounds, and supported by legal arguments. A motion *in limine* is made before trial to settle important evidentiary issues and permit the parties to adjust their cases to account for the presence or absence of certain evidence at trial. Motions *in limine* can be made either formally, with a written motion and supporting legal briefs, or informally, with a verbal motion and supporting arguments based on the rules. Many jurisdictions require written motions, but some jurisdictions — particularly in state courts — operate more informally and permit verbal motions and arguments.

Advocates may also make 403 objections to evidence during trial. In some jurisdictions, pretrial discovery in criminal cases is limited, and the defense might not learn of certain items of evidence until trial. Sometimes, the prejudicial or cumulative impact of evidence does not become apparent until it is presented in context with other evidence during the trial. In addition, an advocate might decide for tactical reasons to wait until trial to object to evidence on 403 grounds.

A good 403 objection, whether at trial or in a pretrial *motion in limine*, focuses on the detrimental impact the evidence has on the trial process: the evidence either encourages the jury to make decisions for the wrong reasons, or it wastes the court's time. A 403 objection should include more than the conclusory language, "the evidence is unfairly prejudicial." It should explain *how* and *why* the evidence violates 403 and the values of the adversarial trial system. It should also specifically explain the detrimental impact the evidence will have on the objecting attorney's case and client.

A good 403 response focuses on the presumptive admissibility of relevant evidence under Rule 403. In general, Rule 403 contemplates that parties will admit evidence at trial that favors their side and/or is prejudicial to the other side. The key, of course, is to avoid unfair prejudice. Thus, the responding advocate should be able to explain the probative value of the evidence at trial, how it fits into the theory of the case and overall plan of proof, and how its use is necessary at trial. If the objection focuses on the cumulative nature of the evidence or its tendency to waste time, the responding advocate should point out the unique nature of a particular exhibit or the necessity to paint a full picture of proof for the jury.

The Exercise

Objective: To demonstrate proficiency in making and responding to a pretrial verbal Rule 403 motion *in limine*.

Factual Scenario: On June 15, police responded to a call from a resident of the Shady Acres trailer park. The resident, concerned that her elderly neighbor had not been seen for several days, broke into the trailer and found her neighbor's body, along with blood spatters and a lot of gore. Investigator Irving, from the Calamity Bureau of Investigation, arrived at the crime scene and conducted an investigation. He found the body on a chair in the living room and surmised from the condition of the body and the blood spatter evidence that the victim had been shot. He took samples of blood, found bloody fingerprints on the victim's belongings, and collected evidence related to the crime. A police photographer took multiple photographs of the crime scene. Running the fingerprint led him to find Darla Defendant, the victim's niece and a known meth addict. During an interview, Darla confessed to the murder and said she had done it for money. Darla subsequently pled not guilty and is on trial for murder. The confession, although contested, is admissible. The prosecution intends to offer the crime scene photographs into evidence.

Advance Preparation: The instructor will provide electronic copies of crime scene photographs on the course home page. Prepare a verbal defense *motion in limine* to exclude the photographs from evidence under Rule 403. Also prepare a prosecution response to that motion.

In-Class Exercise: Three students will participate in this exercise: Prosecutor, defense counsel, and a judge. The defense counsel will make a verbal motion *in limine* to exclude the photographs under Rule 403. The prosecutor will respond. The judge will rule. Note: each photograph must be addressed individually.

Chapter 7

RULES 407–411: EXTRINSIC SOCIAL POLICIES AND THE EXCLUSION OF RELEVANT EVIDENCE

Chapter Objectives:

- Introduce and explain the concept of excluding relevant evidence in order to support extrinsic social policies and Rules 407-411

- Analyze and discuss issues pertaining to Rules 407- 411 through case law and hypothetical problems

- Apply the concepts from this chapter in a teaching application exercise

---

I. BACKGROUND AND EXPLANATORY MATERIAL

Social Policy and the Exclusion of Evidence

In Chapters Five and Six, we learned that Federal Rules of Evidence 401-402 establish a policy favoring the introduction of relevant evidence at trial. Rule 403 permits the exclusion of relevant evidence whose probative value is substantially outweighed by the danger of unfair prejudice, confusion of the issues, misleading the jury, undue delay, waste of time, or needless presentation of cumulative evidence. Rule 403 is primarily concerned with evidence that jeopardizes the intrinsic integrity or efficiency of the fact-finding process. In this sense, the rule's primary function is to ensure that juries make decisions for the right reasons; what happens outside the courtroom — the *extrinsic* impact of the evidence[1] — is outside the ambit of Rule 403.

As the excerpt from Professor Imwinkelreid's article demonstrated, it is inappropriate for judges to make Rule 403 decisions based on bias, prejudice, social policy or other factors extrinsic to the courtroom decision-making process. To bring external policies or factors into play would jeopardize the intent of Rule 403, place an unwarranted amount of power in the hands of trial judges and thrust into disarray the uniformity and predictability of a codified evidentiary system.

---

[1] Throughout this chapter, I will use the term "extrinsic" in reference to the impact of evidence outside the courtroom. The term "intrinsic" refers to the immediate effect of evidence on the fact-finding process inside the courtroom.

And yet, the evidentiary decisions made by judges in the courtroom can impact relationships and behavior outside the courtroom. Thus, the common law excluded a wide variety of relevant evidence for extrinsic policy reasons. The types of excluded evidence included evidence of subsequent remedial measures, statements made during settlement negotiations, offers to pay medical expenses, statements made during withdrawn offers to plead guilty or *nolo contendere*, and the existence or absence of liability insurance.[2] These types of evidence were excluded from courtrooms in order to promote and support salutary out-of-court behaviors, such as offering to settle claims, purchasing insurance, making repairs, and so forth.[3]

To illustrate, consider the common law rule excluding subsequent remedial measure, such as repairs, to prove the liability or negligence of the alleged tortfeasor. Suppose that a plaintiff trips over a loose floorboard in the defendant's residence and suffers an injury. After being made aware of the plaintiff's injury, the defendant has two basic choices: (1) he could leave the floorboard in its dangerous condition, thus risking additional injuries to others; or (2) he could repair the floorboard to avoid similar accidents in the future.

A plaintiff who learned about a subsequent repair might seek to introduce it into evidence to help prove the defendant's liability or negligence. The evidence is unquestionably relevant: a repair made after an accident is in many respects a conduct-based admission of responsibility for the dangerous condition that caused the accident. It would do no violence to the concept of relevance for a party to introduce evidence of the subsequent repair to support an inference of liability or negligence.

On the other hand, it is in the best interests of society for these repairs to be made so as to minimize the likelihood of future unfortunate incidents. If the defendant knew that the fact of making the repair could be used against him in court to prove liability, he would, at least theoretically, have a disincentive to make the repair. Thus, the common law excluded evidence of subsequent remedial measures in order to promote an external social policy of encouraging such measures to be taken. The rules represented a value judgment that the potential cost to the jury's fact-finding ability or excluding the evidence paled in comparison to the external social and behavioral impact of admitting the evidence.

The common law's exclusion of certain types of relevant evidence for reasons of social policy was codified in Rules 407-411 of the Federal Rules of Evidence.[4] The categories include subsequent remedial measures (Rule 407), evidence of compromise and offers to compromise (Rule 408), payment of medical expenses (Rule 409), evidence of guilty pleas and plea discussions in criminal cases (Rule 410), and liability insurance (Rule 411). These rules are reproduced below:

---

[2] Evidentiary privileges also exclude evidence at trial for extrinsic policy reasons, primarily related to the preservation of relationships that are considered beneficial to society, such as attorney-client, priest-penitent, or spousal relationships. Privileges will be covered separately in this book.

[3] For an excellent discussion of the pre-Rules approach to excluding evidence for extrinsic social policies, *see* Judson F. Falknor, *Extrinsic Policies Affecting Admissibility*, 10 RUTGERS L. REV. 574 (1956).

[4] There are, of course, some differences between the common law rules and the Federal Rules.

Through Dec. 1, 2011	After Dec. 1, 2011
Rule 407. Subsequent Remedial Measures When, after an injury or harm allegedly caused by an event, measures are taken that, if taken previously, would have made the injury or harm less likely to occur, evidence of the subsequent measures is not admissible to prove negligence, culpable conduct, a defect in a product, a defect in a product's design, or a need for a warning or instruction. This rule does not require the exclusion of evidence of subsequent measures when offered for another purpose, such as proving ownership, control, or feasibility of precautionary measures, if controverted, or impeachment.	**Rule 407. Subsequent Remedial Measures** When measures are taken that would have made an earlier injury or harm less likely to occur, evidence of the subsequent measures is not admissible to prove: • negligence; • culpable conduct; • a defect in a product or its design; or • a need for a warning or instruction. But the court may admit this evidence for another purpose, such as impeachment or — if disputed — proving ownership, control, or the feasibility of precautionary measures.

Through Dec. 1, 2011	After Dec. 1, 2011
Rule 408. Compromise and Offers to Compromise **(a) Prohibited uses**. Evidence of the following is not admissible on behalf of any party, when offered to prove liability for, invalidity of, or amount of a claim that was disputed as to validity or amount, or to impeach through a prior inconsistent statement or contradiction: (1) furnishing or offering or promising to furnish—or accepting or offering or promising to accept—a valuable consideration in compromising or attempting to compromise the claim; and (2) conduct or statements made in compromise negotiations regarding the claim, except when offered in a criminal case and the negotiations related to a claim by a public office or agency in the exercise of regulatory, investigative, or enforcement authority. **(b) Permitted uses**. This rule does not require exclusion if the evidence is offered for purposes not prohibited by subdivision (a). Examples of permissible purposes include proving a witness's bias or prejudice; negating a contention of undue delay; and proving an effort to obstruct a criminal investigation or prosecution.	**Rule 408. Compromise Offers and Negotiations** **(a) Prohibited Uses**. Evidence of the following is not admissible - on behalf of any party - either to prove or disprove the validity or amount of a disputed claim or to impeach by a prior inconsistent statement or a contradiction: (1) furnishing, promising, or offering - or accepting, promising to accept, or offering to accept - a valuable consideration in compromising or attempting to compromise the claim; and (2) conduct or a statement made during compromise negotiations about the claim - except when offered in a criminal case and when the negotiations related to a claim by a public office in the exercise of its regulatory, investigative, or enforcement authority. **(b) Exceptions**. The court may admit this evidence for another purpose, such as proving a witness's bias or prejudice, negating a contention of undue delay, or proving an effort to obstruct a criminal investigation or prosecution.

Through Dec. 1, 2011	After Dec. 1, 2011
Rule 409. Payment of Medical and Similar Expenses Evidence of furnishing or offering or promising to pay medical, hospital, or similar expenses occasioned by an injury is not admissible to prove liability for the injury.	**Rule 409. Offers to Pay Medical and Similar Expenses** Evidence of furnishing, promising to pay, or offering to pay medical, hospital, or similar expenses resulting from an injury is not admissible to prove liability for the injury.

Through Dec. 1, 2011	After Dec. 1, 2011
Rule 410. Inadmissibility of Pleas, Plea Discussions, and Related Statements Except as otherwise provided in this rule, evidence of the following is not, in any civil or criminal proceeding, admissible against the defendant who made the plea or was a participant in the plea discussions: (1) a plea of guilty which was later withdrawn; (2) a plea of nolo contendere; (3) any statement made in the course of any proceedings under Rule 11 of the Federal Rules of Criminal Procedure or comparable state procedure regarding either of the foregoing pleas; or (4) any statement made in the course of plea discussions with an attorney for the prosecuting authority which do not result in a plea of guilty or which result in a plea of guilty later withdrawn. However, such a statement is admissible (i) in any proceeding wherein another statement made in the course of the same plea or plea discussions has been introduced and the statement ought in fairness be considered contemporaneously with it, or (ii) in a criminal proceeding for perjury or false statement if the statement was made by the defendant under oath, on the record and in the presence of counsel.	**Rule 410. Pleas, Plea Discussions, and Related Statements** **(a) Prohibited Uses**. In a civil or criminal case, evidence of the following is not admissible against the defendant who made the plea or participated in the plea discussions: (1) a guilty plea that was later withdrawn; (2) a nolo contendere plea; (3) a statement made during a proceeding on either of those pleas under Federal Rule of Criminal Procedure 11 or a comparable state procedure; or (4) a statement made during plea discussions with an attorney for the prosecuting authority if the discussions did not result in a guilty plea or they resulted in a later-withdrawn guilty plea. **(b) Exceptions**. The court may admit a statement described in Rule 410(a)(3) or (4): (1) in any proceeding in which another statement made during the same plea or plea discussions has been introduced, if in fairness the statements ought to be considered together; or (2) in a criminal proceeding for perjury or false statement, if the defendant made the statement under oath, on the record, and with counsel present.

Through Dec. 1, 2011	After Dec. 1, 2011
Rule 411. Liability Insurance	**Rule 411. Liability Insurance**
Evidence that a person was or was not insured against liability is not admissible upon the issue whether the person acted negligently or otherwise wrongfully. This rule does not require the exclusion of evidence of insurance against liability when offered for another purpose, such as proof of agency, ownership, or control, or bias or prejudice of a witness.	Evidence that a person was or was not insured against liability is not admissible to prove whether the person acted negligently or otherwise wrongfully. But the court may admit this evidence for another purpose, such as proving a witness's bias or prejudice or proving agency, ownership, or control.

Rules 407-411 as Individual Applications of Rule 403

Rule 403 provides for the exclusion of relevant evidence that could be used for improper purposes by a jury. As discussed in the last chapter, Rule 403 gives a tremendous amount of discretion to trial judges. In this respect, Rule 403 differs considerably from the rest of the Federal Rules of Evidence, which limit judicial discretion by codifying the rules and establishing standards and procedures for admissibility.

The question naturally arises: given the broad scope of Rule 403, why not trust judges to use their discretion and make the right decisions regarding the evidentiary categories covered by Rules 407-411? Rules 407-411 exist separately from Rule 403 for two important reasons. First, at its core, Rule 403 is more concerned with the intrinsic impact of evidence on the decision-making process at trial than with the promotion of extrinsic social policies. Second, the drafters of these rules felt that the underlying extrinsic social policies were important enough that uniformity of application should trump judicial discretion.

Rules 407 through 411 can still, however, usefully be conceptualized as specific applications of Rule 403's core principle: relevant evidence should not be admitted at trial if its probative value would be substantially outweighed by the danger of unfair prejudice, confusing the issues or misleading the jury. Some of the evidence covered by Rules 407-411 has limited probative value compared with the danger of a jury making decisions for the wrong reason. For instance, Rule 408 prohibits evidence of compromise or offers to compromise. If jurors learned that the defendant in a civil case had initiated settlement negotiations with the plaintiff, they could improperly decide that the primary reason for doing so was that the defendant was admitting liability. In reality, of course, parties offer to settle cases for reasons entirely unrelated to liability, including good will, management of risk, and the desire to avoid litigation.

In other cases, the probative value of evidence might be high and the danger of unfair prejudice to the parties at trial fairly low. The prejudicial impact of admitting evidence under these rules would occur *outside* the courtroom. The earlier example of the loose floorboard and Rule 407's exclusion of subsequent remedial measures demonstrates this principle.

A Template for Analyzing Evidence Under Rules 407-411

A standard four-step template applies to analyzing evidence under each of these Rules: (1) identify the social policy or value underlying the rule; (2) evaluate whether the proposed use of the evidence violates the social policy or value; (3) determine whether there is an exception to the general rule of exclusion; (4) apply an independent Rule 403 analysis to any apparent exceptions. Each of these steps will be discussed in turn below.

First, each rule recognizes, reinforces and promotes an underlying social policy or value by prohibiting the introduction of a certain type of evidence for improper purposes. The theory is that excluding the evidence will promote behavior that is beneficial to society. For example, Rule 409, like its common-law predecessor, prohibits admitting evidence of a person's offer to pay another's medical expenses as proof of liability or negligence. From a Rule 401 standpoint, such evidence is relevant to the issue of liability or negligence. Offering to pay someone's medical expenses could be viewed as an indirect admission of wrongdoing or responsibility. The offer to pay medical expenses could also be made from purely humanitarian impulses, or even from a misdirected sense of guilt not related to legal liability. If that evidence could be admitted at trial by an opposing party to prove fault, the theory is that individuals would be discouraged from offering to pay the medical expenses of others. Thus, to encourage socially valuable behavior, Rule 407 strikes a balance in favor of an extrinsic policy, even at the expense of excluding relevant, probative evidence from trial.

Second, it is important to determine why the evidence is being offered. In the end, Rules 407-411 exist to ensure that the jury does not draw improper inferences from the categories of evidence covered by these rules. The rules do not, however, necessarily bar introduction of the evidence at trial for all purposes. Provided that the inference to be drawn from the evidence does not violate the social policy of the rule, there is no impediment to offering it at trial.

For instance, Rule 410 prohibits the introduction into evidence of "any statement made [by a criminal accused during a plea negotiation]." The social policy of Rule 410 is to encourage the efficient practice of plea bargaining. But, like many other human endeavors, plea bargaining is not always successful. If the prosecution could introduce into evidence statements made by criminal defendants in unsuccessful plea bargaining negotiations, there would be little incentive for defendants to participate meaningfully in the plea bargaining process. Prosecutors could theoretically obtain incriminating evidence from defendants, then withdraw from plea negotiations and use the evidence at trial. The rule's underlying social policy would not apply, however, if the accused introduced favorable out-of-context statements from those negotiations. If that occurred, the prosecution could safely introduce the remaining statements in order to ensure that the jury did not receive a misleading impression from the defendant's evidence. Thus, if there is another reason for offering the evidence that does not violate the rule's underlying social policy, the evidence may well be admissible.

Third, each rule contains numerous exceptions that permit the introduction of the evidence but limit its permissible uses at trial. These exceptions are derived from common-law doctrines that developed over the centuries. Rule 411, for example, prohibits introducing evidence that "a person was or was not insured against liability . . . upon the issue of whether the person acted negligently or otherwise wrongfully." The social policy is to encourage the purchase of insurance by precluding the misleading inference that people who purchase liability insurance behave less carefully than those who do not. Nonetheless, the rule does permit evidence of insurance "when offered for another purpose, such as proof of agency, ownership, or control, or bias or prejudice of a witness."

The fourth and final step in the template is to conduct an independent Rule 403 analysis of evidence that may otherwise be admissible under Rules 407-411. Suppose, for example, that a party wants to introduce evidence of insurance in order to prove agency or control in a case, an exception that is within the plain language of Rule 411. Looking at the other evidence in the case — both what is offered and what is potentially available — a judge could still apply a Rule 403 analysis and decide that the probative value of the evidence would be substantially outweighed by the factors listed in Rule 403.

Exclusion of Relevant Evidence for Extrinsic Social Policies: Quick Hits

- Rule 403 permits the exclusion of evidence at trial if it would have an unfairly detrimental impact on a party or on the efficiency of the trial process when compared to the probative value of the evidence. Rules 407-411, in contrast, exclude relevant evidence from trial based on the desire to support social policies outside the courtroom.

- The evidence covered in Rules 407-411 is generally of marginal probative value, but it is thought that its introduction at trial could discourage parties from engaging in socially valuable behavior such as repairing damaged property, settling disputes, offering to pay medical expenses, plea bargaining or obtaining insurance.

- Rules 407-411 contain numerous exceptions that permit the introduction of the otherwise prohibited evidence for purposes unrelated harm valuable behaviors such as reparing 403 is a rule of presumptive admissibility for relevant evidence. This means the opponent of the evidence must demonstrate that it somehow violates Rule 403 in order for it to be excluded.

Chapter References

Christopher B. Mueller & Laird C. Kirkpatrick, Evidence §§ 4.23–4.31 (4th ed. 2009).

Glen Weissenberger & James J. Duane, Federal Rules of Evidence: Rules, Legislative History, Commentary and Authority §§ 407–11 (6th ed. 2009).

Jack B. Weinstein & Margaret A. Berger, Weinstein's Federal Evidence §§ 407–11 (Joseph M. McLaughlin ed., Matthew Bender 2d ed. 1997).

STEVEN GOODE & OLIN GUY WELLBORN III, COURTROOM HANDBOOK ON FEDERAL EVIDENCE Ch. 5 (West 2010).

II. APPLICATION EXERCISE

Objective: To demonstrate proficiency in researching, preparing written materials, and teaching one of the 407-411 rules to other students.

Factual Scenario: This exercise is different from most in the book. Instead of a courtroom scenario, this is a small-group teaching exercise in which students will research and prepare materials on a rule of evidence, then present their materials to the rest of the class.

Advance Preparation. As assigned by the professor, students work in small groups to research and prepare teaching materials on one of the 407-411 rules. Each group is assigned one of the rules for research and presentation. The group will create a one-page handout for distribution to the class and will prepare a 15-minute presentation (including time for questions and answers) on the rule.

The handout must contain the following components:

a.   The underlying extrinsic policy expressed by the rule.

b.   Common applications of the rule.

c.   The primary exceptions to the rule.

d.   A short case brief from any jurisdiction construing the rule or one of its exceptions.

e.   A hypothetical problem that helps illustrate the rule.

In-Class Exercise. During class, each group will present and teach its assigned rule to the rest of the class.

Chapter 8

THE RAPE SHIELD RULE: EXCLUSION OF A SEXUAL ASSAULT VICTIM'S PRIOR SEXUAL HISTORY

Chapter Objectives:

- Introduce and explain Rule 412 and the concept of excluding evidence of an alleged sexual assault victim's sexual history in criminal and civil cases

- Analyze and discuss issues pertaining to Rule 412 through case law and hypothetical problems

- Apply the concepts from this chapter in a courtroom application exercise

---

I. BACKGROUND AND EXPLANATORY MATERIAL

The Common Law Evidentiary Rules in Rape and Sexual Assault Cases

From an evidentiary perspective, the common law treated victims of rape and sexual assault quite harshly. A victim — typically a woman — could expect to be re-victimized by the criminal justice system if she filed a sexual assault complaint with the authorities. Her initial complaint would be treated with skepticism at best or outright disbelief at worst. At trial, assuming she was able to endure the process and press forward with her complaint, her entire sexual history was considered fair game for the defense to exploit in the presence of the jury.[1] The law permitted, and arguably even encouraged, the jury to make decisions based on misogynistic

---

[1] *The Accused*, a 1988 film starring Jodie Foster, powerfully depicts the re-victimization suffered by rape victims at the hands of the criminal justice system. Based on an actual event, the film tells the story of a woman named Sarah Tobias, who is brutally gang-raped by three men in a bar as a crowd of bystanders cheered on and encouraged the rapists. Because of Tobias's checkered past and her provocative dress the night of the incident, the prosecution gives a lenient plea bargain deal to the rapists. Angered by her treatment, Tobias confronts the DA (played by Kelly McGillis) and convinces her to prosecute the bystanders for criminal solicitation. *See generally The Accused* (Paramount 1988).

stereotypes and prejudice; a woman whose sexual history included consensual premarital or extramarital sex could expect to see her credibility on a sexual assault claim called into question based solely on her voluntary participation in past sexual activity.

In many respects, the common law put the victim on trial every bit as much as the alleged perpetrator. The basis for the common law evidentiary approach can be summarized in a famous quote by Sir Matthew Hale, a British jurist in the 18th century. He wrote:

> It is true rape is a most detestable crime, and therefore ought severely and impartially to be punished with death;[2] but it must be remembered, that *it is an accusation easily to be made and hard to be proved, and harder to be defended by the party accused, tho never so innocent.*[3]

The following excerpt from an article by Professor Clifford Fishman explains the types of defenses available in a sexual assault case and the types of evidence (and inferences to be drawn therefrom) in a common law trial.

Clifford S. Fishman, *Consent, Credibility, and the Constitution: Evidence Relating to a Sex Offense Complainant's Past Sexual Behavior*
44 Cath. U. L. Rev. 711 (1995)

Rape is perhaps the most difficult aspect of criminal law to discuss rationally. At one extreme, some scholars maintain, in self-righteous rejection of reality, that all heterosexual sex is rape. At the other extreme, troglodytical judges still occasionally express reluctance to sentence a convicted rapist who was "led astray" by a woman who was "asking for it." In balancing these extremes, difficult legal questions inevitably intermix with strongly held beliefs and powerful emotions, presenting daunting challenges to reasoned discourse.

Within this controversy, a key evidentiary question arises in rape cases: to what extent, if at all, should a defendant, or a prosecutor, offer evidence of the complainant's prior sexual history. Fortunately, the days have passed when a rape accusation automatically would open the courtroom door to whatever gossip about the complainant the defendant could scrape up. . . .

---

[2] Rape was a capital offense under the common law. The United States Supreme Court ruled in 1977 that the death sentence for raping an adult woman was excessive under the Eighth Amendment. *See* Coker v. Georgia, 433 U.S. 584 (1977). In 2008, the United States Supreme Court ruled that the Eighth Amendment prohibits the death penalty for the rape of a child where the crime did not result, and was not intended to result, in the death of the victim. *See* Kennedy v. Louisiana, 554 U.S. 407, *modified on denial of rehearing*, 554 U.S. 945 (2008).

[3] Sir Matthew Hale, 1 The History of the Pleas of the Crown 634 (Small 1847) (emphasis added).

I. Traditional Theories of Relevance; "Rape Shield" Legislation

Although definitions of sexual offenses vary considerably in their details, the essence of these crimes is that (1) the defendant engaged in a statutorily designated sexual activity with the complainant (2) without her consent and (3) against her will. Some rape statutes also require the prosecutor to prove that the defendant used force.

As a practical matter, a man charged with a sexual offense has four defenses available: (1) The complainant mistakenly has identified the defendant as the perpetrator; (2) No sexual activity occurred; i.e., the complainant is either lying or confused; (3) The complainant consented to the sexual activity, and currently is lying; (4) If the complainant did not consent, the defendant nevertheless reasonably believed she did. If the defendant asserts the second or third defense, a jury will want to know the complainant's motivation for falsely accusing the defendant. The failure to provide a plausible answer may weigh very heavily against him.

A. Traditional Theories of Relevance

Until recently, a defendant who asserted any of the latter three defenses routinely would offer evidence, assuming such evidence existed or could be manufactured, of the complainant's prior nonmarital or extramarital sexual activity. A defendant might elicit such information by cross-examining the complainant about her prior sexual activity, by calling one or more men to testify about their prior sexual relations with her, or by calling witnesses to testify about the complainant's reputation of unchastity or promiscuity. Even if such evidence had no direct relevance to the specific facts of the case, it was considered relevant for the following reasons:

1. Credibility. It was considered "a matter of common knowledge that the bad character of a man for chastity does not even in the remotest degree affect his character for truth . . . while it does that of a woman."[4] In other words, evidence that a woman was unchaste was thought relevant to prove that she was also a liar.[5]

2. Consent; the "yes/yes inference." Evidence that the complainant engaged in nonmarital sex was considered relevant to support a defendant's claim that she consented to have sex with him on the occasion in question because "common experience teaches us that the woman who has once departed from the paths of virtue is far more apt to consent to another lapse than is the one who has never stepped aside from that path."[6] In essence, the evidence that the complainant

---

[4] [n. 17] State v. Sibley, 33 S.W. 167, 171 (Mo. 1895).

[5] [n.18] 3A JOHN H. WIGMORE, EVIDENCE IN TRIALS AT COMMON LAW s 924a (Chadbourn rev. ed. 1970). Consider the following passage:

> [Rape complainants'] psychic complexes are multifarious, distorted partly by inherent defects, partly by diseased derangements or abnormal instincts, partly by bad social environment, partly by temporary physiological or emotional conditions. . . . The unchaste . . . mentality finds incidental but direct expression in the narration of imaginary sex incidents of which the narrator is the heroine or the victim. Id.

[6] [n. 19] State v. Wood, 122 P.2d 416, 418 (Ariz. 1942). This belief has been previously articulated. One

consented to have sex with some men on some occasions makes it more probable that she would consent to have sex with any man at any time. This is referred to hereinafter as the "yes/yes inference,"[7] i.e., the inference that "yes to some men sometimes means yes to any man any time."

3. Defendant's reasonable belief that complainant consented. Even if the complainant did not in fact consent to intercourse, information concerning the complainant's prior sexual activity, if known to the defendant prior to the events giving rise to the rape accusation, was considered relevant on the question whether the defendant reasonably believed that she consented.

The result of the common law's evidentiary approach to sexual assault claims was a system whose hostility to victims resulted in the underreporting of crimes, the exoneration of guilty defendants, and the shattering of victim's lives. Recognizing these problems, lawmakers on both the state and federal levels began enacting "rape shield" statutes, which limited the evidentiary use at trial of an alleged victim's sexual history.

Rule 412: the Federal "Rape Shield" Rule

Historical Background of Rule 412

Congress enacted Federal Rule of Evidence 412 in 1978, as part of Public Law 95-540, the Privacy Protection for Rape Victims Act of 1978. In her remarks to the House of Representatives, Representative Elizabeth Holtzmann of New York highlighted the problems posed by the common law's treatment of rape victims and the need for a rape shield statute:

> Too often in this country victims of rape are humiliated and harassed when they report and prosecute the rape. Bullied and cross-examined about their prior sexual experiences, many find the trial almost as degrading as the rape itself. Since rape trials become inquisitions into the victim's morality, not trials of the defendant's innocence or guilt, it is not surprising that it is the least reported crime. It is estimated that as few as one in ten rapes is ever reported.[8]

By enacting Rule 412, Congress demonstrated a manifest intent to protect victims of rape and sexual assault from humiliation, degradation and re-victimization at trial.

Congress was also, however, mindful of the legal and constitutional rights of criminal defendants. Recognizing that under appropriate circumstances, an alleged

---

court noted that "it is certainly more probable that a woman who has done these things voluntarily in the past would be much more likely to consent than one whose past reputation was without blemish, and whose personal conduct could not truthfully be assailed." People v. Johnson, 39 P. 622, 623 (Cal. 1895).

[7] [n.21] See generally Frank Tuerkheimer, *A Reassessment and Redefinition of Rape Shield Laws*, 50 Ohio St. L.J. 1245, 1266 (1989) (discussing this inference in the context of whether the accused's knowledge of prior sexual activity should have a bearing on admissibility).

[8] 124 Cong. Rec. H11,944 (remarks of Representative Elizabeth Holtzmann). Pub. L. No. 95-540.

victim's sexual history could indeed be relevant and probative on the issue of the defendant's innocence, Congress sought to strike a balance between protecting victims and ensuring a fair trial for defendants. Representative Holtzman, the drafter and principal sponsor of the bill that created Rule 412, explained how the rule achieved Congress's goals:

> First, this evidence can be introduced if it deals with the victim's past sexual relations with the defendant and is relevant to the issue of whether she consented. Second, when the defendant claims he had no relations with the victim, he can use evidence of the victim's past sexual relations with others if the evidence rebuts the victim's claim that the rape caused certain physical consequences, such as semen or injury. Finally, the evidence can be introduced if it is constitutionally required. This last exception, added in subcommittee, will insure that the defendant's constitutional rights are protected.[9]

Thus, in criminal cases, Rule 412 shields victims from embarrassment and harassment, but not completely. Under some circumstances, the defense can insist that the shield be lowered.

In 1994, Rule 412 was amended to provide coverage in civil cases as well as criminal cases. The explosion of civil sexual harassment claims and other civil actions involving sexual matters necessitated an expansion of the rule to protect the alleged victims in those cases as well. According to the Advisory Committee

> The reason for extending Rule 412 to civil cases is equally obvious. The need to protect alleged victims against invasions of privacy, potential embarrassment, and unwarranted sexual stereotyping, and the wish to encourage victims to come forward when they have been sexually molested do not disappear because the context has shifted from a criminal prosecution to a claim for damages or injunctive relief. There is a strong social policy in not only punishing those who engage in sexual misconduct, but in also providing relief to the victim. Thus, Rule 412 applies in any civil case in which a person claims to be the victim of sexual misconduct, such as actions for sexual battery or sexual harassment.[10]

The types of available evidence and the balancing test for excluding evidence of past sexual activity are different in civil cases than in criminal cases. The differences will be discussed in detail in the next subsection of this chapter.

Rule 412 in Application

Rule 412 is a lengthy rule, somewhat complicated by its efforts to protect victims in both criminal and civil cases, preserve necessary differences in application between the criminal and civil justice systems, and ensure fair trials for defendants. In order to assist in better understanding Rule 412, this subsection breaks the rule into several parts. First, the section introduces the general prohibitions of the rule, which apply equally to criminal and civil cases. Next, the section examines the three

---

[9] 124 Cong. Rec. H11,944 (remarks of Representative Elizabeth Holtzmann). Pub. L. No. 95-540.

[10] Fed. R. Evid. 412, advisory committee note.

exceptions under which sexual history can be admitted in criminal cases, and the standards employed by courts in evaluating each of the exceptions. The section then looks at the provisions of the rule that apply only in civil cases. Finally, the section discusses the procedural aspects of the rule, which apply equally to criminal and civil cases.

General Prohibitions of Rule 412

Through Dec. 1, 2011	After Dec. 1, 2011
Rule 412. Sex Offense Cases; Relevance of Alleged Victim's Past Sexual Behavior or Alleged Sexual Predisposition	**Rule 412. Sex-Offense Cases: The Victim's Sexual Behavior or Predisposition**
(a) Evidence Generally Inadmissible. The following evidence is not admissible in any civil or criminal proceeding involving alleged sexual misconduct except as provided in subdivisions (b) and (c):	**(a) Prohibited Uses**. The following evidence is not admissible in a civil or criminal proceeding involving alleged sexual misconduct:
(1) Evidence offered to prove that any alleged victim engaged in other sexual behavior.	(1) evidence offered to prove that a victim engaged in other sexual behavior; or
(2) Evidence offered to prove any alleged victim's sexual predisposition.	(2) evidence offered to prove a victim's sexual predisposition.

Rule 412 generally prohibits evidence of an alleged victim's prior sexual behavior or sexual predisposition. As discussed in the subsection above, the rule is based on external policy concerns. But the rule also has sound justifications in helping to maintain the intrinsic integrity of the proof process at trial. The evidence prohibited by Rule 412 might technically satisfy the minimal relevance requirements of Rule 401, but it has limited probative value on the issue of whether the alleged sexual misconduct actually occurred. The danger of unfair prejudice to the victim, coupled with the real possibility of the jury deciding the case for the wrong reasons — to punish the victim for a promiscuous lifestyle, for example — are good reasons for excluding the evidence at trial.

The rule is broadly written so as to encompass all types of criminal and civil proceedings that involve allegations of sexual misconduct. The rule carefully uses the adjective "alleged" to describe the status of the victim as well as the validity of the charge. This helps to maintain the constitutional presumption of innocence to which the defendant is entitled in a criminal case.

In cases involving sexual misconduct, Rule 412 protects all alleged victims, regardless of whether they are parties to the litigation.[11] The term "alleged sexual misconduct" refers to actual physical misconduct or Title VII sexual harassment allegations. It does not, however, apply to evidence offered in a defamation action "in which the evidence is offered to show that the alleged defamatory statements

---

[11] FED. R. EVID. 412, advisory committee note to 1994 Amendment.

were true or did not damage the plaintiff's reputation."[12] According to the Advisory Committee, there is no requirement that the sexual misconduct be alleged in the pleadings.[13]

If a case does not involve alleged sexual misconduct — in other words, if the case is about something else altogether — the rule does not shield third-party witnesses from disclosure of evidence of their prior sexual activities. Where applicable, other rules of evidence may protect third-party witnesses in such situations.[14]

The first category is evidence that the victim engaged in other sexual behavior. The term "other sexual behavior" includes actual sexual activity (such as sexual intercourse or other physical sexual behavior), conduct that suggests or implies sexual activity (such as use of contraceptives, birth of an illegitimate child, or treatment for a venereal disease), and even evidence of sexual fantasies and "activities of the mind" (such as might be the topic of conversation or the subject of journal entries or on-line activity).[15] Excluding this type of evidence helps avoid the "yes/yes" inference that a person who has consented to sexual activity in the past is likely to have done so in the case at bar.

The second category is evidence of an alleged victim's sexual predisposition. This can include evidence of specific acts (including activities of the mind), as well as the victim's sexual reputation. Excluding this type of evidence also helps avoid the "yes/yes" inference, as well as the "chastity/veracity" problem, in which jurors discount the testimony of an alleged victim because of her sexual character or predisposition.

It should be noted that the rule applies equally to both parties in a dispute. The most common application of the rule is to shield alleged victims from the indignity or embarrassment of having their sexual history and/or reputation dragged into the courtroom. The rule also prevents the prosecution or plaintiff from introducing evidence of the victim's chastity or virginity to suggest a reduced likelihood of consent.

---

[12] *Id.*

[13] *Id.*

[14] Other rules can be used to protect witnesses, including Rules 403 (unfairly prejudicial or misleading evidence), 404 (improper character evidence), 608 (improper impeachment evidence) and 611 (the court's inherent ability to protect witnesses from harassment or undue embarrassment).

[15] *See* GLEN WEISSENBERGER & JAMES J. DUANE, FEDERAL RULES OF EVIDENCE: RULES, LEGISLATIVE HISTORY, COMMENTARY AND AUTHORITY § 412.3 (6th ed. 2009).

Exceptions to the General Rule of Exclusion in Criminal Cases

Through Dec. 1, 2011	After Dec. 1, 2011
Rule 412, cont'd	**Rule 412, cont'd**
(b) Exceptions.	**(b) Exceptions.**
(1) In a criminal case, the following evidence is admissible, if otherwise admissible under these rules:	(1) *Criminal Cases.* The court may admit the following evidence in a criminal case:
(A) evidence of specific instances of sexual behavior by the alleged victim offered to prove that a person other than the accused was the source of semen, injury or other physical evidence;	(A) evidence of specific instances of a victim's sexual behavior, if offered to prove that someone other than the defendant was the source of semen, injury, or other physical evidence;
(B) evidence of specific instances of sexual behavior by the alleged victim with respect to the person accused of the sexual misconduct offered by the accused to prove consent or by the prosecution; and	(B) evidence of specific instances of a victim's sexual behavior with respect to the person accused of the sexual misconduct, if offered by the defendant to prove consent or if offered by the prosecutor; and
(C) evidence the exclusion of which would violate the constitutional rights of the defendant.	(C) evidence whose exclusion would violate the defendant's constitutional rights.

As previously discussed, Rule 412 attempts to strike a balance between the interests of alleged victims and criminal defendants. The three exceptions to Rule 412 are designed to do just that.

The first exception recognizes and validates the defense that someone else might have been responsible for a sexual assault or rape. It permits the accused to introduce evidence of the alleged victim's specific acts of conduct with another person or persons "to prove that a person other than the accused was the source of semen, injury, or other physical evidence." The accused may not introduce reputation or opinion evidence that would suggest past acts; the rule requires evidence of actual conduct. Injuries can include not only sexual injuries, but injuries that might have been incurred in defending against a sexual assault, such as bruises, cuts, scratches, and the like. By using the words "physical evidence," the rule precludes evidence of psychological or mental injuries that might have occurred as the result of a sexual assault. The Advisory Committee note makes clear that evidence offered under this section must survive analysis under Rules 401 and 403.[16]

The second exception applies only to instances of past sexual behavior by the victim with respect to the accused. There are two primary applications of this

---

[16] FED. R. EVID. 412, advisory committee note.

exception. The first permits the accused to raise the defense of mistake of fact as to consent. The basis of this defense is that something in the victim's past sexual behavior toward the accused contributed to the accused's reasonable (but mistaken) belief that the alleged victim consented on the charged occasion. The rule is carefully written to encompass not only past sexual acts between the alleged victim and the accused, but also more ambiguous behavior such as the alleged victim's fantasies about the accused or expressions of desire to participate in sexual activity with the accused.

The second application of this exception is that the prosecution can introduce specific instances of the alleged victim's sexual behavior with respect to the accused for any purpose that would otherwise be permitted by the rules of evidence. The Advisory Committee lists one such example in the Advisory Committee Notes to Rule 412:

> In a prosecution for child sexual abuse, for example, evidence of uncharged sexual activity between the accused and the alleged victim offered by the prosecution may be admissible pursuant to Rule 404(b) to show a pattern of behavior. Evidence relating to the victim's alleged sexual predisposition is not admissible pursuant to this exception.[17]

Thus, evidence of specific acts involving the alleged victim and the accused could be used to demonstrate the increased likelihood of the accused having committed the charged offense in the case at bar.

The third exception is evidence that is constitutionally required. There are two primary constitutional rights implicated by this exception: (1) the Fifth Amendment right to due process in criminal trials; and (2) the Sixth Amendment right of confrontation. This exception often comes into play at trial when a criminal accused wants to reveal evidence of the alleged victim's bias or motivation to lie. A common example is the allegation that the victim has claimed rape or sexual assault in order to protect her status in another relationship; introducing evidence of the other relationship could require a discussion of the alleged victim's sexual activity in the relationship. The key to using this exception at trial is the defense's ability to plausibly tie evidence of the alleged victim's past sexual activity *or disposition* to an articulable constitutional purpose.

The Balancing Test for Evidence in Civil Cases

The victim of alleged sexual misconduct faces similar risks of humiliation or degradation in both civil and criminal cases if her sexual history or predisposition is brought into the courtroom. Because there is no possibility of deprivation of life or liberty in a civil case, the stakes for a defendant are much lower than they are for an accused in a criminal case. Accordingly, the bar is set much higher in a civil case for introducing evidence of an alleged victim's past sexual behavior or predisposition.

The text of subsection(b)(2) of Rule 412 is as follows:

---

[17] *Id.*

Through Dec. 1, 2011	After Dec. 1, 2011
Rule 412, cont'd	**Rule 412, cont'd**
(2) In a civil case, evidence offered to prove the sexual behavior or sexual predisposition of any alleged victim is admissible if it is otherwise admissible under these rules and its probative value substantially outweighs the danger of harm to any victim and of unfair prejudice to any party. Evidence of an alleged victim's reputation is admissible only if it has been placed in controversy by the alleged victim.	(2) *Civil Cases.* In a civil case, the court may admit evidence offered to prove a victim's sexual behavior or sexual predisposition if its probative value substantially outweighs the danger of harm to any victim and of unfair prejudice to any party. The court may admit evidence of a victim's reputation only if the victim has placed it in controversy.

The civil exception creates a heightened admissibility test that inverts the traditional 403 balancing test. Recall that Rule 403 is a rule of presumptive admissibility under which evidence is admitted *unless* its probative value is substantially outweighed by the danger of unfair prejudice or the other considerations listed in the rule. Rule 403's primary concern is with the integrity of the trial process itself; prejudice is measured by its impact on a party's ability to present its case. Rule 412, on the other hand, is a rule of presumptive exclusion. In civil cases, evidence cannot be admitted unless its probative value substantially outweighs the danger of harm to any victim and of unfair prejudice to any party. In practical terms, this means that the defendant faces a nearly insurmountable barrier in attempting to admit evidence of the alleged victim's sexual behavior or predisposition in a civil case.

Procedural Aspects of Rule 412

Through Dec. 1, 2011	After Dec. 1, 2011
Rule 412, cont'd	**Rule 412, cont'd**
(c) Procedure To Determine Admissibility.	**(c) Procedure to Determine Admissibility.**
(1) A party intending to offer evidence under subdivision (b) must—	*(1) Motion.* If a party intends to offer evidence under Rule 412(b), the party must:
(A) file a written motion at least 14 days before trial specifically describing the evidence and stating the purpose for which it is offered unless the court, for good cause requires a different time for filing or permits filing during trial; and	(A) file a motion that specifically describes the evidence and states the purpose for which it is to be offered;
	(B) do so at least 14 days before trial unless the court, for good cause, sets a different time;
(B) serve the motion on all parties and notify the alleged victim or, when appropriate, the alleged victim's guardian or representative.	(C) serve the motion on all parties; and
	(D) notify the victim or, when appropriate, the victim's guardian or representative.
(2) Before admitting evidence under this rule the court must conduct a hearing in camera and afford the victim and parties a right to attend and be heard. The motion, related papers, and the record of the hearing must be sealed and remain under seal unless the court orders otherwise.	*(2) Hearing.* Before admitting evidence under this rule, the court must conduct an in camera hearing and give the victim and parties a right to attend and be heard. Unless the court orders otherwise, the motion, related materials, and the record of the hearing must be and remain sealed.
	(d) Definition of "Victim." In this rule, "victim" includes an alleged victim.

Most rules of evidence do not speak to procedure, but Rule 412 is an exception. Rule 412 lists specific procedures that must be followed before evidence can be offered under one of the exceptions to the rule's general prohibitions. These procedures, like the rule itself, are designed to balance the privacy interests of the alleged victim with the defendant's interests in defending himself at trial. The procedural section of Rule 412 applies alike in civil and criminal cases.

To protect against surprise or prejudice to the victim's privacy interests, the defendant must provide written notice of intent to offer evidence covered by Rule 412 at least 14 days prior to trial. Recognizing that judicial independence and evidentiary surprises are a reality at trial, the rule permits a judge to waive the 14-day requirement or even permit filing during trial for good cause shown.

What cannot be waived, however, is the *in camera* hearing about the evidence. An *in camera* hearing is closed to the public. The victim and parties have a right to attend the hearing, and the evidence obtained during the hearing is placed under seal. This procedure protects the privacy of the victim and ensures that evidence which may be inadmissible at trial is not published or broadcast to the public at large.

II. CASES, DISCUSSION QUESTIONS AND PROBLEMS

OLDEN v. KENTUCKY
Supreme Court of the United States
488 U.S. 227 (1988)

PER CURIAM. [Starla Matthews, the alleged victim in this case, was a white woman. She claimed at trial that the petitioner, a black man, had raped and sodomized her at knifepoint near Princeton, Kentucky. Prior to trial, she had told several versions of the story that were inconsistent with her trial testimony (for instance, she originally claimed that she had been raped by four men; then amended the story to two men; and then at trial said that Olden was the sole rapist). She was cross-examined on these inconsistencies. The defense raised the issue of consent and claimed that after the consensual activity, he dropped Matthews off at the home of Bill Russell, at her request.]

Although Matthews and Russell were both married to and living with other people at the time of the incident, they were apparently involved in an extramarital relationship. By the time of trial the two were living together, having separated from their respective spouses. Petitioner's theory of the case was that Matthews concocted the rape story to protect her relationship with Russell, who would have grown suspicious upon seeing her disembark from Harris' car. In order to demonstrate Matthews' motive to lie, it was crucial, petitioner contended, that he be allowed to intro-duce evidence of Matthews' and Russell's current cohabitation. Over petitioner's vehement objections, the trial court nonetheless granted the prosecutor's motion in limine to keep all evidence of Matthews' and Russell's living arrangement from the jury. Moreover, when the defense attempted to cross-examine Matthews about her living arrangements, after she had claimed during direct examination that she was living with her mother, the trial court sustained the prosecutor's objection.

Based on the evidence admitted at trial, the jury acquitted Petitioner [of] kidnapping and rape. However, in a somewhat puzzling turn of events, the jury convicted petitioner alone [note: he was tried jointly with Harris, a co-accused, who was acquitted of all charges] of forcible sodomy. He was sentenced to 10 years' imprisonment.

Petitioner appealed, asserting, inter alia, that the trial court's refusal to allow him to impeach Matthews' testimony by introducing evidence supporting a motive to lie deprived him of his Sixth Amendment right to confront witnesses against him. The Kentucky Court of Appeals upheld the conviction. No. 86-CR-006 (May 11, 1988). The court specifically held that evidence that Matthews and Russell were living together at the time of trial was not barred by the State's rape shield law. Ky. Rev. Stat. Ann. § 510.145 (Michie 1985). Moreover, it acknowledged that the evidence in question was relevant to petitioner's theory of the case. But it held, nonetheless, that the evidence was properly excluded as "its probative value [was] outweighed by its possibility for prejudice." App. to Pet. for Cert. A6. By way of explanation, the court stated: "[T]here were the undisputed facts of race; Matthews was white and Russell was black. For the trial court to have admitted into evidence testimony that Matthews and Russell were living together at the time of the trial may have created extreme prejudice against Matthews." Judge Clayton, who dissented but did not address the evidentiary issue, would have reversed petitioner's conviction both because he believed the jury's verdicts were "manifestly inconsistent," and because he found Matthews' testimony too incredible to provide evidence sufficient to uphold the verdict. Id., at A7.

The Kentucky Court of Appeals failed to accord proper weight to petitioner's Sixth Amendment right "to be confronted with the witnesses against him." That right, incorporated in the Fourteenth Amendment and therefore available in state proceedings, Pointer v. Texas, 380 U.S. 400 (1965), includes the right to conduct reasonable cross-examination. Davis v. Alaska, 415 U.S. 308, 315-316 (1974).

In Davis v. Alaska, we observed that, subject to "the broad discretion of a trial judge to preclude repetitive and unduly harassing interrogation . . . , the cross-examiner has traditionally been allowed to impeach, i. e., discredit, the witness." Id., at 316. We emphasized that "the exposure of a witness' motivation in testifying is a proper and important function of the constitutionally protected right of cross-examination." Id., at 316-317. Recently, in Delaware v. Van Arsdall, 475 U.S. 673 (1986), we reaffirmed Davis, and held that "a criminal defendant states a violation of the Confrontation Clause by showing that he was prohibited from engaging in otherwise appropriate cross-examination designed to show a prototypical form of bias on the part of the witness, and thereby 'to expose to the jury the facts from which jurors . . . could appropriately draw inferences relating to the reliabiity of the witness.' " 475 U.S., at 680, quoting Davis, supra, at 318.

In the instant case, petitioner has consistently asserted that he and Matthews engaged in consensual sexual acts and that Matthews — out of fear of jeopardizing her relationship with Russell — lied when she told Russell she had been raped and has continued to lie since. It is plain to us that "[a] reasonable jury might have received a significantly different impression of [the witness'] credibility had [defense counsel] been permitted to pursue his proposed line of cross-examination." Delaware v. Van Arsdall, supra, at 680.

The Kentucky Court of Appeals did not dispute, and indeed acknowledged, the relevance of the impeachment evidence. Nonetheless, without acknowledging the significance of, or even adverting to, petitioner's constitutional right to confrontation, the court held that petitioner's right to effective cross-examination was outweighed by the danger that revealing Matthews' interracial relationship would prejudice the jury against her. While a trial court may, of course, impose reasonable limits on defense counsel's inquiry into the potential bias of a prosecution witness, to take account of such factors as "harassment, prejudice, confusion of the issues, the witness' safety, or interrogation that [would be] repetitive or only marginally relevant," Delaware v. Van Arsdall, supra, at 679, the limitation here was beyond reason. Speculation as to the effect of jurors' racial biases cannot justify exclusion of cross-examination with such strong potential to demonstrate the falsity of Matthews' testimony.

In Delaware v. Van Arsdall, supra, we held that "the constitutionally improper denial of a defendant's opportunity to impeach a witness for bias, like other Confrontation Clause errors, is subject to Chapman [v. California, 386 U.S. 18 (1967)] harmless-error analysis." Id., at 684. Thus we stated:

> "The correct inquiry is whether, assuming that the damaging potential of the cross-examination were fully realized, a reviewing court might none-theless say that the error was harmless beyond a reasonable doubt. Whether such an error is harmless in a particular case depends upon a host of factors, all readily accessible to reviewing courts. These factors include the importance of the witness' testimony in the prosecution's case, whether the testimony was cumulative, the presence or absence of evidence corroborating or contradicting the testimony of the witness on material points, the extent of cross-examination otherwise permitted, and, of course, the overall strength of the prosecution's case." Ibid.

Here, Matthews' testimony was central, indeed crucial, to the prosecution's case. Her story, which was directly contradicted by that of petitioner and Harris, was corroborated only by the largely derivative testimony of Russell, whose impartiality would also have been somewhat impugned by revelation of his relationship with Matthews. Finally, as demonstrated graphically by the jury's verdicts, which cannot be squared with the State's theory of the alleged crime, and by Judge Clayton's dissenting opinion below, the State's case against petitioner was far from over-whelming. In sum, considering the relevant Van Arsdall factors within the context of this case, we find it impossible to conclude "beyond a reasonable doubt" that the restriction on petitioner's right to confrontation was harmless.

The motion for leave to proceed in forma pauperis and the petition for certiorari are granted, the judgment of the Kentucky Court of Appeals is reversed, and the case is remanded for further proceedings not inconsistent with this opinion.

It is so ordered.

RODRIGUEZ-HERNANDEZ v. MIRANDA-VELEZ
United States Court of Appeals, First Circuit
132 F.3d 848 (1st Cir. 1998)

Sandra Rodriguez-Hernandez was discharged from her job at Occidental International after complaining to her employer about being subjected to the sexual demands of a high-level executive at Occidental's most important customer. . . .

Rodriguez worked as an office manager for Occidental International, a Florida company with offices in Florida and Puerto Rico. Rodriguez started working for Occidental in December of 1988 in the Traffic and Claims division of the Puerto Rico office. She was twice promoted, and was put in charge of overseeing the daily operations of her office in February of 1990. While she was never formally evaluated during her employment, Rodriguez received regular praise for her work, and before the suspension and dismissal that led to this lawsuit, she had never been the subject of disciplinary action.

[Occidental's president was known for employing young, attractive women, who were known to customers as "Occidental Gals." One of Occidental's main customers was the Puerto Rico Electric Power Authority (PREPA). Edwin Miranda-Velez was PREPA's chief of its Materials Management Division. Rodriguez's duties required her to interact frequently with Miranda.]

Miranda began to make unwelcome approaches and suggestive comments to Rodriguez. He invited her out to dinner. He asked her to visit his office after hours and on Friday evenings. He anonymously sent her flowers for her birthday and included a sexually explicit card. Rodriguez complained to Chavez about this behavior; Chavez responded by stressing that Miranda was an important client, but assured her that he would deal with the problem.

The culmination, as it were, of Miranda's advances came on February 28, 1992. Miranda called Rodriguez and told her he would come pick her up to take her to a motel. Rodriguez, upset by Miranda's latest advance, called Chavez to complain about Miranda's call. Chavez responded by defending Miranda, and saying that Rodriguez should respond to Miranda "as a woman." Rodriguez told Chavez that if he would do nothing about the situation, she would take her complaints to the Director of PREPA.

That weekend, Chavez flew to Puerto Rico. On March 9, 1992, Chavez gave Rodriguez a letter informing her that she was suspended from work for thirty days. The letter stated the reasons for her suspension as unauthorized use of company property, contracting for services in the company name without authorization, and absenteeism. On April 6, Rodriguez received a second letter dismissing her from employment at Occidental. The grounds for her dismissal were an unexplained imbalance of $157.00 in petty cash funds and negligence in executing daily functions such as picking up company mail, as well as the problems noted in the March 9 letter. Rodriguez had never been notified of any such deficiencies before.

[Rodriguez filed a complaint with the EEOC and received a right-to-sue letter to sue Miranda, PREPA, Chavez and Occidental under Title VII of the Civil Rights Act of 1964. The trial was hotly contested by both sides.]

1. Rulings under Rule 412

Defendants continually sought to make an issue of plaintiff's sexual history. In the course of this litigation, defendants attempted to paint the plaintiff as sexually insatiable, as engaging in multiple affairs with married men, as a lesbian, and as suffering from a sexually transmitted disease.[18] Defendants claimed that plaintiff had an affair with a married man that caused her to become distracted from work, and led to the lapses for which she was fired.

---

[18] [n.2] During discovery, defendants requested that plaintiff submit to an AIDS test, apparently to substantiate their allegations of promiscuity. The request was denied.

Fed. R. Evid. 412 was designed to prevent misuse of a complainant's sexual history in cases involving "alleged sexual misconduct." In a civil case, the sole exception to Rule 412's prohibition of evidence offered to prove "that any alleged victim engaged in other sexual behavior" or "any alleged victim's sexual predisposition" is that

> evidence offered to prove the sexual behavior or sexual predisposition of any alleged victim is admissible if it is otherwise admissible under these rules and its probative value substantially outweighs the danger of harm to any victim and of unfair prejudice to any party. Evidence of an alleged victim's reputation is admissible only if it has been placed in controversy by the alleged victim. Fed. R. Evid. 412(b)(2) (emphasis added).

Rule 412 thus reverses the usual approach of the Federal Rules of Evidence on admissibility by requiring that the evidence's probative value "substantially out-weigh" its prejudicial effect. . . .

The district court ruled that evidence concerning plaintiff's moral character or promiscuity and the marital status of her boyfriend was inadmissible under Rule 412. But the court allowed defendants to introduce evidence directly relevant to their theory that plaintiff's relationship distracted her from work. The court also held that evidence concerning plaintiff's allegedly flirtatious behavior toward Miranda was admissible to determine whether Miranda's advances were in fact "unwanted."

These evidentiary rulings were well within the district court's discretion. The court struck an acceptable balance between the danger of undue prejudice and the need to present the jury with relevant evidence, particularly in light of Rule 412's special standard of admissibility.

DISCUSSION QUESTIONS

1. Setting aside the social policy considerations of Rule 412, what is the logical chain of relevance for the following types of evidence under Rule 401, and what is the probative value of each type of evidence?

    a. Evidence that the victim is a virgin or a chaste married person.

    b. Evidence that the victim has been in a consensual sexual relationship with another person besides the defendant in the past.

    c. Evidence that the victim has a reputation for promiscuity either (1) known to the accused; or (2) not known to the accused.

    d. Evidence that the victim has made false claims of rape in the past.

2. What are the dangers of Rule 412(b)(1)(C)'s exception to admit evidence when constitutionally required? In a "gray area" case, should the judge adhere to the purpose of Rule 412 or bend towards the defendant in ruling on the evidence?

3. Given the original purpose of Rule 412 to protect crime victims, does it make sense to extend the rule to plaintiffs or alleged victims of sexual misconduct in civil cases? Why or why not?

PROBLEMS

Problem 8-1. While driving on a remote rural interstate highway, Defendant stops to pick up a female hitchhiker. While traveling down the highway, they talk amicably for an hour or so, then Defendant takes an exit and parks his car in a wooded area near a frontage road. Two hours later, the hitchhiker appears at the door of a nearby farmhouse and asks to use the telephone. She calls the police and reports that she has been raped by Defendant. In an interview with police, Defendant acknowledges having sexual intercourse with the hitchhiker but claims it was consensual. He is indicted and tried for rape. In accordance with Rule 412, his attorney provides notice to the prosecution of intent to offer the following evidence:

(1) A defense investigator discovered that Hitchhiker was using oral contraceptives at the time she met the defendant.

(2) The contents of a conversation between Defendant and Hitchhiker in which she told him about breaking up with an old boyfriend who was unable to meet her sexual needs.

(3) A conversation — also discovered by the investigator — in which Hitchhiker told a friend of her plan to pick up a stranger, seduce him, and write a short story about the experience.

(4) Hitchhiker's arrest two years earlier for indecent exposure and prostitution.

What arguments should the defense make in support of each of these types of evidence? How should the prosecution respond? What ruling should the judge make?

Problem 8-2. Velma works for the Calamity State Highway Patrol, an organization dominated both in numbers and influence by men. Two years ago, she suffered a knee injury that required her to be assigned to desk duty at Troop 55 Headquarters. Tom Troglodyte, her immediate supervisor at Troop 55, thinks she is malingering, hates the idea of women on the force, and also finds Velma irresistibly attractive. He attempts to woo her by displaying pornography at his work station, telling dirty jokes in her presence, brushing up against her, and lewdly (and loudly) propositioning her for various sex acts. She endures his actions without complaint for a year. He then escalates his actions by touching her inappropriately, following her home, and attempting to have sexual intercourse with her. Wanting to keep her job, she does not complain, although she does manage to avoid having intercourse with Troglodyte. She files a complaint with the EEOC and sues Troglodyte and the State Highway Patrol under Title VII of the Civil Rights Act of 1964. Prior to trial, Troglodyte files notice under Rule 412 of his intent to introduce the following evidence at trial:

(1) An incident that occurred six months after Velma moved to Troop 55 HQ in which she invited another male officer to her home for dinner, modeled lingerie for him, and attempted unsuccessfully to seduce him.

(2) Velma's reputation throughout the Highway Patrol for promiscuity.

(3) Dirty stories and jokes that Velma told around the water cooler at Troop 55 HQ, including stories involving her own sexual exploits.

What arguments should Troglodyte make in support of this evidence? How should Velma respond? How should the judge rule?

Rape Shield Rule: Quick Hits

- Rule 412 protects alleged victims of sexual assaults from being humiliated at trial by excluding evidence of their sexual history to prove sexual disposition or behavior.

- In criminal cases, the rule balances the interests of the victim with the constitutional rights provided to a criminal accused. The rule permits introduction of specific acts of the victim for three limited purposes: (1) to prove alternative source of injury or semen; (2) to provide evidence of mistake of fact as to consent based on past sexual behavior between the defendant and victim; (3) if otherwise constitutionally required.

- In civil cases, evidence of the victim's sexual disposition or behavior is admissibly only if its probative value substantially outweighs prejudice to the victim.

- In all cases, the rule requires pretrial notice to the opposing side and the alleged victim and an in-camera hearing on the issues to protect the privacy of the alleged victim.

Chapter References

CHRISTOPHER B. MUELLER & LAIRD C. KIRKPATRICK, EVIDENCE §§ 4.32–4.34 (4th ed. 2009).

GLEN WEISSENBERGER & JAMES J. DUANE, FEDERAL RULES OF EVIDENCE: RULES, LEGISLATIVE HISTORY, COMMENTARY AND AUTHORITY § 412 (6th ed. 2009).

JACK B. WEINSTEIN & MARGARET A. BERGER, WEINSTEIN'S FEDERAL EVIDENCE § 412 (Joseph M. McLaughlin ed., Matthew Bender 2d ed. 1997).

KENNETH S. BROUN, MCCORMICK ON EVIDENCE § 193 (6th ed. 2006).

STEVEN J. GOODE & OLIN GUY WELLBORN III, COURTROOM HANDBOOK ON FEDERAL EVIDENCE Ch. 5 (West 2010).

III. APPLICATION EXERCISE

The application exercise for this chapter is a Rule 412 motion and supporting legal memorandum. The assignment, including the fact pattern, format and due date, will be given to you by your professor under separate cover.

PART THREE

CHARACTER EVIDENCE

Chapter 9

INTRODUCTION TO EVIDENCE OF CHARACTER & HABIT EVIDENCE; USE OF SUCH EVIDENCE IN CRIMINAL CASES

Chapter Objectives:

- Introduce and explain Rules 404(a), 405, 406 and the concepts of character evidence, forms of character evidence, and habit evidence in criminal cases.
- Analyze and discuss issues pertaining to Rules 404(a), 405 and 406 through case law and hypothetical problems
- Apply the concepts from this chapter in a courtroom application exercise

---

I. BACKGROUND AND EXPLANATORY MATERIAL

Introduction to Character Evidence

Human beings use character evidence constantly in their everyday decision-making processes and evaluations of others. And yet, because of the strong Anglo-Saxon tradition that a person should be tried only for the case at bar and not for their entire life's history, character evidence is strongly disfavored at trial. The danger is that a jury might use character evidence to fill in evidentiary gaps at trial, thereby circumventing the legitimate order of proof and burdens of persuasion at trial. Thus, in most instances, the jury never gets to hear some of the most relevant and highly probative evidence that might be available in a case, the type of evidence the jurors would probably consider particularly valuable in weighing the evidence. Ironically, habit evidence, which is closely related to character evidence, has no such restrictions and where applicable, can be freely admitted even if uncorroborated.

Understanding character evidence is a three-step process. The first step is to learn what character evidence is, what it represents, and why it is both valuable and dangerous. The second step is to learn the forms through which character evidence can be introduced at trial. The third step is to understand how to test or rebut character evidence and the forms available for doing so.

The foundational concepts of character evidence are the same in criminal and civil cases. The circumstances and specific applications of character evidence, however, differ greatly between criminal and civil cases. This chapter will introduce the foundational concepts of character evidence but will then focus exclusively on their application in a criminal context.

The Conceptual Underpinnings of Character and Habit Evidence

Character Evidence

The term "character" is used to describe personality traits that are deeply ingrained in a person's psyche. The noted evidence scholar Charles McCormick defined character as "a generalized description of one's disposition, or of one's disposition in respect to a general trait, such as honesty, temperance, or peacefulness." Individuals develop character traits through years of thoughts and decisions translated into words and deeds. Thus, for example, a person who has the character trait of honesty likely earned the trait label as the result of hundreds or thousands of decisions and actions over a period of years, and it would be difficult to conceive of such a person behaving in a dishonest manner, contrary to his character. The generalized terms that are used to define character traits sweep with a broad brush, but they are useful in providing a quick shorthand snapshot of an individual's personality.

As previously mentioned, character is an important component of our everyday decision-making process. People tend to rely on character evidence to make decisions, because "[p]ast conduct or performance is usually thought to be one of the best predictors of future behavior." Most people would not, for example, hire a babysitter with the character trait of carelessness, entrust their money to a banker with the character trait of dishonesty, or pick a fight with a person who has the character trait of violence or turbulence. People make conclusions about the character of others by seeking information about their specific actions, their reputations, or the opinions held by their friends, acquaintances and enemies.

The logical structure that people typically follow in making character-based decisions is simple to understand and follow. Step one is gathering the information to conclude that an individual has a particular character trait. Step two is a logical inference that the character trait is evidence of the individual's propensity to behave in a particular manner. Step three is the conclusion that the character trait has predictive value in determining how the individual acted on a particular occasion. Suppose that John is on trial for assaulting another patron at a bar and that John has a character trait of violence. Following the logical pathway established above, if the prosecution were permitted to introduce character evidence at trial, a juror could use John's character as follows: (1) John has a character trait for violence; (2) people who have the character trait of violence are likely to behave in a violent manner; (3) John's character trait for violence makes it more likely that he acted in accordance with it and committed the charged offense.

There are several recognized dangers associated with the use of character evidence at trial. First, because the use of character evidence is so prevalent in everyday life, the danger exists that the jury will overvalue its importance at trial; in the words of Justice Jackson, "[character evidence] is not rejected because character is irrelevant; on the contrary, it is said to weigh too much with the jury and to so overpersuade them as to prejudge one with a bad general record and deny him a fair opportunity to defend against a particular charge." Second, the use of character evidence could perhaps cause the jury to disregard the burden of proof at trial. For example, if the prosecution in a criminal case presents weak evidence, but introduces a character trait of the defendant consistent with the charged offense, the jury might conclude that the defendant acted consistently with his character on the charged occasion and convict despite the absence of proof beyond a reasonable doubt. Third, while character evidence may provide a generally accurate picture of an individual's decisions and actions, "[it is] less accurate when used to decide what happened on one particular occasion because people do not always act in accordance with their propensities." Fourth, the introduction of character evidence could potentially complicate and considerably lengthen trial proceedings; a man on trial who must answer for his entire life, as opposed simply to the charged offenses, might want to contest and introduce counterproof of some of the character evidence introduced against him.

Because of these dangers, the common law broadly prohibited the use of character evidence at trial, with some specific exceptions that will be discussed later in this chapter. Rule 404(a) adopted the common law approach to character evidence. As a general rule, character evidence is not admissible at trial to prove propensity or conforming conduct.

The text of Rule 404(a) follows:

Through Dec. 1, 2011	After Dec. 1, 2011
Rule 404. Character Evidence Not Admissible to Prove Conduct; Exceptions; Other Crimes	**Rule 404. Character Evidence; Crimes or Other Acts**
(a) **Character evidence generally**. Evidence of a person's character or a trait of character is not admissible for the purpose of proving action in conformity therewith on a particular occasion, except:	(a) **Character Evidence**.
	(1) *Prohibited Uses*. Evidence of a person's character or character trait is not admissible to prove that on a particular occasion the person acted in accordance with the character or trait.
(1) **Character of accused**. In a criminal case, evidence of a pertinent trait of character offered by an accused, or by the prosecution to rebut the same, or if evidence of a trait of character of the alleged victim of the crime is offered by an accused and admitted under Rule 404(a)(2), evidence of the same trait of character of the accused offered by the prosecution;	(2) *Exceptions for a Defendant or Victim in a Criminal Case*. The following exceptions apply in a criminal case:
	(A) a defendant may offer evidence of the defendant's pertinent trait, and if the evidence is admitted, the prosecutor may offer evidence to rebut it;
(2) **Character of alleged victim**. In a criminal case, and subject to the limitations imposed by Rule 412, evidence of a pertinent trait of character of the alleged victim of the crime offered by an accused, or by the prosecution to rebut the same, or evidence of a character trait of peacefulness of the alleged victim offered by the prosecution in a homicide case to rebut evidence that the alleged victim was the first aggressor;	(B) subject to the limitations in Rule 412, a defendant may offer evidence of an alleged victim's pertinent trait, and if the evidence is admitted, the prosecutor may:
	(i) offer evidence to rebut it; and
	(ii) offer evidence of the defendant's same trait; and
(3) **Character of witness**. Evidence of the character of a witness, as provided in Rules 607, 608, and 609.	(C) in a homicide case, the prosecutor may offer evidence of the alleged victim's trait of peacefulness to rebut evidence that the victim was the first aggressor.
	(3) *Exceptions for a Witness*. Evidence of a witness's character may be admitted under Rules 607, 608, and 609.

Habit

Evidence of habit is similar to character evidence, but with an important distinction. Rather than inferentially suggesting a person's behavior based on general character traits, habit evidence focuses on a person's consistent actions in certain situations. The jury is permitted to conclude that a person who always acts in a particular way would have done so on the occasion in question. The Advisory

Committee Notes to Rule 406 explain the difference between character and habit evidence by quoting the noted evidence scholar Charles McCormick:

> Character and habit are close akin. Character is a generalized description of one's disposition, or of one's disposition in respect to a general trait, such as honesty, temperance, or peacefulness. 'Habit,' in modern usage, both lay and psychological, is more specific. It describes one's regular response to a repeated specific situation. If we speak of character for care, we think of the person's tendency to act prudently in all the varying situations of life, in business, family life, in handling automobiles and in walking across the street. A habit, on the other hand, is the person's regular practice of meeting a particular kind of situation with a specific type of conduct, such as the habit of going down a particular stairway two stairs at a time, or of giving the hand-signal for a left turn, or of alighting from railway cars while they are moving. The doing of the habitual acts may become semi-automatic. . . . Character may be thought of as the sum of one's habits though doubtless it is more than this. But unquestionably the uniformity of one's response to habit is far greater than the consistency with which one's conduct conforms to character or disposition. Even though character comes in only exceptionally as evidence of an act, surely any sensible man in investigating whether X did a particular act would be greatly helped in his inquiry by evidence as to whether he was in the habit of doing it.[1]

Because habits are behaviors that are practically automatic, habit evidence is thought to present fewer dangers at trial than character evidence. Accordingly, subject to strict foundational requirements that will be explained later, parties are permitted to introduce habit evidence at trial to prove conforming conduct. For example, in a case involving a vehicle hitting a pedestrian crossing the road, evidence that the pedestrian habitually looked both ways before crossing the street could be used to prove that the pedestrian did so in the incident in question.

The habit rules are codified in Rule 406:

Through Dec. 1, 2011	After Dec. 1, 2011
Rule 406. Habit; Routine Practice	**Rule 406. Habit; Routine Practice**
Evidence of the habit of a person or of the routine practice of an organization, whether corroborated or not and regardless of the presence of eyewitnesses, is relevant to prove that the conduct of the person or organization on a particular occasion was in conformity with the habit or routine practice.	Evidence of a person's habit or an organization's routine practice may be admitted to prove that on a particular occasion the person or organization acted in accordance with the habit or routine practice. The court may admit this evidence regardless of whether it is corroborated or whether there was an eyewitness.

Habit evidence pertains to individuals, and evidence of routine practice pertains to

---

[1] FED. R. EVID. 406, advisory committee notes, *quoting* McCormick § 162, at 340–41.

organizations and corporations. The rules for habit and routine practice at trial are the same.

Types of Evidence Used to Prove Character and Habit

Proof of Pertinent Character Traits

Rule 404 contains a general prohibition against the use of character evidence but recognizes that it is admissible under limited circumstances. The threshold inquiry under Rule 404 is whether the proposed character evidence is pertinent to the case. The term "pertinent" is similar to relevance under Rule 401, but is more narrowly construed. For example, in a homicide or assault case, pertinent character traits include peacefulness, turbulence, violence or aggression, but not honesty, integrity, or chastity. There is a tendency at trial for advocates to attempt to introduce character traits that are not strictly pertinent to the case at hand, and opponents should watch carefully to ensure that this threshold character requirement is not abused.

Rule 404 does not stand alone; it must be read in conjunction with Rule 405, which delineates the forms of evidence that can be used to prove character.

Through Dec. 1, 2011	After Dec. 1, 2011
Rule 405. Methods of Proving Character	**Rule 405. Methods of Proving Character**
(a) Reputation or opinion. In all cases in which evidence of character or a trait of character of a person is admissible, proof may be made by testimony as to reputation or by testimony in the form of an opinion. On cross-examination, inquiry is allowable into relevant specific instances of conduct.	**(a) By Reputation or Opinion**. When evidence of a person's character or character trait is admissible, it may be proved by testimony about the person's reputation or by testimony in the form of an opinion. On cross-examination of the character witness, the court may allow an inquiry into relevant specific instances of the person's conduct.
(b) Specific instances of conduct. In cases in which character or a trait of character of a person is an essential element of a charge, claim, or defense, proof may also be made of specific instances of that person's conduct.	**(b) By Specific Instances of Conduct**. When a person's character or character trait is an essential element of a charge, claim, or defense, the character or trait may also be proved by relevant specific instances of the person's conduct.

According to Rule 405, there are three forms of character evidence that are available at trial: reputation evidence, opinion testimony, and specific acts. The use of specific acts evidence is strictly limited to cases where character evidence is an "essential element of a charge, claim, or defense." In the criminal context, as will be discussed in more detail infra, such circumstances are rare indeed. Each form of evidence and its foundational requirements will be discussed in turn.

Reputation evidence consists of testimony about what others in the community think about the person whose character is at issue. It is in reality a form of shorthand hearsay in which a witness is allowed to tell the jury what other people think about the person about whose character the witness is testifying. Whether good or bad, the reputation earned by a person within a community is the result of specific acts, omissions, and words of that person over a period of years, as well as the gossip and reports about that person generated by others. Reputation testimony neatly distills all that into a compact statement, such as, "Mother Theresa has a reputation for kindness and charity in the world community." A reputation witness can testify only about the broad character trait and is not allowed to testify about specific underlying facts that helped form the reputation. Thus, a reputation witness could not talk about the work Mother Theresa did in the slums of India — only the reputation that she earned in doing this work.

The foundation for reputation testimony is simple. The witness testifies that she belongs to a certain community, along with the person whose character is at issue. She testifies that the person has developed a reputation in the community for a pertinent character trait. She then testifies what that reputation is. It should be noted that the term "community" is broadly defined. It includes not only towns and cities, but also workplaces, social organizations, military units, and the like.

Of the forms of character evidence, reputation is considered the weakest. This is because it is essentially distilled hearsay, devoid of almost any informational value but the labeled character trait.

Opinion testimony is considered slightly stronger than reputation testimony. Like reputation testimony, it distills the person's words and actions over a period of time into a general character trait. It is more powerful than reputation testimony because it represents the witness's direct observations over time, rather than what the witness has heard others say about the person whose character is at issue.

The foundation for opinion testimony is as follows. The witness testifies that she has known the person whose character is at issue for a particular length of time. The witness next testifies that during that time, she has had the opportunity to form an opinion of the person as to a pertinent character trait. The witness then testifies as to what her opinion is, but without being able to tell the jury the basis for her opinion — in other words, leaving out the specific incidents that helped her reach an opinion about the person's character. For example, the witness could testify, "I have known Mother Theresa for six years. During that time, I have had the opportunity to develop an opinion regarding her character for kindness and charity. In my opinion, she has a good character for kindness and charity."

Specific acts evidence is the strongest form of character evidence under the Rules. The underlying premise of this type of evidence is that past acts define one's character and also serve as a predictor of future acts. The logic of specific acts is as follows: X commits an act; the act is proof of X's character; therefore, X's future acts will be in accordance with his character.

In reality, most everyday character decisions are made on the basis of specific acts. For example, a parent who learns that a babysitter had permitted young children to play in the street while she talked on the phone with her boyfriend would likely determine that the babysitter had the character trait of carelessness or irresponsibility and would refuse to hire the babysitter. The specific act would serve as a much more powerful indicator of character and predictor of future actions than the generalized trait labels "careless" or "irresponsible."

Because specific acts evidence is so strong, and the overall probative value of character evidence at trial is considered so slight, the use of specific acts evidence at trial is limited under Rule 405 to cases in which character forms "an essential element of a charge, claim, or defense." As will be discussed in the next chapter, there are a number of instances in which character evidence is an essential part of a civil case. Other than the entrapment defense, in which a criminal defendant makes his own character an essential part of the defense by claiming he never would have committed an offense but for the government's inducement, there are virtually no instances in which character forms an essential element of a charge, claim, or defense in a criminal case. This is so even if character evidence forms the bulk of a defendant's defense strategy at trial.

Specific acts evidence includes not only affirmative evidence of acts, but also evidence of the absence of acts. If a witness testifies that the person whose character is at issue has never done a particular thing, that testimony is specific acts evidence. For example, in a speeding case, the defendant may not call a witness to testify that the defendant has never before gotten a speeding ticket.

When permitted at trial, the foundation for specific acts is as follows. The witness testifies that he or she is familiar with a pertinent specific act or instance of conduct committed by the person whose character is at issue. The witness testifies as to the foundational factors that demonstrate personal knowledge of the act. The witness then testifies as to the act itself.

Proof of Habit or Routine Practice

Habit evidence does not have to be corroborated and can be proved by reputation, opinion or specific acts. The key foundational words of habit testimony are words such as "always," "habitually," "invariably," or the like. A person who "usually" or "generally" does something in a particular way does not have a habit, but merely a tendency, and such testimony is inadmissible as habit evidence to prove conforming conduct.

Testing Character Witnesses and Rebutting Character Evidence

Testing Character Witnesses

The vast majority of character evidence introduced at trial is in the form of reputation or opinion testimony. Besides the previously discussed weaknesses of these forms of evidence, they carry with them some additional dangers. Opinion witnesses are susceptible to bias and may have formed their opinions based on an isolated specific instance. Reputation witnesses, who are essentially introducing filtered hearsay into the courtroom, are no better than the sources of their information when it comes to giving meaningful testimony about a person's reputation for a pertinent character trait.

Rule 405, therefore, contains a mechanism for testing the knowledge of a reputation or opinion witness by cross-examination on specific acts. The purpose of this cross-examination is not to circumvent Rule 405's general prohibition on specific acts evidence. The specific acts inquired into on cross-examination cannot be considered by the jury for their truth, and if the witness denies knowledge of them or claims they can't possibly be true, the examiner is not permitted to provide extrinsic proof of the acts; the examiner is bound by the witness's answer. In closing argument, the examiner can only discuss the specific acts as they pertain to the credibility or bias of the character witness.

Testing a witness's testimony under Rule 405 functions in the following manner. First, in the pretrial preparation and discovery process, the parties explore character issues and prepare to introduce or respond to pertinent character evidence. Second, the proponent of the character witness introduces reputation or opinion testimony of a pertinent character trait. Third, the opponent cross-examines the character witness's knowledge by asking about specific acts that run counter to the reputation or opinion testimony. The opponent must have a good-faith basis to believe that the specific acts are true and must be prepared to make an offer of proof to the judge and opposing counsel. The form of these questions is also critical; the opponent must use the phrases "have you heard," "were you aware," or "did you know," when introducing the specific acts. Fourth, the opponent appropriately uses the cross-examination results on closing argument.

There are only two appropriate uses for the information derived from cross-examination on specific acts. First, a witness's lack of knowledge of the specific acts suggests an inadequate basis for their reputation or opinion testimony. Second, a witness may reveal bias by admitting knowledge of the specific acts but insisting the reputation or opinion is nonetheless true.

The following examples illustrate the operation of this rule. Suppose that in a criminal assault case, the defendant calls a witness to testify that the defendant has a reputation for peacefulness in the community. Having appropriately prepared for trial, and armed with a good-faith belief that the specific instances are in fact true, the defendant's counsel might cross-examine the character witness as follows:

Q: *You have testified that the defendant has a reputation for peacefulness?*

A: *Yes.*

Q: *Have you heard that the defendant started a bar fight at the Wild West Bar and Grill on September 15 last year?*

A: *No, I hadn't heard that.*

Q: *Were you aware that the defendant beat up his girlfriend on October 15 of last year?*

A: *No, I wasn't aware of that.*

Counsel can then argue on closing that the character witness's testimony should be discounted because the witness obviously knew very little about the defendant.

A variation follows.

Q: *You have testified that, in your opinion, the defendant is a peaceful man?*

A: *Yes.*

Q: *Have you heard that the defendant started a bar fight at the Wild West Bar and Grill on September 15 last year?*

A: *Yes, I heard that.*

Q: *Were you aware that the defendant beat up his girlfriend on October 15 of last year?*

A: *Yes, I was aware of that.*

Counsel can then argue on closing that the character witness's testimony should be discounted because it is incredible or biased. A witness may well be biased who persists in testifying that a person has a peaceful character despite the witness's admitted knowledge countervailing acts such as starting bar fights or domestic violence.

Rebutting Character Evidence

When a party introduces pertinent character evidence under Rule 404, the opponent is entitled to rebut with pertinent countervailing character evidence. Under Rule 405, the form of the evidence is generally limited to reputation or opinion testimony, except in the rare cases when character is an essential element of a charge, claim or defense. Thus, if the defendant in a case introduces evidence that the victim had a turbulent character, the prosecution could introduce evidence that the victim had a peaceful character. It would then be up to the jury to weigh and balance the evidence.

Character Evidence in Criminal Cases

Rule 404(a) applies exclusively to criminal cases, although it must be read in conjunction with Rule 405 for the forms of evidence. The key concept pertaining to character evidence in criminal cases is that the criminal defendant holds all the keys to character evidence. The defendant chooses whether to introduce evidence of his own good character or the victim's bad character. Once that decision is made, Rule 404(a) permits the prosecution to respond in particular ways.

To help understand the criminal character rules, it is appropriate to review the historical development of the rules. The following excerpt and table from a law review article explain the character evidence rules in criminal cases:

Christopher W. Behan, *When Turnabout is Fair Play: Character Evidence and Self-Defense in Homicide and Assault Cases*
86 OR. L. REV. 733 (2007)

Under the common law, the criminal defendant held the key to the admission of character evidence pertaining to his own character. According to the so-called "mercy rule," a criminal accused could introduce evidence of his own good character to suggest reasonable doubt as to the charges against him. The prosecution could rebut the defendant's character evidence either by calling character witnesses of its own, or by cross examining the defendant's character witnesses with specific instances of the defendant's conduct to test their knowledge. If the defendant elected to say nothing about his character, the subject was off-limits to the prosecution. In Michelson v. United States, a famous character evidence case from the mid-twentieth century, the Supreme Court explained that the law does not "invest[] the defendant with a presumption of good character, but it simply closes the whole matter of character . . . disposition and reputation on the prosecution's case-in-chief."

There appear to be two broad historical justifications for placing the decision to use character evidence in the hands of the defendant, rather than the prosecutor. First, the common law had a well-documented mistrust of the jury's ability to use character evidence properly. If affirmatively introduced by the prosecution, character evidence could influence the jury to make decisions for improper reasons, possibly relieving the prosecution of the burden to prove guilt on the particular charge beyond a reasonable doubt. Prosecutorial introduction of character evidence would also flout a foundational principle of Anglo-American law, the concept that a criminal defendant should be tried on the charges against him rather than for his life's character.

The second primary reason for placing the character decision in the hands of the defendant was to preserve balance. "There is reason to believe," wrote a nineteenth-century American court, "that this exception [the exclusion of character evidence against the defendant] originated in a usurpation of legislative power by English judges, led by a merciful impulse to mitigate the cruelty of a bloody criminal code by throwing obstacles in the way of its operation." In other words, giving the defendant exclusive control over character evidence was intended to serve as a shield against the power of the state.

One scholar has referred to the policy of letting the defendant use character evidence in his defense as "the inborn sporting instinct of Anglo-Normandom–the instinct of giving the game fair play even at the expense of efficiency of procedure." The policy, which provides that a man on trial for his life or liberty ought to have a sporting chance to defend himself, permits the accused to enjoy a small advantage over the government in matters related to character evidence. Its significance does not rest on its utility to the accused or on its handicapping effect on the prosecution. Rather, the policy is important because of its implied message that criminal justice is concerned not only with convicting the guilty, but also with ensuring that the innocent are not improperly found guilty using inappropriate evidence.

If the decision to introduce character evidence rests with the state, the potential prejudice to the defendant and the interests of justice is considerable: not only might the defendant suffer an unjust conviction, but the values at the bedrock of the criminal justice system suffer if juries are permitted to make decisions for the wrong reasons, and using the wrong evidence. On the other hand, the state suffers relatively little prejudice when the character evidence decision rests with the accused: if the accused is convicted in the absence of negative character evidence against him, the likelihood is higher that the jury reached its decision for the proper reasons. In the final analysis, leaving the character evidence decision up to the defendant may lead to verdicts that are more just than they would otherwise be.

Victim Character Evidence

No one would seriously argue with the proposition that a criminal justice system should provide fairness and due process to the defendant. There is a legitimate question, however, whether that should occur at the expense of an alleged crime victim. As Richard Uviller has observed, permitting the defendant to offer proof of the victim's bad character could damage a person (the victim) who has not placed his or her character in issue at trial. Nevertheless, evidence of the victim's character can play a valuable role at trial, particularly in homicide or assault cases, in helping the jury determine what happened in the incident at bar. As with the rules governing evidence of the defendant's character, the hallmark of the common law rules was a balancing of the relative interests of the defendant and the victim at trial. In the words of Benjamin Tillers, "It should not be forgotten that the accused is on trial, whereas in a criminal prosecution the victim, except in a metaphorical and literal sense, is not."

Thus, the common law gave the criminal defendant the ability to introduce evidence pertaining to the victim's bad character in certain instances, primarily homicide, assault, and rape cases. These attacks could be rebutted with evidence of the victim's good character. Taking this concept further, Dean John Henry Wigmore believed that if the defendant was permitted to attack the victim's character for violence, "the same principle would then justify the prosecution (or plaintiff) in introducing the defendant's character for violence." Significantly, however, the majority of American jurisdictions have not historically permitted the prosecution to rebut an attack on the victim's character with a counterattack on the defendant's character. . . .

When the Federal Rules of Evidence were promulgated, the common law character evidence system was adopted without significant change. In fact, as will be discussed later in this section, the methods of proving character and the purposes for which character evidence may be introduced at trial were virtually the same under the common law and the Federal Rules of Evidence until the Advisory Committee's 2000 amendment to Rule 404(a)(1). . . .

Federal Rule of Evidence 404 provides that "[e]vidence of a person's character or trait of character is not admissible for the purpose of proving action in conformity therewith on a particular occasion." Prior to the 2000 amendment, there were two exceptions to this rule: (1) the accused could offer evidence of a pertinent trait of his own character (which could be rebutted by the prosecution); and (2) the accused could offer evidence of a pertinent character trait of the victim (which could be rebutted by the prosecution). What is noteworthy about both of these exceptions is that the criminal accused had complete control over the introduction of character propensity evidence at trial and could selectively use it to bolster his own character or attack that of the victim. There was only one minor (and highly particularized) exception to this rule. When the defense introduced factual evidence that the alleged victim of a homicide was the first aggressor–for instance, a witness who testified that the victim threw the first punch–the prosecution could introduce propensity evidence of the victim's peaceful character to rebut the factual implication that the victim was the aggressor.

Prior to the 2000 amendment, Rule 404 employed a character evidence formula that relied on strict compartmentalization of character evidence by category of witness: the criminal defendant, the alleged crime victim, and other witnesses. Those categories, particularly the criminal defendant and the alleged crime victim, were akin to apples and oranges. An attack on an apple had to be met with a defense of the apple, but oranges were kept strictly out of the picture. For example, an attack on the victim's character could only be rebutted by defending the victim's character; the prosecution was not permitted to attack the defendant's character for the same pertinent trait. . . .

If there was a competitive edge to one side, it was slight, and belonged to the defense. The rule expressly permitted the defendant to attack the victim's character in a self-defense case without fear of prosecutorial retaliation against his own character. Indeed, conventional wisdom held that a defendant did not put his whole character at issue merely by claiming self- defense, because "that would make mincemeat of the limitations in Rule 404(a) on the use of character evidence."

Post-2000 Character Evidence Rules

. . . In response to a proposal by the Justice Department to link the character of the defendant and the alleged victim, the Committee amended the rule. Mixing apples and oranges for the first time, the new rule permits the prosecution to respond to defense attacks on the alleged victim's character by attacking the defendant's character for the same trait.

Rule	Defendant Action	Prosecution Response
404(a)(1) & 405	Introduce evidence (reputation or opinion) of defendant's character for peacefulness.	Rebut with evidence (reputation or opinion) of defendant's character for violence.
404(a)(2) & 405	Introduce evidence (reputation or opinion) of victim's character for violence.	Rebut with evidence (reputation or opinion) of victim's character for peacefulness. Rebut with evidence (reputation or opinion) of the defendant's character for violence.

Rule	Defendant Action	Prosecution Response
404(a)(2) & 405	Introduce factual evidence that the victim was the first aggressor.	Rebut with counter-factual evidence. Rebut with evidence (reputation or opinion) of victim's peaceful character.

II. CASES, DISCUSSION QUESTIONS AND PROBLEMS

UNITED STATES v. JOHN
United States Court of Appeals, Fifth Circuit
309 F.3d 298 (5th Cir. 2002)

John, a Choctaw Indian, was alleged to have engaged in sexual contact with his eleven-year-old female foster child on the Choctaw Indian Reservation. [The child alleged that John had sexual contact with her on two different occasions, neither of which were witnessed by a third person.]

John denied that the incidents occurred. His defense strategy was twofold. He claimed the child fabricated both incidents as a way of obtaining release from the foster home because she thought she was assigned a disproportionate share of household chores. One of her friends testified she had overheard a conversation in which the complainant and another friend discussed framing John so that she would be removed from the home.

John introduced several witnesses who testified to his good character. Although the court permitted the introduction of this evidence, it denied John's request for a jury instruction regarding character. . . .

The district court committed reversible error in refusing John's request for a character instruction. Unlike the situation in cases in which we have found a character instruction unnecessary, character was a vital part of John's theory of defense. Without any witnesses or other corroborating evidence supporting the child's accusations, guilt hinged entirely on credibility. Given these circumstances and the closeness of the case, the court should have given a character instruction.

The proposed instruction would have informed the jury it should consider evidence of "good general reputation for truth and veracity, or honesty and integrity, or [being a] law abiding-citizen." More importantly, the instruction would have informed the jury that character evidence "may give rise to a reasonable doubt, since you may think it improbable that a person of good character in respect to those traits would commit such a crime." The court apparently rejected the character instruction because it thought that John's only proffered character evidence was the testimony of Sara Lynn John, and that her testimony alone was insufficient to warrant the instruction.[2]

---

[2] [n.8] The court, by referring to character evidence as "reputation" evidence and stating that Sara Lynn John's testimony was the only "reputation" evidence adduced at trial, overlooked the fact that

A.

A character instruction is warranted only if the defendant first introduces admissible character evidence. See United States v. Tannehill, 49 F.3d 1049, 1057-58 (5th Cir. 1995). An accused may offer evidence of a pertinent character trait to prove action in conformity with that trait. FED R. EVID. 404(a)(1). In the criminal context, a pertinent character trait is one that is relevant to the offense charged. United States v. Hewitt, 634 F.2d 277, 279 (5th Cir. Unit A Jan. 1981). Where admissible, proof of character may be made by testimony as to the defendant's reputation or by testimony in the form of an opinion. FED. R. EVID. 405.

John offered a host of admissible character evidence. Geraldine John, his wife, testified that she and John had a good marriage and a normal sexual relationship. Marion Wesley, a social service worker, testified that she knew the Johns, had placed eight foster children with them, and considered them to be "very good parents [who were] willing to do whatever needs to be done for the children." John testified that he was fifty-one years old and had never been accused of sexual misconduct.[3] Finally, Sara Lynn John, John's thirty-three-year-old daughter, testified that John had a "good" reputation for sexual morality and decency in the community.[4]

This character evidence, if believed, might have swayed the jury that John was incapable of engaging in sexual contact with his foster child. The fact that this testimony was given in the form of personal opinion, rather than John's reputation in the community, does not defeat its admissibility.

B.

A defendant may introduce character testimony to show that "the general estimate of his character is so favorable that the jury may infer that he would not be likely to commit the offense charged." Michelson v. United States, 335 U.S. 469, 476, 69 S.

---

character evidence also may be proven by a witness's opinion of the defendant. FED. R. EVID. 405(a). As we will discuss, several witnesses testified to their opinion of John without mentioning his reputation in the community.

[3] [n.9] We have located no authority stating that a defendant's own testimony cannot be considered character evidence within the meaning of rule 404(a)(1). Instead, at least one court has concluded that it can. See United States v. Daily, 921 F.2d 994, 1010-11 (10th Cir. 1991) (considering the defendant's own testimony as character evidence).

[4] [n.10] A language barrier apparently prevented Sara Lynn John from initially comprehending defense counsel's questions regarding John's reputation for sexual morality and decency. After being asked three times whether she had heard people in the community discussing John's reputation for sexual morality and decency, Sara Lynn John responded "yes." When asked whether John was a "good man or a bad man," she responded "good."

The government argues that her acknowledgement on cross-examination that she gathered John's reputation only from the opinions of persons connected to the case, and only after the complainant's allegations were raised, defeats its admissibility. We disagree, noting that rule 405 (a) imposes no requirement beyond the limitation that reputation be limited to the community in which one resides.

"The defendant may introduce evidence of his reputation . . . , and such a witness not only may but must base his testimony upon hearsay, in effect summarizing what he has heard in the community." United States v. Duke, 492 F.2d 693, 695 (5th Cir. 1974). We know of no authority suggesting that a "community" cannot be made up, in whole or in part, of persons interested in the case.

Ct. 213, 93 L. Ed. 168 (1948). Unlike an affirmative defense, character evidence is never legally sufficient to render a defendant not guilty. Standing alone, however, character evidence may create a reasonable doubt regarding guilt. Edgington v. United States, 164 U.S. 361, 366, 17 S. Ct. 72, 41 L. Ed. 467 (1896). "In some circumstances, evidence of good character may of itself create a reasonable doubt as to guilt, and the jury must be appropriately instructed." Hewitt, 634 F.2d at 278 (citations omitted).

We review for abuse of discretion the refusal to give a defense-tendered instruction. United States v. Correa-Ventura, 6 F.3d 1070, 1076 (5th Cir. 1993). A court commits reversible error where (1) the requested instruction is substantially correct; (2) the requested issue is not substantially covered in the charge; and (3) the instruction "concerns an important point in the trial so that the failure to give it seriously impaired the defendant's ability to effectively present a given defense." United States v. Grissom, 645 F.2d 461, 464 (5th Cir. Unit A May 1981).

The government does not argue that the instruction is an improper statement of the law or that the issue of character was otherwise covered in the instructions. We are left to determine whether the omission of the character instruction "impaired the defendant's ability to present" his defense of good character.

A defendant "is usually entitled to have the court instruct the jury on the defense's 'theory of the case.' " United States v. Robinson, 700 F.2d 205, 211 (5th Cir. 1983) (internal citation omitted). Importantly, in cases where we have determined that the lack of a character instruction did not impair the defendant's ability to present his defense, character was not his main theory of defense.

For instance, in United States v. Baytank (Houston), Inc., 934 F.2d 599 (5th Cir. 1991), in holding that a character instruction was unnecessary where a defendant company accused of violating environmental regulations offered character evidence, we stressed that it did "not appear that character evidence was central or crucial." Id. at 614. Similarly, in United States v. Hunt, 794 F.2d 1095 (5th Cir. 1986), we found a character instruction unnecessary where the defendant was convicted of mail fraud. In that case, the defendant argued good faith as his main theory of defense and did not deny that he had solicited customers through mail, but contended only that he lacked the specific intent to defraud.

By contrast, John's theory of defense was that he did not commit the act at all. Character was necessarily a vital part of that defense, along with the credibility of the victim. Without corroborating evidence or an eyewitness, the case boiled down to a "swearing-match" between the victim and the accused. Indeed, defense counsel argued, in his opening statement and closing argument, that John's character made it unlikely that he would have engaged in sexual contact with his foster child.

The fact that character evidence may create a reasonable doubt as to guilt, Edgington, 164 U.S. at 366, is most compelling in cases such as this, where the only evidence linking the defendant to the crime is the victim's word. Therefore, under these narrow circumstances, the court's treatment of character as a non-issue was tantamount to impairing John's ability to present his defense. Grissom, 645 F.2d at 464. Given the closeness of the case, had the jury been told that character evidence might create a reasonable doubt as to guilt, the outcome may well have been different.

DISCUSSION QUESTIONS

1. The issue of character evidence in criminal cases goes directly to the heart of the jury's role in the adversarial trial process. Much of the historical prohibition was based on mistrust of the jury. Knowing what you do about juries, do you think this mistrust was warranted? Why or why not?

2. Does the current system, in which the defense holds the keys to the use of character evidence at trial, continue to make sense? What would happen if both sides had equal opportunities to decide whether or not to introduce defendant or victim character evidence?

3. Did the Johns court get it right in ruling that the defendant's character evidence entitled him to a reasonable-doubt instruction? Why or why not?

PROBLEMS

Problem 9-1. Paul is a clergyman who enjoys a reputation in the community as a peaceful person. During a walk through the bad side of town, Paul becomes involved in a doctrinal argument with Terry, a local hoodlum, drug dealer, and self-anointed sidewalk preacher. Terry has a reputation for violence in his neighborhood, although Paul does not know this at the time of their encounter. Angry at Terry's interpretation of the Sermon on the Mount, Paul draws his .44 magnum handgun and shoots Terry, killing him. There are no eyewitnesses. Several weeks after the incident, Paul learns for the first time about Terry's reputation for violence in his neighborhood. Terry earned this reputation by slapping around a series of his live-in girlfriends while intoxicated. Paul is charged with second-degree murder. At trial, he wants to raise the defense of self-defense.

1. What evidence (and in what form) do Rules 404(a) and 405 permit Paul to raise in his defense?

2. What inferences can the jury draw from this evidence?

Problem 9-2. Flint Huffner is an amateur pornographer who enjoys making video recordings of his sexual escapades and saving them in an elaborate file system on his computer. In December, while at the Stayin' Alive Nightclub in Calamity City, he met a young woman named Desiree, who agreed to go home with him. Huffner and Desiree had sexual intercourse with each other. Huffner recorded the event on a video camera mounted on a tripod in his bedroom. He did not ask Desiree's permission to record the event, and she was not aware of the camera's existence. The next day, Desiree lodged a rape complaint with the police, alleging that she told Huffner "no" but he had sexual intercourse with her anyway. The police visited Huffner's home, and he invited them in, telling them he has nothing to hide. An officer entered Huffner's room and saw the video camera pointed toward the bed. "Did you record this?" he asked. "I did," replied Huffner, "but I thought it was boring, so I deleted the file from the video card and reformatted it." "You know we can recover that file," said the police officer. The officer did not believe it was possible to recover a file from a reformatted video card. "Good," said Huffner. "I hope you can. You'll see I'm telling the truth." Huffner did not know whether a file can be recovered from a reformatted card but thought the officer is probably telling the truth. The file could not be recovered, and Huffner was charged with rape.

At trial, he testifies in his own behalf. His attorney asks this question: "Was it your habit to delete files you thought were boring?" The prosecution immediately objects. Assume that Huffner would answer yes to the question, but that there is no corroborating evidence available.

> 1. What is the basis for the prosecution's objection? How should the defense respond? How should the judge rule?

> 2. Assume you are Huffner's attorney. Draft a proposed instruction for the jury that you think would let them properly consider the evidence.

Character and Habit Evidence in Criminal Cases: Quick Hits

- The common law prohibited the prosecution from introducing evidence of the defendant's bad character to prove conformity therewith on the charged occasion.

- Under Rule 404(a), the defendant holds the key to evidence of his own character or that of the victim in a criminal case.

- The defendant may introduce reputation or opinion testimony related to a pertinent character trait of character.

- If the defendant opens the door, the prosecution may rebut on the same character trait with reputation or opinion testimony.

- If character evidence is introduced, the opposing party may cross-examine character witnesses using specific instances of conduct pertaining to the character trait.

- Habit evidence refers to the invariable or routine practice of an individual.

- Habit evidence does not have to be corroborated and can be proved by evidence of reputation, opinion or specific acts.

Chapter References

CHRISTOPHER B. MUELLER & LAIRD C. KIRKPATRICK, EVIDENCE §§ 4.11–4.14, 4.19–4.22 (4th ed. 2009).

GLEN WEISSENBERGER & JAMES J. DUANE, FEDERAL RULES OF EVIDENCE: RULES, LEGISLATIVE HISTORY, COMMENTARY AND AUTHORITY §§ 404.1–404.10, 405–06 (6th ed. 2009).

JACK B. WEINSTEIN & MARGARET A. BERGER, WEINSTEIN'S FEDERAL EVIDENCE §§ 404.01–404.13, 405–06 (Joseph M. McLaughlin ed., Matthew Bender 2d ed. 1997).

KENNETH S. BROUN, McCORMICK ON EVIDENCE §§ 186–95 (6th ed. 2006).

STEVEN GOODE & OLIN GUY WELLBORN III, COURTROOM HANDBOOK ON FEDERAL EVIDENCE Ch. 5 (West 2010).

III. APPLICATION EXERCISE

Character Evidence in a Criminal Case

The criminal defendant holds the key to introducing character evidence pertaining either to himself or the victim in a criminal case. Evidence offered by a criminal defendant must (1) be pertinent to the proceedings, and (2) in the proper form under Rule 405. The criminal defendant is not required to provide advance notice of intent to offer character evidence under Rule 404. In a case involving homicide or assault, character evidence can be probative to help determine the identity of the aggressor in the incident, and thus, whether the defendant was entitled to claim the defense of self-defense.

It is incumbent on prosecuting attorneys to be prepared to counter defense criminal evidence on cross-examination and also through witness testimony on rebuttal. This is part of the case analysis and preparation process.

The Exercise

Objective: To demonstrate mastery of the techniques used to introduce character evidence in a defense case and prosecution cross-examination of a defense character witness.

Factual Scenario. Use problem 9-1 above.

Advance Preparation. Using the hypothetical problem above, prepare the defense case for Pastor Paul, using both Paul's good character and Terry's bad character. Also, prepare to play the role of the prosecutor with appropriate cross-examination questions. Assume at trial that the jury has already heard the prosecution's case in chief, as well as Paul's testimony about the facts of the case, and they are consistent with problem 8-1.

Paul's good character witness is named Pat. Pat does not personally know Paul, but has known of him for over 15 years and is familiar with his reputation in the community. Paul's bad character witness for Terry is named Jan. Jan knows Terry by reputation and is familiar not only with his general reputation, but the acts upon which it was based.

Additional facts for the prosecution cross-examination. You have a good-faith belief regarding the following facts:

1. Paul has stolen money from the church offering plate on three occasions in order to take trips to visit brothels in Nevada.

2. At the age of 35 (Paul is now 45), Paul and an associate pastor at the church got into a violent disagreement about the meaning of the phrase, "blessed are the peacemakers." Paul beat up the associate pastor, who forgave him and refused to press charges. Few people are aware of the incident.

3. Paul has a reputation in the local pastoral community for being a hothead on doctrinal matters and has on at least a dozen occasions challenged other ministers to fight about various doctrinal issues.

4. Terry once saved an elderly woman from being run over by a bus.

5. Terry is generally thought of as a peaceful man by the patrons of the Wild West Bar and Grill, where he is a regular. On at least 5 occasions, he has stopped fights by grabbing the karaoke microphone and preaching about nonviolence and forgiveness.

In-Class Exercise. Two prosecutors, two defense counsel, and a judge will participate in this exercise. Defense Counsel A will call Pat to testify about Paul's reputation for peacefulness in the community. Prosecutor A will cross-examine Pat. Defense Counsel B will call Jan to testify about Terry's bad character. Prosecutor B will cross-examine Jan.

Chapter 10

CHARACTER & HABIT EVIDENCE IN CIVIL CASES

Chapter Objectives:

- Introduce and explain the character and habit rules in the context of civil cases
- Analyze and discuss issues pertaining to civil applications of Rules 404(a), 405 and 406 through case law and hypothetical problems
- Apply the concepts from this chapter in a courtroom application exercise

I. BACKGROUND AND EXPLANATORY MATERIAL

The use of character evidence in civil cases is markedly different from its use in criminal cases. Until 2006, there was some confusion about the applicability of Rule 404(a) in civil cases. Rule 404(a) was designed with the criminal law in mind, but the rule neither prohibited the use of character evidence in civil cases nor provided guidelines for introducing it at trial. Rule 405(b) allowed the use of specific instances of conduct when such use was "an essential element of a charge, claim, or defense." Reading between the lines, courts crafted doctrines for the use of character evidence in civil cases under some circumstances. The evidence scholar Glen Weissenberger has referred to this practice as the "interstitial admissibility of character evidence."[1]

In 2006, Rule 404(a) was amended to make clear that it applied only to criminal cases. This amendment overruled a line of appellate cases that had permitted the use of character evidence in civil tort cases involving the use of force or violence. Courts had analogized these cases to criminal homicide and assault cases and had permitted character evidence to be used to help juries decide the identity of the first aggressor in those cases.

---

[1] *See generally* Glen Weissenberger, *Character Evidence Under the Federal Rules: A Puzzle with Missing Pieces*, 48 U. Cin. L. Rev. 1 (1979).

The amendments to Rule 404(a) did not, however, end the use of character evidence in civil cases. Rule 405(b) was not amended, and it provides continued authority for the use of specific-acts character evidence in civil cases when it is an "essential element of a charge, claim, or defense."

The rules of evidence do not speak directly to when character is essential to a case. Advocates, therefore, must rely heavily on precedent. Courts have found character essential in the following main types of cases: the character of the plaintiff in a libel or defamation case; character of an employee in a negligent hiring case; character of the entrustee in a negligent entrustment case; and character of the parents in a child-custody case.

Identifying the type of case is only part of the process of deciding whether character is "essential" or "in issue." Another important aspect of determining when character is essential in a civil case is its proposed use at trial. Consider the analysis proposed by Glen Weissenberger in his treatise on the Federal Rules of Evidence:

It should be strongly emphasized, however, that the nature of the case is not determinative of whether character is "in issue." Instead, the question is always whether character or a trait of character is the basis for an inference to prove conforming conduct. Quite simply, if character is used in an inferential manner to prove conforming conduct in any case, then the prohibition of Rule 404 applies. Where 404 applies, character is admissible only pursuant to the express exceptions in the Rule.[2] If, on the other hand, character or a trait of character is an essential element of a party's case, character is "in issue" as compelled by the substantive law, and its use is not prohibited by Rule 404.

The "essential element" formulation, which finds its source in Rule 405, however, can be misleading if it is not fully appreciated. The cause of the problem is that the term "essential" can have various connotations. For example, "essential" evidence could be construed to mean evidence that is necessary because alternative, sufficient means of proof are unavailable for some unforeseen reason. This, however, is not the intent of the Rule or the "character in issue" principle. The essential element test demands that character evidence be substantively required as the terminal point of proof. The substantive law must give the party no choice but to prove character if the claim or defense is to be substantiated. For example, where plaintiff charges defendant with a slander claiming that the defendant said "Plaintiff is dishonest, and the defendant subsequently pleads truth as a defense, the defendant must prove plaintiff's dishonesty (a trait of character) in order to prevail. The dishonesty trait of the plaintiff becomes an element of the defendant's affirmative defense. Plaintiff's dishonesty is not being utilized

---

[2] Please note that the exceptions in subsections (a)(1) and (a)(2) apply only in criminal cases, whereas the exception in subsection (a)(3) applies to the character of witnesses in any case. The exception in subsection (a)(3) will be discussed in the chapter on witness impeachment.

as proof of any conforming conduct. Rather, it is an essential element of the defense, and plaintiff's trait of character is properly "in issue."[3]

There are several important differences between civil and criminal cases pertaining to the use of character evidence. In a civil case, advocates cannot think in terms of "opening the door" as they do in criminal cases. In civil cases, the historical incentive to protect the character of the criminal defendant from prosecutorial attack simply does not exist. Character is either an essential element of a charge, claim, or defense — or it is not. Whereas the criminal defendant holds the key to the use of character evidence in a criminal trial, there is no such limitation in a civil trial; if essential to a claim, the plaintiff in a civil case can introduce character evidence without waiting for the defendant to open the door.

Another significant difference between civil and criminal character evidence is that, unlike in criminal cases,[4] character evidence in a civil case is not limited to reputation or opinion testimony. Rule 405(a) provides for the use of reputation or opinion testimony "in all cases in which evidence of character or a trait of character of a person is admissible." Rule 405(b) permits the use of specific acts evidence in cases where character or a trait of character "is an essential element of a charge, claim, or defense." Thus, in a civil case, all three forms of evidence, including specific acts, are available to prove character.

Evidence of Habit or Routine Practice in Civil Cases

There are no special distinctions between criminal and civil cases pertaining to evidence of habit or routine practice. The opportunities for using such evidence are, however, considerably greater in civil cases than in criminal cases. This is because of the wide variety of causes of action, the increased presence of corporations and other organizations as parties, and the lesser constitutional protections afforded in civil cases.

Advocates in civil cases should be aware of the subtle differences between evidence offered to prove an individual person's habits and evidence offered to prove the routine practice of an organization. These distinctions are the subject of the following article.

Daniel D. Blinka, *Evidence of Character, Habit, and "Similar Acts" in Wisconsin Civil Litigation*
73 Marq. L. Rev. 283 (1989)

The cases and commentary discussing habit and routine practice use the terms in two different, sometimes conflicting ways. First, the narrow psychological denotation describes a classic conditioned response: a semi-

---

[3] Glen Weissenberger & James J. Duane, Federal Rules of Evidence: Rules, Legislative History, Commentary and Authority § 404.10 (6th ed. 2009).

[4] With the possible exception, of course, of entrapment evidence, discussed in the previous chapter.

automatic reaction repeated almost unvaryingly in the face of certain specific circumstances. Second, a broader, probabilistic conception addresses the frequency and specificity of the occurrence of an act. That is, the more often a person or organization has behaved in a certain way in a particular context in the past, the more likely it is that the individual or organization will behave the same way when confronted with the same circumstances on another occasion. . . .

[C]ourts must first give discernable rigor to the meanings of "habit" and "routine practice." It is suggested that when the issue involves the conduct of a particular human being, the behavior should be analyzed to determine whether it is a "habit;" here, the psychological perspective should govern. The trial court should be satisfied that the behavior in question actually implicates a semi-automatic, virtually unconscious response to a specific set of circumstances. Examples are the use of directionals when turning a car or putting on a wristwatch in the morning. Conduct such as lecherous advances by a landlord toward female tenants in a sexual harassment lawsuit, even on four or five different occasions, points more towards a reprehensible character flaw than it does a prurient Pavlovian response to female tenants. The narrow psychological perspective is the only principled way of assuring that the rule barring the circumstantial use of character to prove conduct is not absorbed by the rule allowing the use of habit.

When assessing the conduct of an organization, the focus should be on whether it is a "routine practice" and the probabilistic perspective should govern. This approach is a more liberal standard favoring admissibility than is the psychological approach, as it requires less in the way of specificity of the conduct or frequency of its occurrence. The focus is on the customs, practices, and rules which are followed in the normal functioning of the organization, such as the routing of various business decisions or the handling of mail. At issue is not what a particular human being did on a given occasion, but what the organization normally or regularly does with respect to some recurring conduct. Administrative efficiency alone motivates the regularity of a great deal of group behavior. Such routine practices are more susceptible to proof than are individual habits and it seems less likely that jurors would overvalue such evidence. . . .

A number of civil cases have discussed the admissibility of an organization's routine practice in order to prove that the entity behaved in accordance with that practice. These cases reveal how important it is for lawyers to think through exactly what it is they are trying to prove with the evidence in question. Just because a certain fact pattern recurs does not mean that it constitutes a habit or routine practice. The evidence may very well be admissible, but it is admissible under the rules governing the introduction of other act evidence, not those rules relating to routine practice evidence.

Evidence of routine practice or custom to show conduct in conformity is proper only where the behavior is such that it naturally recurs within the organization. A routine practice involves a finding that there is sufficient evidence to conclude that whenever the organization is confronted with A, it does, or very likely does, B. Conduct such as the routing of mail is one obvious example. Another example concerns the practice of informing prospective employees about various company policies at the time they are hired. Moreover, this kind of evidence may be used to prove the absence of something. For instance, a nurse may testify that when taking a history from a patient she asks about any present pain or other symptoms and then records the complaints in her chart. This testimony may then be relevant to prove the absence of such symptoms, or the patient's failure to mention them, where the chart is silent as to any specific complaints by the patient.

The point is that the routine practice should be a regular and recurring activity. It may be proven through opinion testimony or by specific instances. Although no magic number of proven instances is necessary to establish a practice as "routine," the trial court is not obligated to accept the witness' conclusion that a given course of conduct is routine. It must be remembered that the probative value of this evidence is derived in large measure from the fact that the business or other organization requires regularity in the conduct of its business and that deviations are subject to internal scrutiny or sanction; therefore, one can infer that the entity will generally follow its regular procedures. Any deviation generally goes to the weight of the evidence and is a proper issue for resolution by the trier of fact.

The concept of "routine practice" has, in some instances, been stretched to the point of breaking. In particular, one should not lose sight of the importance of the "regularity" component. Just because something occurs more than once does not mean it is therefore "routine" or "customary." The temptation to draw this erroneous inference is especially tempting in cases involving prior, similar accidents.

For instance, in one case, plaintiff brought suit against a telephone company for injuries received from an improperly grounded phone. The injuries occurred when plaintiff, while holding the improperly grounded phone, received an electrical shock caused by lightning transmitted through the receiver. The court upheld the admission of ten other such incidents as proof of negligence and causation. It specifically held that the evidence was admissible under [Wisconsin's version of Rule 406].

Although ten similar accidents is a shockingly high number of accidents and certainly relevant to negligence and the question of cause, it is difficult to see how they constituted a "routine practice." Corporations may routinely route their mail, but one hopes that they do not routinely electrocute or otherwise maim their customers. It should be recognized that the ten prior accidents were probative of the probability of a defect in the phone system that plaintiff's injury was caused by this defect, and that defendant was aware, or should have been aware, of the defect entirely apart from whether its negligence was "routine." In short, the admissibility of this evidence should have been channeled through subsection [the character evidence rules and Rule 403], not routine practice under [Rule 406]. Such an analysis allows the trial court to focus not on whether the conduct is routine, which is a side-issue at best, but on the propositions for which the evidence is properly admissible: the probability of a defect, the causal relation between the defect and the injury, and whether defendant was aware of the defect. In summary, the label "routine practice" should not be applied as a substitute for thinking about hard evidentiary problems.

II. CASES, DISCUSSION QUESTIONS AND PROBLEMS

HALL v. SSF, INC.
Supreme Court of Nevada
930 P.2d 94 (Nev. 1996)

Appellant Lawrence Hall filed a complaint against respondents alleging several causes of action, including the negligent training, supervision, and retention of employees. Hall sought compensatory and punitive damages, including future medical damages, for injuries sustained when respondent John Handka, a security guard employed by respondent SSF, Inc. (SSF), hit Hall in the jaw. The district judge found for Hall and against respondents Handka and SSF on theories of intentional assault and battery and respondeat superior, awarded Hall damages for past medical bills, but refused to award him damages for future medical expenses. The district judge also refused to hear certain evidence regarding the negligent hiring, training, supervision, and retention claim and ultimately found against Hall on that claim. . . .

[In 1992, Hall and a group of friends attended a nightclub, the Limelite, in Reno. Angry about having to pay a cover charge, they demanded a refund when they decided to leave the nightclub shortly after entering it. The manager refused, and when the group became belligerent, he directed bouncers, including Handka, to remove the group.]

Handka testified that in response to Paul's request, he and the two other doormen began escorting the group from the club. The group engaged in heated words with the bouncers while inside the club and continued to argue with Handka after they were escorted outside of the club. Handka testified that when he perceived someone approaching him in what he thought was a menacing manner, he struck out with his fist, hitting Hall in the right jaw area. Handka further testified that he believed he was in danger and struck out in self-defense. Hall testified that when he turned around to see who had hit him, Handka was jumping up and down, challenging Hall to a fight.

[Hall suffered severe injuries to his jaw as a result of this encounter.] . . .

[R]espondents were on notice that the issues of negligent hiring, training, supervision, and retention were being litigated.

The district judge also stated that even if the pleadings were sufficient, Hall presented insufficient evidence on this issue. "The tort of negligent hiring imposes a general duty on the employer to conduct a reasonable back-ground check on a potential employee to ensure that the employee is fit for the position." Burnett v. C.B.A. Security Service, 107 Nev. 787, 789, 820 P.2d 750, 752 (1991). An employer breaches this duty when it hires an employee even though the employer knew, or should have known, of that employee's dangerous propensities. Kelley v. Baker Protective Services, Inc., 198 Ga.App. 378, 401 S.E.2d 585, 586 (1991).

By the very nature of the job, a bouncer has significant interaction with the public and is routinely placed in confrontational situations with patrons. Therefore, hiring a bouncer who is known to have violent propensities would likely be a breach of the duty to ensure that the employee is fit for the job. See Connes v. Molalla Transport System, Inc., 831 P.2d 1316, 1321 (Colo.1992) (stating that "liability [for negligent hiring] is predicated on the employer's hiring of a person under circumstances antecedently giving the employer reason to believe that the person, by reason of some attribute of character or prior conduct, would create an undue risk of harm to others in carrying out his or her employment responsibilities"); Yunker v. Honeywell, Inc., 496 N.W.2d 419, 422 (Minn.Ct.App.1993) (stating that negligent hiring liability is imposed "when the employer knew or should have known that the employee was violent or aggressive and might engage in injurious conduct").

Hall attempted to discover facts regarding the circumstances surrounding Handka's hiring but was frustrated in his attempts because SSF had been dissolved shortly after the incident at issue and its records and files had been destroyed. At trial, Hall attempted to introduce into evidence the fact that Handka had been discharged less than honorably from the military for striking a superior officer. The district judge sustained respondents' objection that the evidence was inadmissible as irrelevant and as improper character evidence. The district judge permitted Hall to make an offer of proof on this issue, which Hall did.

The decision to admit or exclude testimony rests within the sound discretion of the trial court and will not be disturbed unless it is manifestly wrong. Daly v. State, 99 Nev. 564, 567, 665 P.2d 798, 801 (1983). We conclude that the district judge's decision to exclude the testimony was manifestly wrong. The evidence, which may have been improper character evidence regarding the issue of whether Handka tortiously hit Hall, was still relevant to the issue of negligent hiring because it would have aided the district judge in determining whether Handka had violent propensities and whether SSF knew or should have known of those violent propensities. Therefore, the case must be remanded for a new trial on the issue of negligent hiring, and the district judge must consider evidence of Handka's alleged prior violence as part of the determination of whether SSF was negligent when it hired Handka.

2. Negligent training, supervision, and retention

Hall also alleged that SSF failed to use reasonable care in training, supervising, and retaining Handka. In Nevada, a proprietor owes a general duty to use reasonable care to keep the premises in a reasonably safe condition for use. Moody v. Manny's Auto Repair, 110 Nev. 320, 331-33, 871 P.2d 935, 942-43 (1994). As is the case in hiring an employee, the employer has a duty to use reasonable care in the training, supervision, and retention of his or her employees to make sure that the employees are fit for their positions. See 27 Am.Jur.2d Employment Relationship §§ 475-76 (1996).

Hall tried to question Handka regarding five other fights that Handka had been in, but the judge sustained opposing counsel's objection on the ground that the question called for improper character evidence and did not let Handka answer the question. We conclude that such a ruling was manifestly wrong because while the evidence might have been improper character evidence regarding the issue of whether Handka tortiously hit Hall, it was certainly relevant on the issue of negligent training, supervision, and retention. Handka's testimony regarding when and where the fights occurred would have provided the district judge with information needed to determine whether SSF was aware of Handka's actions and whether SSF had acted negligently in training, supervising, and retaining Handka. Therefore, the case must be remanded for a new trial on the issues of negligent training, supervision, and retention, the district judge must permit testimony regarding Handka's prior fights, and the district judge must consider such evidence when determining whether SSF acted negligently in training, supervising, and retaining Handka.

PERRIN v. ANDERSON
United States Court of Appeals, Tenth Circuit
784 F.2d 1040 (10th Cir. 1986)

This is a 42 U.S.C. § 1983 civil rights action for compensatory and punitive damages arising from the death of Terry Kim Perrin. Plaintiff, administratrix of Perrin's estate and guardian of his son, alleged that defendants, Donnie Anderson and Roland Von Schriltz, members of the Oklahoma Highway Patrol, deprived Perrin of his civil rights when they shot and killed him while attempting to obtain information concerning a traffic accident in which he had been involved. The jury found in favor of defendants. . . .

A simple highway accident set off the bizarre chain of events that culminated in Perrin's death. The incident began when Perrin drove his car into the back of another car on an Oklahoma highway. After determining that the occupants of the car he had hit were uninjured, Perrin walked to his home, which was close to the highway.

Trooper Von Schriltz went to Perrin's home to obtain information concerning the accident. He was joined there by Trooper Anderson. They knocked on and off for ten to twenty minutes before persuading Perrin to open the door. Once Perrin opened the door, the defendant officers noticed Perrin's erratic behavior. The troopers testified that his moods would change quickly and that he was yelling that the accident was not his fault. Von Schriltz testified that he sensed a possibly dangerous situation and slowly moved his hand to his gun in order to secure its hammer with a leather thong. This action apparently provoked Perrin who then slammed the door. The door bounced open and Perrin then attacked Anderson. A fierce battle ensued between Perrin and the two officers, who unsuccessfully applied several chokeholds to Perrin in an attempt to subdue him. Eventually Anderson, who testified that he feared he was about to lose consciousness as a result of having been kicked repeatedly in the face and chest by Perrin, took out his gun, and, with-out issuing a warning, shot and killed Perrin. Anderson stated that he was convinced Perrin would have killed both officers had he not fired.

I.

At trial the court permitted four police officers to testify that they had been involved previously in violent encounters with Perrin. These officers testified to Perrin's apparent hatred or fear of uniformed officers and his consistently violent response to any contact with them. For example, defendants presented evidence that on earlier occasions Perrin was completely uncontrollable and violent in the presence of uniformed officers. On one occasion he rammed his head into the bars and walls of his cell, requiring administration of a tranquilizer. Another time while barefoot, Perrin kicked loose a porcelain toilet bowl that was bolted to the floor. One officer testified that he encountered Perrin while responding to a public drunk call. Perrin attacked him, and during the following struggle Perrin tried to reach for the officer's weapon. The officer and his back-up had to carry Perrin handcuffed, kicking and screaming, to the squad car, where Perrin then kicked the windshield out of the car. Another officer testified that Perrin attacked him after Perrin was stopped at a vehicle checkpoint. During the ensuing struggle three policemen were needed to subdue Perrin, including one 6'2" officer weighing 250 pounds and one 6'6" officer weighing 350 pounds.

Defendants introduced this evidence to prove that Perrin was the first aggressor in the fight — a key element in defendants' self-defense claim. The court admitted the evidence over objection, under Federal Rules of Evidence provisions treating both character and habit evidence. Plaintiff contends this was error. . . .

B

Character and habit are closely akin. The district court found, alternatively, that the testimony recounting Perrin's previous violent encounters with police officers was admissible as evidence of a habit under Fed. R. Evid. 406. Here, we concur.

[The Court quotes Rule 406.]

The limitations on the methods of proving character set out in Rule 405 do not apply to proof of habit. Testimony concerning prior specific incidents is allowed. See McCormick § 195, at 577.

This court has defined "habit" as "a regular practice of meeting a particular kind of situation with a certain type of conduct, or a reflex behavior in a specific set of circumstances." Frase v. Henry, 444 F.2d 1228, 1232 (10th Cir. 1971) (defining "habit" under Kansas law). The advisory committee notes to Rule 406 state that, "while adequacy of sampling and uniformity of response are key factors, precise standards for measuring their sufficiency for evidence purposes cannot be formulated." Fed. R. Evid. 406 advisory committee note. That Perrin might be proved to have a "habit" of reacting violently to uniformed police officers seems rather extraordinary. We believe, however, that defendants did in fact demonstrate that Perrin repeatedly reacted with extreme aggression when dealing with uniformed police officers.

Four police officers testified to at least five separate violent incidents, and plaintiff offered no evidence of any peaceful encounter between Perrin and the police. Five incidents ordinarily would be insufficient to establish the existence of a habit. See Reyes v. Missouri Pacific Railway Co., 589 F.2d 791, 794-95 (5th Cir. 1979) (four convictions for public intoxication in three and one-half years insufficient to prove habit). But defendants here had made an offer of proof of testimony from eight police officers concerning numerous different incidents. To prevent undue prejudice to plaintiff, the district court permitted only four of these witnesses to testify, and it explicitly stated that it thought the testimony of the four officers had been sufficient to establish a habit. Id. We hold that the district court properly admitted this evidence pursuant to Rule 406. There was adequate testimony to establish that Perrin invariably reacted with extreme violence to any contact with a uniformed police officer.

DISCUSSION QUESTIONS

1. The court in *Hall* said that character evidence would have been inadmissible to prove that the bouncer threw the first punch, but it was admissible to prove the negligent hiring case against his employer. Is this a distinction without a difference? If you were the judge, how would you draft a limiting instruction that would help the jury use the evidence for the proper purposes?

2. Keeping in mind what you know and have read about habit evidence, do you agree with the *Perrin* court regarding the use of the decedent's past interactions with the police in this case? Why or why not? What number should be sufficient to establish a habit?

PROBLEMS

Problem 10-1. Pat Plaintiff is suing the Calamity City Police Department for negligent training and supervision. The lawsuit stems from an incident in which Officer Dan Diabalo pulled Pat Plaintiff over for a minor traffic violation. When

Plaintiff failed to produce her automobile insurance card quickly enough to satisfy Diabalo, Diabalo allegedly pulled Plaintiff out of her car, bruising her arm. Diabalo also allegedly struck Plaintiff in the face with his open hand, called her a foul name, and told her he could ruin her life forever. After Plaintiff refused Diabalo's offer to drop the traffic and insurance violations in return for $100 cash, he violently shoved her into the vehicle, during which her head struck the roof of the car, resulting in a gash that required 15 stitches to close.

During discovery, Plaintiff's attorney learned that Diabalo has been a member of the police department for 15 years. During that time frame, the department has received 25 complaints of excessive violence from Diabalo during arrests; 5 of those complaints claimed that Diabalo had offered to drop charges in return for $100 cash.

At trial, Plaintiff claims that the Calamity City Police Department negligently supervised Diabalo.

1.   What evidence can Plaintiff present under Rule 405?

2.   Is Rule 406 a viable option for presenting evidence?

Problem 10-2. Paul Plaintiff suffered severe side effects after receiving a vaccination for swine flu at the Calamity County Health Department. The side effects included a lengthy hospital stay and a condition known as "drop foot," which required plaintiff to use a brace on his foot in order to walk properly. In his lawsuit against the Health Department, plaintiff alleged that he never received sufficient notice of the dangers associated with swine flu vaccinations. He claims instead that he received nothing more than a small blue card advising him that he might suffer from some relatively minor side effects in the 48 hours after the administration of the vaccination. He no longer has a copy of the card. In the Health Department files, there is, in fact, no record of an informed consent form signed by Plaintiff. At trial, the defense proposes to call Nurse Ratchet, the coordinator for the vaccination program to testify that it was the Health Department's routine practice to give each person a registration (consent) form and a national fact sheet containing information about swine flu and the immunization program; and that the signed consent form was exchanged for a blue card which informed the person administering the vaccine the specific type of vaccine the patient was supposed to receive. The Plaintiff objects to this testimony because it is uncorroborated and contradicts the absence of Plaintiff's informed consent form in the Health Department files. How should the defense respond to this objection? How should the judge rule?

Quick Hits: *Character Evidence and Evidence of Habit or Routine Practice in Civil Cases*

- Character evidence may be admitted in civil cases when it is an essential element of a charge, claim or defense

- The substantive law of the cause of action or defense governs when character evidence is "essential"

- Rule 405 permits the use of all three forms of character evidence — reputation, opinion or specific acts — in civil cases

- Habit evidence generally applies to people

- Evidence of routine practice generally applies to organizations

- Evidence of habit or routine practice may not be used as a subterfuge to avoid character evidence prohibitions at trial

---

Chapter References

Christopher B. Mueller & Laird C. Kirkpatrick, Evidence §§ 4.11–4.14, 4.19–4.22 (4th ed. 2009).

Glen Weissenberger & James J. Duane, Federal Rules of Evidence: Rules, Legislative History, Commentary and Authority §§ 404.1–404.10, 405–06 (6th ed. 2009).

Jack B. Weinstein & Margaret A. Berger, Weinstein's Federal Evidence §§ 404.01–404.13, 405–06 (Joseph M. McLaughlin ed., Matthew Bender 2d ed. 1997).

Kenneth S. Broun, McCormick on Evidence §§ 186–95 (6th ed. 2006).

Steven Goode & Olin Guy Wellborn III, Courtroom Handbook on Federal Evidence Ch. 5 (West 2010).

III. APPLICATION EXERCISE

Objective: To demonstrate mastery and understanding of the relevance, character and habit rules in civil cases in a pretrial verbal motion in limine.

Factual Scenario: Use problem 10-1 above. Before trial, the plaintiff's counsel makes clear that they intend to call each of the complainants who had filed a complaint with the department against Officer Diabalo.

Advance Preparation. In this exercise, you should prepare the plaintiff and defense arguments as follows:

Defendant. Prepare a verbal motion in limine to exclude evidence of past complaints pertaining to Officer Diabalo. Use the rules of evidence we have discussed so far in this course to support your arguments.

Plaintiff. Prepare a response to the motion in limine. In particular, be prepared to discuss why you should be able to admit this evidence at trial, and use the rules of evidence we have discussed so far in this course to support your arguments. Be prepared to make an offer of proof about the evidence you will present.

To assist both sides with making and responding to the motion, here is some additional evidence.

1. You have located 20 of the 25 complainants. All are in the area and are willing to testify against Diabalo. Every single case involved a traffic arrest. The alleged facts are practically identical.

3. You have located 5 of the 5 complainants who alleged Diabalo offered to drop charges in return for $100 cash. All are willing to testify. All are women about the same age, height, build and race as Plaintiff. The alleged facts are practically identical.

4. You also have copies (obtained in discovery) of all the complaint reports and their dispositions.

5. Out of the 25 reports, 20 complaints were unfounded, including all of the $100 bribery complaints.

6. Plaintiff is personal friends with 3 claimants, each of whom alleged Diabalo offered to drop charges in return for $100 in cash.

7. Plaintiff's emergency room medical records do not mention anything about Officer Diabalo. She claimed in those records that she injured herself at home when she tripped over a toy one of her children had left on the floor.

Chapter 11

EVIDENCE OF OTHER CRIMES, WRONGS OR ACTS

Chapter Objectives:

- Introduce and explain Rule 404(b) and the process, structure and balancing tests for using Rule 404(b) evidence at trial
- Analyze and discuss issues pertaining to Rule 404(b)
- Apply the concepts from this chapter in a courtroom application exercise

I. BACKGROUND AND EXPLANATORY MATERIAL

Rule 404(b) is a powerful weapon at trial. The rule permits a party to introduce specific instances of past misconduct by the opposing party at trial for appropriate non-character purposes. These purposes include proof of motive, opportunity, intent, preparation, plan, knowledge, identity, absence of mistake or accident, and so forth. Although the rule is most frequently used in criminal cases, it is also applicable in civil cases. In cases involving prior sexual misconduct of an opposing party, Rules 413 and 414 have superseded Rule 404(b) in criminal cases, and Rule 415 has superseded it in civil cases.

The text of Rule 404(b) is as follows:

Through Dec. 1, 2011	After Dec. 1, 2011
Rule 404(b), Other Crimes, Wrongs or Acts	**Rule 404(b), Crimes, Wrongs, or Other Acts**
(b) Other crimes, wrongs, or acts. Evidence of other crimes, wrongs, or acts is not admissible to prove the character of a person in order to show action in conformity therewith. It may, however, be admissible for other purposes, such as proof of motive, opportunity, intent, preparation, plan, knowledge, identity, or absence of mistake or accident, provided that upon request by the accused, the prosecution in a criminal case shall provide reasonable notice in advance of trial, or during trial if the court excuses pretrial notice on good cause shown, of the general nature of any such evidence it intends to introduce at trial.	**(b) Crimes, Wrongs, or Other Acts**. *(1) Prohibited Uses*. Evidence of a crime, wrong, or other act is not admissible to prove a person's character in order to show that on a particular occasion the person acted in accordance with the character. *(2) Permitted Uses; Notice in a Criminal Case*. This evidence may be admissible for another purpose, such as proving motive, opportunity, intent, preparation, plan, knowledge, identity, absence of mistake, or lack of accident. On request by a defendant in a criminal case, the prosecutor must: (A) provide reasonable notice of the general nature of any such evidence that the prosecutor intends to offer at trial; and (B) do so before trial — or during trial if the court, for good cause, excuses lack of pretrial notice.

The Structure of Rule 404(b)

Careful attention to the structure of Rule 404(b) is critical to ensuring the correct use of uncharged misconduct at trial. There are three critical structural aspects of Rule 404(b): the first sentence/subsection, which prohibits the use of prior acts to prove propensity; the second sentence/subsection, which permits the use of prior acts for particular non-character purposes; and the procedural requirements, which are designed to prevent unfair surprise at trial. Please note that this text uses the phrase "sentence/subsection" to account for the language in the rule both before and after December 1, 2011. This is because, at the time the book went to press, the older version of the rule was still used in most of the state codes that are based on the Federal Rules of Evidence.

The First Sentence/Subsection: A Prohibition of Propensity Evidence

The most important part of Rule 404(b) is its first sentence/subsection, which seeks to avoid an impermissible set of logical inferences at trial: 1) the party against whom the evidence is offered committed a particular act of misconduct in the past;

2) that act is evidence of a character trait; 3) the character trait represents the party's propensity to act in a certain way; 4) the party likely acted in accordance with his propensity in the incident at trial. This sentence recognizes the grave danger posed at trial — particularly in criminal cases, where the rule is most frequently applied — by the introduction of uncharged acts.

At first blush, the rule appears to strip from the criminal accused many of the protections granted by Rule 404(a). Under virtually all circumstances, the character of the accused is off-limits to the prosecution unless the accused chooses to introduce evidence of his character or that of the victim. Rule 404(b), however, shifts the decision to admit what seems remarkably similar to character evidence from the accused to the prosecution. Furthermore, the list of permissible purposes is broad, not far removed from some of the impermissible character inferences prohibited by Rule 404(a). Finally, Rule 404(b) uses specific instances of conduct, the strongest form of proof available in the character evidence context.

If Rule 404(b) is used as a pretext for the introduction and misuse of character evidence at trial, the potential prejudice to the accused is substantial. The jury could decide the case based on propensity evidence, short-circuiting the burden of proof and effectively holding the accused liable for all his past misdeeds. The constraints posed by Rule 404(a) and Rule 405 could, moreover, prevent the accused from mounting an effective defense by first requiring him to identify a pertinent character trait to defend and then limiting him to proof by reputation or opinion testimony.

Advocates should be aware of the potential dangers posed by the misuse of Rule 404(b). Vigorous advocacy and insistence on compliance with the purposes of the rule and its procedural protections, coupled with the additional filter of an exacting Rule 403 analysis, is essential in prohibiting the inappropriate use of uncharged acts at trial.

The Second Sentence: Permissible Non-Character Uses of Uncharged Misconduct

The second sentence of Rule 404(b) contains a non-exclusive list of permissible non-character uses of uncharged acts at trial: "It may, however, be admissible for other purposes, such as proof of motive, opportunity, intent, preparation, plan, knowledge, identity, or absence of mistake or accident." Contrary to actual practice by some attorneys and judges, this list is not a mantra, the formulaic chanting of which magically opens the door to the introduction of otherwise inadmissible character evidence at trial. Instead, each of the non-character categories identified in the rule has a particular set of proof requirements that must be met before evidence can be introduced under that category. The proponent of the evidence must, therefore, be able to explain how the uncharged act actually helps prove, for example, motive; it is not enough merely to claim that the evidence somehow falls under one categorical label or multiple labels under the rule.

The following subsections explain some of the permissible non-character uses of uncharged misconduct at trial, as well as the underlying theories that justify their use.

Intrinsic Uncharged Acts

For various reasons, prosecutors do not always charge every single possible offense at trial. These reasons include proof issues, the desire for efficiency at trial, and even an instinct to show some mercy to the accused. Nonetheless, the prosecution must still present a cohesive theory of its case and a compelling story at trial. This often requires introducing evidence of uncharged acts that are closely intertwined with or intrinsic to the charged acts to be proved at trial.

For example, suppose the accused in a criminal case is being tried for the armed robbery of a bank. During his attempted escape from the scene of the crime, he jaywalked to get to his getaway car, and once in the car, violated several traffic laws before finally pulling over and submitting to arrest by the police. The prosecutor may choose not to prosecute the accused for jaywalking, speeding and running red lights, but the introduction of these uncharged acts would be intrinsic to the offense and a necessary part of the story at trial.

The 404(b) Categories

Rule 404(b) provides a non-exclusive list of permissible non-character uses for specific acts evidence at trial. Each of these will be briefly discussed in turn.

(1) *Motive.* With the exception of hate crimes, motive is almost never an element of a criminal offense or a civil cause of action. Nonetheless, evidence of motive helps tell a complete story and explain to the fact-finder why an individual might have acted in a certain way. For example, suppose that Darryl Dimebag is charged with robbing the OK Corral Convenience Store. Darryl is addicted to the prescription drug Vicodin. He has been purchasing Vicodin from a criminal prescription-drug network and is behind on his payments. At the embezzlement trial, the prosecution could admit evidence of Darryl's Vicodin purchases and abuse to help prove his motive for robbery.

(2) *Opportunity.* Evidence of other acts can be used to place an individual near the alleged incident at trial to prove opportunity to commit an act or offense. Suppose that Darryl presents an alibi defense to his robbery charge, claiming he could not have committed the robbery on the charged occasion because he was actually on vacation in Europe. The prosecution has evidence that Darryl was arrested for a DUI in Calamity City the morning after the robbery, but the charges were dropped because his blood sample was mishandled. Rule 404(b) would permit the prosecution to admit evidence of the DUI arrest to show that Darryl had the opportunity to commit the robbery.

(3) *Intent.* Evidence of other acts to prove intent is frequently offered in rebuttal to counter a defendant's claim that he did not possess a particular intent. Similar instances of conduct may also be offered in the prosecution's case in chief to prove the defendant's intent. Suppose that Carl Creeper is charged in federal court with kidnapping Vonda under 18 U.S.C. § 1201(a)(1) and transporting her across state lines. An element of the federal kidnapping statute requires the prosecution to prove that Creeper abducted Vonda for "any reason which would in any way be of benefit to him." The prosecution's theory is that the kidnapping was for the purpose of Creeper's sexual gratification. After his arrest for that incident, state

authorities learn that Creeper kidnapped and sexually assaulted Anna just one week before the alleged kidnapping of Vonda. The state brings charges against Creeper and convicts him of the offenses before he is brought to trial in federal court. Federal prosecutors can offer evidence of Creeper's prior acts against Anna to help prove his intent in kidnapping Vonda.

(4) *Preparation.* Many defendants violate a variety of criminal laws as they prepare to commit their ultimate offense. Proof of these other offenses can be offered to show preparation for the charged offense. Return to the Darryl Dimebag robbery of the OK Corral Convenience Store. Suppose that in the week before committing the offense, Darryl purchased a handgun and ammunition from a neighbor without registering it, in violation of state gun registration laws. In Darryl's robbery trial, the prosecution can offer evidence of the violation to show Darryl was preparing to commit the robbery by obtaining a handgun.

(5) *Common Plan or Scheme.* Evidence of other acts can be used to help prove that the charged offense was part of a common plan or scheme. The prosecution must be able to demonstrate the common plan or scheme and illustrate how the uncharged and charged acts were part of the scheme. A mere circumstantial similarity between the acts will not suffice. To illustrate, suppose that Carl Creeper is charged with using a dangerous pesticide to kill his wife. The prosecution finds evidence that a year earlier, Creeper administered the pesticide to his mother in exactly the same manner, causing his mother's death. The two incidents show a common plan or scheme to employ a dangerous pesticide, administered in a particular manner, to cause the death of another individual.

In contrast, suppose that Creeper is charged with stealing money from a bar by sweeping cash tips into his pocket when he thought no one was looking. The prosecution finds evidence that two years earlier, Creeper stole money from a bar by taking it out of a cash register when he thought no one was looking. The two incidents are not linked closely enough in time or method of commission to constitute a common plan or scheme to steal money from bars in a particular manner.

(6) *Knowledge or Absence of Mistake or Accident.* Other acts can be used to prove the defendant's knowledge of an element of the charged offense, or to rebut a claim of lack of knowledge. Suppose that Dana Druggie is charged with smuggling marijuana in the back of his pickup truck from one state to another. At trial, his defense is that he was just hauling some boxes as a favor for a friend and had no idea they contained marijuana. The prosecution can offer evidence of Dana's prior conviction for transporting marijuana to help rebut his claim of ignorance at trial.

(7) *Identity.* Under this theory, evidence of another act is used to help prove that the same person committed the charged offense and thereby to establish the identity of the defendant as the perpetrator. Commonly known as *modus operandi* evidence, the theory only comes into play if the charged offense and the other acts share distinctive characteristics that are not generic to the crime. For instance, many bank robberies feature a perpetrator wearing a mask, armed with a gun, who passes a note to the teller demanding cash. These are generic features. Suppose, however, that in the charged offense the assailant wore a Spiderman outfit, carried

a nickel-plated.44 magnum pistol, and played the Judas Priest song *Breakin' the Law* through a portable stereo while robbing the bank. If the prosecution had evidence that the defendant had committed a prior bank robbery while wearing a Spiderman outfit and carrying a nickel-plated.44 magnum pistol, the prosecution could offer the prior robbery as proof that the defendant had committed the charged offense. There is no requirement that every detail be identical, only that the charged offense and other acts share distinctive, identifying characteristics.

The Doctrine of Chances

Another theory supporting the introduction of uncharged acts is the doctrine of chances. In a nutshell, the doctrine of chances stands for the proposition that lightning doesn't often strike twice, and that it would be improbable for remarkably similar instances in a defendant's life to be the cause of coincidence.

The following excerpt from a law review article by Professor Imwinkelried gives the historical background of the doctrine of chances and explains its reasoning.

Edward J. Imwinkelried, *An Evidentiary Paradox: Defending the Character Evidence Prohibition by Upholding a Non-Character Theory of Logical Relevance, the Doctrine of Chances*
40 U. RICH. L. REV. 419 (2006)

The case became curiouser and curiouser. Paul Woods was barely eight months old at the time of his death. The death of any child is a tragedy; but, to say the least, the facts surrounding Paul's death were suspicious. Paul died of a cyanotic episode. The Woods household was his second foster placement. During his initial placement, he never suffered any breathing problems. Moreover, when he began experiencing such problems after his placement with the Woods family, he was treated at several different hospitals. He had never had an episode during any of those periods of hospitalizations. When Paul died, the physicians were unable to identify a cause of death. Yet, a forensic pathologist, Dr. Vincent DiMaio, suspected foul play. He would eventually testify at Martha's trial that he thought that Paul's death was homicidal. In his expert opinion, someone had smothered Paul to death. However, Dr. DiMaio was candid. On the witness stand, he testified that although he believed there was a seventy-five percent chance that someone had murdered Paul, there was a remaining twenty-five percent chance that the cause of death was some unknown disease. Dr. DiMaio even went to length of conceding that the forensic evidence did not prove a murder beyond a reasonable doubt.

Given Dr. DiMaio's concessions, his testimony standing alone probably would not have produced a conviction. Indeed, the prosecution's case might never have reached a jury; a trial judge might have been forced to find the case legally insufficient and grant a defense motion for a directed verdict. However, the prosecution had additional, potent evidence. During the preceding twenty-five years, in one way or another, Martha had taken care of many children, both her own and those of relatives and friends. During that period, nine children had suffered at least twenty cyanotic episodes while in Martha's custody. Seven of those children had died. As in Paul's case, none of those children had experienced breathing difficulties while they were in a hospital away from Martha; and, again as in Paul's case, the treating physicians had been unable to identify a definitive medical cause for the fatal episodes. The presentation of the testimony about the other twenty incidents sealed Martha's fate. The jury convicted, and the appellate court affirmed.

On the civil side, plaintiffs' attorneys in civil rights actions often encounter evidentiary challenges similar to the problem faced by the prosecutor in United States v. Woods. For example, the plaintiff's attorney representing a discharged employee may need to establish that the employer was motivated by a discriminatory animus. Unless the employer is stupid as well as biased, the plaintiff's attorney may have no "smoking gun" - no documentary evidence establishing the discriminatory motivation for the plaintiff's discharge. Just as the prosecution might well have suffered a directed verdict in Woods without the benefit of the testimony about the other twenty cyanotic episodes, the dearth of evidence of discriminatory animus in a civil rights action may doom the plaintiff's case. The parallel continues, though. The plaintiff may be able to survive a nonsuit motion and gain a favorable verdict if he or she can find evidence of other instances in which the same employer took adverse personnel actions against similarly situated employees, that is, employees of the same race, gender, or age.

In these cases, when the other incidents are sufficiently numerous and similar to the alleged misconduct, any reasonably intelligent lay juror would find evidence of the other incidents convincing. Indeed, it would be "an affront to common sense" to exclude such evidence. The rub is that, at first blush, there is a plausible objection to the introduction of such evidence. The objection is that the testimony amounts to inadmissible evidence of the defendant's bad character. In the United States, it is a venerable, common-law principle that the proponent may not treat an opposing litigant's other misconduct as circumstantial proof of the misconduct alleged in the pleadings. Today, that principle is expressly codified in the Federal Rules of Evidence. The first sentence of Rule 404(b) reads: "Evidence of other crimes, wrongs, or acts is not admissible to prove the character of a person in order to show action in conformity therewith." The proponent may not argue that: (1) the other incidents demonstrate the person's bad character; and (2) in turn, that character increases the probability that the person committed the misdeed alleged in the pleadings - in other words, the person acted "characteristically" or "true to character" on that alleged occasion.

Fortunately for both prosecutors and plaintiffs, however, most courts have prevented an affront to common sense by recognizing a theory for rationalizing the admission of this critical type of evidence. Immediately after announcing the character evidence prohibition, Rule 404(b) continues: Evidence of other misconduct "may, however, be admissible for other purposes, such as proof of motive, opportunity, intent, preparation, plan, knowledge, identity, or absence of mistake or accident." As at common law, the statute permits the proponent to introduce the evidence so long as there is a tenable non-character theory of logical relevance. Indeed, every federal circuit has construed Rule 404(b) to mean that the proponent may rely on any alternative theory - that is, any theory other than the character theory forbidden in the first sentence of the statute.

In cases such as Woods and the hypothetical civil rights action described above, the courts often invoke the doctrine of objective chances as the non-character theory to legitimate the introduction of the evidence. In the criminal arena, the doctrine has become a mainstay of child abuse and drug prosecutions. If, as in Woods, the defendant claims that the child's death was an accident, the government may introduce evidence of other injuries inflicted on the child to prove the commission of an actus reus. Or in a drug prosecution in which the defendant claims that he was "merely present" at or an "innocent bystander" to a drug transaction, the government may present evidence of the defendant's involvement in other drug trafficking to show mens rea. Innocent persons sometimes accidentally become enmeshed in suspicious circumstances, but it is objectively unlikely that will happen over and over again by random chance. By the same token, evidence of a defendant's other discriminatory acts serves as the backbone of the plaintiff's case in many civil rights actions. . . .

[T]he doctrine of chances differs at least superficially from a character theory of logical relevance. Initially, under the doctrine the proponent does not offer the evidence of the uncharged misconduct to establish an intermediate inference as to the defendant's personal, subjective bad character. Rather, the proponent offers the evidence to establish the objective improbability of so many accidents befalling the defendant or the defendant becoming innocently enmeshed in suspicious circumstances so frequently. The proponent must establish that, together with the uncharged incident, the charged incident would represent an extraordinary coincidence. In some cases, that will be obvious. Smith is a case in point. In a fact situation such as Smith, the jury hardly needs an expert's testimony to appreciate that, on average, finding one's spouse drowned in the family bathtub is at most a " 'once in a lifetime' " experience. In other cases, though, the proponent may need to introduce independent evidence to establish the ordinary incidence of the type of event in which the defendant was involved.

Like the intermediate inference, the final conclusion under the doctrine of chances differs from the ultimate conclusion in character reasoning. If the jury finds the requisite extraordinary coincidence under the doctrine of chances, the proponent may invite the jury to finally conclude that, as a matter of common sense, the coincidence is evidence that one or some of the incidents were not accidents. Under the doctrine, the final inference is a very limited conclusion. The final conclusion is not that all the incidents were the product of an actus reus or mens rea. Rather, the final inference is merely that one or some of the incidents were not accidents. The doctrine posits that some incidents can and, in the normal course of events, do occur accidentally. Moreover, there is nothing about the internal logic of the doctrine which singles out the charged incident as the product of an actus reus or mens rea. At most, all that the doctrine establishes is that one or some of the incidents were probably the product of an actus reus or mens rea.

The doctrine of chances not only comes to a different final conclusion than a character theory; the doctrine also takes a different route to its final conclusion. Under a character theory, the second inference entails using the defendant's subjective character as a predictor of conduct. The second inference under the doctrine of chances is quite different. At trial, the litigants present the jury with at least two competing hypotheses: one that all the incidents are accidents, and the other that one or some of the incidents were not accidents. When a jury is presented with competing versions of the events, the jury is expected to use its common sense to gauge the relative plausibility of the versions. In many jurisdictions, the pattern jury instructions both authorize and encourage the petit jurors to use their common sense in choosing among the competing hypotheses advanced by the litigants.

In this light, it becomes clear that the doctrine is not merely superficially different than a character theory. Far more importantly, the doctrine is distinguishable from a character theory in terms of the policies which inspire the character prohibition.

First, while a true character theory forces the jurors to consciously address the question of the type or kind of person the defendant is, there is no such necessity under the doctrine. Thus, the doctrine reduces the risk that the jurors will in effect penalize the defendant because of his or her status. The judge's instruction on the doctrine should expressly direct the jurors that they may not treat the uncharged evidence as proof of the defendant's personal bad character. It is true that it might occur to an individual juror that the evidence is also logically relevant on a character theory and to vote against the defendant for that reason. However, under the doctrine there is much less risk that that probative danger will materialize. The instruction on the doctrine not only does not compel the jurors to focus on the defendant's character or disposition; the instruction ought to bluntly tell them not to do so. Thus, the doctrine creates a markedly lower danger of misdecision.

Second, the doctrine presents less risk of overvaluation of the evidence. As Part I explained, that risk can be acute when the jury must use the defendant's character as a predictor of conduct on a specific occasion. However, under the doctrine the final inferential step is different. The doctrine does not ask the jurors to utilize the defendant's propensity as the basis for a prediction of conduct on the alleged occasion. Instead, the doctrine asks the jurors to consider the objective improbability of a coincidence in assessing the plausibility of a defendant's claim that a loss was the product of an accident or that he or she was accidentally enmeshed in suspicious circumstances. This common sense mode of reasoning is not only legitimate; indeed, the pattern jury charges in many jurisdictions urge the jurors to resort to precisely that type of reasoning.

The Second Sentence: Procedural Requirements

There is no such thing as a trial by ambush with Rule 404(b) evidence. The rule specifically requires the proponent to provide pretrial notice of intent to introduce prior misconduct, if requested by the accused; consequently, best practices for defense counsel include requesting notice in every case. The court can excuse this requirement for good cause at trial, for example, if the prosecution does not discover the uncharged prior misconduct in enough time to meet the pretrial notice requirements.

Frequently, Rule 404(b) evidence is introduced by the prosecution as part of its rebuttal case. This practice makes it much easier to identify appropriate non-character uses for the evidence: the prosecution can point to the defense theory of the case and rebut it with specific evidence. For example, if the accused's theory of the case is absence of knowledge or intent, the prosecution can wait until rebuttal to introduce past uncharged acts that would tend to prove the accused's knowledge or intent.

Prior misconduct can be proved through witnesses or documents. In cases where the prior misconduct resulted in a criminal conviction, introduction of the conviction itself is the strongest and surest form of proof.

Special Balancing Tests

Most courts apply specific balancing tests to Rule 404(b) evidence. These tests typically require the proponent of the evidence to be able to demonstrate a proper non-character use for the evidence and provide proof that the uncharged acts were actually committed. In addition, although Rule 404(b) does not specifically refer to Rule 403, the balancing tests consistently apply a rigorous Rule 403 analysis to uncharged acts evidence. This is because of the dangers associated with the improper introduction of character evidence at trial.

Many federal circuits apply an enhanced Rule 403 balancing test to uncharged acts evidence, requiring judges to make specific findings on the record before admitting such evidence at trial. A few circuits apply a balancing test that reverses the traditional presumptive admissibility standards of Rule 403, holding that uncharged acts evidence must be more probative (or even substantially more probative) than prejudicial before it can be admitted.

II.   CASES, DISCUSSION QUESTIONS AND PROBLEMS

UNITED STATES v. OLIVO
United States Court of Appeals, Tenth Circuit
69 F.3d 1057 (10th Cir. 1995)

[Among other things, Olivo was convicted of conspiracy to possess with intent to distribute 1,000 kilograms or more of marijuana.]

From 1987 through 1992, Emilio Castillo imported into Oklahoma approximately 8,320 pounds of marijuana from Mexico and Texas. Olivo and his father, Elisar Olivo, transported some of the marijuana from Texas to Oklahoma. Olivo worked as a truck driver for Scrivner Trucking. Because the company sealed the doors to the freight containers on its trucks, law enforcement officers rarely examined its trucks for contraband. Olivo concealed marijuana, which first had been compressed, wrapped, dipped in tar, and rewrapped, in boxes similar to those shipped by Scrivner, and hid the boxes on northbound trucks. After the trucks safely passed through the checkpoints, they stopped at a prearranged destination where the marijuana was removed and then delivered to David Shanks' farm for weighing and distribution. . . .

II. Subsequent bad act

Count one of the superseding indictment alleged Olivo conspired to possess with intent to distribute 1,000 kilo-grams or more of marijuana. The indictment alleged the conspiracy began on or about January 1, 1987, and continued until January 1993. Olivo contends the conspiracy ended no later than April 1992. At trial, the court admitted 185 pounds of marijuana seized from Olivo's vehicle on November 9, 1993, a date subsequent to the dates charged in the superseding indictment and that argued by Olivo. Olivo argues the court erred by admitting the marijuana. We review an evidentiary decision for abuse of discretion. Accordingly, we review the court's admission of evidence under Rule 404(b) to determine whether the court abused its discretion.

Fed. R. Evid. 404(b) provides, in part, that "evidence of other crimes, wrongs, or acts is not admissible to prove the character of a person in order to show action in conformity therewith." Rule 404(b) does not flatly prohibit introduction of evidence of other crimes, wrongs, or acts, but instead limits the purpose for which such evidence may be introduced. Huddleston v. United States, 485 U.S. 681, 687, 108 S. Ct. 1496, 99 L. Ed. 2d 771 (1988). Cf. United States v. Cuch, 842 F.2d 1173, 1176 (10th Cir. 1988) (explaining that the rule is one of inclusion unless the evidence is introduced for an impermissible purpose or undue prejudice is shown). This court has held that a defendant is presumed to be protected against undue prejudice if (1) the evidence is offered for a proper purpose, (2) the evidence is relevant, (3) the trial court makes a Rule 403 determination, and (4) the trial court, upon request, instructs the jury that the evidence is to be considered only for the proper purpose for which it was admitted.

The government notified the court and Olivo prior to trial of its intent to introduce 185 pounds of marijuana seized from Olivo by Texas police on November 9, 1993. The transcript submitted with the record does not contain admission of the challenged evidence. Apparently, Texas authorities, after receiving a tip from a confidential informant, arranged a meeting with Olivo and seized approximately 185 pounds of marijuana from his automobile. Some of the marijuana was in boxes in the trunk and some in a suitcase in the back seat. The marijuana was not packaged uniformly.

Olivo does not specifically direct his argument on appeal to any of the four requirements for admissibility. He argues neither that the court failed to make a Rule 403 determination nor that it failed to give a cautionary instruction. The record contains the court's final jury charge in which the jury was instructed it could not infer guilt from evidence of other unlawful conduct "of a like or similar nature" but could consider it as to "any question of intent or knowledge or lack of accident or mistake regarding the charged crimes."

Olivo notes that this court's cases addressing the admissibility of a subsequent bad act focus upon the similarity and proximity of the charged and subsequent acts. He argues the court abused its discretion because his subsequent misconduct was insufficiently similar and proximate to the crime charged in count one of the superseding indictment.

The subsequent misconduct involved Olivo's association with others to transport and distribute a large quantity of marijuana. His role in the subsequent offense apparently was to transport marijuana allegedly fronted him by another. The fact that the individuals involved in the two offenses packaged the marijuana somewhat differently is not dispositive. Nor is it dispositive that the subsequent conduct involved an automobile whereas the charged conduct involved a commercial vehicle. Differences in the details of subsequent and charged conduct go to whether the evidence is relevant to a particular proper purpose. When the issue is intent, subsequent evidence may be highly probative of intent.

Here, the subsequent conduct was sufficiently similar to the charged conduct to make the existence of Olivo's intent to conspire to possess marijuana with intent to distribute more or less probable. Further, the two instances were not so dissimilar as to make admission of the evidence an abuse of the court's ample discretion under Rule 403. The only potentially troubling aspect here is that Olivo engaged in the subsequent conduct more than one year after the conspiracy ended. Obviously, remoteness may decrease the probative value of extrinsic evidence. However, extrinsic evidence separated by more than a year from the charged conduct has been found probative of intent. See United States v. Terebecki, 692 F.2d 1345, 1349 (11th Cir. 1982) (fraudulent transaction fifteen months after charged fraudulent transaction not too remote to show intent). Cf. Cuch, 842 F.2d at 1178 (assault committed seven and one-half years prior to crime charged probative and admissible to show intent). But see United States v. Betts, 16 F.3d 748, 757-60 (7th Cir. 1994) (abuse of discretion to admit evidence of possession of large quantities of marijuana two years subsequent to charged act of conspiracy to distribute marijuana). Although it is a close question, we find that, under the facts of the instant case, the court did not abuse its discretion.

III. Prior bad acts

Olivo argues the court twice erred in admitting evidence regarding prior bad acts. He challenges portions of testimony given by two witnesses: LaDonna Staehle and Wales. Olivo argues their testimony violated Rule 404(b) because it placed him in a negative light; more specifically, he argues Staehle's testimony tended to show he was the type of person who would smuggle drugs, and Wales' testimony tended to show he was the type of person who would participate in illegal monetary transactions. We review the court's admission of evidence under Rule 404(b) for abuse of discretion.

Staehle admitted early in her testimony that she previously had a drug problem and had used marijuana, cocaine, and Valium. The government developed her association with Castillo and her role in his operation. Shortly before the offending testimony, Staehle explained she and her husband spent one week in a motel waiting for Castillo to instruct them regarding an upcoming marijuana transaction. The government asked what she and her husband did that week and Staehle responded, "we were staying in a motel room and we were doing some cocaine." The government inquired about her association with Olivo. She explained that although she did not meet him in connection with Castillo's marijuana operation, she did attend a party at Olivo's house the day before she and her husband were arrested. When asked what kind of party it was, Staehle answered, "they were drinking beer. Me and my husband, we were doing some cocaine." Olivo moved for mistrial arguing that Staehle's testimony connected him to "the cocaine trade." The court denied the motion explaining, "there is no basis there. She said she was the one taking cocaine."

Wales testified he was a passenger in Winkle's Corvette when it was driven to Olivo's house. He stated that he showed the Corvette to Olivo, who drove it, and the car was left at Olivo's house. He also admitted Winkle later re-ported the vehicle stolen and collected the insurance money. At a bench conference requested by Olivo's counsel, the court indicated the manner in which the government developed Wales' testimony "certainly left an impression with me that [Olivo] was involved [in the fraud scheme]." The government asked for an opportunity to clarify that Olivo was not involved, and the court assented and withheld decision on Olivo's motion for a mistrial. The government asked Wales: "Mr. Wales, listen to me very closely. Mr. Nuco [Arnulfo] Olivo, did he have any knowledge or information relating to the scheme involving the Corvette that you took down there?" Wales responded, "No, Nuco thought we were trying to sell the Corvette." The court then denied Olivo's motion.

Olivo did not participate in the objectionable conduct about which Staehle and Wales testified. Even if Staehle's and Wales' conduct can be attributed to Olivo, the government argues it elicited the testimony to impeach its own witnesses. See Fed. R. Evid. 607 (stating that "the credibility of a witness may be attacked by any party, including the party calling the witness"). Neither the court nor the government adhered to United States v. Kendall, 766 F.2d 1426, 1436 (10th Cir. 1985), cert. denied, 474 U.S. 1081, 106 S. Ct. 848, 88 L. Ed. 2d 889 (1986), which requires both to identify the purpose for which the evidence is offered and admitted. We consider a failure to adhere to Kendall harmless error if "the purpose for admitting the other acts testimony is apparent from the record, and the district court's decision to admit was correct." United States v. Orr, 864 F.2d 1505, 1511 (10th Cir. 1988).

We find no abuse of discretion in admitting the challenged testimony. The government offered the testimony to impeach its own witnesses. Impeachment may be a permissible "other purpose" within the meaning of Rule 404(b). The testimony was relevant to credibility and, although we agree with Olivo that the testimony may have had some spillover effect, we do not believe it was so great that the court's decision was an abuse of discretion under Rule 403. Finally, despite the court's apparent failure to instruct the jury with respect to this testimony, there is no indication in the record before us that Olivo requested either a contemporaneous cautionary instruction or a final limiting instruction. See United States v. Record, 873 F.2d 1363, 1376 (10th Cir. 1989) (failure to instruct harmless absent a request by counsel).

DISCUSSION QUESTIONS

1. If the doctrine of chances predates the Federal Rules of Evidence, why do you think the drafters of the rules left it out of Rule 404(b)? Should its absence from the Rules affect its use at trial? Why or why not?

2. Do you agree with Professor Imwinkelried that the doctrine of chances avoids the dangers posed by the improper introduction and use of character evidence at trial? Why or why not?

3. What does the Olivo court say about post-offense uncharged misconduct? Is it more or less prejudicial than prior uncharged misconduct?

4. Identify the special balancing test used in the 10th Circuit for the admission of Rule 4049(b) evidence. Did the prosecution satisfy the balancing test in this case?

PROBLEMS

Problem 11-1. On a cold winter day in December, a frantic Darryl Defendant brought his 18-month-old son, Barry, into the emergency room of the hospital. Darryl claimed that he had been holding Barry in his arms, trying to rock him to sleep, when Barry suddenly went limp and became nonresponsive. Resuscitation efforts failed, and Barry was pronounced dead at the hospital. The autopsy as to cause of death was inconclusive. There was no apparent cause of death, although Barry did have some suspicious subcutaneous bruises under his scalp. The autopsy did reveal, however, that Barry had suffered, sometime in the previous year, several broken ribs and a broken leg, none of which had ever been treated but had healed on their own. These broken bones were not the cause of Barry's death.

This was not Barry's first visit to the hospital. Two weeks earlier, his parents had brought him in for facial burns he suffered when Darryl held him directly over a hot-steam nebulizer to clear Barry's clogged nasal passages. The autopsy findings triggered attention from the State of Calamity Children's Death Review Board, a board set up by statute to examine suspicious deaths in young children. The Board concluded that Barry's death was a homicide, and the Calamity State's Attorney indicted Darryl for second-degree murder.

Before trial, the prosecution provided notice of intent to introduce evidence of Barry's broken ribs and leg under Rule 404(b) under the "doctrine of chances" theory. The defense filed a motion in limine to exclude the evidence. In a pretrial hearing, the defense claimed that those injuries could have come from several other people who had access to Barry during the time frame the injuries occurred: Darryl's wife, Suzette; Darryl's babysitter, Margaret; and Darryl's maternal grandparents, Bob and Barbie. The prosecution conceded that no one knew for sure the source of Barry's injuries, but the doctrine of chances mandated admitting the evidence. Evaluate the prosecution's "doctrine of chances" argument. How should the judge rule on the defense's motion, and why?

Problem 11-2. Defendant Lester Lee is charged with the second-degree murder of another motorist, stemming from an accident in which he veered into a lane of oncoming traffic and hit another car. At the time of the accident, he had a blood alcohol content of .25. The jurisdiction's murder statute requires "malice aforethought" for second-degree murder, which is defined as "conduct which is reckless and wanton, and a gross deviation from a reasonable standard of care, of such a nature that a jury is warranted in inferring that defendant was aware of a serious risk of death or serious bodily harm."

Defendant has four prior convictions for Driving Under the Influence within the past five years, in two different jurisdictions. In each case, defendant pled guilty in return for a favorable disposition in his case. None of the prior incidents involved an accident or harm to other people.

1. What arguments should the prosecution make in support of admitting evidence of Mr. Lee's prior DUI convictions at trial under Rule 404?

2. What arguments should the defense make to exclude the evidence under Rule 404?

Problem 11-3. Paula brings a wrongful death action against Railroad for the death of her husband at a railroad crossing when his car was hit by a train. She claims the crossing was unsafe. At trial, she seeks to introduce evidence under FRE 404(b) that on two prior occasions within the last six months, Railroad's trains have hit vehicles at this crossing in exactly the same manner as her husband's was hit. How should the judge rule, and why?

Evidence of Uncharged Misconduct or Other Acts Evidence: Quick Hits

- Rule 404(b) permits the use of uncharged or other acts evidence at trial for non-character purposes

- The rule applies in both civil and criminal cases

- The proponent of the evidence must be able to explain on the record a non-character theory for the use of the evidence

- The doctrine of chances is a non-character theory that helps explain the non-coincidental nature of repeated similar acts, or results in an individual's life

- Parties desiring to admit evidence under Rule 404(b) must provide pretrial notice to their opponents

- Judges must apply a Rule 403 balancing test to evidence admitted under Rule 404(b), and many jurisdictions require enhanced balancing tests with additional factors

---

Chapter References

CHRISTOPHER B. MUELLER & LAIRD C. KIRKPATRICK, EVIDENCE §§ 4.15–4.18 (4th ed. 2009).

GLEN WEISSENBERGER & JAMES J. DUANE, FEDERAL RULES OF EVIDENCE: RULES, LEGISLATIVE HISTORY, COMMENTARY AND AUTHORITY §§ 404.11–404.22 (6th ed. 2009).

JACK B. WEINSTEIN & MARGARET A. BERGER, WEINSTEIN'S FEDERAL EVIDENCE §§ 404.20–404.23 (Joseph M. McLaughlin ed., Matthew Bender 2d ed. 1997).

KENNETH S. BROUN, MCCORMICK ON EVIDENCE §§ 186–95 (6th ed. 2006).

STEVEN GOODE & OLIN GUY WELLBORN III, COURTROOM HANDBOOK ON FEDERAL EVIDENCE Ch. 5 (West 2010).

III. APPLICATION EXERCISE

Objective: To conduct a Rule 404(b) hearing in a pretrial *motion in limine* in a murder case.

Factual Scenario: Return to Problem 9-1 and the Pastor Paul hypothetical for the basic facts. Pastor Paul is being charged with murder in the death of Terry, the street preacher. The jurisdiction defines murder as the "purposeful, knowing or reckless killing of one human being by another." The jurisdiction uses the Model Penal Code definitions for the culpability states of purpose, knowledge, and reckless.

The prosecution has given proper notice to the defense of its intent to introduce uncharged acts against Pastor Paul under Rule 404(b). In its notice to the defense, the prosecution identified the following uncharged acts:

> 1. At the age of 35 (Paul is now 45), Paul and an associate pastor at the church got into a violent disagreement about the meaning of the phrase, "blessed are the peacemakers." Paul beat up the associate pastor, who forgave him and refused to press charges. The pastor, whose name is Van, is available to testify about the incident. Paul has always denied that the incident occurred.

> 2. On at least five occasions in the past two years, Paul challenged other ministers to fight about various doctrinal issues during local pastoral association meetings. Every single one of these incidents was precipitated by a discussion on different verses in the Sermon on the Mount. Paul considers himself a leading expert on the Sermon on the Mount, having written a dissertation on it during his seminary days. The president of the pastoral Association, Elmore Leonard, is available to testify about these incidents.

The defense has filed a written motion in limine to preclude the use of this evidence at trial. The motion alleges that the uncharged acts are improper character evidence under Rule 404(a) and that introduction of the evidence would be unfairly prejudicial under Rule 403. The prosecution's response claims that the evidence is proper for a non-character purpose under Rule 404(b) and that its probative value is not substantially outweighed by the evidence of unfair prejudice. We are now at a pretrial hearing on this motion in limine. Van and Elmore Leonard are available to testify.

Advance Preparation: Prepare for both the defense and prosecution roles in this case.

<u>Defense:</u> Be prepared to verbally renew the motion in limine in the presence of the judge. The defense should carry its burden of production by identifying the problems with the evidence under Rule 404(a) and 403 and requesting that the evidence be excluded from trial. The defense should also be prepared to cross-examine prosecution witnesses. After the prosecution has called its witnesses, the

defense must present argument on the motion in light of the evidence raised.

Prosecution: The prosecution has the burden of persuasion and should be prepared to (1) identify a proper non-character purpose for the evidence under Rule 404(b), (2) call Van and Elmore Leonard to provide proof on the record that the prior incidents actually occurred (the defense should be prepared to cross-examine them), and (3) satisfy the Rule 403 balancing test. The prosecution should also be prepared to present argument on the motion.

In-Class Exercise. Students A and B will play the role of defense counsel. Student A will make the initial motion and cross examine Van. Student B will cross-examine Elmore Leonard and will make the final defense arguments. Students 1 and 2 will play the prosecutorial roles. Student 1 will respond to the defense motion and call Van on direct examination. Student 2 will call Elmore Leonard on direct and will present argument on the motion. Student 3 will play the role of the judge. Other students will play the roles of Elmore Leonard and Van.

Chapter 12

DEFENDANT'S SEXUAL PROPENSITY EVIDENCE IN SEXUAL ASSAULT AND CHILD MOLESTATION CASES

Chapter Objectives:

- Introduce and explain Rules 413-415 and the process, structure and balancing test for admitting evidence of the defendant's sexual propensity in sexual assault and child molestation cases
- Analyze and discuss issues pertaining to Rules 413-415
- Apply the concepts from this chapter in a courtroom application exercise

---

I. BACKGROUND AND EXPLANATORY MATERIAL

Introduction to Rules 413-415

In cases of alleged sexual assault or child molestation, Rules 413-415 turn all the other character evidence rules inside out. Rules 413 and 414 allow the prosecution to introduce into evidence prior instances of sexual assault or child molestation committed by the accused. They further permit the prosecution to use that evidence for "its bearing on any matter to which it is relevant," including character or propensity. In criminal cases, Rules 413 and 414 do away with two significant protections available to the defendant: (1) the tradition that the defendant holds the key to the introduction of character evidence at trial, as codified in Rule 404(a); and (2) the prohibition against using evidence of specific acts to prove character under Rule 404(b). In civil cases, Rule 415 permits the use of specific acts evidence of prior sexual misconduct, even if it is not essential to a charge, claim or defense, thus circumventing the normal functions of Rule 405.

In discussing these rules, Section I first examines the controversial creation of Rules 413-415. The section next evaluates the validity of these rules' departure from traditional character evidence rules. Finally, the section explains the framework of the rules and the procedures for their use at trial.

The Controversial Creation of Rules 413-415

Few evidentiary rules have been as engendered as much controversy as Rules 413-415. Almost universally scorned and disliked by judges, professors, and advocacy groups — including feminist advocacy groups — the rules are based on questionable justifications that lack empirical support. Furthermore, the rules create procedural, evidentiary and potential constitutional problems at trial.

Congressional Justification for the Rules

Rules 413-415 were directly enacted by Congress as part of the Violent Crime Control and Law Enforcement Act of 1994. The bill was co-sponsored by Senator Robert Dole and Representative Susan Molinari. The rules are premised on the concept that past instances of sexual misconduct are probative on the issue of whether a criminal accused committed the charged acts and require special rules differentiating them from other types of uncharged criminal misconduct.

The legislative history of the rule demonstrates Congress's thought process in adopting these rules. In her floor statement to the House, Representative Molinari described the rules as

> [G]eneral rules of admissibility in sexual assault and child molestation cases for evidence that the defendant has committed offenses of the same type on other occasions. The enactment of the reform is first and foremost a triumph for the public — for the women who will not be raped and the children who will not be molested because we have strengthened the legal system's tools for bringing the perpetrators of these atrocious crimes to justice.[1]

In his speech to the Senate, Senator Dole described the necessity for the rules as follows:

> [T]oo often, crucial evidentiary information is thrown out at trial because of technical evidentiary rulings. This amendment is designed to clarify the law and make clear what evidence is admissible, and what evidence is not admissible, in sex crime cases. . . .

> I think if somebody is a repeat offender, if you brought in eight or nine women, for example, . . . and he had one offense after another, it would be probative. If it had not happened for 10 years, it probably would not have any value. . . .

> [I]f we are really going to get tough, and if we are really going to try to make certain that justice is provided for the victim as well as the defendant, of course, then I think we ought to look seriously at this.

Thus, from the outset, Congress intended to adopt evidentiary rules for sexual assault cases that were much different from the character and propensity rules that were already a part of the Federal Rules of Evidence. The goal was to make it

---

[1] Floor Statement of Representative Susan Molinari Concerning the Prior Crimes Evidence for Sexual Assault and Child Molestation Cases (Congressional Record, Aug. 21, 1994, H8991–H8992).

easier for prosecutors to obtain convictions.

Procedures for Adopting the Rules

Congress did not apply the normal procedures for amending or adding new rules of evidence under the Rules Enabling Act, 28 U.S.C. §§ 2071–2077. Under these procedures, proposed rules are considered by the Advisory Committee, published for public comment, reconsidered by the Advisory Committee in light of the public comments, transmitted to the Judicial Conference's Standing Committee on Rules of Practice and Procedure for approval, transmitted to the Judicial Conference for approval, then transmitted to the Supreme Court. The Supreme Court approves the rule change, then transmits it to the Congress by May 1 of the year in which the rule is supposed to take effect. Congress has at least 7 months to act on any rules prescribed by the Supreme Court, and if the Congress takes no legislative action to reject, modify or defer the proposed rule, it takes effect on December 1.[2]

Under normal circumstances, rule changes are the result of a deliberative process that takes into account the differing viewpoints of judges, lawyers, professors and members of the public. The procedures Congress used to create Rules 413–415 circumvented this process. Instead, Congress provided the Judicial Conference with 150 days to review the rules *after* they had already been enacted. Although the statute created a mechanism for Congress to review any recommendations made by the Judicial Conference, Congress took no action on any of the Conference's suggested changes.

The Judicial Conference solicited input from all federal judges, 900 evidence professors, 40 women's rights organizations, and approximately 1,000 other individuals and interested organizations.[3] Public responses to the rules included 84 written comments representing 112 individuals and 16 local and national legal organizations.[4] The overwhelming majority of responses opposed the new rules, on two grounds: (1) the rules would permit the admission of unfairly prejudicial evidence at trial; and (2) careless draftsmanship would lead to problems not intended by the authors.[5] The Judicial Conference submitted a report to Congress recommending that it reconsider its policy bases for the rules. In the alternative, the report recommended amending Rules 404[6] and 405[7] to preserve "the substance

---

[2] James C. Duff, *The Rulemaking Process: A Summary for Bench and Bar* (Oct. 2007), *available at* http://www.uscourts.gov/rules/procedures.htm.

[3] Report of the Judicial Conference of the United States.

[4] *Id.*

[5] *See id.*

[6] *Id.* Here are the proposed changes to Rule 404(a):

(4) Character in sexual misconduct cases. Evidence of another act of sexual assault or child molestation, or evidence to rebut such proof or an inference therefrom, if that evidence is otherwise admissible under these rules, in a criminal case in which the accused is charged with sexual assault or child molestation, or in a civil case in which a claim is predicated on a party's alleged commission of sexual assault or child molestation.

(A) In weighing the probative value of such evidence, the court may, as part of its rule 403 determination, consider:

(i) proximity in time to the charged or predicate misconduct;

of the congressional enactment but . . . clarify drafting ambiguities and eliminate possible constitutional infirmities."[8]

Despite the overwhelming criticism of Rules 413-415, Congress neither changed them nor adopted the Judicial Conference's recommended amendments to Rules 404 and 405. In the absence of further Congressional action, the rules became operative on July 9, 1995.

Theoretical Flaws of Rules 413-415

One of the most salient flaws in Rules 413-415 is the underlying premise that sex offenders are substantially different from other criminals and are thereby not entitled to the same evidentiary protections at trial. Another weakness of Rules 413-415 is their failure to differentiate types of sex offenses. In other words, the rules themselves do not require any degree of similarity between the uncharged acts introduced at trial and the charged offenses. Although their purpose is to provide protection from crimes of sexual violence, the Rules may actually indicate a profound misunderstanding about what rape is and what motivates sex offenders.

The following excerpt from an article by James Duane makes a powerful argument against the rules and illustrates some of its fundamental flaws.

———————

      (ii) similarity to the charged or predicate misconduct;

      (iii) frequency of the other acts;

      (iv) surrounding circumstances;

      (v) relevant intervening events; and

      (vi) other relevant similarities or differences.

(B) In a criminal case in which the prosecution intends to offer evidence under this subdivision, it must disclose the evidence, including statements of witnesses or a summary of the substance of any testimony, at a reasonable time in advance of trial, or during trial if the court excuses pretrial notice on good cause shown.

(C) For purposes of this subdivision,

      (i) "sexual assault" means conduct — or an attempt or conspiracy to engage in conduct — of the type proscribed by chapter 109A of title 18, United States Code, or conduct that involved deriving sexual pleasure or ratification from inflicting death, bodily injury, or physical pain on another person irrespective of the age of the victim — regardless of whether that conduct would have subjected the actor to federal jurisdiction.

      (ii) "child molestation" means conduct — or an attempt or conspiracy to engage in conduct — of the type proscribed by chapter 110 of title 18, United States Code, or conduct, committed in relation to a child below the age of 14 years, either of the type proscribed by chapter 109A of title 18, United States Code, or that involved deriving sexual pleasure or gratification from inflicting death, bodily injury, or physical pain on another person — regardless of whether that conduct would have subjected the actor to federal jurisdiction.

[7] *Id.* Here are the proposed changes to Rule 405:

      (c) Proof in sexual misconduct cases. In a case in which evidence is offered under rule 404(a)(4), proof may be made by specific instances of conduct, testimony as to reputation, or testimony in the form of an opinion, except that the prosecution or claimant may offer reputation or opinion testimony only after the opposing party has offered such testimony.

[8] *Id.*

James Joseph Duane, *The New Federal Rules of Evidence on Prior Acts of Accused Sex Offenders: A Poorly Drafted Version of a Very Bad Idea,* 157 F.R.D. 95 (1994)

A. The New Rules Create a Terrible Risk of Unfair Prejudice to Innocent Defendants with a Criminal History

[T]he new rules will probably accomplish only one of their intended objectives: to increase, at least slightly, the number of convictions of sex offenses. That is, however, the most profound and compelling reason to reject the new rules. At the risk of stating what should have been obvious, a mere increase in the rate of convicting accused sex offenders is not necessarily a good thing, unless those additional convictions obtained under the new rules are all (or at least substantially all) obtained in the case of guilty defendants. If any significant number of those found guilty under the new rules are actually innocent of the crime charged, their hasty adoption will have been a horrible mistake.

Of course, if we were determined to increase the conviction rate for guilty offenders at all costs, there are certain reforms we could theoretically pursue that would do so with little or no risk to innocent defendants. But abolition of the "propensity rule" in sex offense cases is not such a reform. It is self-evident that allowing juries to learn of a defendant's prior criminal history will not increase the chances of convicting all guilty defendants, although it will increase the chances of convicting all those accused defendants who have been convicted (or least accused) of sexual offenses in the past — regardless of whether those defendants are guilty or innocent. That is the simple reality lying at the very heart of Federal Rule of Evidence 404, and the reason why our law has universally condemned such attempts to convict a man by attacking his character for centuries. Nor is the rule a relic from the ancient past; the logic behind the rule was recently and unanimously reaffirmed by the Supreme Court.[9] Indeed, the use of propensity evidence in this manner carries such an inherent risk of convicting the innocent that there is substantial authority to suggest that such use of character evidence against a criminal defendant would violate the Constitutional guarantees of Due Process and the presumption of innocence.

The legislative history of the new rules contains no acknowledgment of the undeniable fact that they can possibly lead to additional convictions only in the case of those defendants who (1) are acquitted under current law, and (2) have some sort of alleged history of sexual assault. Given that inevitable reality, would that change result in a net improvement or reduction in the overall accuracy and integrity of our system for determining guilt and innocence? The answer to that crucial question — which was barely even mentioned in the Congressional debates leading

---

[9] [n.70] In Huddleston v. United States, 485 U.S. 681, 108 S.Ct. 1496, 99 L.Ed.2d 771 (1988), the Supreme Court unanimously noted its "concern" that evidence of prior bad acts and crimes admitted under the present exceptions of Rule 404(b) might carry a risk of "unfair prejudice," but for a number of detailed safeguards contained in the current Rules of Evidence against the possible misuse of such evidence to prove a defendant's bad character. Id. at 691, 108 S.Ct. at 1502.

to the passage of the rules — depends entirely on one's assumptions about the group of accused sex offenders who are acquitted under current law but have a suspect background: how many of them are innocent, and how many are guilty? Even if only 10% of that group are actually innocent, increasing the chances of convicting them all runs afoul of our society's fundamental constitutional value determination "that it is far worse to convict an innocent man than to let a guilty man go free."[10]

Proponents of the new rules anticipated but dismissed this objection with the absurd assumption that an accused sex offender with a criminal record is virtually certain to be guilty of the crime charged. The sponsors of the new rules relied on the rather dogmatic assumption that:

> It is inherently improbable that a person whose prior bad acts show that he is in fact a rapist or child molester would have the bad luck to be later hit with a false accusation of committing the same type of crime, or that a person would fortuitously be subject to multiple false accusations by a number of different victims. . . .. For example, consider a case in which the defense attacks the victim's assertion that she did not consent, or represents that the whole incident was made up by the victim. Suppose further that there is practically conclusive evidence that the defendant has in fact committed one or more sexual assaults on other occasions, such as a prior conviction of the defendant on a charge of rape. In the presence of such evidence, the defense's claim of consent, or claim that the whole incident did not occur, would usually amount to a contention that the victim fabricated a false charge of rape against a person who just happened to be a rapist. The improbability of such a coincidence gives similar crimes evidence a high degree of probative value, and supports its admission, in such a case.[11]

As a justification for the new rules, this account is utterly unrealistic, for two distinct reasons. First, it greatly exaggerates the value of the new rules by focusing on a hypothetical case in which the evidence of prior offenses is "practically conclusive," when the new rules require no such thing. Under new Rule 413, prosecutors are not even restricted to conclusive evidence, much less convictions, and are free to use even unproven (and perhaps false) allegations of sexual misconduct that may be many years old. Old convictions admittedly cannot be created out of whole cloth after a suspect has been accused, but antagonistic accusers with stale, uncertain, and possibly false allegations can easily come out of the woodwork after it becomes widely known that an accused rapist is heading for trial on either civil or criminal charges.

Moreover, even if the new rules were applied only to defendants who have been conclusively shown to have committed sexual offenses in the past, it is by no means

---

[10] [n. 72] Francis v. Franklin, 471 U.S. 307, 313, 105 S.Ct. 1965, 1970, 85 L.Ed.2d 344 (1985) (citation omitted). In the well-known estimate of Blackstone, "it is better that ten guilty persons escape than that one innocent suffer." Coffin v. United States, 156 U.S. 432, 455-56, 15 S.Ct. 394, 403, 39 L.Ed. 481 (1895) (quoting 2 WILLIAM BLACKSTONE, COMMENTARIES, c.27).

[11] [n.73] 137 CONG. REC. S3191-02, 3240-41 (Mar. 13, 1991) (section-by-section analysis of proposed Rules of Evidence 413-415) (emphasis added).

"inherently improbable" that such defendants would never find themselves the victim of an erroneous accusation of rape. The quoted passage exaggerates the apparent implausibility of that result by focusing on the situation in which the defendant admits sexual contact but claims there was consent, or maintains that the rape was entirely fabricated. In that case, it is true, it would be an odd coincidence for a woman to make such mistaken charges against a man who happened to have a prior record for such offenses. But in the common case where the defendant maintains that the victim has simply identified the wrong man — which includes virtually all rape cases in which the victim has been threatened with a weapon or caused serious physical injury — it is altogether likely that an innocent accused who has been mistakenly identified as the victim's rapist or abuser would also have a record of similar criminal accusations or convictions. Such a scenario would hardly amount to a "coincidence" if, as is often the case, the wrong man first became a suspect because he was known to the police (and then brought to the attention of the victim) due to his record of prior complaints, arrests, or convictions. . . .

When jurors are advised that an accused has a record of prior sexual offenses, including perhaps some for which he had never previously been charged or convicted, the danger is not merely that they will take that evidence as a decisive reason to believe he is guilty now. On the contrary, such evidence has widely been presumed to carry the risk of unfair prejudice because of the grave possibility that the jurors, even if they do not conclude that the defendant is guilty of the crime charged beyond a reasonable doubt, will be inclined to convict him (at least in part) on the basis of their disapproval of his prior crimes, or their hunch that he has committed other crimes for which he was never caught, or their fear of letting him remain on the streets to commit future crimes — especially if he was never punished or the jurors feel that he was not punished enough. To an innocent defendant attempting to protect himself from the risk of such prejudice, it is utterly beside the point to claim that he is free to "impeach" the complaining witness by suggesting that her identification of him in this case was tainted by her knowledge of his criminal background. That is no protection at all.

Incredibly, the hurried Congressional debate leading to the passage of the new rules apparently does not contain any serious discussion — much less hard empirical evidence — as to the percentage of accused sexual offenders with criminal records who are nevertheless innocent, or as to how that percentage might possibly increase under the new rules. Given the enormous stakes that hang in the balance with the new rules, it is astonishing that Congress chose to adopt those rules with little or no empirical evidence as to their likely effect on innocent suspects. It is even more troublesome in light of the ample evidence that even the leading Congressional sponsors of the new rules had a very confused understanding of the nature of, and the reasons for, the current rules. That is, by itself, a decisive reason to reject the adoption of these ill-conceived rules.

B. The New Rules Will Make the Federal Rules of Evidence Hopelessly Inconsistent and Utterly Inexplicable

Without a doubt, the most ironic "justification" which has been offered for the adoption of the new rules has been the criticism that the current body of law reflected in Federal Rule of Evidence 404(b) "has never been a model of clarity and consistency."[12] In support of their arguments in favor of the new rules, the proponents of this legislation cited a passage from a leading evidence treatise, Wigmore on Evidence, describing the "strong tendency" of many State courts in sex offense prosecutions "to admit evidence of the accused's sexual proclivities," which supposedly suggests that "the general rule against the use of propensity evidence against an accused is not honored in sex offense prosecutions."[13]

It is unspeakably ironic that the proponents of these new rules would cite Wigmore in support of their recommendation that federal law ought to retain a general ban on the use of character evidence to show criminal propensity, while at the same time adopting a special exception for the use of such evidence in sexual offense cases. In fact, although Wigmore acknowledges that several state courts have taken such an approach, that treatise just as clearly rejects that approach as hopelessly inconsistent. In language that was not included in the Congressional record of the legislative history, Wigmore goes on to conclude — correctly — that:

> If the rule against the use of character evidence [Federal Rule of Evidence 404] means anything, a broad sexual proclivity exception, available in all sex offense prosecutions [such as new Federal Rule 413], is utterly inexplicable. . . . [I]f character evidence generally is excluded because its prejudicial impact normally outweighs its probative value, this theory of exclusion arguably applies to evidence of prior sexual misconduct — evidence of a most inflammatory sort. . . . If we wish to use sexual propensity evidence against an accused, consistency demands that we abolish the propensity rule [Federal Rule 404] in its entirety.[14]

As Wigmore's treatise correctly predicted years ago, the adoption of a rule such as the new Federal Rules of Evidence 413 and 414, while simultaneously retaining Federal Rule 404, would be "utterly inexplicable," and inconsistent with the fundamental demands of basic logical consistency. It would be the height of absurdity and hypocrisy for the Federal government to revise its rules of evidence in order to model an inconsistent and illogical pattern adopted by a small number of states, especially in order to abolish a centuries-old system in the name of "clarity and consistency."

The supporters of the new federal rules, however, show no sign of taking Wigmore's suggestion that we "abolish the propensity rule in its entirety." On the contrary, the legislative history contains numerous suggestions that the new rules are designed to reflect some supposedly unique features of sexual offenders, and to create special "rules of admission tailored to the distinctive characteristics of sex offense cases."[15]

---

[12] [n.82] 137 CONG. REC. S3191-02, S3240 (Mar. 13, 1991).

[13] Id. at S3238 (quoting 1A WIGMORE ON EVIDENCE, § 62.2 at 1334-35 (Tillers rev. 1983)). This use of criminal records "to show a passion or propensity for unusual and abnormal sexual relations" has been approved in some states, but it has been subjected to serious criticism and its permissibility under the current Federal Rules of Evidence "is highly doubtful." MCCORMICK ON EVIDENCE, supra note 22, § 190 at 803 & n.24 (4th ed. 1992). See supra note 47.

[14] 1A WIGMORE ON EVIDENCE, § 62.2 at 1345 (Tillers rev. 1983) (emphasis added).

[15] [n.87] 137 CONG. REC. S3191-02, S3240 (Mar. 13, 1991).

One of the leading sponsors of the new rules, Senator Dole, evidently spoke for a number of Congressmen in stating that "when someone is out there committing sex crime after sex crime, committing child molestation after child molestation, it is this Senator's view that this evidence should be admitted at trial without a protracted legal battle over what is admissible or what is not."[16]

There appears to have been a widespread Congressional assumption that a special rule of evidence is justified by some unusually high rate of recidivism among sexual offenders, which would make evidence of such criminal histories of unusually great probative value. But the legislative history contains no empirical evidence to support that crucial assumption, and there is good reason to question it. Wigmore, for one, emphatically rejects that assumption.[17] Moreover, there is a substantial body of empirical research that flatly contradicts that critical assumption, and suggests that the recidivism rate for sex offenders is actually lower than for most other categories of serious crimes. For example, a recent Bureau of Justice Statistics study that followed 100,000 prisoners for three years following release found that 31.9% of released burglars were rearrested for burglary, 24.8% of drug offenders were rearrested for drug offenses, 19.6% of violent robbers were rearrested for robbery, but only 7.7% of rapists were rearrested for rape.

These statistics raise profound questions about the logical basis for allowing evidence of criminal propensity in sexual offense cases but not in other criminal cases. If there is in fact a generally lower rate of recidivism for sex offenders, as much of the available data suggests, then general propensity evidence would presumably have the least probative value in sex offense and child molestation cases, where it would also carry the greatest danger of unfair prejudice and inflaming the jury. There may be room for questioning such data, but the failure of the Congress to adduce any statistical evidence for its contrary assumption speaks volumes about the thoughtless manner in which these rules were adopted. . . .

D. The New Rules are Unnecessarily Ambiguous as to the Scope of their Reach and the Number of Current Federal Rules that they will Effectively Override

The legislative history contains numerous explicit indications that Congress saw the only effect of the new rules as creating a special exception, in sex offense cases, to the provisions of Federal Rule of Evidence 404(b). In most (if not all) other respects, the primary proponents of the new rules asserted that "the general standards of the rules of evidence will continue to apply" to propensity evidence of a defendant's prior sexual misconduct.

Despite these facile assurances, it is clear that the new rules, by their plain language, would have an impact on existing rules of evidence that is not limited to Federal Rule 404(b). For the most obvious example, although the legislative history gives no mention of such an intention, the new rules inevitably create a special

---

[16] [n.88] 140 CONG. REC. S10273-03, S10276 (Aug. 2, 1994).

[17] [n.89] "[U]nder any theory, the distinctive treatment of sexual propensity evidence is warranted only if such evidence has particularly great probative value, but it surely is true that some other types of character evidence have equally great probative value." 1A WIGMORE ON EVIDENCE, § 62.2 at 1345 (Tillers rev. 1983).

exception to the provisions of Rule 405 in sex offense cases. In its current form, Rule 405 provides that, even in those limited situations where character evidence is admissible as circumstantial proof of a party's conduct, such evidence may only be admitted in the form of reputation and opinion testimony, and may not include extrinsic evidence of specific acts. This limitation reflected a careful and deliberate legislative choice, in recognition of the fact that "evidence of specific instances of conduct . . . possesses the greatest capacity to arouse prejudice, to confuse, to surprise, and to consume time."[18] That careful policy choice has now been unceremoniously jettisoned in all sexual abuse cases, in which the new rules now explicitly authorize the admission of "evidence of the defendant's commission of another offense or offenses" of sexual assault or child molestation.

Likewise, it is equally clear that the new rules have also (albeit perhaps unwittingly) created a special exception, again limited to sexual abuse cases, to the carefully balanced provisions of Federal Rules of Evidence 608 and 609, which govern the use of prior bad acts and crimes for impeachment purposes if the defendant chooses to take the witness stand. Those two rules contain a number of thoughtfully crafted limits on the use of such evidence which seem to be in irreconcilable conflict with the provisions of the new rules for sex cases: for example, the rule precluding the use of extrinsic evidence of specific instances of misconduct that have not furnished the basis for a prior conviction, and the rule allowing such use of prior convictions only if their probative value outweighs its prejudicial effect to the accused and presumptively excluding convictions more than ten years old. All of those restrictions have evidently now been discarded if the accused is charged with sexual assault or child molestation, because evidence of specific prior acts of such misconduct — regardless of its age and whether it was the basis for a conviction — has now categorically been deemed admissible "for its bearing on any matter to which it is relevant." Given the deliberately broad definition of "relevant" evidence under the Federal Rules, of course, the conclusion is unavoidable that extrinsic evidence of specific acts of prior uncharged sexual offenses is now admissible not merely to prove the defendant's actions, but also to impeach his testimony by attacking his character for veracity, contrary to the otherwise generally applicable provisions of Rules 608 and 609.

Slightly less clear, but equally troublesome, is the fact that the new rules would apparently also entail a special exception — again, limited to sex cases — to Federal Rule 105, which authorizes a court, in its discretion, to give the jury a limiting instruction that they may consider evidence for some purposes but not for others. In language that is without parallel in the other Federal Rules of Evidence, the new rules state that evidence of prior acts of sexual misconduct "may be considered" — not merely admitted — for "its bearing on any matter to which it is relevant." By speaking in terms of how the evidence may be "considered" (which is something done by the jury), the new rules seem to create a right in favor of the jury to use the evidence as it sees fit, and a corresponding restriction of the judge's liberty to tell them otherwise. Although this reading is arguably not compelled by the language of the new rules, it draws unambiguous support from the legislative history, which recites that "there is no risk that evidence admitted under the

---

[18] [n.105] Advisory Comm. Notes to FED. R. EVID. 405.

proposed new rules will be considered for a prohibited purpose, since the rules do not limit the purposes for which such evidence may be considered."[19]

It seems clear, therefore, that the plain language of the new rules will require the implied creation of exceptions to at least five existing Federal Rules of Evidence, including some conflicts Congress evidently did not envision. But there is even room for serious doubt as to whether the new rules will entail implied exceptions to a great number of other rules as well. . . .

CONCLUSION

The new Rules 413-415 are among the very worst proposed amendments ever given serious consideration for the Rules of Evidence. They are largely unnecessary, because they are designed primarily to attain objectives that can already be accomplished as well, if not better, by current law. Even more important, the new rules carry a number of serious and potentially constitutional dangers, including a virtual certainty of increasing the risk of convicting an innocent man, despite the apparent absence of any hard evidence that even one guilty man has been set free because of the limits placed upon federal prosecutors by current Federal Rule of Evidence 404(b). Indeed, the rules rest largely upon a collection of dubious and unsupported assumptions about recidivism and other variables, most of which assumptions are called into serious question by the best available data. The adoption of the new rules while retaining the general ban on propensity evidence will also introduce an irreconcilable inconsistency into federal law, and will send out a confusing and mixed message to the States. And they will unavoidably create at least the appearance of terrible racial injustice, because their impact will be felt almost entirely by the Native Americans who now comprise the overwhelming majority of all defendants in federal sex offense prosecutions.

---

[19] [n.112] 137 CONG. REC. S3191-02, S3242 (Mar. 13, 1991) (emphasis added).

Rules 413-415 in Operation

Through Dec. 1, 2011	After Dec. 1, 2011
Rule 413. Evidence of Similar Crimes in Sexual Assault Cases	**Rule 413. Similar Crimes in Sexual-Assault Cases**
(a) In a criminal case in which the defendant is accused of an offense of sexual assault, evidence of the defendant's commission of another offense or offenses of sexual assault is admissible, and may be considered for its bearing on any matter to which it is relevant.	(a) **Permitted Uses**. In a criminal case in which a defendant is accused of a sexual assault, the court may admit evidence that the defendant committed any other sexual assault. The evidence may be considered on any matter to which it is relevant.
(b) In a case in which the Government intends to offer evidence under this rule, the attorney for the Government shall disclose the evidence to the defendant, including statements of witnesses or a summary of the substance of any testimony that is expected to be offered, at least fifteen days before the scheduled date of trial or at such later time as the court may allow for good cause.	(b) **Disclosure to the Defendant**. If the prosecutor intends to offer this evidence, the prosecutor must disclose it to the defendant, including witnesses' statements or a summary of the expected testimony. The prosecutor must do so at least 15 days before trial or at a later time that the court allows for good cause.
(c) This rule shall not be construed to limit the admission or consideration of evidence under any other rule.	(c) **Effect on Other Rules**. This rule does not limit the admission or consideration of evidence under any other rule.
(d) For purposes of this rule and Rule 415, "offense of sexual assault" means a crime under Federal law or the law of a State (as defined in section 513 of title 18, United States Code) that involved—	(d) **Definition of "Sexual Assault."** In this rule and Rule 415, "sexual assault" means a crime under federal law or under state law (as "state" is defined in 18 U.S.C. § 513) involving:
(1) any conduct proscribed by chapter 109A of title 18, United States Code;	(1) any conduct prohibited by 18 U.S.C. chapter 109A;
(2) contact, without consent, between any part of the defendant's body or an object and the genitals or anus of another person;	(2) contact, without consent, between any part of the defendant's body — or an object — and another person's genitals or anus;
(3) contact, without consent, between the genitals or anus of the defendant and any part of another person's body;	(3) contact, without consent, between the defendant's genitals or anus and any part of another person's body;
(4) deriving sexual pleasure or gratification from the infliction of death, bodily injury, or physical pain on another person; or	(4) deriving sexual pleasure or gratification from inflicting death, bodily injury, or physical pain on another person; or
(5) an attempt or conspiracy to engage in conduct described in paragraphs (1)–(4).	(5) an attempt or conspiracy to engage in conduct described in subparagraphs (1)–(4).

Through Dec. 1, 2011	After Dec. 1, 2011
Rule 414. Evidence of Similar Crimes in Child Molestation Cases	**Rule 414. Similar Crimes in Child-Molestation Cases**
(a) In a criminal case in which the defendant is accused of an offense of child molestation, evidence of the defendant's commission of another offense or offenses of child molestation is admissible, and may be considered for its bearing on any matter to which it is relevant.	**(a) Permitted Uses**. In a criminal case in which a defendant is accused of child molestation, the court may admit evidence that the defendant committed any other child molestation. The evidence may be considered on any matter to which it is relevant.
(b) In a case in which the Government intends to offer evidence under this rule, the attorney for the Government shall disclose the evidence to the defendant, including statements of witnesses or a summary of the substance of any testimony that is expected to be offered, at least fifteen days before the scheduled date of trial or at such later time as the court may allow for good cause.	**(b) Disclosure to the Defendant**. If the prosecutor intends to offer this evidence, the prosecutor must disclose it to the defendant, including witnesses' statements or a summary of the expected testimony. The prosecutor must do so at least 15 days before trial or at a later time that the court allows for good cause.
(c) This rule shall not be construed to limit the admission or consideration of evidence under any other rule.	**(c) Effect on Other Rules**. This rule does not limit the admission or consideration of evidence under any other rule.
(d) For purposes of this rule and Rule 415, ''child'' means a person below the age of fourteen, and ''offense of child molestation'' means a crime under Federal law or the law of a State (as defined in section 513 of title 18, United States Code) that involved—	**(d) Definition of "Child" and "Child Molestation."** In this rule and Rule 415:
	(1) "child" means a person below the age of 14; and
(1) any conduct proscribed by chapter 109A of title 18, United States Code, that was committed in relation to a child;	(2) "child molestation" means a crime under federal law or under state law (as "state" is defined in 18 U.S.C. § 513) involving:
(2) any conduct proscribed by chapter 110 of title 18, United States Code;	(A) any conduct prohibited by 18 U.S.C. chapter 109A and committed with a child;
(3) contact between any part of the defendant's body or an object and the genitals or anus of a child;	(B) any conduct prohibited by 18 U.S.C. chapter 110;
(4) contact between the genitals or anus of the defendant and any part of the body of a child;	(C) contact between any part of the defendant's body — or an object — and a child's genitals or anus;
(5) deriving sexual pleasure or gratification from the infliction of death, bodily injury, or physical pain on a child; or	(D) contact between the defendant's genitals or anus and any part of a child's body;
(6) an attempt or conspiracy to engage in conduct described in paragraphs (1)–(5).	(E) deriving sexual pleasure or gratification from inflicting death, bodily injury, or physical pain on a child; or
	(F) an attempt or conspiracy to engage in conduct described in subparagraphs (A)–(E).

Through Dec. 1, 2011	After Dec. 1, 2011
Rule 415. Evidence of Similar Acts in Civil Cases Concerning Sexual Assault or Child Molestation	**Rule 415. Similar Acts in Civil Cases Involving Sexual Assault or Child Molestation**
(a) In a civil case in which a claim for damages or other relief is predicated on a party's alleged commission of conduct constituting an offense of sexual assault or child molestation, evidence of that party's commission of another offense or offenses of sexual assault or child molestation is admissible and may be considered as provided in Rule 413 and Rule 414 of these rules.	**(a) Permitted Uses.** In a civil case involving a claim for relief based on a party's alleged sexual assault or child molestation, the court may admit evidence that the party committed any other sexual assault or child molestation. The evidence may be considered as provided in Rules 413 and 414.
(b) A party who intends to offer evidence under this Rule shall disclose the evidence to the party against whom it will be offered, including statements of witnesses or a summary of the substance of any testimony that is expected to be offered, at least fifteen days before the scheduled date of trial or at such later time as the court may allow for good cause.	**(b) Disclosure to the Opponent.** If a party intends to offer this evidence, the party must disclose it to the party against whom it will be offered, including witnesses' statements or a summary of the expected testimony. The party must do so at least 15 days before trial or at a later time that the court allows for good cause.
(c) This rule shall not be construed to limit the admission or consideration of evidence under any other rule.	**(c) Effect on Other Rules.** This rule does not limit the admission or consideration of evidence under any other rule.

Despite the controversy over Rules 413-415, they have been in use for over a decade now and have survived constitutional challenges in the federal courts of appeal. This subsection discusses how they are used at trial. There are several factors to consider at trial when attempting to introduce or exclude evidence under this rule.

Subject Matter of Rules

FREs 413-415 come into play only when the case at bar involves a charge of sexual assault or child molestation in criminal cases, or in a civil case, when a claim for relief is predicated on a party's alleged commission of a sexual assault or child molestation. In cases not involving sexual assault or child molestation, the defendant's past acts of sexual misconduct are not admissible under FREs 413-415, although, depending on the purpose for their admission, they may be under other rules. In their commentary on the Federal Rules, Saltzburg, Capra and Martin use the offense of kidnapping as an example of when prior sexual assaults would be inadmissible under the rules: "So for example, if the defendant is charged with kidnapping, a prior sexual assault on the victim (or on any other victim, for that matter), is not covered by this Rule. Presumably the Rule is inapplicable even if the defendant kidnapped the victim with a motive of sexual assault."[20]

No Time Limit for Prior Acts of Assault or Misconduct

Case law has made it clear that there is no presumptive time limit for prior acts of assault or misconduct. The passage of time is an issue that goes to the weight, not the admissibility, of the evidence. Evidence that might not be admissible for a non-character purpose under Rule 404(b) might nonetheless be admissible to prove character under Rules 413-415. For example, if a defendant accused of child molestation had molested a child thirty years earlier, the passage of time would make it difficult to find a non-character use for the evidence under Rule 404(b). The evidence would, however, face no such hurdles under Rule 414.

Proof Requirements

Evidence of prior sexual assaults or incidents of child molestation can be proved in a variety of ways. Past convictions, of course, are the strongest form of proof, but they are by no means the only form available. Victims of past offenses can come to the courtroom and directly testify about their experiences with the accused, regardless of whether the incidents were ever reported to officials or whether any legal action was taken against the accused. Witnesses to the past acts could also testify about them in court.

The testimony must, however, come in the form of specific acts; reputation and/or opinion testimony are impermissible forms of proof under the rules. The existence of the prior acts is a matter of conditional relevance under Rule 104(b), although some commentators have suggested that since the evidence is being used to prove propensity, the issue is one for the judge to find by a preponderance of the evidence under Rule 104(a).[21] In civil cases, Rule 415 trumps Rule 405, requiring the use of specific acts to prove the prior incidents of sexual assault or child molestation.

Procedural Requirements

Because of the dangerous nature of evidence concerning prior sexual misconduct, the procedural requirements of the rule are particularly important. The prosecution (or in a civil case, the party offering the evidence), must provide notice at least 15 days before trial or as otherwise directed by a judge. This is to permit the party against whom the evidence will be offered the opportunity to contest its validity at a Rule 104 hearing or to prepare for cross-examination and confrontation.

In constitutional challenges, federal appellate courts have consistently ruled that Rule 403 balancing tests are the one factor that preserves the constitutionality of Rules 413 and 414 in criminal cases. Appellate courts have created enhanced Rule

---

[20] Stephen A. Saltzburg, Daniel J. Capra, and Michael M. Martin, *Commentary to FRE 413.*

[21] Mueller & Kirkpatrick, § 4.35, at 283.

403 balancing tests for sexual propensity evidence offered under these rules, holding that judges should consider the following factors: (1) how clearly the prior act has been proved, (2) how probative the evidence is of the material fact it has been admitted to prove, (3) how seriously disputed the material fact is, and (4) the availability of less prejudicial evidence.[22] Evidence scholars Christopher Mueller and Laird Kirkpatrick have identified several additional factors that judges should consider in their 403 balancing tests: length of time since the prior conduct occurred; similarity of prior conduct to charged offense; number of occurrences of prior conduct; presence or absence of relevant intervening events; and the inflammatory nature of the prior conduct.[23]

As with all other applications of Rule 403, evidence that meets the criteria of Rules 413-415 is presumptively admissible. In fact, it can be argued that Rules 413-415 skew the probative value/prejudice balance even more strongly in favor of admissibility than under other rules; this is because Rules 413-415 create a strong presumption of probative value for prejudicial evidence that would otherwise have low probative value under the rules of evidence.

II.   CASES, DISCUSSION QUESTIONS AND PROBLEMS

UNITED STATES v. ROGERS
United States Court of Appeals, Seventh Circuit
587 F.3d 816 (7th Cir. 2009)

I

Rogers has an unfortunate habit of chatting with minor girls on the Internet. In 2005, he used the Internet to initiate chats with a 14-year-old girl in Wisconsin. In addition to frequently raising the topic of sex, Rogers encouraged the girl to send him pictures of herself, which she did. These pictures included a closely cropped picture of the 14-year-old's genitalia and a picture of her naked breasts. In addition, Rogers repeatedly urged the girl to meet him for a sexual encounter. As a result of this conduct, the government charged Rogers with knowingly receiving child pornography, in violation of 18 U.S.C. § 2252A(a)(2)(A), and persuading a minor to engage in sexually explicit conduct for the purpose of producing child porn, in violation of 18 U.S.C. § 2251(a).

In 2006, Rogers again used the Internet to strike up a conversation with someone whom he believed was a minor girl; this time, however, he was chatting with a police officer pretending to be a 13-year-old girl named "Emily." Over the course of two months, Rogers used email and instant messenger to persuade "Emily" to meet him for sex. Rogers arranged dates, times, and places to meet, but he never showed up at any of the arranged meetings. He continued, however, to have sexually explicit communications with "Emily." He also emailed "Emily" a cell phone picture of a hand holding an erect penis. For this conduct, the government

---

[22]   United States v. Enjady, 134 F.3d 1427, 1433 (10th Cir. 1998).

[23]   MUELLER & KIRKPATRICK, § 4.35, at 281–82.

charged Rogers with attempting to entice a minor to engage in sexual activity, 18 U.S.C. § 2442(b), and using the Internet to attempt to transfer obscene material to a minor, 18 U.S.C. § 1470.

Rogers has one prior conviction for using the Internet to persuade someone whom he believed was a minor to have sex. In 2001, Rogers initiated a chat-room conversation with "Loren," a police officer pretending to be a 15-year-old girl. Rogers arranged to meet "Loren" at her house for sex, and the police arrested Rogers as he walked toward the address supplied by the officer. Rogers pleaded guilty in state court to indecent solicitation of a child in violation of 720 ILCS 5/11-6.

In the lead-up to Rogers's trial for his 2005 and 2006 conduct, the government filed a motion to admit evidence of the 2001 conviction. During a hearing on January 31, 2008, the district court orally denied the motion. The judge found that, while the 2001 conviction falls within Rule 413, the danger of unfair prejudice to Rogers from inferences based on his propensity to commit this sort of crime substantially outweighs the minimal probative value of the 2001 conviction. The court commented that the conviction "creates exactly the kind of concern that propensity evidence is always worried about," and then ruled that it would exclude the conviction under Rule 403.

After this decision, the government filed a superseding indictment that charged the four counts discussed above. The latest indictment added the child-pornography count based on new information provided by the Wisconsin minor. In response, Rogers asked the court to bifurcate the trial: he wanted one proceeding for his interactions with the 14-year-old girl and one for his interactions with "Emily." The district court granted his request. The government then filed its second Rule 413 motion, asking the court to admit evidence of both his 2001 conviction and the 2005 conduct relating to Rogers's interactions with the 14-year-old Wisconsin girl. In that motion, it took the position that the 2005 conduct fell within the definition of an "offense of sexual assault" provided by Rule 413(d)(1) and (5), insofar as it went beyond the mere sending of pictures and included concrete attempts to meet the minor for purposes of sexual intercourse. The 2005 conduct, it argued, thus involved attempted sexual contact with a minor and qualified as "conduct proscribed by Chapter 109A of title 18, United States Code." See Doe v. Smith, 470 F.3d 331, 342 & n.20 (7th Cir. 2006). The government made a similar argument with respect to the conduct underlying the 2001 conviction.

During a hearing on February 29, 2008, the district court denied this second Rule 413 motion. This time, the district court found that the conduct failed to qualify as an "offense of sexual assault" under Rule 413 because the Wisconsin minor willingly participated in the conversations. Alternatively, the district court found that the danger from propensity inferences substantially outweighed the minimal probative value and excluded the evidence under Rule 403. Invoking this court's jurisdiction over an interlocutory appeal by the United States from a decision to exclude evidence, see 18 U.S.C. § 3731 P 2, the government appeals the exclusion of both the 2001 conviction and the 2005 conduct with the minor.

II

The government challenges the court's decisions on two grounds: first, with respect to the 2005 conduct, it argues that the district court erred by interpreting "offense of sexual assault" to exclude attempted, non-forcible sexual contact with a minor; and second, with respect to both of its proffers, it argues that the district court abused its discretion by excluding the evidence under Rule 403 because it failed to recognize that Rule 413 reversed the presumption that prior crimes pose a danger of unfair prejudice from propensity inferences. We review a district court's interpretation of the rules of evidence de novo and we review its decision to admit or exclude evidence for abuse of discretion. United States v. LeShore, 543 F.3d 935, 939, 941 (7th Cir. 2008).

[Court quotes FRE 413]

Two criteria must be satisfied for this rule to apply: first, the defendant must be accused of an offense of sexual assault, second, the prior act must be an offense of sexual assault. . . . Nobody disputes that the first criterion is met: the government charged Rogers with an attempt to entice a minor to engage in sexual activity. And nobody disputes that the second criterion is satisfied for the 2001 conviction, as Rogers pleaded guilty to knowingly soliciting a person he believed to be a minor to perform an act of sexual penetration. See 720 ILCS 5/11-6.

The first question we must address is whether the district court correctly found that the 2005 conduct does not qualify as an "offense of sexual assault" because there was no "contact, without consent." . . .

To reach this conclusion, the district court interpreted "consent" to mean literal consent rather than legal consent. Under this interpretation, an attempt to have sex with a minor could be consensual for the purpose of Rule 413 if the minor willingly participated. Looking at Rogers's conversations with the 14-year-old girl in 2005, the district court decided that they were not "without consent" and therefore did not qualify under Rule 413. We cannot agree with the district court's interpretation of the word "consent." Rule 413 uses that word without qualifying it as actual or literal, and nothing suggests that Congress meant "consent" to mean anything other than its general legal definition. Minors lack the capacity to consent, and so sexual contact with a minor is always "without consent." See Doe v. Smith, 470 F.3d at 345 (holding that a defendant attempts to assault a minor sexually when he solicits the child's acquiescence in the sex act). Attempting to have sexual contact with the 14-year-old girl therefore qualifies as an "offense of sexual assault" under Rule 413, and thus the second criterion of the rule is satisfied for the 2005 behavior as well.

But, as the district court recognized, whether Rule 413 evidence is admissible neither begins nor ends with the text of that rule. Rule 413, after all, is permissive; it allows, but does not compel, the admission of evidence falling within its sweep. Accordingly, we must also consult Rules 401, 402, and 403. Evidence is admissible only if it is relevant. FED. R. EVID. 402. In other words, the evidence must have at least some "tendency to make the existence of any fact that is of consequence to the determination of the action more probable or less probable than it would be without the evidence." FED. R. EVID. 401. Before considering whether evidence is admissible under a more specific rule, such as Rule 413, courts must consider why the evidence is relevant.

Here, we see at least three ways Rogers's prior conduct makes it more likely that Rogers, by chatting with "Emily," was attempting to entice a minor to engage in sexual activity and to send obscene material to a minor. [These are: (1) proof of intent to send an obscene picture to and persuade a minor to engage in sexual acts; (2) Proof of motive; (3) Propensity to repeat the conduct.]

Relevance, in short, is necessary, but not sufficient, for admissibility. . . . Rule 413 alters [the general character evidence] prohibition by permitting the admission of a prior offense of sexual assault "for its bearing on any matter to which it is relevant" in a criminal case where the defendant is accused of sexual assault. The rule expressly allows the government to use a defendant's prior conduct to prove the defendant's propensity to commit the types of crime described in the rule. Congress intended, in passing Rule 413, to provide an exception to Rule 404(b)'s general bar and to permit the trier of fact to draw inferences from propensity evidence.

We have explicitly said, and both parties agree, that after a Rule 413 analysis the court must next consider whether it should exclude the evidence under Rule 403. See Hawpetoss, 478 F.3d at 824. The question therefore becomes whether Rule 413's permission to use propensity evidence in sexual assault trials affects a court's Rule 403 analysis of evidence falling within that rule. Under Rule 403, a court may exclude evidence "if its probative value is substantially outweighed by the danger of unfair prejudice, confusion of the issues, or misleading the jury, or by considerations of undue delay, waste of time, or needless presentation of cumulative evidence." Evidence poses a danger of "unfair prejudice" if it has "an undue tendency to suggest decision on an improper basis, commonly, though not necessarily, an emotional one." FED. R. EVID. 403 advisory committee's note.

The government argues that Rule 413 reverses "any presumption, applicable in other cases not involving sexual offense, that evidence of other crimes poses an unfair prejudice." But this cannot be right, because it takes as a premise a presumption that does not exist. Rule 404(b) bans the use of prior bad acts to show action in conformity with the past behavior. The rule bans not the evidence, but the propensity inference. It also says that other inferences that might be drawn from prior bad acts, such as intent or motive, are permissible. Rule 404(b) neither creates any presumption nor tells a court what to do when prior-act evidence gives rise to both a propensity inference and an intent interference. The rule instead identifies which inferences are improper and which are proper. It is Rule 403 — not Rule 404 — that gives a court discretion to exclude prior-act evidence if the danger of the improper inferences substantially outweighs the probity of the proper ones. Rule 404(b) is thus nothing more than a rule that bars one particular inference from prior-act evidence; it is Rule 403 that gives a court discretion to exclude evidence that is problematic because it will be difficult to confine it to proper bounds, because of "the danger of unfair prejudice, confusion of the issues, or misleading the jury," or similar concerns.

But while we reject the government's argument, we nonetheless agree with the broader position that Rule 413 affects the Rule 403 analysis of past sexual offenses introduced in sexual assault cases. As we outlined above, the danger of unfair prejudice comes from the risk that a jury will base its decision on improper inferences. Rule 404(b) identifies the propensity inference as improper in all circumstances, and Rule 413 makes an exception to that rule when past sexual offenses are introduced in sexual assault cases. Congress has said that in a criminal trial for an offense of sexual assault, it is not improper to draw the inference that the defendant committed this sexual offense because he has a propensity to do so. Because Rule 413 identifies this propensity inference as proper, the chance that the jury will rely on that inference can no longer be labeled as "unfair" for purposes of the Rule 403 analysis. While Rule 403 remains the same, a court's Rule 403 analysis of prior conduct differs if the evidence falls under Rule 404(b) versus Rule 413; in the former analysis, the rule has decreed that the propensity inference is too dangerous, while in the latter, the propensity inference is permitted for what it is worth.

That said, evidence of prior sexual offenses may still pose significant dangers against which the district court must diligently guard. Even if the evidence does not create unfair prejudice solely because it rests on propensity, it may still risk a decision on the basis of something like passion or bias — that is, an improper basis. Even though Congress has made the propensity inference permissible, it has not said that evidence falling within Rule 413 is per se non-prejudicial. To the contrary, a jury might use such evidence, for example, to convict a defendant because it is appalled by a prior crime the defendant committed rather than persuaded that he committed the crime charged. See Old Chief, 519 U.S. at 180-81. Or a jury, uncertain of guilt, may convict a defendant because they think the defendant is a bad person generally deserving of punishment. See id. We mention these dangers only as examples; our list does not purport to be exhaustive. Rule 403 remains an important safeguard against the admission of prejudicial evidence, and courts enjoy wide discretion in applying the rule. Julian, 427 F.3d at 487. When exercising that discretion, however, courts must recognize that, for Rule 413 evidence, the propensity inference must be viewed differently.

While the danger of prejudice may well substantially outweigh the probative value of Rogers's 2001 conviction and 2005 conduct, it is unclear from the record whether the district court took the approach that we have outlined here. In excluding the 2001 conviction and the 2005 conversations, the court expressed concern that proof of past acts would improperly distract a jury's attention away from the charges at hand. The court explained that the evidence that the government had proffered "increase[s] enormously the danger that the jury might convict upon — not upon what the actual charges are here, but because this guy is a terrible guy as evidenced by this earlier occurrence." While the court properly identified an illegitimate and prejudicial form of inference, it also discussed the substantial danger posed by "propensity evidence" and stated there was the "strongest kind of prospect for a jury to be making a propensity determination." A decision to exclude evidence based on the prejudicial effect of the propensity inference would be problematic.

The court also balanced the dangers of prejudice against the probative value, which it considered minimal. The court did not however acknowledge the probative value of the propensity inference, nor did it explain what about Rogers's particular prior sexual offenses made them more prejudicial than probative. Thus, although the court worked admirably to comply with Rules 403 and 413, we are not convinced that it fully appreciated the finely tuned balancing that the Rules require.

Although, after conducting the appropriate analysis, the district court may come to the same conclusion, we conclude that we must remand this case so that it can reconsider its ruling on these two sets of prior-act evidence. If we thought that a list of "factors" would be helpful in this process, we would offer one, but, unlike our colleagues in the Ninth Circuit, we believe that lists are unhelpful in the end for this inquiry. Rule 403 balancing depends on the context and individual circumstances of each case, and we prefer not to "cabin artificially the discretion of the district courts." Hawpetoss, 478 F.3d at 825.

*   *   *

We REVERSE the exclusion of the 2001 conviction and the 2005 conduct and Remand for further proceedings consistent with this opinion.

DISCUSSION QUESTIONS

1. If the recidivism rate for sex offenses is low, what empirical justification exists for Rules 413-415?

2. Why did the 7th Circuit reverse the trial judge in *Rogers*? Knowing what you do about Rule 403 tests, judicial discretion, and the abuse of discretion standard of review, did 7th Circuit get this right?

3. What are the special considerations a judge must make when applying a Rule 403 balancing test to a Rule 413 case? Where did the judge go wrong in this case?

PROBLEMS

Problem 12-1. Carl Creeper, a 23-year-old college student at Calamity State University, is on trial for the attempted rape of a female college student. The prosecution alleges that Creeper met the woman at a bar, plied her with alcohol until she was close to passing out, then took her to his off-campus apartment, where he removed her underclothing. As he was on the verge of penetrating her, his roommate walked in the front door with a group of friends who were planning to watch a basketball game on the roommate's television. The roommate called the police, who took statements from everyone and arrested Creeper. The woman agreed to press charges against him.

Fifteen days before trial, the prosecution gives notice to the defense under Rule 413 of its intention to introduce prior acts of sexual assault and child molestation committed by Creeper. The prior acts are as follows:

1. Ten years earlier, when Creeper was 13 years old, he persuaded the six-year-old little brother of a friend to perform oral sodomy on Creeper. Creeper gave the child a pack of gum and some baseball cards to help persuade him. No charges were ever filed. The 16-year-old boy is available and willing to testify.

2. Three years earlier, Creeper was arrested for indecent exposure outside a nightclub in Calamity City. Creeper showed up for court, but neither the arresting officer nor any witnesses were present, and the charges were dropped. The arrest record is available.

3. Two years earlier, Creeper, who was severely intoxicated, met a woman on the dance floor of a local club and groped her. She called security, and Creeper was arrested and charged with misdemeanor sexual assault under the Calamity state penal code. Creeper pled no contest and received 90 days' probation as a sentence. The public record of the case is available.

4. Last year, Creeper purchased a keg of beer for a local sorority party and helped several of the coeds do keg stands with the beer. Two sorority members are available to testify that they observed him indecently fondling and touching some of their sorority sisters. Two other sorority members are available to testify that Creeper has a reputation for living up to his name.

a. What arguments should the prosecution make in support of admitting evidence these acts against Creeper under Rule 413?

b. What arguments should the defense make to exclude the evidence under Rule 413?

c. How should the judge rule?

Problem 12-2. Pete O'Phile is sixty-five years old. He has three grown children, ages 35, 37 and 40, all daughters. He and his wife, Maggie, have recently taken a foster child, Annie, into their home. Annie is eleven years old. The Calamity Department of Health and Human Services has just removed Annie from the O'Phile home after Annie complained to a school counselor that Pete had watched her bathe several times, had climbed into bed with her, and had fondled her breasts and genitals on several occasions. The Calamity State's Attorney has charged Pete with sexual assault of a minor under the Calamity Criminal Code. Before trial, the prosecutor files notice of intent under Rule 414 to call two of Pete's daughters (the 35-year-old and the 37-year-old) to testify that Pete had taken indecent liberties with them while bathing them when they were five years old and seven years old, respectively. The incidents were never reported to police, nor were they reported to Maggie. The daughters had both separately called the prosecutor's office when they read in the paper of the charges against their father to report the past offenses.

a. What arguments should the prosecution make in support of admitting evidence these acts against Pete under Rule 414?

b. What arguments should the defense make to exclude the evidence under Rule 414?

c. How should the judge rule?

Rules 413-415: Quick Hits

- Rules 413-415 were created to make prosecuting sexual assault and/or child molestation cases easier

- The rules permit the prosecutor or plaintiff to use sexual propensity evidence for any purpose at trial, without having to wait for the defendant to open the door to the use of such evidence

- The broad consensus of commentators and practitioners is that the justification for the rules is deeply flawed and contrary to available social science and empirical data

- The rules do not recognize a time limit for prior acts of sexual assault or child molestation

- Procedural notice requirements prevent trial by ambush with evidence covered by the rule

- Many jurisdictions require enhanced Rule 403 balancing tests in order to preserve the constitutionality of these rules.

Chapter References

CHRISTOPHER B. MUELLER & LAIRD C. KIRKPATRICK, EVIDENCE §§ 4.35–4.36 (4th ed. 2009).

GLEN WEISSENBERGER & JAMES J. DUANE, FEDERAL RULES OF EVIDENCE: RULES, LEGISLATIVE HISTORY, COMMENTARY AND AUTHORITY §§ 413–15 (6th ed. 2009).

JACK B. WEINSTEIN & MARGARET A. BERGER, WEINSTEIN'S FEDERAL EVIDENCE §§ 413–15 (Joseph M. McLaughlin ed., Matthew Bender 2d ed. 1997).

KENNETH S. BROUN, MCCORMICK ON EVIDENCE §§ 192–93 (6th ed. 2006).

STEVEN GOODE & OLIN GUY WELLBORN III, COURTROOM HANDBOOK ON FEDERAL EVIDENCE Ch. 5 (West 2010).

III. APPLICATION EXERCISE

Objective: To demonstrate the use of sexual propensity evidence admitted under Rules 413-415 in a closing argument at trial.

Factual Scenario: We will use the facts in problem 12-1, above.

Advance Preparation: Analyze problem 12-1 and anticipate how a judge might rule on these issues. Prepare a prosecution closing argument that integrates the admissible facts in problem 12-1 and uses them to help persuade a jury of Creeper's guilt. Also prepare a defense argument to counter the prosecution argument.

In-Class Exercise. We will discuss this problem in class. As a class, we will decide on an appropriate ruling on the defense's motion in limine in the problem. To begin the application exercise, students will be divided into small groups to finalize closing arguments based on the ruling in the case. After a few minutes of finalization and preparation, the instructor will designate some students to give prosecution closing arguments to the class and others to give defense closing arguments.

PART FOUR

THE LAW OF WITNESSES AND IMPEACHMENT

Chapter 13

WITNESS COMPETENCY

Chapter Objectives:

- Introduce and explain Rules 602-603, 605-606 and the concepts of witness qualification and testimonial competency
- Analyze and discuss issues pertaining to Rules 602-603, 605-606
- Apply the concepts from this chapter in a courtroom application exercise

I. BACKGROUND AND EXPLANATORY MATERIAL

Introduction

The law of witnesses under Article VI of the Federal Rules of Evidence controls who is allowed to testify in the courtroom, the general subject matter of their testimony, and the conditions under which they are permitted to testify. These rules are rooted in the purposes of the adversarial trial: the search for truth and the desire for fair verdicts. No one can simply walk into a courtroom, sit down on the witness stand, and tell the court his or her story. The law requires that a witness satisfy certain fundamental requirements before taking the stand.

In order to testify, a witness must have personal knowledge of an issue in the case, be competent to testify, and be willing to take an oath or make an affirmation. These are merely the threshold requirements to testify; the witness's testimony must also be relevant and otherwise admissible under the Rules. As discussed in Chapter One, witness testimony must be presented in the framework of direct or cross examination.

This section begins with an explanation of competency, its historical antecedents and modern application in Rule 601. The section then discusses Rule 602 and the requirement that witnesses must have personal knowledge in order to testify. Next, the section examines the role of an oath or affirmation under Rule 603. Finally, the section discusses the categorical disqualification of judges and jurors as witnesses under Rules 605 and 606.

Competency

In normal usage, the term "competency" suggests a certain level of proficiency or expertise. When we say someone is competent, we mean that she is fully capable of facing a challenge or performing a task. As used at trial, the term "competency" has a similar, but subtly different, connotation. A competent witness is not one who has achieved a certain level of proficiency as a witness, but rather one who is able to appreciate the duty to testify truthfully and has at least some capacity to observe, recall and communicate events.

Under the common law, witnesses were considered incompetent for a wide variety of reasons, including age, religion, conviction of a crime, personal interest, and mental capacity, as explained in the following passage:

> In addition to barring certain mentally disordered persons from testifying, the common law rendered certain categories of persons per se incompetent as witnesses: interested persons, persons who had previously suffered specified felony convictions, and persons with aberrant religious beliefs. The common law did so on the theory that the integrity of these persons was questionable. Bentham put the matter bluntly when he wrote that the early common law altogether prevented these persons from testifying because it presumed that persons in the prohibited categories were "liars."[1]

Although the common law incompetency rules were simple to understand and easy to apply, they deprived the fact-finder of valuable evidence. As the roles of the judge and jury developed over time, so did the concept of competency. The focus began to shift from witness competency to witness credibility.[2]

In federal courts, Rule 601 controls the issue of witness competency:

Through Dec. 1, 2011	After Dec. 1, 2011
Rule 601. General Rule of Competency	**Rule 601. Competency to Testify in General**
Every person is competent to be a witness except as otherwise provided in these rules. However, in civil actions and proceedings, with respect to an element of a claim or defense as to which State law supplies the rule of decision, the competency of a witness shall be determined in accordance with State law.	Every person is competent to be a witness unless these rules provide otherwise. But in a civil case, state law governs the witness's competency regarding a claim or defense for which state law supplies the rule of decision.

Rule 601's default position is that witnesses are presumed competent to testify. In other words, Rule 601 does away with the common law's categorical disqualification of certain categories of witnesses. Under Rule 601, cross-examination and impeachment take the place of disqualification on grounds of incompetence. Defects

---

[1] Edward J. Imwinkelried, *The Worst Evidence Principle: The Best Hypothesis as to The Logical Structure of Evidence Law*, 46 U. MIAMI L. REV. 1069 (1992).

[2] *See* GLEN WEISSENBERGER & JAMES J. DUANE, FEDERAL RULES OF EVIDENCE: RULES, LEGISLATIVE HISTORY, COMMENTARY AND AUTHORITY §§ 601.3–601.5 (2009).

or shortcomings related to any of the traditional competency disqualifiers such as bias or interest may be pointed out on cross-examination, and the finder of fact can consider their effect in weighing the testimony of the witness.

As with almost every evidentiary rule, there are exceptions to the general rule of competency. First, in civil cases under the *Erie* doctrine, where the law of a state supplies the rule of decision, Federal courts must use state rules related to competency. Some states still retain vestiges of the common law competency disqualifiers, such as Dead Man's Acts. A Dead Man's Act prohibits claimants to the estate of a deceased from testifying about their conversations with the deceased relating to the claim.

Second, even in Federal court, a party can move to have a witness declared incompetent. This typically happens in cases involving intoxication, insanity, or young children who are witnesses to or victims of a crime.

C. The Requirement of Personal Knowledge

Broadly speaking, witnesses can be divided into two categories: percipient (or fact) witnesses and opinion witnesses. A percipient witness is one who has seen, heard, touched, felt, otherwise perceived with her senses, or has personal experience with, a factual matter relevant to the case. This type of testimony runs the gamut from eyewitness testimony to hearsay testimony.

Rule 602 controls the testimony of percipient witnesses at trial.

Through Dec. 1, 2011	After Dec. 1, 2011
Rule 602. Lack of Personal Knowledge	**Rule 602. Need for Personal Knowledge**
A witness may not testify to a matter unless evidence is introduced sufficient to support a finding that the witness has personal knowledge of the matter. Evidence to prove personal knowledge may, but need not, consist of the witness' own testimony. This rule is subject to the provisions of rule 703, relating to opinion testimony by expert witnesses.	A witness may testify to a matter only if evidence is introduced sufficient to support a finding that the witness has personal knowledge of the matter. Evidence to prove personal knowledge may consist of the witness's own testimony. This rule does not apply to a witness's expert testimony under Rule 703.

For the vast majority of witnesses at trial, personal knowledge is a threshold requirement to testify; a witness without personal knowledge has nothing relevant to offer to the jury. The requirement of personal knowledge is an issue of conditional relevancy under Rule 104. The judge does not find that the witness has personal knowledge, but rather that a reasonable juror could find that the witness has personal knowledge. The foundational requirement is generally satisfied when an advocate asks brief foundational questions of the witness, such as, "Did you see a car accident on July fifth of last year?" A judge can order a more searching inquiry if she deems it necessary.

The second main category is opinion witnesses. An opinion witness, as the label suggests, is one who shares his or her opinion about an issue in the case with a jury. Opinion witnesses are further divided into two categories: lay opinion witnesses and expert witnesses. Under Rule 701, the testimony of lay opinion witnesses must be based on their own personal observations and experience. Rules 702 and 703 permit qualified expert witnesses to testify based on hearsay and other materials that are generally relied on by experts in their field. The opinion testimony rules will be covered in greater detail in a subsequent chapter.

Witnesses with personal knowledge are only permitted to testify to the reasonable limits of their perceptive ability; they cannot, in other words, speculate or offer improper opinion testimony. Questions that ask a witness about the motives of other witnesses, what someone else was thinking, or the like, violate the personal knowledge rule and may be objected to on grounds that the questions call for speculation.

The Oath

The final condition a witness must satisfy before being permitted to testify is the oath or affirmation. This requirement is contained in Rule 603.

Through Dec. 1, 2011	After Dec. 1, 2011
Rule 603. Oath or Affirmation Before testifying, every witness shall be required to declare that the witness will testify truthfully, by oath or affirmation administered in a form calculated to awaken the witness' conscience and impress the witness' mind with the duty to do so.	**Rule 603. Oath or Affirmation to Testify Truthfully** Before testifying, a witness must give an oath or affirmation to testify truthfully. It must be in a form designed to impress that duty on the witness's conscience.

The witness oath is a solemn promise, formally administered by a person with legal authority, to tell the truth. The person taking the oath raises his right arm and faces the administrator, whose hand is also raised in similar fashion. A typical witness oath contains language such as the following: "Do you solemnly swear (or affirm) that the testimony you shall give in the case now in hearing shall be the truth, the whole truth, and nothing but the truth, so help you God?" The language of the oath is designed to prick the witness's conscience and impress upon him not only the importance of telling the truth, but the existence of penalties, whether earthly or divine, for failing to do so.

When courts first began requiring witnesses to take oaths, society was much different than it is today. Religious belief and practice were closely intertwined with everyday life and constantly emphasized by frequent attendance at worship services, the liturgical calendar, and the mixed religious and secular authority of the clergy. Most people believed in divine judgment and punishment. The formal oath impressed upon them the likelihood of divine retribution for telling a lie and violating their oath; in many cases, the witness had to place one hand on the Bible and raise the other to the square while facing the administrator, thus acknowledging both earthly and divine authority. The common law showed flexibility towards those who did not recognize the Bible as authoritative, permitting individuals to use other sacred books (such as the Quran) or to engage in ritualistic behavior (such as the Chinese practice of breaking a plate) to show their acknowledgement of a higher authority.

Although society has changed, the basic elements of the oath remain the same. In practice, however, courts have permitted modifications of the oath in order to accommodate individuals who do not recognize divine authority or have religious beliefs that prevent them from taking either an oath or an affirmation. The most important function of an oath is for the witness to make a serious public commitment to testify truthfully or to acknowledge the penalty of perjury for false testimony.

E. Presumed Incompetency of Judges and Jurors

Although Rule 601 states that witnesses are generally competent to testify, Rules 605 and 606 provide two important exceptions to this rule for judges and jurors.

Judges

Through Dec. 1, 2011	After Dec. 1, 2011
Rule 605. Competency of Judge as Witness	**Rule 605. Judge's Competency as a Witness**
The judge presiding at the trial may not testify in that trial as a witness. No objection need be made in order to preserve the point.	The presiding judge may not testify as a witness at the trial. A party need not object to preserve the issue.

Rule 605 is a short, common-sense rule that is premised on maintaining the appropriate role of the judge in an adversarial trial system. The judge in an adversarial trial is the lawgiver and a neutral arbiter who is not permitted to show favoritism or partiality to either side. If a judge were to testify in a trial over which she presided, serious questions would arise concerning the judge's ability to maintain fairness to both sides, control of the courtroom, and appropriate decorum. For example, if one of the parties found the judge's testimony objectionable, the party would be faced with the Hobson's choice of objecting and enraging the judge, or remaining silent and forfeiting the issue.

In order to avoid putting counsel and judges in this situation, the prohibition against judicial testimony cannot be waived or forfeited. If a judge does choose to testify, no objection is necessary to preserve the issue.

Jurors

Through Dec. 1, 2011	After Dec. 1, 2011
Rule 606. Competency of Juror as Witness	**Rule 606. Juror's Competency as a Witness**
(a) At the trial. A member of the jury may not testify as a witness before that jury in the trial of the case in which the juror is sitting. If the juror is called so to testify, the opposing party shall be afforded an opportunity to object out of the presence of the jury.	**(a) At the Trial**. A juror may not testify as a witness before the other jurors at the trial. If a juror is called to testify, the court must give a party an opportunity to object outside the jury's presence.
(b) Inquiry into validity of verdict or indictment. Upon an inquiry into the validity of a verdict or indictment, a juror may not testify as to any matter or statement occurring during the course of the jury's deliberations or to the effect of anything upon that or any other juror's mind or emotions as influencing the juror to assent to or dissent from the verdict or indictment or concerning the juror's mental processes in connection therewith. But a juror may testify about (1) whether extraneous prejudicial information was improperly brought to the jury's attention, (2) whether any outside influence was improperly brought to bear upon any juror, or (3) whether there was a mistake in entering the verdict onto the verdict form. A juror's affidavit or evidence of any statement by the juror may not be received on a matter about which the juror would be precluded from testifying.	**(b) During an Inquiry into the Validity of a Verdict or Indictment**. *(1) Prohibited Testimony or Other Evidence*. During an inquiry into the validity of a verdict or indictment, a juror may not testify about any statement made or incident that occurred during the jury's deliberations; the effect of anything on that juror's or another juror's vote; or any juror's mental processes concerning the verdict or indictment. The court may not receive a juror's affidavit or evidence of a juror's statement on these matters. *(2) Exceptions*. A juror may testify about whether: (A) extraneous prejudicial information was improperly brought to the jury's attention; (B) an outside influence was improperly brought to bear on any juror; or (C) a mistake was made in entering the verdict on the verdict form.

There are two aspects of juror testimony encompassed in Rule 606. The first, similar in basis and reasoning to Rule 605, is a prohibition against serving as a juror and testifying in the same trial. Unlike the testimony of a judge, however, the issue of a juror in a trial being called as a witness can be forfeited or waived by the parties.

The second aspect of juror testimony in the rule is a prohibition against improperly impeaching the jury's verdict. The common law holds a jury's verdict to be sacrosanct, free from outside inquiry or impeachment. Juries have the power to render verdicts that are contrary to the law and the evidence, a concept called jury nullification, and to do so without fear of retribution or second-guessing. Members of the jury are free to cast their vote for any reason. A juror who has been outvoted or who later questions or regrets his vote, his reasons for voting, or the factors considered by his fellow jurors, should not have the power to derail justice by an *ex post facto* impeachment of the deliberations.

Rule 606 does permit testimony about certain types of juror misconduct. Jurors are not allowed to independently investigate the case, find their own evidence, conduct legal research, or use evidence that has been excluded from trial. In the adversarial system, a jury renders its decision by bringing its collective experience, common sense and wisdom to analyze evidence presented by the advocates in the light of legal instructions provided by the judge. Unlike the earliest juries, which required personal knowledge of an event as a prerequisite for jury service and welcomed extraneous juror fact-finding, modern jury law draws a strict line of demarcation between the proper roles of counsel and the jurors. If a jury has considered extraneous information, jurors may testify about the fact that they did so. They may not, however, testify about how the extraneous information impacted the jury's deliberative process.

II. CASES, DISCUSSION QUESTIONS AND PROBLEMS

PEOPLE v. WILLIAMS
Supreme Court of Illinois
147 Ill. 2d 173, 588 N.E.2d 983 (1991)

[Defendant was convicted of murder, aggravated kidnapping, and rape and sentenced to death. One of the primary government witnesses was a woman named Gray, who helped the police with the investigation and testified at a grand jury hearing that she had been present when one of the victims was raped and when another one was shot in the head by the defendant and others. Along with her family, Gray later went to live with the defendant's mother. She exhibited bizarre behavior and was examined by a physician for mental problems and hospitalized from May 22-24, 1978. She recanted her grand jury testimony against the defendant at a preliminary hearing.]

[When recanting her testimony] She either failed to respond to questioning or simply repeated, when referred by defense counsel to each of her previous statements before the grand jury, "[T]hat is a lie," "[I] don't know nothing," or "[I] didn't see nothing." Defendant [and others] were subsequently charged by information with murder, rape, and aggravated kidnapping.

Shortly thereafter, Gray was indicted for her participation in the crimes, and for perjury. She was subsequently arrested and taken into custody. At a suppression hearing in her own case in October 1978, Gray repeated her recantation. Gray was tried simultaneously with defendant [and others] although a separate jury was empaneled to hear Gray's case. [Defendant's attorney] represented Gray, following her indictment, at every hearing wherein she recanted her grand jury testimony (her suppression hearing and trial, defendant's first trial and sentencing hearing), although neither Gray nor her family hired him.

At her trial, Gray claimed that the authorities had forced her to lie before the grand jury and continued to flatly deny that defendant [and others] raped Schmal. Defendant [and others] were subsequently convicted of murder, rape and aggravated kidnapping. Gray was also convicted of perjury.

[Defendant successfully appealed and was granted a new trial. Gray also appealed and was granted a new trial. She testified at defendant's trial while her second trial remained pending.]

Defendant contends that the trial court improperly refused to allow Gray to testify at a pretrial competency hearing, despite the existence of medical testimony that Gray had been diagnosed and hospitalized with an "acute schizophrenic reaction" immediately after the killings.

Defendant filed a pretrial motion styled "Motion in Limine to Bar the Testimony of Paula Gray," on the basis of her alleged incompetency. Attached to the motion were copies of Gray's hospital records for May 22-24, 1978, written and signed by Dr. Watkins.

Prior to hearing on the motion, the trial court ruled that Gray would not testify [at the hearing] because the mere fact of defendant's challenge to her competency did not, by itself, justify a competency hearing. The trial court determined, however, that if defendant made a sufficient showing which would call Gray's competency into question, the court would then conduct a hearing as to competency and her testimony would be allowed. Defendant failed to make such a showing, however, and no competency hearing was held.

Factors warranting a decision to conduct a preliminary inquiry as to competency must necessarily call into question the witness' ability to observe, recollect, and communicate. Even where a competency determination is to be made, due process does not require an examination of the witness by the challenging party.

In the present case, medical records produced by the defense in support of its motion and the testimony of Dr. Watkins failed to establish a connection between Gray's past mental problem and her ability to give competent testimony. Hospitalization itself does not reflect on Gray's competence to testify at trial; at most it established that she had once been treated for an acute schizophrenic reaction, albeit shortly after the killings, a fact the State conceded. In addition, there was no showing that Gray continued to suffer from such disability, or that she was thus disabled at the time of the killings. Consequently, we find that the trial court's denial of defendant's request to examine Gray was in the exercise of sound discretion.

Defendant maintains, however, as a related matter, that the subsequent admission of Gray's testimony at trial was plain error because she was incompetent. A witness is competent to testify if he has the capacity to observe, recollect, and communicate, and his mental deficiency is considered only insofar as it affects credibility. Thus, sanity is not the test of competency. Likewise, an individual suffering from mental retardation is legally competent to testify so long as he possesses the requisite capacities, and the burden to show otherwise is upon the party questioning competency. The determination of whether a witness is competent to testify is within the sound discretion of the trial court and may be arrived at either through preliminary inquiry or by observing the witness' demeanor and ability to testify during trial.

Our review reveals that the trial court's subsequent admission of Gray's testimony at trial was proper. Gray's testimony in toto indicates that Gray was a competent witness. Any inconsistency regarding whether Gray had previously lied under "oath" obviously concerned her inability to understand the meaning of the term "oath," rather than a failure to understand any moral duty to tell the truth. It is true that Gray displayed a marked tendency to remember events under direct examination, and to forget matters unrelated to the crime itself during cross-examination. Yet, this tendency appears somewhat justified given the fact that much of that cross-examination concerned whether she remembered making certain specific statements during any of several, previous separate hearings. In total, we believe that Gray's memory lapses, however, reflect more upon her credibility than her capacities. She even admitted that her memory improved "a little bit" upon redirect examination.

In the final analysis, the trial court is in the best position to ascertain a witness' competence based upon her appearance and conduct at trial and we will not disturb that finding absent an abuse of discretion. We find none here.

TANNER v. UNITED STATES
Supreme Court of the United States
483 U.S. 107 (1987)

JUSTICE O'CONNOR delivered the opinion of the Court. [Defendants were convicted of conspiring to defraud the United States and mail fraud in connection with the construction of a coal-fired power plant. After defendants were convicted, one of their attorneys received an unsolicited telephone call from a juror alleging that several of the jurors were intoxicated during trial and consequently slept their way through important parts of the trial. The judge refused to call any jurors as witnesses, but instead invited testimony of anyone who might have independently observed such behavior by the jurors. In support of a subsequent motion for a new trial based on jury misconduct, attorneys included additional information regarding juror misconduct, including extensive alcohol use, marijuana and cocaine use, and jurors selling drugs to each other. The trial court denied the motion for a new trial, the 11th Circuit affirmed, and the Supreme Court granted certiorari to consider whether the trial court was required to hold an evidentiary hearing about the juror misconduct.]

Petitioners argue that the District Court erred in not ordering an additional evidentiary hearing at which jurors would testify concerning drug and alcohol use during the trial. Petitioners assert that, contrary to the holdings of the District Court and the Court of Appeals, juror testimony on ingestion of drugs or alcohol during the trial is not barred by Federal Rule of Evidence 606(b). Moreover, petitioners argue that whether or not authorized by Rule 606(b), an evidentiary hearing including juror testimony on drug and alcohol use is compelled by their

Sixth Amendment right to trial by a competent jury.

By the beginning of this century, if not earlier, the near-universal and firmly established common-law rule in the United States flatly prohibited the admission of juror testimony to impeach a jury verdict. See 8 J. Wigmore, Evidence § 2352, pp. 696-697 (J. McNaughton rev. ed. 1961) (common-law rule, originating from 1785 opinion of Lord Mansfield, "came to receive in the United States an adherence almost unquestioned").

Exceptions to the common-law rule were recognized only in situations in which an "extraneous influence," Mattox v. United States, 146 U.S. 140, 149, 13 S.Ct. 50, 53, 36 L.Ed. 917 (1892), was alleged to have affected the jury. In Mattox, this Court held admissible the testimony of jurors describing how they heard and read prejudicial information not admitted into evidence. The Court allowed juror testimony on influence by outsiders in [several cases]. . . . In situations that did not fall into this exception for external influence, however, the Court adhered to the common-law rule against admitting juror testimony to impeach a verdict.

Lower courts used this external/internal distinction to identify those instances in which juror testimony impeaching a verdict would be admissible. The distinction was not based on whether the juror was literally inside or outside the jury room when the alleged irregularity took place; rather, the distinction was based on the nature of the allegation. Clearly a rigid distinction based only on whether the event took place inside or outside the jury room would have been quite unhelpful. For example, under a distinction based on location a juror could not testify concerning a newspaper read inside the jury room. Instead, of course, this has been considered an external influence about which juror testimony is admissible. Similarly, under a rigid locational distinction jurors could be regularly required to testify after the verdict as to whether they heard and comprehended the judge's instructions, since the charge to the jury takes place outside the jury room. Courts wisely have treated allegations of a juror's inability to hear or comprehend at trial as an internal matter.

Most significant for the present case, however, is the fact that lower federal courts treated allegations of the physical or mental incompetence of a juror as "internal" rather than "external" matters. In United States v. Dioguardi . . . the Court of Appeals noted "[t]he strong policy against any post-verdict inquiry into a juror's state of mind," and observed:

"The quickness with which jury findings will be set aside when there is proof of tampering or external influence, . . . parallel the reluctance of courts to inquire into jury deliberations when a verdict is valid on its face. . . . Such exceptions support rather than undermine the rationale of the rule that possible internal abnormalities in a jury will not be inquired into except 'in the gravest and most important cases.' "

*   *   *

Substantial policy considerations support the common-law rule against the admission of jury testimony to impeach a verdict. As early as 1915 this Court explained the necessity of shielding jury deliberations from public scrutiny:

"[L]et it once be established that verdicts solemnly made and publicly returned into court can be attacked and set aside on the testimony of those who took part in their publication and all verdicts could be, and many would be, followed by an inquiry in the hope of discovering something which might invalidate the finding. Jurors would be harassed and beset by the defeated party in an effort to secure from them evidence of facts which might establish misconduct sufficient to set aside a verdict. If evidence thus secured could be thus used, the result would be to make what was intended to be a private deliberation, the constant subject of public investigation-to the destruction of all frankness and freedom of discussion and conference." McDonald v. Pless, 238 U.S., at 267-268, 35 S.Ct., at 784.

The Court's holdings requiring an evidentiary hearing where extrinsic influence or relationships have tainted the deliberations do not detract from, but rather harmonize with, the weighty government interest in insulating the jury's deliberative process. The Court's statement in Remmer that "[t]he integrity of jury proceedings must not be jeopardized by unauthorized invasions," could also be applied to the inquiry petitioners seek to make into the internal processes of the jury.

There is little doubt that postverdict investigation into juror misconduct would in some instances lead to the invalidation of verdicts reached after irresponsible or improper juror behavior. It is not at all clear, however, that the jury system could survive such efforts to perfect it. Allegations of juror misconduct, incompetency, or inattentiveness, raised for the first time days, weeks, or months after the verdict, seriously disrupt the finality of the process. Moreover, full and frank discussion in the jury room, jurors' willingness to return an unpopular verdict, and the community's trust in a system that relies on the decisions of laypeople would all be undermined by a barrage of postverdict scrutiny of juror conduct.

Federal Rule of Evidence 606(b) is grounded in the common-law rule against admission of jury testimony to impeach a verdict and the exception for juror testimony relating to extraneous influences.

Petitioners have presented no argument that Rule 606(b) is inapplicable to the juror affidavits and the further inquiry they sought in this case, and, in fact, there appears to be virtually no support for such a proposition. . . . Rather, petitioners argue that substance abuse constitutes an improper "outside influence" about which jurors may testify under Rule 606(b). In our view the language of the Rule cannot easily be stretched to cover this circumstance. However severe their effect and improper their use, drugs or alcohol voluntarily ingested by a juror seems no more an "outside influence" than a virus, poorly prepared food, or a lack of sleep.

[The Court extensively reviewed the legislative history of rule 606(b)]. Thus, the legislative history demonstrates with uncommon clarity that Congress specifically understood, considered, and rejected a version of Rule 606(b) that would have allowed jurors to testify on juror conduct during deliberations, including juror intoxication. This legislative history provides strong support for the most reasonable reading of the language of Rule 606(b)-that juror intoxication is not an outside influence" about which jurors may testify to impeach their verdict.

Finally, even if Rule 606(b) is interpreted to retain the common-law exception allowing post-verdict inquiry of juror incompetence in cases of "substantial if not wholly conclusive evidence of incompetency," Dioguardi, 492 F.2d, at 80, the showing made by petitioners falls far short of this standard. The affidavits and testimony presented in support of the first new trial motion suggested, at worst, that several of the jurors fell asleep at times during the afternoons. The District Court Judge appropriately considered the fact that he had "an unobstructed view" of the jury, and did not see any juror sleeping. The juror affidavit submitted in support of the second new trial motion was obtained in clear violation of the District Court's order and the court's local rule against juror interviews; on this basis alone the District Court would have been acting within its discretion in disregarding the affidavit. In any case, although the affidavit of juror Hardy describes more dramatic instances of misconduct, Hardy's allegations of incompetence are meager. Hardy stated that the alcohol consumption he engaged in with three other jurors did not leave any of them intoxicated. App. to Pet. for Cert. 47 ("I told [the prosecutor] that we would just go out and get us a pitcher of beer and drink it, but as far as us being drunk, no we wasn't"). The only allegations concerning the jurors' ability to properly consider the evidence were Hardy's observations that some jurors were "falling asleep all the time during the trial," and that his own reasoning ability was affected on one day of the trial. App. to Pet. for Cert. 46, 55. These allegations would not suffice to bring this case under the common-law exception allowing post-verdict inquiry when an extremely strong showing of incompetency has been made.

* * *

As described above, long-recognized and very substantial concerns support the protection of jury deliberations from intrusive inquiry. . . . Indeed, in this case the District Court held an evidentiary hearing giving petitioners ample opportunity to produce nonjuror evidence supporting their allegations.

In light of these other sources of protection of petitioners' right to a competent jury, we conclude that the District Court did not err in deciding, based on the inadmissibility of juror testimony and the clear insufficiency of the nonjuror evidence offered by petitioners, that an additional post-verdict evidentiary hearing was unnecessary.

DISCUSSION QUESTIONS

1. What are the key factors in witness competence?

2. If the judge had granted the motion in *Williams* and held the hearing, do you think the Illinois Supreme Court would have found this action within the judge's discretion? Why or why not?

1. Identify the interests at stake in a juror misconduct allegation. Should the finality of verdicts trump the other interests at trial? Why or why not?

2. Suppose the district judge had granted the hearing in *Turner* and called jurors to testify about the alcohol and drug use during deliberations. Would such a hearing have been within the district court's discretion under Rule 606(b)?

PROBLEMS

Problem 13-1. Defendant is on trial for molesting his seven-year-old stepdaughter, Annie, who suffers from mild mental retardation. The alleged incident occurred one evening while Annie's mother was out shopping. When the mother returned, the child reported that she and Defendant played a game and Defendant touched her "pee-pee." The mother immediately reported the incident to the police. A day later, Annie told the same story to a criminal investigator and demonstrated what the defendant had done to her using anatomically correct dolls. At trial, on motion of the defense, the judge holds a competency hearing, which reveals the following facts: (1) Annie was of below-average intelligence; (2) Annie understood that it was "bad to lie"; (3) Annie was not sure what her address was; (4) Annie knew she went to school but did not remember what grade she was in; (5) Annie knew the names of several of her friends at school; (6) Annie did not know the year, month, date or time of the incident; (7) Annie was able to understand questions and reply to them.

How should the judge rule on the motion to declare the victim incompetent? Why? What factors would change your decision?

Problem 13-2. Pat sues Donald for rear-ending her car at a busy intersection in the city. Pat alleges that Donald was using his cell phone at the time of the accident and was not paying attention to traffic conditions. At trial, Donald calls his best friend Wayne, who was a passenger in the car, to testify that Donald was not using a cell phone and that Pat suddenly slammed on her brakes, making the accident unavoidable. In discovery, Pat's attorney learned the following: (1) Wayne is a felon and Donald's best friend from their time together in prison for drug trafficking; (2) Wayne is also a chronic alcoholic and a drug addict and had been drinking the day of the accident; (3) Wayne and Donald are both members of a prison gang whose members have taken an oath to defend each other at all costs, including perjury; (4) Wayne has been diagnosed as a paranoid schizophrenic, is under the care of a psychiatrist, and has been prescribed medication for his condition. At trial, Pat's attorney moves to disqualify Wayne as incompetent.

Should the judge grant the motion? Why or why not?

Problem 13-3. Same facts as Problem 13-2. Assume that the judge agrees to conduct a competency hearing and attempts to place Wayne under oath. Wayne refuses to raise his right hand, swear, or affirm. Instead, Wayne offers to take this oath: "Although I recognize the authority of neither God or man, I am guided by a strong internal compass and will remain true to my convictions through my words." Pat's attorney objects that the oath is insufficient and that Wayne should be disqualified as a witness.

Is this oath sufficient to satisfy the requirements of Rule 603? Why or why not?

Problem 13-4. The case of *Smith v. Ferocious Firearms, Inc.*, is one of the biggest cases in recent memory. The plaintiff in the case is the grieving mother of a five-year-old child who was playing basketball in the family's driveway, when the loaded shotgun that his father kept in the back window of his locked pickup truck spontaneously discharged, killing the child. Both sides have called metallurgists and engineers as expert witnesses to testify about whether there were design defects that would cause a weapon to spontaneously discharge, or whether the discharge was due to improper maintenance of the firearm. Because of the emotions involved in the case, the jurors have been sequestered for several weeks.

After 10 days of deliberations, the jury renders a verdict for the plaintiffs and awards substantial damages. A day or so later, Juror 2 executes the following affidavit.

I, Juror 2, am concerned about the way this jury reached its verdict. Four of us — *myself, Juror 5, Juror 6, and Juror 9, thought the plaintiffs were lying about the* *gun, but we couldn't prove it to anyone. I think the truck wasn't locked and one of* *the other kids touched the gun. Juror 12 ridiculed us throughout the deliberations,* *calling us "stupid morons" and threatening to tell reporters how stupid we were* *after the trial. Also, some of the jurors didn't seem to care about the trial very* *much and were more concerned with getting home to their families. Juror 3 said* *during the deliberations that she didn't care what happened because her daughter* *was sick and could we please just get things over with. Jurors 7 and 8 were having* *an affair with each other, and it was disgusting. Once, they even made out while* *everyone else was arguing during deliberations.*

The thing that bothers me the most, is that everyone ignored the judge's *instructions about liability. The jury foreman said, "I'm in charge here; who cares* *what the judge said. We'll do the right thing. That's a family that lost a kid, and* *someone has to pay." Also, Juror 11 kept looking stuff up on his smartphone.* *Everyone hated him because of his body odor and the way he picked his nose* *during breaks, so we didn't really pay much attention to him, at least I didn't, but* *he did seem to know a lot more about guns and metal than anyone else. He was* *always telling us how the experts on both sides had got it wrong and explaining* *the whole thing about metal, engineering, and that coefficient of expansion thing* *everyone was arguing about at trial.*

The day we reached our verdict, about half of the jurors were drinking. The jury *foreman had brought in some alcohol in his briefcase. It was a bottle of Jack* *Daniel's. I'm embarrassed to say that I took a drink, but I don't think it affected* *my vote. I do think it affected some people's votes, though. Some people were* *looking pretty tanked and they were doing whatever the jury foreman told them to* *do. I think he got it from the plaintiff's attorneys. I didn't trust them, and I'm* *pretty sure they would cheat to win. The only reason I voted for the plaintiff's was* *that a bunch of the jurors ganged up on me and started screaming at me because* *there were only two of us left that were voting for the defense. They called me some* *really foul names and said I was just trying to be difficult and ignoring all the* *evidence because I'm a racist. Which I'm not. Some of my best friends are the* *same race as the plaintiffs. That sounds like juror intimidation to me.*

Identify the issues raised in this hypothetical problem. If you were the judge, what would you do with this affidavit? Should you trust this verdict?

Witness Competency: Quick Hits

- All witnesses are presumed competent to testify at trial.

- The traditional competency disqualifiers have been replaced by cross-examination, with the jury making the ultimate decisions about witness credibility.

- Judges retain the authority to conduct competency hearings for small children or people who are psychologically or mentally impaired.

- Witnesses are qualified to testify based on personal knowledge of a matter in the case and taking an oath or affirmation.

- Judges are incompetent to testify in a case over which they are presiding.

- Jurors are incompetent to testify about the deliberative process but may testify about juror misconduct involving the improper consideration of extraneous information.

Chapter References

CHRISTOPHER B. MUELLER & LAIRD C. KIRKPATRICK, EVIDENCE §§ 6.5–6.15 (4th ed. 2009).

GLEN WEISSENBERGER & JAMES J. DUANE, FEDERAL RULES OF EVIDENCE: RULES, LEGISLATIVE HISTORY, COMMENTARY AND AUTHORITY §§ 602–03, 605–06 (6th ed. 2009).

JACK B. WEINSTEIN & MARGARET A. BERGER, WEINSTEIN'S FEDERAL EVIDENCE §§ 602–03, 605–06 (Joseph M. McLaughlin ed., Matthew Bender 2d ed. 1997).

KENNETH S. BROUN, MCCORMICK ON EVIDENCE §§ 61–71 (6th ed. 2006).

STEVEN GOODE & OLIN GUY WELLBORN III, COURTROOM HANDBOOK ON FEDERAL EVIDENCE Ch. 5 (West 2010).

III. APPLICATION EXERCISE

Procedures for Competency Hearings

A competency hearing is a Rule 104(a) hearing. Under the Federal Rules of Evidence, judges have considerable discretion to use whatever procedures they deem necessary to determine competency at trial. Competency to testify is a legal decision that is solely within the decision-making province of the judge; competency is not a matter for the jury.

1. We will assume that a party (generally a defendant, but not always), has filed a written motion to declare a witness incompetent, and that the other party has replied. Both the motion and reply may include affidavits attesting to the witness's competency or lack thereof to testify. These affidavits could include lay witnesses who have observed the witness and also professionals (such as psychologists or psychiatrists) who have examined the witness.

2. After entertaining brief arguments on the issue, the judge will decide whether to conduct a hearing. We will assume that the parties have witnesses available to testify immediately should the judge require further inquiry into the issue of competence.

3. At this hearing, the witness can testify *in camera* (in a proceeding not open to the public). The witness may be examined by the witness proponent or the judge, and may be subject to cross-examination at the judge's discretion. The direct examination will focus on what makes a witness competent to testify: the ability to observe, recall and testify about matters personally known to the witness.

4. The judge may also choose to hear testimony from experts who have examined the witness and developed an opinion about the witness's competence.

5. At the close of the hearing, the judge will announce findings of fact and conclusions of law about the witness's competency.

The Exercise

1. *Objective*: To conduct a competency hearing in a criminal case involving a co-defendant and witness who was found criminally insane and incompetent to stand trial for the same incident.

2. *Factual Scenario*. This case involves a stabbing that occurred in the Calamity State Penitentiary. The government alleges that Victim was attacked and stabbed by Darryl Defendant and Mike McNasty, fellow inmates at the facility. This allegation is consistent with Victim's story about what happened. Darryl Defendant is on trial for the stabbing. Mike McNasty, his erstwhile co-defendant, was declared insane and incompetent to stand trial. McNasty was subsequently transferred to a state mental hospital. In addition to being insane, McNasty also suffers from hallucinations. McNasty told prison psychiatrists that extraterrestrial beings had ordered him to kill Victim because Victim was planning to take over the prison and release all the prisoners.

Defendant's defense is that he was walking by Victim's cell and saw McNasty and Victim fighting. He claims that the only reason he was in the cell was to try and stop McNasty from stabbing Victim. No other witnesses have come forward. After being declared insane and incompetent to stand trial, McNasty now claims that he was totally responsible for the attack on Victim and that Defendant had nothing to do with it. The defense wants to call McNasty to testify, but the prosecution opposes this on grounds that if McNasty is insane and incompetent to stand trial, he is also incompetent to testify. The government has filed a motion to declare McNasty incompetent.

3. *Additional Information.* The government intends to rely on the trial judge's earlier finding that McNasty is insane and incompetent to stand trial. The defense has available Dr. Pat Psychiatrist, who has examined McNasty and concluded that McNasty was able to observe, remember and communicate about the incident in the cell.

4. *Advance Preparation.* Prepare prosecution and defense arguments about McNasty's competency to testify. Prepare defense direct examinations of Dr. Psychiatrist and McNasty. Prepare prosecution cross-examinations of Psychiatrist and McNasty.

5. *In-Class Exercise.* Student will play the roles of prosecutor, defense attorney, and judge. Pursuant to the procedures discussed above, we will assume that both sides have filed the appropriate paperwork for a competency hearing. The prosecution will address the judge and ask for a declaration of incompetency, relying on the judge's earlier ruling. The defense will respond to the prosecution's argument and offer to call witnesses on the matter. Defense attorney will offer to call Dr. Psychiatrist and McNasty. The prosecutor will cross-examine both witnesses. The judge will rule on McNasty's competency to testify. The class will determine whether the judge's ruling was an abuse of discretion.

Chapter 14

REFRESHING THE RECOLLECTION OF THE FORGETFUL WITNESS

Chapter Objectives:

- Introduce and explain Rule 612, the concept of refreshing witness recollection, and the procedures and types of information that can be used to refresh a witness's recollection
- Analyze and discuss issues pertaining to Rule 612
- Apply the concepts from this chapter in a courtroom application exercise

I. BACKGROUND AND EXPLANATORY MATERIAL

Refreshing the Recollection of a Forgetful Witness

Occasionally, even the best witnesses forget parts of their testimony. Forgetfulness can be caused by a number of factors, including nervousness, fear, the passage of time, or the inability to recall specific details such as manifest lists, license plate numbers, exact weights and measures, and the like. Many witnesses do not appreciate the significance of an event at the time of its occurrence enough to keep it at the forefront of their minds. By the time a case comes to trial, even facts perceived at the time as important may have faded into the mind's remotest recesses. The process of refreshing recollection can help revive the memory of these facts.

A witness who cannot testify from memory has little of relevance to say in a courtroom. Recall from our discussion of Rule 602 that personal knowledge is a threshold factor for a witness to testify. A witness's ability to observe, recall and communicate is a critical component of competence. In general, witnesses are not permitted to sit on the witness stand and read aloud to the jury from documents either they or others have created. There is a hearsay exception for the introduction of a witness's recorded past recollections of an event under Rule 803(5), but this is not always a satisfactory solution to the problem of the forgetful witness; not all witnesses have "made or adopted" a "memorandum or record" while the event was fresh in their minds, as required by Rule 803(5).

Rule 612 provides a mechanism for advocates to help refresh the recollection of forgetful witnesses using written materials or other items calculated to assist the recall process and help the witness testify from memory. It also contains procedural protections that permit the opponent to introduce into evidence other portions of writings used to refresh a witness's testimony.

Through Dec. 1, 2011	After Dec. 1, 2011
Rule 612. Writing Used To Refresh Memory	**Rule 612. Writing Used to Refresh a Witness's Memory**
Except as otherwise provided in criminal proceedings by section 3500 of title 18, United States Code, if a witness uses a writing to refresh memory for the purpose of testifying, either—	**(a) Scope**. This rule gives an adverse party certain options when a witness uses a writing to refresh memory:
(1) while testifying, or	(1) while testifying; or
(2) before testifying, if the court in its discretion determines it is necessary in the interests of justice, an adverse party is entitled to have the writing produced at the hearing, to inspect it, to cross-examine the witness thereon, and to introduce in evidence those portions which relate to the testimony of the witness. If it is claimed that the writing contains matters not related to the subject matter of the testimony the court shall examine the writing in camera, excise any portions not so related, and order delivery of the remainder to the party entitled thereto. Any portion withheld over objections shall be preserved and made available to the appellate court in the event of an appeal. If a writing is not produced or delivered pursuant to order under this rule, the court shall make any order justice requires, except that in criminal cases when the prosecution elects not to comply, the order shall be one striking the testimony or, if the court in its discretion determines that the interests of justice so require, declaring a mistrial.	(2) before testifying, if the court decides that justice requires the party to have those options. **(b) Adverse Party's Options; Deleting Unrelated Matter**. Unless 18 U.S.C. § 3500 provides otherwise in a criminal case, an adverse party is entitled to have the writing produced at the hearing, to inspect it, to cross-examine the witness about it, and to introduce in evidence any portion that relates to the witness's testimony. If the producing party claims that the writing includes unrelated matter, the court must examine the writing in camera, delete any unrelated portion, and order that the rest be delivered to the adverse party. Any portion deleted over objection must be preserved for the record. **(c) Failure to Produce or Deliver the Writing**. If a writing is not produced or is not delivered as ordered, the court may issue any appropriate order. But if the prosecution does not comply in a criminal case, the court must strike the witness's testimony or — if justice so requires — declare a mistrial.

A variety of materials and resources can permissibly be used to refresh recollection, and this can be done either before or during trial.

Resources Available to Refresh Recollection

As the following excerpts from classic evidence cases illustrate, literally anything can be used to refresh a witness's recollection: "Anything may in fact revive a memory: a song, a scent, a photograph, and allusion, even a past statement known to be false."[1]

> "The memory aid itself need not even be a writing. What may it be? It may be anything. It may be a line from Kipling or the dolorous refrain of "The Tennessee Waltz"; a whiff of hickory smoke; the running of the fingers across a swatch of corduroy; the sweet carbonation of a chocolate soda; the sight of a faded snapshot in a long-neglected album. All that is required is that it may trigger the Proustian moment. It may be anything which produces the desired testimonial prelude, "It all comes back to me now."[2]

The practice of hauling cases of chocolate soda into court to refresh recollection is rare; few attorneys, moreover, burn hickory briquettes,[3] play music, or read poetry to help their witnesses remember important facts. In practice, written documents and photographs are the items of evidence most commonly used to refresh recollection.

Writings can include the witness's own written materials, whether sworn or unsworn, including diaries, post-it notes, affidavits and sworn statements; depositions; official documents and records; business records created by others; notes taken by attorneys or investigators; letters, notes, e-mails, labels, cereal boxes, and so forth, without limitation. Even untrue writings can be used to refresh recollection. The following case excerpt eloquently explains why there are few restrictions on the types of documents that can be used to refresh memory:

> Common experience, the work of Proust and other keenly observant literary men, and recondite psychological research, all teach us that memory of things long past can be accurately restored in all sorts of ways. The creaking of a hinge, the whistling of a tune, the smell of seaweed, the sight of an old photograph, the taste of nutmeg, the touch of a piece of canvas, may bring vividly to the foreground [of] consciousness the recollection of events that happened years ago and which would otherwise have been forgotten. If a recollection thus reawakened be then set down on paper, why should not that paper properly serve in the courtroom, as it does in everyday life, to prod the memory at still a later date? The memory-prodder may itself lack meaning to other persons as a symbol of the past event, as everyone knows who has ever used a knot in his handkerchief as a reminder. Since the workings of the human memory still remain a major mystery after centuries of study, courts should hesitate before they glibly contrive dogmatic rules concerning the reliability of the ways of provoking it.[4]

---

[1] United States v. Rappy, 157 F.2d 964, 967 (2d Cir. 1946).

[2] Baker v. State, 371 A.2d 699, 705 (Md. Ct. Spec. App. 1977).

[3] This could potentially set up a conflict between court security rules and the right to a fair trial.

[4] Fanelli v. United States Gypsum Co., 141 F.2d 216, 217 (2d Cir. 1944).

In rare instances, attorneys can also use hypnotism to help refresh a witness's recollection. This occurs as part of the pretrial preparation process, outside the courtroom, and is subject to jurisdiction-specific rules.

Refreshing Recollection Pretrial

As part of the pretrial process of preparing witnesses to testify, attorneys often permit witnesses to review their deposition transcripts, sworn statements, financial records, or other relevant documents. In addition, many attorneys practice direct and cross examinations of with their witnesses. Pretrial witness preparation often serves to refresh recollection of past events that the witness may have forgotten. In addition, witnesses are frequently given the opportunity to review their past statements just before going on the stand.

There is nothing unethical about refreshing a witness's recollection prior to trial. Attorneys cross the line when they create memories for witnesses, but not when they help witnesses remember what they once knew. In order to help ensure the integrity of the pretrial preparation process and the in-court presentation of refreshed testimony, Rule 612 contains provisions granting opposing counsel the right to inspect, cross-examine upon, and introduce into evidence portions of documents used to refresh recollection.

Refreshing Recollection at Trial

When a witness forgets something important while testifying, an advocate may attempt to refresh her testimony while she is still on the stand. Any of the memory-stimulating items discussed above are available for this purpose. The document or item itself is not evidence; as the court observed in *Baker v. State*, "the stimulus itself is never evidence. . . . Of such mere stimuli or memory-prods, McCormick says, at 18, '[T]he cardinal rule is that they are not evidence, but only aids in the giving of evidence.' " If the effort is successful, the document or other item is taken away from the witness, who then testifies from memory.

The most significant concern with refreshing a witness's recollection is ensuring that the witness is in fact testifying from revived memory and not simply parroting the contents of a document. For this reason, opposing counsel is permitted to inspect the document and offer other portions of it into evidence. For example, if a witness's deposition contains marginal notes from an attorney, such as "make sure to emphasize the word 'red' when you repeat this to the jury," opposing counsel might want to make the jury aware of the notes to help them evaluate the witness's credibility.

One way to avoid questions about witness memory is to strictly follow the foundational elements for refreshing recollection. The process for doing this is discussed in the next section.

Opponent's Right to Inspect and Use Refreshing Materials

When a witness's memory is refreshed with a document during her testimony, it is a relatively simple matter to ensure that opposing counsel has the opportunity to inspect the document and cross-examine the witness concerning it. All the proponent has to do is walk across the aisle and hand the document to opposing counsel, who is then free to use it as she sees fit.

As originally drafted by the Advisory Committee, Rule 612 would have treated statements used to refresh a witness's testimony *before* trial exactly the same as statements to refresh a witness's testimony *during* trial. In other words, opposing counsel would have free reign to examine whatever documents might have been used to help prepare a forgetful witness. The House Committee on the Judiciary, however, was concerned that untrammeled access to these materials could lead to fishing expeditions by opposing counsel. The rule as written leaves the production of statements used before trial to the discretion of a judge, if necessary in the interests of justice.

Rule 612 treats witnesses who testify in criminal cases differently from witnesses in other cases. In criminal cases, the normal disclosure procedures of Rule 612 are subordinated to 18 U.S.C. § 3500, the Jencks Act. The Jencks Act has been incorporated into Rule 26.2 of the Federal Rules of Criminal Procedure, which states:

Rule 26.2. Producing a Witness's Statement

(a) Motion to Produce. After a witness other than the defendant has testified on direct examination, the court, on motion of a party who did not call the witness, must order an attorney for the government or the defendant and the defendant's attorney to produce, for the examination and use of the moving party, any statement of the witness that is in their possession and that relates to the subject matter of the witness's testimony.

(b) Producing the Entire Statement. If the entire statement relates to the subject matter of the witness's testimony, the court must order that the statement be delivered to the moving party.

(c) Producing a Redacted Statement. If the party who called the witness claims that the statement contains information that is privileged or does not relate to the subject matter of the witness's testimony, the court must inspect the statement in camera. After excising any privileged or unrelated portions, the court must order delivery of the redacted statement to the moving party. If the defendant objects to an excision, the court must preserve the entire statement with the excised portion indicated, under seal, as part of the record.

(d) Recess to Examine a Statement. The court may recess the proceedings to allow time for a party to examine the statement and prepare for its use.

(e) Sanction for Failure to Produce or Deliver a Statement. If the party who called the witness disobeys an order to produce or deliver a statement, the court must strike the witness's testimony from the record. If an attorney for the government disobeys the order, the court must declare a mistrial if justice so requires.

(f) "Statement" Defined. As used in this rule, a witness's "statement" means: (1) a written statement that the witness makes and signs, or otherwise adopts or approves; (2) a substantially verbatim, contemporaneously recorded recital of the witness's oral statement that is contained in any recording or any transcription of a recording; or (3) the witness's statement to a grand jury, however taken or recorded, or a transcription of such a statement.

(g) Scope. This rule applies at trial, at a suppression hearing under Rule 12, and to the extent specified in the following rules: (1) Rule 5.1(h) (preliminary hearing); (2) Rule 32(i)(2) (sentencing); (3) Rule 32.1(e) (hearing to revoke or modify probation or supervised release); (4) Rule 46(j) (detention hearing); and (5) Rule 8 of the Rules Governing Proceedings under 28 U.S.C. § 2255.[5]

It is beyond the scope of this text to discuss in any further detail the process of requesting production and use of statements used to prepare witnesses before trial.

Foundational Issues

One of the best ways to avoid problems in the courtroom with refreshing a witness's recollection is to strictly follow the foundational elements for doing so. There are two primary methods that can be used to refresh recollection: using a gently-leading question to prod the witness's memory, or using the formal foundation for refreshing recollection. It should be noted that the formal foundation for refreshing recollection is a required part of the foundation for introducing past recollection recorded under Rule 803(5) for a witness whose memory cannot be refreshed. Each of the two foundations is listed below.

(1) *The Gently Leading Question*

During direct examination, Rule 611 requires the use of non-leading questions. There is an exception for foundational matters, and there is also an unwritten exception for refreshing a witness's recollection on non-material matters. The use of leading questions to refresh should be used when it is obvious that a witness has misspoken. For example, if the witness has consistently stated that the accident occurred at 12 p.m., but says on direct examination that it occurred at 12 a.m, the examiner could quickly and gently correct him with a leading question: "you meant to say 12 p.m." The steps for doing so follow:

1. The witness misstates a non-material fact on direct examination.

2. Noticing that the witness has done so, the attorney quickly corrects the witness with a leading question.

3. If the attorney draws an objection, the attorney rephrases the question as a non-leading question and gives the witness the opportunity to try again.

(2) *The Formal Foundation for Refreshing Recollection*

1. The witness forgets an important fact.

---

[5] FED. R. CRIM. P. 26.2.

2. The attorney rephrases the question in order to clarify that the witness has in fact forgotten.

3. The attorney asks if anything will refresh the witness's recollection.

4. The witness says yes.

5. The attorney marks the document or item as an exhibit for identification, shows it to opposing counsel, and then gives it to the witness. [Note, in some cases, having established that the witness has forgotten something, the attorney might skip steps 3 and 4 and go directly to step 5.]

6. After the witness has finished examining the item or document, the attorney retrieves it from the witness and asks whether it has refreshed the witness's recollection.

7. If the witness replies affirmatively, the attorney re-asks the question from before.

8. The witness replies from memory.

II. CASES, DISCUSSION QUESTIONS AND PROBLEMS

BAKER v. STATE
Court of Special Appeals of Maryland
371 A.2d 699 (Md. Ct. Spec. App. 1977)

[During a murder trial, the testifying police officer forgot some details of the case on cross-examination. The defendant's attorney attempted to refresh his recollection through the use of another officer's report. The judge sustained the prosecutor's objection to the use of another officer's report, and the defendant appealed.]

On so critical an issue as possible exculpation from the very lips of the crime victim, appellant was entitled to try to refresh the memory of the key police witness. She was erroneously and prejudicially denied that opportunity. . . .

When we are dealing with an instance of Present Recollection Revived, the only source of evidence is the testimony of the witness himself. The stimulus may have jogged the witness's dormant memory, but the stimulus itself is not received in evidence. Dean McCormick makes it clear that even when the stimulus is a writing, when the witness "speaks from a memory thus revived, his testimony is what he says, not the writing." Id., at 15. . . .

The psychological community is in full agreement with the legal community in assessing the mental phenomenon. See Cairn, Law and the Social Sciences 200 (1935):

> "In permitting a witness to refresh his recollection by consulting a memorandum, the courts are in accord with present psychological knowledge. A distinction is drawn, in the analysis of the memory process, between recall, which is the reproduction of what has been learned, and recognition, which is recall with a time-factor added, or an awareness that

the recall relates to past experience. It is with recognition that the law is principally concerned in permitting a witness to revive his recollection. The psychological evidence is clear that in thus allowing to be brought to mind what has been forgotten, the law is following sound psychological procedure."

And see Hutchins and Slesinger, Some Observations on the Law of Evidence — Memory, 41 Harv. L. Rev. 860 (1928).

The catalytic agent or memory stimulator is put aside, once it has worked its psychological magic, and the witness then testifies on the basis of the now-refreshed memory. The opposing party, of course, has the right to inspect the memory aid, be it a writing or otherwise, and even to show it to the jury. This examination, however, is not for the purpose of testing the competence of the memory aid (for competence is immaterial where the thing in question is not evidence) but only to test whether the witness's memory has in truth been refreshed. As McCormick warns, "But the witness must swear that he is genuinely refreshed. . . . And he cannot be allowed to read the writing in the guise of refreshment, as a cloak for getting in evidence an inadmissible document." . . .

In solid accord with both the psychological sciences and the general common law of evidence, Maryland has long established it that even when a writing of some sort is the implement used to stir the embers of cooling memory, the writing need not be that of the forgetful witness himself, need not have been adopted by him, need not have been made contemporaneously with or shortly after the incident in question, and need not even be necessarily accurate. The competence of the writing is not in issue for the writing is not offered as evidence but is only used as a memory aid. . . .

When the writing in question is to be utilized simply "to awaken a slumbering recollection of an event" in the mind of the witness, the writing may be a memorandum made by the witness himself, 1) even if it was not made immediately after the event, 2) even if it was not made of firsthand knowledge and 3) even if the witness cannot now vouch for the fact that it was accurate when made. It may be a memorandum made by one other than the witness, even if never before read by the witness or vouched for by him. It may be an Associated Press account. It may be a highly selective version of the incident at the hands of a Hemingway or an Eliot. All that is required is that it ignite the flash of accurate recall — that it accomplish the revival which is sought. . . .

Although the use of a memorandum of some sort will continue quantitatively to dominate the field of refreshing recollection, we are better able to grasp the process conceptually if we appreciate that the use of a memorandum as a memory aid is not a legal phenomenon unto itself but only an instance of a far broader phenomenon. . . . [T]he process could just as well proceed, "Your Honor, I am pleased to present to the court Miss Rosa Ponselle who will now sing 'Celeste Aida' for the witness, for that is what was playing on the night the burglar came through the window.' Whether by conventional or unconventional means, precisely the same end is sought. One is looking for the effective elixir to revitalize dimming memory and make it live again in the service of the search for truth.

Even in the more conventional mode, it is quite clear that in this case the appropriate effort of the appellant to jog the arguably dormant memory of the key police witness on a vital issue was unduly and prejudicially restricted.

Judgments reversed; case remanded for a new trial; costs to be paid by Mayor and City Council of Baltimore.

DISCUSSION QUESTIONS

1. Although the rule on refreshing recollection technically permits the use of such things as the smell of perfume or the sound of music, this is a rare phenomenon. How might an advocate go about using a non-conventional method to refresh recollection? What foundational standards would have to be satisfied? How would the record be preserved on appeal?

2. One requirement of refreshing recollection is that the witness hand back the document and be able to testify from memory. To what extent do you think this realistically occurs? In other words, do witnesses tend to testify about their short-term memory of the document they've just read, or does the document genuinely trigger the recall of a long-term memory?

PROBLEMS

Problem 14-1. Special Agent Smith works for the Calamity Bureau of Investigation. He was the lead investigator in the case of *People v. Darla Defendant*, a white collar crime case involving complex financial transactions and money laundering. Smith's investigation was complete more than one year prior to the trial. The day before trial, Smith spent the entire day reviewing his lengthy investigative report. The next day, just before he began testifying, the defense objected that Smith's earlier review of the report meant that he was not testifying from independent recollection. How should the judge rule in this case?

Problem 14-2. Special Agent Jane Jones also works for the CBI as an investigator. In the same case, while testifying, Jones forgot some key facts pertaining to the investigation. The prosecutor showed Jones a summary of her agent's notes taken during the investigation. The defense requested to see the actual agent's notes, rather than the summary of the notes that the prosecutor showed Jones, to prepare for cross-examining Jones. What arguments should the defense make in support of this request? What arguments should the prosecutor make in response? How should the judge rule?

Refreshing Recollection: Quick Hits

- All witnesses at trial must testify from memory.

- When witnesses forget things they once knew, either before testifying or while testifying, Rule 612 provides a mechanism to refresh recollection.

- Advocates can use documents prepared by the witness, documents prepared by others, or any other available means to refresh the witness's recollection.

- The opposing party is entitled to inspect materials used to refresh recollection, cross-examine the witness on them, and introduce in evidence those portions that relate to the testimony of the witness.

Chapter References

CHRISTOPHER B. MUELLER & LAIRD C. KIRKPATRICK, EVIDENCE §§ 6.66–6.69 (4th ed. 2009).

GLEN WEISSENBERGER & JAMES J. DUANE, FEDERAL RULES OF EVIDENCE: RULES, LEGISLATIVE HISTORY, COMMENTARY AND AUTHORITY § 612 (6th ed. 2009).

JACK B. WEINSTEIN & MARGARET A. BERGER, WEINSTEIN'S FEDERAL EVIDENCE § 612 (Joseph M. McLaughlin ed., Matthew Bender 2d ed. 1997).

KENNETH S. BROUN, MCCORMICK ON EVIDENCE § 9 (6th ed. 2006).

STEVEN GOODE & OLIN GUY WELLBORN III, COURTROOM HANDBOOK ON FEDERAL EVIDENCE Ch. 5 (West 2010).

III. APPLICATION EXERCISE

Procedures for Refreshing Recollection

Refer to the Foundational Issues subsection above for the procedures to be used in refreshing recollection.

The Exercise

Objective: To demonstrate mastery of the procedures for refreshing a witness's recollection.

Factual Scenario: An expert witness at trial is testifying about the credentials, past scholarly activity, and other activities of a faculty member at your law school.

Advance Preparation. As assigned by your professor, visit the faculty member's webpage, review his or her curriculum vitae, and prepare a brief (3-5 minute) direct examination on any aspect of their professional life discussed in the CV.

There is no need for you to print out a hard copy of the CV; one will be provided to you in class.

In-Class Exercise. Students will play the roles of witness, judge and direct examiner in this exercise. An attorney will be called upon to conduct a direct examination of the witness. During direct examination, the witness will forget various details of the other faculty member's curriculum vitae, and students may be called upon to use various methods to refresh recollection: gently leading questions, use of a document, use of an object (provided by the professor in class as part of the exercise), and use of a song (also provided in class as part of the exercise).

Chapter 15

INTRODUCTION TO IMPEACHMENT

> **Chapter Objectives:**
>
> - Introduce and explain Rules 607-609 and the basic theories and concepts of character-based impeachment, impeachment by prior convictions, and bias or motive impeachment
> - Analyze and discuss issues pertaining to Rules 607-609 and bias or motive impeachment
> - Apply the concepts from this chapter in a courtroom application exercise

I. BACKGROUND AND EXPLANATORY MATERIAL

Introduction to Impeachment

In the interests of shielding the jury from false testimony, the common law competency rules kept entire suspect groups of people — such as convicts, interested persons, or children — from testifying at trial. Over time, the competency rules were replaced by the philosophy that the adversarial trial system could provide the jury with enough information to decide what value to give a witness's testimony. Under the Federal Rules, witnesses are generally presumed competent to testify, but the parties are free to attack the credibility, perception or motives of opposing witnesses.

The term "impeachment" describes the process used at trial to discredit witnesses or call into question the accuracy of their testimony. Traditionally, the reasons for impeaching witnesses fall into five broad categories: (1) the witness has an untruthful character; (2) the witness is biased or has a motive to falsify testimony; (3) the witness has a defective capacity to observe, recall or communicate; (4) the witness has made prior statements that are inconsistent with his trial testimony; (5) the witness's testimony can be contradicted by other witnesses or evidence.[1] Each of these reasons will be explored in greater detail in

---

[1] *See* United States v. Collicott, 92 F.3d 973, 980 n.5 (9th Cir. 1996) (*citing* STRONG, MCCORMICK ON

this chapter and the following chapter.

Attorneys can impeach a witness in a variety of ways: on direct examination, on cross-examination, by the use of prior convictions, or through the testimony of other witnesses. The category of impeachment plays a significant role in the selection of an impeachment method. For example, impeachment by prior inconsistent statement almost always occurs on cross-examination. After a witness has been impeached during trial, the attorney can explain the significance of the impeachment and the effect it should have on the jury's decision-making process during closing argument.

This chapter will discuss the methods of impeachment for untruthful character, prior convictions, bias or motive, defective capacity, and contradiction. Chapter Sixteen will cover impeachment based on prior inconsistent statements.

Who Can Impeach: Rule 607

A threshold issue in impeaching a witness concerns who is entitled to impeach, and when. Under the common law voucher rule, attorneys were presumed to vouch for the credibility of the witnesses they called to the witness stand. As a general rule, therefore, attorneys were not permitted to impeach their own witnesses on direct examination. Impeachment was reserved for hostile witnesses, those affiliated with and called by the other side.

The voucher rule is logically consistent with the underlying precepts of the adversarial trial, which places upon the parties the responsibility to present the best possible witnesses and evidence to the jury. For reasons of persuasion and advocacy, there are powerful disincentives to calling witnesses whose credibility or trustworthiness is suspect. No courtroom advocate would set out deliberately to undermine his case with problematic witnesses.

Over time, the common law developed exceptions to the voucher rule. The primary exception was for surprise, when the witness's testimony was "authentically unanticipated and affirmatively damaging to the party's case."[2] At representative example of this is *State v. Moutray*,[3] in which the defendant was alleged to have shot and killed his adult daughter's ex-husband during an altercation at the defendant's home. The defendant claimed that the victim had started the fight by attacking him when the defendant walked through the front door after returning home from a party. A critical issue in the trial concerned the defendant's actions when he first walked through the door. In a pretrial statement to police, the defendant's daughter — who was also the victim's ex-wife — testified that the defendant had shoved her mother into the television set trying to push past her when he first saw the victim in the house. At trial, however, the daughter changed her testimony. The trial occurred in Missouri, a common-law evidence jurisdiction that continued to use the voucher rule at the time of trial. The following

---

EVIDENCE § 33 (1992)), *cited in* STEVEN GOODE AND GUY WELLBORN III, COURTROOM EVIDENCE HANDBOOK 178 (West 2010-2011 Student Edition).

[2] GLEN WEISSENBERGER & JAMES J. DUANE, FEDERAL RULES OF EVIDENCE: RULES, LEGISLATIVE HISTORY, COMMENTARY AND AUTHORITY § 607.1 (6th ed. 2009).

[3] 728 S.W.2d 256 (Mo. Ct. App. 1987).

colloquy from the trial shows the dilemma faced by an attorney at trial when his own witness changes testimony in order to help the other side:[4]

Q.   *[Prosecutor] So, are you saying your dad didn't push your mom into the TV set?*

A.   *Well, I don't really remember because I was, you know, just kind of waking up.*

Q.   *Do you recall telling the police — giving a statement to the police back on January 21, 1985?*

A.   *Do I remember — Yeah, but I was all shooken up. I don't remember saying too much on it.*

Q.   *Well, do you recall telling the police officer —*

MR. RANDOLPH [attorney for appellant]: Just a minute. Your Honor, we object to this. May we approach the bench?

THE COURT: Yes.

(Counsel approached the bench and the following proceedings were had:)

MR. ROBB: Your Honor, I'm surprised by this testimony. I've got a statement from her which — and I'll read it in effect: "Statement of Cherisse Moutray. Marvin opened the door, and dad pushed mom through the door into the TV. Dad was drunk and he started swinging at Marvin." And I feel I'm surprised by that testimony. I would like to cross-examine this witness.

MR. RANDOLPH: Well, she certainly didn't testify to that at the preliminary hearing.

THE COURT: Well, I don't know about that. If he has an inconsistent statement, he — and he's surprised, he can —

MR. RANDOLPH: Well, he can lay a proper foundation for it. I object —

THE COURT: For the statement?

MR. RANDOLPH: Yes.

THE COURT: Okay. Sustained.

(Proceedings returned to open court.)

BY MR. ROBB: [Assistant Prosecuting Attorney] Q. You do you [sic] recall giving the statement to the police; is that correct?

A.   *I didn't really say anything on the statement. I could — I was so shook up. And, you know, they wanted it right then and there. And I told them I really didn't want to talk to them. They said, "Well, how about if we ask you questions and then, you know, you can yes or no on what you recall." But I didn't really, you know, give them*

---

[4] State v. Moutray, 728 S.W.2d 256, 260–61 (Mo. Ct. App. 1987).

any word specifics. I was saying yes and no. And they were doing the questioning. You know, they were asking me the questions.

Q. *They were asking you yes and no about somebody pushing somebody into the TV set, and they weren't even there to know any of that?*

A. *Yeah. They — No, they just — They, like, they'd ask me certain questions, like on the TV set. I couldn't even really remember.*

Q. *All right. Well, let me show you –*

A. *He was probably pushing. You know, they were probably getting out of the way because Marvin was coming towards my dad, and dad was coming towards him. So, yeah, you know, probably to get mom out of the way.*

Q. *So, you're not denying that your dad could have pushed your mom into the TV set now; is that correct?*

A. *He could have, yeah.*

The examination continued in this vein for several more minutes, the witness making every attempt to deny that she had actually said that the defendant had pushed her mother into the television set. The Court of Appeals summarized the situation:

> [W]ithin some 40-45 minutes of the shooting of the victim, appellant's daughter gave her statement to the local police. It is obvious from the record herein that the daughter, by her trial testimony, attempted to assist the appellant, her father. This produced inconsistencies between the statement she had given the police and her trial testimony.[5]

The Court went on to explain that the prosecutor had followed the proper technique for impeaching his own witness:

> As a general rule, the state may not impeach its own witness. The rule is equally applicable to any party to a case, whether civil or criminal. A witness may be impeached as hostile, however if two requirements are met. First, the witness must, by reason of answers which are inconsistent with previous statements, surprise the party propounding the questions. Second, the answers as given must state facts which in effect make the witness a witness for the other side.[6]

As illustrated by the above example from the *Moutray* case, the voucher rule presents serious difficulties at trial. The primary flaw is the premise that parties have a meaningful choice in the selection of witnesses. This premise is defective. As the Advisory Committee put it, "A party does not hold out his witnesses as worthy of belief, since he rarely has a free choice in selecting them. Denial of the [right to impeach] leaves the party at the mercy of the witness and the adversary."[7] A

---

[5] State v. Moutray, 728 S.W.2d 256, 262 (Mo. Ct. App. 1987).

[6] State v. Moutray, 728 S.W.2d 256, 262 (Mo. Ct. App. 1987).

[7] FED. R. EVID. 607, advisory committee notes.

reluctant, mendacious, biased, deliberately forgetful, or unreliable witness could sabotage an attorney's case, not to mention the attorney's credibility, with the jury.

The Federal Rules of Evidence did away with the common law voucher rule because of "doubts as to its basic soundness and workability."[8] It was replaced by Rule 607, which permits any party to impeach a witness.

Through Dec. 1, 2011	After Dec. 1, 2011
Rule 607. Who May Impeach	**Rule 607. Who May Impeach a Witness**
The credibility of a witness may be attacked by any party, including the party calling the witness.	Any party, including the party that called the witness, may attack the witness's credibility.

Rule 607 grants flexibility to advocates at trial by dispensing with the artificial conventions and exceptions of the voucher rule.

Rule 607 is, however, potentially vulnerable to abuse at trial. Oftentimes, an advocate will know what to expect from a witness before trial. Unfettered by the voucher rule, some advocates might be tempted to call a witness to testify for the sole purpose of impeaching that witness. An advocate might want to do this for a couple of reasons: (1) to discredit a witness who is clearly aligned with the opposing side, hoping thereby to cast doubt on the overall validity of the opposing side's case; or (2) to impeach the witness using prior inconsistent statements that might otherwise be inadmissible under the rules of evidence. Although Rule 607 does not forbid such tactics on its face, case law holds that impeachment cannot be used as a subterfuge to place otherwise inadmissible evidence before the jury.[9] Rules 403 (excluding evidence whose probative value is substantially outweighed by the danger of unfair prejudice) and 611 (permitting a judge to exercise control over the court in order to protect witnesses from harassment or undue embarrassment) also operate to prevent improper subterfuge impeachment of witnesses at trial.

Character-Based Impeachment

Every witness who testifies at trial is required to take an oath to testify truthfully. The twin acts of testifying and taking the oath make relevant issues pertaining to the witness's veracity. Rule 608 is a character rule that applies only to witnesses. In most respects, it functions exactly like Rules 404(a) and 405 at trial.

---

[8] FED. R. EVID. 607, advisory committee notes.

[9] *See* United States v. Buffalo, 358 F.3d 519, 522–23 (8th Cir. 2004); United States v. Johnson, 802 F.2d 1459, 1466 (D.C. Cir. 1986).

Through Dec. 1, 2011	After Dec. 1, 2011
Rule 608. Evidence of Character and Conduct of Witness	**Rule 608. A Witness's Character for Truthfulness or Untruthfulness**
(a) Opinion and reputation evidence of character. The credibility of a witness may be attacked or supported by evidence in the form of opinion or reputation, but subject to these limitations: (1) the evidence may refer only to character for truthfulness or untruthfulness, and (2) evidence of truthful character is admissible only after the character of the witness for truthfulness has been attacked by opinion or reputation evidence or otherwise.	**(a) Reputation or Opinion Evidence**. A witness's credibility may be attacked or supported by testimony about the witness's reputation for having a character for truthfulness or untruthfulness, or by testimony in the form of an opinion about that character. But evidence of truthful character is admissible only after the witness's character for truthfulness has been attacked.
(b) Specific instances of conduct. Specific instances of the conduct of a witness, for the purpose of attacking or supporting the witness' character for truthfulness, other than conviction of crime as provided in rule 609, may not be proved by extrinsic evidence. They may, however, in the discretion of the court, if probative of truthfulness or untruthfulness, be inquired into on cross-examination of the witness (1) concerning the witness' character for truthfulness or untruthfulness, or (2) concerning the character for truthfulness or untruthfulness of another witness as to which character the witness being cross-examined has testified. The giving of testimony, whether by an accused or by any other witness, does not operate as a waiver of the accused's or the witness' privilege against self-incrimination when examined with respect to matters that relate only to character for truthfulness.	**(b) Specific Instances of Conduct**. Except for a criminal conviction under Rule 609, extrinsic evidence is not admissible to prove specific instances of a witness's conduct in order to attack or support the witness's character for truthfulness. But the court may, on cross-examination, allow them to be inquired into if they are probative of the character for truthfulness or untruthfulness of: (1) the witness; or (2) another witness whose character the witness being cross-examined has testified about. By testifying on another matter, a witness does not waive any privilege against self-incrimination for testimony that relates only to the witness's character for truthfulness.

The rule contains some important limitations. First, veracity, or character for truthfulness, is the only permissible trait for which a witness's character may be attacked or supported. Second, the form of evidence for attacking or supporting character is limited to reputation or opinion testimony. Third, a party may not introduce evidence of a witness's character for truthfulness unless and until the opponent has launched an attack on the same witness's character for untruthfulness. The practice of offering evidence of truthful character in advance of an attack is referred to as "bolstering," and it is forbidden under Rule 608(a).

A party may not introduce extrinsic evidence of a witness's specific acts in attacking or supporting a witness's character for veracity. Similar to Rule 405(b), Rule 608(b) does, however, permit an advocate to use specific acts, if probative of truthfulness or untruthfulness, on cross-examination of a witness who has offered reputation or opinion testimony of another witness's character for veracity. The purpose of this cross-examination is not to introduce specific acts into evidence, but rather to test the basis of the character witness's knowledge or opinion.

To illustrate the interplay of sections (a) and (b) of Rule 608, suppose that Monica testified during the plaintiff's case in chief in a personal injury case. The defendant could call Veronica to testify that in Monica has a reputation in the community for being untruthful. On cross-examination, the plaintiff's counsel could cross-examine Veronica with "did you know" or "have you heard" questions that are probative of truthfulness, such as "have you heard that Monica voluntarily admitted to making a mistake on her state income tax form and had to pay extra taxes because of it?" If Veronica has not heard of this incident, the fact-finder might conclude that perhaps Veronica does not know much about Monica's reputation, after all. If Veronica had heard of the incident but nevertheless testified about Monica's reputation for untruthfulness, the fact-finder might conclude that Veronica is an untrustworthy or biased witness. Finally, during the plaintiff's rebuttal case, the plaintiff could call a witness to offer evidence, in the form of reputation or opinion testimony, of Monica's character for truthfulness.

Impeachment by Proof of Prior Convictions

Felons were considered incompetent to testify under the common law. Over time, competency rules were liberalized; categorical exclusions disappeared, replaced by a rule of general competency. Rule 609, which allows impeachment of a witness's character for truthfulness by evidence that the witness has been convicted of a crime, is a vestige of the old common law rule that declared felons incompetent to testify.

Through Dec. 1, 2011	After Dec. 1, 2011
Rule 609. Impeachment by Evidence of Conviction of Crime	**Rule 609. Impeachment by Evidence of a Criminal Conviction**
(a) General rule. For the purpose of attacking the character for truthfulness of a witness,	**(a) In General**. The following rules apply to attacking a witness's character for truthfulness by evidence of a criminal conviction:
(1) evidence that a witness other than an accused has been convicted of a crime shall be admitted, subject to Rule 403, if the crime was punishable by death or imprisonment in excess of one year under the law under which the witness was convicted, and evidence that an accused has been convicted of such a crime shall be admitted if the court determines that the probative value of admitting this evidence outweighs its prejudicial effect to the accused; and	(1) for a crime that, in the convicting jurisdiction, was punishable by death or by imprisonment for more than one year, the evidence:
	(A) must be admitted, subject to Rule 403, in a civil case or in a criminal case in which the witness is not a defendant; and
(2) evidence that any witness has been convicted of a crime shall be admitted regardless of the punishment, if it readily can be determined that establishing the elements of the crime required proof or admission of an act of dishonesty or false statement by the witness.	(B) must be admitted in a criminal case in which the witness is a defendant, if the probative value of the evidence outweighs its prejudicial effect to that defendant; and
	(2) for any crime regardless of the punishment, the evidence must be admitted if the court can readily determine that establishing the elements of the crime required proving — or the witness's admitting — a dishonest act or false statement.
(b) Time limit. Evidence of a conviction under this rule is not admissible if a period of more than ten years has elapsed since the date of the conviction or of the release of the witness from the confinement imposed for that conviction, whichever is the later date, unless the court determines, in the interests of justice, that the probative value of the conviction supported by specific facts and circumstances substantially outweighs its prejudicial effect. However, evidence of a conviction more than 10 years old as calculated herein, is not admissible unless the proponent gives to the adverse party sufficient advance written notice of intent to use such evidence to provide the adverse party with a fair opportunity to contest the use of such evidence.	**(b) Limit on Using the Evidence After 10 Years**. This subdivision (b) applies if more than 10 years have passed since the witness's conviction or release from confinement for it, whichever is later. Evidence of the conviction is admissible only if:
	(1) its probative value, supported by specific facts and circumstances, substantially outweighs its prejudicial effect; and
	(2) the proponent gives an adverse party reasonable written notice of the intent to use it so that the party has a fair opportunity to contest its use.

Through Dec. 1, 2011	After Dec. 1, 2011
Rule 609, cont'd	**Rule 609, cont'd**
(c) Effect of pardon, annulment, or certificate of rehabilitation. Evidence of a conviction is not admissible under this rule if (1) the conviction has been the subject of a pardon, annulment, certificate of rehabilitation, or other equivalent procedure based on a finding of the rehabilitation of the person convicted, and that person has not been convicted of a subsequent crime that was punishable by death or imprisonment in excess of one year, or (2) the conviction has been the subject of a pardon, annulment, or other equivalent procedure based on a finding of innocence.	**(c) Effect of a Pardon, Annulment, or Certificate of Rehabilitation**. Evidence of a conviction is not admissible if: (1) the conviction has been the subject of a pardon, annulment, certificate of rehabilitation, or other equivalent procedure based on a finding that the person has been rehabilitated, and the person has not been convicted of a later crime punishable by death or by imprisonment for more than one year; or (2) the conviction has been the subject of a pardon, annulment, or other equivalent procedure based on a finding of innocence.
(d) Juvenile adjudications. Evidence of juvenile adjudications is generally not admissible under this rule. The court may, however, in a criminal case allow evidence of a juvenile adjudication of a witness other than the accused if conviction of the offense would be admissible to attack the credibility of an adult and the court is satisfied that admission in evidence is necessary for a fair determination of the issue of guilt or innocence.	**(d) Juvenile Adjudications**. Evidence of a juvenile adjudication is admissible under this rule only if: (1) it is offered in a criminal case; (2) the adjudication was of a witness other than the defendant; (3) an adult's conviction for that offense would be admissible to attack the adult's credibility; and (4) admitting the evidence is necessary to fairly determine guilt or innocence.
(e) Pendency of appeal. The pendency of an appeal therefrom does not render evidence of a conviction inadmissible. Evidence of the pendency of an appeal is admissible.	**(e) Pendency of an Appeal**. A conviction that satisfies this rule is admissible even if an appeal is pending. Evidence of the pendency is also admissible.

Analytical Template for Rule 609

At first blush, Rule 609 is a lengthy and daunting rule, but when the proper analytical template is applied, it is actually fairly easy to understand and apply. As a starting point, it is important to remember the following organizational factors about Rule 609: (1) it differentiates between felonies and *crimen falsi* crimes; (2) it treats ordinary witnesses and criminal defendants differently; and (3) it contains a relatively strict time limit for offenses. This section will examine each of these factors in turn.

(1) *Felonies v. Crimen Falsi Crimes.* Rule 609 addresses two categories of crimes. The first is crimes "punishable by death or imprisonment in excess of one year under the law under which the witness was convicted." In most jurisdictions, these crimes constitute felonies. The key is not whether a jurisdiction has categorized an offense as a low-level felony or a high-level misdemeanor, but rather the maximum potential punishment for the offense. With respect to the first category of offenses, the judge is permitted to exercise discretion in deciding whether to admit evidence of conviction.

The second category is crimes that require "proof or admission of an act of dishonesty or false statement by the witness." These offenses are known as *crimen falsi* crimes. Crimen falsi crimes are those whose elements include some form of dishonesty or false statement, such as "perjury or subornation of perjury, false statement, criminal fraud, embezzlement or false pretenses, or any other offense, in the nature of crimen falsi the commission of which involves some element of untruthfulness, deceit or falsification."[10] It is important to distinguish crimen falsi crimes from other crimes — such as theft, robbery or burglary — in which proof of falsehood is not an element of proof. This is so even if the individual was untruthful or dishonest while committing the crime. With respect to *crimen falsi* crimes, the judge is not permitted to exercise discretion in deciding whether to admit evidence of conviction: all *crimen falsi* convictions that meet Rule 609's time limit are admissible.

(2) *Ordinary Witnesses v. the Accused in a Criminal Case.* For an ordinary witness, defined in the rule as "a witness other than the accused," evidence of serious offenses is admissible subject to a Rule 403 balancing test. This means that evidence of these convictions is presumptively admissible, unless for some reason the probative value of the evidence is substantially outweighed by the danger of unfair prejudice. Evidence of *crimen falsi* convictions is admissible without a balancing test, provided that the convictions occurred within Rule 609's time limit.

Even if he testifies on his own behalf, the accused in a criminal case is in a different position from all other witnesses at trial. This is because his freedom is at stake. Thus, Rule 609 shifts the balancing test for the accused's past convictions for serious offenses. The accused's convictions are admissible only if the judge "determines that the probative value of admitting this evidence outweighs its prejudicial effect to the accused." This provision erects a high bar for admission and is exactly the opposite of Rule 403's presumptive approach to admissibility. The enhanced balancing test applies only to convictions for serious offenses. The accused is treated like any other witness with respect to the admissibility of *crimen falsi* convictions: evidence of such convictions is admissible without a balancing test.

(3) *The 10-year Time Limit.* Rule 609 imposes a 10-year time limit on convictions. This is calculated from the date of conviction or release from confinement, whichever is later. With proper notice to the opposing party, a party can petition the

---

[10] S. Rep. No. 93-122, at 14 (1977).

court to admit a conviction more than 10 years old. Rule 609 imposes an enhanced balancing test on older convictions, permitting admissibility only if "the court determines, in the interests of justice, that the probative value of the conviction supported by specific facts and circumstances substantially outweighs its prejudicial effect."

Proving Convictions under Rule 609

Rule 609 does not specify the form of proof for convictions. One method of impeaching with a prior conviction is to ask the witness about the conviction on cross examination. Another method is to introduce a public record of the conviction. The name of the crime and the date of commission, as well as the punishment, are sufficient for impeachment. In fact, it is considered improper to explore the details of the crime.

Bias and Motivational Impeachment

One of the most effective ways to impeach a witness is to demonstrate that the witness is biased against a party or has an ulterior motive to testify. According to the Supreme Court,

> Bias is a term used in the "common law of evidence" to describe the relationship between a party and a witness which might lead the witness to slant, unconsciously or otherwise, his testimony in favor of or against a party. Bias may be induced by a witness' like, dislike, or fear of a party, or by the witness' self-interest. Proof of bias is almost always relevant because the jury, as finder of fact and weigher of credibility, has historically been entitled to assess all evidence which might bear on the accuracy and truth of a witness' testimony. The "common law of evidence" allowed the showing of bias by extrinsic evidence, while requiring the cross-examiner to "take the answer of the witness" with respect to less favored forms of impeachment.[11]

Such impeachment has always been permissible at trial, but it is not specifically written into the Federal Rules of Evidence. Nonetheless, because of the importance and potential constitutional implications of impeachment on bias or motive, the Supreme Court has held that "it is permissible to impeach a witness by showing his bias under the Federal Rules of Evidence just as it was permissible to do so before their adoption."[12]

Bias can be shown on cross-examination. It can also be shown through the introduction of extrinsic evidence tending to show the nature of the witness's bias or his motive to shade or slant his testimony against one of the parties at trial.

---

[11] United States v. Abel, 469 U.S. 45, 52 (1984) (citations omitted).

[12] *Id.*

Impeachment for Defects in Capacity

Impeachment for defective capacity is not contained in the Federal Rules of Evidence but is a core method of impeachment. It relates closely to witness competency under Rule 601. Recall that the law has replaced categorical declarations of witness incompetence with a presumption of competence, coupled with cross-examination to expose defects in the witness's ability to observe, recall and testify.

Common defects in capacity include the influence of drugs or alcohol, vision problems, mental illness, diseases or accidents affecting observational capacity or memory, and structural impairments (such as the witness's inability to see an event because of buildings or other obstacles in the way). Defects in capacity can be shown on cross examination or through the introduction of extrinsic evidence.

Impeachment by Contradiction

Impeachment by contradiction is another mode of impeachment that is not contained in the Federal Rules of Evidence but is still an important part of trial practice. This mode of impeachment is explained in the following excerpt from a legal journal.

Christopher W. Behan, *The Thrill and Excitement of Impeachment by Contradiction*
ARMY LAW., Oct. 2004, at 10–16

Impeachment by contradiction, or impeachment by specific contradiction as it is sometimes known, is one of the five primary modes of impeachment at trial. In concept, impeachment by contradiction is rather simple. When a witness makes an assertion of fact, the attorney can impeach him by showing that the fact is not true; this can be done either by cross examining the witness, using extrinsic evidence, or both. For example, if the witness testifies that an incident occurred at "high noon at the OK Corral," the attorney can show by cross-examination or by calling witnesses that the incident actually occurred at midnight at the Circle K convenience store. If the fact-finder believes the counterproof offered by the attorney, the witness has been impeached in two ways. First, the fact-finder will believe that the witness lied or made a mistake on the specific fact contradicted. But second, and perhaps more significantly, the fact-finder may begin to doubt everything else the witness has said. Because the attorney can use extrinsic evidence rather than simply relying on cross-examination, impeachment by contradiction can be devastating to a witness's credibility. . . .

In order for an attorney to use impeachment by contradiction, the witness must make a statement of fact that is significant to the case at hand. The normal rule, drawn from the common law, is that impeachment by contradiction should not be used for collateral matters. Thus, if a complaining witness testifies that on the morning of the alleged rape she had oatmeal for breakfast, defense counsel would probably not be permitted to use impeachment by contradiction to demonstrate that the witness actually had cornflakes. A good rule of thumb is that the statement should either relate closely to the facts of the case or be so closely tied to the witness's credibility that impeachment by contradiction is necessary. The statement can arise either on direct examination or cross-examination.

Counsel should be particularly alert for broad, gratuitous statements in which a witness attempts to bolster his own character or credibility. For example, in *United States v. Trimper*,[13] the accused, an Air Force JAG captain, was on trial for cocaine use. He made a broad statement on direct that he had never in his life used cocaine. This permitted trial counsel to introduce extrinsic evidence as impeachment by contradiction that the accused had gone to an off-base hospital and requested a private urinalysis to screen for cocaine metabolites. . . .

Listen at trial for broad factual assertions on direct that cry out for impeachment by contradiction. Words such as "always," "never," or "not since [insert date or event]" are statements of fact that, in many cases, beg for contradiction. Counsel who have carefully prepared their case will recognize these phrases as the red flags that they are.

Cross-examination can also be a fruitful source for impeachment by contradiction opportunities. Consider the O.J. Simpson trial, when F. Lee Bailey set up Mark Furman, the LAPD detective, for impeachment by getting Mr. Furman to state unequivocally on cross-examination that he had never used a particular racial epithet during the previous ten years.[14] The defense was then able to call witnesses who testified that they had heard Mr. Furman use that epithet within the ten-year period. . . .

In most cases, an attorney using impeachment by contradiction will seek to introduce extrinsic evidence to complete the impeachment. It is critical to remember, however, that the rules of evidence still apply. A document that impeaches a factual assertion made by a witness, for example, is not independently admissible in evidence unless it has been properly authenticated under Section IX of the [Federal Rules of Evidence]. Hearsay rules, privileges, and [Rule 412] still apply to impeachment by contradiction evidence.

II.   CASES, DISCUSSION QUESTIONS AND PROBLEMS

UNITED STATES v. McMILLON
United States Court of Appeals, Fourth Circuit
14 F.3d 948 (4th Cir. 1994)

Julia McMillon was in charge of a crack distribution organization in the Washington, D.C. area. Her indictment and arrest resulted from a domino-effect series of arrests and cooperation agreements involving individuals below her in the organization, each of whom provided evidence regarding people above them. . . .

---

[13] [n.8] 28 M.J. 460 (C.M.A. 1989).

[14] [n.25] *See Live Report: Simpson Trial* (CNN television broadcast, July 27, 1995) (transcript #120-1) (LEXIS, Newsgroup All). In the transcript of the court hearing, Mr. Gerald Uelman, a member of O.J. Simpson's defense team, told the judge that the impeachment witnesses were intended not to prove that Mr. Furman was a racist, but rather that he was a liar. *See id.*

McMillon had left the Washington, D.C. area in early 1989 and moved to Miami following a police raid on her house in Maryland. In the late spring of 1990, she returned to the D.C. area, accompanied by Jacques Beckwith. McMillon indicated to Toni Williams, whom she had known since 1980 and out of whose house she began to sell drugs in 1987, that she had returned to do some more business, and Williams agreed to act as a broker and finder for McMillon.

In the months covered by the conspiracy charge, the basic procedure was for Beckwith to travel to Miami to obtain cocaine and return with it to Maryland; once a supply arrived, Toni Williams would inform Hammonds or others, who would then come to Ms. Williams' house for the transaction. McMillon herself never handled the cocaine in plain sight; this job usually was handled by Beckwith or Ms. Williams in the living room, while McMillon remained in the upstairs bedroom where she would measure out the quantity sold and count the money. Hammonds would purchase an eighth or quarter kilo of cocaine, which he then would cook into crack and separate into small, street-level quantities for further sale. After Hammonds' arrest, he provided information against Rodney and Toni Williams and Beckwith, and these three named McMillon, eventually testifying against her at trial.

Finally, McMillon assigns error to the district court's ruling preventing her attorney from cross examining Jacques Beckwith on certain topics. As an evidentiary matter, we review the district court's ruling only to determine whether it has abused its discretion. United States v. Gravely, 840 F.2d 1156, 1162 (4th Cir. 1988).

At a bench conference directly prior to cross examination of Beckwith, defense counsel indicated that he intended to obtain testimony that Beckwith used drugs in order to force people to engage in sexual acts with him and that he used and manipulated them based on their addiction and his access to drugs. That the people allegedly manipulated were men is worth noting, for a review of the transcript discloses that it was part of the defense strategy to highlight Beckwith's sexuality as part of the effort to impeach his credibility. The government objected to this line of questioning, and the district judge sustained the objection.

Under Federal Rule of Evidence 611(b), "cross-examination should be limited to the subject matter of the direct examination and matters affecting the credibility of the witness." When credibility is the issue, as in this instance, under Rule 608(b), specific instances of the conduct of a witness may be inquired into on cross-examination only if probative of truthfulness or untruthfulness.

In a criminal context, cross-examination is an important element of the right of confrontation. Smith v. Illinois, 390 U.S. 129, 88 S. Ct. 748, 19 L. Ed. 2d 956 (1968). But while it is "essential to a fair trial," United States v. Cole, 622 F.2d 98 (4th Cir.), cert. denied, 449 U.S. 956, 101 S. Ct. 363, 66 L. Ed. 2d 221 (1980), the trial court is vested with broad discretion to control the mode of interrogation and presentation of evidence to insure that witnesses are treated fairly and the search for truth is not impaired by presentation of extraneous, prejudicial or confusing material. United States v. Gravely, 840 F.2d 1156 (4th Cir. 1988). Indeed, "there is a duty to protect [the witness] from questions which go beyond the bounds of proper cross-examination merely to harass, annoy or humiliate him." Alford v. United States, 282 U.S. 687, 694, 51 S. Ct. 218, 75 L. Ed. 624 (1931).

McMillon argues on appeal that the prohibited inquiry met these standards because it was probative of Beckwith's truthfulness. We disagree. The cornerstone for McMillon's argument is the contention that Beckwith portrayed himself in his direct testimony as being manipulated by McMillon. This, it is argued, allows the defense to show that Beckwith himself is a manipulator. The first difficulty lies in the fact that a review of the transcript shows that Beckwith admired and at times adulated McMillon as a wealthy, successful black woman, not that he portrayed himself as manipulated by her. The second difficulty with this approach is that it simply strays too far from the matter at hand: the testimony regarding Beckwith's sexual life is not probative of his character for truthfulness. Instead, it is exactly the type of cross-examination strategy, warned against in Gravely and Alford, that impairs the search for the truth and harasses, annoys or humiliates the witness in the process.

UNITED STATES v. BRACKEEN
United States Court Of Appeals, Ninth Circuit
969 F.2d 827 (9th Cir. 1992)

PER CURIAM:

This court has convened en banc to determine whether bank robbery necessarily involves "dishonesty," as that term is used in Federal Rule of Evidence 609(a)(2). The question arises in the context of whether a witness can be impeached by evidence of prior convictions. Faced with intra-circuit precedents which provide irreconcilably conflicting answers to the question, the original panel called sua sponte for en banc review. . . .

FACTS AND PROCEEDINGS BELOW

Robert Nello Brackeen robbed three different banks, one bank a day on each of three separate days in July 1990. In the first robbery, Brackeen and an accomplice, Jermaine Moore, presented a threatening note to a teller. Bank surveillance photos showed Moore with a pistol, which he pointed at the teller. During the robbery, Brackeen and Moore acted in close proximity to each other. In the other two robberies, Brackeen was unarmed and apparently acted alone.

Brackeen was charged in a single indictment with one count of aiding and abetting an armed bank robbery, in violation of 18 U.S.C. §§ 2, 2113(a), 2113(d) (1988), and two counts of unarmed bank robbery, in violation of 18 U.S.C. § 2113(a). On September 24, 1990, Brackeen pleaded guilty to both unarmed bank robberies. On October 2, 1990, Brackeen went to trial on count one of the indictment, aiding and abetting Moore in the armed bank robbery. He claimed he did not know Moore had a gun.

On the second day of the two-day trial, Brackeen indicated he would testify, and objected before taking the stand to the use for impeachment of his guilty pleas to the two unarmed bank robberies. The court reserved its ruling on the objection until after Brackeen testified. Brackeen was the sole defense witness. On cross-examination, the court allowed impeachment with the guilty pleas.

The trial court's basis for admitting the prior guilty pleas as impeachment evidence was Federal Rule of Evidence 609(a)(2), which allows impeachment of a defendant by any crime involving "dishonesty or false statement." The court expressly refused to admit the pleas under Rule 609(a)(1), which allows impeachment using any felony "if the court determines that the probative value of admitting this evidence outweighs its prejudicial effect to the accused. . . . " The court stated: "No. I don't think under Rule 609(a)(1) that I would let it in. . . . I don't think I could make that analysis under Rule 609(a)(1) so I'm going to base my ruling on Rule 609(a)(2) that this is a crime involving dishonesty and the government has an absolute right to use it to impeach him." The court made this ruling after reading aloud relevant portions of United States v. Kinslow, 860 F.2d 963, 968 (9th Cir. 1988), cert. denied, 493 U.S. 829, 110 S. Ct. 96, 107 L. Ed. 2d 60 (1989).

Brackeen appeals, claiming the impeachment was improper because . . . (2) the guilty pleas were to bank robbery, a crime that does not involve "dishonesty or false statement" as required by Rule 609(a)(2). The original panel called for en banc proceedings to decide the second issue, and the full court granted en banc review.

ANALYSIS

Rule 609 provides in part: [Court quotes FRE 609(a)]

Brackeen's bank robberies did not involve any "false statements," id., and were not "actually committed by fraudulent or deceitful means." United States v. Glenn, 667 F.2d 1269, 1273 (9th Cir. 1982). Accordingly, the only issue in this case is whether bank robbery is per se a crime of "dishonesty" under Rule 609, regardless of the means by which it is perpetrated. Our circuit has not spoken with one voice on this question. Compare, e.g., Kinslow, 860 F.2d at 968 (holding armed robbery is per se a crime of "dishonesty" under Fed. R. Evid. 609(a)(2),) with, e.g., Glenn, 667 F.2d at 1272-73 (holding bank robbery is not per se a crime of "dishonesty" under Fed. R. Evid.609(a)(2)). We now disapprove and reject Kinslow on this issue, and adopt the holding in Glenn: bank robbery is not per se a crime of "dishonesty" under Federal Rule of Evidence 609(a)(2).

Our first step in interpreting any statute or rule is to consider the plain meaning of the provision in question. Often, this will be the end of the analysis, because the words of the provision allow but one interpretation and preclude others.

Unfortunately, "dishonesty" has more than one meaning. In the dictionary, and in everyday use, "dishonesty" has two meanings, one of which includes, and one of which excludes, crimes such as bank robbery. In its broader meaning, "dishonesty" is defined as a breach of trust, a "lack of . . . probity or integrity in principle," "lack of fairness," or a "disposition to . . . betray." Webster's Third New International Dictionary 650 (1986 unabridged ed.). This dictionary states, under the heading "synonyms," that "dishonest may apply to any breach of honesty or trust, as lying, deceiving, cheating, stealing, or defrauding." Id. Bank robbery fits within this definition of "dishonesty" because it is a betrayal of principles of fairness and probity, a breach of community trust, like stealing.

In its narrower meaning, however, "dishonesty" is defined as deceitful behavior, a "disposition to defraud . . . [or] deceive," id., or a "disposition to lie, cheat, or defraud," Black's Law Dictionary 421 (5th ed. 1979). Bank robbery does not fit within this definition of "dishonesty" because it is a crime of violent, not deceitful, taking. Everyday usage mirrors the dictionary: we use "dishonesty" narrowly to refer to a liar, and broadly to refer to a thief.

Fortunately, we are not operating in a vacuum: while nothing in the text of Rule 609 indicates precisely what Congress meant when it used the term "dishonesty," we find guidance in the legislative history of the rule. As the Supreme Court has stated in another context, "we begin by considering the extent to which the text of Rule 609 answers the question before us. Concluding that the text is ambiguous . . . we then seek guidance from legislative history. . . ." Green v. Bock Laundry Machine Co., 490 U.S. 504, 508-09, 109 S. Ct. 1981, 104 L. Ed. 2d 557 (1989). We look to the Advisory Committee's Note to the Rule, and to the relevant House and Senate Conference Committee Reports, which are legitimate sources of legislative history. See id. at 511-24.

The legislative history of Rule 609 makes clear that Congress used the term "dishonesty" in the narrower sense, to mean only those crimes which involve deceit. The House Conference Committee Report on Rule 609 states:

By the phrase "dishonesty and false statement" the Conference means crimes such as perjury or subornation of perjury, false statement, criminal fraud, embezzlement, or false pretense, or any other offense in the nature of crimen falsi, the commission of which involves some element of deceit, untruthfulness, or falsification bearing on the accused's propensity to testify truthfully.

Fed. R. Evid. 609 Advisory Committee's Note (Notes of Conference Committee, House Report No. 93-1597) (emphasis added). The Senate Judiciary Committee Report contains substantially the same language. Id. (Notes of Committee of the Judiciary, Senate Report No. 93-1277) ("crimen falsi . . . untruthfulness, deceit, or falsification").

Bank robbery is not "in the nature of crimen falsi." Black's Law Dictionary defines "crimen falsi" as follows: "Term generally refers to crimes in the nature of perjury or subornation of perjury, false statement, criminal fraud, embezzlement, false pretense, or any other offense which involves some element of deceitfulness, untruthfulness, or falsification bearing on witness' propensity to testify truthfully." Black's Law Dictionary 335 (5th ed. 1979).

Other circuits have reached similar conclusions. The Tenth Circuit has stated:

Of course, robbery, burglary and theft are ordinarily considered to be dishonest, but the term as used in Rule 609(a)(2) is more restricted. We think the legislative history of this provision shows that Congress intended to limit the term to prior convictions involving some element of deceit, untruthfulness, or falsification which would tend to show that an accused would be likely to testify untruthfully. United States v. Seamster, 568 F.2d 188, 190 (10th Cir. 1978) (emphasis added).

See United States v. Farmer, 923 F.2d 1557, 1567 (11th Cir. 1991) ("It is established in this Circuit . . . that crimes such as theft, robbery, or shoplifting do not involve 'dishonesty or false statement' within the meaning of Rule 609(a)(2)" (quotation omitted)); McHenry v. Chadwick, 896 F.2d 184, 188 (6th Cir. 1990) ("shoplifting does not fall into the category" described by Rule 609(a)(2)); Altobello v. Borden Confectionary Products, Inc., 872 F.2d 215, 216-17 (7th Cir. 1989) ("agreeing with those dicta" from cases such as Glenn); United States v. Yeo, 739 F.2d 385, 388 (8th Cir. 1984) ("we believe that the better view is that theft is not a crime of 'dishonesty or false statement' as that term is used in Rule 609(a)(2)"); United States v. Lipscomb, 702 F.2d 1049, 1057 nn.32-33 (D.C. Cir. 1983) (prior conviction for larceny not admissible under Rule 609(a)(2)); Shows v. M/V Red Eagle, 695 F.2d 114, 119 (5th Cir. 1983) ("admissibility of a prior bank robbery conviction for impeachment purposes requires the balancing exercise of Rule 609(a)(1)"); United States v. Grandmont, 680 F.2d 867, 871 & n.3 (1st Cir. 1982) ("the robberies were not admissible under 609(a)(2)"); United States v. Cunningham, 638 F.2d 696, 698-99 (4th Cir. 1981) (noting "Rule 609(a)(2) . . . is confined to a narrow class of crimes," and holding a state conviction for writing "worthless checks" is not admissible under Rule 609(a)(2)); United States v. Hawley, 554 F.2d 50, 53 n.7 (2d Cir. 1977) (dicta) (noting an "exhaustive opinion" by the D.C. Circuit concluding robbery was not a crime of " 'dishonesty or false statement' within the meaning of 609(a)(2)," but not reaching the issue); but see United States v. Del Toro Soto, 676 F.2d 13, 18 (1st Cir. 1982) ("The grand larceny conviction could certainly have been introduced under Federal Rule of Evidence 609(a)(2) on the general question of the defendant's credibility").

CONCLUSION

Congress intended Rule 609(a)(2) to apply only to those crimes that factually or by definition entail some element of misrepresentation or deceit, and not to " 'those crimes which, bad though they are, do not carry with them a tinge of falsification.' " Glenn, 667 F.2d at 1273 (quoting United States v. Ortega, 561 F.2d 803, 806 (9th Cir. 1977)). We must follow Congress' intent. See Green, 490 U.S. at 508 ("Our task in deciding this case . . . is not to fashion the rule we deem desirable but to identify the rule that Congress fashioned"). Brackeen's conviction is REVERSED, and the case is REMANDED for a new trial.

DISCUSSION QUESTIONS

1. Do you agree with the 4th Circuit in *McMillon* that evidence regarding someone's sexual life is not probative of character for truthfulness? Why or why not?

2. What is the relationship between FRE 611 and FRE 608 when it comes to cross-examining a witness? What role does the judge play?

3. In *Brackeen*, why did the district court deny the government's effort to introduce the convictions under FRE 609(a)(1)? Doesn't the evidence meet the standard of FRE 609(a)(1)?

4. Do you agree with the *Brackeen* court's narrow reading of "dishonesty?" Why or why not?

PROBLEMS

Problem 15-1. Minnie Phalzhud has been called to testify as a witness in an automobile accident case. Ms. Phalzhud was a passenger in Paul Plaintiff's SUV, which hit Dan Defendant's pickup truck from behind at an intersection. Plaintiff alleged that Defendant's brake lights were defective and he had no warning when Defendant came to a complete stop. Ms. Phalzhud intends to testify at trial that she did not see Defendant's brake lights flash.

Evaluate the following additional facts and determine whether, and in what form, they could be used at trial on the issue of credibility.

1. Ms. Phalzhud and Mr. Plaintiff have been dating for several years and are, in fact, engaged to be married.

2. Ms. Phalzhud did not see Defendant's brake lights because she was typing a text message into her cellphone at the time of the accident. Carl Contractor, who was parked at the intersection in the next lane waiting for the traffic light to change, saw her texting at the time of the accident. He also saw that the traffic light was red and that Defendant's brake lights were on.

3. When Ms. Phalzhud was a student at Calamity State University, she was academically dismissed for failing to complete a mandatory Freshman Ethics course at the university.

4. Ms. Phalzhud was fired from her previous two jobs for taking sick days off when she was not actually sick. In both cases, other employees turned her in.

5. A private investigator has learned that Ms. Phalzhud has cheated on Mr. Plaintiff three times, including the night before the accident.

6. Wilma Witness, an acquaintance of Ms. Phalzhud, is aware that Ms. Phalzhud has a reputation for being a "frickin' liar" in the community, and also has an opinion, based on Ms. Phalzhud cheating on Mr. Plaintiff, that she is a dishonest person.

Problem 15-2. Charlie "Killer" Ross is a long-haul trucker who also happens to be a cannibal. Over the years, he has developed a standard modus operandi for luring victims into his truck: He walks into a truckstop with a banjo, starts playing a bluegrass song, and offers free bluegrass CDs to the first person who can recite in order all the songs on the O Brother Where Art Thou soundtrack. When he gets a winner, he invites the person to accompany him to his truck to get the CD. There is, of course, no CD. If there are no witnesses in the area, Ross injects the victim with a knockout drug, shoves him or her into his truck, and drives off to a secluded location, where he kills, cooks and eats his victim. If there are witnesses in the area, Ross pretends to look for the CD and then regretfully announces that he must be out of them.

Ross has been caught and convicted three times for luring victims into his truck, murdering them and eating them. In each case, he received a light sentence by convincing the judge that he was sorry, had learned his lesson, and would never do it again.

This time is different. The Calamity State Police caught him in the act of dismembering and cooking a law student from the Calamity State University School of Law. At Ross's trial for murder and cannibalism, he is the sole witness for the defense. The prosecution wants to impeach him with evidence of his prior convictions. The judge applies the balancing test of FRE 609(a)(1) and refuses to permit the questions. The prosecutor next attempts to get the evidence in under FRE 609(a)(2). What are the prosecution's best arguments for using FRE 609(a)(2)? What are the best counterarguments?

Introduction to Impeachment: Quick Hits

- Impeachment is calling into question a witness's believability or credibility.

- The five traditional modes of impeachment include untruthful character, bias, prior inconsistent statement, defects in capacity and contradiction.

- Rule 608 permits attacks on any witness's character for truthfulness. The form of evidence is reputation or opinion testimony, and cross-examination on specific instances of conduct related to truthfulness is permitted. Rule 608 prohibits bolstering a witness's credibility before it has been attacked.

- Rule 609 allows the use of prior convictions to attack a witness's character for truthfulness. The rule permits evidence of felonies or crimen falsi crimes within a 10-year window. Ordinary witnesses and criminal defendants are treated differently under the rules.

- When impeaching, parties can use cross-examination, extrinsic evidence, to introduce evidence of bias or motive, defective capacity, or contradiction.

Chapter References

CHRISTOPHER B. MUELLER & LAIRD C. KIRKPATRICK, EVIDENCE §§ 6.16–6.39 (4th ed. 2009).

GLEN WEISSENBERGER & JAMES J. DUANE, FEDERAL RULES OF EVIDENCE: RULES, LEGISLATIVE HISTORY, COMMENTARY AND AUTHORITY §§ 607–09 (6th ed. 2009).

JACK B. WEINSTEIN & MARGARET A. BERGER, WEINSTEIN'S FEDERAL EVIDENCE §§ 607–09 (Joseph M. McLaughlin ed., Matthew Bender 2d ed. 1997).

KENNETH S. BROUN, MCCORMICK ON EVIDENCE §§ 33–50 (6th ed. 2006).

STEVEN GOODE & OLIN GUY WELLBORN III, COURTROOM HANDBOOK ON FEDERAL EVIDENCE Ch. 5 (West 2010).

III. APPLICATION EXERCISE

Impeaching Witnesses at Trial

Cross-examination and impeachment are at the heart of the adversarial trial system. A well-planned and effectively executed impeachment can discredit a witness and knock the legs out from under an opponent's case. As part of discovery and case analysis, attorneys actively seek information that could cast doubt on the believability of a witness's story or the witness's personal credibility.

During the trial preparation process, attorneys prepare their impeaching materials. It is necessary to decide whether to conduct the impeachment on cross-examination, call an impeaching character witness, or offer extrinsic proof of a relationship, motive or contradictory fact. Attorneys should also anticipate attacks against their own witnesses and make plans to object, call rebuttal witnesses or offer other counterproof to combat their opponent's impeachment efforts.

In addition to planning the impeachment itself, the attorney should draft any necessary limiting instructions for the jury. Finally, the attorney should integrate the impeachment into the closing argument, explaining to the jury how the impeachment makes the witness less worthy of belief.

The Exercise

Objective: To demonstrate proficiency in impeaching a witness using a variety of techniques at trial.

Factual Scenario: Use Problem 15-1 for the basic facts of this exercise. Assume that Ms. Phalzhud has testified on direct in the plaintiff's case that she did not see Defendant's brake lights and that the traffic light was green.

Advance Preparation. For the defense, prepare a cross-examination of Ms. Phalzhud focusing on permissible impeachment under Rule 608 and other impeachment doctrines (bias, motive to testify falsely) discussed in your reading materials. Prepare a brief (2-3) minute direct examination of Carl Contractor (impeachment by contradiction) and Wilma Witness (character for untruthfulness). For the plaintiff, prepare to defend your witness from attack by making proper objections to the defense efforts to impeach. Prepare also to cross-examine Wilma Witness with specific instances of conduct pertaining to Ms. Phalzhud's truthfulness. Make up some specific instances of conduct for your cross-examination.

In-Class Exercise. Students will play the following roles: defense attorney, witness, plaintiff's attorney, and judge. The professor will conduct a brief direct examination of Ms. Phalzhud, following which the defense attorney will cross. The defense will then call Carl Contractor to the stand, followed by Wilma Witness. The plaintiff's attorney will cross.

Chapter 16

IMPEACHMENT BY PRIOR INCONSISTENT STATEMENTS: RULE 613

Chapter Objectives:

- Introduce and explain Rule 613 and the basic theory and concept of impeachment by prior inconsistent statements
- Analyze and discuss issues pertaining to Rules 613 and impeachment by prior inconsistent statements
- Apply the concepts from this chapter in a courtroom application exercise

I. BACKGROUND AND EXPLANATORY MATERIAL

One of the most common forms of impeachment at trial is impeachment by prior inconsistent statements under Rule 613. The text of the rule follows:

Through Dec. 1, 2011	After Dec. 1, 2011
Rule 613. Prior Statements of Witnesses	**Rule 613. Witness's Prior Statement**
(a) Examining witness concerning prior statement. In examining a witness concerning a prior statement made by the witness, whether written or not, the statement need not be shown nor its contents disclosed to the witness at that time, but on request the same shall be shown or disclosed to opposing counsel.	**(a) Showing or Disclosing the Statement During Examination**. When examining a witness about the witness's prior statement, a party need not show it or disclose its contents to the witness. But the party must, on request, show it or disclose its contents to an adverse party's attorney.
(b) Extrinsic evidence of prior inconsistent statement of witness. Extrinsic evidence of a prior inconsistent statement by a witness is not admissible unless the witness is afforded an opportunity to explain or deny the same and the opposite party is afforded an opportunity to interrogate the witness thereon, or the interests of justice otherwise require. This provision does not apply to admissions of a party-opponent as defined in rule 801(d)(2).	**(b) Extrinsic Evidence of a Prior Inconsistent Statement**. Extrinsic evidence of a witness's prior inconsistent statement is admissible only if the witness is given an opportunity to explain or deny the statement and an adverse party is given an opportunity to examine the witness about it, or if justice so requires. This subdivision (b) does not apply to an opposing party's statement under Rule 801(d)(2).

The Concept

The rationale for this form of impeachment is that a witness who makes inconsistent statements is unworthy of belief: inconsistent statements are indicative of a witness's unreliability, instability, or outright deception.

As a threshold matter, it is important to understand what is meant by the terms "prior statement" and "inconsistent statement." A "prior statement" is one made by the witness before trial. There is no requirement that the prior statement be under oath or subject to any formal acknowledgements of accuracy or validity by its maker. Furthermore, there is no requirement that the statement be reduced to writing or recorded using any form of audiovisual equipment.

The following is a non-exclusive list of types of prior statements:

1. A casual remark made by a witness to another person prior to trial.

2. A verbal statement made to a police officer or investigator.

3. An audio or audiovisual recording of a verbal statement made to a police officer or investigator.

4. A sworn statement, reduced to writing and signed under oath.

5. A deposition, either transcribed into writing or recorded using audiovisual equipment.

6. A blog entry or written statement made on a social networking site.

7. Statements made in e-mails, letters, and diary or journal entries.

8. Written entries on official forms or applications.

An "inconsistent statement" is determined by comparing a witness's prior statement with the testimony actually given in court. Rule 613 seeks for true inconsistencies on material matters. An actual inconsistency exists if, "taken as a whole, either by what it says or by what it omits to say affords some indication that the fact was different from the testimony of the witness whom it sought to contradict."[1] Inconsistencies on trivial or collateral matters, such as whether the witness had oatmeal or cold cereal on the day of the incident, do not truly impeach the witness and have limited probative value at trial.

A witness's prior statements can be directly inconsistent with in-court statements, or they can be inconsistent by omission or implication. A prior statement is inconsistent by omission with in-court testimony if it is missing material details that the witness testified to in court, of the type one would expect to be included in the prior statement. Similarly, an in-court statement that conveniently leaves out important details found in a prior statement is inconsistent by implication with the prior statement. If a witness testifies in court about an event, but previously claimed to have no memory of the event, such testimony would be inconsistent with the prior statement.

It is important to distinguish inconsistent omissions from actual lapses in memory. If a witness at trial experiences a genuine failure of memory concerning a prior event or statement, this is not an inconsistency; anyone can forget, especially in the tense atmosphere of the courtroom. The appropriate in-court remedy for a memory lapse is to refresh the witness's recollection under Rule 612, or, failing that, to introduce the prior statement under Rule 803(5), the hearsay exception for past recollection recorded.

Impeaching witnesses with prior inconsistent statements is a dramatic and effective technique to use at trial; it is difficult for a witness to run away from his own words. The more stark and significant the inconsistency, the greater its impeachment value at trial. The theatrical value cannot be underestimated: attorneys enjoy doing it, jurors love watching it, and witnesses hate enduring it.

Attorneys who are involved in litigation should master impeachment by inconsistent statements as a matter of fundamental competence. The possibility of finding and exploiting inconsistent statements forms much of the justification for the pre-trial discovery rules in both civil and criminal cases, as well as a reason to depose witnesses and obtain their prior sworn and unsworn statements. Attorneys who understand the concept and can apply the techniques used in this form of impeachment will do a better job not only at trial, but also in case investigation and case analysis prior to trial.

---

[1] United States v. Barile, 286 F.3d 749, 755 (4th Cir. 2002).

The Method

During case investigation and analysis, attorneys gain a thorough knowledge of the facts of the case and the expected testimony of each potential witness. Through the process of discovery and investigation, attorneys often identify in advance areas of potential testimonial inconsistency for a witness. Once these areas are identified, an attorney can prepare in advance for impeachment. Sometimes, of course, a witness's inconsistent statement at trial comes as a complete surprise to all parties. An attorney who has learned her case and prepared to examine each witness will be prepared to exploit opportunities that arise at trial to impeach a witness with prior inconsistent statements or omissions.

There are three primary ways to impeach a witness with prior inconsistent statements: (1) an intrinsic impeachment (in other words, an impeachment that occurs *during* an examination of that witness) using the witness's prior inconsistent written and/or recorded statements; (2) an intrinsic impeachment in which the witness is questioned about the omission of important information from prior written and/or recorded statements; and (3) extrinsic proof of a prior inconsistent statement by introducing a document or calling another witness to testify as to the inconsistency. This section discusses each of these techniques in turn.

Intrinsic Impeachment with Prior Inconsistent Statement

This method is useful for all types of prior inconsistent statements, but it is particularly valuable when the witness's prior statement has been sworn, transcribed, written or recorded. The more formal the process, the better, because the formal steps taken to preserve, acknowledge or validate the prior statement can be used to magnify its significance at trial. This type of impeachment usually occurs on cross-examination of an opposing or hostile witness, although Rule 607 would also permit its use on direct examination. There are three components to the in-court confrontation, each of which will be discussed in turn: (1) commit the witness to her in-court testimony; (2) credit or validate the prior statement; (3) confront with the inconsistency.

(1) *Commit.* The first step is to commit the witness to her in-court testimony. This is done by asking the witness to commit to the precise words she just used in court. The purpose of this step is to ensure that the witness cannot, when later confronted with the prior inconsistency, claim to have misspoken or to have been misunderstood in the courtroom.

(2) *Credit or Validate.* The second step is to credit or validate the prior statement. This is done by asking the witness questions about the circumstances surrounding the making of the earlier statement, including that the witness made the statement closer in time to the incident and that at the time of making the prior statement the witness had an interest in telling the truth and/or accurately recalling the incident. These questions "credit" or "validate" the prior statement, making it difficult for the witness to deny or explain away inconsistencies, and ensuring that the witness cannot legitimately claim to have misspoken or to have been misunderstood in the prior statement.

The first two steps — commit and credit — build a sense of drama in the courtroom, heightening the jurors' expectations that something important is about to happen.

(3) *Confront.* The third step provides a climax to the dramatic moment by confronting the witness, in the presence of the jury, with his own prior inconsistent words — words he has just validated and now cannot lightly dismiss or explain away. These words can be read aloud by the attorney, published on a screen using an overhead projector or presentation software such as Powerpoint or Sanction, or even be heard to come from the witness's own mouth if there is an audio or video recording of the prior statement. In fact, some commercial trial presentation software uses split-screen technology that permits an attorney to click a button and show the written transcript of the prior statement scrolling underneath a video of the witness giving testimony at a deposition.

To illustrate these techniques in action, we will use a civil personal injury case involving a car accident at the intersection. The accident occurred in Year One. The trial is taking place in Year Three. One of the critical issues at trial is whether the light at the intersection was red or green.

(Direct Examination)

Q: *What color was the light?*

A: *It was red.*

(The direct examination continues until it is complete.)

(Cross Examination)

Q: *On direct examination, you testified that the light was red, didn't you?* [COMMIT]

A: *Yes.*

Q: *Do you recall giving deposition testimony on this case in July of Year Two?* [CREDIT or VALIDATE]

A: *Yes.*

Q: *That deposition occurred in my office?*

A: *Yes.*

Q: *I was there?*

A: *Yes.*

Q: *The plaintiff's attorneys were there?*

A: *Yes.*

Q: *And there was a court reporter?*

A: *Yes.*

Q: *Before you testified, you took an oath, didn't you?*

A: *Yes.*

Q: *And in that oath, you swore to tell the truth?*

A: *Yes.*

Q: *And you knew it was important to tell the truth, didn't you?*

A: *Yes.*

Q: *We asked you if you were under the influence of any medication, alcohol, or drugs, correct?* [Note: it is wise practice to begin a deposition by asking these sorts of questions, not only to ensure that the witness is not under the influence, but also to have this colloquy available to use in a later impeachment.]

A: *Yes.*

Q: *And you said you were not under the influence of any of these substances?*

A: *Yes.*

Q: *And we asked you if you were feeling sick or unwell, didn't we?*

A: *Yes.*

Q: *And you said you were not?*

A: *Yes.*

Q: *You testified truthfully at the deposition?*

A: *Yes.*

Q: *You had the chance to tell your entire story, correct?*

A: *Yes.*

Q: *And you would agree with me that Year Two was closer in time to the accident than today is, correct?*

A: *Yes.*

Q: *And when the deposition was over, the court reporter sent you the transcript, right?*

A: *Yes.*

Q: *You had the opportunity to read it and make corrections, didn't you?*

A: *Yes.*

Q: *You signed the last page of the deposition, indicating that it was correct?*

A: *Yes.*

Q: *Now, I'd like to turn to page 55, lines 14 and 15 of the deposition. [The attorney approaches the witness and hands him a copy of the deposition.]*

Q: *Read silently to yourself as I read aloud lines 14 and 15. "Question: What color was the light? Answer: The light was green." Those were your words, correct?"* [CONFRONT] [Note that the <u>attorney</u> reads the questions and answers; this way the attorney maintains control of the witness and is able to put the appropriate inflection on both the question and the answer. Further note that if presentation software is available, the transcript could be projected on a screen for the jury to read silently as the attorney reads aloud, and, if it is available, an actual audio or videorecording of the witness could be played instead of the attorney reading the words aloud.]

A: *Yes.*

Q: *Let's move to another topic. . . .*

The foregoing example is relatively lengthy, illustrating a more formal approach to impeaching with a prior inconsistent statement. If there are numerous impeachments occurring during one witness's testimony, attorneys will often use a formal approach the first time, and a less formal approach the second time. Note what is missing from this impeachment is a sarcastic exchange with the witness such as, "Well, were you lying then, or are you lying now?" Although this sort of question is often asked during courtroom impeachments, it is objectionable because it is argumentative.

The same sort of impeachment can occur with far fewer steps, as illustrated below. Assume that the direct examination testimony is the same.

(Cross Examination)

Q: *You just testified on direct that the light was red?* [COMMIT]

A: *Yes.*

Q: *Do you recall giving a deposition in this case on July of Year Two?* [CREDIT/VALIDATE]

A: *Yes.*

Q: *In this deposition you swore to tell the truth?*

A: *Yes.*

Q: [handing the witness a copy of the deposition]. *I'm showing you your deposition, page 55, lines 14 and 15. Please read silently to yourself as I read aloud. "Question: What color was the light? Answer: It was green." Those were your words?* [CONFRONT]

A: *Yes.*

The same basic impeachment technique can be used even if the prior statement is less formal than a deposition. The key is to establish during the Credit/Validate stage the reliability of the prior statement. The example below uses a Facebook wall entry in illustration.

Q: *You just testified on direct that the light was red?* [COMMIT]

A: *Yes.*

Q: *You have a Facebook page, don't you?* [CREDIT/VALIDATE]

A: *Yes.*

Q: *You use this to keep in touch with friends and family?*

A: *Yes.*

Q: *You post information on the page about what's going on in your life?*

A: *Yes.*

Q: *And you have an interest in posting accurate information on your page, correct?*

A: *Yes.*

Q: *And you created an entry on your wall the day of the accident, didn't you?*

A: *Yes.*

Q: *In fact, you made the entry right after the accident?*

A: *Yes.*

Q: *When the memory of the accident was still fresh in your mind?*

A: *Yes.*

Q: *I'm showing you a printout of your Facebook wall from the day of the accident. Please read silently to yourself as I read aloud. "Damn! Just saw a car accident at 5th and Vine. I was waiting to cross the street. A car got hit from behind at the intersection. I actually got hit by a piece of glass! Weird thing? Light was GREEN. Who stops at a green light? The world is full of stupid people." Those are your words, correct?* [CONFRONT]

A: *Yes.*

There is no requirement to actually show or disclose the inconsistent statement to the witness during the impeachment. Instead, Rule 613 merely requires that the statement be shown or disclosed to opposing counsel upon request. This represents a change from the common rule (also known as the Rule in the Queen's Case, after the name of the English case that first recognized the rule), which required the cross-examiner to show the witness the prior statement prior to questioning the witness about it.

Intrinsic Impeachment by Omission

This method is appropriate when a witness has just testified in court, giving details that were never provided in previous statements or depositions. The key foundational element is that the details must be of the type that a witness would normally have been expected to provide in a previous statement or deposition. The details must also be material to the case.

The technique for impeaching on a prior omission is quite similar to impeaching on a prior inconsistent statement. The witness commits to the in-court testimony. The attorney then gets the witness to credit or validate a prior statement. The confrontation occurs when the attorney asks the witness to examine the prior statement and identify where in that statement the witness discussed the details just testified to in court. The witness has to admit that the details were not provided in the prior statement.

To illustrate, we will use the same red light/green light example as before. Assume that the witness has testified on direct examination that the light was red, but made no mention of the light at all in the prior deposition.

(Cross Examination)

Q: *You just testified on direct that the light was red?* [COMMIT]

A: *Yes.*

Q: *This accident occurred in December of Year One, right?*

A: *Yes.*

Q: *And in July of Year Two, just six months later, you gave a deposition in my office, didn't you?* [CREDIT/VALIDATE]

A: *Yes*

    [At this point, the attorney would CREDIT/VALIDATE, either in greater or lesser detail, the steps involved in the deposition.]

Q: *During that deposition, you were instructed to include all relevant details about the accident, weren't you?*

A: *Yes.*

Q: *And after the deposition was over, you were provided with a copy of the transcript and told that you could make any necessary corrections, additions or deletions?*

A: *That's right.*

Q: *And you signed the deposition, indicating that it was complete.*

A: *Yes.*

Q: *Now, you would agree with me that the color of the light at the intersection is an important detail in this case, isn't it?*

A: *Yes.*

Q: *I'm handing you your deposition. Please take a few minutes to read through it. Let me know when you come to the part in your deposition where you testified about the color of the light.* [CONFRONT]

A: *(After paging through the deposition). There's nothing in there.*

Q: *Nothing about the color of the light. Let's move on to discuss your relationship with the plaintiff in this case . . .*

A variation of impeachment by omission is impeachment by evidence of silence when the circumstances called for an explanation. This will be discussed later in this chapter in the *Jenkins v. Anderson* case.

Impeachment by Extrinsic Proof of Prior Inconsistent Statement

This form of impeachment generally occurs after the witness has been excused from the stand. The method of impeachment is to offer extrinsic proof that the witness made prior statements inconsistent with the witness's in-court testimony. The proof may consist of documents or the verbal testimony of another witness who heard and can testify about the inconsistency.

Rule 613 mandates that the witness whose testimony is being impeached with extrinsic evidence be "afforded an opportunity to explain or deny the same and the opposite party is afforded an opportunity to interrogate the witness thereon." The common law required the impeaching attorney to do this while the witness was still on the stand, which limited the dramatic impact and effectiveness of this method of impeachment.

In most cases, the impeaching attorney can comply with Rule 613 simply by requesting that the witness be excused subject to recall. This sends a signal to opposing counsel and the judge that the attorney may be planning an extrinsic impeachment. The judge is still free to regulate the order of proof under Rule 611 — and in some cases, particularly where the requirement to remain available would create a hardship for the witness — may require the impeaching attorney to provide the witness with the opportunity to explain or deny the statement prior to being excused.

It is important to understand that extrinsic evidence offered under Rule 613 is admitted not for its truth, but for its tendency to impeach the witness's prior testimony. Thus, unless the statement is also independently admissible under another rule of evidence, the jury cannot consider it for its truth.

II.   CASES, DISCUSSION QUESTIONS AND PROBLEMS

UNITED STATES v. MITCHELL
United States Court Of Appeals, Tenth Circuit
113 F.3d 1528 (10th Cir. 1997)

Defendant Thomas Mitchell was convicted of bank robbery by intimidation in violation of 18 U.S.C. § 2113(a) and sentenced to 210 months imprisonment. . . .

I. SUFFICIENCY OF THE EVIDENCE

Mitchell first contends that there was insufficient evidence to support his conviction of bank robbery by intimidation. "We review the sufficiency of the evidence in the light most favorable to the government to determine whether any rational trier of fact could have found the essential elements of the crime beyond a reasonable doubt." United States v. Spring, 80 F.3d 1450, 1459 (10th Cir.), cert. denied, 117 S. Ct. 385, 136 L. Ed. 2d 302 (1996) (quotation omitted).

Mitchell argues that the evidence only supports a conviction for the lesser crime of bank larceny, rather than bank robbery by intimidation, because Ms. Angela

Muller, the only employee in the bank at the time of the robbery, could not have been intimidated by his actions. Mitchell asserts that after he entered the bank and approached the teller's window, he merely said, "this is a holdup" and "get back." He also asserts that he did not have a weapon or claim to have a weapon, never yelled, never threatened Ms. Muller with injury, and never touched her at any time during the course of his offense. Mitchell maintains that in this situation, the evidence was insufficient to support a finding of intimidation.

In determining whether the evidence is sufficient to support a finding of intimidation in the context of a bank robbery, we look to three factors: (1) whether the situation appeared dangerous, (2) whether the defendant in-tended to intimidate, and (3) whether the bank personnel were reasonable in their fear of death or injury. United States v. Smith, 10 F.3d 724, 729 (10th Cir. 1993) (citing United States v. Slater, 692 F.2d 107, 109 (10th Cir. 1982)).

Applying these factors, we conclude that Mitchell's conduct was "aggressive behavior which very well could have been considered as intimidating by the jury." Slater, 692 F.2d at 109. Ms. Muller testified that Mitchell's tone was serious and that she felt threatened by his actions. After Mitchell took the money, he instructed Ms. Muller to go with him. Ms. Muller complied. As they walked toward the back door of the bank, Mitchell "yanked" the phone out of the wall. Once outside, Mitchell ordered Ms. Muller to go back into the bank. She again complied. Ms. Muller testified that because she thought Mitchell might come back inside, she locked the back door and left through the front of the bank to call the police. Under these circumstances, there was ample evidence supporting the element of intimidation.

II. ADMISSIBILITY OF IMPEACHMENT EVIDENCE

Mitchell next contends that the district court erred in refusing to admit extrinsic evidence of a prior inconsistent statement to impeach Ms. Muller's testimony. We review questions concerning the admission of evidence under an abuse of discretion standard. United States v. Bowser, 941 F.2d 1019, 1021 (10th Cir. 1991). "In reviewing a court's determination for abuse of discretion, we will not disturb the determination absent a distinct showing it was based on a clearly erroneous finding of fact or an erroneous conclusion of law or manifests a clear error of judgment." Cartier v. Jackson, 59 F.3d 1046, 1048 (10th Cir. 1995).

At trial, the defense sought to impeach Ms. Muller's testimony by introducing a statement contained in a psychological counseling record. The record stated that Ms. Muller "did report that she had some problems with forgetfulness since the above listed event." R. Vol. II, at 120. The defense sought to question Ms. Muller regarding the statement in order to impeach her testimony that she has no trouble remembering the events that took place during the course of the bank robbery. During cross examination of Ms. Muller, the defense counsel asked the following questions:

Q: *Your memory, however, has not been the best, has it?*

A: *I think it's been pretty good.*

Q: *Okay. But isn't it true that you do have trouble sometimes with your memory and suffer from forgetfulness?*

A: *No.*

R. Vol. II, at 52. At this point, the district court refused to allow defense counsel to question Ms. Muller about the statement contained in the psychological record because of the court's concern that the statement might be privileged. R. Vol. II, at 56. After later concluding that the statement was not privileged, the court allowed the defense to recall Ms. Muller to question her regarding whether she had made the statement. R. Vol. II, at 127. The court stated that if Ms. Muller denied making the statement, then the defense could introduce the statement to impeach her testimony.

After the defense recalled Ms. Muller and asked her about the statement, she testified that she could not recall making the statement to her psychologist. Thereafter, the court refused to allow the statement to be put into evidence. The court stated, "She has not denied making this statement. She basically doesn't think she said so but she can't remember. That's not sufficient in the Court's opinion to have a statement made into the record . . . without the explanation of the person who made the statement." R. Vol. II, at 149-150. The defense objected to the court's ruling.

After reviewing the record, we conclude that the statement is properly character-ized as a prior inconsistent statement and should have been admitted under Federal Rule of Evidence 613(b). During cross-examination, Ms. Muller denied having problems with her memory and suffering from forgetfulness. This testimony is directly inconsistent with the statement Ms. Muller allegedly made to her psycholo-gist. Pursuant to Rule 613(b), Ms. Muller was given an opportunity to explain or deny making the prior statement, R. Vol. II, at 146-47, and the prosecution was permitted to interrogate Ms. Muller regarding the statement and her recollection of the events surrounding the bank robbery, R. Vol. II, at 147-48. Ms. Muller testified that she could not remember making the statement, but she confirmed — at the behest of the prosecution — that she clearly remembers the events on the day of the robbery. R. Vol. II, at 146-48. Under Rule 613(b), the defense should have been allowed to introduce extrinsic evidence of the statement to impeach Ms. Muller's testimony. Therefore, the court abused its discretion in excluding extrinsic evidence of the statement.

We conclude, however, that the error was harmless in the context of the entire case against defendant Mitchell. "Error in the admission or exclusion of evidence is harmless if it does not affect the substantial rights of the parties, and the burden of demonstrating that substantial rights were affected rests with the party asserting error." United States v. Arutunoff, 1 F.3d 1112, 1118 (10th Cir. 1993) (quotation omitted). A nonconstitutional error is harmless unless it had a substantial influence on the jury's verdict in the context of the entire case, or leaves one in grave doubt whether it had such an effect. United States v. Walker, 107 F.3d 774, 785 (10th Cir. 1997) (citing Kotteakos v. United States, 328 U.S. 750, 764-65, 66 S. Ct. 1239, 90 L. Ed. 1557 (1946)).

The overwhelming evidence against Mitchell on the element of intimidation included his own testimony regarding his words and actions after he entered the bank. This testimony alone was sufficient for the jury to find the element of intimidation. Moreover, despite the court's exclusion of the extrinsic evidence regarding Ms. Muller's statement, the defense nevertheless was permitted to ask Ms. Muller in the presence of the jury whether she had told her psychologist that she suffered from forgetfulness. Thus, the jury was aware of this attack on Ms. Muller's credibility but apparently chose to believe Ms. Muller when she testified that she was intimidated. In the context of the entire trial, we cannot say that the error had a substantial influence in determining the jury's verdict. Accordingly, we hold that the error was harmless.

JENKINS v. ANDERSON
Supreme Court of the United States
447 U.S. 231 (1980)

MR. JUSTICE POWELL delivered the opinion of the Court.

I

On August 13, 1974, the petitioner stabbed and killed Doyle Redding. The petitioner was not apprehended until he turned himself in to governmental authorities about two weeks later. At his state trial for first-degree murder, the petitioner contended that the killing was in self-defense.

The petitioner testified that his sister and her boyfriend were robbed by Redding and another man during the evening of August 12, 1974. The petitioner, who was nearby when the robbery occurred, followed the thieves a short distance and reported their whereabouts to the police. According to the petitioner's testimony, the next day he encountered Redding, who accused him of informing the police of the robbery. The petitioner stated that Redding attacked him with a knife, that the two men struggled briefly, and that the petitioner broke away. On cross-examination, the petitioner admitted that during the struggle he had tried "[to] push that knife in [Redding] as far as [I] could," App. 36, but maintained that he had acted solely in self-defense.

During the cross-examination, the prosecutor questioned the petitioner about his actions after the stabbing:

Q.   *And I suppose you waited for the Police to tell them what happened?*

A.   *No, I didn't.*

Q.   *You didn't?*

A.   *No.*

Q.   *I see. And how long was it after this day that you were arrested, or that you were taken into custody?*

After some discussion of the date on which petitioner surrendered, the prosecutor continued:

Q.   *When was the first time that you reported the things that you have told us in Court today to anybody?*

A.   *Two days after it happened.*

Q.   *And who did you report it to?*

A.   *To my probation officer.*

Q.   *Well, apart from him?*

A.   *No one.*

Q.   *Who?*

A.   *No one but my —*

Q.   *(Interposing) Did you ever go to a Police Officer or to anyone else?*

A.   *No, I didn't.*

Q.   *As a matter of fact, it was two weeks later, wasn't it?*

A.   *Yes.*

In closing argument to the jury, the prosecutor again referred to the petitioner's prearrest silence. The prosecutor noted that petitioner had "waited two weeks, according to the testimony — at least two weeks before he did anything about surrendering himself or reporting [the stabbing] to anybody." Id., at 43. The prosecutor contended that the petitioner had committed murder in retaliation for the robbery the night before.

The petitioner was convicted of manslaughter and sentenced to 10 to 15 years' imprisonment in state prison. [Following direct review in state court, the petitioner filed a habeas corpus petition, which was denied by federal district court and affirmed by the 6th Circuit. The Supreme Court granted certiorari on the constitutional issues under the 5th and 14th amendments raised by the prosecutor's comments on the petitioner's pre-arrest silence.]

II

At trial the prosecutor attempted to impeach the petitioner's credibility by suggesting that the petitioner would have spoken out if he had killed in self-defense. The petitioner contends that the prosecutor's actions violated the Fifth Amendment as applied to the States through the Fourteenth Amendment. The Fifth Amendment guarantees an accused the right to remain silent during his criminal trial, and prevents the prosecution from commenting on the silence of a defendant who asserts the right. Griffin v. California, 380 U.S. 609, 614 (1965). In this case, of course, the petitioner did not remain silent throughout the criminal proceedings. Instead, he voluntarily took the witness stand in his own defense.

This Court's decision in Raffel v. United States, 271 U.S. 494 (1926), recognized that the Fifth Amendment is not violated when a defendant who testifies in his own defense is impeached with his prior silence. The defendant in *Raffel* was tried twice. At the first trial, a Government agent testified that *Raffel* earlier had made an inculpatory statement. The defendant did not testify. After the first trial ended in deadlock the agent repeated his testimony at the second trial, and *Raffel* took the stand to deny making such a statement. Cross-examination revealed that *Raffel* had not testified at the first trial. Id., at 495, n. The Court held that inquiry into prior silence was proper because "[the] immunity from giving testimony is one which the defendant may waive by offering himself as a witness. . . . When he takes the stand in his own behalf, he does so as any other witness, and within the limits of the appropriate rules he may be cross-examined. . . ." Id., at 496-497. Thus, the *Raffel* Court concluded that the defendant was "subject to cross-examination impeaching his credibility just like any other witness." Grunewald v. United States, 353 U.S. 391, 420 (1957). . . .

In determining whether a constitutional right has been burdened impermissibly, it also is appropriate to consider the legitimacy of the challenged governmental practice. See Chaffin v. Stynchcombe, supra, at 32, and n. 20. Attempted impeachment on cross-examination of a defendant, the practice at issue here, may enhance the reliability of the criminal process. Use of such impeachment on cross-examination allows prosecutors to test the credibility of witnesses by asking them to explain prior inconsistent statements and acts. A defendant may decide not to take the witness stand because of the risk of cross-examination. But this is a choice of litigation tactics. Once a defendant decides to testify, "[the] interests of the other party and regard for the function of courts of justice to ascertain the truth become relevant, and prevail in the balance of considerations determining the scope and limits of the privilege against self-incrimination." Brown v. United States, 356 U.S. 148, 156 (1958).

Thus, impeachment follows the defendant's own decision to cast aside his cloak of silence and advances the truth-finding function of the criminal trial. We conclude that the Fifth Amendment is not violated by the use of prearrest silence to impeach a criminal defendant's credibility.

III

The petitioner also contends that use of prearrest silence to impeach his credibility denied him the fundamental fairness guaranteed by the Fourteenth Amendment. We do not agree. Common law traditionally has allowed witnesses to be impeached by their previous failure to state a fact in circumstances in which that fact naturally would have been asserted. 3A.J. Wigmore, Evidence § 1042, p. 1056 (Chadbourn rev. 1970). Each jurisdiction may formulate its own rules of evidence to determine when prior silence is so inconsistent with present statements that impeachment by reference to such silence is probative. For example, this Court has exercised its supervisory powers over federal courts to hold that prior silence cannot be used for impeachment where silence is not probative of a defendant's credibility and where prejudice to the defendant might result.

Only in Doyle v. Ohio, 426 U.S. 610 (1976), did we find that impeachment by silence violated the Constitution. In that case, a defendant received the warnings required by Miranda v. Arizona, supra, at 467-473, when he was arrested for selling marihuana. At that time, he made no statements to the police. During his subsequent trial, the defendant testified that he had been framed. The prosecutor impeached the defendant's credibility on cross-examination by revealing that the defendant remained silent after his arrest. The State argued that the prosecutor's actions were permissible, but we concluded that "the Miranda decision compels rejection of the State's position." 426 U.S., at 617. Miranda warnings inform a person that he has the right to remain silent and assure him, at least implicitly, that his subsequent decision to remain silent cannot be used against him. Accordingly, " 'it does not comport with due process to permit the prosecution during the trial to call attention to his silence at the time of arrest and to insist that because he did not speak about the facts of the case at that time, as he was told he need not do, an unfavorable inference might be drawn as to the truth of his trial testimony.' " Id., at 619, quoting United States v. Hale, supra, at 182-183 (WHITE, J., concurring in judgment).

In this case, no governmental action induced petitioner to remain silent before arrest. The failure to speak occurred before the petitioner was taken into custody and given Miranda warnings. Consequently, the fundamental unfairness present in Doyle is not present in this case. We hold that impeachment by use of prearrest silence does not violate the Fourteenth Amendment.

IV

Our decision today does not force any state court to allow impeachment through the use of prearrest silence. Each jurisdiction remains free to formulate evidentiary rules defining the situations in which silence is viewed as more probative than prejudicial. We merely conclude that the use of prearrest silence to impeach a defendant's credibility does not violate the Constitution. The judgment of the Court of Appeals is affirmed.

DISSENT

MR. JUSTICE MARSHALL, with whom MR. JUSTICE BRENNAN joins, dissenting.

Today the Court holds that a criminal defendant's testimony in his own behalf may be impeached by the fact that he did not go to the authorities before his arrest and confess his part in the offense. The decision thus strikes a blow at two of the foundation stones of our constitutional system: the privilege against self-incrimination and the right to present a defense.

I

The Court's decision today is extraordinarily broad. It goes far beyond a simple holding that the common-law rule permitting introduction of evidence of silence in the face of accusation or in circumstances calling for a response does not violate the privilege against self-incrimination. For in this case the prosecution was allowed to cast doubt on an acused's testimony that he acted in self-defense by forcing him to testify that he did not go to the police of his own volition, before he had been indicted, charged, or even accused of any offense, and volunteer his version of the events.

The Court's holding that a criminal defendant's testimony may be impeached by his prearrest silence has three patent — and, in my view, fatal — defects. First, the mere fact of prearrest silence is so unlikely to be probative of the falsity of the defendant's trial testimony that its use for impeachment purposes is contrary to the Due Process Clause of the Fourteenth Amendment. Second, the drawing of an adverse inference from the failure to volunteer incriminating statements impermissibly infringes the privilege against self-incrimination. Third, the availability of the inference for impeachment purposes impermissibly burdens the decision to exercise the constitutional right to testify in one's own defense.

A

The use of prior silence for impeachment purposes depends, as the majority recognizes, ante, at 238, on the reasonableness of an inference that it is inconsistent with the statements that are to be impeached. If the defendant's prior silence does not make it more likely that his trial testimony was false, the evidence is simply irrelevant. Such an inference cannot fairly be drawn from petitioner's failure to go to the police before any charges were brought, admit that he had committed a homicide, and offer an exculpatory explanation.

In order for petitioner to offer his explanation of self-defense, he would necessarily have had to admit that it was he who fatally stabbed the victim, thereby supplying against himself the strongest possible proof of an essential element of criminal homicide. It is hard to imagine a purer case of self-incrimination. Since we cannot assume that in the absence of official warnings individuals are ignorant of or oblivious to their constitutional rights, we must recognize that petitioner may have acted in reliance on the constitutional guarantee. In fact, petitioner had most likely been informed previously of his privilege against self-incrimination, since he had two prior felony convictions. App. 28. One who has at least twice before been given the Miranda warnings, which carry the implied promise that silence will not be penalized by use for impeachment purposes, Doyle v. Ohio, 426 U.S. 610 (1976), may well remember the rights of which he has been informed, and believe that the promise is still in force. Accordingly, the inference that petitioner's conduct was inconsistent with his exculpatory trial testimony is precluded. See Doyle v. Ohio, supra; United States v. Hale, 422 U.S. 171, 176-177 (1975).

Moreover, other possible explanations for silence spring readily to mind. It is conceivable that a person who had acted in self-defense might believe that he had committed no crime and therefore had no call to explain himself to the police. Indeed, all the witnesses agreed that after the stabbing the victim ran across the street and climbed a flight of stairs be-fore collapsing. Initially, at least, then, petitioner might not have known that there was a homicide to explain. More-over, petitioner testified that he feared retaliation if he went to the police. One need not be persuaded that any of these possible explanations represents the true reason for petitioner's conduct to recognize that the availability of other plausible hypotheses vitiates the inference on which the admissibility of the evidence depends. See United States v. Hale, supra, at 176-177, 180.

The Court implies that its decision is consistent with the practice at common law; but at common law silence is admissible to contradict subsequent statements only if the circumstances would naturally have called for a response. For example, silence was traditionally considered a tacit admission if a statement made in the party's presence was heard and understood by the party, who was at liberty to respond, in circumstances naturally calling for a response, and the party failed to respond. Silence was not considered an admission if any of the prerequisites were absent, for in such a case the failure to speak could be explained other than as assent. Similarly, failure to assert a fact could be used for impeachment if it would have been natural, under the circumstances, to assert the fact. But the authority cited by the majority in support of this proposition, ante, at 239, makes it clear that the rule cannot be invoked unless the facts affirmatively show that the witness was called on to speak, circumstances which are not present in this case.[2]

Plainly, the omission to seek out an opportunity to speak is not included within these categories. Of all the cases cited by Wigmore involving silence by a criminal defendant, not one involves prearrest silence by a suspect not in the presence of law enforcement officers.

Since petitioner's failure to report and explain his actions prior to his arrest was not probative of the falsity of his testimony at trial, it was fundamentally unfair and a deprivation of due process to allow the jury to draw from that silence an inference that his trial testimony was false. Doyle v. Ohio, supra.

DISCUSSION QUESTIONS

1. After reading the *Mitchell* opinion, why would extrinsic evidence of an inconsistent statement be necessary to impeach the witness?

2. What was the inconsistency in *Mitchell*? Why was it an inconsistency and not simply a witness being forgetful on the stand? What standards should a court use to differentiate between true inconsistencies and mere forgetfulness?

3. Having read the majority and dissenting opinions in *Jenkins*, which approach do you think more fairly captures the spirit of the common law doctrine of impeachment by silence? Why?

4. Notice the connection in *Jenkins* between the impeachment on cross-examination and the prosecution's closing argument. What advocacy lessons can you draw from that linkage?

---

[2] [n.3] The Wigmore treatise lists three categories of cases in which silence may be used for impeachment:

"(1) Omissions in legal proceedings to assert what would naturally have been asserted under the circumstances.

"(2) Omissions to assert anything . . . when formerly narrating, on the stand or elsewhere, the matter now dealt with.

"(3) Failure to take the stand at all. . . ." 3A Wigmore, supra, § 1042, pp. 1056–1058 (footnotes omitted, emphasis in original). As we have previously observed, "[in] most circumstances silence is so ambiguous that it is of little probative force." United States v. Hale, supra, at 176.

PROBLEMS

Problem 16-1. Minnie Phaltzhud testified for the plaintiff on direct examination in an automobile accident trial. She was a passenger in a car driven by her fiancée, the plaintiff in the case. The plaintiff claimed that the defendant came to an abrupt stop at an intersection with a green light, and that the defendant's brake lights were not working. Ms. Phaltzhud testified that she was paying careful attention to road conditions and that she had a clear view of the defendant's brake lights. Following her testimony, she was permanently excused from the proceedings. On the defendant's case-in-chief, the defendant called Bonnie Bell, a friend of Ms. Phaltzhud, to testify that she received a text from Ms. Phaltzhud immediately after the accident that said, "OMG! Paul just hit truck in front of us! We r ok, lol. :) IDK what happened yet."

What grounds does the plaintiff have for objection under Rule 613? How should the defendant respond? Are there alternative grounds for impeachment?

Problem 16-2. Using the same facts as the previous problem, assume that Ms. Phaltzhud was excused from trial subject to recall. Following Ms. Bell's testimony, Ms. Phaltzhud took the stand and denied sending a text message with that content to Ms. Bell. Instead, she testified that her text said, "OMG! Paul just hit truck in front of us! We r ok, lol. :) Dumbass in truck had broken taillights." Neither side preserved the text messages, and no proof of their content is available.

How should the judge address the discrepancy between the stories told by Ms. Bell and Ms. Phaltzhud? What sort of evidentiary instruction would be appropriate for the jury? What should the parties be able to say about the differing versions of the text in closing arguments?

Impeachment by Prior Inconsistent Statements: Quick Hits

- Inconsistent statements cast doubt on a witness's credibility whose in-court testimony is different from prior statements.

- To qualify for this method of impeachment, the prior statement must be genuinely inconsistent.

- Intrinsic impeachments occur on cross-examination. The witness is questioned about a prior inconsistent statement or omission.

- The impeaching attorney can also, or in the alternative, offer extrinsic evidence of a prior inconsistent statement.

- In cases of extrinsic impeachment, Rule 613 requires that the witness be given the opportunity to explain or deny the statement. This is usually accomplished by excusing the witness subject to recall and shifting to the party that originally called the witness the responsibility and decision to re-call the witness.

- To complete impeachment by prior inconsistent statement, counsel should mention the impeachment in closing argument and

---

> discuss its effect on the witness's credibility.

Chapter References

Christopher B. Mueller & Laird C. Kirkpatrick, Evidence §§ 6.40–6.42 (4th ed. 2009).

Glen Weissenberger & James J. Duane, Federal Rules of Evidence: Rules, Legislative History, Commentary and Authority § 613 (6th ed. 2009).

Jack B. Weinstein & Margaret A. Berger, Weinstein's Federal Evidence § 613 (Joseph M. McLaughlin ed., Matthew Bender 2d ed. 1997).

Kenneth S. Broun, McCormick on Evidence §§ 33–38 (6th ed. 2006).

Steven Goode & Olin Guy Wellborn III, Courtroom Handbook on Federal Evidence Ch. 5 (West 2010).

III. APPLICATION EXERCISES

Intrinsic Impeachment by Prior Inconsistent Statement

We will use the facts of the red light/green light case that are used throughout this chapter. No advance preparation is required for this exercise.

Impeachment with Extrinsic Evidence of Prior Statement

Impeaching a witness with extrinsic evidence of a prior inconsistent statement is rarely as dramatic as an intrinsic impeachment. The impeaching attorney may, in fact, desire to take a very low key approach to this impeachment. One strategy is to let the witness tell the story, then request excusal of the witness subject to recall to comply with the requirements of Rule 613. The impeachment itself will occur much later in the trial.

In order to take full advantage of this method of impeachment, it is also necessary to plan how to exploit it on closing argument.

The Exercise

Objective: To demonstrate proficiency in conducting an impeachment with extrinsic evidence and integrating the impeachment in a closing argument.

Factual Scenario: The rock group Genocidal Interlude recently broke up after being together nearly 20 years. As is typical of such breakups, the lead guitarist, Armind Hamner, took about half the band with him and formed a new group. The lead singer, Bëik Änsoda, took the other half and formed another group. Both groups are using the name Genocidal Interlude, which has, of course, created some confusion in the music industry and among music fans everywhere. Mr. Hamner has brought suit against Mr. Änsoda for the rights to the name Genocidal Interlude.

At trial, Mr. Hamner called Dirk Stonefeather, his agent, to testify about the breakup. Stonefeather testified in substance as follows:

> *In 2007, it became obvious that the group weren't getting along with each other anymore. Armind Hamner, Bëik Änsoda — they were at each other's throats all the time. Musical differences, personal differences, choice in clothing, women, drugs — you name it, they fought about it. Finally, the group all sat down with me backstage at an arena in the US. I want to say it was Cleveland. It was like something out of Spinal Tap. What we basically agreed was that everyone would go their separate ways, as quickly and peacefully as possible. Everyone thought the right thing to do would be to let Armind keep the band name. I mean, after all, the whole thing had started in his garage, and, as I recall, his mother had thought of the name. It wasn't until later that Bëik Änsoda decided to try to cash in on the name and start another band and call it Genocidal Interlude. I guess his band, The Bëik Änsoda Massacre, just didn't have the right ring to it.*

During pretrial investigation, Bëik Änsoda's attorney tracked down noted rock journalist Sandy Sartain. Sartain conducted an unpublished interview with Dirk Stonefeather that occurred just six weeks before the breakup. The interview took place in a sidewalk café in Greenwich Village. As per Stonefeather's interview policy, no tape recorders were allowed, but Sartain was permitted to take notes. Sartain is prepared to testify substantially as follows:

> *I asked Dirk Stonefeather if the band would ever break up, and he said no. I asked about the rumors of fighting on tour, and he said it was just rumors; the band were like brothers. So I said, hypothetically, if the band did break up, who would own the name Genocidal Interlude? There's a lot of money in that name. Stonefeather laughed and said, "Bëik Änsoda would keep the name. Everyone agreed on that years ago. He's the one who thought of the name and talked everyone into it. Armind Hamner has always said he hated the name but went along with it to make Bëik Änsoda happy."*

Advance Preparation: Assume that Sartain is available to testify. Prepare a direct examination of Sartain to impeach Stonefeather's trial testimony. Also prepare a brief closing argument incorporating the impeachment and explaining its impact on the case.

In-class Exercise: Students will play the following roles: Plaintiff's attorney, Dirk Stonefeather, Sandy Sartain, defense attorney, and judge. The plaintiff's attorney will conduct a brief examination of Stonefeather. The defense attorney will decline cross-examination and request excusal of Stonefeather subject to recall. The plaintiff will rest its case, and the defense will call Sandy Sartain as a witness to conduct an extrinsic impeachment. The plaintiff will receive an opportunity to recall Stonefeather to explain or deny the statement. Finally, the defense will make a short closing argument integrating the impeachment.

PART FIVE

THE LAW OF EXHIBITS: AUTHENTICATION AND THE BEST EVIDENCE RULE

Chapter 17

AUTHENTICATION

> **Chapter Objectives:**
>
> - Introduce and explain Rules 901-902 and the concepts of authentication and self-authentication
> - Analyze and discuss issues pertaining to Rules 901-902
> - Apply the concepts from this chapter in a courtroom application exercise

I. BACKGROUND AND EXPLANATORY MATERIAL

Introduction to the Concept of Authentication

To authenticate evidence is to demonstrate that it is what it purports to be. The requirement to authenticate evidence under Rule 901 is functionally similar to the requirement that a witness have personal knowledge under Rule 602. Both are rules of relevance. Just as a witness without personal knowledge of a matter in a case has nothing relevant to offer the fact-finder, an item of evidence that cannot be authenticated is practically and legally worthless at trial.

Rule 901(a) contains the general requirement of authentication for the Federal Rules of Evidence:

Through Dec. 1, 2011	After Dec. 1, 2011
Rule 901. Requirement of Authentication or Identification	**Rule 901. Authenticating or Identifying Evidence**
(a) General provision. The requirement of authentication or identification as a condition precedent to admissibility is satisfied by evidence sufficient to support a finding that the matter in question is what its proponent claims.	**(a) In General.** To satisfy the requirement of authenticating or identifying an item of evidence, the proponent must produce evidence sufficient to support a finding that the item is what the proponent claims it is.

Authentication under Rule 901 is also a question of conditional relevance under Rule 104. In other words, the ultimate decision is up to the fact-finder; the judge is required only to find that a reasonable fact-finder *could* conclude that the item is what it purports to be. With particular exceptions that will be discussed later in this chapter, most items of evidence require a witness to authenticate them. These witnesses — often referred to as *foundation witnesses* — testify about an item's authenticity based on their personal knowledge or experience with either the item itself, or with the processes or systems that generated or created the item.

For example, assume that the prosecutor in a murder case wanted to introduce the murder weapon into evidence at trial. To authenticate the weapon, she would have to prove that it was the actual weapon used to commit the killing. Possible authentication witnesses could include a witness to the murder, the detective who processed evidence at the crime scene, or even a confession or admission by the defendant identifying the weapon.

Another example is a bank robbery case. Assume that the robbery was captured on surveillance video from a bank. In order to authenticate the video, the prosecutor could call a security specialist to testify about the video surveillance system and the process used to record and preserve surveillance footage.

Categories of Evidence and Basic Foundational Elements

Broadly speaking, admissible evidence at trial can be divided into several categories, including live witness testimony, real evidence, writings, illustrative evidence and silent witness exhibits (sound and video recordings). Although there are specific foundational requirements for each category of evidence, there are two threshold authentication elements common to all: the proponent must demonstrate that (1) the evidence is relevant, and (2) the evidence is what it purports to be.

The previous chapter discussed the foundational rules for live witness testimony. The other major categories of evidence and the elements required to authenticate them are explained below.

Real Evidence

Real evidence consists of tangible objects such as guns, drugs, bodily fluids, etc. Real evidence is further subdivided into fungible and non-fungible evidence. Fungible evidence consists of things that are freely interchangeable with other things of the same kind or that lack visually identifiable distinguishing characteristics. For example, a standard fast-food hamburger from a particular chain is virtually indistinguishable from all other similar hamburgers sold by that chain. Visually, one blood or urine sample looks much like any other blood or urine sample. Fungible evidence is frequently introduced in criminal cases. In order to authenticate fungible evidence, the proponent establishes a chain of custody that accounts for the evidence from the time it was seized until its appearance in the courtroom.

Non-fungible real evidence has distinguishing characteristics or features that make it readily identifiable. An example is a gun with serial number stamped on the receiver; other guns of the same make and manufacture can be distinguished because of their different serial numbers. A witness with personal knowledge of the item can identify it. A key aspect of the foundation for non-fungible real evidence is that the item is in the same or substantially the same condition as it was at the time of the incident.

Writings

This category includes business records, diaries, letters, contracts, official government documents, and the like. Writings can be printed or handwritten. Electronic documents such as e-mails or text messages are also classified as writings for evidentiary purposes. To authenticate a writing, the proponent must prove authorship. In the case of government records, the proponent can prove institutional authorship. Authenticating a writing does not guarantee its admissibility; it must still be relevant to the proceedings and satisfy other evidentiary rules and doctrines, including the best evidence and hearsay rules. Rule 902 provides for the self-authentication of many writings, eliminating the need to prove authorship in the courtroom.

Illustrative Evidence

This category includes photographs, maps, models, and movies. Illustrative evidence is designed to help the fact-finder visually understand what happened in the case and is relevant so long as it fairly and accurately depicts the portrayed scene or incident. There are two key foundational elements for illustrative evidence: (1) the evidence fairly and accurately depicts something the witness observed; and (2) the evidence will be helpful to assist the fact-finder in understanding the witness's testimony.

Silent Witness Exhibits

Silent witness exhibits include surveillance videotapes or wiretap recordings. The term silent witness comes from the fact that there is typically no live witness who can actually authenticate the contents of the recording. Instead, the law creates a fiction that the recording is a silent witness to the proceedings. To authenticate recordings, the proponent must call a witness who can testify that the recording system is in good mechanical order, and that the process or system used produces accurate results.

The Process of Authentication

The process of authenticating evidence is becoming a lost art. The rules of civil procedure,[1] pretrial admissibility orders,[2] verbal or written stipulation agreements between counsel, and the self-authentication provisions of Rule 902 have largely

---

[1] Applicable rules include FED. R. CIV. P. 26(a) (production of documents under the rule authenticates the evidence; the opposing party has 14 days to object); FRCP 36 (a party can request admission of facts, including the genuineness of documents); FRCP 33 (a party can use interrogatories to establish authenticity or genuineness of documents); FED. R. CIV. P. 30–31 (procedure for authenticating documents in a deposition).

[2] Many judges require pretrial authentication and admissibility of all evidence to spare the jury from having to listen to technical evidentiary foundations, objections and responses. Common practice is for

eliminated the need to comply with technical authentication requirements. Many advocates voluntarily stipulate to the authenticity of exhibits: knowing that opposing counsel is capable of laying a foundation, they desire to save time at trial and to earn similar consideration from their opponents. Nonetheless, authentication remains a condition precedent to admitting evidence, and advocates should be prepared to authenticate any evidentiary exhibit they intend to introduce at trial.

Rule 901(b) provides a non-exclusive list of authentication methods available at trial for different types of exhibit. Each of these will be discussed in turn.

Authentication by a Witness

Through Dec. 1, 2011	After Dec. 1, 2011
Rule 901. Requirement of Authentication or Identification	**Rule 901. Authenticating or Identifying Evidence**
(b) Illustrations. By way of illustration only, and not by way of limitation, the following are examples of authentication or identification conforming with the requirements of this rule:	**(b) Examples.** The following are examples only — not a complete list — of evidence that satisfies the requirement:
(1) Testimony of witness with knowledge. Testimony that a matter is what it is claimed to be.	*(1) Testimony of a Witness with Knowledge.* Testimony that an item is what it is claimed to be.

The easiest and most common method of authenticating evidence is through the testimony of a witness with personal knowledge. To satisfy the requirements of relevance and personal knowledge, the witness must explain his or her basis for knowledge of the exhibit. For example, in a contract dispute, the witness would identify the contract and explain, "I saw the parties sign this document."

A second step is for the witness to testify whether the evidence is in substantially the same condition as when the witness last saw it. This lets the fact-finder know that the evidence has not been tampered with or altered. If there are changes, the proponent must introduce testimony to explain what the changes were and why they were made. An example of this is the chemical testing of contraband samples or bodily fluids. As part of the testing process, portions of the sample are used up or destroyed. Explaining the process to the jury helps them understand why, for example, a fluid sample's volume is decreased or part of an item of clothing has been cut out.

In some cases, more than one authenticating witness may be necessary. This is particularly true in cases involving a chain of custody. As previously mentioned, virtually all chain of custody cases are criminal cases. To strictly establish the chain

---

the judge to issue a pretrial order listing all the evidence that is authentic and admissible. *See* Fed. R. Civ. P. 16. Opposing parties often facilitate this process by stipulating to authenticity when they know their opponent would be able to establish authenticity by "strict proof" if called upon to do so.

of custody, the proponent is required to call each person who had custody of the item from the time it was seized until trial. Each witness must testify about the following: (1) when and from whom they took custody of the item; (2) what they did to preserve and safeguard the item (for example, put it in an evidence bag or locker); (3) that the item was not altered or tampered with while it was in their possession; and (4) when and to whom they relinquished custody. As a practical matter, provided that documentary evidence can establish the links in the chain of custody, most jurisdictions do not require the proponent to call each witness in the chain.

Another issue with chain of custody concerns gaps. There are times when one of the witnesses in a chain of custody is unavailable, or the evidence has not been accounted for during a particular period of time. Gaps in the chain of custody do not automatically defeat authentication, but normally are considered for the weight of the evidence.

Identification of Writings by Opinion, Comparison, or Testimony of Distinctive Characteristics

Through Dec. 1, 2011	After Dec. 1, 2011
Rule 901(b), cont'd	**Rule 901(b), cont'd**
(2) Nonexpert opinion on handwriting. Nonexpert opinion as to the genuineness of handwriting, based upon familiarity not acquired for purposes of the litigation.	*(2) Nonexpert Opinion About Handwriting.* A nonexpert's opinion that handwriting is genuine, based on a familiarity with it that was not acquired for the current litigation.
(3) Comparison by trier or expert witness. Comparison by the trier of fact or by expert witnesses with specimens which have been authenticated.	*(3) Comparison by an Expert Witness or the Trier of Fact.* A comparison with an authenticated specimen by an expert witness or the trier of fact.
(4) Distinctive characteristics and the like. Appearance, contents, substance, internal patterns, or other distinctive characteristics, taken in conjunction with circumstances.	*(4) Distinctive Characteristics and the Like.* The appearance, contents, substance, internal patterns, or other distinctive characteristics of the item, taken together with all the circumstances.

In order to establish the authenticity of a writing, the proponent must prove authorship. The ease with which documents can be forged or fabricated requires specialized doctrines to help aid the fact-finder in making this determination.

(1) *Nonexpert Opinion*

The first of these doctrines is that a lay witness who is familiar with someone's handwriting can give an opinion as to the authorship of a handwritten document. A key constraint is that the witness's basis for familiarity cannot have been obtained solely for the purposes of litigation. Thus, a police officer or private investigator cannot compare handwriting samples as part of their investigation and testify concerning the authorship of a document.

There are several ways to establish familiarity. Family members, close friends, work associates, and others who seen an individual's handwriting in the course of business, personal or professional dealings have sufficient familiarity to testify under this rule. Likewise, individuals who have engaged in handwritten correspondence have sufficient familiarity to meet this requirement.

(2) *Comparison by Trier of Fact or Expert*

The second doctrine is comparison by the trier of fact or an expert witness. The key to this type of analysis is the existence of genuine and authentic handwriting exemplars — that is, known handwriting samples of the individual to whom the proponent is attempting to attribute authorship of documents at trial. The genuineness of the exemplars is a matter of conditional relevancy; the judge need only find that a reasonable jury could believe the exemplars to be genuine. There are many ways to establish the genuine nature of exemplars. First, the parties can stipulate. Second, the proponent of the evidence can introduce known exemplars such as tax returns or other writings from official files. Third, the court can order the production of exemplars. In criminal cases, the accused can be compelled to provide exemplars without violating his privilege against self-incrimination.

Once the exemplars have been deemed authentic, the process of comparison can take place. In a practice dating back to the earliest days of the common law, the jury itself can compare the disputed handwriting sample with the exemplar to determine whether there is common authorship.

Experts who have been specially trained in handwriting analysis and are otherwise qualified under the rules of evidence can compare the disputed sample with the exemplars and render an opinion as to whether there is common authorship. As with any other opinion evidence, the jury is free to accept or reject the expert's conclusion.

It should be noted that the expert witness provisions of Rule 901(b)(3) apply not only to handwriting, but also to the authentication of fingerprints and genetic material such as DNA or blood samples. The process involves obtaining known exemplars and comparing them to the disputed material to determine whether there is a common source.

(3) *Distinctive Characteristics and the Like*

This method of proof involves using circumstantial evidence to determine the authorship of a writing. Several types of evidence are commonly used for this type of authentication.

The first is content. A writing can be authenticated by reference to its content, including information known to the author, code words, or distinctive language patterns used by the author. Distinctive language patterns include word choice, punctuation, spelling peculiarities, paragraph structure, or identifiable characteristics in the use of slang, jargon or vulgarities.

The second is the reply letter doctrine. If A writes a letter to B, and B replies, referencing A's letter in his reply, the reply is evidence of B's authorship. A variation that essentially combines the content and reply letter doctrines has also been used to authenticate e-mail and text messages. The proponent introduces evidence of e-mail addresses, replies, and content to establish authorship of the messages.

The third is the use of letterhead. Rules 901(b)(4) and 902(7) suggest that letterhead can be used to authenticate a writing. Letterhead evidence is more valuable if the letterhead is distinctive and not generally available to outsiders.

The fourth is circumstantial evidence related to the discovery of a writing. Suppose, for example, that law enforcement agents seize a stack of written materials from the basement bedroom of a social recluse. Suppose further that the writings reference people known to the recluse, as well as things of interest to the recluse. The circumstances of discovery point to the recluse as the author of the materials.

Voice Identification & Telephone Calls

Through Dec. 1, 2011	After Dec. 1, 2011
Rule 901(b), cont'd.	**Rule 901(b), cont'd**
(5) Voice identification. Identification of a voice, whether heard firsthand or through mechanical or electronic transmission or recording, by opinion based upon hearing the voice at any time under circumstances connecting it with the alleged speaker.	*(5) Opinion About a Voice*. An opinion identifying a person's voice — whether heard firsthand or through mechanical or electronic transmission or recording — based on hearing the voice at any time under circumstances that connect it with the alleged speaker.
(6) Telephone conversations. Telephone conversations, by evidence that a call was made to the number assigned at the time by the telephone company to a particular person or business, if (A) in the case of a person, circumstances, including self-identification, show the person answering to be the one called, or (B) in the case of a business, the call was made to a place of business and the conversation related to business reasonably transacted over the telephone.	*(6) Evidence About a Telephone Conversation*. For a telephone conversation, evidence that a call was made to the number assigned at the time to: (A) a particular person, if circumstances, including self-identification, show that the person answering was the one called; or (B) a particular business, if the call was made to a business and the call related to business reasonably transacted over the telephone.

Rule 901(b)(5) provides for voice identification as a means of authentication. This often occurs in the context of wiretap recordings, which are not relevant to a proceeding if the recorded voices have nothing to do with the case at hand. The witness who identifies a voice must have personal knowledge. This knowledge can be acquired prior to or after the incident in question. Familiarity can be acquired from face-to-face communication or from listening to voice exemplars. As with handwriting exemplars or bodily fluid samples, there is no self-incrimination privilege against the compelled production of voice exemplars in criminal cases.

Rule 901(b)(5) is also an acceptable method for authenticating the source of an incoming telephone call. Self-identification of the caller is not a sufficient means of authentication, as anyone who has ever unsuccessfully attempted a prank telephone call knows. Thus, voice identification under Rule 901(b)(5) or identification based on the contents of the conversation under 901(b)(4) must be used to authenticate the source of an incoming call.

Outgoing telephone calls are easier to authenticate and have their own procedure under Rule 901(b)(6). Authentication under this rule is accomplished by showing that a certain number was assigned by the telephone company, that the witness called the number, and that the person answering identified himself as the one called, or circumstances and content of the conversation identify the answerer as the person called. Similarly, if the call is to a business, the proponent must show that the number called was assigned to the business and that someone answered the phone and either identified themselves as being from the business, or the circumstances and content of the call were such as would be reasonably expected in a telephone call to this business.

Public Records or Reports

Through Dec. 1, 2011	After Dec. 1, 2011
Rule 901(b), cont'd.	**Rule 901(b), cont'd**
(7) Public records or reports. Evidence that a writing authorized by law to be recorded or filed and in fact recorded or filed in a public office, or a purported public record, report, statement, or data compilation, in any form, is from the public office where items of this nature are kept.	*(7) Evidence About Public Records*. Evidence that: (A) a document was recorded or filed in a public office as authorized by law; or (B) a purported public record or statement is from the office where items of this kind are kept.

If a proponent wishes to authenticate a public record, Rule 901(b)(7) makes the process simple. The proponent need only show that the document was retrieved from the correct place of custody. There is no requirement to call a witness to authenticate the document or a custodian to testify as to the method of storage and retrieval.

The rule covers two types of documents. The first type is writings that are (1) authorized to be recorded and filed and are (2) actually recorded and filed. These documents include deeds, contracts, tax returns, and so forth. The second type is a purported public record, report, statement or data compilation in any form. This can include police reports, court orders or judgments, property tax assessments and the like.

Ancient Documents

Through Dec. 1, 2011	After Dec. 1, 2011
Rule 901(b), cont'd.	**Rule 901(b), cont'd**
(8) Ancient documents or data compilation. Evidence that a document or data compilation, in any form, (A) is in such condition as to create no suspicion concerning its authenticity, (B) was in a place where it, if authentic, would likely be, and (C) has been in existence 20 years or more at the time it is	***(8) Evidence About Ancient Documents or Data Compilations.*** For a document or data compilation, evidence that it: (A) is in a condition that creates no suspicion about its authenticity; (B) was in a place where, if authentic, it would likely be; and (C) is at least 20 years old when offered.

Under the common law, ancient documents could be admitted into evidence if they were at least 30 years old and were found in a place where one might expect such a document to be found if authentic. Rule 901(b)(8) changes the time frame from 30 years to 20 years, but otherwise continues common law practice in this area. The rule includes not only public records and writings, but also private writings, personal correspondence, private deeds and contracts, and computer records. It also applies to foreign as well as domestic documents and records.

The biggest authentication hurdle under this rule is proving the age of the document or recording. This can be done through the testimony of witnesses with knowledge, expert testimony regarding age, circumstantial evidence relating to the surrounding circumstances, analysis of contents, and/or physical appearance.

Process or System

Through Dec. 1, 2011	After Dec. 1, 2011
Rule 901(b), cont'd.	**Rule 901(b), cont'd**
(9) Process or system. Evidence describing a process or system used to produce a result and showing that the process or system produces an accurate result.	***(9) Evidence About a Process or System.*** Evidence describing a process or system and showing that it produces an accurate result.

Rule 901(b) is a useful way to solve the authentication problem presented by wiretap sound recordings, surveillance video camera footage, X-rays, and some types of computer output. The issue all these types of evidence have in common is that there may not be an authenticating witness who can testify that the matters recorded or produced fairly and accurately represent what they depict. In the matter of X-rays, for example, the X-ray technician has no personal knowledge about the interior of a patient's body. Likewise, in the case of a surveillance camera, the person watching the video recording of an incident has no personal knowledge of the incident; the camera serves as a sort of silent witness to the proceedings.

Under Rule 901(b)(9), an authenticating witness can establish that the equipment was in good working order, the operator was qualified to operate it and did so properly, that no changes were made to the recording, and that the process used by the equipment produces a certain type of result. The exact procedures for this type of authentication vary by jurisdiction.

Other Methods Provided by Statute or Rule

Some types of evidence can be authenticated by compliance with provisions established in other statutes, rule of civil or criminal procedure, or local court rules. These rules encourage efficiency in proof at trial and reduce the need for advocates to find foundation witnesses or rely on other doctrines to authenticate evidence.

Rule 901(b)(10) provides for authentication of evidence pursuant to other rules or statutes.

Through Dec. 1, 2011	After Dec. 1, 2011
Rule 901(b), cont'd.	**Rule 901(b), cont'd**
(10) Methods provided by statute or rule. Any method of authentication or identification provided by Act of Congress or by other rules prescribed by the Supreme Court pursuant to statutory authority.	*(10) Methods Provided by a Statute or Rule.* Any method of authentication or identification allowed by a federal statute or a rule prescribed by the Supreme Court.

Examples of other rules include Rule 44 of the Federal Rules of Civil Procedure, which provides for the authentication of public documents or copies of public documents accompanied by a seal; FRCP 30(f), which provides for prima facie authentication of depositions and documents attached to depositions, provided that the deponent identifies the documents during the deposition; and FRCP 80(c), authenticating transcripts of prior trials or hearings.

Self Authentication

Among the most useful evidentiary rules is Rule 902, with its laundry list of self-authentication provisions. The premise of the rule is that certain categories of evidence are inherently unlikely to be anything other than what they purport to be. Rather than force litigants to spend time and money authenticating these types of evidence, the rule dispenses with the requirement by declaring that the evidence is self-authenticating. For most of these items, the proponent can offer a certificate from a custodian or other responsible person attesting to the authenticity of the attached documents.

Through Dec. 1, 2011	After Dec. 1, 2011
Rule 902. Self-authentication	**Rule 902. Evidence That Is Self-Authenticating**
Extrinsic evidence of authenticity as a condition precedent to admissibility is not required with respect to the following:	The following items of evidence are self-authenticating; they require no extrinsic evidence of authenticity in order to be admitted:
(1) Domestic public documents under seal. A document bearing a seal purporting to be that of the United States, or of any State, district, Commonwealth, territory, or insular possession thereof, or the Panama Canal Zone, or the Trust Territory of the Pacific Islands, or of a political subdivision, department, officer, or agency thereof, and a signature purporting to be an attestation or execution.	**(1)** *Domestic Public Documents That Are Sealed and Signed.* A document that bears: (A) a seal purporting to be that of the United States; any state, district, commonwealth, territory, or insular possession of the United States; the former Panama Canal Zone; the Trust Territory of the Pacific Islands; a political subdivision of any of these entities; or a department, agency, or officer of any entity named above; and
(2) Domestic public documents not under seal. A document purporting to bear the signature in the official capacity of an officer or employee of any entity included in paragraph (1) hereof, having no seal, if a public officer having a seal and having official duties in the district or political subdivision of the officer or employee certifies under seal that the signer has the official capacity and that the signature is genuine.	(B) a signature purporting to be an execution or attestation. **(2)** *Domestic Public Documents That Are Not Sealed but Are Signed and Certified.* A document that bears no seal if: (A) it bears the signature of an officer or employee of an entity named in Rule 902(1)(A); and (B) another public officer who has a seal and official duties within that same entity certifies under seal — or its equivalent — that the signer has the official capacity and that the signature is genuine.

Through Dec. 1, 2011	After Dec. 1, 2011
Rule 902, cont'd	**Rule 902, cont'd**
(3) Foreign public documents. A document purporting to be executed or attested in an official capacity by a person authorized by the laws of a foreign country to make the execution or attestation, and accompanied by a final certification as to the genuineness of the signature and official position (A) of the executing or attesting person, or (B) of any foreign official whose certificate of genuineness of signature and official position relates to the execution or attestation or is in a chain of certificates of genuineness of signature and official position relating to the execution or attestation. A final certification may be made by a secretary of an embassy or legation, consul general, consul, vice consul, or consular agent of the United States, or a diplomatic or consular official of the foreign country assigned or accredited to the United States. If reasonable opportunity has been given to all parties to investigate the authenticity and accuracy of official documents, the court may, for good cause shown, order that they be treated as presumptively authentic without final certification or permit them to be evidenced by an attested summary with or without final certification.	**(3) Foreign Public Documents**. A document that purports to be signed or attested by a person who is authorized by a foreign country's law to do so. The document must be accompanied by a final certification that certifies the genuineness of the signature and official position of the signer or attester — or of any foreign official whose certificate of genuineness relates to the signature or attestation or is in a chain of certificates of genuineness relating to the signature or attestation. The certification may be made by a secretary of a United States embassy or legation; by a consul general, vice consul, or consular agent of the United States; or by a diplomatic or consular official of the foreign country assigned or accredited to the United States. If all parties have been given a reasonable opportunity to investigate the document's authenticity and accuracy, the court may, for good cause, either: (A) order that it be treated as presumptively authentic without final certification; or (B) allow it to be evidenced by an attested summary with or without final certification.
(4) Certified copies of public records. A copy of an official record or report or entry therein, or of a document authorized by law to be recorded or filed and actually recorded or filed in a public office, including data compilations in any form, certified as correct by the custodian or other person authorized to make the certification, by certificate complying with paragraph (1), (2), or (3) of this rule or complying with any Act of Congress or rule prescribed by the Supreme Court pursuant to statutory authority.	**(4) Certified Copies of Public Records**. A copy of an official record — or a copy of a document that was recorded or filed in a public office as authorized by law — if the copy is certified as correct by: (A) the custodian or another person authorized to make the certification; or (B) a certificate that complies with Rule 902(1), (2), or (3), a federal statute, or a rule prescribed by the Supreme Court.
(5) Official publications. Books, pamphlets, or other publications purporting to be issued by public authority.	**(5) Official Publications**. A book, pamphlet, or other publication purporting to be issued by a public authority.
(6) Newspapers and periodicals. Printed materials purporting to be newspapers or periodicals	**(6) Newspapers and Periodicals**. Printed material purporting to be a newspaper or periodical.

Through Dec. 1, 2011	After Dec. 1, 2011
Rule 902, cont'd	**Rule 902, cont'd**
(7) Trade inscriptions and the like. Inscriptions, signs, tags, or labels purporting to have been affixed in the course of business and indicating ownership, control, or origin.	*(7) Trade Inscriptions and the Like.* An inscription, sign, tag, or label purporting to have been affixed in the course of business and indicating origin, ownership, or control.
(8) Acknowledged documents. Documents accompanied by a certificate of acknowledgment executed in the manner provided by law by a notary public or other officer authorized by law to take acknowledgments.	*(8) Acknowledged Documents.* A document accompanied by a certificate of acknowledgment that is lawfully executed by a notary public or another officer who is authorized to take acknowledgments.
(9) Commercial paper and related documents. Commercial paper, signatures thereon, and documents relating thereto to the extent provided by general commercial law.	*(9) Commercial Paper and Related Documents.* Commercial paper, a signature on it, and related documents, to the extent allowed by general commercial law.
(10) Presumptions under Acts of Congress. Any signature, document, or other matter declared by Act of Congress to be presumptively or prima facie genuine or authentic.	*(10) Presumptions Under a Federal Statute.* A signature, document, or anything else that a federal statute declares to be presumptively or prima facie genuine or authentic.
(11) Certified domestic records of regularly conducted activity. The original or a duplicate of a domestic record of regularly conducted activity that would be admissible under Rule 803(6) if accompanied by a written declaration of its custodian or other qualified person, in a manner complying with any Act of Congress or rule prescribed by the Supreme Court pursuant to statutory authority, certifying that the record— (A) was made at or near the time of the occurrence of the matters set forth by, or from information transmitted by, a person with knowledge of those matters; (B) was kept in the course of the regularly conducted activity; and (C) was made by the regularly conducted activity as a regular practice. A party intending to offer a record into evidence under this paragraph must provide written notice of that intention to all adverse parties, and must make the record and declaration available for inspection sufficiently in advance of their offer into evidence to provide an adverse party with a fair opportunity to challenge them.	*(11) Certified Domestic Records of a Regularly Conducted Activity.* The original or a copy of a domestic record that meets the requirements of Rule 803(6)(A)-(C), as shown by a certification of the custodian or another qualified person that complies with a federal statute or a rule prescribed by the Supreme Court. Before the trial or hearing, the proponent must give an adverse party reasonable written notice of the intent to offer the record — and must make the record and certification available for inspection — so that the party has a fair opportunity to challenge them.

Through Dec. 1, 2011	After Dec. 1, 2011
Rule 902, cont'd	**Rule 902, cont'd**
(12) Certified foreign records of regularly conducted activity. In a civil case, the original or a duplicate of a foreign record of regularly conducted activity that would be admissible under Rule 803(6) if accompanied by a written declaration by its custodian or other qualified person certifying that the record—	*(12) Certified Foreign Records of a Regularly Conducted Activity.* In a civil case, the original or a copy of a foreign record that meets the requirements of Rule 902(11), modified as follows: the certification, rather than complying with a federal statute or Supreme Court rule, must be signed in a manner that, if falsely made, would subject the maker to a criminal penalty in the country where the certification is signed. The proponent must also meet the notice requirements of Rule 902(11).
(A) was made at or near the time of the occurrence of the matters set forth by, or from information transmitted by, a person with knowledge of those matters;	
(B) was kept in the course of the regularly conducted activity; and	
(C) was made by the regularly conducted activity as a regular practice.	
The declaration must be signed in a manner that, if falsely made, would subject the maker to criminal penalty under the laws of the country where the declaration is signed. A party intending to offer a record into evidence under this paragraph must provide written notice of that intention to all adverse parties, and must make the record and declaration available for inspection sufficiently in advance of their offer into evidence to provide an adverse party with a fair opportunity to challenge them.	

Rules 902(11) and 902(12), provide for the self-authentication of records of regularly conducted activities. These provisions allow advocates to introduce business records at trial without having to call foundation witnesses. Rules 902(11) and 902(12) combine the foundation requirements of the business records exception to the hearsay rule — Rule 803(6) with the traditional authentication requirement that a proponent must prove that a document is what it purports to be. Thus, the certificate must attest that the record was (1) made at or near the time of the occurrence; (2) by a person with knowledge of the matter or from information transmitted from such a person; (3) was kept in the course of a regularly conducted activity (e.g., a business); and (4) was made by the regularly conducted activity as a regular practice. Paragraphs 11 and 12 of Rule 902 each contain a notice provision so that an opponent can contest authentication or whether the record was actually kept in the course of a regularly conducted activity.

II. CASES, DISCUSSION QUESTIONS AND PROBLEMS

UNITED STATES v. SKIPPER
United States Court of Appeals, Fifth Circuit
74 F.3d 608 (5th Cir. 1996)

[The accused was convicted for possession of crack cocaine with intent to distribute. At trial, the government introduced evidence of his past convictions.]

At trial, pursuant to Federal Rule of Evidence 404(b), the district court admitted into evidence two state-court convictions for crimes allegedly committed by Skipper. Government Exhibit # 3 was a certified copy of a judgment against "John Derrick Skipper" indicating that Appellant pled guilty to possession of a controlled substance. An expert testified that the fingerprints on this conviction matched Appellant's fingerprints. Government Exhibit # 2 was a certified copy of a deferred adjudication order indicating that "John D. Skipper" was placed on ten years probation for possession of a controlled substance. However, this order did not bear any fingerprints, and the government did not otherwise identify Appellant as the person named in the order. . . .

II. Admissibility of Deferred Adjudication Order

We review the admission of evidence only for an abuse of discretion. Furthermore, even if we find an abuse of discretion in the admission or exclusion of evidence, we review the error under the harmless error doctrine. Finally, we must affirm evidentiary rulings unless they affect a substantial right of the complaining party. Fed. R. Evid. 103(a).

The district court admitted into evidence a deferred adjudication order indicating that a "John D. Skipper" was placed on ten years probation for possession of a controlled substance. However, the court erred in admitting this evidence because the government should have been required to produce evidence proving that Appellant was the actual "John D. Skipper" named in the deferred adjudication order. Rule 901(a) of the Federal Rules of Evidence provides: "The requirement of authentication or identification as a condition precedent to admissibility is satisfied by evidence sufficient to support a finding that the matter in question is what its proponent claims." We hold that the mere similarity in name between a criminal defendant and a person named in a prior conviction alone does not satisfy Rule 901's identification requirement.

Nevertheless, we find the court's error harmless. "In a harmless error examination, 'we must view the error, not in isolation, but in relation to the entire proceedings.' " United States v. Williams, 957 F.2d 1238, 1244 (5th Cir. 1992) (quoting United States v. Brown, 692 F.2d 345, 350 (5th Cir. 1982)). "We must decide whether the inadmissible evidence actually contributed to the jury's verdict." United States v. Gadison, 8 F.3d 186, 192 (5th Cir. 1993). Because the court properly admitted a similar possession conviction and instructed the jury on its limited purpose, the improperly admitted order did not actually contribute to the jury's verdict.

[The court reversed on other grounds, vacated the sentence and remanded for a new trial.]

UNITED STATES v. MILLER
United States Court Of Appeals, Eighth Circuit
994 F.2d 441 (8th Cir. 1993)

[The defendant was convicted by a jury of possession with intent to distribute cocaine base. During a search of defendant's premises pursuant to a warrant, officers caught the accused trying to stuff a matchbox full of cocaine rocks into his couch. Detective Turner seized the box.]

Turner gave the match box and its contents to Detective Jamie Dean, the case agent on the search warrant application.

After Dean inspected and examined the contents of the match box, he packaged and sealed it in an evidence envelope. Thereafter, he initialed it to insure that the contents were not tampered with. Dean's testimony is not too clear as to when he delivered the sealed evidence envelope to Sergeant McCurdy, the evidence officer. In any event, Sergeant McCurdy testified that he received the sealed evidence envelope from Dean on January 3, 1992. McCurdy further testified that he hand carried the evidence to the Arkansas State Crime Laboratory on January 7, 1992.

Linda Burdick, a forensic chemist at the Arkansas State Crime Laboratory, testified that on January 10, 1992, she removed the sealed evidence envelope from the evidence storage room and analyzed it. According to her testimony she found the match box to contain 1.095 grams of cocaine base with a purity level of 89%. After Burdick completed her examination of the drug package, she put her initials on it, the laboratory case number and the date she resealed the package. The evidence package was then returned to the Pine Bluff Police Department where it remained until produced for Appellant's trial.

Appellant's sole contention on appeal is that the district court abused its discretion by permitting the government to introduce the match box and its contents into evidence as its exhibit No. 1 without a proper showing of the chain of custody. Specifically, Appellant complains that the government failed to show where exhibit No. 1 was between December 5, 1991, and January 3, 1992.

We review a district court's rulings on the admission of evidence on a clear abuse of discretion standard. Where a real or physical object is offered as evidence in a criminal prosecution, an adequate foundation for the admission of that object requires testimony first, that such object is the same object which was involved in the alleged incident, and that the condition of that object is substantially unchanged. Charles T. McCormick et al., McCormick on Evidence, § 212, at 527 (2nd ed. 1972). If the object sought to be introduced into evidence is one impervious to change, the discretion of the trial judge is very broad; on the other hand, where the object is one not readily identifiable, or susceptible to alteration by tampering or contamination, the trial judge's discretion may require a substantially more elaborate foundation. Id.

The district court may admit a piece of physical evidence if it is satisfied that there is a reasonable probability that such evidence has not been changed or altered.

Moreover, the integrity of such evidence is presumed to be preserved unless there is a showing of bad faith, ill will, or proof that the evidence has been tampered with. See United States v. Brown, 482 F.2d 1226, 1228 (8th Cir. 1973) (where no evidence indicating otherwise is produced, the presumption of regularity supports the official acts of public officers, and courts presume that they have properly discharged their official duties).

The government could have easily avoided the problem presented here, by having each officer who handled exhibit No. 1 identify his or her initials on the exhibit and to state whether the exhibit was in substantially the same physical condition at the time he or she first saw it and at the time of trial. Nonetheless, the testimony presented by the government beginning with Detective Dean who placed the match box in the sealed package and initialed it, reasonably shows that exhibit No. 1 was unchanged: Dean gave it to Sergeant McCurdy, who testified that exhibit No. 1 was sealed and taped; McCurdy took it to The Arkansas State Crime Laboratory; Miss Burdick testified that she removed the evidence from storage room, opened and tested it, and then initialed and resealed it. The evidence package was then returned to the Pine Bluff Police Department where it was kept until brought into court for Appellant's trial. On this showing alone, we hold that the district court did not abuse its discretion in allowing into evidence the government's exhibit No. 1.

Furthermore, where, as in the present case, the Appellant made no showing that none of the police officers or laboratory employees tampered or altered the evidence, the officials are entitled to the presumption of integrity. United States v. Doddington, 822 F.2d 818, 822 (8th Cir. 1987) (citations omitted).

Accordingly, the judgment of the district court is affirmed.

PEOPLE v. HOWARD
Appellate Court of Illinois, Second District
387 Ill. App. 3d 997 (2009)

[Defendant was convicted of delivery of more than 15 but less than 100 grams of cocaine. During a controlled buy on June 26, 2006, police officers purchased a baggie containing 53 grams of a white powder from the accused. An officer named Gately took the baggie into custody and packaged it for evidence. Another officer, Wellbank, testified that he took the evidence to Monroe and put it in a safe to which only he had the key. He did not, however, note this on the chain of custody form. Two days later, on June 28, Wellbank retrieved the evidence and dropped it into an evidence chute for the Illinois State Crime Lab Zone 16 vault in Rockport. Trooper Renaldo signed the chain of custody form for the Crime Lab on July 3 or July 5 (the entry was unclear). There was testimony that the evidence was handled another time on July 5, but no explanation about who handled it, or why. Wellbank later retrieved the bag from Renaldo. Officer Madigan of the Freeport Police Department retrieved it from Wellbank in the Zone 2 investigations office. There was no satisfactory explanation for how the evidence was transported from Zone 16 to Zone 2. Madigan took it to the state police crime lab on October 3, where it was tested by Skelcy and repackaged. Skelcy stored it in a secure evidence vault until October 18, when Madigan retrieved the evidence from the crime lab and placed it in an evidence locker at the Freeport police department.]

On appeal, defendant argues that the State failed to establish a sufficient chain of custody for the admission of the cocaine exhibit and its associated evidence, making the evidence insufficient to sustain his conviction. He asserts that, because the State did not explain the two times the evidence bag was handled when Wellbank put it in the drop box and when he retrieved it for Madigan to take it to the lab, the State failed to show that the police took reasonable protective measures. He also argues that the lack of evidence of a unique inventory number means that the police failed to use adequate measures to prevent the accidental substitution of samples. The State argues that the two weight measurements of the contraband, in combination with the officers' badge numbers and initials and the date, adequately identified it. Further, it argues that the evidence adequately explained the "extra" entries on the chain-of-custody form. We agree with defendant on one point; we deem that the State failed to provide proper evidence that no accidental substitution of the evidence occurred, so that the court should not have admitted the exhibit and related evidence. This was reversible error. . . .

The rules of evidence require that, before the State can introduce results of chemical testing of a purported controlled substance, it must provide a foundation for their admission by showing "that the police took reasonable protective measures to ensure that the substance recovered from the defendant was the same substance tested by the forensic chemist." People v. Woods, 214 Ill. 2d 455, 467, 293 Ill. Dec. 277, 828 N.E.2d 247 (2005). . . . Further, before admitting the physical evidence and the test results, the trial court must determine whether the State has met its "burden to establish a custody chain that is sufficiently complete to make it improbable that the evidence has been subject to tampering or accidental substitution." Woods, 214 Ill. 2d at 467. " '[A] trial court's ruling on the sufficiency of a chain of custody is subject to reversal only for an abuse of discretion.' " People v. Dixon, 228 Ill. App. 3d 29, 38, 170 Ill. Dec. 424, 592 N.E.2d 1104 (1992).

Illinois decisions endorse the use of one unique identifier to show that each person in a chain of custody is describing the same piece of evidence; the unique identifier is typically a police inventory number. Use of one unique identifier is the simplest, and so the most satisfactory, method of showing that each person was handling the same evidence. Indeed, if police and crime lab procedure has been reasonable, we can see no reason that the State would present its foundational evidence in another form. That said, if the State does ignore the standard, but nevertheless establishes "a custody chain that is sufficiently complete to make it improbable that the evidence has been subject to tampering or accidental substitution" (Woods, 214 Ill. 2d at 467), a trial court arguably would have discretion to accept the foundation. Despite that possible flexibility, the absence here of adequate protection against accidental substitution precludes our holding that the foundation was sufficient.

Wellbank and Gately described marking the evidence bag with their initials and badge numbers, the date, and other unspecified information. They also described weighing the baggie before placing it in the evidence bag, resulting in a measurement similar to Skelcy's. The State argues that the weight measurements, taken with the initials, badge numbers, and date, are sufficient to show that accidental substitution was improbable. We disagree. The State would have shown that accidental substitution was improbable only if it showed that it was improbable that the same officers would have handled another bag of white powder of similar weight on that day. Narcotics enforcement is SLANT's function, so we are not prepared to assume that two SLANT officers would not make two or more similar drug purchases in one day. Gately's vague testimony that this was "one of the higher purchases for the Freeport area" is insufficient to support that assumption.

Careful reading of the testimony suggests that the case for the foundation having been sufficient is stronger than the State's arguments on appeal would indicate. Several custodians' testimony raised points suggesting that the police labeled the evidence bag more thoroughly than the State's brief (and initial impressions) would suggest. Those additional points favoring admission are not enough, however, to change the result here. The additional points give only a fragmented view of the police treatment of the evidence. To meld and form those points into a basis for affirmance — even assuming that to be possible — would require us to engage in outright advocacy for the State's position. Such advocacy by the court is inappropriate. We now review those points and explain why they do not form a clear basis for admission.

Madigan mentioned that the police had designated — and labeled — the cocaine exhibit as exhibit No. 6. (Gately mentioned this as well, but only after the court had already admitted the exhibit.) Wellbank's and Gately's testimony shows that, after the rendezvous, Gately wrote in an area at the top of the bag information to which he did not testify. If we assume that Gately added the exhibit number after the rendezvous or that what Gately wrote at the top of the bag contained unique identifiers, our concerns about identification would be much alleviated. However, either assumption would be based on an inference that itself would be based on the assumption that the police acted reasonably. However fair that latter assumption is, it would be improper in this context. We cannot assume reasonable procedure; it is the State's burden to establish the use of such procedure. Woods, 214 Ill. 2d at 467.

We are aware that, unlike us, the trial court most likely could actually see the information on the evidence bag when it made its ruling. The court may have known what Gately wrote on the bag but that possibility does not compel a finding of admissibility, because the court did not make a record of any observations that led it to conclude that admission was proper. Furthermore, the State could have supplemented the record on appeal to indicate the unexplained information on the evidence bag, but the State failed to do so. Absent a complete record of the trial court's observations or any other record of the information on the bag, our review of the admissibility issue is limited to the witnesses' vague testimony in the transcript.

The State's "burden [was] to establish a custody chain that is sufficiently complete to make it improbable that the evidence has been subject to tampering or accidental substitution." Woods, 214 Ill. 2d at 467. The initials, badge numbers, date, and weight measurements fail that standard as a matter of law. For us to accept other information as overcoming the weaknesses of that information would require us to become advocates for the State's position. Thus, despite the deference we accord the trial court under an abuse of discretion standard, we must hold that admission of the exhibit was improper.

Although we conclude, based on the record before us, that the trial court erred in admitting the cocaine exhibit and related evidence, defendant is not entitled to an outright reversal; the State may retry him without offending double jeopardy principles.

DISCUSSION QUESTIONS

1. What lessons about authentication and documents can you draw from *Skipper*?

2. Suppose the only prior bad act evidence available in *Skipper* was the deferred adjudication order. Would the court have held differently on the issue of harmless error?

3. What legal standards does the court apply to: (1) the judge's ruling; (2) the errors, if any?

4. Compare the *Miller* and *Howard* cases, which involve similar chain of custody issues. Which court has the better analysis? Why did the *Howard* court reverse?

2. When dealing with fungible evidence such as cocaine, does it make sense for chain of custody evidence to be broadly construed or narrowly construed? Why?

3. What are the dangers, if any, of sloppy chain of custody management and presentation?

PROBLEMS

Problem 17-1. On October 13, the Calamity County Sheriff's department responded to the report of a fight in progress in the stands at the Calamity 500, a NASCAR race. Bobby Best and Jimmie Garrett, both intoxicated, were fighting over whether the Calamity 500 should adopt restrictor plate racing. During the altercation, Best struck Garrett on the head with a portable scanner that he used to listen to radio conversations between his favorite driver and the pit crew. Garrett suffered a gash to his head, bruising and a concussion. Deputy Sheriff Patty Ham arrested Best and took the radio into evidence. She scratched her initials and badge number — "PH 06" — on a metal plate on the case of the radio and took it to the Sheriff's Department evidence locker. Because of faulty wiring, the radio caught on fire while in storage. The radio's cheap plastic case melted, rendering the radio unrecognizable. The metal where Ham had scratched her initials was bent and twisted, but the initials were still there.

Best is charged with aggravated battery for his use of the radio against Garrett. At trial, the prosecutor attempts to offer the radio into evidence. The defense objects, claiming that the object is not in the same condition as it was when received into evidence and therefore cannot be authenticated. How should the prosecution respond? How should the judge rule?

Problem 17-2. Beef McGraw was a large, powerful, jealous man who couldn't stand the thought of his girlfriend, Mary Jane, spending time with or talking to other men. Mary Jane's job as a sales clerk at an automotive parts store made it difficult for her to avoid other men. On several occasions, Beef angrily confronted men who were flirting with Mary Jane at the checkout stand. Tired of Beef's jealous rages, Mary Jane finally broke up with him. Two weeks later, Mary Jane disappeared after work. Her badly battered body was found in a field a few days later. There was no DNA evidence, fingerprint evidence, eyewitness evidence or anything else that could link her death to Beef. Beef publicly expressed his grief about Mary Jane's death and vowed not to rest until the killer was found.

During its investigation of the murder, the Calamity Bureau of Investigation found an undated, typewritten letter in the glovebox of Mary's car. There was nothing special or distinguishing about the font. The letter had no signature, fingerprints or other identifying material, other than Mary Jane's fingerprints. The text of the letter read as follows:

MJ,

You know bad things happen to people who dis me. Remember Shorty, cause you don't want anything like that to happen to you. I don't want anything like that to happen to you, I promise, but I can't guarantee I can stop it if my heart is broken, just like with Shorty. I would never hurt you on purpose but if you hurt me that bad I can't say what would happen. Think about that song Can't Let You Go, because it's a true song. If we could just talk it would be better but u won't talk to me and that hurts more than you know.

Think about it.

Love,

Me

The CBI believed the letter was a threat from Beef McGraw. Beef, however, was not cooperating with the investigation, on the advice of famed defense attorney Graybeard Schroeder. None of the CBI's usual informants knew anything about Shorty. The CBI finally showed the letter to Mary Jane's sister, Jenny Jane. Jenny read it and said, "This is from Beef. I'm sure of it. First, he always called her MJ. And Shorty? Shorty was his dog. He took Shorty hunting one day with Mary Jane and me, and Shorty ate the picnic lunch that Beef had made for us. Beef went into a rage and snapped Shorty's neck. Then he just broke down sobbing like a baby. And the song — Can't Let You Go? — that was one of Beef's favorite songs. He used to listen to it all the time. It's a Rainbow song from the '80's about a guy who can't let go of a relationship even though it's over."

Beef is charged with murder. The letter is the prosecution's main item of evidence against him. Can this letter be authenticated at trial? Why or why not?

Problem 17-3. Darryl "Dimebag" Defendant is on trial for possession of 100 pounds of marijuana with intent to distribute. The marijuana was found in the trunk of his car pursuant to a valid search warrant. Darryl was nowhere near the car when the marijuana was found. His good friend, Carl Co-Defendant, was arrested a few days before police found Darryl. Pursuant to a cooperation agreement with the police, Carl agreed to call Darryl on the telephone. The conversation was recorded and monitored by Special Agent Jeff Hagler. During the conversation, Darryl said, "It sucks to lose 100 pounds of marijuana, but that's the breaks. I'll just lay low for a couple of months and try again." At trial, Carl is not available to identify Darryl's voice. Instead, the prosecution calls Hagler to identify the voice.

> *Prosecutor: Are you familiar with the voice on the tape?*
>
> *Hagler: I am*
>
> *Prosecutor: And how did you become familiar with this voice?*
>
> *Hagler: I attended Mr. Defendant's arraignment and heard him answer the judge's questions.*

The defense objects that Hagler's testimony is insufficient to authenticate Darryl's voice. How should the judge rule, and why?

Problem 17-4. Pat Plaintiff is suing Ramona Realtor for injuries she sustained in an automobile accident while riding in Realtor's CarCo Luxuriant automobile as a passenger. Plaintiff alleges that Realtor negligently maintained her car's computerized braking system and did not have the car repaired pursuant to a recall notice from the manufacturer, CarCo. The brakes caught fire and were destroyed in the accident. **(1)** At trial, plaintiff wants to introduce a model of the brake system used in Realtor's vehicle. What must plaintiff do to authenticate the model? **(2)** In her responsive pleadings, Realtor alleges that she never received a copy of the recall notice from the manufacturer. At trial, Plaintiff offers to admit into evidence a letter that a local dealership received on Realtor's letterhead. Ramona's attorney counters that the letter is not authenticated and could have been written by anyone. Should the judge admit the letter? Why or why not?

Ramona Realty
"If We Can't Sell It, You Should Condemn It"
3115 Pike Boulevard
Calamity City, Calamity 12345

Aug. 1, Current Year

Local Automobiles
Attn: Service Manager
5255 Robertson Lane
Calamity City, Calamity 12345

Dear Sir,

I just received a recall notice from CarCo about the computerized braking system in my brand-new Luxuriant. The letter was dated July 15. Since I just had my car serviced at your dealership on July 10, I am wondering if it is really necessary for me to bring the car in. The mechanic said everything was running great. Unless I hear back from you, I won't bring it in. I'm a busy woman, time is money, and I can't afford to keep bringing my car back in and losing it for a day at a time.

Sincerely,
Ramona Realtor

Authentication: Quick Hits

- There are several types of evidence that must be authenticated at trial: real evidence (both fungible and non-fungible), documents, voice recordings, photographs, video recordings, and the like

- Authentication, which establishes that an item of evidence is in fact what it purports to be, is a condition precedent to introducing evidence at trial

- Attorneys must identify the proper foundational witnesses and questions in order to authenticate evidence

- Parties can stipulate to the authentication of evidence but should be prepared to offer "strict proof" of authentication if necessary

- Fungible evidence requires establishing a chain of custody accounting for the evidence from the time of seizure to its appearance in court

- Rule 902 contains numerous self-authentication provisions for evidence — such as public records and business documents — that is unlikely to be anything other than what it purports to be

Chapter References

CHRISTOPHER B. MUELLER & LAIRD C. KIRKPATRICK, EVIDENCE §§ 9.1–9.30 (4th ed. 2009).

GLEN WEISSENBERGER & JAMES J. DUANE, FEDERAL RULES OF EVIDENCE: RULES, LEGISLATIVE HISTORY, COMMENTARY AND AUTHORITY §§ 901–02 (6th ed. 2009).

JACK B. WEINSTEIN & MARGARET A. BERGER, WEINSTEIN'S FEDERAL EVIDENCE §§ 901–02 (Joseph M. McLaughlin ed., Matthew Bender 2d ed. 1997).

KENNETH S. BROUN, McCORMICK ON EVIDENCE §§ 221–29 (6th ed. 2006).

STEVEN GOODE & OLIN GUY WELLBORN III, COURTROOM HANDBOOK ON FEDERAL EVIDENCE Ch. 5 (West 2010).

III. APPLICATION EXERCISE

Procedures for Chain of Custody

In authenticating an item of evidence through chain of custody, the proponent must account for the evidence from the time it was seized to its introduction into the courtroom. Provided that the chain of custody paperwork is in order, it is generally not necessary to call every person who may have handled the evidence. The witness who establishes the chain of custody can testify about the procedures used and can explain each step in the chain of custody. When there are issues with the chain of custody, however, as in the *Howard* case above, it may be necessary to call each person in the chain to explain their handling and transfer of the evidence.

If the opponent believes the proponent has not established a sufficient chain of custody, the opponent should object and explain the deficiencies. The opponent can request the opportunity to cross-examine (or *voir dire*) the witness in aid of objection.

The Exercise

1. *Objective*: To demonstrate the chain of custody for fungible evidence and establish a complete chain of custody in a courtroom exercise.

2. *Factual Scenario.* As part of the Anti-Obesity Act, the State of Calamity has criminalized possession of Oreo cookies with intent to distribute. Possession of two or more Oreos creates a presumption of intent to distribute. The arresting officer will run a sting operation and arrest the accused for violating Calamity law. The Oreos will be tagged, bagged, taken into custody and tested using the scientifically valid "consumption taste test." A standard Calamity chain of custody voucher will be used to account for the Oreos at each stage of the process. After we have seen all these steps take place, we will then shift to the courtroom, where a prosecuting attorney will attempt to establish a chain of custody for the evidence.

3. *Advance Preparation.* Familiarize yourself with the procedures for establishing a chain of custody in the courtroom.

4. *In-Class Exercise.* Students will play the following roles: (1) undercover agent/arresting officer; (2) crime lab evidence custodian; (3) lab technician (taste test); (4) prosecuting attorney; (5) defense attorney; (6) judge.

Chapter 18

BEST EVIDENCE (ORIGINAL DOCUMENTS) RULE

Chapter Objectives:

- Introduce and explain Rules 1001-1008, the "best evidence" rule, and the methods used in admitting originals and duplicates, and in successfully challenging evidence on best evidence grounds
- Analyze and discuss issues pertaining to Rules 1001-1008
- Apply the concepts from this chapter in a courtroom application exercise

---

I. BACKGROUND AND EXPLANATORY MATERIAL

Introduction to the Best Evidence Rule

The Best Evidence Rule is inaptly named. It has almost nothing at all to do with ensuring the presentation of the highest quality evidence possible at trial, a concept known as the best evidence principle.[1] Instead, the Best Evidence Rule requires the introduction of original documents or recordings under relatively narrow circumstances, when the contents of the document or recording are in question. The rule ought to be called the Original Document Rule. (In fact, many evidence scholars and advocacy teachers refer to it by that name to enhance clarity and alleviate confusion.)

Many centuries ago, the Best Evidence Rule encompassed both the original documents rule and the best evidence principle. Over time, however, the Best Evidence Rule shifted its focus to documents. The quality of evidence introduced at trial became a discretionary decision for advocates. While it might be desirable for an advocate always to present the highest quality evidence, it is not always possible, and there is no ironclad requirement to do so. An advocate may choose to introduce circumstantial evidence, descriptions, photographs, or similar representations of the evidence. Thus, if a key item of real evidence is not available at trial (for instance, in a criminal case where the murder weapon is never found),

---

[1] For an excellent explanation of the best evidence principle, see generally Dale A. Nance, *The Best Evidence Principle*, 73 Iowa L. Rev. 227 (1988).

the parties can introduce testimonial or secondary evidence about the item of evidence. Similarly, there is no requirement to produce audio or video recordings of conversations, even if they are available; an attorney can simply present testimony from a witness recounting the conversation to the best of the witness's recollection.

The modern Best Evidence Rule reflects an era long since past, when documents were laboriously duplicated by hand and the possibilities for error were legion. If everyone agreed on the content of the document, the use of secondary evidence presented no problems. In fact, it promoted judicial economy and efficiency. If, however, the parties could not agree on the content of a document, common law courts applied the logical doctrine that the original document itself was the best evidence of its content. Hence the name "Best Evidence Rule."

Rule 1002 codifies the common law Best Evidence Rule. According to the rule, the original of a writing, recording or photograph is required in order to prove its contents. An important corollary to the best evidence rule is Rule 1003, which treats duplicates the same as originals unless there are questions concerning the authenticity of the original or duplicate or it would be unfair to admit a duplicate. The text of these rules follows:

Through Dec. 1, 2011	After Dec. 1, 2011
Rule 1002. Requirement of Original	**Rule 1002. Requirement of the Original**
To prove the content of a writing, recording, or photograph, the original writing, recording, or photograph is required, except as otherwise provided in these rules or by Act of Congress.	An original writing, recording, or photograph is required in order to prove its content unless these rules or a federal statute provides otherwise.
Rule 1003. Admissibility of Duplicates	**Rule 1003. Admissibility of Duplicates**
A duplicate is admissible to the same extent as an original unless (1) a genuine question is raised as to the authenticity of the original or (2) in the circumstances it would be unfair to admit the duplicate in lieu of the original.	A duplicate is admissible to the same extent as the original unless a genuine question is raised about the original's authenticity or the circumstances make it unfair to admit the duplicate.

Definitions

Definitions are the key to understanding the Best Evidence Rule. The definitions for writings, recordings, and photographs are self-explanatory, although it should be noted that the rule broadly defines photographs to include X-rays, videotapes, and motion pictures. The most important terms the rule defines are "originals" and "duplicates."

Rule 1001 defines the necessary terms to understand and apply the Best Evidence Rule.

Through Dec. 1, 2011	After Dec. 1, 2011
Rule 1001. Definitions	**Rule 1001. Definitions That Apply to This Article [Article X]**
For purposes of this article the following definitions are applicable:	In this article:
(1) Writings and recordings. "Writings" and "recordings" consist of letters, words, or numbers, or their equivalent, set down by handwriting, typewriting, printing, photostating, photographing, magnetic impulse, mechanical or electronic recording, or other form of data compilation.	(a) A "writing" consists of letters, words, numbers, or their equivalent set down in any form.
	(b) A "recording" consists of letters, words, numbers, or their equivalent recorded in any manner.
(2) Photographs. "Photographs" include still photographs, X-ray films, video tapes, and motion pictures.	(c) A "photograph" means a photographic image or its equivalent stored in any form.
(3) Original. An "original" of a writing or recording is the writing or recording itself or any counterpart intended to have the same effect by a person executing or issuing it. An "original" of a photograph includes the negative or any print therefrom. If data are stored in a computer or similar device, any printout or other output readable by sight, shown to reflect the data accurately, is an "original".	(d) An "original" of a writing or recording means the writing or recording itself or any counterpart intended to have the same effect by the person who executed or issued it. For electronically stored information, "original" means any printout — or other output readable by sight — if it accurately reflects the information. An "original" of a photograph includes the negative or a print from it.
(4) Duplicate. A "duplicate" is a counterpart produced by the same impression as the original, or from the same matrix, or by means of photography, including enlargements and miniatures, or by mechanical or electronic re-recording, or by chemical reproduction, or by other equivalent techniques which accurately reproduces the original.	(e) A "duplicate" means a counterpart produced by a mechanical, photographic, chemical, electronic, or other equivalent process or technique that accurately reproduces the original.

Originals

In the case of writings, an original is either the writing itself or a counterpart intended to have the same effect. The term "original" may seem almost too obvious to merit comment; the fair connotation of the word "original" has a chronological component, suggesting the first document produced in time. There are circumstances, however, when the first document chronologically is not actually the original. Weinstein's Federal Evidence, an influential evidence treatise, explains some of these nuances:[2]

> This technical definition may be quite different from what "original" means in lay terms. When a particular writing reproduces the terms of another document, ordinary usage would call the former the "copy" or "duplicate," while the latter would be termed the "original." In this "lay" sense, the term "original," "duplicate," and "copy" have a chronological dimension. Under Rule 1001(3), however, chronology is not decisive.
>
> For purposes of the best evidence rule, the "original" is simply the writing or recording whose contents are to be proved. This jural significance is what determines whether a writing or recordng is an original, regardless of whether it was (1) written or recorded before or after another, (2) copied from another, or (3) itself used to make further copies. For example, in one case, the appellate court concluded that a corporate officer had complied with a subpoena seeking the production of "original records" by submitting photocopies.
>
> Part of the problem is simply semantic because of the ambiguity of the word "copy." Since the term "copy" is sometimes applied to what is really an original writing or recording, the mere fact that a writing or recording is referred to as a "copy" is not conclusive. However, the question of what is an original is essentially one of relevancy and not semantics. If we ask, "what is the writing or recording being offered to prove?" the identity of the original often becomes apparent. If it is the terms of a contract, then the signed agreement is the contract containing its terms. If we are trying to show delivery of goods, the original is the signed receipt. If we are trying to show shipment of goods, the original may be the shipping clerk's tally sheet. If we are trying to show an offer, the original may be the signed letter received. If we are trying to show authority to make the offer, the original may be a carbon copy of the agent's letter in the principal's file.
>
> Depending on the issue, a writing or recording may be both a copy and an original in the same case. For example, to show an offer, the original signed copy of a letter is the original; however, to show that someone knew of the offer, a carbon copy in his or her file would be the original. On the other hand, the carbon would be a copy when seeking to show what was received by the offeree, and the signed letter a copy to show what was in the file.

A counterpart is a writing that both parties intend to serve as the original. It could be a specific duplicate or copy made later in time, so long as the parties intend for it to be treated as if it were the original.

An original writing also includes computer printouts of information stored on a computer. This is important to understand, because the information actually stored on the computer is in binary form and does not actually exist in the format that appears on the printout. Nonetheless, for all practical and reasonable purposes, the printout should be treated as the original, because without the translation medium provided by the computer operating system and software, the 1's and 0's of a

---

[2] 6 Jack B. Weinstein & Margaret A. Berger, Weinstein's Federal Evidence § 1001.08 (2d ed.)

computer record would be meaningless to a juror.

With respect to photographs, the definition of original includes both the negative and prints produced from it. As Weinstein points out, though, if the negative contains details that are not visible in a print, there is a preference for the negative to be treated as the original.[3] With respect to X-rays, the negative is preferred as an original, although there is some authority for the use of a print made from an X-ray negative.

Duplicates

Simply put, a duplicate is a faithful and accurate reproduction of the original. Rule 1001 lists several duplicating techniques that are common for various types of media, but the key phrase is "other equivalent techniques which accurately reproduce[] the original." This phrase is broad enough to encompass technological changes that improve the speed and accuracy of the duplication process.

Rule 1003 states that duplicates are admissible to the same extent as originals unless there is a genuine question as to the authenticity of the original or it would be unfair to admit the duplicate in lieu of the original. Although the rule does not specifically state it, a corollary principle is that a duplicate is inadmissible if there are significant questions about the authenticity and accuracy of the duplicate itself.

For all intents and purposes, a duplicate is treated exactly as an original at trial.

The Best Evidence Rule in Application

The Best Evidence Rule only comes into play when the contents of a writing, recording or photograph are at issue. If the contents are not at issue, there is no need to produce an original document (or a duplicate that is treated as an original) at trial. The question for advocates thus becomes — when are the contents of a writing, recording or photograph actually at issue? Some situations are obvious, such as proving the terms of a written contract or a will. If the terms of the contract or will are at issue, then the contents of a writing are involved, and the Best Evidence Rule applies. If, however, the issue is slightly different — such as whether a will or contract exists — the terms of a writing are not at issue and the rule doesn't apply.

If a fact or an event has been recorded or reduced to writing, the Best Evidence Rule does not require that the proponent introduce the actual recording or document. This is because what is at issue is the fact or event itself, not the contents of the recording or document that captured it. Thus, a party can call a witness with actual knowledge of the fact or event and does not have to produce the actual document or recording. If, however, the witness only gained his knowledge of the event from the document or recording, the Best Evidence Rule is implicated: the witness is essentially testifying about the contents of the document or recording and lacks personal knowledge within the meaning of Rule 602.

---

[3] Weinstein'S Federal Evidence § 1001.08[10][b].

Secondary Evidence

Rule 1004 trumps the Best Evidence Rule if the original document or recording is lost, destroyed, unobtainable, in the possession of an opponent, or so unrelated to the central issue at trial as to be insignificant. Under those circumstances, a party can introduce other evidence of the contents of a document or recording. This evidence typically consists of testimony from a witness with knowledge of the writing or recording. It can also consist of other types of proof, such as hand-made copies that the parties have certified to be accurate, the transcript of a recording, or the like.

The text of Rule 1004 follows:

Through Dec. 1, 2011	After Dec. 1, 2011
Rule 1004. Admissibility of Other Evidence of Contents	**Rule 1004. Admissibility of Other Evidence of Content**
The original is not required, and other evidence of the contents of a writing, recording, or photograph is admissible if—	An original is not required and other evidence of the content of a writing, recording, or photograph is admissible if:
(1) Originals lost or destroyed. All originals are lost or have been destroyed, unless the proponent lost or destroyed them in bad faith; or	(a) all the originals are lost or destroyed, and not by the proponent acting in bad faith;
(2) Original not obtainable. No original can be obtained by any available judicial process or procedure; or	(b) an original cannot be obtained by any available judicial process;
(3) Original in possession of opponent. At a time when an original was under the control of the party against whom offered, that party was put on notice, by the pleadings or otherwise, that the contents would be a subject of proof at the hearing, and that party does not produce the original at the hearing; or	(c) the party against whom the original would be offered had control of the original; was at that time put on notice, by pleadings or otherwise, that the original would be a subject of proof at the trial or hearing; and fails to produce it at the trial or hearing; or
(4) Collateral matters. The writing, recording, or photograph is not closely related to a controlling issue.	(d) the writing, recording, or photograph is not closely related to a controlling issue.

A key foundational prerequisite to the use of secondary evidence under Rule 1004 is a finding that the original once existed, or exists and cannot be obtained. This is a question of preliminary admissibility under FRE 104(a), and the judge must find by a preponderance of the evidence that there was an original and that it has been lost, destroyed, or cannot be obtained.

There are a variety of reasons to support a finding that an original cannot be obtained. It might be infeasible to produce an original, as in the case of "an inscription on a 30-ton piece of heavy equipment or an item of personal property which should be promptly returned to the owner." The original may be beyond the reach of judicial process, as might be the case for documents that are located in foreign jurisdictions that do not recognize the subpoena power of a US court.

Rule 1004 also has an equitable component. If a proponent has lost or destroyed documents or recordings in bad faith, the proponent does not get the benefit of using secondary evidence to prove its contents; he gets no benefit from his wrongdoing. On the other hand, if the opponent of the document or recording refuses to produce it at trial, he cannot complain when the proponent is permitted to introduce secondary evidence of its contents.

Finally, Rule 1004 recognizes that a court does not have unlimited time or resources to require strict proof in collateral matters. Thus, if a document or recording is not central to the case — not closely related to a controlling issue — the rule is flexible enough to permit secondary proof of contents in order to spare everyone the unnecessary time and expense of production.

Copies of Public Records

Through Dec. 1, 2011	After Dec. 1, 2011
Rule 1005. Public Records	**Rule 1005. Copies of Public Records to Prove Content**
The contents of an official record, or of a document authorized to be recorded or filed and actually recorded or filed, including data compilations in any form, if otherwise admissible, may be proved by copy, certified as correct in accordance with rule 902 or testified to be correct by a witness who has compared it with the original. If a copy which complies with the foregoing cannot be obtained by the exercise of reasonable diligence, then other evidence of the contents may be given.	The proponent may use a copy to prove the content of an official record — or of a document that was recorded or filed in a public office as authorized by law — if these conditions are met: the record or document is otherwise admissible; and the copy is certified as correct in accordance with Rule 902(4) or is testified to be correct by a witness who has compared it with the original. If no such copy can be obtained by reasonable diligence, then the proponent may use other evidence to prove the content.

Rule 1005 presents a slight twist to the doctrines contained in the Best Evidence Rule and Rule 1004. The rule encompasses two strongly held values: (1) the significant role of public records in the judicial process; and (2) the importance of retaining the originals of public records in their normal locations to ensure their availability to the public and to avoid their loss or damage. To accommodate those values, Rule 1005 turns the Best Evidence Rule on its head by establishing a preference for a certified copy over the original: either a copy that complies with the self-authentication provisions of Rule 902, or one whose correctness is established by a witness with knowledge of the original.

If copies that comply with Rule 1005 cannot be obtained "by the exercise of reasonable diligence," the rule then permits secondary evidence to prove the contents of the document. Significantly, the rule does not require findings of loss, destruction, or improper behavior by the parties as a condition precedent to introducing secondary evidence. As with the predicate findings for Rule 1004, the question of whether a proponent has exercised reasonable diligence is a preliminary finding for the judge under Rule 104(a).

On the rare occasions when a dispute about a public record rages on to the extent that it can only be solved by production of the original, the judge does, of course, retain the ability to order the production, safeguarding, and quick return to its repository of the original to help settle the dispute.

Summaries

Through Dec. 1, 2011	After Dec. 1, 2011
Rule 1006. Summaries	**Rule 1006. Summaries to Prove Content**
The contents of voluminous writings, recordings, or photographs which cannot conveniently be examined in court may be presented in the form of a chart, summary, or calculation. The originals, or duplicates, shall be made available for examination or copying, or both, by other parties at reasonable time and place. The court may order that they be produced in court.	The proponent may use a summary, chart, or calculation to prove the content of voluminous writings, recordings, or photographs that cannot be conveniently examined in court. The proponent must make the originals or duplicates available for examination or copying, or both, by other parties at a reasonable time and place. And the court may order the proponent to produce them in court.

Rule 1006 presents another wrinkle to the Best Evidence Rule. The sheer volume of documents in modern litigation can be staggering. In many instances, it would be neither desirable nor practicable to produce and examine the originals or duplicates in the courtroom. Rule 1006 permits the use of charts, summaries or calculations in the courtroom, provided that the source documents are made available for examination and/or copying by the other parties.

Rule 1006 is not available unless there is a predicate finding under Rule 104(a) that the original writings, recordings or photographs are "voluminous" and cannot be conveniently examined in court. The underlying items would themselves have to be authentic and admissible before a Rule 1006 summary could be used in court.

There is an important distinction between a summary under Rule 1006 and demonstrative evidence such as a chart or diagram that is used merely to illustrate a point or help educate the jury. Demonstrative exhibits are not received into evidence and usually do not go back into the jury room during deliberations. Summaries under Rule 1006, in contrast, are treated as substantive evidence and are given to the jury for use during deliberations.

Proof by Admission

Through Dec. 1, 2011	After Dec. 1, 2011
Rule 1007. Testimony or Written Admission of Party	**Rule 1007. Testimony or Statement of a Party to Prove Content**
Contents of writings, recordings, or photographs may be proved by the testimony or deposition of the party against whom offered or by that party's written admission, without accounting for the nonproduction of the original.	The proponent may prove the content of a writing, recording, or photograph by the testimony, deposition, or written statement of the party against whom the evidence is offered. The proponent need not account for the original.

One of the most venerable principles of evidence law is that a party cannot complain if his own words are used against him at trial. The doctrine of admissions will be discussed in greater detail in the chapter on hearsay, *infra*, but the basic principle is easy enough to understand: relevant words that a party to the litigation has said or written are admissible against him at trial.

Rule 1007 is another exception to the Best Evidence Rule. The proponent of evidence does not have to produce an original document, recording or photograph if the other party has already testified concerning its contents at a proceeding or in a deposition. A proceeding includes a current or former trial, grand jury testimony, administrative proceedings or legislative hearings.

Likewise, if the other party has created a written admission of the item's contents, there is no need to produce the original at trial to prove its contents. A written admission can be a note, letter, any other writing, or responses to interrogatories or requests for admission under the applicable rules of civil procedure.

Role of Judge and Jury

Through Dec. 1, 2011	After Dec. 1, 2011
Rule 1008. Functions of Court and Jury	**Rule 1008. Functions of the Court and Jury**
When the admissibility of other evidence of contents of writings, recordings, or photographs under these rules depends upon the fulfillment of a condition of fact, the question whether the condition has been fulfilled is ordinarily for the court to determine in accordance with the provisions of rule 104. However, when an issue is raised (a) whether the asserted writing ever existed, or (b) whether another writing, recording, or photograph produced at the trial is the original, or (c) whether other evidence of contents correctly reflects the contents, the issue is for the trier of fact to determine as in the case of other issues of fact.	Ordinarily, the court determines whether the proponent has fulfilled the factual conditions for admitting other evidence of the content of a writing, recording, or photograph under Rule 1004 or 1005. But in a jury trial, the jury determines — in accordance with Rule 104(b) — any issue about whether: (a) an asserted writing, recording, or photograph ever existed; (b) another one produced at the trial or hearing is the original; or (c) other evidence of content accurately reflects the content.

Rule 1008 clarifies the functions of the judge and the jurors when dealing with the Best Evidence Rule and its exceptions. As has been frequently mentioned throughout this section, the judge must decide under Rule 104(a) whether a condition precedent exists that would permit secondary evidence to prove the contents of a writing, recording, or photograph. The rule clarifies, however, that the jury must decide the ultimate factual issues pertaining to original documents: whether the original ever existed at all; whether another document produced at trial is actually the original; or whether secondary evidence correctly reflects the contents of the original. The provisions of Rule 1008 pertaining to the jury's role are, of course, subject to judicial findings of conditional relevance under Rule 104(b): if, for example, a judge determines that no reasonable juror could find that a particular document was actually an original, the issue will never be presented to the jury because it failed to meet the standards for conditional relevance.

II.   CASES, DISCUSSION QUESTIONS AND PROBLEMS

UNITED STATES v. BENNETT
United States Court of Appeals, Ninth Circuit
363 F.3d 947 (9th Cir. 2004)

[The accused in this case was convicted of importation of marijuana after Customs officials seized his boat in US territorial waters, heading north away from Mexico.]

Here, although Bennett's boat was heading north (away from Mexico) when officers first spotted it, the boat was in U.S. waters at the time. Thus, the government on appeal relies chiefly on three other items of evidence that Bennett imported drugs from outside the United States. First, U.S. Customs Officer Malcolm McCloud Chandler testified that he discovered a global positioning system ("GPS") while searching Bennett's boat and that the GPS revealed that Bennett's boat had traveled from Mexican waters to San Diego Bay. Second, during his testimony, Chandler indirectly introduced Bennett's admission that he had been navigating in Mexican waters looking for scuba-diving sites. Third, a jailmate of Bennett's testified that Bennett told him that he had been arrested for transporting drugs from Mexico, which he used to do several times per week. Bennett claims that the admission of Chandler's GPS-related testimony violated the rules of evidence and that the introduction of his statement to Chandler violated his Miranda rights. He does not contest the admissibility of his jailmate's testimony.

A.

Bennett's most serious challenge to the evidence supporting his importation conviction relates to Chandler's testimony about the global positioning system he discovered during his search of Bennett's boat. A GPS device uses global positioning satellites to track and record the location of the device and, therefore, the location of any object to which it is attached. The GPS came with a "backtrack" feature that graphed the boat's journey that day. Chandler testified that the backtrack feature mapped Bennett's journey from Mexican territorial waters off the coast of Rosarito, Mexico, to the Coronado Islands and then north to San Diego Bay. Less significantly, Chandler also retrieved "way points" — navigational points programmed into the GPS to assist the captain in navigating to a particular destination. Chandler testified that within the previous year, someone had programmed way points into the GPS that included points in Mexican waters. Chandler acknowledged on cross-examination that he had not taken possession of the GPS device itself or obtained any record of the data contained therein.

At trial, the district court overruled Bennett's foundation, best evidence rule and hearsay objections to this testimony, along with his request for a side bar conference. We review these evidentiary rulings for abuse of discretion.

The best evidence rule provides that the original of a "writing, recording, or photograph" is required to prove the contents thereof. Fed. R. Evid. 1002. A writing or recording includes a "mechanical or electronic recording" or "other form of data compilation." Fed. R. Evid. 1001(1). Photographs include "still photographs, X-ray films, video tapes, and motion pictures." Fed. R. Evid. 1001(2). An original is the writing or recording itself, a negative or print of a photograph or, "if data are stored in a computer or similar device, any printout or other output readable by sight, shown to reflect the data accurately." Fed. R. Evid. 1001(3).

Where the rule applies, the proponent must produce the original (or a duplicate, see Fed. R. Evid. 1003) or explain its absence. Fed. R. Evid. 1002, 1004. The rule's application turns on "whether contents are sought to be proved." Fed. R. Evid. 1002 Advisory Committee's note. "An event may be proved by nondocumentary evidence, even though a written record of it was made." Id. Accordingly, the rule is inapplicable when a witness merely identifies a photograph or videotape "as a correct representation of events which he saw or of a scene with which he is familiar." Id.; see also United States v. Workinger, 90 F.3d 1409, 1415 (9th Cir. 1996) ("[A] tape recording cannot be said to be the best evidence of a conversation when a party seeks to call a participant in or observer of the conversation to testify to it. In that instance, the best evidence rule has no application at all."). However, the rule does apply when a witness seeks to testify about the contents of a writing, recording or photograph without producing the physical item itself — particularly when the witness was not privy to the events those contents describe. See Fed. R. Evid. 1002 Advisory Committee's note.

That is the nature of Chandler's GPS testimony here and why his testimony violated the best evidence rule. First, the GPS display Chandler saw was a writing or recording because, according to Chandler, he saw a graphical representation of data that the GPS had compiled about the path of Bennett's boat. See Fed. R. Evid. 1001(1). Second, Chandler never actually observed Bennett's boat travel the path depicted by the GPS. Thus, Chandler's testimony concerned the "content" of the GPS, which, in turn, was evidence of Bennett's travels. Fed. R. Evid. 1002. At oral argument, the government admitted that the GPS testimony was offered solely to show that Bennett had come from Mexico. Proffering testimony about Bennett's border-crossing instead of introducing the GPS data, therefore, was analogous to proffering testimony describing security camera footage of an event to prove the facts of the event instead of introducing the footage itself.

This is precisely the kind of situation in which the best evidence rule applies. See, e.g., L.A. News Serv. v. CBS Broad., Inc., 305 F.3d 924, 935 (9th Cir. 2002) ("We think that Fox's report of what he saw on the label . . . was inadmissible under the best evidence rule."), amended by 313 F.3d 1093 (9th Cir. 2002); see also 14 Am. Jur. Proof of Facts 2d 173 § 14 (1977) ("The reported cases show that proponents of computer-produced evidence occasionally founder on the best evidence rule by presenting oral testimony based on the witness' review of computer printouts without actually introducing the printouts themselves into evidence." (citing State v. Springer, 283 N.C. 627, 197 S.E.2d 530 (N.C. 1973)). Yet the government did not produce the GPS itself — or a printout or other representation of such data, see Fed. R. Evid. 1001(3) — which would have been the best evidence of the data showing Bennett's travels. Instead, the government offered only Chandler's GPS-based testimony about an event — namely, a border-crossing — that he never actually saw.

Other evidence" of the contents of a writing, recording or photograph is admissible if the original is shown to be lost, destroyed or otherwise unobtainable. Fed. R. Evid. 1004. But the government made no such showing. When asked on cross-examination to produce the GPS or its data, Chandler simply stated that he was not the GPS's custodian. He further testified that "there was no need to" videotape or photograph the data and that he had nothing other than his testimony to support his assertions about the GPS's contents. Moreover, the government has not offered any record evidence that it would have been impossible or even difficult to download or print out the data on Bennett's GPS. On the record before us, the government is not excused from the best evidence rule's preference for the original. We therefore hold that Chandler's GPS-based testimony was inadmissible under the best evidence rule.

When an error is not constitutional in magnitude, as in the admission of Chandler's GPS-based testimony, we will consider the error to be prejudicial unless it is more probable than not that the error did not materially affect the verdict. See United States v. Seschillie, 310 F.3d 1208, 1214 (9th Cir. 2002). Here, we conclude that the error was indeed prejudicial.

Putting aside Chandler's GPS-based testimony, the other items of evidence the government cites in support of the importation conviction are not overwhelming. First, Chandler obliquely referred to Bennett's having been in Mexican waters to scuba dive. Specifically, when asked whether finding scubadiving equipment on Bennett's boat struck him as unusual, Chandler testified that it seemed odd for someone to scuba dive alone in Mexican waters. Even assuming that this testimony did not violate Bennett's Miranda rights, Chandler never actually testified that Bennett had admitted navigating Mexican waters. Moreover, the government did not even argue Chandler's scuba-related testimony to the jury as evidence of importation. Second, the jailmate's testimony that Bennett admitted transporting drugs from Mexico is equally problematic. Bennett's jailmate was a multiply convicted felon who admitted on cross-examination that he hoped his testimony against Bennett would earn him a reduced sentence for a recent conviction. Third, the government points to other evidence that only circumstantially suggests that Bennett imported the marijuana from Mexico — specifically, that his boat was first spotted near Mexican waters and that he was carrying Mexican pesos with him on the boat. Taken together, these items of evidence are not so compelling that the jury would likely have found importation even without Chandler's GPS-based testimony.

More importantly, there is compelling evidence that the jury in fact relied on the GPS-based testimony to conclude that Bennett imported marijuana from Mexico. During its deliberations, Bennett's jury asked court about the GPS data and Chandler's GPS-based testimony. In response, the court ordered a read back of the GPS-related portions of Chandler's testimony. Shortly thereafter, the jury returned with a guilty verdict.

On this record, we cannot say the erroneous admission of Chandler's GPS testimony was more probably than not immaterial to the jury's verdict. We hold, accordingly, that Bennett was prejudiced by the erroneous admission of the GPS testimony and that, although his possession conviction survives this appeal, his importation conviction does not.

DISCUSSION QUESTIONS

1. Why was Agent Chandler not qualified to testify under FRE 602 about Bennett's travels on the day in question?

2. Why not apply Rule 1004 and permit secondary proof of the contents of the GPS receiver?

3. Using the other evidence in the opinion, can you make the case for conviction without the GPS evidence? How?

4. Why not simply call this harmless error and affirm the conviction? What does the court's decision tell you about the significance of jury questions in weighing the importance of evidentiary exhibits at trial?

PROBLEMS

Problem 18-1. Plaintiff and Defendant are co-workers. Plantiff is suing Defendant for libel based on an e-mail Defendant sent to co-workers. The e-mail contained an unflattering Photoshop image of Plaintiff, as well as libelous written content. The e-mail still exists and is available for use at trial. However, instead of introducing the e-mail, Plaintiff calls Witness, another co-worker, to testify about the picture and the libelous statements.

Should Defendant object? If so, on what grounds? How should the judge rule?

Problem 18-2. Darren Devious is on trial for securities fraud. During his trial, the prosecutor calls Connie Informant to testify about a conversation she and Devious had. CI was wired during this conversation, and a poor-quality recording and transcript are available. Prosecutor decides to call CI and not introduce the recording. Devious objects on Best Evidence grounds. How should the judge rule?

Later in Devious's trial, the prosecutor plays a CD of a wiretap recording between Devious and CI. The CD is of poor quality, so the prosecutor provides a transcript for the jury to read as they listen to the CD. The wiretap was originally recorded on an audiotape, but the prosecutor felt it would be easier to play a CD in the courtroom.

Devious objects to the transcript and the CD on Best Evidence grounds. How should the judge rule?

Problem 18-3. Svetlana, a Russian translator, is suing Bob for breach of her employment contract to translate for tour groups in Calamity City. The original contract was written in Russian and placed in a safe-deposit box in Moscow. To prove the terms of the contract, Svetlana introduces a photocopy of the first two pages of the contract, along with a certified translation. The contract is five pages long.

Bob objects on Best Evidence grounds. How should the judge rule?

> ### *Best Evidence Rule, Original Documents and Duplicates: Quick Hits*
>
> - The so-called "best evidence rule" applies only when the content of a writing, recording or photograph is in dispute
>
> - The "best evidence principle" refers to the general desire of parties in an adversarial proceeding to present the highest-quality available evidence in presenting their cases
>
> - In general, duplicates are admissible to the same extent as originals
>
> - Secondary evidence of an original's contents can be introduced when is lost, destroyed, unobtainable, in the possession of an

> opponent, or so unrelated to the central issue at trial as to be insignificant
>
> • Summaries may be used in place of introducing voluminous documents, recordings, photographs and the like
>
> • The contents of a document are a question of fact for the jury

Chapter References

CHRISTOPHER B. MUELLER & LAIRD C. KIRKPATRICK, EVIDENCE §§ 10.1–10.18 (4th ed. 2009).

GLEN WEISSENBERGER & JAMES J. DUANE, FEDERAL RULES OF EVIDENCE: RULES, LEGISLATIVE HISTORY, COMMENTARY AND AUTHORITY §§ 1001–08 (6th ed. 2009).

JACK B. WEINSTEIN & MARGARET A. BERGER, WEINSTEIN'S FEDERAL EVIDENCE §§ 1001–08 (Joseph M. McLaughlin ed., Matthew Bender 2d ed. 1997).

KENNETH S. BROUN, McCORMICK ON EVIDENCE §§ 230–243.1 (6th ed. 2006).

STEVEN J. GOODE & OLIN GUY WELLBORN III, COURTROOM HANDBOOK ON FEDERAL EVIDENCE Ch. 5 (West 2010).

III. APPLICATION EXERCISE

Objective: To demonstrate mastery of the best evidence rule in application.

Factual Scenario. The factual scenario for this exercise is provided through an assigned video clip, which you must watch in preparation for the courtroom exercise. Part One of the exercise involves conducting direct examinations of the participants in an event. Part Two of the exercise is a direct examination of a person playing the role of a security manager whose company captured the event on a surveillance videocamera.

Advance Preparation. You will be given a supplemental assignment memorandum for this exercise. Watch the video clip and prepare short (2-3 minute) direct examinations of the principal witnesses, who are characters in the video clip. Also prepare a longer (4-7 minute) direct examination of Sal Security, the security manager, testifying about what he saw on the video.

In-Class Exercise. Students will play the role of Sal Security, the assigned characters from the video clip, the proponent attorney (conducting the direct examination), the opposing counsel (objecting as appropriate), and the judge.

Chapter 19

AUTHENTICATION OF ELECTRONIC AND COMPUTER-GENERATED EVIDENCE

Chapter Objectives:

- Introduce and explain authentication of electronic and computer-generated evidence within the framework of the Federal Rules of Evidence
- Analyze and discuss issues pertaining to the authentication of electronic and computer-generated evidence
- Apply the concepts from this chapter in a courtroom application exercise

---

I. BACKGROUND AND EXPLANATORY MATERIAL

Introduction

There are no special rules for the authentication of electronic evidence such as digital images, e-mails, text messages, chat-room transcripts or web pages. Considering the prevalence of these items in everyday life, this is somewhat surprising. Attorneys and judges use a combination of precedent, analogy and creative mixing of evidentiary doctrines to authenticate — or contest the authentication of — electronic evidence at trial.

The following excerpt from a law review article does an excellent job of introducing the issues pertaining to the admissibility of electronic evidence at trial.

Hon. Paul W. Grimm, Michael V. Ziccardi, Esq., Alexander W. Major, Esq., *Back to the Future:* Lorraine v. Markel American Insurance Co. *and New Findings on the Admissibility of Electronically Stored Information*
42 AKRON L. REV. 357 (2009)

It is not a frivolous question to ask, "Do the existing rules of evidence adequately deal with admissibility of electronic evidence?" In a thoughtful, recently published book, attorney George Paul, who has extensive experience dealing with evidentiary issues associated with ESI/digital evidence, made the following observations:

> The current evidentiary scheme comprises three main historical policies: (1) the notion of authentic writings, exemplified by the search for an "original" object tying certain people, acting at a certain time, to certain permanently recorded information; (2) the rule against hearsay, giving litigants the right to test factual statements through cross-examination, unless there was an accepted policy reason not to do so; and (3) the notion that evidence, particularly evidence implicating specialized knowledge, be generally scientific in that it be subject to a "test" of its hypotheses or methodologies. These policies are all stressed by digital evidence. . . . There is now a new world of [digital] evidence. New foundations are necessary.

While this may be true, and a "new world order" of admitting and weighing electronic evidence an inevitable outcome, this will not occur overnight, and in the interim there must be a method of dealing with the ever changing forms of digital or electronic evidence in court proceedings. This means that the existing law of evidence must be applied to the admissibility of electronic evidence, and courts that have been asked to do so have expressed no significant concerns about the adequacy of those rules to accomplish this task. As one court noted, "Essentially, appellant would have us create a whole new body of law just to deal with e-mails or instant messages. . . . We believe that e-mail messages and similar forms of electronic communications can be properly authenticated within the existing framework of [the rules of evidence]." Recognizing this, the *Lorraine* opinion identifies the following five evidentiary "hurdles" that must be evaluated in order to assess the admissibility of electronically stored or digital evidence:

Whether ESI is admissible into evidence is determined by a collection of evidence rules that present themselves like a series of hurdles to be cleared by the proponent of the evidence. Failure to clear any of these evidentiary hurdles means that the evidence will not be admissible. Whenever ESI is offered as evidence, either at trial or in summary judgment, the following evidence rules must be considered: (1) is the ESI relevant as determined by Rule 401 (does it have any tendency to make some fact that is of consequence to the litigation more or less probable than it otherwise would be); (2) if relevant under 401, is it authentic as required by Rule 901(a) (can the proponent show that the ESI is what it purports to be); (3) if the ESI is offered for its substantive truth, is it hearsay as defined by Rule 801, and if so, is it covered by an applicable exception (Rules 803, 804 and 807); (4) is the form of the ESI that is being offered as evidence an original or duplicate under the original writing rule, or if not, is there admissible secondary evidence to prove the content of the ESI

(Rules 1001-1008); and (5) is the probative value of the ESI substantially outweighed by the danger of unfair prejudice or one of the other factors identified by Rule 403, such that it should be excluded despite its relevance.

III. AUTHENTICATION OF ESI

In actuality, the authentication of evidence is a relatively straightforward concept: "A piece of paper or electronically stored information, without any indication of its creator, source, or custodian may not be authenticated under Federal Rule of Evidence 901." Nevertheless, in the two years since *Lorraine* was issued, courts and counsel still seem to struggle with the basic principles of authentication as it applies to electronic evidence. Some courts are still permitting only rudimentary admissibility standards and counsel are still, at times, failing to meet that low bar. As electronic evidence becomes more ubiquitous at trial, it is critical for courts to start demanding that counsel give more in terms of authentication — and counsel who fail to meet courts' expectations will do so at their own peril.

It may come as no surprise to the readers of this Article that *Lorraine* was drafted, in part, as a "how to" for the authentication of electronic evidence. It was written to assist counsel in better preparing themselves for the use of electronic evidence during trial by clarifying how Rules 901 and 902 might apply. As Lorraine demonstrates, electronic evidence comes in many forms and it is no secret that someone highly adept with computers has the ability to make viewers see whatever he or she wants them to see. But it is also a very real possibility that someone inept with computers may also alter electronic evidence so as to make it unusable or inadmissible. Therefore, as technology continues creating relevant evidence while, simultaneously, outpacing the working knowledge and ability of most lawyers and judges to deal with it, ensuring proper authentication of electronic evidence becomes a greater responsibility for attorneys and judges alike.

In practice, there are several keys to authenticating electronic evidence or computer-generated evidence. First, the proponent must understand and be able to explain the system used to generate the evidence. In this respect, Rule 901(b)(9) — process or system authentication — is a critical rule, especially for new types of evidence. Second, the proponent must understand the weaknesses and vulnerabilities of the evidence. For example, if the data in a computer file can be easily manipulated, the trustworthiness of reports or images generated from that file could be suspect. Third, the proponent must understand the law of authentication well enough to analogize the new evidence with well-established categories of evidence.

The following table lays out some of the most common types of electronic evidence and the rules used to authenticate them. [Author's note: this table is derived from the Grimm and Zaccardi article above. It merely lays out in tabular form information that exists textually in that article.]

Type of Electronic Evidence	Applicable Rules
E-mail	• Rule 901(b)(1), Testimony of a Witness with Knowledge • Rule 901(b)(3), Comparison by Trier or Expert Witness • Rule 901(b)(4), Distinctive Characteristics and the Like
Internet Websites	• Rule 901(b)(1), Testimony of a Witness with Knowledge • Rule 901(b)(3), Comparison by Trier or Expert Witness • Rule 901(b)(4), Distinctive Characteristics and the Like • Rule 901(b)(7), Public Records or Reports" • Rule 901(b)(9), Process or System"
Chat Room and Text Messages	• Rule 901(b)(1), Testimony of a Witness with Knowledge • Rule 901(b)(4), Distinctive Characteristics and the Like
Computerized Records or Data	• Rule 901(b)(1), Testimony of a Witness with Knowledge • Rule 901(b)(3), Comparison by Trier or Expert Witness • Rule 901(b)(4), Distinctive Characteristics and the Like • Rule 901(b)(9), Process or System
Computer Animations	• Rule 901(b)(1), Testimony of a Witness with Knowledge • Rule 901(b)(3), Comparison by Trier or Expert Witness
Computer Simulations	• Rule 901(b)(1), Testimony of a Witness with Knowledge • Rule 901(b)(3), Comparison by Trier or Expert Witness
Digital Photographs	• Rule 901(b)(9), Process or System

Differences Between Writings and Computer-Generated Evidence

J. Shane Givens, *Comment, The Admissibility of Electronic Evidence at Trial: Courtroom Admissibility Standards*
34 CUMB. L. REV. 95 (2003)

Electronic evidence has been broadly defined as "any information created or stored in digital form whenever a computer is used to accomplish a task." As this definition implies, electronic evidence may be found in several situations: when someone enters data into a computer; when a computer generates an output in response to an operator's request; or when a computer uses or processes information. Therefore, "electronic evidence . . . may include information databases, operating systems, applications programs, "computer-generated models', electronic and voice mail messages and records, and other information or "instructions residing in computer memory.'" With this change in media, naturally come changes in evidentiary procedures. In order to understand these procedures, however, it is first necessary to explore the major differences between electronic and traditional paper evidence.

Obtainability

One primary difference between electronic and paper evidence is that electronic data, because of the convenience and ease of electronically transferring and storing information, is often easier to obtain than traditional paper evidence. To illustrate this point, imagine a situation involving two different employees faced with relaying information to a co-worker. Assume that employee A chooses to send his communication via e-mail and employee B chooses to send his communication through traditional mail. One major difference that can be noted right away between the two modes of communication is that employee B might not word his written letter in the same manner employee A would word his e-mail. To explain, while e-mail transmissions are virtually instantaneous, sending a letter is a good deal slower in process and delivery; as a result, the extra time involved in writing a letter and mailing it leaves employee B more time for thought and reconsideration of the content. Consequently, e-mails may contain "uncensored" or "off-the-cuff" remarks that a writer may not include in a written letter. In all actuality, the extra effort required to write a letter often means that employee B might not even take the time to send his correspondence. This means that if not for e-mail, many communications would simply never happen and would not be available for evidentiary purposes at all.

Availability

A second major difference between paper and electronic evidence lies in the availability of the evidence. For example, assume that an employee needs to transmit an important communication to his supervisor. If the employee chooses to put his thoughts down on paper and that transmission is needed at a later time for use at trial, several problems immediately arise. First, the supervisor would have had to keep the letter. Second, if the supervisor did keep the letter, he would then have to remember having received the letter. Third, the supervisor would have to remember where he stored the letter. If all of this occurs, an additional problem arises in that the supervisor would then have the liberty to decide whether he wanted the letter to be found, or whether the shredder was the more appropriate place for the document. As can be seen, sometimes several obstacles lie in the way of the party wishing to discover paper records.

On the other hand, the destruction or misplacement of an electronic file is much more difficult, making electronic evidence more readily available for trial. In most cases, the durability of electronic evidence even stands in the way of the "book burner" or other spoliation rogue. For example, communications sent via e-mail are ordinarily routed through a third party computer system or a centralized back-up system. Consequently, a third party computer system or back-up system could store and save all e-mails passing through it. This means that a simple search of the third party system could turn up several "deleted" or otherwise misplaced files.

Further, deleting an electronically stored file is not equivalent to throwing out or shredding paper documents. Instead, when an electronic file is "deleted," the computer actually earmarks the unwanted file to be overwritten with other information at a later time. The "deleted" file may not be overwritten with new data for "seconds, days, or even months." Moreover, even when new data has overwritten the unwanted file, the old file still may not be completely wiped out. Fragments of a "deleted" file sometimes survive because software programs usually allocate more space than is necessary to a given file. In other words, the computer assigns a certain block of space on the hard drive to each file; therefore, if the old "deleted" file is larger than the file assigned to overwrite it, then fragments of the old file will not be overwritten and may be recovered by a "competent computer forensics technician."

Content

Still another difference between paper and electronic evidence lies in the content of each type of medium. Even though a handwritten letter (or a computer printout of electronically stored or transmitted data) and the actual electronic file may contain the same visible words and thoughts, electronically stored data can potentially contain "hidden" information. The United States District Court for the District of Columbia recognized the presence of this "hidden" information when questioned about the differences between printouts of e-mails and e-mails in their electronic state:

> Both the recipient and the author of a note can print out a "hard copy" of the electronic message containing essentially all the information displayed on the computer screen. That paper rendering will not, however, necessarily include all the information held in the computer memory as part of the electronic document. Directories, distribution lists, acknowledgements of receipts and similar materials do not appear on the computer screen - and thus are not reproduced when users print out the information that appears on the screen. Without this "non-screen" information, a later reader may not be able to glean from the hard copy such basic facts as who sent or received a particular message or when it was received.

Electronic data in its original form, therefore, often contains vital information that is not present in paper records or even computer printouts of the same electronic evidence.

DISCUSSION QUESTIONS

1. What are some of the primary differences between electronic evidence and paper evidence?

2. What significance do these differences hold for the process of authenticating evidence?

3. Does the presence of additional information, hidden to the naked eye, complicate the task of authenticating electronic evidence? Is an electronically generated document the same as a traditional document? Why or why not?

Issues Associated with Digital Images

Jill Witkowski, *Note, Can Juries Really Believe What They See? New Foundational Requirements for the Authentication of Digital Images*
10 Wash. U. J. L. & Pol'y 267 (2002)

Digital imaging presents the most recent trend in photographic technology. Digital cameras operate by principles similar to traditional cameras. There are significant differences, however, between traditional photographs and digital images that may necessitate different evidentiary treatment than that normally given to traditional photographs. The digital image creation process and the susceptibility of digital images to manipulation make digital images sufficiently different from photographs to necessitate different treatment under the Federal Rules of Evidence.

A. Digital Image Creation Process

Two facets of the digital image creation process separate digital images from traditional photographs: initial image quality and compression.

The quality of the initial images produced by photographs and digital images distinguishes the two technologies. Images taken by a digital camera vary dramatically from those taken by a traditional film camera. Digital cameras produce lower quality images than those produced by 35mm film. Typically, 35mm film yields better resolution, a higher dynamic range, and better color range and fidelity than digital images. In contrast, digital images tend to have relatively lower resolution, and therefore poor image quality in the brightest portions of the scene being recorded.

The possibility of digital image compression also distinguishes digital images from photographs. Unlike a traditional camera that limits the number of photographs taken to the amount of film in the camera, digital cameras allow users to choose the number of images they want to capture and store on a storage medium. Through a process called "compression," users can choose to store a greater number of images of lesser quality by permanently discarding some of the information originally contained in the digital image. When the user wants to view the image, the decompression process "guesses" what information was discarded to produce a complete image.

Although compression may seem a convenient way to store more images per unit of storage medium, complications arise when a user wants to print the digital image. The larger the print desired, the larger the file necessary to preserve the image integrity and produce a useable image. Even though certain types of removable storage media hold insufficient data to support even one five-by seven-inch print, some digital cameras allow the user to store between twenty and twenty-four images. Such large compression ratios discard a significant amount of information so that the image viewing software must then "guess" the lost information during reversal. A very high compression ratio, which saves only a small portion of the information contained in the original image, limits the size of the print a user can produce because there is not enough information within the image file; larger prints are too "grainy" to be useful. A lower compression ratio still produces an image that is less accurate than a traditional photograph. For example, compression of a digital image of a wound could, by inserting artifacts and altering colors within the image, exaggerate the wound and "create" bruises or other wounds that did not exist.

B. Digital Images are Highly Susceptible to Manipulation

Digital images are easier to manipulate than traditional photographs and digital manipulation is more difficult to detect.

Digital images are highly susceptible to manipulation. Manipulation, as distinct from enhancement, consists of changing the elements of a photograph or image by changing the colors, moving items from place to place on the image, or otherwise altering the original image. Individuals without training or specialized equipment may easily manipulate digital images. In fact, users do not even need specialized software to manipulate images; the same programs that allow users to view images or adjust contrast also allow users to cut and paste items with a click of the mouse. Digital camera users also have a greater opportunity to manipulate images than those using traditional cameras because digital camera users process the image themselves, while traditional camera users generally take the film to a professional developer to produce the prints.

While manipulation tools are both accessible and easy to use for those without training, those who have training may make even more convincing manipulations. Hollywood's increasing use of digital technology is an excellent illustration of the ease of manipulation and variety of alterations possible with digital imaging.

The electronic nature of the image file makes undetectable manipulation of a digital image easy, in part because no traditional "original image" is made. Unlike traditional cameras, which produce one negative, digital cameras create an electronic file from which the image can be generated. Because the image file contains a finite set of ones and zeros, exact copies of the image file can be made with no loss of image quality between generations. Thus, it is impossible to determine which image is a first generation image and is therefore the "original." The lack of an "original" for comparison with the offered image reduces the opportunity to verify that the image has not been altered or has only been altered in an acceptable manner, thereby increasing the likelihood that changes will not be discovered unless the proponent of the image reveals them.

Some proponents of digital images argue that it is just as easy to manipulate a photograph as it is to manipulate a digital image. Although photographs may be manipulated, the potential for making subtle but significant alterations to digital images gives cause for concern that digital images may be unfit for use as evidence in a court of law.

DISCUSSION QUESTIONS

1. What are some of the issues that exist with digitally produced images?

2. If a digital image can be easily altered and manipulated, how can it be of value in a courtroom?

3. What additional steps do you think ought to be taken to authenticate digital evidence?

II.   CASES, DISCUSSION QUESTIONS AND PROBLEMS

ANTOINE LEVAR GRIFFIN v. STATE OF MARYLAND
Court of Special Appeals of Maryland
995 A.2d 791 (Md. Ct. Spec. App. 2010)

[Appellant was convicted of murdering Guest by shooting the unarmed Guest seven times in the women's room at a bar. At appellant's first trial, his cousin, Gibbs, an eyewitness, testified that he did not see appellant pursue Guest into the restroom. At appellant's second trial, Gibbs testified that appellant and Guest were the only two people in the bathroom when the shots were fired. He said he had testified differently at the first trial because appellant's girlfriend, Barber, had threatened him via a MySpace message.]

Thereafter, the court permitted the State to introduce into evidence a redacted printout obtained in December 2006 from a MySpace profile page allegedly belonging to Ms. Barber. The profile page, introduced for the limited purpose of corroborating Gibbs's testimony, said, in part: "JUST REMEMBER, SNITCHES GET STITCHES!! U KNOW WHO YOU ARE!!" . . .

II. DISCUSSION

A.

Appellant contends that the court erred in admitting the MySpace evidence. He complains that the evidence was not properly authenticated and that its prejudicial effect outweighed its probative value. . . .

The State also called Ms. Barber. She testified that, on the night in question, appellant was her boyfriend, and he lived with her and their two children. Ms. Barber identified appellant's nickname as "Boozy." . . .

On the day after Ms. Barber testified, the prosecutor sought to introduce five pages printed on December 5, 2006, from an Internet Web site for a MySpace profile in the name of "SISTASOULJAH," who was described on that Web page as a 23 year-old female from Fort Deposit. The profile page listed the member's birthday as "10-2-83." It also contained a photograph posted next to the description, showing a "three-quarter view" of an embracing couple. Counsel and the court agreed that the couple appeared to be appellant and Ms. Barber. A "blurb" posted on the profile stated as follows:

I HAVE 2 BEAUTIFUL KIDS. . . . FREE BOOZY!!!! JUST REMEMBER SNITCHES GET STITCHES!! U KNOW WHO YOU ARE!!

The State offered the printout to rehabilitate Gibbs's credibility, and to bolster Gibbs's claim that Ms. Barber had threatened him before the first trial. Defense counsel objected, arguing that the State had not sufficiently established a "connection" to Ms. Barber, and had failed to question her about the MySpace profile. In response, the prosecutor asserted that the profile could be authenticated as belonging to Barber through the testimony of Sergeant John Cook, the Maryland State police investigator who printed the document.

The trial court then allowed defense counsel to voir dire Sergeant Cook, outside the presence of the jury. The following transpired:

[DEFENSE COUNSEL]: How do you know that this is her web page? . . .

[SGT. COOK]: Through the photograph of her and Boozy on the front, through the reference to Boozy, to the reference of the children, and to her birth date indicated on the form.

[DEFENSE COUNSEL]: How do you know she sent it?

[SGT. COOK]: I can't say that.

Sergeant Cook acknowledged that he could not determine when any particular posting was made. But, he indicated that he visited the Web site on December 5, 2006, the date that appeared on the printout.

The court ruled that it would admit a single, redacted page from the MySpace printout, containing only the photo next to a description of the page creator as a 23 year-old female from Fort Deposit, and a portion of the blurb, stating: "FREE BOOZY!!!! JUST REMEMBER SNITCHES GET STITCHES!! U KNOW WHO YOU ARE!!"

Without waiving appellant's objection, defense counsel agreed [a stipulation in lieu of Cook's testimony, to the effect that Cook had downloaded some information from MySpace, that it contained a photograph of Barber and her birthdate, and the phrase, "just remember snitches get stitches."

Thereafter, the court promptly instructed the jury regarding the limited evidentiary purpose of the MySpace printout, [telling them they could use it for the limited purpose of corroborating what Gibbs said about being threatened by Barber, that they did not have to find it corroborated Gibbs' claim, and that they were free to believe or disbelieve Gibbs' claim.]

The defense did not present any testimonial evidence. But, it introduced various documents. . . .

In closing argument, the State relied upon the MySpace page to explain the inconsistencies in Gibbs's testimony. . . .

In closing argument, the defense argued, in part, [that Gibbs had given inconsistent statements in two different trials].

B.

As noted, appellant contends that the trial court erred in admitting the redacted printout from the MySpace page. He asserts: "The State came nowhere near authenticating the contents of the MySpace page as statements by Barber." . . .

Maryland Rule 5-901 governs authentication. Notably, the authentication concerns attendant to the use of evidence printed from a social networking Web site such as MySpace is a topic on which there is no Maryland precedent and scant case law from other jurisdictions.

[Maryland Rule 5-901 is the general rule of authentication. Circumstantial evidence can play an important role in establishing authentication. The judge's decision for authentication is whether a jury could reasonably find that the evidence is what it purports to be.] . . .

The design and purpose of social media sites make them especially fertile ground for "statements involving observations of events surrounding us, statements regarding how we feel, our plans and motives, and our feelings (emotional and physical)[.]" Lorraine, 241 F.R.D. at 569. For that reason, both prosecutors and criminal defense attorneys are increasingly looking for potential evidence on the expanding array of Internet blogs, message boards, and chat rooms. As indicated, users of social media Web sites, blogs, chat rooms, and discussion forums may post messages anonymously or under pseudonyms. See Wilson, supra, at 1220. The Court observed in Brodie, 407 Md. at 425: "Since the early 1990's, when Internet communications became available to the American public, anonymity or pseudonymity has been a part of the Internet culture."

The MySpace profile at issue here illustrates that a user "can choose not to provide" the user's real name. See id. at 424 n.3. Instead, users may join the online community anonymously, by registering under password and user names that are self-selected and confidential. Access to the profile may be obtained by logging in on the Web site with the confidential user name and password. Other social networking site features preserve the veil of anonymity or pseudonymity, by allowing members to communicate electronically using their chosen screen names, both via private message sent to other members, as an alternative to traditional e-mail in which "users generally know with whom they are communicating[,]" id. at 422, and via an "in-house" instant messaging option that allows members to conduct real-time "chats" with other members, by use of their screen names. See Wilson, supra, at 1220. . . .

The anonymity features of social networking sites may present an obstacle to litigants seeking to authenticate messages posted on them. That is the issue we encounter here: whether the State adequately established the author of the cyber message in question.

Despite the pervasive popularity of social networking sites and their potential as treasure troves of valuable evidence, Maryland appellate courts have not yet addressed the issue of authenticating anonymous or pseudonymous documents printed from social media Web sites. Notably, neither the Maryland Rules of Evidence nor the Maryland Rules of Procedure specifically address the authentication of such evidence. Perhaps this is because courts that have generally considered the issue of authentication of electronic communications have concluded that they may be authenticated under existing evidentiary rules governing authentication by circumstantial evidence.

In the leading case of Lorraine v. Markel Am. Ins. Co., 241 F.R.D. 534 (D. Md. 2007), Magistrate Judge Paul Grimm, a noted authority on electronic discovery, offered well-reasoned methods to authenticate various types of electronically stored information, including e-mails, text messages, chat room logs, and "Internet Website Postings." Although Lorraine recognized that such evidence "may require greater scrutiny than that required for the authentication of 'hard copy' documents," the court suggested that the existing rules governing authentication provide an adequate analytical framework to determine the admissibility of such evidence. Id. at 542-43. . . .

We have found only a handful of reported cases involving evidence specifically pertaining to social networking Web sites. . . . Our research reveals only one reported decision directly resolving an authentication challenge to evidence printed from a social media Web site. However, it involved a printout of MySpace instant messages rather than a MySpace profile page, and was authored by a trial court; we have not found a reported appellate decision addressing the authentication of a printout from a MySpace or Facebook profile.

[That decision, Ohio v. Bell, 882 N.E.2d 502, 511 (Ohio C.P. 2008), aff'd, 2009], is consistent with other decisions affirming the admission of transcripts of chat room conversations on the basis of similar authenticating testimony by the other party to the online conversation. [The court cites examples of internet chat logs being authenticated by participants, content, external circumstantial evidence, and timing.]

To be sure, profile information posted on social networking Web pages differs from chat logs of instant message correspondence conducted through such sites. A chat log is a verbatim transcript of a private "real time" online conversation between site members, which can be authenticated by either of the two participants. In contrast, social networking profiles contain information posted by someone with the correct user name and password, with the intent that it be viewed by others. Therefore, a proponent should anticipate the concern that someone other than the alleged author may have accessed the account and posted the message in question. Cf., e.g., In re K.W., 192 N.C. App. 646, 666 S.E.2d 490, 494 (2008) (although victim admitted that the proffered MySpace page was hers, she claimed that her friend posted the answers to the survey questions that defendant sought to introduce as impeachment evidence with respect to her claims of rape). See also St. Clair v. Johnny's Oyster & Shrimp, Inc., 76 F. Supp. 2d 773, 774-75 (S.D. Tex. 1999) ("There is no way Plaintiff can overcome the presumption that the information he discovered on the Internet is inherently untrustworthy. Anyone can put anything on the Internet . . . hackers can adulterate the content on any website. . . .").

A pseudonymous social networking profile might be authenticated by the profiled person, based on an admission. That did not occur here, however, because the State never questioned Ms. Barber about the profile. Nevertheless, we regard decisions as to authentication of evidence from chat rooms, instant messages, text messages, and other electronic communications from a user identified only by a screen name as instructive to the extent that they address the matter of authentication of pseudonymous electronic messages based on content and context. We see no reason why social media profiles may not be circumstantially authenticated in the same manner as other forms of electronic communication — by their content and context.

The inherent nature of social networking Web sites encourages members who choose to use pseudonyms to identify themselves by posting profile pictures or descriptions of their physical appearances, personal background information, and lifestyles. This type of individualization may lend itself to authentication of a particular profile page as having been created by the person depicted in it. That is precisely what occurred here.

The My Space profile printout featured a photograph of Ms. Barber and appellant in an embrace. It also contained the user's birth date and identified her boyfriend as "Boozy." Ms. Barber testified and identified appellant as her boyfriend, with the nickname of "Boozy." When defense counsel challenged the State to authenticate the MySpace profile as belonging to Ms. Barber, the State proffered Sergeant Cook as an authenticating witness. He testified that he believed the profile belonged to Ms. Barber, based on the photograph of her with appellant; Ms. Barber's given birth date, which matched the date listed on the profile; and the references in the profile to "Boozy," the nickname that Ms. Barber ascribed to appellant. . . .

On the record before us, we have no trouble concluding that the evidence was sufficient to authenticate the MySpace profile printout. Therefore, the trial court did not err or abuse its discretion in admitting that document into evidence.

DISCUSSION QUESTIONS

1. What was the court's solution for authenticating the MySpace printout? Does this solution resolve the concern that someone else could have posted the information?

2. What are some reasons that attorneys might want to use information gained from social networking sites in either civil or criminal cases? Besides Rule 901, what other evidentiary rules would come into play in authenticating or using this information at trial?

3. The *Griffin* court essentially cobbled together an authentication doctrine for social networking sites. From your reading of this opinion and the other materials in this chapter, do you believe the current authentication rules are flexible enough

to handle electronic evidence, or should specific rules be developed for this sort of evidence?

PROBLEMS

Problem 19-1. Harold is on trial as an accomplice in the murder of Vernon and the theft of Vernon's pickup truck. Neither Harold nor Carl, the co-defendant, has admitted to being involved in the killing. The prosecution's primary exhibit linking Harold to the murder is a digital photograph of Harold and two other men standing next to Vernon's pickup truck. The foundation witness for the photograph is Paula. Paula is a friend of Vernon's and has hated Harold since Harold broke up with her during the middle of a high school prom dance. Paula claims that the picture fairly and accurately represents the three men standing near the truck after the killing. Harold claims that his image was digitally added to the scene and that he did not know the two men in the picture. Is Paula's testimony sufficient to authenticate the picture? How can Harold contest the picture's authenticity? What sort of finding must the judge make under FREs 901 and 104? If the judge rules that the picture is authentic, is the ruling binding on the jurors?

Problem 19-2. Dan Defendant has been accused of shoplifting by Retailer. Unhappy with his treatment at the hands of the store detective, he decided to write a letter of complaint to Smith, the manager of the store. Prior to sending the letter, he e-mailed an electronic copy of it, as a file attachment, to his attorney. His attorney edited the letter and sent it back. Defendant was pleased with his attorney's edits and forwarded the file to Smith. Unknown to Defendant, his attorney had not removed the metadata from the file. Smith, who was much more computer savvy than either Defendant or his lawyer, was able to view the metadata.

The letter Defendant thought he was sending and the version with metadata follow:

Dear Mr. Smith,

I am unhappy with the treatment I received at your retail establishment. I hope we can meet soon to discuss an acceptable solution to your organization's customer service problem. The problems I experienced are likely being experienced by other customers as well, and I feel strongly that we should meet so others are not treated in a similar manner. If you cannot arrange a time of mutual convenience, I would be happy to send my assistant.

Sincerely,

Dan Defendant.

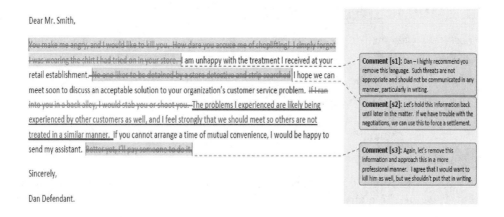

Dear Mr. Smith,

~~You make me angry, and I would like to kill you. How dare you accuse me of shoplifting! I simply forgot I was wearing the shirt I had tried on in your store.~~ I am unhappy with the treatment I received at your retail establishment. ~~No one likes to be detained by a store detective and strip searched.~~ I hope we can meet soon to discuss an acceptable solution to your organization's customer service problem. ~~If I ran into you in a back alley, I would stab you or shoot you.~~ The problems I experienced are likely being experienced by other customers as well, and I feel strongly that we should meet so others are not treated in a similar manner. If you cannot arrange a time of mutual convenience, I would be happy to send my assistant. ~~Better yet, I'll pay someone to do it.~~

Sincerely,

Dan Defendant.

Comment [s1]: Dan – I highly recommend you remove this language. Such threats are not appropriate and should not be communicated in any manner, particularly in writing.

Comment [s2]: Let's hold this information back until later in the matter. If we have trouble with the negotiations, we can use this to force a settlement.

Comment [s3]: Again, let's remove this information and approach this in a more professional manner. I agree that I would want to kill him as well, but we shouldn't put that in writing.

Assume that Defendant has sued the store in tort for false imprisonment. Retailer wants to introduce the metadata version of the letter against Defendant at trial. How could the letter be authenticated? What arguments could Defendant make against admitting the metadata version? Based on what you know about the other rules of evidence so far, how could this letter be used in evidence?

Electronic and Computer-Generated Evidence: Quick Hits

- There are no special authentication rules for the admission of electronic and computer-generated evidence.

- Advocates must use analogy and other established rules to authenticate electronic evidence.

- Electronic and computer-generated exhibits can contain hidden information and are subject to manipulation and alteration that may affect the admissibility or limit the use of the exhibits.

Chapter References

CHRISTOPHER B. MUELLER & LAIRD C. KIRKPATRICK, EVIDENCE §§ 9.13–9.17 (4th ed. 2009).

GLEN WEISSENBERGER & JAMES J. DUANE, FEDERAL RULES OF EVIDENCE: RULES, LEGISLATIVE HISTORY, COMMENTARY AND AUTHORITY § 901 (6th ed. 2009).

JACK B. WEINSTEIN & MARGARET A. BERGER, WEINSTEIN'S FEDERAL EVIDENCE § 901 (Joseph M. McLaughlin ed., Matthew Bender 2d ed. 1997).

KENNETH S. BROUN, McCORMICK ON EVIDENCE § 227 (6th ed. 2006).

STEVEN GOODE & OLIN GUY WELLBORN III, COURTROOM HANDBOOK ON FEDERAL EVIDENCE Ch. 5 (West 2010).

III. APPLICATION EXERCISES

Objective: To demonstrate the principles and processes for authenticating electronic evidence.

Factual Scenario: None

Advance Preparation: Prior to class, please think through the steps you might take to authenticate (and contest the authentication of) the following. Prepare an authentication foundation for the e-mail and web page assignments.

1. E-mails.

— An e-mail replying to an earlier e-mail of yours. Bring the e-mail with you to class. It can be from anyone.

— An e-mail sent by the instructor through the course website (I will send an e-mail to you before class). Hint: see if you can get your e-mail program to show all the data pertaining to the e-mail.

2. A web page. Use any non-pornographic web page, social media page, blog page, or the course home page.

3. A digital photograph. The instructor will provide a digital photograph in class.

In Class Exercise. The instructor will play the role of a cooperative witness. Students will be called on to play the roles of proponent and opponent for the authentication of each of the above-listed items.

PART SIX

HEARSAY

Chapter 20

INTRODUCTION TO HEARSAY

> **Chapter Objectives:**
>
> - Introduce and explain the concept of hearsay, the hearsay definitions and exclusions of Rule 801, and the "hearsay hierarchy" of out-of-court statements
> - Analyze and discuss issues pertaining to the admissibility of out-of-court statements for non-hearsay purposes
> - Apply the concepts from this chapter in a courtroom application exercise

I. BACKGROUND AND EXPLANATORY MATERIAL

Introduction to Hearsay: Definitions and Dangers

It is almost universally acknowledged that hearsay is less valuable than other forms of information. This belief applies not only in the courtroom, but out of it as well. For example, even the most casual eavesdropper cannot help but overhear comments such as, "well, that's all just hearsay anyway," to dismiss arguments or observations made about the circumstances or events of another's life.

Hearsay is commonly defined as an "out-of-court statement offered for the truth of the matter asserted." Rule 801(c) gives a slightly more precise definition: " 'Hearsay' is a statement, other than one made by the declarant while testifying at the trial or hearing, offered in evidence to prove the truth of the matter asserted." Conceptually, these definitions seem to suggest that all statements made outside the courtroom and quoted within it are hearsay, but in application, defining hearsay becomes somewhat more complicated. For instance, some forms of assertive conduct (such as pointing or head-nodding) qualify as statements, not all out-of-court statements qualify as hearsay under the rules, and some statements that seem like hearsay are not actually offered for their truth. These concepts will be explored in greater detail later in this chapter.

Rule 801 of the Federal Rules of Evidence defines hearsay and the key concepts related to it. Rule 802, in turn, creates a general prohibition on the use of hearsay evidence in the courtroom: the rule states that hearsay is not admissible unless it meets an exception under the Federal Rules of Evidence or other rules prescribed by the Supreme Court or Congress.

This chapter will focus exclusively on defining hearsay and identifying out-of-court assertions and conduct that are admissible for non-hearsay purposes under the Rules. The definitional sections of Rule 801 follow:

Through Dec. 1, 2011	After Dec. 1, 2011
Rule 801. Definitions	**Rule 801. Definitions That Apply to This Article; Exclusions from Hearsay**
The following definitions apply under this article:	**(a) Statement.** "Statement" means a person's oral assertion, written assertion, or nonverbal conduct, if the person intended it as an assertion.
(a) Statement. A "statement" is (1) an oral or written assertion or (2) nonverbal conduct of a person, if it is intended by the person as an assertion.	**(b) Declarant.** "Declarant" means the person who made the statement.
(b) Declarant. A "declarant" is a person who makes a statement.	**(c) Hearsay.** "Hearsay" means a statement that:
(c) Hearsay. "Hearsay" is a statement, other than one made by the declarant while testifying at the trial or hearing, offered in evidence to prove the truth of the matter asserted.	(1) the declarant does not make while testifying at the current trial or hearing; and
	(2) a party offers in evidence to prove the truth of the matter asserted in the statement.

As a threshold matter, it is important to understand **who** is involved in hearsay evidence, **what** constitutes a statement under the rules, **when** a statement is being offered for the truth of the matter asserted, and **why** hearsay is considered dangerous in the courtroom. Each of these topics will be addressed in turn.

The Who of Hearsay

There are two people involved in every hearsay statement: the declarant and the witness. Rule 801(b) defines a declarant as "a person who makes a statement." The witness is the person who will be introducing the declarant's statement into the courtroom, either by testifying about it or introducing it in the form of a document.

For example, assume that Danielle is a spectator at a NASCAR race and that she observes a crash between two race cars. In a state of excitement, she turns to her boyfriend, Wayne, and exclaims, "Did you see that? The number 6 car drove right into the number 15 car!" If Wayne were called to testify about Danielle's statement at the race, Wayne would be the witness and Danielle would be the declarant, as in the following dialogue:

Q: *How did you learn of the crash between the two cars?*

A: *From my girlfriend, Danielle.*

Q: *What did she say?*

A: *She said, "Did you see that? The number 6 car drove right into the number 15 car!"*

Q: *Please describe her emotional state at the time she said this.*

A: *She was pretty excited. I think it was her first time seeing a crash.*

What would happen if Danielle testified in the courtroom and was asked to quote herself, as in the following scenario?

Q: *When you saw the crash, what did you say to Wayne?*

A: *I said to Wayne, I said, "Wayne! Did you see that? The number 6 car drove right into the number 15 car!"*

Q: *Why did you say that?*

A: *It was my first NASCAR race, and I was surprised to see that one driver would hit another one on purpose.*

In this scenario, Danielle is both the declarant (the person who made the out-of-court statement) and the witness (the person who is introducing it into the courtroom). If she is simply quoting herself — even though she is present in the courtroom and can be cross-examined — her out-of-court statements must be analyzed under the hearsay rules as such to see whether they can be admitted at trial.

The What of Hearsay

Rule 801(a) defines a statement as "(1) an oral or written assertion or (2) nonverbal conduct of a person, if it is intended by the person as an assertion." Black's Law Dictionary defines assertion as "[a] person's speaking, writing, acting, or failing to act with the intent of expressing a fact or opinion; the act or an instance of engaging in communicative behavior."

In the courtroom, assertions come in two primary flavors: verbal statements and documents. The most common situations involve a witness coming into the courtroom to either quote a declarant's verbal statement or authenticate a document containing written statements by the declarant.

Assertive conduct also meets the definition of a statement under Rule 801(a). The key to defining conduct as a statement under the rule is the intended message of the conduct. If the conduct sends a clear and unambiguous message that does not require intermediate inferences or interpretation, chances are good that it is intended as an assertion under the rule. Most cases of assertive conduct are context-specific: a nod, pointing in response to a question, signaling another person with gestures or other behavior, and the like.

Implied assertions, whether verbal or by gesture, are not statements under the rule and are, therefore, not prohibited. The reason for this is that the alleged message must be inferred from the statement or conduct. In other words, the statement or conduct is not an assertion. The meaning comes not from the declarant, but from a logical chain inferred by the witness (and, perhaps, implied by the declarant). A famous example of an implied assertion occurs in the movie *The Pink Panther Strikes Again*.[1] In that movie, Inspector Clouseau, standing in front of a small dog, turns to a hotel clerk and asks, "Does your dog bite?" The clerk replies, "No." Clouseau bends down to pet the dog, which immediately bites him. Indignant, Clouseau exclaims, "I thought you said your dog did not bite!" The clerk answers, "That is not my dog." The implied assertion in this example occurs when the clerk says his dog does not bite; given the context of the question, the implied assertion is, *and that is my dog.*

When a Statement is Hearsay

According to FRE 801(c), a declarant's out-of-court statement is hearsay when it is offered for the truth of the matter asserted. This requires careful attention to the substance of the statement and the purpose for which it is being offered. Many attorneys fail to analyze the substance of out-of-court statements, erroneously objecting on hearsay grounds to any out-of-court statements. When faced with such objections, the proponent of the evidence must be able to explain the substance of the statement and why it is not being offered for its truth.

There are many reasons to offer an out-of-court statement that are independent from whether the statement itself is true. Those reasons include context, such as to show why a police officer went to particular location; notice, such as to prove that an employer was aware of an employee's words or actions in the workplace; and effect on the listener, such as the impact of a threatening statement made by the declarant to a witness. Verbal acts, including the words necessary to complete a contract, are another category of statements that are not considered hearsay under the rule.

When analyzing an out-of-court statement, it helps to isolate the substance of the statement and determine whether the information contained in the statement has any relevance other than its truthfulness. If it is relevant for some other purpose, chances are good it is admissible for a non-hearsay purpose. Consider, for example, the statement from a police radio dispatcher, "Robbery in progress at 5th and Vine." If the statement is being offered to prove that there was in fact a robbery in progress at 5th and Vine, it is being offered for its truth and is hearsay. If, however, the statement is being offered to help give context to a police officer's story of responding to a crime scene, the jury does not need to believe there was actually a robbery in progress; it simply helps explain why the police officer showed up at 5th and Vine.

Why Hearsay is Dangerous in the Courtroom

The law of evidence treats hearsay evidence with a great deal of suspicion; it is presumptively inadmissible. It is viewed as being not only unreliable, but also potentially dangerous to the jury's fact-finding function and the rights of the parties. This suspicion is rooted in the values at the core of the adversarial trial process: the role of the jury in assessing the credibility of witnesses and the

---

[1] THE PINK PANTHER STRIKES AGAIN (Amjo 1976).

probative value of evidence, and — especially in criminal cases — the importance of cross-examination and face-to-face confrontation in testing witness testimony.

Live testimony permits the jury to measure directly a witness's credibility and value as a witness. According to the Advisory Committee, the three primary factors to be considered in evaluating a witness's testimony are "perception, memory, and narration," with "sincerity" sometimes added as a fourth factor.[2] To aid this process, "the Anglo-American tradition has evolved three conditions under which witnesses will ideally be required to testify as witnesses: (1) under oath, (2) in the personal presence of the trier of fact, (3) subject to cross-examination."[3]

Every hearsay statement involves a declarant (who is usually not present in the courtroom) and a witness. The witness is subject to cross-examination about her competence, the quality of her observations, her biases, and her character for truthfulness, but the hearsay declarant is not. If the statements quoted in court by the witness are considered for their truth, there is no way to test them in the crucible of cross-examination.

In addition to making it more difficult for the jury to gauge the credibility of the hearsay declarant, the use of hearsay in criminal cases creates a potential constitutional problem. The Sixth Amendment to the Constitution guarantees the criminal accused the right to be "confronted with the witnesses against him." An absent declarant makes it virtually impossible to comply with the confrontation guarantee. The concept of confrontation and hearsay will be explored in greater detail in a subsequent chapter.

Rule 801(d): Out-of-Court Statements, Admitted for Their Truth, That Are Not Hearsay

Rule 801(d) exempts several categories of evidence from the hearsay rule: (1) prior inconsistent statements made under oath at a trial, hearing, other proceeding, or deposition; (2) prior consistent statements offered to rebut an express or implied charge of recent fabrication; (3) out-of-court identification; and (4) admissions, including personal, agency, and co-conspirator admissions. Every category of statement covered by the rule meets the traditional common-law definition of hearsay; all of them are out-of-court statements offered for the truth of the matter asserted.[4] Yet Rule 801(d) performs a sort of definitional alchemy that declares them not to be hearsay at all.

There are sound reasons that the statements covered by Rule 801(d) should be exempt from the constraints of the hearsay rule. In the case of statements under Rule 801(d)(1), the declarant is actually in court and subject to cross-examination concerning the prior statements, thereby mitigating (although not entirely eliminating) the recognized dangers of hearsay. Statements under Rule 801(d)(2) all involve admissions — whether direct, adoptive, or vicarious — and they

---

[2] Advisory Committee Notes, Article VIII, Hearsay.

[3] Advisory Committee Notes, Article VIII, Hearsay.

[4] In fact, common-law evidence jurisdictions treat these categories of statements as hearsay and admit them as specific exceptions to the general hearsay prohibition.

implicate one of the most strongly held values in the adversary trial system: a party to a lawsuit cannot be heard to complain about having its own words used against it at trial.

Each of the categories listed in Rule 801(d) will be treated by this chapter in turn.

Prior Statements

The first major category of exemptions under Rule 801(d) is prior statements. This category is divided into three subcategories: (1) prior inconsistent statements under oath, made at a trial, hearing, other proceeding or deposition; (2) prior consistent statements offered to rebut an express or implied charge of recent fabrication or improper influence or motive; and (3) prior out-of-court identifications. Each of the three subcategories under Rule 801(d)(1) requires that the declarant — the person who made the prior statement — be at the trial or hearing in which the statement is offered, and subject to cross-examination. The text of the rule follows:

Through Dec. 1, 2011	After Dec. 1, 2011
Rule 801(d)	**Rule 801(d)**
(d) Statements which are not hearsay. A statement is not hearsay if—	**(d) Statements That Are Not Hearsay**. A statement that meets the following conditions is not hearsay:
(1) Prior statement by witness. The declarant testifies at the trial or hearing and is subject to cross-examination concerning the statement, and the statement is (A) inconsistent with the declarant's testimony, and was given under oath subject to the penalty of perjury at a trial, hearing, or other proceeding, or in a deposition, or (B) consistent with the declarant's testimony and is offered to rebut an express or implied charge against the declarant of recent fabrication or improper influence or motive, or (C) one of identification of a person made after perceiving the person; or	*(1) A Declarant-Witness's Prior Statement*. The declarant testifies and is subject to cross-examination about a prior statement, and the statement: (A) is inconsistent with the declarant's testimony and was given under penalty of perjury at a trial, hearing, or other proceeding or in a deposition; (B) is consistent with the declarant's testimony and is offered to rebut an express or implied charge that the declarant recently fabricated it or acted from a recent improper influence or motive in so testifying; or (C) identifies a person as someone the declarant perceived earlier.

(1) *Prior Inconsistent Statements*

The concept of prior inconsistent statements is a familiar one: as discussed in Chapter 15, Rule 613 permits impeaching witnesses with their prior inconsistent statements and even provides for extrinsic proof of the prior statement if the witness denies it on cross-examination. The trier of fact cannot consider statements offered under Rule 613 for their truth, but rather for the effect of the inconsistency on the credibility of the witness. The proponent of these statements cannot argue their truth to a jury, and the opponent is entitled to a limiting instruction on the proper uses of prior inconsistent statements to impeach.

Rule 801(d)(1)(A) permits the introduction of testimonial prior inconsistent statements at trial, and it also allows the trier of fact to consider these statements for their truth. The proponent of prior inconsistent statements under Rule 801(d)(1)(A) may argue their truth to the jury, and the opponent is not entitled to a limiting instruction. Furthermore, statements offered under Rule 801(d)(1)(A) may also be considered for their impeachment value, thereby conferring a dual benefit on the proponent: the proponent can argue that (1) the prior inconsistent statement is true; and (2) because the witness is inconsistent, the witness's in-court testimony is not credible.

Rule 801(d)(1)(A) applies only to testimonial prior inconsistent statements. These are statements that were given under oath at a trial, hearing, other proceeding, or deposition. The opportunity for prior cross-examination is a key foundational element to admitting these statements at trial. Thus, affidavits, sworn statements, and other similar types of prior statements would not qualify for admission under Rule 801(d)(1)(A).

(2) *Prior Consistent Statements*

Rule 801(d)(1)(B) permits the introduction of any prior consistent statement made by a witness, in order to rebut an express or implied charge of recent fabrication or improper influence or motive. The prior consistent statement must have been made prior to the alleged fabrication, influence or motive. The theory is that a witness's credibility can be bolstered by offering evidence that the witness consistently told the same story, and told it before the alleged motive to fabricate arose.

For example, suppose that a teenager reported her parents for child abuse after having her cellphone taken away as a disciplinary measure. At trial, her parents' attorney might well impeach her for an improper motive to testify: revenge against her parents for punishing her. If the teenager had complained to friends or otherwise reported the abuse *prior to the cellphone being taken away*, that evidence could be offered under Rule 801(d)(1)(B) as a prior consistent statement. In essence, the proponent of her testimony could argue, "yes, she was being punished by her parents, but she's telling the truth about the child abuse, because she made the report *before* the cellphone was taken away from her."

(3) *Prior Out-of-Court Identification*

Rule 801(d)(1)(C) permits a proponent to introduce evidence of prior out-of-court identifications made by a witness. The prior identification can take place during a line-up, show-up, photo array or lineup, a prior hearing, or any other circumstance.

The rule is necessary because witnesses — especially in criminal cases — may suffer real or feigned amnesia regarding the identification of a suspect, or otherwise demonstrate reluctance to cooperate at trial. If a prior identification exists, Rule 801(d)(1)(C) provides the prosecutor with the necessary tools to introduce evidence of the identification to the jury. This can be done through examination of the witness, or by calling a police officer or other witness who was present when the prior identification was made.

Admissions

Through Dec. 1, 2011	After Dec. 1, 2011
Rule 801(d)	**Rule 801(d)**
(2) Admission by party-opponent. The statement is offered against a party and is (A) the party's own statement, in either an individual or a representative capacity or (B) a statement of which the party has manifested an adoption or belief in its truth, or (C) a statement by a person authorized by the party to make a statement concerning the subject, or (D) a statement by the party's agent or servant concerning a matter within the scope of the agency or employment, made during the existence of the relationship, or (E) a statement by a coconspirator of a party during the course and in furtherance of the conspiracy. The contents of the statement shall be considered but are not alone sufficient to establish the declarant's authority under subdivision (C), the agency or employment relationship and scope thereof under subdivision (D), or the existence of the conspiracy and the participation therein of the declarant and the party against whom the statement is offered under subdivision (E).	*(2) An Opposing Party's Statement.* The statement is offered against an opposing party and: (A) was made by the party in an individual or representative capacity; (B) is one the party manifested that it adopted or believed to be true; (C) was made by a person whom the party authorized to make a statement on the subject; (D) was made by the party's agent or employee on a matter within the scope of that relationship and while it existed; or (E) was made by the party's coconspirator during and in furtherance of the conspiracy. The statement must be considered but does not by itself establish the declarant's authority under (C); the existence or scope of the relationship under (D); or the existence of the conspiracy or participation in it under (E).

One of the most venerable traditions of the adversarial trial system is that a party to the proceedings cannot be heard to complain about his own words being used against him at trial. For the purposes of Rule 801(d)(2), an admission is *any statement* made or adopted by a party, by someone authorized by the party, by a party's agent or employee within the scope of employment, or, in criminal cases, by a co-conspirator within the scope and in furtherance of the conspiracy. The statement does not have to be in the nature of a confession, nor does it have to be against interest at the time it is made. The statement can be verbal or written.

Statements that qualify as admissions under Rule 801(d)(2) may be offered into evidence by an opponent and used for any legitimate purpose. The only real constraints on the use of these statements come from Rules 401 through 405: the statements must be relevant and not unfairly prejudicial or detrimental to the integrity of the fact-finding process; furthermore, they cannot be used to undermine the character evidence doctrines of Rules 404 and 405.

(1) *Statements Made or Adopted by a Party*

Any statement — verbal or written — made or adopted by a party at any time qualifies under this rule. The statement can be made in the party's individual or representative capacity; in other words, a statement that a party makes while purporting to speak in a representative capacity for someone else can still be used against the party. There are no requirements to prove that the statement was true, or even that the party believed it to be true at the time it was made. Simply put, the value from these statements comes from the fact that they were made by a party to the proceedings.

Of course, the party against whom the admission is offered is not bound by the contents of the admission. The party can repudiate it, explain it, or argue that it has minimal probative value. The trier of fact makes the final decision about the value of the admission.

It is important to understand that this rule applies only to statements by the party against whom the evidence is being offered. In civil cases involving multiple defendants, one defendant's admission cannot be offered against the other defendants in the case. This requires careful attention by attorneys and appropriate limiting instructions from judges.

In criminal cases, the issues involving admissions are a bit more complex. First, the timing of an admission affects its admissibility. If made prior to arrest, admissions are freely admissible against an accused. If made after arrest, the admission must first be filtered through the lens of *Miranda* before it can be offered;[5] in other words, the defendant must have received the rights warnings to which he was entitled by law.

Second, the *Bruton* doctrine applies to cases in which one defendant's confession or admission implicates another defendant.[6] In many criminal cases, the defendant elects not to testify, and prosecutors admit his admissions or confessions against him under Rule 801(d)(2). In a multiple-defendant case, particular dangers are presented when none of the defendants elect to testify. If a defendant's admission or confession implicates his co-defendants, and that defendant does not testify, the consequences to co-defendants could be devastating: they could be convicted without ever having the opportunity to confront the witness whose admission or confession was used against them. *Bruton* stands for the proposition that a limiting instruction to the effect that one defendant's admission cannot be used against

---

[5] *See generally* Miranda v. Arizona, 384 U.S. 436 (1966).

[6] Bruton v. United States, 391 U.S. 123 (1968).

another is inadequate to prevent a jury from misusing the evidence. The cleanest way to solve the *Bruton* problem is to sever trials of co-defendants that involve these types of statements.

(2) *Adoptive Admissions*

An adoptive admission occurs when a party manifests an adoption or belief of a statement made by someone else. A party can adopt an admission through the use of statements, by actions, or by acquiescence or silence in the face of an accusation that would by its terms demand a response.

For example, suppose that the Calamity High School football team has lost all of its football games for the past three seasons. The coach of the team could admit his team's ineptitude in a number of ways:

Example 1: Direct Admission. *Well, we're not very good. We might be the worst team in the state right now.*

Example 2: Adoptive Admission by Verbal Statement. *It says here in this newspaper article that we're not very good and we might be the worst team in the state. The author is right.*

Example 3: Adoptive Admission by Action. Sending a copy of the above-mentioned article to the booster club, along with a note: *Until we get funding for better facilities and uniforms, this is the future of our football team.*

Example 4: Adoptive Admission by Silence. At the annual Calamity City High School Athletic Association Dinner, silence in response to an accusation by an opposing coach. *Not only do y'all suck, but you're a bunch of dirty cheaters. Your offensive line can't do anything but hold.* The silence would be an adoptive admission of the cheating accusation.

(3) *Statements by Authorized Persons, or Agents or Servants Within Scope of Agency or Employment*

The first two subsections of Rule 801(d)(2) deal with admissions either personally made or directly adopted by the declarant. Subsections (C) and (D) add admissions that are made by authorized persons, or by agents or servants within the scope of employment and during the existence of the relationship. For each of the admissions encompassed by (C) and (D), the judge must make a preliminary finding under Rule 104(a) of the agency relationship or the existence of authorization. The proponent of the evidence bears the burden of proof. To prove the relationship, the proponent may use the statement itself but must corroborate it with other evidence.

The following issues frequently arise with respect to these types of admissions: the authority of the agent or servant to speak and bind the principal, the scope of the agency, and the duration of the relationship. Courts look beyond formal titles or declarations of authority to the substance of the statement, and whether it was offered during the scope of employment.

Suppose, for example, that the Calamity Heavy Construction Company had a strict policy that employees were not allowed to speak to insurance adjusters, police, the public or the press about any accidents or incidents unless a Company attorney or officer was present. This policy would not hinder a court from admitting — against the Company — statements made by employees within the scope of their employment, including statements of fault, negligence, improper maintenance of Company equipment, and the like.

Attorneys should be aware that statements they make in the course of representing a client could be admissible against the client under these rules. Attorneys should pay careful attention to supervisory court opinions in their jurisdictions to avoid making statements that could be used as admissions against their clients. Special rules apply to government attorneys; in criminal cases, courts have held that out-of-court statements by government agents are not admissible against the government under these rules.

(4) *Statements of Co-Conspirators*

One of the most troubling and controversial aspects of Rule 801(d) is subsection (E), which permits the admissibility of statements "made by a co-conspirator of a party during the course and in furtherance of the conspiracy." These types of statements are considered to be admissible under an agency theory that each conspirator is an agent of the others. The admission of these statements is consistent with the generally harsh treatment of conspirators under the criminal law.

Pursuant to Rule 104(a), the existence of a conspiracy, its scope, its membership, and whether the statement was made in furtherance of it, are preliminary matters for the judge. The statement itself can be used to prove the conspiracy, but it must be corroborated with some other independent evidence.

II.   CASES, DISCUSSION QUESTIONS AND PROBLEMS

SIMPLE v. WALGREEN
United States Court of Appeals, Seventh Circuit
511 F.3d 668 (7th Cir. 2007)

The district court granted summary judgment in favor of the defendant in this suit for racial discrimination in employment in violation of Title VII and 42 U.S.C. § 1981, and the plaintiff appeals. He had been hired by Walgreen in 1995, initially as a management trainee. Four years later he was promoted to assistant store manager and two years after that he was offered the job of manager of a Walgreens store in Kankakee, Illinois. He declined the offer because the store was in a "socioeconomically challenged" area with a high "shrink," which means a gap between expected and actual profits that is due to shoplifting. The offer was made by Michael Palmer, the district manager for the region in Northern Illinois that includes Kankakee. The following year Palmer offered the plaintiff a store manager job in Normal, but the plaintiff rejected that offer too. Walgreen's demographic tracking records show that the average annual income of the customers of both the Kankakee store and another store, in Peoria, that the plaintiff was also offered and declined is "low" (defined as less than $40,000) and that more than 40 percent of the customers are black. Although the store in Normal that the plaintiff was also offered had a more affluent customer base and 80 percent of its customers were white, the defendant makes nothing of the demographic differences between that store and the ones in Kankakee and Peoria.

A few years later, Palmer, though aware of the plaintiff's wanting to manage a store in Palmer's district (which contains 28 Walgreen stores), hired a white woman, Melissa Jonland, as manager of a store in Pontiac, Illinois, without notifying the plaintiff of the opening. The customers of this store have an average income of $40,000 to $60,000 and more than 80 percent of them are white. It is a more desirable store to manage than the Kankakee and Peoria stores that had been offered to the plaintiff — it is more profitable (in part because of less shrinkage), and store managers' bonuses are based on their stores' profits. . . .

By the time Jonland was appointed to manage the Pontiac store, the plaintiff had been an assistant store manager for four years and Jonland for only two. (Only assistant store managers are eligible for promotion to store manager.) The company considered both to be highly qualified for appointment as store managers. Only the difference in experience — which favored the plaintiff — seems to have distinguished them. Jonland had not expressed interest in the Pontiac store, and Palmer had not offered her a store manager's job at one of the pre-dominantly black/low-income stores.

Shortly after Jonland's appointment, Leanne Turley, the manager of the store of which the plaintiff was assistant manager, had a conversation with him in which, she testified in her deposition, "I may have stated that Pontiac was possibly not ready to have a black manager. It is well known in this area that some of the smaller, outlying towns have some very racist tendencies, and I was simply trying to make [the plaintiff] feel better because my feeling was he may not have been very happy working there." Turley had previously been the manager of a store of which Jonland had been assistant manager; and in an answer to an interrogatory propounded by the plaintiff, Palmer stated that his assessment of Jonland's performance, in deciding to promote her to store manager, had been "supported by" Turley. . . .

[T]he defendant was unable to give a coherent reason for appointing Jonland rather than the plaintiff. Palmer gave inconsistent explanations, on one occasion saying that Jonland "outshines you [the plaintiff] in market appeal" and on another that she would be better at improving "employee morale." The inconsistency is suggestive of pretext and thus is evidence of discrimination, and it does not stand alone, but instead reinforces the other evidence of a racial motive. A finding of pretext can complete the prima facie case under McDonnell Douglas, but it can also be independent evidence of discrimination.

[I]t is apparent that the district judge should not have granted summary judgment. A reasonable jury, if the evidence gathered in the summary judgment proceedings were the evidence at a trial, could find that the plaintiff was denied the promotion to manage the store in Pontiac because he is black. The evidence suggests that Palmer wanted to steer his highly regarded black assistant manager to a store in a predominantly black, low-income neighborhood; when the plaintiff balked, Palmer suggested that he might prefer to move to a big city, where there are more Walgreens stores.

There is no evidence that Jonland was more qualified to manage the store in Pontiac than the plaintiff, who had twice her experience as an assistant manager, the mandatory stepping stone to store manager. But she is white, and the store is in a predominantly white neighborhood, while the plaintiff is black and so was twice offered a "black" store — and when the store manager's job at the "white" store fell vacant he was ignored. The significance of Turley's remark about racism in Pontiac lies in the fact that as an experienced Walgreens store manager (it appears that she had been one for at least four years) she was undoubtedly aware of what Palmer was looking for in a store manager in Pontiac, and one interpretation of the remark is that the plaintiff's race would bar him from consideration by Palmer. The plaintiff would not feel "happy" among Pontiac's white racists, which is a standard euphemism for refusing a job to someone of a different race from the people he would be associating with. Racial segregation is obviously a form of racial discrimination.

Turley's statement was an admission by Walgreen because it was a statement about a matter within the scope of her employment, Fed. R. Evid. 801(d)(2)(D) — remember that she had been consulted by Palmer about the appointment of a manager for the Pontiac store. And this means that the plaintiff's deposition testimony that Turley had also told him that "race played a factor" in the decision to appoint Jonland to manage the Pontiac store was another admission that race had played a role in Palmer's decision to appoint Jonland rather than the plaintiff. "[A] subordinate's [in this case, the plaintiff's] account of an explanation of the supervisor's [Turley's] understanding regarding the criteria utilized by management in making decisions on hiring, firing, compensation, and the like is admissible against the employer, regardless of whether the declarant has any involvement in the challenged employment action." Marra v. Philadelphia Housing Authority, 497 F.3d 286, 298 (3d Cir. 2007). . . .

We acknowledge that in apparent contradiction to the passage from Marra and to the other decisions that we have just cited (including our own Williams v. Pharmacia, Inc.), some of our decisions say that "the declarant must [for his evidence to be treated as an admission of his employer] be involved in the decisionmaking process affecting the employment action." [citations omitted] But the contradiction dissolves when we note the difference between "employment action" and "decisionmaking process affecting the employment action." Turley was not involved in the employment action — appointing Jonland to be the Pontiac store manager. But . . . she was involved in the process that led up to that action, by being consulted about the appointment. That was enough to make her statement — which was confirmed, moreover, by an internal investigation by Walgreen — an admission by her employer.

The trial may cast the facts in a different light; we do not mean to prejudge the outcome. But there is enough evidence of discrimination to entitle the plaintiff to a trial.

REVERSED AND REMANDED.

UNITED STATES OF AMERICA v. GARCIA
United States Court of Appeals, Eighth Circuit
893 F.2d 188 (8th Cir. 1990)

Alexander Garcia is a sixty-three year-old resident of the Philippines who ran an auto repair shop with his sons. His son Dante is a Philippine national who is in the U.S. Air Force, and is stationed at Clark Air Force Base in the Philippines. Both had been to the United States prior to the trip in 1988 involved in this case.

In late 1988, Alexander, Dante and Remedios [Alexander's mother-in-law] planned a trip to the United States. Both Alexander and Remedios were scheduled for heart treatment in Honolulu, but also intended to go to Missouri to do some Christmas shopping. Dante was to join them in Honolulu, and travel to Missouri with them, where he intended to obtain a divorce from his wife. Dante arrived first in Honolulu, where all three were to spend the night with Alexander's daughter, Carmelita. Dante arrived in the early morning, and Rolito Garcia Junio, Carmelita's son, testified at trial that Dante arrived with a suitcase and a black briefcase. Dante opened the briefcase in Rolito's presence, and he could see that it contained brown envelopes full of United States currency, in $20 and $100 bills. When Rolito left for work that morning, Dante was counting money.

When Rolito arrived home in mid-afternoon, Alexander and Remedios were there as well. The family had dinner together, and then Dante and Rolito went out. They found two prostitutes in Honolulu, took them to a hotel, and attempted to pay them with counterfeit money, which money the prostitutes refused. While in the hotel room, Dante indicated to Rolito to keep quiet about the money. Once outside in the parking lot, Dante told Rolito that the money was indeed counterfeit, and that he had brought it into the United States for his father, Alexander.

Alexander, Remedios and Dante left together the next morning for the mainland. They spent a few days in San Francisco. They then traveled to Kansas City, and to Neosho, Missouri, where Dante was to obtain a divorce, and Alexander and Remedios were to go shopping before returning to Honolulu for heart treatment. All three went to the North Park Mall in Joplin. Dante attempted to pass a counterfeit $20 bill. The store clerk refused it, and after Dante left, the clerk called mall security. A mall security guard then stopped Dante and asked him about the money. Dante denied having the bill, and said he had given it back to his father. Since Dante and the security guard could not find Alexander, Dante was released. Soon after, Alexander and Remedios were arrested at a Wal-Mart store, where Remedios had attempted to pass a counterfeit $100 bill, while Alexander waited outside. When arrested, Alexander had on his person fifty-three $100 bills and four $20 bills, all counterfeit. Any other counterfeit bills brought into the United States from the Philippines were not recovered.

II. DISCUSSION

Alexander argues that the district court erroneously admitted several statements made by Dante, since the statements were not made "in furtherance of the conspiracy" as required by Rule 801(d)(2)(E). The first statements at issue were made by Dante to Rolito. Rolito testified that after Dante attempted to pay the prostitutes with the counterfeit money, Dante told him "that the money was not real." Trial Transcript, vol. 1, at 45. Dante also told him, in Rolito's words, that "only me, my grandpa and him knows about the money." Id. In addition, Dante also said that he brought the money into Honolulu for his father, that he brought it because it was easier for him, as a member of the armed forces, to get the money through customs, and that he brought $ 40,000 to $50,000. Id. at 46. The other statements at issue were made by Dante to David Lee Jones, the Joplin mall security guard. Dante simply told him that he had given the refused $20 bill to Alexander. Id. vol 2, at 77. Alexander argues that these statements were not made in furtherance of the conspiracy.

Rule 801(d)(2)(E) provides that a statement is not hearsay if it is "a statement by a coconspirator of a party during the course and in furtherance of the conspiracy." This circuit has held that for a statement to be admissible, the government must prove (1) that a conspiracy existed, (2) that the defendant and the declarant were members of the conspiracy, and (3) that the statements were made in furtherance of the conspiracy. [Citations omitted.]

At issue here is only the "in furtherance" requirement, and it is satisfied if the statements "somehow advance the objectives of the conspiracy." DeLuna, 763 F.2d at 909. Thus, in United States v. Bentley, 706 F.2d 1498 (8th Cir. 1983), cert. denied, 467 U.S. 1209, 104 S. Ct. 2397, 81 L. Ed. 2d 354 (1984), we held that statements designed to enlist a third party's assistance were in furtherance of the conspiracy. Id. at 1506-07. It was sufficient that the statements were made in "an effort to induce the listener's aid in achieving some objectives" of the conspiracy. Id. at 1507. Similarly, in United States v. Handy, 668 F.2d 407 (8th Cir. 1982), we held that "statements of a coconspirator identifying a fellow conspirator are considered to be in furtherance of the conspiracy." Id. at 408.

Alexander argues that the statements admitted were not in furtherance of the conspiracy, but were mere conversation, or simple, narrative statements which in no way advanced the objectives of the conspiracy. See, e.g., DeLuna, 763 F.2d at 909 (statements which "merely inform the listener . . . of the declarant's activities" are not in furtherance); United States v. Snider, 720 F.2d 985, 992 (8th Cir. 1983), cert. denied, 465 U.S. 1107, 104 S. Ct. 1613, 80 L. Ed. 2d 142 (1984) (statements merely describing a marijuana-growing operation were meant to impress the listener, but not to advance the objects of the conspiracy); United States v. Green, 600 F.2d 154, 158 (8th Cir. 1979) (distinguishing statements found to be "casual comments which were neither intended to further, nor had the effect of furthering the conspiracy in any way.").

We conclude that the statements at issue in this case were not casual comments or mere conversation. The "in furtherance" language of Rule 801(d)(2)(E) is to be read broadly, Bentley, 706 F.2d at 1506, and here the statements advanced the objects of the conspiracy. The statements made by Dante to the mall security guard were necessary to delay or prevent Dante's arrest, and thus to allow the conspiracy to continue. The statements to Rolito were in furtherance because they identified a fellow conspirator, see Handy, 668 F.2d at 408, and also because they revealed the existence and progress of the conspiracy. Id. Moreover, the statements made to Rolito could be construed as meant to enlist Rolito's assistance by not unintentionally revealing the existence of the conspiracy. See Bentley, 706 F.2d at 1506. While still in the Honolulu hotel room, Dante signaled to Rolito to be quiet, and then made the statement at issue, explaining his actions. The statement was meant to keep Rolito quiet by revealing to him the conspiracy. Therefore, we find no error in the district court's rulings.

We also note that even if the statements were not in furtherance of the conspiracy, the evidence against Alexander was so compelling that the admission of these statements was harmless error. See Snider, 720 F.2d at 993; Green, 600 F.2d at 158.

DISCUSSION QUESTIONS

1. What is the standard test to determine when a company is bound by the admissions of one of its employees?

2. Are you convinced that Turley's statement should be used against her employer? Why or why not?

3. Imagine a situation in which a rogue manager, just to stir up trouble, makes untrue statements about a company's decision-making process. What protections, if any, does the company have under the rules? What protections should they have? What strategy should the company follow at a 104(a) hearing to keep the statements out?

4. With respect to statements of co-conspirators, what evidence can the government use to prove the existence, scope and membership of a conspiracy?

5. What does *Alexander* tell you about the way courts interpret statements of co-conspirators? Should courts interpret these statements narrowly or broadly? What policies support your answer?

PROBLEMS

Problem 20-1. While watching a baseball game at Calamity State University, Pat Plaintiff was injured when a splinter from a broken bat was impaled in his eye. A day after the accident, Pat made a sworn statement to a university police officer, admitting that he was not sitting in the seat or section assigned to his ticket. Pat sued the university, alleging negligent failure to install safety netting. At trial, when asked whether he was sitting in his assigned seat, Pat said "yes." Evaluate whether the sworn statement to the police officer is admissible under Rule 801?

Add the following additional facts: In a pretrial deposition, Pat was asked whether he was sitting in his assigned seat. He answered no. At trial, he said he was sitting in his assigned seat. Is the deposition admissible under FRE 801(d)(1)?

Problem 20-2. Paula Plaintiff is suing her employer, Big Box Retail, for sexual harassment. When Paula testified at trial, the attorney for Big Box Retail suggested on cross-examination that Paula's allegations were a convenient and predictable response to the company's denial of her application for promotion to manager. At trial, Paula calls Debbie to testify about a conversation Paula and Debbie had six months before Paula applied for promotion. In that conversation, Paula allegedly said, "I'm so sick of getting treated like a sex object and a piece of meat at this place." The plaintiff objects on hearsay grounds. How should the judge rule, and why?

Problem 20-3. Victim, a convenience store clerk, is robbed at gunpoint. At the police station, he picks Defendant out of a photo lineup and says, "that's the guy that robbed me." At trial one year later, when asked whether he can identify Defendant as the robber, Victim truthfully testifies that he is not sure. What options does the prosecution have under Rule 801(d)(1)?

Problem 20-4. Professor Malcolm Tendt, a professor at Calamity State University, files a grievance against the university, alleging that the dean retaliated against him for comments he made at a faculty meeting by not giving him an annual raise. A committee examines the allegations, reports, and forwards a report to the CSU President. The President reads the report, fires the dean, and follows the committee's recommendations to restructure the annual review process. The President does not, however, give Tendt back pay. Tendt sues the university and offers the report into evidence. The defense attorney objects: "Hearsay." How should the plaintiff reply? What ruling should the judge make?

Problem 20-5. Sarah's Salad Dressing Shoppe is the subject of a story in the Calamity City Clarion. The article makes several true and false claims about Sarah's salad dressings. One such claim is that Sarah's Herbal Essence Delight dressing cures cancer. Sarah's reprints the article and includes it in an advertising circular. Wayne, a Calamity resident who as just diagnosed with curable early-stage cancer, reads the article and buys a case of the dressing. He quits going to the doctor and dies three months later. The estate sues Sarah's and attempts to introduce the circular as an admission. How should the judge rule?

Problem 20-6. Scott is a manager at a struggling paper company. In 2008, he fired Toby, the HR rep, allegedly for insubordination. On December 23, 2009, Scott was fired for incompetence. In early 2010, Scott sends Toby a letter: "I am sorry for hating you and treating you badly for so many years. You need to know that corporate ordered me to fire you because you were divorced and the company thought all HR reps should be married." Toby sued the paper company. At trial, he attempted to offer Scott's letter as an admission against the company. The judge excluded the letter. Toby appealed, arguing that the judge abused her discretion in excluding the letter. How should the appellate court rule?

Introduction to Hearsay: Quick Hits

- Hearsay is an out of court statement or assertion offered in-court to prove the truth of the matter asserted.

- The law has traditionally viewed hearsay with suspicion because it interferes with the traditional methods used by fact-finders to gauge witness credibility.

- Many out of court statements are admitted for non-hearsay purposes such as notice, effect on the listener, and *res gestae*.

- Rule 801 excludes several categories of out-of-court statements offered for their truth from the hearsay rule: prior testimonial inconsistent statements, consistent statements, admissions of a party opponent, adoptive admissions, and co-conspirator statements.

- When evaluating the admissibility of an out-of-court statement, consider the "hearsay hierarchy":

  - Non-hearsay: not offered for its truth, but for some other purpose.

  - Hearsay Exclusions: fits within a hearsay exemption under Rule 801(d).

  - Hearsay: being offered for the truth of the matter asserted.

Chapter References

Christopher B. Mueller & Laird C. Kirkpatrick, Evidence §§ 8.1–8.34 (4th ed. 2009).

Glen Weissenberger & James J. Duane, Federal Rules of Evidence: Rules, Legislative History, Commentary and Authority § 801 (6th ed. 2009).

Jack B. Weinstein & Margaret A. Berger, Weinstein's Federal Evidence § 801 (Joseph M. McLaughlin ed., Matthew Bender 2d ed. 1997).

Kenneth S. Broun, McCormick on Evidence §§ 244–53 (6th ed. 2006).

Steven Goode & Olin Guy Wellborn III, Courtroom Handbook on Federal Evidence Ch. 5 (West 2010).

III. APPLICATION EXERCISE

Preparing to Identify, Object and Respond to Objections Regarding Out-of-Court Statements

In a trial setting, the introduction of hearsay evidence is rarely a spontaneous event that takes everyone by surprise. This is not to say that the advocates sit down and inform each other of the out-of-court statements each intends to offer at trial. Rather, through the process of case analysis, discovery and trial preparation, advocates learn the sources of information at trial and the probable scope of each witness's testimony. In many cases, advocates have already deposed witnesses and can make fairly accurate predictions of any given witness's testimony at trial.

One of the most important parts of case analysis is evaluating a file to determine potential sources of hearsay. Keeping in mind the basic definition of hearsay — an out of court statement offered to prove the truth of the matter asserted — counsel should carefully read witness statements, depositions, reports and documents to determine the *source* of the witness's knowledge about an issue. In many cases, a witness's knowledge comes from an outside source: another person, a document, a rumor. Some witnesses have a combination of personal knowledge and reported knowledge: a police officer who investigates an incident generally makes personal observations and also receives information from the reports of others.

Advocates should be prepared to contest or defend statements that are based on information originally provided by out-of-court declarants. Frequently, Rule 801(d) permits the introduction of evidence that would otherwise be excluded under the rule.

The Exercise

Objective: To demonstrate proficiency in identifying, objecting to, and defending out-of-court statements under Rules 801 and 802.

Factual Scenario: The Kramers have been involved in a bitter child custody battle for the past several years. Bertha Kramer, the children's mother, has custody of the children. Karl Kramer believes that Bertha is an unfit mother who has placed his children in moral, physical and spiritual danger. Karl Kramer has recently raised the stakes in the battle by hiring a private investigator, Irving, to spy on his ex-wife, Bertha Kramer, and her live-in boyfriend, Beef McGraw. Irving wrote a report and gave it to Karl Kramer as part of his employment. After reading the report, Kramer filed an action to obtain sole custody of his children. He intends to call Irving to testify at trial.

Following is the text of Irving's report:

> **12 October, Last Year**
> **Memorandum To: Karl Kramer**
> **From: Irving**
> **Subject: Investigation of Bertha Kramer and Beef McGraw**

On October 10, Last Year, the undersigned, pursuant to the employment agreement between the undersigned and Karl Kramer, conducted an on-site investigation of the property at 1314 Mockingbird Lane, currently occupied by Bertha Kramer (33), Beef McGraw (34), and the minor children Lydia Kramer (11), Tanner Kramer (9) and Hobart Kramer (5). The undersigned obtained the address of the residence from Karl Kramer and went there at his request.

The undersigned did dress in the uniform of a satellite TV wiring inspector and knocked on the door of the said residence at approximately 10 am, the day being a school day and the children presumably being in school, which latter presumption turned out to be an incorrect presumption, as the undersigned did learn when the door was answered by one Tanner Kramer, who was wearing a Green Bay Packers T-shirt, Power Rangers briefs and one sock, on his left foot. The undersigned did ask the above-mentioned Tanner his name, to which he replied Tanner Kramer, and then asked for the location of Bertha Kramer, and was advised that "Bertha and Beef are in the bedroom and won't let us come in." The "us" he identified as Lydia Kramer, Hobart Kramer and Macon McGraw (7). The undersigned learned in subsequent conversation with Bertha McGraw that the said Macon was the illegitimate child of Beef McGraw and his former consort, Bubbles Divine, a local dancer at a gentleman's club. It was Beef McGraw's week to have custody of the child.

The house was in an unkempt condition with clothing strewn about, dirty dishes on the couch, and the television running constantly in the background. The undersigned observed that the children were watching Cartoon Network and asked one of the children how long they had been watching, and obtained an answer, to wit: three days. All of the children were in their pajamas. The children reported that none of them were sick but that "Beef is cool and makes Mom let us stay home whenever Macon is in town."

Beef and Bertha came downstairs in a disheveled state of undress, he wearing a pink terrycloth women's robe and she wearing a long, blue cotton men's robe. "Got dressed quickly?" said the undersigned. "Must've been a little hanky panky going on, eh?" To which neither of them replied at all but blushed. Then Beef asked who I was and what my business was.

I answered I was there to check the satellite wiring, in response to which Beef said they had cable. "Isn't this 1313 Mockingbird Lane?" asked the undersigned, to which Bertha answered, "No, that's across the street. That's where Dana Druggie lives." I commented on the name and she said, "His real name is Dana, but we call him Dana Druggie because he sells drugs. Everyone knows it."

The undersigned commented that it must be rough to live so near a drug dealer, and Bertha said, "It's tough." Then one of the children, Lydia, said, "It isn't so bad. We play there all the time. And they come over here all the time. Those people are nice. They have cool stuff at their house, and cool people are always coming over. And Beef and Dana go on business trips together all the time. They gave us a boat." Bertha and Beef looked embarrassed but said nothing. The undersigned asked Beef about his employment, and Beef said he was looking for work. Bertha likewise indicated looking for work. The undersigned indicated that many people are living out of work and asked how they were making it, and Bertha replied "food stamps, unemployment and child support." The undersigned commented that the house was nice and she must have a rich ex-husband, and she said, "well, I had to get something out of the divorce besides Beef," and pointed at Beef McGraw. The undersigned took this to confirm the divorce allegation that she was unfaithful to Beef before the dissolution of the marriage.

The undersigned asked about the children and why they were home. Bertha indicated who each child was and who Macon was, then said the children were ill with "a virus" and the doctor had said they should not go to school for a week.

The undersigned noticed a bruise on Hobart's face about the size of a hand and said, "Is that child a boxer?" Beef said, "no, he isn't a boxer, you dumba*!, he's only seven years old." And then Bertha said, "He's five, Beef, but he can take a pretty good slap, can't he?" Beef glared at her and said, "let's take a look at his back and see who's good at dishing it out." To which Bertha said nothing but walked into the kitchen.

Beef said the undersigned should probably be on my way. On the way out the door, the undersigned noticed a hookah by the door. "Middle Eastern tobacco?" the undersigned asked. To which Beef replied, "I think you'd better go now."

Irving Investigator

Advance Preparation. Assume that Irving will testify pursuant to his report. Identify possible out-of-court statements that might be admitted in evidence. Be prepared to object to them and respond to objections.

In-Class Exercise. The professor will conduct a plaintiff's direct examination of Irving. Students will play the role of Irving, defense counsel (making objections), plaintiff's counsel (responding to objections), and judge (ruling on objections).

Chapter 21

RULE 802 AND THE PROBLEM OF
CONFRONTATION IN CRIMINAL CASES

Chapter Objectives:

- Introduce and explain Rule 802, the problem of confrontation and hearsay and the Supreme Court's Confrontation Clause hearsay cases
- Analyze and discuss issues pertaining to hearsay and confrontation
- Apply the concepts from this chapter in a courtroom application exercise

---

I. BACKGROUND AND EXPLANATORY MATERIAL

The Basic Hearsay Prohibition of Rule 802

In the courtroom, hearsay is presumptively inadmissible. We have already seen that the law of evidence treats hearsay evidence with a great deal of suspicion. It is viewed as being not only unreliable, but also potentially dangerous to the jury's fact-finding function and the rights of the parties.

Rule 801 of the Federal Rules of Evidence defines hearsay. Rule 802 creates a general prohibition on the use of hearsay evidence in the courtroom. The text of Rule 802 follows:

Through Dec. 1, 2011	After Dec. 1, 2011
Rule 802. Hearsay Rule	**Rule 802. The Rule Against Hearsay**
Hearsay is not admissible except as provided by these rules or by other rules prescribed by the Supreme Court pursuant to statutory authority or by Act of Congress.	Hearsay is not admissible unless any of the following provides otherwise: • a federal statute; • these rules; or • Other rules prescribed by the Supreme Court.

In essence, Rule 802 codifies the common-law prohibition of hearsay in the courtroom. When evidence qualifies as hearsay under Rule 801 (an out-of-court statement or assertion offered for its truth and not exempt under Rule 801(d)), it is presumptively inadmissible under Rule 802.

There are, of course, exceptions to the hearsay rule, many of which will be discussed in forthcoming chapters. But the basic rule, founded on centuries of courtroom hostility to hearsay, is exclusion. This suspicion is rooted in the values at the core of the adversarial trial process: the jury's role in assessing the credibility of witnesses and determining what weight to assign evidence; the judge's role as a evidentiary gatekeeper to protect the jury from inadmissible evidence; and — especially in criminal cases — the importance of cross-examination and face-to-face confrontation in testing witness testimony.

The Problem of Hearsay and Confrontation in Criminal Cases

The Confrontation Clause of the Sixth Amendment to the Constitution provides that "in all criminal prosecutions, the accused shall enjoy the right . . . to be confronted with the witnesses against him." The clause suggests face-to-face confrontation between the accused and the witness in open court, with the witness's testimony subject to the testing crucible of cross-examination.

All of the hearsay dangers discussed in the previous chapter are magnified in a criminal trial. Mistaken, misleading or malicious hearsay testimony could lead to wrongful or tainted convictions. For the criminal defendant, the stakes are high: personal freedom, liberty and even life itself may be on the line in a criminal case. When hearsay statements are admitted in a criminal trial, the adversarial process provides few protections to a criminal accused. Because of the abuse of discretion standard of review, evidentiary mistakes are not easily rectified. Furthermore, during the pendency of an appeal, a criminal accused is likely to be incarcerated; even if he is eventually exonerated, no one can ever replace the lost days and years of confinement.

As we will see in the *Crawford* case below, there is some evidence that the Framers intended the Confrontation Clause to require actual confrontation in most cases. The clause was written to ensure that abusive practices such as trial by affidavit or *ex parte* examination of prosecution witnesses would never be permitted in American courtrooms.

Over time, however, American appellate courts adopted a loose interpretation of the Confrontation Clause when applied to hearsay statements in criminal cases. The landmark Supreme Court case of *Ohio v. Roberts* held that the Confrontation Clause was satisfied if the hearsay statements being offered bore "adequate indicia of reliability."[1] The reliability test could be satisfied if the hearsay statement fell within a firmly-rooted hearsay exception, or, in the alternative, demonstrated

---

[1] Ohio v. Roberts, 448 U.S. 56, 66 (1980). For a description of *Roberts*, see GLEN WEISSENBERGER & JAMES J. DUANE, FEDERAL RULES OF EVIDENCE: RULES, LEGISLATIVE HISTORY, COMMENTARY AND AUTHORITY § 801.2 (6th ed. 2009).

"particularized guarantees of trustworthiness."[2] According to Weissenberger and Duane, "As a practical matter, this test rendered the Confrontation Clause largely duplicative of the hearsay rules, and greatly minimized the incentive for criminal defense attorneys to object on constitutional grounds to the admission of hearsay."[3] In other words, if the proponent of hearsay evidence (typically the prosecutor in a criminal case) could demonstrate that a statement met a hearsay exception, there was no real Confrontation Clause analysis.

For statements that did not meet standard hearsay exception, courts would apply a "particularized guarantees of trustworthiness" test. If evidence had sufficiently particularized guarantees of trustworthiness, it would satisfy the Confrontation Clause, even if the accused never had the opportunity to confront the witness in court.

In 2004, the Supreme Court revitalized the Confrontation Clause as applied to the introduction of hearsay statements against the accused in criminal cases. The Court held that when the prosecution seeks to introduce a testimonial hearsay statement against a criminal accused, the Confrontation Clause requires that the accused be provided the opportunity for confrontation and cross-examination, either at the trial itself or in a prior proceeding.

The next section of this chapter will introduce the two seminal Supreme Court cases on hearsay and confrontation in criminal cases. As you read the cases, pay particular attention to the Court's discussion of the history of the Confrontation Clause. Ask yourself whether the "testimonial hearsay" formulation developed by the Court falls within the meaning of the Confrontation Clause. Pay attention to the potential issues and problems raised by the Court's approach.

II.   CASES, DISCUSSION QUESTIONS AND PROBLEMS

CRAWFORD v. WASHINGTON
Supreme Court of the United States
541 U.S. 36 (2004)

Justice Scalia delivered the opinion of the Court. . . .

On August 5, 1999, Kenneth Lee was stabbed at his apartment. Police arrested petitioner later that night. After giving petitioner and his wife Miranda warnings, detectives interrogated each of them twice. Petitioner eventually confessed that he and Sylvia had gone in search of Lee because he was upset over an earlier incident in which Lee had tried to rape her. The two had found Lee at his apartment, and a fight ensued in which Lee was stabbed in the torso and petitioner's hand was cut. . . .

[Petitioner told police he had acted in self-defense because Lee was drawing a knife on him. Sylvia generally corroborated petitioner's story about the events leading up to the fight, but in her account of the fight, Petitioner struck first, and

---

[2] *Roberts*, 448 U.S. at 66.

[3] Weissenberger & Duane § 801.2.

Lee had no weapon in his hands, which were, in fact, open.] . . .

The State charged petitioner with assault and attempted murder. At trial, he claimed self-defense. [He was able to keep Sylvia from testifying against him using the state's marital privilege, which bars a spouse from testifying without the other spouse's consent. In Washington, the privilege does not extend to the spouse's out-of-court statements available under a hearsay exception. The State introduced Sylvia's out-of-court statements as statements against penal interest. The trial court admitted Sylvia's statements and found that they had "particularized guarantees of trustworthiness" under the *Ohio v. Roberts* framework.]

The prosecution played the tape for the jury and relied on it in closing, arguing that it was "damning evidence" that "completely refutes [petitioner's] claim of self-defense." Tr. 468 (Oct. 21, 1999). The jury convicted petitioner of assault.

The Washington Court of Appeals reversed. [And applied a 9-factor test based on *Roberts* to determine the statement was not reliable.]

The Washington Supreme Court reinstated the conviction, [and determined the statement was reliable under *Roberts*]. . . .

II

The Sixth Amendment's Confrontation Clause provides that, "[i]n all criminal prosecutions, the accused shall enjoy the right . . . to be confronted with the witnesses against him." We have held that this bedrock procedural guarantee applies to both federal and state prosecutions. Pointer v. Texas, 380 U.S. 400, 406, 85 S. Ct. 1065, 13 L. Ed. 2d 923 (1965). As noted above, Roberts says that an unavailable witness's out-of-court statement may be admitted so long as it has adequate indicia of reliability — i.e., falls within a "firmly rooted hearsay exception" or bears "particularized guarantees of trustworthiness." 448 U.S., at 66, 13 L. Ed. 2d 923, 85 S. Ct. 1065. Petitioner argues that this test strays from the original meaning of the Confrontation Clause and urges us to reconsider it.

A

The Constitution's text does not alone resolve this case. One could plausibly read "witnesses against" a defendant to mean those who actually testify at trial, those whose statements are offered at trial, or something in-between. We must therefore turn to the historical background of the Clause to understand its meaning.

The right to confront one's accusers is a concept that dates back to Roman times. The founding generation's immediate source of the concept, however, was the common law. English common law has long differed from continental civil law in regard to the manner in which witnesses give testimony in criminal trials. The common-law tradition is one of live testimony in court subject to adversarial testing, while the civil law condones examination in private by judicial officers. See 3 W. Blackstone, Commentaries on the Laws of England 373-374 (1768).

Nonetheless, England at times adopted elements of the civil-law practice. Justices of the peace or other officials examined suspects and witnesses before trial. These examinations were sometimes read in court in lieu of live testimony, a practice that "occasioned frequent demands by the prisoner to have his 'accusers,' i.e. the witnesses against him, brought before him face to face." 1 J. Stephen, History of the Criminal Law of England 326 (1883). In some cases, these demands were refused. [citations omitted] . . .

[The court traces the extensive history of civil-law examinations by affidavit.]

The most notorious instances of civil-law examination occurred in the great political trials of the 16th and 17th centuries. One such was the 1603 trial of Sir Walter Raleigh for treason. Lord Cobham, Raleigh's alleged accomplice, had implicated him in an examination before the Privy Council and in a letter. At Raleigh's trial, these were read to the jury. Raleigh argued that Cobham had lied to save himself: "Cobham is absolutely in the King's mercy; to excuse me cannot avail him; by accusing me he may hope for favour." 1 D. Jardine, Criminal Trials 435 (1832). Suspecting that Cobham would recant, Raleigh demanded that the judges call him to appear, arguing that "[t]he Proof of the Common Law is by witness and jury: let Cobham be here, let him speak it. Call my accuser before my face. . . ." 2 How. St. Tr., at 15-16. The judges refused, id., at 24, and, despite Raleigh's protestations that he was being tried "by the Spanish Inquisition," id., at 15, the jury convicted, and Raleigh was sentenced to death. . . .

[In the aftermath of Raleigh's death, use of affidavits was disfavored and face-to-face confrontation preferred.]

One recurring question was whether the admissibility of an unavailable witness's pretrial examination depended on whether the defendant had had an opportunity to cross-examine him. [History, according to the court, indicates yes.] . . .

B

Controversial examination practices were also used in the Colonies. [The Court cites admiralty court jurisdiction over Stamp Act Offenses. The courts followed civil-law procedures and took testimony by depositions or private judicial examinations.] John Adams, defending a merchant in a high-profile admiralty case, argued: "Examinations of witnesses upon Interrogatories, are only by the Civil Law. Interrogatories are unknown at common Law, and Englishmen and common Lawyers have an aversion to them if not an Abhorrence of them." Draft of Argument in Sewall v Hancock (1768-1769), in 2 Legal Papers of John Adams 194, 207 (K. Wroth & H. Zobel eds. 1965).

Many declarations of rights adopted around the time of the Revolution guaranteed a right of confrontation. [Historical references omitted.]

Early state decisions shed light upon the original understanding of the common-law right. State v. Webb, 2 N. C. 103 (1794) (per curiam), decided a mere three years after the adoption of the Sixth Amendment, held that depositions could be read against an accused only if they were taken in his presence. Rejecting a broader reading of the English authorities, the court held: "[I]t is a rule of the common law, founded on natural justice, that no man shall be prejudiced by evidence which he had not the liberty to cross examine." Id., at 104.

Similarly, in State v. Campbell, 30 S.C.L. 124 (1844), South Carolina's highest law court excluded a deposition taken by a coroner in the absence of the accused. It held: "[I]f we are to decide the question by the established rules of the common law, there could not be a dissenting voice. For, notwithstanding the death of the witness, and whatever the respectability of the court taking the depositions, the solemnity of the occasion and the weight of the testimony, such depositions are ex parte, and, therefore, utterly incompetent." Id., at 125. The court said that one of the "indispensable conditions" implicitly guaranteed by the State Constitution was that "prosecutions be carried on to the conviction of the accused, by witnesses confronted by him, and subjected to his personal examination." Ibid.

Many other decisions are to the same effect. Some early cases went so far as to hold that prior testimony was inadmissible in criminal cases even if the accused had a previous opportunity to cross-examine. See Finn v. Commonwealth, 26 Va. 701, 708 (1827); State v. Atkins, 1 Tenn. 229 (1807) (per curiam). Most courts rejected that view, but only after reaffirming that admissibility depended on a prior opportunity for cross-examination. [Citations omitted.] . . .

III

This history supports two inferences about the meaning of the Sixth Amendment.

A

First, the principal evil at which the Confrontation Clause was directed was the civil-law mode of criminal procedure, and particularly its use of ex parte examinations as evidence against the accused. It was these practices that the Crown deployed in notorious treason cases like Raleigh's; that the Marian statutes invited; that English law's assertion of a right to confrontation was meant to prohibit; and that the founding-era rhetoric decried. The Sixth Amendment must be interpreted with this focus in mind.

Accordingly, we once again reject the view that the Confrontation Clause applies of its own force only to in-court testimony, and that its application to out-of-court statements introduced at trial depends upon "the law of Evidence for the time being." 3 Wigmore § 1397, at 101; accord, Dutton v. Evans, 400 U.S. 74, 94, 91 S. Ct. 210, 27 L. Ed. 2d 213 (1970) (Harlan, J., concurring in result). Leaving the regulation of out-of-court statements to the law of evidence would render the Confrontation Clause powerless to prevent even the most flagrant inquisitorial practices. Raleigh was, after all, perfectly free to confront those who read Cobham's confession in court.

This focus also suggests that not all hearsay implicates the Sixth Amendment's core concerns. An off-hand, overheard remark might be unreliable evidence and thus a good candidate for exclusion under hearsay rules, but it bears little resemblance to the civil-law abuses the Confrontation Clause targeted. On the other hand, ex parte examinations might sometimes be admissible under modern hearsay rules, but the Framers certainly would not have condoned them.

The text of the Confrontation Clause reflects this focus. It applies to "witnesses" against the accused — in other words, those who "bear testimony." 2 N. Webster, An American Dictionary of the English Language (1828). "Testimony," in turn, is typically "[a] solemn declaration or affirmation made for the purpose of establishing or proving some fact." Ibid. An accuser who makes a formal statement to government officers bears testimony in a sense that a person who makes a casual remark to an acquaintance does not. The constitutional text, like the history underlying the common-law right of confrontation, thus reflects an especially acute concern with a specific type of out-of-court statement.

Various formulations of this core class of "testimonial" statements exist: "ex parte in-court testimony or its functional equivalent — that is, material such as affidavits, custodial examinations, prior testimony that the defendant was unable to cross-examine, or similar pretrial statements that declarants would reasonably expect to be used prosecutorially," Brief for Petitioner 23; "extrajudicial statements . . . contained in formalized testimonial materials, such as affidavits, depositions, prior testimony, or confessions," White v. Illinois, 502 U.S. 346, 365, 112 S. Ct. 736, 116 L. Ed. 2d 848 (1992) (Thomas, J., joined by Scalia, J., concurring in part and concurring in judgment); "statements that were made under circumstances which would lead an objective witness reasonably to believe that the statement would be available for use at a later trial," Brief for National Association of Criminal Defense Lawyers et al. as Amici Curiae 3. These formulations all share a common nucleus and then define the Clause's coverage at various levels of abstraction around it. Regardless of the precise articulation, some statements qualify under any definition — for example, ex parte testimony at a preliminary hearing.

Statements taken by police officers in the course of interrogations are also testimonial under even a narrow standard. Police interrogations bear a striking resemblance to examinations by justices of the peace in England. The statements are not sworn testimony, but the absence of oath was not dispositive. Cobham's examination was unsworn, see 1 Jardine, Criminal Trials, at 430, yet Raleigh's trial has long been thought a paradigmatic confrontation violation, see, e.g., Campbell, 30 S.C.L., at 130. Under the Marian statutes, witnesses were typically put on oath, but suspects were not. See 2 Hale, Pleas of the Crown, at 52. Yet Hawkins and others went out of their way to caution that such unsworn confessions were not admissible against anyone but the confessor.

That interrogators are police officers rather than magistrates does not change the picture either. Justices of the peace conducting examinations under the Marian statutes were not magistrates as we understand that office today, but had an essentially investigative and prosecutorial function. See 1 Stephen, Criminal Law of England, at 221; Langbein, Prosecuting Crime in the Renaissance, at 34-45. England did not have a professional police force until the 19th century, see 1 Stephen, supra, at 194-200, so it is not surprising that other government officers performed the investigative functions now associated primarily with the police. The involvement of government officers in the production of testimonial evidence presents the same risk, whether the officers are police or justices of the peace.

In sum, even if the Sixth Amendment is not solely concerned with testimonial hearsay, that is its primary object, and interrogations by law enforcement officers fall squarely within that class.[4]

B

The historical record also supports a second proposition: that the Framers would not have allowed admission of testimonial statements of a witness who did not appear at trial unless he was unavailable to testify, and the defendant had had a prior opportunity for cross-examination. The text of the Sixth Amendment does not suggest any open-ended exceptions from the confrontation requirement to be developed by the courts. Rather, the "right . . . to be confronted with the witnesses against him," Amdt. 6, is most naturally read as a reference to the right of confrontation at common law, admitting only those exceptions established at the time of the founding. As the English authorities above reveal, the common law in 1791 conditioned admissibility of an absent witness's examination on unavailability and a prior opportunity to cross-examine. The Sixth Amendment therefore incorporates those limitations. The numerous early state decisions applying the same test confirm that these principles were received as part of the common law in this country. . . .

We do not read the historical sources to say that a prior opportunity to cross-examine was merely a sufficient, rather than a necessary, condition for admissibility of testimonial statements. They suggest that this requirement was dispositive, and not merely one of several ways to establish reliability. This is not to deny, as the Chief Justice notes, that "[t]here were always exceptions to the general rule of exclusion" of hearsay evidence. Post, at ____, 158 L. Ed. 2d, at 206. Several had become well established by 1791. See 3 Wigmore § 1397, at 101; Brief for United States as Amicus Curiae 13, n 5. But there is scant evidence that exceptions were invoked to admit testimonial statements against the accused in a criminal case. Most of the hearsay exceptions covered statements that by their nature were not testimonial — for example, business records or statements in furtherance of a conspiracy. We do not infer from these that the Framers thought exceptions would apply even to prior testimony.

IV

Our case law has been largely consistent with these two principles. Our leading early decision, for example, involved a deceased witness's prior trial testimony. Mattox v. United States, 156 U.S. 237, 15 S. Ct. 337, 39 L. Ed. 409 (1895). In allowing the statement to be admitted, we relied on the fact that the defendant had had, at the first trial, an adequate opportunity to confront the witness: "The substance of the constitutional protection is preserved to the prisoner in the advantage he has once had of seeing the witness face to face, and of subjecting him to the ordeal of a cross-examination. This, the law says, he shall under no circumstances be deprived of. . . ." Id., at 244, 39 L. Ed. 409, 15 S. Ct. 337.

Our later cases conform to Mattox's holding that prior trial or preliminary hearing

---

[4] [n.4] We use the term "interrogation" in its colloquial, rather than any technical legal, sense. Cf. Rhode Island v. Innis, 446 U.S. 291, 300-301, 100 S. Ct. 1682, 64 L. Ed. 2d 297 (1980) . . .

testimony is admissible only if the defendant had an adequate opportunity to cross-examine. Even where the defendant had such an opportunity, we excluded the testimony where the government had not established unavailability of the witness. We similarly excluded accomplice confessions where the defendant had no opportunity to cross-examine. In contrast, we considered reliability factors beyond prior opportunity for cross-examination when the hearsay statement at issue was not testimonial.

Even our recent cases, in their outcomes, hew closely to the traditional line. Ohio v. Roberts admitted testimony from a preliminary hearing at which the defendant had examined the witness. Lilly v Virginia, supra, excluded testimonial statements that the defendant had had no opportunity to test by cross-examination. And Bourjaily v. United States, admitted statements made unwittingly to an FBI informant after applying a more general test that did not make prior cross-examination an indispensable requirement.

[The Court distinguishes a case involving interlocking confessions and their admissibility.]

Our cases have thus remained faithful to the Framers' understanding: Testimonial statements of witnesses absent from trial have been admitted only where the declarant is unavailable, and only where the defendant has had a prior opportunity to cross-examine.

Finally, we reiterate that, when the declarant appears for cross-examination at trial, the Confrontation Clause places no constraints at all on the use of his prior testimonial statements. It is therefore irrelevant that the reliability of some out-of-court statements " 'cannot be replicated, even if the declarant testifies to the same matters in court.' " Post, at ___, 158 L. Ed. 2d, at 206-207 (quoting United States v. Inadi, 475 U.S. 387, 395, 106 S. Ct. 1121, 89 L. Ed. 2d 390 (1986)). The Clause does not bar admission of a statement so long as the declarant is present at trial to defend or explain it. The Clause also does not bar the use of testimonial statements for purposes other than establishing the truth of the matter asserted.

V

Although the results of our decisions have generally been faithful to the original meaning of the Confrontation Clause, the same cannot be said of our rationales. Roberts conditions the admissibility of all hearsay evidence on whether it falls under a "firmly rooted hearsay exception" or bears "particularized guarantees of trustworthiness." 448 U.S., at 66, 65 L. Ed. 597, 100 S. Ct. 2531. This test departs from the historical principles identified above in two respects. First, it is too broad: It applies the same mode of analysis whether or not the hearsay consists of ex parte testimony. This often results in close constitutional scrutiny in cases that are far removed from the core concerns of the Clause. At the same time, however, the test is too narrow: It admits statements that do consist of ex parte testimony upon a mere finding of reliability. This malleable standard often fails to protect against paradigmatic confrontation violations.

A

Where testimonial statements are involved, we do not think the Framers meant to leave the Sixth Amendment's protection to the vagaries of the rules of evidence, much less to amorphous notions of "reliability." Certainly none of the authorities discussed above acknowledges any general reliability exception to the common-law rule. Admitting statements deemed reliable by a judge is fundamentally at odds with the right of confrontation. To be sure, the Clause's ultimate goal is to ensure reliability of evidence, but it is a procedural rather than a substantive guarantee. It commands, not that evidence be reliable, but that reliability be assessed in a particular manner: by testing in the crucible of cross-examination. The Clause thus reflects a judgment, not only about the desirability of reliable evidence (a point on which there could be little dissent), but about how reliability can best be determined. Cf. 3 Blackstone, Commentaries, at 373 ("This open examination of witnesses . . . is much more conducive to the clearing up of truth"); M. Hale, History and Analysis of the Common Law of England 258 (1713) (adversarial testing "beats and bolts out the Truth much better").

The *Roberts* test allows a jury to hear evidence, untested by the adversary process, based on a mere judicial determination of reliability. It thus replaces the constitutionally prescribed method of assessing reliability with a wholly foreign one. . . .

The Raleigh trial itself involved the very sorts of reliability determinations that Roberts authorizes. In the face of Raleigh's repeated demands for confrontation, the prosecution responded with many of the arguments a court applying Roberts might invoke today: that Cobham's statements were self-inculpatory, 2 How. St. Tr., at 19, that they were not made in the heat of passion, id., at 14, and that they were not "extracted from [him] upon any hopes or promise of Pardon," id., at 29. It is not plausible that the Framers' only objection to the trial was that Raleigh's judges did not properly weigh these factors before sentencing him to death. Rather, the problem was that the judges refused to allow Raleigh to confront Cobham in court, where he could cross-examine him and try to expose his accusation as a lie.

Dispensing with confrontation because testimony is obviously reliable is akin to dispensing with jury trial because a defendant is obviously guilty. This is not what the Sixth Amendment prescribes.

B

The legacy of *Roberts* in other courts vindicates the Framers' wisdom in rejecting a general reliability exception. The framework is so unpredictable that it fails to provide meaningful protection from even core confrontation violations. [The Court cites numerous examples.]

It is not enough to point out that most of the usual safeguards of the adversary process attend the statement, when the single safeguard missing is the one the Confrontation Clause demands.

C

Roberts' failings were on full display in the proceedings below. [Court reviews the facts and discusses the opposite findings of the trial court, Court of Appeals, and Washington Supreme Court as to reliability.] The case is thus a self-contained demonstration of *Roberts'* unpredictable and inconsistent application. . . .

We readily concede that we could resolve this case by simply reweighing the "reliability factors" under *Roberts* and finding that Sylvia Crawford's statement falls short. But we view this as one of those rare cases in which the result below is so improbable that it reveals a fundamental failure on our part to interpret the Constitution in a way that secures its intended constraint on judicial discretion. Moreover, to reverse the Washington Supreme Court's decision after conducting our own reliability analysis would perpetuate, not avoid, what the Sixth Amendment condemns. The Constitution prescribes a procedure for determining the reliability of testimony in criminal trials, and we, no less than the state courts, lack authority to replace it with one of our own devising. . . .

Where nontestimonial hearsay is at issue, it is wholly consistent with the Framers' design to afford the States flexibility in their development of hearsay law — as does *Roberts*, and as would an approach that exempted such statements from Confrontation Clause scrutiny altogether. Where testimonial evidence is at issue, however, the Sixth Amendment demands what the common law required: unavailability and a prior opportunity for cross-examination. We leave for another day any effort to spell out a comprehensive definition of "testimonial." Whatever else the term covers, it applies at a minimum to prior testimony at a preliminary hearing, before a grand jury, or at a former trial; and to police interrogations. These are the modern practices with closest kinship to the abuses at which the Confrontation Clause was directed.

In this case, the State admitted Sylvia's testimonial statement against petitioner, despite the fact that he had no opportunity to cross-examine her. That alone is sufficient to make out a violation of the Sixth Amendment. *Roberts* notwithstanding, we decline to mine the record in search of indicia of reliability. Where testimonial statements are at issue, the only indicium of reliability sufficient to satisfy constitutional demands is the one the Constitution actually prescribes: confrontation.

The judgment of the Washington Supreme Court is reversed, and the case is remanded for further proceedings not inconsistent with this opinion.

It is so ordered.

DISCUSSION QUESTIONS

1. What are the dangers of using hearsay in a criminal trial?

2. Having read Justice Scalia's opinion in light of what you know about the traditionally recognized dangers of hearsay testimony, do you agree that confrontation trumps reliability? Why or why not?

3. What does "testimonial" mean? Is Scalia's definition helpful? Why or why not?

4. What problems could you predict arising from this opinion's failure (or refusal) to define the term "testimonial?"

DAVIS v. WASHINGTON
Supreme Court of the United States
547 U.S. 813 (2006)

[The court considered two cases in this opinion, *Davis v. Washington* and *Hammon v. Indiana*. In *Davis*, the issue involved statements obtained during a 911 call to police. In *Hammon*, the issue involved statements given to a police officer who responded to a domestic violence complaint, when the complainant was safe from the defendant and talking to the police at the kitchen table.]

Justice Scalia delivered the opinion of the Court.

II

The Confrontation Clause of the Sixth Amendment provides: "In all criminal prosecutions, the accused shall enjoy the right . . . to be confronted with the witnesses against him." In Crawford v. Washington, 541 U.S. 36, 53-54, 124 S. Ct. 1354, 158 L. Ed. 2d 177 (2004), we held that this provision bars "admission of testimonial statements of a witness who did not appear at trial unless he was unavailable to testify, and the defendant had had a prior opportunity for cross-examination." A critical portion of this holding, and the portion central to resolution of the two cases now before us, is the phrase "testimonial statements." Only statements of this sort cause the declarant to be a "witness" within the meaning of the Confrontation Clause. See id., at 51. It is the testimonial character of the statement that separates it from other hearsay that, while subject to traditional limitations upon hearsay evidence, is not subject to the Confrontation Clause.

Our opinion in *Crawford* set forth "[v]arious formulations" of the core class of " 'testimonial' " statements, ibid., but found it unnecessary to endorse any of them, because "some statements qualify under any definition," id., at 52. Among those, we said, were "[s]tatements taken by police officers in the course of interrogations," ibid.; see also id., at 53. The questioning that generated the deponent's statement in *Crawford* — which was made and recorded while she was in police custody, after having been given Miranda warnings as a possible suspect herself — "qualifies under any conceivable definition" of an " 'interrogation,' " 541 U.S. We therefore did not define that term, except to say that "[w]e use [it] . . . in its colloquial, rather than any technical legal, sense," and that "one can imagine various definitions . . . , and we need not select among them in this case." Ibid. The character of the statements in the present cases is not as clear, and these cases require us to determine more precisely which police interrogations produce testimony.

Without attempting to produce an exhaustive classification of all conceivable statements — or even all conceivable statements in response to police interrogation — as either testimonial or nontestimonial, it suffices to decide the present cases to hold as follows: Statements are nontestimonial when made in the course of police interrogation under circumstances objectively indicating that the primary purpose of the interrogation is to enable police assistance to meet an ongoing emergency. They are testimonial when the circumstances objectively indicate that there is no such ongoing emergency, and that the primary purpose of the interrogation is to establish or prove past events potentially relevant to later criminal prosecution.

III

A

In *Crawford*, it sufficed for resolution of the case before us to determine that "even if the Sixth Amendment is not solely concerned with testimonial hearsay, that is its primary object, and interrogations by law enforcement officers fall squarely within that class." Id., at 53. Moreover, as we have just described, the facts of that case spared us the need to define what we meant by "interrogations." The *Davis* case today does not permit us this luxury of indecision. The inquiries of a police operator in the course of a 911 call are an interrogation in one sense, but not in a sense that "qualifies under any conceivable definition." We must decide, therefore, whether the Confrontation Clause applies only to testimonial hearsay; and, if so, whether the recording of a 911 call qualifies.

The answer to the first question was suggested in *Crawford*, even if not explicitly held:

"The text of the Confrontation Clause reflects this focus [on testimonial hearsay]. It applies to 'witnesses' against the accused — in other words, those who 'bear testimony.' 1 N. Webster, An American Dictionary of the English Language (1828). 'Testimony,' in turn, is typically 'a solemn declaration or affirmation made for the purpose of establishing or proving some fact.' Ibid. An accuser who makes a formal statement to government officers bears testimony in a sense that a person who makes a casual remark to an acquaintance does not." 541 U.S., at 51.

A limitation so clearly reflected in the text of the constitutional provision must fairly be said to mark out not merely its "core," but its perimeter.

We are not aware of any early American case invoking the Confrontation Clause or the common-law right to confrontation that did not clearly involve testimony as thus defined. Well into the 20th century, our own Confrontation Clause jurisprudence was carefully applied only in the testimonial context. [Citations and examples omitted.]

Even our later cases, conforming to the reasoning of Ohio v. Roberts, 448 U.S. 56 (1980), never in practice dispensed with the Confrontation Clause requirements of unavailability and prior cross-examination in cases that involved testimonial hearsay, see Crawford, 541 U.S., at 57-59 (citing cases), with one arguable exception, see id., at 58, n. 8, 124 S. Ct. 1354 (discussing White v. Illinois, 502 U.S. 346 (1992)). Where our cases did dispense with those requirements — even under the *Roberts* approach — the statements at issue were clearly nontestimonial. See, e.g., Bourjaily v. United States, 483 U.S. 171 (1987) (statements made unwittingly to a Government informant); Dutton v. Evans, 400 U.S. 74, 87-89 (1970) (plurality opinion) (statements from one prisoner to another).

Most of the American cases applying the Confrontation Clause or its state constitutional or common-law counterparts involved testimonial statements of the most formal sort — sworn testimony in prior judicial proceedings or formal depositions under oath — which invites the argument that the scope of the Clause is limited to that very formal category. But the English cases that were the progenitors of the Confrontation Clause did not limit the exclusionary rule to prior court testimony and formal depositions, see Crawford, supra, at 52. In any event, we do not think it conceivable that the protections of the Confrontation Clause can readily be evaded by having a note-taking policeman recite the unsworn hearsay testimony of the declarant, instead of having the declarant sign a deposition. Indeed, if there is one point for which no case — English or early American, state or federal — can be cited, that is it.

The question before us in *Davis*, then, is whether, objectively considered, the interrogation that took place in the course of the 911 call produced testimonial statements. When we said in *Crawford*, supra, at 53, that "interrogations by law enforcement officers fall squarely within [the] class" of testimonial hearsay, we had immediately in mind (for that was the case before us) interrogations solely directed at establishing the facts of a past crime, in order to identify (or provide evidence to convict) the perpetrator. The product of such interrogation, whether reduced to a writing signed by the declarant or embedded in the memory (and perhaps notes) of the interrogating officer, is testimonial. It is, in the terms of the 1828 American dictionary quoted in *Crawford*, " '[a] solemn declaration or affirmation made for the purpose of establishing or proving some fact.' " 541 U.S., at 51. (The solemnity of even an oral declaration of relevant past fact to an investigating officer is well enough established by the severe consequences that can attend a deliberate falsehood. [Citations and examples omitted.] A 911 call, on the other hand, and at least the initial interrogation conducted in connection with a 911 call, is ordinarily not designed primarily to "establis[h] or prov[e]" some past fact, but to describe current circumstances requiring police assistance.

The difference between the interrogation in *Davis* and the one in *Crawford* is apparent on the face of things. In *Davis*, McCottry was speaking about events as they were actually happening, rather than "describ[ing] past events," Lilly v. Virginia, 527 U.S. 116 (1999) (plurality opinion). Sylvia Crawford's interrogation, on the other hand, took place hours after the events she described had occurred. Moreover, any reasonable listener would recognize that McCottry (unlike Sylvia Crawford) was facing an ongoing emergency. Although one might call 911 to provide a narrative report of a crime absent any imminent danger, McCottry's call was plainly a call for help against a bona fide physical threat. Third, the nature of what was asked and answered in *Davis*, again viewed objectively, was such that the elicited statements were necessary to be able to resolve the present emergency, rather than simply to learn (as in *Crawford*) what had happened in the past. That is true even of the operator's effort to establish the identity of the assailant, so that the dispatched officers might know whether they would be encountering a violent felon. And finally, the difference in the level of formality between the two interviews is striking. Crawford was responding calmly, at the station house, to a series of questions, with the officer-interrogator taping and making notes of her answers; McCottry's frantic answers were provided over the phone, in an environment that was not tranquil, or even (as far as any reasonable 911 operator could make out) safe.

We conclude from all this that the circumstances of McCottry's interrogation objectively indicate its primary purpose was to enable police assistance to meet an ongoing emergency. She simply was not acting as a witness; she was not testifying. What she said was not "a weaker substitute for live testimony" at trial, like Lord Cobham's statements in Raleigh's Case, or Jane Dingler's ex parte statements against her husband in *King v. Dingler*, or Sylvia Crawford's statement in *Crawford*. In each of those cases, the ex parte actors and the evidentiary products of the ex parte communication aligned perfectly with their courtroom analogues. McCottry's emergency statement does not. No "witness" goes into court to proclaim an emergency and seek help.

Davis seeks to cast McCottry in the unlikely role of a witness by pointing to English cases. None of them involves statements made during an ongoing emergency. In *King v. Brasier*, for example, a young rape victim, "immediately on her coming home, told all the circumstances of the injury" to her mother. The case would be helpful to Davis if the relevant statement had been the girl's screams for aid as she was being chased by her assailant. But by the time the victim got home, her story was an account of past events.

This is not to say that a conversation which begins as an interrogation to determine the need for emergency assistance cannot, as the Indiana Supreme Court put it, "evolve into testimonial statements," 829 N. E. 2d, at 457, once that purpose has been achieved. In this case, for example, after the operator gained the information needed to address the exigency of the moment, the emergency appears to have ended (when Davis drove away from the premises). The operator then told McCottry to be quiet, and proceeded to pose a battery of questions. It could readily be maintained that, from that point on, McCottry's statements were testimonial, not unlike the "structured police questioning" that occurred in *Crawford*, 541 U.S., at 53, n. 4. This presents no great problem. Just as, for Fifth Amendment purposes, "police officers can and will distinguish almost instinctively between questions necessary to secure their own safety or the safety of the public and questions designed solely to elicit testimonial evidence from a suspect," New York v. Quarles, 467 U.S. 649, 658-659 (1984), trial courts will recognize the point at which, for Sixth Amendment purposes, statements in response to interrogations become testimonial. Through in limine procedure, they should redact or exclude the portions of any statement that have become testimonial, as they do, for example, with unduly prejudicial portions of otherwise admissible evidence. Davis's jury did not hear the complete 911 call, although it may well have heard some testimonial portions. We were asked to classify only McCottry's early statements identifying Davis as her assailant, and we agree with the Washington Supreme Court that they were not testimonial. That court also concluded that, even if later parts of the call were testimonial, their admission was harmless beyond a reasonable doubt. Davis does not challenge that holding, and we therefore assume it to be correct.

B

Determining the testimonial or nontestimonial character of the statements that were the product of the interrogation in *Hammon* is a much easier task, since they were not much different from the statements we found to be testimonial in *Crawford*. It is entirely clear from the circumstances that the interrogation was part of an investigation into possibly criminal past conduct — as, indeed, the testifying officer expressly acknowledged, App. in No. 05-5705, at 25, 32, 34. There was no emergency in progress; the interrogating officer testified that he had heard no arguments or crashing and saw no one throw or break anything, id., at 25. When the officers first arrived, Amy told them that things were fine, id., at 14, and there was no immediate threat to her person. When the officer questioned Amy for the second time, and elicited the challenged statements, he was not seeking to determine (as in *Davis*) "what is happening," but rather "what happened." Objectively viewed, the primary, if not indeed the sole, purpose of the interrogation was to investigate a possible crime — which is, of course, precisely what the officer should have done.

It is true that the *Crawford* interrogation was more formal. It followed a *Miranda* warning, was tape-recorded, and took place at the station house. While these features certainly strengthened the statements' testimonial aspect — made it more objectively apparent, that is, that the purpose of the exercise was to nail down the truth about past criminal events — none was essential to the point. It was formal enough that Amy's interrogation was conducted in a separate room, away from her husband (who tried to intervene), with the officer receiving her replies for use in his "investigat[ion]." App. in No. 05-5705, at 34. What we called the "striking resemblance" of the *Crawford* statement to civil-law ex parte examinations, is shared by Amy's statement here. Both declarants were actively separated from the defendant — officers forcibly prevented Hershel from participating in the interrogation. Both statements deliberately recounted, in response to police questioning, how potentially criminal past events began and progressed. And both took place some time after the events described were over. Such statements under official interrogation are an obvious substitute for live testimony, because they do precisely what a witness does on direct examination; they are inherently testimonial.

As for the charge that our holding is not a "targeted attempt to reach the abuses forbidden by the [Confrontation] Clause," post, at 842, at 249, which the dissent describes as the depositions taken by Marian magistrates, characterized by a high degree of formality, see post, at 835-836,: We do not dispute that formality is indeed essential to testimonial utterance. But we no longer have examining Marian magistrates; and we do have, as our 18th-century forebears did not, examining police officers, see L. Friedman, Crime and Punishment in American History 67-68 (1993) — who perform investigative and testimonial functions once performed by examining Marian magistrates, see J. Langbein, The Origins of Adversary Criminal Trial 41 (2003). It imports sufficient formality, in our view, that lies to such officers are criminal offenses. Restricting the Confrontation Clause to the precise forms against which it was originally directed is a recipe for its extinction.

Both Indiana and the United States as amicus curiae argue that this case should be resolved much like *Davi* s. For the reasons we find the comparison to *Crawford* compelling, we find the comparison to *Davis* unpersuasive. The statements in *Davis* were taken when McCottry was alone, not only unprotected by police (as Amy Hammon was protected), but apparently in immediate danger from Davis. She was seeking aid, not telling a story about the past. McCottry's present-tense statements showed immediacy; Amy's narrative of past events was delivered at some remove in time from the danger she described. And after Amy answered the officer's questions, he had her execute an affidavit, in order, he testified, "[t]o establish events that have occurred previously." App. in No. 05-5705, at 18.

Although we necessarily reject the Indiana Supreme Court's implication that virtually any "initial inquiries" at the crime scene will not be testimonial, see 829 N. E. 2d, at 453, 457, we do not hold the opposite — that no questions at the scene will yield nontestimonial answers. We have already observed of domestic disputes that "[o]fficers called to investigate . . . need to know whom they are dealing with in order to assess the situation, the threat to their own safety, and possible danger to the potential victim." Hiibel, 542 U.S., at 186, 124 S. Ct. 2451, 159 L. Ed. 2d 292. Such exigencies may often mean that "initial inquiries" produce nontestimonial statements. But in cases like this one, where Amy's statements were neither a cry for help nor the provision of information enabling officers immediately to end a threatening situation, the fact that they were given at an alleged crime scene and were "initial inquiries" is immaterial.

IV

Respondents in both cases, joined by a number of their amici, contend that the nature of the offenses charged in these two cases — domestic violence — requires greater flexibility in the use of testimonial evidence. This particular type of crime is notoriously susceptible to intimidation or coercion of the victim to ensure that she does not testify at trial. When this occurs, the Confrontation Clause gives the criminal a windfall. We may not, however, vitiate constitutional guarantees when they have the effect of allowing the guilty to go free. Cf. Kyllo v. United States, 533 U.S. 27 (2001) (suppressing evidence from an illegal search). But when defendants seek to undermine the judicial process by procuring or coercing silence from witnesses and victims, the Sixth Amendment does not require courts to acquiesce. [The Court affirms the doctrine that an accused who intimidates a witness into silence, arranges for their absence from a proceeding, or kills the witness, cannot later be heard to complain about the lack of confrontation.]

We have determined that, absent a finding of forfeiture by wrongdoing, the Sixth Amendment operates to exclude Amy Hammon's affidavit. The Indiana courts may (if they are asked) determine on remand whether such a claim of forfeiture is properly raised and, if so, whether it is meritorious.

We affirm the judgment of the Supreme Court of Washington in No. 05-5224. We reverse the judgment of the Supreme Court of Indiana in No. 05-5705, and remand the case to that court for proceedings not inconsistent with this opinion.

It is so ordered.

DISCUSSION QUESTIONS

1. How does the Court distinguish between testimonial and non-testiomonial statements? Is this a workable test?

2. How should courts draw the line between a government agent who is merely gathering information to help meet an on-going emergency, and one who is collecting testimonial evidence?

3. What happens in hybrid cases that begin with emergency information and morph into testimonial information?

PROBLEMS

Problem 21-1. In the case of Kramer v. Kramer, Karl Kramer attempts to introduce testimony from a police officer about statements taken from his children about conditions in his wife Bertha's home. Specifically, the children alleged that Bertha's live-in boyfriend exposed himself to them. The other side objects that this evidence should be excluded under *Crawford* because it is testimonial. How should the judge rule, and why?

Problem 21-2. Millicent, a five-year-old child, complained to her mother about pain in her vaginal and rectal areas. Her mother immediately took her to the emergency room. An emergency room physician examined Millicent and asked her what happened. Millicent replied, "Bobby did it," referring to her mother's boyfriend. When the physician asked what Bobby did, Millicent, using age-appropriate language, explained that Bobby had inserted his penis into her vagina and rectum. At Bobby's trial for rape and forcible sodomy of a child, the prosecution calls the physician to testify about what Millicent said about Bobby during the exam. The defense objects that the evidence is testimonial. How should the judge rule, and why?

Problem 21-3. Melissa, a cab driver, was brutally assaulted and raped by two men. After the attack, Melissa approached a house and rang the doorbell. When Dorothy, the owner of the home, opened the door, Melissa quickly told her what had happened and asked for help. Dorothy then called 911, requested an ambulance, and relayed on behalf of Melissa several pieces of information to include Melissa's injuries, Melissa's age, her location, a description of the vehicle of the assailants, and direction which the assailants fled. Testimonial or not?

Hearsay and Confrontation: Quick Hits

- Rule 802 generally prohibits the introduction of hearsay at trial, unless it meets an exception under the rules.

- In criminal cases, testimonial hearsay is inadmissible unless the defendant's Sixth Amendment Confrontation Clause rights have been satisfied. Confrontation means a face-to-face opportunity for the defendant to cross-examine the witnesses against him, either at or before trial.

- Testimonial statements describe past events and are either given or elicited for the purpose of assisting law enforcement.

- Nontestimonial statements to police officers are informal statements made for the purpose of resolving an emergency.

Chapter References

Glen Weissenberger & James J. Duane, Federal Rules of Evidence: Rules, Legislative History, Commentary and Authority § 802 (6th ed. 2009).

Kenneth S. Broun, McCormick on Evidence §§ 244–45 (6th ed. 2006).

Steven Goode & Olin Guy Wellborn III, Courtroom Handbook on Federal Evidence Ch. 5 (West 2010).

III. APPLICATION EXERCISE

Preparing to Make or Meet a Confrontation Clause Challenge to Hearsay

As part of case analysis and the pretrial preparation process, criminal defense attorneys identify hearsay statements the prosecution may wish to introduce against their clients. Confrontation Clause issues exist when a witness is dead, unable or unwilling to attend the proceedings, or incapable of testifying at trial for some reason. Sometimes, these witnesses have made out-of-court statements that the prosecution would like to admit at trial.

Frequently, defense attorneys will file motions in limine to exclude out-of-court hearsay statements on Confrontation Clause grounds. Courts generally follow some variant of the following analysis in evaluating these claims. First, the court will determine whether the statement is hearsay. If it is, the court will then evaluate whether it is testimonial within the meaning of *Crawford* and *Davis.* If the statement is testimonial, it cannot be admitted unless the Confrontation Clause has been satisfied. If the statement is not testimonial, the court will determine whether the statement meets a hearsay exception and can be otherwise admitted at trial.

These motions are usually written, although they can be made orally, depending on practice in a particular jurisdiction. In order to determine whether the statements are testimonial or not, courts frequently require testimony from witnesses about the facts and circumstances surrounding the making of the statement. The court then determines, as a matter of law under Rule 104, whether the statement is testimonial or not.

The Exercise

Objective: To demonstrate applied knowledge of testimonial and non-testimonial statements in the context of a hearing on a defense motion in limine to exclude certain statements on Confrontation grounds.

Factual Scenario: In the case of *State v. Malif Actour*, the accused was charged with aggravated assault of Vernon Victim, a resident of the Sylvan Grove Nursing Home. The accused was employed at Sylvan Grove as a maintenance worker at the time of the assault. The incident occurred, as with most other incidents in the State of Calamity, on July 15 of last year. Two months after the incident was reported, but well before it could be brought to trial, Vernon Victim died of natural causes unrelated to the assault, at the ripe old age of 92.

Management at Sylvan Grove learned of the incident on the evening of July 15. Vernon did not show up for dinner, and attendants found him unconscious in his room, bleeding from a head wound and suffering blunt force trauma. It appeared — at first — that he had tripped and fallen against a radiator near the window of his room.

He received medical treatment and when he first regained consciousness, a nurse asked him what had happened. He replied, "That maintenance man — the one with the Fu Manchu mustache and the goatee — came into my room and tried to rob me. I told him to go to hell, and he took something off his tool belt and hit me with it. That's the last thing I remember." Subsequent medical examination indicated that the wounds could have been caused by a hammer or a wrench.

The nurse called Shady Grove manager, who came to Vernon's room to interview him. When asked what happened, Vernon replied, "You know that maintenance man with the Fu Manchu mustache and the goatee. He's been coming to my room to visit me for the past few weeks. Whenever he comes, I usually give him a dollar to buy himself a soda. He seemed like a nice kid to me and I wanted to give him a break. Well, this afternoon he came in and said he needed 100 dollars. I told him I didn't have it, and that's true — I didn't have any cash. He asked if I would go to the ATM and I told him I wouldn't. He threatened to kill me if I didn't get the money. I was getting afraid of him, but I did tell him to go to hell. Then he reached for his tool belt and grabbed something. I think it was a hammer. And he hit me with it. And that's the last thing I remember."

The manager immediately called 911, while still in the room with Vernon, and reported this information to the dispatcher. The dispatcher asked the manager what Vernon was wearing, and Vernon answered, "a black Mickey Mouse T-shirt and blue jeans." The manager relayed the information to the dispatcher. The manager also provided the accused's name — Malif Actour — and his address —

1315 Mockingbird Lane — to the dispatcher.

About an hour later, Detective Dudley Doright of the Calamity City Police came to interview Vernon. Based on the interview, Doright typed out a sworn statement. He returned to Shady Grove the next morning and Vernon signed the statement. The text of the statement follows:

> *On July 15, Malif Actour, a maintenance worker at Shady Grove, came to my room and demanded $100 in cash. Actour and I had been friendly with each other. I considered him like a grandson, and believe it or not, I have a great grandson who has a Fu Manchu mustache and a goatee just like him. He used to drop by and talk to me. Usually we talked about sports and women. I had been married four times and he was thinking about getting engaged. When he'd leave, I would often give him a dollar or so and tell him to buy himself a soda. I thought he was a nice kid. On the 15th, it was different. He was agitated and nervous. He could have been high on drugs. That's how he was acting. He said he needed $100, and I told him I didn't have it. I was being honest, too, because I didn't have any cash. He told me to go to the ATM and get it, and I said I couldn't. He said he would kill me if I didn't. I was afraid, but I was in World War II as an infantry officer, and I figured if I made it through that, I could deal with him. So I laughed and told him to go to hell. Then he reached for his tool belt to grab something. I'm not sure what it was, but I think it was a hammer. He swung towards me, and that's the last thing I remember.*

Actour denied being present in Vernon's room on July 15. There was no forensic evidence linking him to the offense. The only available evidence is Vernon's medical records, the statements made to the nurse, the manager, and the sworn statement to the police. Experts for both the prosecution and the defense agree that the blunt force trauma could have been caused either by a hammer or other tool, or by Vernon tripping and hitting his head on the radiator.

Advance Preparation. Formulate an oral motion in limine to exclude Vernon's statement on Confrontation Clause grounds. You should incorporate not only the Confrontation Clause, *Crawrford* and *Davis*, but any other relevant state or federal case law you can find in your jurisdiction. Be prepared to cross-examine the witnesses as part of the motion hearing. The prosecution should be prepared to counter the motion and to call witnesses as necessary.

In-Class Exercise. The defense will make an oral motion in limine and will present argument on the issue. The prosecution will respond. The judge will decide that the parties should call witnesses in support of the motion. The prosecution will call all three witnesses (nurse, manager, police officer), and the defense will conduct cross-examination. Following the witnesses, the defense will renew its objection and make such additional arguments as are necessary. The prosecution will respond and the judge will rule.

Chapter 22

HEARSAY EXCEPTIONS UNDER RULES 803(1) TO 803(4)

Chapter Objectives:

- Introduce the *res gestae* exceptions contained in Rules 803(1) to 803(4): present sense impressions, excited utterances, statements of then-existing physical or mental condition, and statements made for the purposes of medical treatment
- Analyze and discuss issues pertaining to the *res gestae* hearsay exceptions
- Apply the concepts from this chapter in a courtroom application exercise

I. BACKGROUND AND EXPLANATORY MATERIAL

Introduction to Hearsay Exceptions under the Rules

To this point in the book, we have defined hearsay, discussed the traditionally accepted hearsay dangers and examined the interplay of the Confrontation Clause and the hearsay rule. We have also identified non-hearsay uses for out-of-court statements and evaluated the hearsay exemptions contained in Rule 801(d); in so doing, we have learned that there are many ways an out-of-court statement can be admitted into evidence without actually implicating the hearsay rule.

When an out-of-court statement cannot be categorized as non-hearsay and does not fall within the hearsay exemptions of Rule 801(d), the next alternative is to analyze it for its admissibility under the hearsay rules contained in Rules 802-807. The default position under the Federal Rules for hearsay is contained in Rule 802, which states that "[h]earsay is not admissible" unless an exception applies.

The exceptions are covered in Rules 803, 804 and 807. Rule 803 identifies twenty-three hearsay exceptions under which evidence can be admitted regardless of whether the declarant is available to testify in court. Rule 804 identifies four hearsay exceptions under which evidence can be admitted only when the declarant is unavailable to testify in court. Rule 807, the residual hearsay rule, creates an additional exception for hearsay that does not meet the criteria listed in Rules 803 and 804, but nevertheless has equivalent circumstantial guarantees of trustworthiness.

All of the codified hearsay exceptions in the Federal Rules are based on the common law. Although the common law prohibited hearsay, it developed a set of doctrinal exceptions that permitted the introduction of out-of-court statements whose trustworthiness and reliability could not reasonably be questioned and where cross-examination could add little or nothing to the jury's evaluation of the declarant's truthfulness. Each common-law hearsay exception solved a practical problem of proof in the courtroom. That same approach to hearsay applies in evaluating hearsay exceptions under the Federal Rules.

Accordingly, the first step in learning a hearsay exception is to understand why it came into being. This text follows a standard template for each hearsay exception: it explains the basis for the exception, lists the key foundational elements of the exception, and provides examples of the rule in application.

Hearsay and the *Crawford* Problem

In criminal cases, the Supreme Court case of *Crawford v. Washington* represented a sea change in the evaluation of out-of-court statements under the Confrontation Clause of the Sixth Amendment in State and Federal courtrooms. The case held that in-court confrontation (or its equivalent, such as a prior opportunity to cross examine at another adversarial proceeding) was required before testimonial evidence could be introduced at trial.

With respect to the hearsay exceptions we are about to examine, the *Crawford* analysis can be applied in one of two ways. Method one analyzes the statement under the Confrontation Clause before evaluating it under the codified hearsay exceptions. The first step is to determine whether the out-of-court statement is testimonial. If it is, the Confrontation Clause must be satisfied before the statement can be admitted into evidence; in other words, the accused must have the opportunity for face-to-face confrontation and cross-examination. If it is not testimonial, the second step is to determine whether the statement meets a recognized hearsay exception.

The second method is to evaluate the statement as hearsay, then apply a Confrontation Clause analysis. The first step in this method is to determine whether the statement meets a recognized hearsay exception that would permit its admission into evidence. The second step is to determine whether the statement is testimonial and the Confrontation Clause must be satisfied before the statement can be introduced.

Although either method ostensibly leads to the same answer, the first method saves time and energy. If a statement is testimonial, it cannot be admitted against an accused at trial in violation of the Confrontation Clause even if it satisfies every element of a codified hearsay exception.

Keep in mind that the *Crawford* analysis applies only to criminal cases. Cross-examination occurs at civil trials, of course, but it is not rooted in the Sixth Amendment Confrontation Clause as it is in criminal trials.

II. ANALYSIS AND DISCUSSION OF INDIVIDUAL HEARSAY EXCEPTIONS

The Present Sense Impression

Through Dec. 1, 2011	After Dec. 1, 2011
Rule 803. Hearsay Exceptions; Availability of Declarant Immaterial	**Rule 803. Exceptions to the Rule Against Hearsay — Regardless of Whether the Declarant Is Available as a Witness**
The following are not excluded by the hearsay rule, even though the declarant is available as a witness:	The following are not excluded by the rule against hearsay, regardless of whether the declarant is available as a witness:
(1) Present sense impression. A statement describing or explaining an event or condition made while the declarant was perceiving the event or condition, or immediately thereafter.	**(1) Present Sense Impression**. A statement describing or explaining an event or condition, made while or immediately after the declarant perceived it.

Basis

The first of the codified hearsay exceptions under Rule 803 — the present sense impression — is not firmly rooted in the common law. In their treatise on the federal rules of evidence, Professors Weissenberger and Duane trace the exception to "the common law concept of res gestae,[1] a term historically denoting words or statements that accompany the principal litigated fact;" they also point out that the concept of res gestae is "vague and imprecise."[2]

According to the Advisory Committee notes, the basis for reliability of present sense impressions "is that substantial contemporaneity of event and statement negative the likelihood of deliberate or conscious misrepresentation." Linking this to the concept of res gestae, this exception is predicated on the theory that individuals are unlikely to lie while describing an event that is occurring or has just occurred; in other words, insufficient time has elapsed to create a distortion or misrepresentation. An additional reliability factor is that the declarant often makes the statement to another person who has an equal opportunity observe the event and check for misstatements. Furthermore, in practice the declarant is often available to testify in court and be cross-examined about the facts and circumstances surrounding the event and the making of the statement.

---

[1] Glen Weissenberger & James J. Duane, Federal Rules of Evidence: Rules, Legislative History, Commentary & Authority § 803.2, at 480–81 (2009).

[2] *Id.*

Key Foundational Elements

Temporal proximity of statement to event is the key to this hearsay exception. There are three commonly accepted foundational elements for this exception:

a. The declarant must make the statement while actually perceiving an event or immediately thereafter. The passage of even a few minutes' time is enough to defeat the exception.

b. The explanation of the event must be a simple description of the observed event or condition.

c. The declarant must have personal knowledge of the described event.

The Rule in Application

In many Federal circuits, courts have added a corroboration requirement to statements introduced under this hearsay exception. This requires some evidence independent of the statement itself that the described event occurred. If the declarant is in-court and quoting himself, corroborating evidence can be introduced through the declarant; otherwise, it can be introduced through another witness. As noted by Saltzburg, Capra and Martin, the corroboration approach is consistent with the Advisory Committee notes, which indicate that under this exception, the testifying witness can be examined "as to the circumstances as an aid in evaluating the statement."[3]

Cases, Discussion Questions and Problem

UNITED STATES v. BLAKEY
United States Court of Appeals, Seventh Circuit
607 F.2d 779 (7th Cir. 1979)

The defendants, Chicago police officers James Blakey and Louis Berry, were convicted by a jury of extortion and conspiracy to commit extortion in violation of the Hobbs Act, 18 U.S.C. § 1951. . . .

On July 31, 1976, a shop operated by Leo Dyer at 6724 South Halsted Street in Chicago was under intensive Federal Bureau of Investigation (F.B.I.) and Chicago Police Department surveillance. The F.B.I., pursuant to court order, had planted microphones inside the shop and had placed a wire tap on the shop's telephone. The Chicago Police Department, investigating suspected police corruption, maintained physical surveillance of the shop. Both operations were conducted from an apartment in a building across the street from Dyer's establishment. Dyer attracted this attention because he was believed to be engaged in the illegal sale of narcotics and stolen property and in "paying off" Chicago police officers.

[The defendants entered the shop, ostensibly to search for narcotics. Both were off-duty at the time and were operating outside their assigned area. The officers searched the people in the shop and then began searching the shop itself.]

---

[3] Saltzburg, Commentary to FRE 803(1).

The defendants then called Dyer to the rear of the shop; one of them picked up Dyer's roll of money and carried it into the rear with him. The two officers and Dyer remained in the rear for almost fifteen minutes when the third officer joined them; all three officers emerged approximately one minute later and began filling paper bags with merchandise from the shop. The officers were observed leaving the shop by the surveillance personnel across the street. Before the officers reached their car, Alphonzo Pitman ran after them, at Dyer's request, to retrieve Dyer's keys, which had been next to the money on the freezer; Officer Blakey gave Pitman the keys.

The F.B.I. electronic surveillance team recorded a number of conversations in the shop during the defendants' visit and after their departure. These recorded conversations will be described where relevant in the discussion that follows. Leo Dyer died of natural causes prior to trial and thus was unavailable for cross-examination as to his recorded statements. The defense theory at trial was that the defendants had taken no cash from Dyer and had paid for the merchandise they carried from the store. Apparently, the jury found this theory unconvincing. . . .

Defendants next object to the trial court's decision to admit into evidence statements made in the tire shop and recorded after the defendants' departure. The following statements are the subject of the objection:

> *2ND WOMAN: I bet they were gonna bribe you anyway.*
>
> *DYER: What'd you say?*
>
> *2ND WOMAN: I bet you were gonna bribe them anyway so we wasn't worried about it (inaudible).*
>
> *DYER: You see one piece they, they take one piece (inaudible) they take everything you got they take everything you got that stuff like tonight cost me a thousand dollars.*

The defendants claim that these statements were a crucial element of the government's case and that their admission violated the rule against hearsay and the Sixth Amendment Confrontation Clause. The trial court admitted the statements as present sense impressions. Fed.R.Evid. 803(1). We will address first the defendants' hearsay objection and then their Confrontation Clause argument.

A

Defendants raise two objections to the use of the present sense impression exception. First, they contend that the statements were not, as required by Rule 803(1), substantially contemporaneous with the event they describe. Second, there were no witnesses, other than Dyer and the three officers, to the relevant event the exchange of $1000 in the rear of the shop. There is no explicit requirement in Rule 803(1) that a witness to the event be available for cross-examination; defendants, however, argue that such a requirement must be considered implicit in the present sense impression exception.

The latter contention need not detain us long. Although Dyer was alone with the three officers in the rear of the shop, there were several witnesses who could testify to all the events leading up to and following that brief meeting. The availability of these witnesses for cross-examination satisfies the *Houston Oxygen* requirement. It is not necessary that the witnesses be in the same position to observe as the declarant; it is only necessary that the witnesses be able to corroborate the declarant's statement. The witnesses in this case supplied substantial corroboration. We note also that the need for such witnesses is somewhat reduced where, due to tape recording, there is no uncertainty as to the content of the declarant's statement.

The defendants' argument that the time lapse between the event and Dyer's statement was too great to comply with Rule 803(1) is less easily resolved. The underlying rationale of the present sense impression exception is that substantial contemporaneity of event and statement minimizes unreliability due to defective recollection or conscious fabrication. There is no per se rule indicating what time interval is too long under Rule 803(1); however, several courts have found particular intervals to be too long under the circumstances of the cases before them. [citations omitted.] Due to factual differences, neither Cain nor Narciso provides much guidance in this case. Defendants rely heavily on Hilyer, in which the District of Columbia Circuit indicated that a 15 to 45 minute interval is longer than contemplated by Rule 803(1). 188 U.S.App.D.C. at 184 n.7, 578 F.2d at 426 n.7. This statement was unnecessary to the decision in Hilyer since that case was resolved on the basis of the excited utterance exception, Fed.R.Evid. 803(2); nonetheless, it is suggestive of the standard to be applied here. We note, however, that the admissibility of statements under hearsay exceptions depends upon the facts of the particular case.

It is difficult, from the record before us, to determine precisely the interval between the event of extortion and Dyer's statement. It is undisputed that the officers left the shop at 6:00 p. m. The statements at issue were recorded after the officers' departure and prior to a telephone conversation which occurred at 6:23 p. m. Government Trial Exhibit A-2. It is clear, therefore, that Dyer's statements were made between several minutes and 23 minutes after the defendants left the shop. A relatively large amount of conversation was recorded, according to the transcript of the tape, between Dyer's statements and the 6:23 p. m. telephone call; the transcript thus would support a finding that Dyer's statements were made soon after defendants' departure. Defendants' Abstract and Excerpts of Record at 226-32. The trial court was justified in finding that the time interval was not so great as to render Rule 803(1) inapplicable to Dyer's statements. This finding, coupled with the substantial circumstantial evidence corroborating the statements' accuracy, indicate that the trial court acted properly in admitting these statements. See Fed.R.Evid. 104(a).

UNITED STATES v. CRUZ
United States Court of Appeals, Eleventh Circuit
765 F.2d 1020 (11th Cir. 1985)

In June, 1983, Alejandro Lage a/k/a Alejandra Perrera, a paid government informant, introduced Eddie Benitez, a special agent of the Bureau of Alcohol, Tobacco, and Firearms, to Eduardo Jaime Rouco. Benitez began conducting an undercover investigation of Rouco for weapons violations. On June 10, 1983, Rouco asked Benitez whether he was interested in purchasing a large quantity of cocaine. Rouco stated the cocaine belonged to a friend and agreed to arrange a meeting between Benitez and his friend.

On June 17, 1983, Benitez and Lage met Rouco at a restaurant. Cruz subsequently joined the meeting and told Benitez that he had a friend who would supply Benitez with the cocaine. After discussing the quantity, quality, and price of the cocaine, Cruz invited Benitez to accompany him to get a sample of the cocaine.

Cruz took Benitez to Hernandez's paint and body shop. Rouco and Lage remained at the restaurant. At Hernandez's shop, a small quantity of cocaine was given to Benitez as a sample of the cocaine which Benitez could expect to receive. Benitez, Cruz, and Hernandez discussed the purity of the cocaine and the date on which the transaction would occur. Hernandez instructed Benitez to telephone him later to confirm the fact that arrangements had been made for the sale.

Benitez and Cruz returned to the restaurant and discussed the purity of the cocaine sample. When the meeting ended, Benitez met his supervising agent, James W. Pherson, and gave Pherson the cocaine sample and one of Hernandez's business cards. Pherson had been outside the restaurant conducting surveillance.

On June 21, 1983, Benitez, Lage, and Jerry Castillo, an undercover special agent of the Drug Enforcement Administration, met with Rouco and Cruz to finalize the details of the cocaine transaction. Benitez introduced Castillo as his partner. After agreeing on a price and experiencing some disagreement as to where the transaction would occur, Rouco and Cruz began to suspect that Benitez and Castillo were federal agents. Cruz decided to "take a chance" with Benitez and Castillo and designated Hernandez's shop as the location for the transaction.

The group later met at Hernandez's shop. Cruz announced that within forty minutes he would receive a telephone call setting up the cocaine delivery. Minutes later Cruz left to get the cocaine. Shortly thereafter, Cruz telephoned the office and told Rouco that police vehicles were in the area, and in a second telephone call postponed the transaction until later that afternoon. Concerned by the change in plans and the possibility that their law enforcement status had been discovered, the agents cancelled the transaction. When Rouco informed Hernandez that the transaction would not be completed, Hernandez appeared upset.

In August, 1983, Cruz and Hernandez were arrested and charged with conspiracy to possess with intent to distribute cocaine, in violation of 21 U.S.C.A. § 846 (West 1981), and distribution of cocaine, in violation of 21 U.S.C.A. § 841(a)(1) (West 1981 and Supp.1985) and 18 U.S.C.A. § 2 (West 1969). A jury found Cruz and Hernandez guilty as charged. By the time of trial, Benitez was deceased. Over defense objection, the district court permitted both Pherson and Castillo to testify as to whom Benitez had said had given him the cocaine. Cruz and Hernandez contend that the admission of Benitez's hearsay statements violated their sixth amendment right to confront the witnesses against them. . . .

The district court admitted Benitez's statements to Pherson and Castillo under the present sense impression exception to the hearsay rule, Fed.R.Evid. 803(1). Cruz and Hernandez argue that Benitez's statements to Pherson and Castillo were not sufficiently contemporaneous with Benitez's receipt of the cocaine to constitute present sense impressions admissible under Fed.R.Evid. 803(1). We agree.

The record does not disclose the distances and time lapses between Benitez's receipt of the cocaine and his statement to Pherson. The record does not reflect how long it took Benitez to travel from the restaurant to Hernandez's paint and body shop, engage in conversation with Cruz and Hernandez, obtain the cocaine sample, and return to the restaurant and engage in further conversation, before turning the cocaine and one of Hernandez's business cards over to Pherson. It is clear, however, that Benitez's statement to Pherson was not made immediately following Benitez's receipt of the cocaine. Benitez's statement to Castillo occurred even later than the statement to Pherson, apparently days later. Clearly, Benitez's statement to Castillo also lacked the contemporaneity required by Fed.R.Evid. 803(1).

We conclude that, under the circumstances, Benitez's statements to Pherson and Castillo as to who had given him the cocaine were not sufficiently contemporaneous with Benitez's receipt of the cocaine to come within the present sense impression exception to the hearsay rule under Fed.R.Evid. 803(1). The lack of consistency in the agents' testimony as to whom Benitez had identified as the source of the cocaine also illustrates the statements' lack of "particularized guarantees of trustworthiness." Roberts, 448 U.S. at 66, 100 S. Ct. at 2539.

[The court conducted a harmless error analysis and sustained the conviction.]

DISCUSSION QUESTIONS

1. From these opinions, what is required to exclude evidence offered under the present sense impression?

2. Why not simply adopt a bright line test? Don't the words "while . . . perceiving . . . or immediately thereafter" provide better guidance than the 7th Circuit seems to believe? Which Circuit gets it right: the 11th or the 7th?

3. Both of these cases are pre-Crawford cases. Is there a Confrontation Clause problem in either of these cases? If so, what is the problem? Could the evidence be admitted anyway?

PROBLEMS

Problem 22-1. Melvin witnessed a slip-and-fall accident at a grocery store in which an elderly woman slipped on a puddle of vegetable oil in an aisle of the store and fell, breaking her hip. Within a short time after the incident, as the paramedics were attending to the woman, Melvin said to the person standing next to him, "I can't understand why people always ignore those signs they put out telling you not to go into the aisle until they can clean it."

A few days after the accident, Melvin went to the store manager and stated that he had seen the warning sign and the woman had walked right past it just before she slipped. He then spoke to the store's insurance company investigator and made a statement to the same effect.

At trial, the store calls Melvin as a witness to quote the statement he made to the unnamed and unknown bystander standing next to him and later repeated to the store manager and insurance investigator. The plaintiff's attorney objects on two grounds: hearsay and Confrontation Clause violation. How should the store's attorney reply, and how should the judge rule?

The Excited Utterance

Through Dec. 1, 2011	After Dec. 1, 2011
Rule 803. Hearsay Exceptions; Availability of Declarant Immaterial	**Rule 803. Exceptions to the Rule Against Hearsay — Regardless of Whether the Declarant Is Available as a Witness**
The following are not excluded by the hearsay rule, even though the declarant is available as a witness:	The following are not excluded by the rule against hearsay, regardless of whether the declarant is available as a witness:
(2) Excited utterance. A statement relating to a startling event or condition made while the declarant was under the stress of excitement caused by the event or condition.	**(2) Excited Utterance.** A statement relating to a startling event or condition, made while the declarant was under the stress of excitement that it caused.

Basis

The excited utterance exception is closely related to the present-sense impression. Both derive from the *res gestae* doctrine discussed in the previous subsection. They differ, however, in their foundational bases. Whereas the present-sense impression relies on the temporal proximity between the observe event and the statement, the excited utterance is based on the theory that a person who is in a state of nervous excitement cannot tell a lie. The noted evidence scholar John Wigmore described the justification for the exception as follows:

> This general principle is based on the experience that, under certain external circumstances of physical shock, a stress of nervous excitement may be produced which stills the reflective faculties and removes their control, so that the utterance which then occurs is a spontaneous and sincere response to the actual sensations and perceptions already produced by the external shock.[4]

Thus, the key to determining reliability under the excited utterance exception is the extent to which the declarant was, in the words of the rule, under the "stress of excitement caused by the event or condition." Time can be important in determining whether the declarant was still under the stress of excitement when making the statement, but it is not dispositive.

As science's understanding of psychology has increased, the theoretical premise for this hearsay exception has come under attack. Consider the following excerpt

---

[4] 5 JOHN HENRY WIGMORE, EVIDENCE IN TRIALS AT THE COMMON LAW 1749, n.199 (James H. Chadbourn ed., 1978).

from a law review article written by I. Daniel Stewart.

I. Daniel Stewart, Jr., *Perception, Memory, and Hearsay: A Criticism of Present Law and the Proposed Federal Rules of Evidence*
1970 Utah L. Rev. 1

The most unreliable type of evidence admitted under hearsay exceptions is the excited utterance. This exception provides an important source of evidence in cases such as criminal and tort actions which often involve events which produce a high level of emotional stress and its attendant distortion. The events are unexpected and episodic, and a person witnessing them is presented with a vast number of stimuli that far transcend the span of apperception.

The theory of the exception was formulated by Wigmore in an effort to synthesize the amorphous res gestae doctrine:

> [U]nder certain external circumstances of physical shock, a stress of nervous excitement may be produced which stills the reflective faculties and removes their control, so that the utterance which then occurs is a spontaneous and sincere response to the actual sensations and perceptions already produced by the external shock. Since this utterance is made under the immediate and uncontrolled domination of the senses, and during the brief period when considerations of self-interest could not have been brought fully to bear by reasoned reflection, the utterance may be taken as particularly trustworthy.[5]

The theory is faulty on every score. Excitement is not a guarantee against lying, especially since the courts often hold that excitement may endure many minutes and even hours beyond the event. More important, excitement exaggerates, sometimes grossly, distortion in perception and memory especially when the observer is a witness to a nonroutine, episodic event such as occurs in automobile collision cases and crimes.

The likelihood of inaccurate perception, the drawing of inferences to fill in memory gaps, and the reporting of nonfacts is high. As one psychologist has observed, the exception "indicates a pragmatic position which prefers the disclosure of deception to the facilitation of accuracy."[6]

Yet in Wigmore's view an excited utterance is such a superior quality of evidence that the declarant need not testify even though available, "a proposition never disputed." In fact, the theory is merely an artifice for the admission of highly unreliable evidence which is often the only type of evidence available. No justification exists for foregoing cross-examination and admitting such evidence if the declarant is available.

Professor Morgan distilled from the res gestae doctrine the element of contempo-

---

[5] [n.125] VI Wigmore § 1747.

[6] [n.129] Fishman, *Some Current Research Needs in the Psychology of Testimony*, 13 J. Social Issues 60, 64 (1951).

raneousness of the narration and the event as an indicum of trustworthiness. Although contemporaneous statements might include contemporaneous excited utterances, the basic rationale is not one that serves to magnify distortion. Like Wigmore, however, Morgan saw the prevention of deliberate falsification as an adequate warrant for admitting hearsay. According to Morgan, a statement describing an event uttered at or near the time the event transpires will not permit adequate time for self-interest to be asserted - a theory with little merit. But even without considering falsification and the distorting effect of excitement, contemporaneous utterances are subject to distortion in the declarant's perception and memory (the declaration need only be substantially contemporaneous) as well as the perception and memory of the reporting witness.

Recognizing the inherent weakness of this type of evidence, Morgan relied upon the likelihood that the witness who related the hearsay declaration could add corroborating evidence, since he too would have perceived the event. "The witness is subject to cross-examination concerning that event as well as the fact and content of the utterance, so that the extrajudicial statement does not depend solely upon the credit of the declarant."[7]

Corroboration, however, has not been a requirement of spontaneous or excited declarations, and, because of Wigmore's monumental, but erroneous, authority, unavailability of the declarant has never been required, despite a few offhand suggestions that it should be.

Foundational Elements

The following elements are necessary to satisfy the excited utterance exception:

> 1. There must be a startling event. Note that this requirement illustrates another difference between the present sense impression and the excited utterance. A present sense impression can relate to an ordinary, unexceptional observation.

> 2. The declarant must perceive the event.

> 3. The event must trigger the "stress of excitement" in the declarant. Generally, descriptions of the declarant's emotional state, physical appearance, behavior and condition suffice to demonstrate the stress of excitement.

> 4. The statement must relate to the startling event itself.

The Rule in Application

There are two primary issues related to the application of this rule in practice. The first is the application of the Confrontation Clause pursuant to *Crawford v. Washington* in criminal cases. Often, police or other officials question witnesses who are still under the stress of excitement of a startling event. Under the holding in *Davis v. Washington*, the interrogational activities of governmental actors can make

---

[7] [n.133] Morgan, *A Suggested Classification of Utterances Admissible As Res Gestae*, 31 YALE L.J. 229, 236 (1922).

some of these statements testimonial. Prior to *Crawford* and *Davis*, the primary concern with introducing hearsay under this section was the emotional state of the declarant, not the Confrontation Clause; thus, in criminal cases, the exception permitted the introduction of considerable testimonial evidence at trial.

The second issue concerns the effect of the passage of time on the declarant's emotional state. Simply put, the lapse of time between the startling event and the declarant's statement increases opportunities for the declarant to reflect on the startling event and to fill in gaps with lies, fabrications or guesses. Courts consider a number of factors in evaluating whether the declarant is under the requisite stress for the hearsay exception to apply, including (1) lapse of time between event and declaration; (2) age of declarant; (3) physical and mental state of the declarant; (4) characteristics of the event; and (5) subject matter of the statement.[8] In cases involving small children, the lapse of time can be considerable.

Cases, Discussion Questions and Problems

UNITED STATES v. GOLDEN
United States Court of Appeals, Tenth Circuit
671 F.2d 369 (10th Cir. 1982)

[The defendant was a police officer charged with depriving an individual of his civil rights. The evidence showed that the defendant pulled the victim over for speeding at 2 am and beat the victim with a flashlight. The victim required eight stitches.]

II. Hearsay Evidence

Mr. Golden alleges that the trial court erroneously admitted into evidence testimony concerning the victim's statements to his grandmother pursuant to the excited utterance exception to the hearsay rule. Fed.R.Evid. 803(2). He also argues that the grandmother's testimony was cumulative, and therefore admitted in violation of Rule 403 of the Federal Rules of Evidence.

Rulings on evidentiary matters are committed to the discretion of the trial judge and will not be reversed on appeal unless it is shown that the ruling was a clear abuse of discretion or that it affected the substantial rights of the defendant. United States v. Carranco, 551 F.2d 1197, 1199-1200 (10th Cir. 1977); Fed.R.Crim.P. 52(a).

An excited utterance is an exception to the general rule that hearsay testimony is not admissible into evidence. It is defined as "(a) statement relating to a startling event or condition made while the declarant was under the stress of excitement caused by the event or condition." Fed.R.Evid. 803(2). The evidence shows that after the altercation, the victim drove twelve miles to his grandmother's house at speeds of approximately 120 miles per hour. Upon his arrival he related what had happened to him and said he feared for his life. Appellant argues that the trial court erred in admitting this testimony because the conversation was hearsay and

---

[8] Morgan v. Foretich, 846 F.2d 941, 947 (4th Cir. 1988), *cited in* GOODE AND WELLBORNE, at 254.

occurred too remote in time from the assault to fall within the excited utterance exception. However, the victim's statement to his grandmother occurred within fifteen minutes of the startling event, immediately after a high-speed flight from the scene of the assault. The facts presented indicate that there was no reason to suspect that the victim was no longer "under the stress of excitement caused by the event" when he spoke with his grandmother. Therefore, the court did not err in admitting testimony concerning this conversation under the excited utterance exception to the hearsay rule.

Section 403 of the Federal Rules of Evidence provides that relevant evidence may be excluded because of "considerations of undue delay, waste of time, or needless presentation of cumulative evidence." Although the grandmother's testimony paralleled that of the victim, we do not believe that the trial judge abused his discretion in refusing to exclude it under Rule 403.

DISCUSSION QUESTIONS

1. If the victim in this case could drive 120 mph for 15 minutes, wouldn't this provide enough time to reflect on events and create a story?

2. How much time do you think is too much under this hearsay exception? In other words, how much time is required before an adult begins to engage in "sad reflection" and perhaps make up facts?

3. If the declarant is present to be cross-examined, wouldn't this cure any problems with the admissibility of evidence under this exception?

4. What do you think of Stewart's contention that the excited utterance exception is the least reliable of the *res gestae* hearsay exceptions?

PROBLEMS

Problem 22-1. Alex, a 21-year-old college student, becomes intoxicated at the Wild West Saloon. Noticing his intoxication, Randy, a stranger, approaches Alex and offers to let him "sleep it off" at his nearby apartment. Alex accepts the offer and falls asleep on the couch. He awakes to discover Randy performing fellatio on him. Alex leaps up, gets dressed, and flees the house. He walks three blocks back to the Wild West, finds his car, and starts the engine. He makes the one-hour drive back to his dorm. Nearly two hours after the event, he walks into his dorm room, sees his roommate, and bursts into angry tears, and tells the sordid story

Is the statement admissible as an excited utterance?

Then-Existing Mental, Emotional or Physical Condition

Through Dec. 1, 2011	After Dec. 1, 2011
Rule 803. Hearsay Exceptions; Availability of Declarant Immaterial	**Rule 803. Exceptions to the Rule Against Hearsay — Regardless of Whether the Declarant Is Available as a Witness**
The following are not excluded by the hearsay rule, even though the declarant is available as a witness:	The following are not excluded by the rule against hearsay, regardless of whether the declarant is available as a witness:
(3) Then existing mental, emotional, or physical condition. A statement of the declarant's then existing state of mind, emotion, sensation, or physical condition (such as intent, plan, motive, design, mental feeling, pain, and bodily health), but not including a statement of memory or belief to prove the fact remembered or believed unless it relates to the execution, revocation, identification, or terms of declarant's will.	**(3) Then-Existing Mental, Emotional, or Physical Condition**. A statement of the declarant's then-existing state of mind (such as motive, intent, or plan) or emotional, sensory, or physical condition (such as mental feeling, pain, or bodily health), but not including a statement of memory or belief to prove the fact remembered or believed unless it relates to the validity or terms of the declarant's will.

Basis

Rule 803(3) is another hearsay exception rooted in the common-law *res gestae* doctrine. According to Weissenberger, "The Rule combines two common-law exceptions, *i.e.*, the relatively simple and less troublesome exception pertaining to statements concerning then existing physical conditions and the complicated and more difficult exception pertaining to statements concerning mental or emotional conditions."[9] Its reliability is premised on the idea that a declarant is likely to be telling the truth when describing his own state of mind, emotions, or physical condition at the time he is experiencing them.

The rule covers four categories of statements. The first is statements of the declarant's present bodily condition. The second is statements pertaining to the declarant's state of mind or emotion at the time the statement was made. The third category, statements of the declarant's present state of mind to prove his subsequent conduct, has been controversial since the Supreme Court created it out of whole cloth in *Mutual Life Insurance Co. v. Hillmon*, an 1892 insurance fraud case.

The first three categories share a requirement that the statement must be a present or contemporaneous statement, that is, a statement directly relating to the declarant's condition at the moment it was made. This applies even to statements of future intent, which essentially indicate the declarant's present state of mind to do something in the future. For example, the statement "I am going to eat lunch at noon," represents the declarant's present intention to have lunch at noon.

---

[9] WEISSENBERGER & DUANE § 803.12, at 490–91.

The fourth category permits statements of memory or belief made by the testator related to "the execution, revocation, identification, or terms of the declarant's [testator's] will." Because the state of mind of the testator (who is obviously going to be unavailable for trial) is of "paramount importance, and the testator's own statements are likely to be the most probative evidence of the import of his or her own will,"[10] statements of memory or belief are permitted. It should be noted that the rule limits such statements only to facts related to the execution, revocation, identification, or terms of the will itself; other past statements of the declarant are not admissible under this category. This category has limited application in federal courts, but there is, according to the Advisory Committee, "ample reinforcement in the decisions, resting on practical grounds of necessity and expediency rather than logic."

Foundational Elements

The following foundational elements are necessary to admit evidence under this exception.

1. First and foremost, the declarant's bodily, emotional or mental condition must be at issue in the case.

2. The statement made must be a present or contemporaneous statement and not a statement of past feelings or conditions. Thus, "I feel a sharp, stabbing pain in my abdomen" would be admissible, whereas "yesterday I felt a sharp, stabbing pain" would not be admissible.

3. The statement must be of the declarant's state of mind, not someone else's. "Bob feels great today" is a statement that is inadmissible unless Bob himself has made the statement.

Cases, Discussion Questions and Problems

MUTUAL LIFE INSURANCE COMPANY v. HILLMON
Supreme Court of the United States
145 U.S. 285 (1892)

There is, however, one question of evidence so important, so fully argued at the bar, and so likely to arise upon another trial, that it is proper to express an opinion upon it.

This question is of the admissibility of the letters written by Walters on the first days of March, 1879, which were offered in evidence by the defendants, and excluded by the court. In order to determine the competency of these letters, it is important to consider the state of the case when they were offered to be read.

The matter chiefly contested at the trial was the death of John W. Hillmon, the insured; and that depended upon the question whether the body found at Crooked Creek on the night of March 18, 1879, was his body, or the body of one Walters.

---

[10] WEISSENBERGER & DUANE § 803.17, at 498.

Much conflicting evidence had been introduced as to the identity of the body. The plaintiff had also introduced evidence that Hillmon and one Brown left Wichita in Kansas on or about March 5, 1879, and travelled together through Southern Kansas in search of a site for a cattle ranch, and that on the night of March 18, while they were in camp at Crooked Creek, Hillmon was accidentally killed, and that his body was taken thence and buried. The defendants had introduced evidence, without objection, that Walters left his home and his betrothed in Iowa in March, 1878, and was afterwards in Kansas until March, 1879; that during that time he corresponded regularly with his family and his betrothed; that the last letters received from him were one received by his betrothed on March 3 and postmarked at Wichita March 2, and one received by his sister about March 4 or 5, and dated at Wichita a day or two before; and that he had not been heard from since.

The evidence that Walters was at Wichita on or before March 5, and had not been heard from since, together with the evidence to identify as his the body found at Crooked Creek on March 18, tended to show that he went from Wichita to Crooked Creek between those dates. Evidence that just before March 5 he had the intention of leaving Wichita with Hillmon would tend to corroborate the evidence already admitted, and to show that he went from Wichita to Crooked Creek with Hillmon. Letters from him to his family and his betrothed were the natural, if not the only attainable, evidence of his intention.

The position, taken at the bar, that the letters were competent evidence, within the rule stated in Nicholls v. Webb, 8 Wheat. 326, 337, as memoranda made in the ordinary course of business, cannot be maintained, for they were clearly not such.

But upon another ground suggested they should have been admitted. A man's state of mind or feeling can only be manifested to others by countenance, attitude or gesture, or by sounds or words, spoken or written. The nature of the fact to be proved is the same, and evidence of its proper tokens is equally competent to prove it, whether expressed by aspect or conduct, by voice or pen. When the intention to be proved is important only as qualifying an act, its connection with that act must be shown, in order to warrant the admission of declarations of the intention. But whenever the intention is of itself a distinct and material fact in a chain of circumstances, it may be proved by contemporaneous oral or written declarations of the party.

The existence of a particular intention in a certain person at a certain time being a material fact to be proved, evidence that he expressed that intention at that time is as direct evidence of the fact, as his own testimony that he then had that intention would be. After his death there can hardly be any other way of proving it; and while he is still alive, his own memory of his state of mind at a former time is no more likely to be clear and true than a bystander's recollection of what he then said, and is less trustworthy than letters written by him at the very time and under circumstances precluding a suspicion of misrepresentation.

The letters in question were competent, not as narratives of facts communicated to the writer by others, nor yet as proof that he actually went away from Wichita, but as evidence that, shortly before the time when other evidence tended to show that he went away, he had the intention of going, and of going with Hillmon, which made it more probable both that he did go and that he went with Hillmon, than if there had been no proof of such intention. In view of the mass of conflicting testimony introduced upon the question whether it was the body of Walters that was found in Hillmon's camp, this evidence might properly influence the jury in determining that question.

The rule applicable to this case has been thus stated by this court: "Wherever the bodily or mental feelings of an individual are material to be proved, the usual expressions of such feelings are original and competent evidence. Those expressions are the natural reflexes of what it might be impossible to show by other testimony. If there be such other testimony, this may be necessary to set the facts thus developed in their true light, and to give them their proper effect. As independent explanatory or corroborative evidence, it is often indispensable to the due administration of justice. Such declarations are regarded as verbal acts, and are as competent as any other testimony, when relevant to the issue. Their truth or falsity is an inquiry for the jury." Insurance Co. v. Mosley, 8 Wall. 397, 404, 405.

In accordance with this rule, a bankrupt's declarations, oral or by letter, at or before the time of leaving or staying away from home, as to his reason for going abroad, have always been held by the English courts to be competent, in an action by his assignees against a creditor, as evidence that his departure was with intent to defraud his creditors, and therefore an act of bankruptcy.

The highest courts of New Hampshire and Massachusetts have held declarations of a servant, at the time of leaving his master's service, to be competent evidence, in actions between third persons, of his reasons for doing so. And the Supreme Court of Ohio has held that, for the purpose of proving that a person was at a railroad station intending to take passage on a train, previous declarations made by him at the time of leaving his hotel were admissible.

In actions for criminal conversation, letters by the wife to her husband or to third persons are competent to show her affection towards her husband, and her reasons for living apart from him, if written before any misconduct on her part, and if there is no ground to suspect collusion. So from a husband to a third person, showing his state of feeling, affection and sympathy for his wife, have been held by this court to be competent evidence, bearing on the validity of the marriage, when the legitimacy of their children is in issue.

Even in the probate of wills, which are required by law to be in writing, executed and attested in prescribed forms, yet where the validity of a will is questioned for want of mental capacity or by reason of fraud and undue influence, or where the will is lost and it becomes necessary to prove its contents, written or oral evidence of declarations of the testator before the date of the will has been admitted, in Massachusetts and in England, to show his real intention as to the disposition of his property, although there has been a difference of opinion as to the admissibility, for such purposes, of his subsequent declarations. . . .

Upon an indictment of one Hunter for the murder of one Armstrong at Camden, the Court of Errors and Appeals of New Jersey unanimously held that Armstrong's oral declarations to his son at Philadelphia, on the afternoon before the night of the murder, as well as a letter written by him at the same time and place to his wife, each stating that he was going with Hunter to Camden on business, were rightly admitted in evidence.

Chief Justice Beasley said: "In the ordinary course of things, it was the usual information that a man about leaving home would communicate, for the convenience of his family, the information of his friends, or the regulation of his business. . . . I think [] that a reference to the companion who is to accompany the person leaving is as natural a part of the transaction as is any other incident or quality of it. If it is legitimate to show by a man's own declarations that he left his home to be gone a week, or for a certain destination, which seems incontestable, why may it not be proved in the same way that a designated person was to bear him company? . . . If it was in the ordinary train of events for this man to leave word or to state where he was going, it seems to me it was equally so for him to say with whom he was going," Hunter v. State, 11 Vroom (40 N.J. Law) 495, 534, 536, 538.

Upon principle and authority, therefore, we are of opinion that the two letters were competent evidence of the intention of Walters at the time of writing them, which was a material fact bearing upon the question in controversy; and that for the exclusion of these letters, as well as for the undue restriction of the defendants' challenges, the verdicts must be set aside, and a new trial had.

As the verdicts and judgments were several, the writ of error sued out by the defendants jointly was superfluous, and may be dismissed without costs; and upon each of the writs of error sued out by the defendants severally the order will be

Judgment reversed, and case remanded to the Circuit Court, with directions to set aside the verdict and to order a new trial.

DISCUSSION QUESTIONS

1. What was the evidentiary significance of these letters?

2. Do you agree with the Court's reasoning in this case that led to the creation of this exception? Why or why not?

3. Does this exception properly account for the standard hearsay dangers discussed earlier in the text?

4. How about using statements of one's own intention to prove the subsequent conduct of a person named in the statement, as the Court approved of in Hillmon? What difficulties are posed by doing this?

PROBLEMS

Problem 21-3. Darla and her best friend Mindy recently became estranged after Mindy treated Darla badly at a party and gossiped about Darla with Darla's arch-enemy, Candace. After two weeks of virtually no contact between the two women, Mindy sent Darla the following e-mail:

Darla,

I am sorry about everything that happened between us at the party. I was wrong to treat you the way I did. It would have hurt my feelings if you had done the same to me. I have been thinking about this for two weeks, and I feel terrible about it. I've even thought about just ending it all, I didn't know I could be so cruel and awful. I feel like I messed up a really good friendship, and I don't know if I can make everything up to you. I guess I was just feeling jealous because of your new job and thinking maybe I wasn't good enough to be your friend anymore. Also, I was angry because you started dating Andy, and you know I've had a crush on him since senior year of high school. I know — stupid. I've thought lots of things. Today I have been looking through some old photo albums and just crying, thinking about all the good times we've had. I'm just so depressed right now. It's all overwhelming. I would like us to get together for a girl's night out at Donovan's Dive tomorrow night. For old times' sake. I will be there, and I hope you will be too.

Darla did not reply to the e-mail, and she did not go to Donovan's Dive. Instead, she went for a weekend trip to Las Vegas with her boyfriend, Andy. Meanwhile, Mindy disappeared without a trace. She left her home at 7 pm the night after sending the e-mail, but did not tell anyone where she was going. Her internet e-mail account was password-protected. After the story of her disappearance hit the news, Darla went to the police with the e-mail. Soon thereafter, Mindy's body was found in a ravine several miles outside of town. The autopsy revealed that she had ingested enough rat poison to kill several people. Acting on a tip from a bartender at Donovan's Den, police arrested Perry, an exterminator who liked to talk about the similarities between killing vermin and people, a few days later and charged him with the murder of Mindy. At Perry's trial, his attorney seeks to admit Mindy's e-mail to Darla as proof that Mindy had actually committed suicide. The prosecution objects. How should the defense respond to the objection? How should the judge rule, and why?

Statements for Purposes of Medical Diagnosis or Treatment

Through Dec. 1, 2011	After Dec. 1, 2011
Rule 803. Hearsay Exceptions; Availability of Declarant Immaterial The following are not excluded by the hearsay rule, even though the declarant is available as a witness: **(4) Statements for purposes of medical diagnosis or treatment**. Statements made for purposes of medical diagnosis or treatment and describing medical history, or past or present symptoms, pain, or sensations, or the inception or general character of the cause or external source thereof insofar as reasonably pertinent to diagnosis or treatment.	**Rule 803. Exceptions to the Rule Against Hearsay — Regardless of Whether the Declarant Is Available as a Witness** The following are not excluded by the rule against hearsay, regardless of whether the declarant is available as a witness: **(4) *Statement Made for Medical Diagnosis or Treatment*.** A statement that: (A) is made for — and is reasonably pertinent to — medical diagnosis or treatment; and (B) describes medical history; past or present symptoms or sensations; their inception; or their general cause.

Basis

Rule 803(4) is the last of the res gestae exceptions to the hearsay rule. The basis for this rule is that individuals who are seeking medical treatment have a powerful motive to be truthful about their symptoms. This rule applies not only to present statements of condition — "my abdomen hurts" — but also to statements regarding past medical history — "my abdomen has been hurting since my neighbor stabbed me last Thursday." The rule covers statements made to a treating physician, associated medical personnel such as doctors, nurses, psychologists and others, as well as statements made to members of the family for the purpose of seeking medical treatment. In some circumstances, depending on the relationship involved, statements made to a physician by others — such as parents or caregivers — on the patient's behalf may be admissible under this exception.

The statement covers only statements made by a patient to a doctor (or a doctor's equivalent under the rule). It does not cover statements made by the doctor to the patient.

Foundational Elements

The following elements must be shown before admitting evidence under the medical hearsay exception:

1. The statement must relate to the cause or condition. Statements describing what happened are admissible insofar as they are related to treatment. For example, it might be related to treatment for the patient to explain that she had been hit by a car, but not related to treatment that the other driver ran a red light.

2. The statement must be made for the purpose of obtaining treatment. Whether made directly to medical personnel or even to a family member or caregiver, the key element is the declarant's understanding that the statement is related to receiving treatment.

The Rule in Application

In practice, the medical hearsay rule is extremely useful but is vulnerable to abuse. The mere fact that information appears in a medical record does not mean that it will be admissible at trial. This is particularly true if the information is not directly related to what is necessary for treatment.

There is a fine line, however, in cases involving psychological or sexual abuse. In those cases, the identity of a perpetrator may be absolutely critical to obtaining proper treatment for the victim. It may be necessary, for example, to move a perpetrator out of the home or remove the victim from a home. Furthermore, if the individual is being treated for psychological or psychiatric conditions, some information pertaining to emotional trauma might be necessary for treatment.

Another issue that often arises in trials has to do with the testimony of child witnesses. This hearsay exception is premised on the patient's belief that providing accurate information to a caregiver results in better treatment. Accordingly, some have argued that a child declarant must understand the "medical significance" of testifying at trial. In practice, this requires a relatively modest quantum of proof. Usually, it is enough to demonstrate that a child thought she was going to the doctor to "get better," or words to that effect.

Cases, Discussion Questions and Problems

UNITED STATES v. GEORGE
United States Court of Appeals, Ninth Circuit
960 F.2d 97 (9th Cir. 1992)

The indictment charged George with causing his 12-year-old stepdaughter to have sexual intercourse with him on three separate occasions in 1988. In her testimony, the victim identified George as her attacker and described the sexual attacks. She testified to the approximate date of the acts alleged in count III of the indictment. However, she was not able to recall the approximate dates of the acts alleged in counts I and II.

Dr. Ortiz-Pino examined the victim on February 22, 1989, approximately five months after the date of the last attack as alleged in the indictment. Over George's objections, the trial court allowed Dr. Ortiz-Pino to testify to a hearsay statement identifying George as the assailant, which the victim made during the course of Dr. Ortiz-Pino's examination of her . . .

After George's conviction, the victim recanted her testimony against him and George moved for a new trial, which was denied after an evidentiary hearing. Appellant was sentenced to a term of 264 months and this appeal followed.

II

A

The trial court admitted Dr. Ortiz-Pino's hearsay testimony pursuant to the hearsay rule's medical examination exception, which permits hearsay testimony regarding:

> Statements made for purposes of medical diagnosis or treatment and describing medical history, or past or present symptoms, pain, or sensations, or the inception or general character of the cause or external source thereof insofar as reasonably pertinent to diagnosis or treatment.

Fed.R.Evid. 803(4). . . .

George contends that statements identifying an assailant do not fall within the medical examination exception. The advisory committee notes to Rule 803(4) observe that statements of fault will not ordinarily be admissible under the exception. However, other circuits have held that statements by a victim identifying her sexual abuser are admissible under the medical examination exception. The critical inquiry is whether such statements are "made for purposes of medical diagnosis or treatment" and are "reasonably pertinent to diagnosis or treatment." Fed.R.Evid. 803(4).

Sexual abuse involves more than physical injury; the physician must be attentive to treating the victim's emotional and psychological injuries, the exact nature and extent of which often depend on the identity of the abuser. Renville, 779 F.2d at 437. Furthermore, depending upon the nature of the sexual abuse, the identity of the abuser may be pertinent to the diagnosis and treatment of sexually transmitted diseases.[11] Dr. Ortiz-Pino testified that she asked about the assailant's identity for the purpose of diagnosing and treating the victim. We hold, therefore, that the district court did not abuse its discretion in admitting Dr. Ortiz-Pino's hearsay testimony pursuant to Fed.R.Evid. 803(4) and that George's rights under the Confrontation Clause were not violated.

That the victim in this case was a 12-year-old child does not change our analysis. Focusing on the personal characteristics of the victim is inconsistent with the categorical approach to "firmly rooted" hearsay exceptions adopted by the Supreme Court. See Wright, 110 S.Ct. at 3147 (reliability requirement satisfied if statement falls within "firmly rooted" hearsay exception). For hearsay statements to be admissible under Rule 803(4), the district court need only determine that they were "made for purposes of medical diagnosis or treatment" and were "reasonably pertinent to diagnosis or treatment." Fed.R.Evid. 803(4). As a general matter, the age of the child and her other personal characteristics go to the weight of the hearsay statements rather than their admissibility.

---

[11] [n.1] If the victim is a child, the physician may also have an obligation under state law to prevent the child from being returned to an environment in which she cannot be adequately protected from abuse. Renville, 779 F.2d at 438.

DISCUSSION QUESTIONS

1. Analyze this opinion under *Crawford*. Would there be a *Crawford* violation in admitting this testimony? Why or why not?

2. If the Confrontation Clause is satisfied, what is it about the victim's statements at issue here that permit them to be admitted under Rule 803(4)? Is the Court's reasoning persuasive?

3. How should judges draw the line between statements made for medical diagnosis and treatment and other statements?

PROBLEM

Problem 22-4. Barry and his roommate David became involved in a violent altercation over who would do the dishes. Each man thought it was the other's responsibility, and before long, they came to blows. During the altercation, David grabbed a dirty electric frying pan and threw it at Barry. The frying pan hit Barry in the head, lacerating his scalp.

David took Barry to the emergency room. As luck would have it, the attending nurse was David's ex-fiancée, Ellen. During her initial examination of Barry's scalp, she asked, "what happened?" Barry replied, "I hit my head on something."

Ellen said, "That's a pretty bad laceration. I'll bet David threw something at you, didn't he?"

Barry nodded his head yes.

"What did he throw?"

"A frying pan," Barry answered. "A big, heavy, electric frying pan."

Further discussion revealed that Ellen knew everything about the frying pan. David had stolen it from her when they broke up. "That's a really heavy-duty pan," she said. "I'm going to tell the doctor I think you might need some X-rays." X-rays showed that Barry had a small fracture on his scalp.

At David's criminal battery trial, Barry was suffering from amnesia and could not remember what had happened to him. The prosecution called Ellen as a witness. The defense objected on hearsay grounds. How should the prosecution respond? How should the judge rule?

The Res Gestae Hearsay Exceptions: Quick Hits

- The key to evaluating hearsay exceptions at trial is to identify the core reliability factors for each exception.

- The reliability basis for the present sense impression, Rule 803(1), is the contemporaneous nature of the declarant's observation and statement.

- The reliability basis for the excited utterance, Rule 803(2), is that the declarant is unlikely to formulate a lie while under the stress of excitement of a startling event.

- The reliability basis for then-existing mental, emotional, or physical condition, Rule 803(3) is the contemporaneous nature of the statement and declarant's observation about her own condition.

- Under Rule 803(3), statements of a then-existing intent to do something are admissible as proof that the declarant acted in accordance with her expressed intention.

- The reliability basis for the medical hearsay exception, Rule 803(4), is the incentive to tell the truth to a medical provider in order to obtain effective medical treatment.

Chapter References

CHRISTOPHER B. MUELLER & LAIRD C. KIRKPATRICK, EVIDENCE §§ 8.35–8.42 (4th ed. 2009).

GLEN WEISSENBERGER & JAMES J. DUANE, FEDERAL RULES OF EVIDENCE: RULES, LEGISLATIVE HISTORY, COMMENTARY AND AUTHORITY §§ 803.1–803.21 (6th ed. 2009).

JACK B. WEINSTEIN & MARGARET A. BERGER, WEINSTEIN'S FEDERAL EVIDENCE §§ 803.01–803.06 (Joseph M. McLaughlin ed., Matthew Bender 2d ed. 1997).

KENNETH S. BROUN, McCORMICK ON EVIDENCE §§ 268–78 (6th ed. 2006).

STEVEN GOODE & OLIN GUY WELLBORN III, COURTROOM HANDBOOK ON FEDERAL EVIDENCE Ch. 5 (West 2010).

III.   APPLICATION EXERCISE

Preparing to Use and Defend Against Hearsay at Trial

Sometimes it is necessary to use hearsay at a trial. For various reasons, the most persuasive, reliable and probative evidence available might be an out-of-court statement, offered for its truth. In such situations, attorneys identify possible hearsay statements and prepare to either introduce them into evidence or to object to them. This is an important part of the case analysis process.

In preparing to introduce or attack hearsay statements, the following template is useful:

1. Identify the out-of-court statement and decide where it fits on the "hearsay hierarchy."

a.   Non-hearsay: not offered for its truth, but for some other purpose.

b.   Not-hearsay: fits within a hearsay exemption under Rule 801(d).

c.   Hearsay: being offered for the truth of the matter asserted.

2. If the case is criminal, determine whether the statement is testimonial, and if so, whether *Crawford* is satisfied.

3. If the case is civil, or in a criminal case, if the statement is non-testimonial, or testimonial but satisfies Crawford, proceed to the next step.

4. Analyze the statement to determine whether it fits a recognized hearsay exception, and consider the following:

    (1)   The basis for reliability of the hearsay exception.

    (2)   Whether the statement fits the foundational requirements of the hearsay exception.

5. Identify and prepare objections and responses to the evidence.

6. If the hearsay is integral to the case, attorneys should consider a motion in limine to ensure that the evidence is admitted or excluded prior to trial.

The Exercise

Objective: To demonstrate proficiency in identifying hearsay statements, preparing to argue their admission or exclusion at trial, and integrating the statements into a direct examination.

Factual Scenario: On July 15 of last year, Paul Plaintiff, a city public works employee, was seriously injured while working on a road resurfacing project on Ventura Boulevard in Calamity City. One lane of the boulevard was being resurfaced, and traffic moving in both directions had to use a single lane. This was accomplished by stopping traffic in one direction and permitting traffic to go in the other direction.

Paul's job was to control traffic by holding up a sign that said "Stop" on one side, and "Slow" on the other. Paul's job was particularly important because the section of road being resurfaced included a curve that made it almost impossible for drivers to see oncoming traffic in the single lane.

Paul was crushed between a blue, northbound minivan driven by Darla Defendant and a concrete lane barrier. Darla was driving the only vehicle headed north on the single lane of traffic. When Darla saw another car coming towards her from the curve, she swerved to avoid it and hit Paul, who was trying to get over the concrete barrier to safety.

Paul suffered a ruptured spleen, a broken leg, and severe head trauma. He was airlifted from the scene by a Liferescue helicopter and transported to the trauma unit at Calamity General Hospital. Rescue personnel spoke briefly to several bystanders about the accident as they worked to stabilize Paul for medical transport.

During the helicopter ride, Paul drifted in and out of consciousness. At one point, he said, "Where am I? Am I dead?" and before anyone could answer, he passed out again. By the time the helicopter reached the hospital, he had been sedated and was unconscious. In the intake statement to the trauma unit, one of the paramedics stated, "Patient hit by northbound minivan. Driver of minivan was texting on a cellphone." This statement was included in Paul's medical records. The statement did not identify the source of the information.

After several hours of surgery, Paul was taken to a recovery room. When he emerged from sedation a day later, he asked the attending nurse, Nurse Ratchet, where he was. She replied that he was in the hospital and had been hit by a car. He asked, "Was it a blue minivan?" She replied that it was, and Paul said, "That's what I thought. I saw it coming and I couldn't get out of the way." Nurse Ratchet entered this information in his medical record.

Paul then lapsed into a coma that lasted for three weeks. After emerging from the coma, his life was no longer in danger, and he recovered sufficiently to return home. Besides losing his spleen, he had a permanent limp and a plate in his head.

Paul has total amnesia related to the day of the accident.

Other than Paul and Darla, the only person who actually saw the accident was Will Witness, whose car was first in line of a long string of cars that had just been released by Paul's counterpart on the other end of the project to travel south on the boulevard. Will was lawfully traveling southbound, was obeying the speed limit and driving carefully, and was not responsible in any way for the accident. After the accident, Will stayed at the scene for 45 minutes. Just before he left, he reported his observations to Officer Oliver, who duly recorded them in the report he made later that evening. Quoting Will, Oliver wrote the following:

> Will Witness, a resident of Bangor Maine, was driving on Ventura Boulevard going southbound. He saw a blue minivan coming towards him in the single lane, driving slowly, maybe 15-20 mph, about the same speed he was driving. The driver appeared to be texting on a cellphone. He remembers saying to himself that there ought to be a law against that kind of thing and that she was really stupid. She looked up and swerved to miss him but hit the flag man into the concrete wall. He stopped right away and called 911. He said the woman got out of her van and was crying, and said, "The sign said Slow and I thought I had the right of way." Will Witness doesn't remember seeing the flagman's sign.

Officer Oliver also interviewed Darla and wrote the following:

> Driver in hysterics. Crying and sobbing. Kept saying, "I'm so sorry this happened. The sign said Slow. It said Slow." This officer asked driver if she was texting or not, and she just started crying even more and shook her head "yes."

Paul sued Darla for causing his injuries, alleging that her negligence in texting while driving contributed to her hitting him.

Advance Preparation. Assume that Officer Oliver and Nurse Ratchet are available to testify. Prepare a brief (3-5) minute direct examination of each of them. Identify any hearsay statements that are necessary to prove the case, and be prepared to lay the proper foundation for their introduction. Also prepare to make proper objections and arguments to exclude these statements from evidence.

In-class Exercise. Students will play the following roles: plaintiff counsel team, defense counsel team, Officer Oliver, Nurse Ratchet, judge. Student A will conduct a direct examination of Officer Oliver as Student B offers objections to hearsay evidence. Student C will conduct a direct examination of Nurse Ratchet as Student D offers objections to hearsay evidence. Student E will serve as a judge.

Chapter 23

HEARSAY WITHIN HEARSAY, PAST RECOLLECTION RECORDED AND BUSINESS RECORDS: RULES 805 AND 803(5)–(7)

> **Chapter Objectives:**
>
> - Introduce and explain the hearsay exceptions for past recollection recorded and records of regularly conducted business
> - Analyze and discuss issues pertaining to the admissibility of recorded recollections and business records
> - Apply the concepts from this chapter in a courtroom application exercise

I. BACKGROUND AND EXPLANATORY MATERIAL

Much of the evidence in modern trials comes in the form of documents or other records. As we have already seen, such exhibits must be authenticated under the 900-series of the Federal Rules of Evidence: the proponent of the evidence must demonstrate that it is what it purports to be. But authentication is only the first step in admitting this evidence. Very often, the evidence contained in documents and records is hearsay, inadmissible under Rule 802 unless it qualifies for an exception under Rules 803 or 804.

To illustrate, suppose an advocate wants to introduce a medical record into evidence at trial. Authenticating the record is easy enough. The advocate can either call a knowledgeable witness to testify that the document is, in fact, an actual medical record (or copy thereof) pertaining to a particular individual, or the advocate can introduce a self-authentication certificate under Rule 902 that accomplishes the same purpose.

The record itself, however, did not spontaneously come into being. It was created as part of a system of records at a hospital or doctor's office. At some stage in the process, human beings — the patient, doctors, nurses, other medical professionals, or clerks — entered information into the record. The record likely contains several types of information: indirect quotes from the patient or a family member, such as *"abdominal pain began two days ago during dinner"*; observations from a doctor, such as *"palpitation revealed large mass in abdominal area"*; human transcriptions of instrument data, such as temperature or blood-pressure readings; and conclusions and diagnoses, such as *"patient has a tumor."* The record was then stored in a regularized system so that the hospital or doctor's office could provide additional treatment, follow up on patient care, bill the patient, and satisfy local and national record-keeping laws.

The record itself, having been prepared outside the courtroom but being offered for its truth inside the courtroom, is a form of hearsay. Recall that every hearsay statement involves two distinct testimonial roles: that of the declarant, who makes the out-of-court statement or assertion that is being offered for its truth; and that of the witness, who quotes the declarant's statement or assertion in court. As we have learned, both roles can be played by the same person. In our medical record example, the declarant is whoever provided the information that appears in the record: the patient, doctor, nurse, or clerk. The "witness" role is played by the record itself, which "quotes" the out-of-court information entered into it by others.

All of the normal hearsay concerns theoretically apply. If the record is admitted into evidence, the declarant (the person who provided, transcribed or input the information in the record) likely will not be present to testify subject to cross-examination. There will be no way for the fact-finder to evaluate the credibility of the declarant or the accuracy of the information. The record itself cannot be cross-examined.

If, however, the record is relevant, has probative value and is not unfairly prejudicial, it will likely be admitted into evidence under one of the record-keeping hearsay exceptions found in Rule 803 — in this case the business records exception of Rule 803(6). This is because the circumstances surrounding the information-gathering process, creation and maintenance of the record ameliorate the traditionally recognized hearsay dangers. Simply put, a medical provider that keeps sloppy or inaccurate medical records will not stay in business; patient health will suffer, and the provider will be shut down by market forces or government regulators. The same factors that motivate the provider to keep accurate records ensure the evidentiary reliability at trial of those records.

The common law contained numerous exceptions permitting the admission of certain types of records as exceptions to the hearsay rule. These exceptions have been codified in Rule 803, which contains a number of hearsay exceptions permitting the introduction of information whose admissibility is predicated on the reliability and regularity of private and public records and record-keeping systems. These exceptions are found in Rules 803(5) through 803(18). This chapter focuses on the exceptions in Rules 803(5) and 803(6).

The Concept of Double Hearsay

As discussed in the previous section, most records consist of information compiled from a variety of sources. This information often includes hearsay, some of which might be independently admissible under exceptions to the hearsay rule, and some of which might simply be altogether inadmissible. Thus, in evaluating whether a record should be admitted into evidence, it is necessary to examine not only the record itself, but the sources and types of information contained in it. If the record meets a hearsay exception, *and* any other hearsay contained within it is independently admissible on its own merits under a hearsay exception, then the record is admissible in evidence.

This concept, known as double hearsay, is contained in Rule 805. It applies not only to records, but to verbal utterances as well. Its most common application pertains to the record-keeping hearsay exceptions. The text of Rule 805 follows:

Through Dec. 1, 2011	After Dec. 1, 2011
Rule 805. Hearsay Within Hearsay	**Rule 805. Hearsay Within Hearsay**
Hearsay included within hearsay is not excluded under the hearsay rule if each part of the combined statements conforms with an exception to the hearsay rule provided in these rules.	Hearsay within hearsay is not excluded by the rule against hearsay if each part of the combined statements conforms with an exception to the rule.

Return to the example of the medical record discussed in the previous section. Assume that the record itself satisfies all the requirements for the business records exception of Rule 803(6) (note: these requirements will be discussed in greater detail later in this chapter). The information contained in the record must be evaluated to determine whether it is hearsay, and if so, whether it satisfies a hearsay exception or should be excluded.

Suppose the record contains the following statements: *"Patient reports abdominal pain and possible internal bleeding. Patient was struck in abdomen with a closed fist and brass knuckles two days ago."* These statements, made by the patient for the purpose of obtaining medical treatment and recorded by a doctor or nurse, are hearsay but would be independently admissible under the medical hearsay exception of Rule 803(4). Under these circumstances, it makes sense to admit the medical record into evidence even though it contains hearsay; after all, the proponent of the evidence could just as easily — but at the cost of efficiency and additional time at trial — call the doctor or nurse to the stand in order to have the information repeated to the jury. As the Advisory Committee notes explain, "In principle it scarcely seems open to doubt that the hearsay rule should *not* call for exclusion of a hearsay statement which includes a further hearsay statement when both conform to the requirements of a hearsay exception."[1]

Our medical record might, however, also include hearsay that would *not* be independently admissible. For example, suppose the statement above continued as follows: *"Patient reports that the assailant was a friend named Bluto who punched him during an argument over a poker game."* This additional information is not necessary for medical treatment and so would not meet the requirements of the medical hearsay exception. Furthermore, the additional information does not meet any other hearsay exceptions. The mere fact that it is contained in an otherwise admissible business record does not cure it of its flaws: it is still hearsay, and it is

---

[1] FED. R. EVID. 805 advisory committee's note (emphasis added).

still inadmissible. If the medical record is to be admitted into evidence, the inadmissible information contained in it must be marked out or redacted.

It should be noted that the concept of "double hearsay" also applies to out-of-court statements, offered for the truth of the matters asserted therein, that are exempted from the hearsay rule under Rule 801. This includes admissions, co-conspirator statements, and the like. Returning to our medical record example, suppose the record contained the following additional statement from a follow-up visit two weeks later: "*Patient reports symptoms have disappeared entirely. Patient has not been taking prescribed medication and did not fill prescription.*" If the patient subsequently sues the doctor for malpractice, the doctor can enter the medical record into evidence as a business record. The patient's statements about the symptoms and not taking medication would be independently admissible as admissions of a party-opponent under Rule 801. Thus, the record and the statements would be admissible in evidence without violating the prohibition against double hearsay.

It is necessary to understand the concept of double hearsay before learning the record-keeping hearsay exceptions. These hearsay exceptions will be discussed in detail throughout the rest of this chapter.

II. ANALYSIS AND DISCUSSION

Recorded Recollection

Through Dec. 1, 2011	After Dec. 1, 2011
Rule 803. Hearsay Exceptions; Availability of Declarant Immaterial	**Rule 803. Exceptions to the Rule Against Hearsay — Regardless of Whether the Declarant Is Available as a Witness**
The following are not excluded by the hearsay rule, even though the declarant is available as a witness:	The following are not excluded by the rule against hearsay, regardless of whether the declarant is available as a witness:
(5) Recorded recollection. A memorandum or record concerning a matter about which a witness once had knowledge but now has insufficient recollection to enable the witness to testify fully and accurately, shown to have been made or adopted by the witness when the matter was fresh in the witness' memory and to reflect that knowledge correctly. If admitted, the memorandum or record may be read into evidence but may not itself be received as an exhibit unless offered by an adverse party.	*(5) Recorded Recollection.* A record that: (A) is on a matter the witness once knew about but now cannot recall well enough to testify fully and accurately; (B) was made or adopted by the witness when the matter was fresh in the witness's memory; and (C) accurately reflects the witness's knowledge. If admitted, the record may be read into evidence but may be received as an exhibit only if offered by an adverse party.

Basis

In an ideal world, all witnesses would be good ones: truthful, unbiased, and blessed with excellent perception, flawless memory, and the ability to clearly and accurately tell their stories on direct examination in a courtroom. In the real world, however, witnesses often fall far short of the ideal in one or more areas, and yet they still must testify at trial. Concerning the fallibility of witnesses, the evidence scholar Edmund Morgan wrote:

> In Utopia, doubtless, a machine of flawless perfection, automatically yielding minutely accurate products, would be provided for this vastly important business of administering justice. In Utopia, too, omniscience would sit upon the bench or in the jury-box. But so long as the adjustment of disputes must be entrusted to mere man, so long will human limitations continue to operate in the process and in the result. And those limitations

powerfully affect the kind of evidence producible as well as the practicability of appraising it.[2]

It occasionally happens that a witness experiences a moment of forgetfulness on the stand. The Rules provide mechanisms for dealing with the forgetful witness, whether that forgetfulness is real or feigned. We have already learned about Rule 612, which permits an advocate to refresh a witness's recollection by using documents or other memory triggers so that the witness is able to testify from memory at trial. In most cases of forgetfulness, Rule 612 is adequate to ensure that the witness is able to carry on and testify from memory, as required by the Rules.

Sometimes, attempts to refresh a witness's recollection fail. This presents the parties and judge with a real problem: the witness perceived something of importance to the trial and made or adopted a record of it, but can no longer remember what she once knew; the information is available, but not in a form normally acceptable at trial.

Although the majority of common law courts ignored the hearsay aspects of recorded recollections,[3] such records — having been prepared outside the courtroom and now being offered into evidence to prove the truthfulness of the matters asserted therein — are indisputably hearsay. Thus, the dilemma: the witness cannot (or will not) remember what she once knew, yet the evidence of what she knew is available in recorded form and may very well be necessary to resolve issues of importance in the case.

Recognizing the problem, Rule 803(5) provides a mechanism, in the form of a hearsay exception, for getting this information into evidence, even when the witness is unable (as in cases of actual forgetfulness) or unwilling (as in cases of feigned forgetfulness) to do so. Rule 803(5) comes into play only when a forgetful witness has been unable to testify from memory and after unsuccessful efforts were made to refresh the witness's recollection under Rule 612. In such cases, Rule 803(5) permits the proponent to read or otherwise publish to the jury a memorandum or record made or adopted by the witness while the matter was still fresh in the witness's memory and accurately reflecting the witness's knowledge.

Rule 803(5) represents long-standing practice under the common law and in the federal court system. According to the Advisory Committee, the basis for the recorded recollection hearsay exception is "the reliability inherent in a record made while events were still fresh in mind and accurately reflecting them."[4]

Key Foundational Elements

There are four primary foundational elements required in order to introduce evidence under Rule 803(5).

---

[2] Edmund S. Morgan, *The Relation Between Hearsay and Preserved Memory*, 40 HARV. L. REV. 712, 713–14 (1927).

[3] *See generally* Edmund S. Morgan, *The Relation Between Hearsay and Preserved Memory*, 40 HARV. L. REV. 712 (1927).

[4] FED. R. EVID. 803(5) advisory committee's note.

a. The witness must demonstrate — on the stand — the inability fully and accurately to remember something about which the witness has actual personal knowledge. On cross-examination, the inability to remember can include feigned forgetfulness or willful efforts to evade answering questions.

b. The advocate's efforts to refresh the witness's recollection under Rule 612 must fail.

c. The advocate must establish that the witness made or adopted a record of the matter while it was still fresh in the witness's mind. There is no set time period for determining whether the matter was still fresh in the witness's mind.

d. The advocate must establish that the record correctly reflects the witness's knowledge.

After the foundational elements have been met, the advocate is permitted to read — or play, as in the case of an audio or video recording — the record to the fact-finder. The hard copy of the record itself is not received into evidence; this is to prevent the fact-finder from giving greater credence to the record than to the live testimony of other witnesses who are testifying from personal knowledge.

The Rule in Application

As previously mentioned, Rule 803(5) is not triggered until after an advocate has attempted unsuccessfully to refresh a witness's recollection under Rule 612. According to the Advisory Committee, there are sound reasons for requiring a showing of impaired memory before introducing a recorded recollection: "the absence of the requirement, it is believed, would encourage the use of statements carefully prepared for purposes of litigation under the supervision of attorneys, investigators, or claim adjusters."[5] These types of statements, if introduced without a showing of genuine memory lapse, would subvert the purposes of the adversary trial by effectively denying cross-examination to opponents of the evidence.

A close examination of Rule 803(5) reveals a potential anomaly. The witness on the stand has no recollection of the matter at hand, and yet the rule requires proof of three important foundational elements: (1) the witness once had knowledge of the now-forgotten matter; (2) the witness made or adopted a record while the matter was fresh in the witness's mind; and (3) the record correctly reflects the witness's knowledge. The person most likely to provide the foundational information is the same person whose inability to remember has created the evidentiary problem in the first place. Rule 803(5) is silent as to how these things can be proven, and the Advisory Committee note indicates that this was a deliberate choice: "No attempt is made in the exception to spell out the method of establishing the initial knowledge or the contemporaneity and accuracy of the record, leaving them to be dealt with as the circumstances of the particular case might indicate."[6]

---

[5] FED. R. EVID. 803(5) advisory committee's note.

[6] FED. R. EVID. 803(5) advisory committee's note.

There are several ways to prove the contemporaneity and accuracy of the record, even if the witness cannot remember what is actually contained in it. First, the witness can directly testify to it: *As soon as I got home, I wrote down everything that had happened. I wanted to make sure I put it on paper and that I had a record of it.* Second, the witness can testify about her habit with respect to recording important information: *I don't have any specific recollection of that day, but I do make a habit of keeping a diary. I write every day, and I always include the important things that happened during the day. If it's in my diary, it's accurate.* Third — particularly in cases where the witness has adopted a memorandum or record made by someone else — the witness can testify about her routine practice: *Whenever I get an accident report, I review it. I won't sign it if there are mistakes or questions. So if my signature is on that report, it means I reviewed it and that it was accurate.*

There are also instances in which multiple people participated in the creation of the record. Suppose, for example, that two cowboys have the responsibility to count and record the number of cattle being taken to market, and that their chosen method of operation is for Cowboy Bob to count out loud as Cowboy Chuck records tick marks in a ledger book. If Cowboy Bob is called to testify at trial about the number of cattle taken to market, cannot remember, and fails to have his memory refreshed, the ledger book could be introduced under Rule 803(5). Both cowboys would have to testify concerning their role in creating the record, and Cowboy Bob would have to further testify that the record accurately reflected his knowledge as to the number of cattle.

Another issue that arises under Rule 803(5) is the meaning of the phrase "when the matter was fresh in the witness' memory." The rule does not define a specific time limit for fresh memories, and case law has demonstrated considerable flexibility with respect to the time between the incident and the recorded recollection of it.[7]

Finally, Rule 803(5) is also available to help solve the problem of the witness whose claim of forgetfulness is in itself a species of deceit; to borrow language from Edmund Morgan, "lack of recollection" can be a "perjurer's sanctuary."[8] When a witness feigns forgetfulness on the stand, Rule 803(5) permits the judge to determine that the witness is not testifying "fully and accurately" and allow opposing counsel to introduce the witness's recorded recollection into evidence.

---

[7] *See* United States v. Patterson, 678 F.2d 774, 779–80 (9th Cir. 1982), *cert. denied*, 459 U.S. 911 (1982) (holding that trial judge did not abuse discretion in admitting grand jury testimony that was given more than ten months after a conversation); United States v. Senak, 527 F.2d 129, 141 (7th Cir. 1975), *cert. denied*, 425 U.S. 907 (1976) (admitting a witness statement made more than three years after the event in a pre-Rules case). *But see* Maxwell's Ex'rs v. Wilkinson, 113 U.S. 656 (1885) (denying use of a memorandum made twenty months after the event).

[8] Edmund M. Morgan, *The Relation Between Hearsay and Preserved Memory*, 40 HARV. L. REV. 712, 719 (1927).

Cases, Discussion Questions and Problems

UNITED STATES v. WILLIAMS
United States Court of Appeals, Sixth Circuit
571 F.2d 344 (6th Cir. 1978)

[Defendant Williams was on trial for cashing government checks with forged endorsements. The main issue at trial was whether the defendant knew the endorsements were forged. The government called witness Gary Ball, who owned a junkyard next to the bar where Williams allegedly cashed the forged checks. Ball knew Williams and, in fact, rented part of his lot to Williams. The proprietor of the bar originally thought Ball had cashed the check, but Ball denied it. On further inquiry, the proprietor learned that Williams had cashed the check.]

The witness then related his conversations with Williams about this check. After stating that Williams admitted that he had cashed the check and was willing to make it good, Ball was asked if Williams had stated where he had gotten the check. The witness answered, "Not to my knowledge, I don't remember him telling me where he got it." When the government attorney asked Ball specifically if he ever had a conversation with Williams "about a deal he had going with his landlord about checks . . . ," counsel for the defendant objected. The court directed that the question be rephrased, and this question and answer followed:

Q: *Mr. Ball, I am going to rephrase my question slightly.*

             Did you have a conversation with Mr. Williams about another check besides this one payable to Mr. Quick?

A: *We had a conversation — I don't remember exactly the time or the day or when — but I asked him about the checks, and he said that he had cashed them for a landlord or a caretaker. One check, he said he had found in a hotel room.*

The witness was then asked to examine a written statement which he had given to a secret service agent 15 months prior to the trial. He identified the signature at the end of the statement as his and made an incomplete reference to a "discrepancy" as he read the statement to himself. Once Ball finished reading the statement, he was asked, "Can you now remember more about these conversations than you just did a moment ago?" Ball answered, "No." The jury was then excused and a "special record" was made. The direct examination of the witness by government counsel included the following:

Q: *Mr. Ball, the statement that you have in front of you now, did you give that statement to Agent Lutz of the Secret Service in about July of '75?*

A: *I did.*

Q: *Were the conversations that you had had with Mr. Williams fairly fresh in your mind at the time you made that statement?*

A: *They were.*

Q: *Did you swear to Agent Lutz that that statement was a true statement?*

A: *I did.*

Q: *You were put under oath, asked to raise your hand and so forth, to tell the truth?*

A: *I don't remember if I was or not.*

Q: *Had you told Agent Lutz before basically the same version about these conversations with Williams orally but not in writing?*

A: *Do you mean from the first time I talked to Mr. Lutz or up until this was taken?*

Q: *On previous occasions when you had talked to Mr. Lutz, did you tell him basically the same version that you put in the statement there?*

A: *When I first met Mr. Lutz, he was accusing me of cashing the checks. And he accused me before I even talked to Tony about this check, the Willington check, or the Quick check. It was after that they told me that I wasn't the one that they were looking for that Tony asked me if I could get his money back for the check, and I told him I would try, I would talk to Glenn about it.*

Q: *But my question is: Did you give basically the same account to Agent Lutz orally on previous occasions before you gave this statement?*

A: *Basically the same account, to the best of my recollection.*

Q: *Was that statement true and accurate to the best of your knowledge?*

A: *Yes.*

Q: *And is that statement true and accurate now to the best of your knowledge?*

A: *It is.*

On cross-examination, still out of the presence of the jury, Ball testified that the statement was in the handwriting of Secret Service Agent Lutz and that it had not been taken down word for word by the agent. Rather, "We talked and then he wrote this out, and then I signed it." While affirming his previous testimony that the statement was true and accurate at the time he gave it, Ball now said it was true and accurate "in general." On the question of what Williams had told him about where he (Williams) had gotten the checks, the testimony was as follows:

Q: *All right. On this paper, here (indicating), it says, "Glenn told me that he and his/or a landlord or caretaker were getting checks before the payee could get his mail."*

        Is that a quote from you?

A: *I think the quote from me would have probably been that something like wherever Glenn stayed at, he got it from his caretaker or*

> *landlord. I don't remember ever putting in there that "before coming from the mail, getting the mail".*

Q: *Did Glenn ever tell you — excuse me — did Mr. Williams ever tell you that these checks were stolen checks?*

A: *No, he didn't.*

Q: *Okay. Did you intimate, did you try to lead Officer Lutz, Agent Lutz, into believing that you believed that Glenn Williams was admitting to you a crime?*

A: *No, I didn't.*

Q: *So, what were you telling Agent Lutz that you knew?*

A: *That he cashed the checks at Tony's bar, and that he had got them from where he was living at to cash them, to the best of my knowledge.*

*   *   *

Q: *Did you tell Mr. — excuse me — Agent Lutz that it was your understanding that someone else was stealing checks and giving them to Glenn?*

A: *I didn't put it in those words. I told him it was my understanding that the checks were coming from an apartment building.*

Q: *Did you tell him that they were stolen checks, that Mr. Williams had told you that?*

A: *No, I didn't.*

Q: *Is there anything else in this statement that is not what you told Officer Lutz but, rather, is what he wrote in here?*

A: *No, there is not; not that I know of.*

Q: *Would you just explain to me, Mr. Ball, did you give Officer Lutz — Agent Lutz the impression that Mr. Williams had told you that he was stealing checks?*

A: *No, I didn't.*

Q: *Did you give Agent Lutz the impression, or did you try to give him the impression, that you believed that Mr. Williams was cashing stolen checks and that he knew it?*

A: *No, I didn't.*

Q: *Did you believe, when you were signing this statement, that you were in any way incriminating Mr. Williams?*

A: *No, I didn't.*

On redirect examination Ball admitted reading the statement before he signed it, and swearing to Agent Lutz that it was true. He contended that he had not told the agent that Williams had told him that he or the landlord or caretaker were getting the checks before the addressees picked up their mail. He also gave an explanation for his comment to Williams, "I thought you told me you had stopped this b.s.," which did not imply that the checks were stolen. He testified that he and Williams remained friends.

The district court then heard arguments of counsel after which it ruled that the statement would be admitted as "recollection of a statement that had been adopted by the witness." The District Judge held that a foundation had been adequately laid for admission of the statement, finding that his (Ball's) "relationship with the defendant here, his demeanor, his selective memory with regard to matters, convinces this Court that he is withholding and that his protestations of failure of recollection are not convincing to the Court." Following the requirements of Rule 803(5), the court did not admit the statement as an exhibit, but permitted it to be read to the jury after deleting the subjective impression, "It was my understanding that someone else was stealing the checks and giving them to Glenn." When the jury returned, and before the statement was read, Ball testified again that the statement was true and accurate at the time he gave it. Ball then read the statement.

On cross-examination, after the jury had heard the statement, Ball testified that the writing and words of the statement were those of Agent Lutz. He stated that he was frightened when the agent first accused him of passing bad checks and that he wanted to cooperate. He testified that Agent Lutz told him that he, Lutz, suspected that the landlord was involved. He didn't remember telling Lutz that Williams told him that he or his landlord was getting the checks before the payees could get their mail.

Agent Lutz testified that the statement was taken from Ball after several discussions, and at the time of the statement there was no suggestion that Ball was under suspicion or was being accused. He said the statement was taken at the Secret Service Office following a review of their prior discussions and that the witness read the statement, asserted that it was correct and said he was satisfied it was accurate when asked if he had any corrections, deletions or additions to make. Lutz testified that Ball then signed and swore to the statement.

Following denial of motions for a mistrial and for a judgment of acquittal the case was submitted to the jury and Williams was found guilty on four counts of the indictment. The only issue on appeal relates to admission of the statement signed by Gary Ball as substantive evidence. We affirm.

The first contention of Williams is that the statement should not have been admitted because it was not Ball's statement. This position is based on the fact that Agent Lutz wrote the statement in his own words. This argument misconstrues the requirements of Rule 803(5). To be admissible the memorandum or record must have been made "or adopted by the witness when the matter was fresh in his mind and to reflect that knowledge correctly." (emphasis added). By signing and swearing to the statement Gary Ball adopted it. This occurred approximately six months after the events recited in the statement. Ball testified unequivocally that his conversations with Williams were fresh in his mind at the time he signed the statement and that it was a true and accurate statement at that time.

As proposed by the Supreme Court Rule 803(5) provided only for reading into evidence a memorandum or record shown to have been made by the witness. The

House of Representatives amended the rule to add "or adopted by the witness." The amendment was explained in the Senate Report to P.L. 93-595, Rules of Evidence, as follows: "When the verifying witness has not prepared the report, but merely examined it and found it to be accurate, he has adopted the [**12] report, and it is therefore admissible." S. Rep. No. 93-1277, 93rd Cong., 2d Sess., 4 U.S. Code Cong. & Admin. News at 7074 (1974). Williams relies on this court's decision in United States v. Shoupe, 548 F.2d 636 (6th Cir. 1977), where we held it was a violation of due process to permit a prosecuting attorney to present the entire substance of an unsworn, oral statement, later disavowed by the witness, in attempting to impeach his in-court testimony. Shoupe does not control the present case. In Shoupe the witness testified he did not even remember making the statement, whereas Gary Ball testified that he read and signed the statement. There was clearly no adoption by the witness in Shoupe of the memorandum of his earlier unsworn, oral statement and the court properly did not consider Rule 803(5).

Appellant's second argument is that it was error to admit a statement "when the witness had clear recollection of his conversations with defendant and when he testified that a statement written by a government investigator following a conversation with the witness was inaccurate." If the record supported the quoted assertion the Ball statement would not be admissible under Rule 803(5). Rule 803(5) applies only to memoranda or records of matters "about which a witness once had knowledge but now has insufficient recollection to enable him to testify fully and accurately. . . ." (emphasis added). There is no doubt that Ball had sufficient recollection to testify generally about his conversations with Williams. However, the critical question about those conversations was whether Williams had told him how the checks came into his possession. This was the very aspect of the conversations which Ball testified he could not recall. Referring to one of the checks which Williams had cashed at the bar, Ball testified, ". . . I don't remember him telling me where he got it." He further testified that Williams said that the checks came from his caretaker or landlord and that he didn't remember stating that they were taken before payees could get their mail. In addition he testified that he didn't remember saying, "I told Glenn he was nuts."

The District Judge, who observed Gary Ball testify before the jury and in the special record proceedings, concluded that the witness was exercising a "selective memory." Regardless of whether it was a deliberate act born of his friendship with the defendant, it is clear that Ball was claiming no recollection of certain features of his conversations with Williams which had been included in the statement that he had previously adopted. Once it was established that Ball's in-court testimony would be incomplete because of his insufficient recollection, the statement which he had adopted when the events were fresh in his mind, and which he repeatedly testified was accurate, became admissible under Rule 803(5). We note that in a case tried before the effective date of the Federal Rules of Evidence, the reviewing court applied the "modern concept of the admissibility of relevant evidence" to approve the admission of an earlier statement which a witness had given F.B.I. agents where the evidence of insufficient recollection was quite similar to that in the present case. United States v. Senak, 527 F.2d 129, 138 (7th Cir. 1975), cert. denied, 425 U.S. 907, 96 S. Ct. 1500, 47 L. Ed. 2d 758 (1976). This result is clearly correct under the rules.

Williams makes much of the fact that Ball disputed portions of the statement on cross-examination. However Ball continued to agree that the statement was accurate "in general." He appeared to question primarily any implication to be drawn from the statement that he considered Williams guilty of a crime, yet his disagreements with the language of the statement were couched in terms of insufficient recollection. We conclude that the matters brought out in cross-examination did not preclude admissibility of the statement, but went only to the weight to be given it. United States v. Senak, supra, 527 F.2d at 139. The jury was free to believe Ball's explanation of his intentions and impressions when he adopted the statement. They were not bound to accept the statement as conclusive evidence of the defendant's guilt. However, they were entitled to hear the statement as an accurate account of Ball's conversations with Williams, given at a time when those conversations were recent events and his memory of them was unimpaired. As Judge Learned Hand wrote in Di Carlo v. United States, 6 F.2d 364, 368 (2d Cir. 1925):

> The possibility that the jury may accept as the truth the earlier statement in preference to those made upon the stand is indeed real, but we find no difficulty in it. If, from all that the jury sees of the witness, they conclude that what he says now is not the truth, but what he said before, they are none the less deciding from what they see and hear of that person and in court.

* * *

Courts and commentators have long recognized the "recorded past recollection" exception which is the subject of Rule 803(5). The Advisory Committee's Note to Exception (5) makes it clear that the method of establishing the initial knowledge of the declarant and the accuracy of the material sought to be introduced must be determined from the circumstances of each case. 28 U.S.C. (1970) App. Supp. V at pp. 2351-52. We find no abuse of discretion in the determination of the District Judge that the statement signed by Gary Ball should be read to the jury. It contained the indicia of trustworthiness required by Rule 803(5) and was never categorically disowned or contradicted by the witness. There being no claim that the Sixth Amendment right to confrontation was violated, see California v. Green, 399 U.S. 149, 90 S. Ct. 1930, 26 L. Ed. 2d 489 (1970), no reversible error has been demonstrated.

The judgment of the district court is affirmed.

DISCUSSION QUESTIONS

1. What role does the passage of time play in determining the freshness of a witness's recollection? Do you think there should be an outer limit for determining freshness, and if so, what would it be?

2. The *Williams* case involves a statement written by an agent and adopted by the witness. What are the dangers in using adoptive statements under Rule 803(5)? From the portions of the record in this case, does the adversarial system provide sufficient protections to ensure such statements are not abused?

3. The statement at issue in *Williams* was introduced by the government to counter its own witness's evidently feigned claim of forgetfulness. Procedurally, how does this differ from the more traditional uses of past recollection recorded under Rule 803(5)? What foundational challenges would an adversary face in introducing the recorded recollection of a hostile witness? How can those challenges be overcome?

PROBLEMS

Problem 23-1. Wil Arthur writes a popular weekly column for the *Calamity Crier* entitled *Amblin' Man*, in which he describes his walking tours to various points of interest in the city and his encounters with the local citizenry. On Father's Day last year, he wrote an emotional column, entitled *Reunited and it Feels So Good*, about a recently released prisoner reuniting with his son in the parking lot of the county jail. The following is an excerpt from the column:

> *I should have known better than to cry, but I couldn't help it. I'm a father myself, and what I saw outside the Calamity City Jail three weeks ago touched me deeply. I'll never forget it. I've thought about it over and over, and there was something about the scene that just won't leave me. It was that poignant. That significant. I think it changed me forever. . . .*
>
> *Dad, a muscular man in his early thirties, heavily tattooed, with a clean-shaven head and sporting a goatee, emerged from the doorway of the jail. He was wearing jail-issue gray sweatpants and a white T-shirt. When he walked out the door and the sunlight hit his eyes, he blinked and blocked the sun with one of his hands. But then he smiled and raised his face to the sky, soaking it all in. Right next to him, holding his hand, was a beautiful young woman of exotic ethnicity, with rich raven hair cascading down her shoulders. She smiled and beamed up at him. It had been a long time. He was missed.*
>
> *As they approached the family car, a brand-new black Camaro with a vanity plate that read DNGR ZON, a little boy could contain himself no longer. He flung the door open and burst out, racing towards his father. I could hear him from across the street. "Daddy! Daddy! You came back!" he shouted. He was probably five years old, no older, and you could tell Dad was the center of his life. . . .*

Arthur's column turned out to be the missing link that helped the police break an auto-theft ring in Calamity City. The vehicle described in the column had been reported stolen a month before the column came out. Detectives looked at jail release records for the approximate time frame of the column, connected the dots and arrested Priscilla Perpetrator, the "Mom" in the column. Priscilla was no youthful exotic beauty, but was rather a plain woman, middle-aged and with unkempt, dishwater-blond hair. She was the girlfriend of a prisoner who had been released from the jail at about the time that Arthur described in his column. They were parents of a five-year old son. The stolen vehicle matched the description of the car in the column; police seized it from Priscilla's driveway. There was no vanity license plate, just the original plate that was on the car when it was stolen. Priscilla was charged with larceny of the automobile and also, based on the column, child neglect for leaving her son in the car while she went into the jail to secure the release of his father.

Arthur was subpoenaed to testify at trial. He was a reluctant witness. "I don't want to be here," he said to the judge as he was being sworn in. "I'm a journalist, not a police snitch." Williams was vague about the description of the people, the car and the vanity plate and said, "It's been a long time." The prosecution showed him a copy of his column to refresh his recollection, but when he handed it back, he said, "I can't really remember much about the day. I'm sorry." The prosecutor asked him if his column was a truthful account of what happened that day, and Arthur replied, "I write columns. Not news. Sometimes I make things up to fill in the gaps or tell a better story. I mean, the column is about my thoughts and impressions; that's the whole point of it. But the basic story of every column is based on something real." The prosecution seeks to admit Arthur's column as past recollection recorded under Rule 803(5). What arguments should the prosecution make? How should the defense counter? How should the judge rule, and why?

Business Records

Through Dec. 1, 2011	After Dec. 1, 2011
Rule 803. Hearsay Exceptions; Availability of Declarant Immaterial The following are not excluded by the hearsay rule, even though the declarant is available as a witness:	**Rule 803. Exceptions to the Rule Against Hearsay — Regardless of Whether the Declarant Is Available as a Witness** The following are not excluded by the rule against hearsay, regardless of whether the declarant is available as a witness:
(6) Records of regularly conducted activity. A memorandum, report, record, or data compilation, in any form, of acts, events, conditions, opinions, or diagnoses, made at or near the time by, or from information transmitted by, a person with knowledge, if kept in the course of a regularly conducted business activity, and if it was the regular practice of that business activity to make the memorandum, report, record or data compilation, all as shown by the testimony of the custodian or other qualified witness, or by certification that complies with Rule 902(11), Rule 902(12), or a statute permitting certification, unless the source of information or the method or circumstances of preparation indicate lack of trustworthiness. The term ''business'' as used in this paragraph includes business, institution, association, profession, occupation, and calling of every kind, whether or not conducted for profit.	*(6) Records of a Regularly Conducted Activity.* A record of an act, event, condition, opinion, or diagnosis if: (A) the record was made at or near the time by — or from information transmitted by — someone with knowledge; (B) the record was kept in the course of a regularly conducted activity of a business, organization, occupation, or calling, whether or not for profit; (C) making the record was a regular practice of that activity; (D) all these conditions are shown by the testimony of the custodian or another qualified witness, or by a certification that complies with Rule 902(11) or (12) or with a statute permitting certification; and (E) neither the source of information nor the method or circumstances of preparation indicate a lack of trustworthiness.

Basis

Rule 803(6), the business records exception, is one of the most important and frequently used of the Federal Rules of Evidence. Modern trials, whether civil or criminal, are replete with documents and records. The business records exception to the hearsay rule, coupled with the self-authentication provisions of Rules 902(11) and 902(12), provides the basis for admitting the vast majority of these records.

The modern-day rule is based on two common-law hearsay exceptions, the *shop-book rule* and its derivative, the *regular entries rule*. The influential treatise *McCormick on Evidence* explains these two rules:

By the 1600s in England, a custom emerged in the common law courts of receiving the "shop books" of tradesmen and craftsmen as evidence of debts for goods sold or services rendered on open accounts. Since most tradesmen were their own bookkeepers, the rule permitted a reasonable means of avoiding the harsh common law rule preventing a party from appearing as its own witness. Nevertheless, theoretical objections to the self-serving nature of this evidence, apparently coupled with abuse of it in practice, led to a statutory curb in 1609 that limited the use of a party's shopbooks to a period of one year after the debt was created unless a bill of debt was given or the transaction was between merchants and trades-men. . . .

During the 1700s a broader doctrine began to develop in the English common law courts. At first, this doctrine permitted only the use of regular entries in the books of a party by a deceased clerk, but it was expanded to cover books regularly kept by third persons who had since died. By 1832, the doctrine was firmly grounded, and its scope was held to include all entries made by a person, since deceased, in the ordinary course of the maker's business.[9]

The shop-book rule applied to one's own records, and the regular entries rule applied to books kept by third parties.[10]

As it eventually evolved, the common law hearsay exception for regularly kept records had four foundational elements, many of which have survived in the modern business records exception. The entries had to be (1) original entries made in the routine of a business; (2) made upon the personal knowledge of the recorder or someone reporting the information; (3) made at or near the time of the transaction recorded; and (4) the recorder had to be unavailable for trial.[11]

The shop-book and regular entries rules were emblematic of the common law's practical and common-sense approach to solving evidentiary problems. The modern-day rule is based on the common law but has expanded the scope of activities and records covered by the rule to include records kept in the regular course of a business activity. The term "business activity" is broadly defined to include "business, institution, association, profession, occupation, and calling of every kind, whether or not conducted for profit." The rule's expansion of scope from its common law roots permits more documents, from a wider variety of entities, to be entered into evidence, but sometimes at the cost of almost unrecognizable variance from the original shop-keeper and regular entries rules.

The basis of reliability for the modern business records exception is the regular practices and incentives that exist for businesses and entities to create and maintain good records in order to be competitive and remain viable. According to the Advisory Committee,

> The element of unusual reliability of business records is said variously to be supplied by systematic checking, by regularity and continuity which

---

[9] 2 McCormick on Evidence § 285.

[10] Charles V. Laughlin, *Business Entries and the Like*, 46 Iowa L. Rev. 276, 278 (1960).

[11] 2 McCormick on Evidence § 286.

produce habits of precision, by actual experience of business in relying upon them, or by a duty to make an accurate record as part of a continuing job or occupation.[12]

Rule 803(7) is similarly based on the reliability of records and the idea that in a well-maintained system of records, what does not appear in the records has independent significance.

Through Dec. 1, 2011	After Dec. 1, 2011
Rule 803. Hearsay Exceptions; Availability of Declarant Immaterial The following are not excluded by the hearsay rule, even though the declarant is available as a witness: **(7) Absence of entry in records kept in accordance with the provisions of paragraph (6).** Evidence that a matter is not included in the memoranda reports, records, or data compilations, in any form, kept in accordance with the provisions of paragraph (6), to prove the nonoccurrence or nonexistence of the matter, if the matter was of a kind of which a memorandum, report, record, or data compilation was regularly made and preserved, unless the sources of information or other circumstances indicate lack of trustworthiness.	**Rule 803. Exceptions to the Rule Against Hearsay — Regardless of Whether the Declarant Is Available as a Witness** The following are not excluded by the rule against hearsay, regardless of whether the declarant is available as a witness: *(7) Absence of a Record of a Regularly Conducted Activity.* Evidence that a matter is not included in a record described in paragraph (6) if: (A) the evidence is admitted to prove that the matter did not occur or exist; (B) a record was regularly kept for a matter of that kind; and (C) neither the possible source of the information nor other circumstances indicate a lack of trustworthiness.

In essence, Rule 803(7) permits a party to prove a negative: "Failure of a record to mention a matter which would ordinarily be mentioned is satisfactory evidence of its nonexistence."[13] The absence of information does not seem to fit within Rule 801's definition of hearsay as "a statement . . . offered in evidence to prove the truth of the matter asserted," because no assertion is involved. The Advisory Committee elected to include it as a hearsay exception, however, because some appellate decisions "may be found which class the evidence not only as hearsay, but also as not within any exception."[14]

Foundational Elements

The following elements are necessary to satisfy Rule 803(6), the business records exception:

---

[12]   FED. R. EVID. 803(6) advisory committee's note.

[13]   FED. R. EVID. 803(7) advisory committee's note.

[14]   FED. R. EVID. 803(7) advisory committee's note.

1. The record must be made and kept in the course of a regularly conducted business activity. And as a corollary to this element, the record must be of the type regularly kept and maintained by that business.

2. The record must be made at or near the time of the event recorded therein.

3. The record must be made by, or from information transmitted by, a person with knowledge who had a business duty to report the information.

The following elements are necessary to satisfy Rule 803(7), absence of entry.

1.   The same elements to establish a business record, plus

2.   The witness must introduce the record that shows absence of entry, or

3.   The witness must testify that a diligent search of files revealed no record at all.

The Rule in Application

(1) *Recorded Recollection v. Business Records*

In some respects, the business records exception is similar to the recorded recollection exception. For instance, both rely to some extent on contemporaneous recording of information: Rule 803(5) states that the record must have been "made or adopted by the witness when the matter was fresh in the witness' memory"; Rule 803(6) requires the record to have been created "at or near the time by, or from information transmitted by, a person with knowledge." In addition, both rules require a showing of accuracy as a precursor to admissibility.

There is inevitable overlap between the two rules: for example, one can easily envision a situation in which a single record could be admissible either as a past recollection recorded or as a business record. But, as one scholar has noted, the two exceptions are not necessarily co-extensive:

> It is especially important to note the requirement [for past recollection recorded] that the witness who qualifies the memorandum must be able to vouch for its accuracy. The most obvious way to prove the accuracy of the memorandum is to show that the witness remembers having made it and testifies that it was accurate when made. However, a witness may not remember having made the specific memorandum but knows that it is a type of document that he customarily makes, or he may recognize his handwriting and have no reason to believe that he recorded anything erroneously. In such cases the argument for admissibility is weaker than it is if the witness can remember having accurately made the document, but there is authority permitting the document to be used in evidence. In any event the facts recorded must be such as the witness knew personally when the record was made, and he must be willing and able, on the stand, to underwrite the accuracy of the record.

It is evident that the problem of past recollection recorded overlaps considerably the problem of business entries. Frequently, courts are not clear as to which ground of admissibility is used, or if the document can be qualified upon either ground the courts do not always clearly so state. Anyone doing research should examine each authority from both points of view. The bases of reliability are quite different. A memorandum used as past recollection recorded is reliable because a witness is willing to testify that it correctly evidences certain facts. On the other hand, a document admitted as a business entry under any of the four bases for admitting such entries is reliable because it is regularly prepared and therefore relied upon by those to whom it matters. There are records which can be admitted on one basis but not on the other. An isolated memorandum may be qualified as past recollection recorded even though it is no part of any system of regular entries. On the other hand, difficulty is presented by the use of a memorandum prepared by more than one person when offered as past recollection recorded, which might be obviated if there is sufficient regularity to get it in as a business entry.[15]

There are other important differences between recorded recollections and business records. The recorded recollection exception is not triggered until the witness has experienced an incurable lapse of memory on the stand; no such limitation exists for the business records exception. Business records can be received directly into evidence and taken back to the jury room during deliberations; a recorded recollection, on the other hand, can only be read or played to the fact-finder and is treated no differently than other verbal testimony in deliberations. The recorded recollection requires personal knowledge by the witness of the recorded events; the business records exception, on the other hand, does not require a testifying witness to have personal knowledge of the recorded event.

(2) *Routine or Regular Practice of a Business Activity*

Rule 803(6) requires the proponent of a record to demonstrate that it was "kept in the course of a regular business activity." The definition of "business activity" in the rule is broad enough to encompass nearly any recognizable activity, including traditional businesses, nonprofit organizations, sole proprietorships, clubs, fraternal organizations, and even illegal enterprises. *McCormick on Evidence* notes the wide variety of business activities that have been held within the scope of the rule:

It has been held to encompass such diverse items as a diary of tips kept by a blackjack dealer, notations on calendar of daily illegal drug sales, performance evaluations of hospital employees, a hospital's scrapbook of newspaper articles showing visiting hours, a restaurant "guest check" with defendant's name written on it, a videotape made by prison of removal of prisoner from his cell, a bill of lading, an automobile lease by dealer, a logbook of malfunctions of a machine, loan counselor's notes of telephone

---

[15] Charles V. Laughlin, *Business Entries and the Like*, 46 Iowa L. Rev. 276, 279–80 (1960).

conversations with defendant, and an appraisal of a painting for purposes of insurance.[16]

The mere fact that a document or record appears in the files of a business activity is not, however, enough to guarantee that it will be admitted into evidence. The proponent must also demonstrate that "it was the regular practice of that business activity to make [the record]." In other words, the proponent must show that this was the type of record routinely created by the business activity. This requirement has a direct bearing on the perceived trustworthiness of the record. As the Advisory Committee notes point out, "Absence of routineness raises lack of motivation to be accurate."[17]

Much of the litigation on the issue of routine practice has focused on such things as accident or investigative reports. The classic example is a pre-Rules case, *Palmer v. Hoffman*,[18] in which the Supreme Court affirmed a trial judge's decision to exclude an accident report offered by the defendant railroad in a collision case. The report had been prepared by the engineer who was driving the train. Using a precursor statute to Rule 803(6) that governed the admissibility of business records in federal courts, the trial court excluded it because it was not in the regular course of the railroad's business to create such reports. The Court affirmed, stating

> The engineer's statement which was held inadmissible in this case falls into quite a different category. It is not a record made for the systematic conduct of the business as a business. An accident report may affect that business in the sense that it affords information on which the management may act. It is not, however, typical of entries made systematically or as a matter of routine to record events or occurrences, to reflect transactions with others, or to provide internal controls. The conduct of a business commonly entails the payment of tort claims incurred by the negligence of its employees. But the fact that a company makes a business out of recording its employees' versions of their accidents does not put those statements in the class of records made "in the regular course" of the business within the meaning of the Act. If it did, then any law office in the land could follow the same course, since business as defined in the Act includes the professions. We would then have a real perversion of a rule designed to facilitate admission of records which experience has shown to be quite trustworthy. Any business by installing a regular system for recording and preserving its version of accidents for which it was poten- tially liable could qualify those reports under the Act. The result would be that the Act would cover any system of recording events or occurrences provided it was "regular" and though it had little or nothing to do with the management or operation of the business as such. Preparation of cases for trial by virtue of being a "business" or incidental thereto would obtain the benefits of this liberalized version of the early shop book rule. The

---

[16] McCormick on Evidence § 288.

[17]   Fed. R. Evid. 803(6) advisory committee's note.

[18] 318 U.S. 109 (1943).

probability of trustworthiness of records because they were routine reflections of the day to day operations of a business would be forgotten as the basis of the rule. . . .

In short, it is manifest that in this case those reports are not for the systematic conduct of the enterprise as a railroad business. Unlike payrolls, accounts receivable, accounts payable, bills of lading and the like, these reports are calculated for use essentially in the court, not in the business. *Their primary utility is in litigating, not in railroading.*[19]

The question of whether a record is kept in the regular course of a business activity can be complicated. Modern businesses and entities keep and maintain an astonishing variety of records. Some of these are directly related to the core business of the entity. For example, to stay operational, a railroad has to purchase supplies, obtain rights of way, bill for services rendered, and the like. Some records are ancillary to the entity's core business but nonetheless critical to its operation. For instance, a railroad cannot operate without employees, so it must keep records pertaining to the hiring, pay, promotion and termination of employees.

The further afield a record falls from the core types of records that are required to keep the entity operational and functional, the less likely the record was made in the regular course of business. The less routine a record is to the normal functions of a business activity, the less likely it is to have the built-in trustworthiness factors that form the foundation of Rules 803(6) and 803(7).

Rule 803(6) permits a judge to exclude a record if there are indications that it lacks trustworthiness. When records, such as accident reports, are created with the possibility of litigation in mind, the record may well be outside the scope of regular business. This is because when an employee fills out an accident report, particularly in cases involving damage or injury to third parties, there is a powerful incentive to write the report in a way that will minimize liability to the employer. In the absence of cross-examination or confrontation, the record is less trustworthy than other types of records in the business's files and can be excluded.

(3) *Personal Knowledge, Business Duty to Report*

In addition to requiring that a record be kept in the regular course of a business activity, Rule 803(6) also requires that the record by created "by, or from information transmitted by, a person with knowledge." The person who places such information into a record is said to have a "business duty" to report the information; in other words, that person's role in the business activity is to supply just the sort of information that the record contains. This requirement is generally satisfied if the informant — the person with a business duty to report — creates the record using first-hand knowledge or observations.

Many records that are created, kept and maintained by business activities contain outside information from people who do not have a business duty to report such information. Much of this information is hearsay and must be evaluated on its own merits under Rule 805, the so-called "double hearsay" rule. If it is indepen-

---

[19] Palmer v. Hoffman, 318 U.S. 109, 113–14 (1943).

dently admissible, it can be admitted as part of the record; if not, the record must be excluded or the outside information redacted. This is because the source of the information is not part of the business activity and therefore lacks the motivation to provide trustworthy information of someone with a business duty to report. In the words of the Advisory Committee, "If, however, the supplier of the information does not act in the regular course, an essential link is broken; the assurance of accuracy does not extend to the information itself, and the fact that it may be recorded with scrupulous accuracy is of no avail."[20]

There are occasions, however, when outside information provided by a person without a business duty to report can become part of the business record. Such information is admissible under the business records exception if the business activity verifies, incorporates this information into its own records and relies upon it as being trustworthy. For example, suppose that a hotel desk clerk is checking in a new guest. In the process of creating a business record related to that guest's stay, the clerk will input different types of information into the record: the date, time, room rate and so forth. At some point, the clerk will ask for the guest's name. The clerk likely has no first-hand knowledge of the guest's identity, but will verify the identity by asking for a form of identification such as a driver's license or passport. The guest who provides the name does not have a business duty to report, but the information will nonetheless satisfy the business records hearsay exception because it was the regular business practice of the clerk to verify the information.

(4) *Custodians and Affidavits*

The classic method for introducing a business record into evidence is to call a witness, known as a custodian, to testify how the record was made and kept. The custodian does not have to be the same person who created the record or who is in charge of keeping or maintaining the activity's records; it is enough for the custodian to be familiar with the processes used to create and store the records.

In 2000, the Rules were amended to permit self-authentication of most business records in the absence of genuine concerns about the trustworthiness of the documents. Rules 902(11) and (12) provide for the self-authentication of domestic and foreign records, respectively. Under these rules, the records may be admitted if accompanied "by a written declaration of its custodian or other qualified person" certifying that the foundational requirements of Rule 803(6) have been met because the record:

(A) was made at or near the time of the occurrence of the matters set forth by, or from information transmitted by, a person with knowledge of those matters.

(B) was kept in the course of the regularly conducted activity; and

(C) was made by the regularly conducted activity as a regular practice.

In addition, the party seeking to offer the record must provide sufficient advance notice to the adverse party and an opportunity to inspect the document so the adverse party has a "fair opportunity to challenge" the document if necessary.

---

[20] FED. R. EVID. 803(6) advisory committee's note.

Cases, Discussion Questions and Problems

UNITED STATES v. GRANT
United States Court of Appeals, Armed Forces
56 M.J. 410 (C.A.A.F. 2002)

On November 22, 1997, appellant was found unconscious at the club complex on Incirlik Air Base in Turkey. He was transported by ambulance to the base hospital, where he was evaluated by the physician on duty, Captain (Capt) Poindexter. Observing that appellant was unconscious and unresponsive to pain stimuli, Capt Poindexter ordered, among other things, a drug screen urinalysis. [The purpose of the drug screen was to help the physician determine treating options for the patient.]

In the two years he had been stationed at the Incirlik hospital, Capt Poindexter never ordered a drug screen prior to this occasion. Consequently, he was unaware that the hospital, unequipped to perform the screen, was required to send appellant's urine sample to the Armstrong Laboratory at Brooks Air Force Base in Texas. It took two weeks for Incirlik to receive results of any drug screen requested from Brooks Air Force Base. Apparently, Capt Poindexter's experience stateside had been that a physician could receive results of a drug screen within an hour of requesting one.

Meanwhile, based on results of other tests requested by Capt Poindexter and received at the time of initial treatment, he diagnosed appellant as suffering from acute alcohol intoxication. Appellant was treated accordingly and released from the hospital the following day, November 23. Although appellant had been released, the hospital continued processing Capt Poindexter's request to test the urine sample.

Armstrong Laboratory subsequently received the sample on November 28, tested it, and notified Incirlik of the results by e-mail on December 5. Senior Airman (SrA) Lynch, a lab technician at the hospital, received the results from Armstrong, downloaded the report, and printed it out. This report contained the "Armstrong Laboratory Epidemiology Division" heading at the top of the page. It also contained the name and Social Security Number of the patient, along with the various drugs tested for and the results of those tests. The result column of the report indicates either "NEGATIVE" or "POSITIVE," depending on what drugs were detected in the patient's urine. This report indicated that appellant's urine tested positive for cannabinoids.

[This information was provided to the Air Force Office of Special Investigations. Confronted with the report, the appellant confessed to using marijuana on three separate occasions. At trial, the prosecution introduced the record under Military Rule of Evidence 803(6) to corroborate the appellant's confession.]

The Government called no witnesses from either Incirlik or Armstrong to testify about the chain of custody regarding appellant's urine sample. Nor did it call any witnesses to testify about the testing procedures used at Armstrong Laboratory. Instead, the Government called Capt Poindexter and SrA Lynch to demonstrate the hospital's reliance on the record and to establish that the record was procured and incorporated in the hospital's records in the normal course of business. Over timely defense objection, the military judge admitted the report to corroborate appellant's confession and subsequently admitted the confession.

I

Appellant's complaint on appeal is that the drug screen report from the Armstrong lab was not admissible as a business record. . . . We review a military judge's ruling admitting or excluding evidence for an abuse of discretion. United States v. Hursey, 55 MJ 34, 36 (2001).

This Court has yet to address the foundation necessary to admit under Mil.R.Evid. 803(6) a business record created by a third party not before the trial court, that is incorporated into the business records of the testifying party. However, as the Military Rules of Evidence are largely derived from the Federal Rules of Evidence, we look to the federal Courts of Appeals for treatment of the issue. Our review reveals that these courts have generally held that a document prepared by a third party is properly admitted as part of a second business entity's records if the second business integrated the document into its records and relied upon it in the ordinary course of its business. See Air Land Forwarders, Inc. v. United States, 172 F.3d 1338 (Fed. Cir. 1999); MRT Construction, Inc. v. Hardrives, 158 F.3d 478 (9th Cir. 1998); United States v. Doe, 960 F.2d 221 (1st Cir. 1992); United States v. Jakobetz, 955 F.2d 786 (2d Cir. 1992); United States v. Ullrich, 580 F.2d 765 (5th Cir. 1978); United States v. Carranco, 551 F.2d 1197 (10th Cir. 1977).

At issue in *Air Land Forwarders, Inc.*, was the trial court's admission of certain repair estimates produced by third parties but maintained in the records of a military transportation office. Air Land Forwarders, Inc., was a common carrier under contract with the Military Traffic Management Command to transport servicemembers' household goods. When a member initiated a claim, he was required to submit a number of documents detailing the circumstances of the loss. Servicemembers could also submit repair estimates prepared by third parties to prove the amount of the claim. The trial court concluded that it was the regular course of the Military Traffic Management Command to collect such information and include it in the entire claims file. It further concluded that the military relied upon the repair estimates to properly adjudicate the claims, indicating the military's interest in the accuracy of the claims records. 172 F.3d at 1341, 1343. Finally, the trial court concluded that the trial record contained assurances of reliability. For instance, servicemembers filed their claims with the knowledge that filing a false claim exposed them to criminal liability. Id. at 1343. The Court of Appeals then held that the repair estimates were "properly admitted. . . even though the government did not produce a witness that could testify with first-hand knowledge as to the procedures used in the original preparation of each of the repair estimates." Id. at 1344.

In *Doe*, the defendant was convicted of being a felon in possession of a firearm that had moved in interstate commerce. The Government's evidence on this issue included, inter alia, an invoice from a South Carolina telemarketing firm admitted through the testimony of a Massachusetts sports shop owner who had ordered the firearm from the firm. The invoice was admitted as a business record of the sports shop owner, and the Court of Appeals found this proper. The court noted as "irrelevant" the fact that the invoice had earlier been the record of a different business. 960 F.2d at 223. The court focused instead on the shop owner's testimony that he relied on such documents to show acquisition of the firearm. In addition, federal law required him to keep an "acquisition and disposition book." Id. Logically, he had a substantial interest in the accuracy of the record. See MRT Const., Inc., supra.

What we conclude from the cited cases is that a record incorporated by a second entity may be admitted under Mil.R.Evid. 803(6) on the testimony of a "qualified witness" of the incorporating entity alone if certain criteria are met. First, the incorporating entity must obviously procure and keep the record in the normal course of its business. Mil.R.Evid. 803(6). Second, the entity must show that it relies on the accuracy of the incorporated record in its business. Air Land Forwarders, Inc., 172 F.3d at 1343. Finally, there must be "other circumstances indicating the trustworthiness of the document." Id.

In this case, both SrA Lynch and Capt Poindexter were qualified witnesses who provided sufficient foundation to show that the Armstrong lab report had been incorporated by the hospital as its own business record. SrA Lynch testified that he was very familiar with the hospital lab's procedures for handling urine samples. He testified how the samples are prepared and shipped to the Armstrong lab and that a record was kept of the shipments. In the past, he had sent samples to Armstrong and had "always gotten back results showing either positive or negative." He testified as to the daily practice of the Armstrong lab of sending results by e-mail and that they did so "all the time" in the course of the Armstrong lab's business. He further testified that it was his practice when he received results to download the e-mail, print it out, and file it. His testimony was that this procedure occurred in the hospital lab "all the time."

Capt Poindexter also testified regarding his familiarity with how medical records were maintained at the hospital. He testified that the hospital had a duty imposed by regulations to maintain documents like the drug screen report in the patient's medical records. As for the specific report in issue, he identified it as a copy of that which was contained in appellant's medical record. He further testified as to his familiarity with Air Force medical testing and stated that he and presumably other physicians rely on such results to be accurate "in order to make the appropriate treatment" in cases where the patient is unresponsive to pain stimuli.

As for indicia of trustworthiness, Capt Poindexter's reliance on the report speaks directly to its trustworthiness. Presumably, those responsible for conducting the test and providing the results at Armstrong are aware that an incorrect result may lead to a patient's failure to receive proper medical treatment, which could be potentially followed by serious medical consequences or even death. 2 McCormick on Evidence, supra, § 293 at 264 (discussing the reasons why modern medical records are generally reliable). Moreover, there is no evidence in the record that suggests the hospital had received false or erroneous results from Armstrong in the past.

Based on this record, we hold that witnesses Lynch and Poindexter provided a sufficient basis for admitting the Armstrong lab report as a business record of the Incirlik hospital, and the military judge did not abuse his discretion in doing so.

UNITED STATES v. HEDMAN
United States Court of Appeals, Seventh Circuit
630 F.2d 1184 (7th Cir. 1980)

The evidence at trial showed that the defendants commenced their employment with the City of Chicago during the 1950's as inspectors for the Department of Buildings. In 1969 and 1970, they were promoted to the positions of Supervisor. In those positions, the defendants were responsible for supervising the inspection, by six district inspectors, of all new construction and remodeling in the geographical areas of the City of Chicago to which they had been assigned. The Chicago Building Code requires that anyone who undertakes any construction work, structural repairs, additions or remodeling in the city, secure a building permit from the Department of Buildings. . . . Once the permit is obtained, the construction may proceed. At various stages of the construction a building inspector from the City of Chicago inspects the project to insure compliance with the building code. Upon completion of the construction, the inspector validates the permit.

A. Counts One through Five

These counts alleged the receipt of extortionate payments by the defendants from the Danley Lumber Company, an Illinois corporation whose principal business is the construction of residential garages. In the course of its business, Danley annually purchases approximately $1,000,000 in building materials from manufacturers outside the State of Illinois.

Since its inception in 1959, Danley has constructed a substantial number of garages in Chicago that violated the Building Code, usually because the garages were too large or too close to the lot line. On such occasions, Danley would either fail to obtain a building permit or obtain one through the submission of a false application. For these jobs, Danley would make illegal payoffs to the defendants.

Between 1959 and the mid-1960's Bentley Weitzman, the President of Danley, would pay $25 to the building inspector for the district in which the non-conforming garage was being erected. The money for these payoffs was obtained from the receipts for construction work that was performed but not recorded on Danley's books. Weitzman testified that these receipts were also not reported on Danley's tax returns. From the mid-1960's until 1976, the task of making payoffs on construction that violated the Chicago Building Code was handled by Bentley Weitzman's father, Harry Weitzman. When a job did not violate the building code, Harry Weitzman would file a permit application and pay the required fee to the City of Chicago.

A routine procedure was established at Danley for processing non-conforming garages. When a job violated the Building Code, the employee at Danley who processed that job order would give Harry Weitzman a slip of paper indicating the address of the job and a notation that a violation existed. Weitzman would then write the name of the area supervisor for that job on the slip, and return the slip to the job file. At the same time, Weitzman would make an entry on a list he maintained of all non-conforming jobs. When the garage was being built, the slip would be returned to Weitzman. He accumulated slips for several days and then gave them to Irving Lazarus, Vice President of Danley. Lazarus would obtain cash from a walk-in safe located in Danley's offices, place $25 per slip in an envelope with the slips, and give the money and slips to Weitzman. Bentley Weitzman testified that, on occasion, he also provided the cash to his father.

When Harry Weitzman received the cash and slips from Lazarus, he would delete the job addresses from his list. He would then write the name of the supervisors on separate envelopes, place the appropriate amount of money in each envelope, and personally deliver them to all four defendants at either their offices in City Hall or their homes. On occasion, Weitzman would give to one supervisor an envelope to be delivered to another supervisor.

From 1968 or 1969 until 1976, Harry Weitzman kept a diary of these payoffs. At the top of each page of the note-book, Weitzman wrote the first name of a supervisor, e. g., "Mike," "Tom," "Hank," and "John." Also listed on these pages were the addresses of the non-conforming job sites, as well as the amounts, the dates, and the places of the payments made to each supervisor for those jobs. The diary detailed payments that were made to all four defendants individually, as well as payments that were made to one supervisor for delivery to another. . . .

In presenting its evidence related to the counts involving the Danley Lumber Company, the government offered into evidence a diary kept by Harry Weitzman, the Danley employee responsible for making payoffs to Chicago Building Inspection Supervisors. Over the vigorous objections of the appellants, the trial court admitted the diary as a business record under Rule 803(6) of the Federal Rules of Evidence. Appellants have renewed their objection on appeal. We conclude that the trial court did not abuse its discretion in admitting the diary into evidence.

Harry Weitzman testified that after several years of making payoffs on behalf of Danley to Building Inspection Supervisors, he began recording these payoffs in a small notebook. The notebook contained an entry for every payoff he had made from 1968 or 1969 until 1976. An entry would be recorded in the office after a payment had been made. Harry Weitzman kept the diary in his desk at work and did not make the diary available to other employees at Danley. Weitzman further testified that the reason for maintaining the diary was to provide documentation if Irving Lazarus, the Vice President of Danley, ever demanded an accounting of the payments made to the supervisors. Despite objections by defense counsel that the diary was inadmissible under Rule 803(6) because it was not used or relied on by other Danley employees, nor required to be kept by Weitzman, and contained inaccuracies, Judge Bua admitted the diary on the basis of the foundation testimony, stating:

> *The Court: I have heard enough. Mr. Newman, I think the key here in deciding this matter is whether the books record a regularly conducted business activity as opposed to some personal matter that the scrivener or the one who keeps the record is recording, and while it is a close case, I think it comes within the purview of 803(6).*
>
> *The court takes the position that really this goes all of your arguments of the defense go, good arguments, go to the weight rather than to the*

admissibility, and the diary may be introduced into the record pursuant to the provisions of 803(6) of the Federal Rules of Evidence.

Tr. at 281-282.

We agree with the district court that the diary was admissible. In that connection, our decision in United States v. McPartlin, 595 F.2d 1321 (7th Cir. 1979), is especially pertinent. In McPartlin, the government sought to admit into evidence desk calendar-appointment dairies authored by and containing records of the daily business activities of a witness. The diaries were kept strictly for the use of the witness and the entries therein were recorded at or near the time of the activity. The defendants in McPartlin objected to the admissibility of the diaries as business records because the entries were not made in sequence and because the diaries were relied on only by the witness. We upheld the admissibility of the diaries under Rule 803(6) on the grounds that they were records kept as part of a business activity and the entries were made with regularity at or near the time of the described event, and that verification by persons other than the one making the entry was unnecessary to establish verification. Moreover, we noted that since the witness had to rely on the entries made, there would be little reason for him to distort or falsify the entries. Finally, we observed that the degree of reliability necessary for the admission of diaries under the business record exception to the hearsay rule was greatly reduced because the declarant testified and was available for cross-examination. McPartlin, supra at 1347-1351.

The ratio decidendi of McPartlin is equally applicable to the contested admissibility of the diary in this case. Harry Weitzman testified that he kept the diary as part of a business activity. The entries were recorded with regularity at or near the date of the payoffs. Since Weitzman believed that he would be required to account to Lazarus for the payments, it was unlikely that he would have made false entries. Similarly, the fact that Weitzman was not told to keep the diary and did not make it available to others at Danley does not affect its admissibility under Rule 803(6). Finally, in this case, as in McPartlin, that the diaries recorded illicit business dealings is of no consequence; the illegal nature of those activities were nevertheless part of the normal business of Danley. McPartlin, supra at 1349.

DISCUSSION QUESTIONS

1. Both *Grant* and *Hedman* involve non-standard uses of the business records exception to help secure convictions in criminal cases. Evaluate the intellectual and theoretical integrity of these two court opinions. Are they true to the letter and spirit of Rule 803(6), or have these two appellate courts stretched the rules to help preserve criminal convictions?

2. What does *Grant* teach about the doctrine of incorporating records or information from outside entities? Based on the holding in *Grant*, what are the outer limits of this doctrine, in other words, when would incorporation *not* be permitted?

3. Are any Confrontation Clause issues implicated by the *Grant* case? If so, what are they? Does it make a difference that the record was created to aid a medical diagnosis rather than to aid in a criminal prosecution? Why or why not?

4. What are some alternative bases of admissibility for the diary entries in *Hedman*? Why choose the business records exception over some of these alternative bases of admissibility?

PROBLEMS

Problem 23-2. Tawdry Trailers, Inc., manufactures mobile homes for use by movie stars. Tawdry is involved in a dispute with B-Grade Entertainment, a major producer of low-budget, low-brow films. Although Tawdry has provided the correct number of trailers, B-Grade claims the trailers lack certain amenities, including carpeted walls and mirrored ceilings. As the dispute grows more heated, but prior to any litigation, Tawdry's VP for Manufacturing produces a memorandum for the president that details the entire history of Tawdry's contracts with B-grade for the past 5 years. At trial, Tawdry seeks to introduce the memorandum as a business record. Should it be admitted? Why or why not?

Problem 23-3. Darrell set up a sham business for the purpose of processing fraudulent credit card transactions. Using stolen credit cards, he created fictitious transactions that caused banks throughout the country to pay funds pursuant to their agreements with cardholders. During Darrell's trial for wire fraud, the government seeks to introduce records from the card-issuing banks regarding the transactions. The records contain, among other things, affidavits from cardholders reporting fraudulent transactions on their accounts. Darrell objects on hearsay grounds. The government counters that the records are admissible under Rule 803(6). Your ruling?

Problem 23-4. Dawn, a customer of Massive Retail, parked her car in the parking lot and went in to shop. While she was in the store, an employee collecting shopping carts accidentally let go of an entire string of carts, which struck Dawn's car and damaged it. Dawn immediately filed a complaint with the store manager. Following established procedures, the manager contacted Massive Retail's insurance company, who sent an insurance adjuster to the store. The adjuster interviewed the employee, who admitted he hadn't been very careful and had let go of the carts. The adjuster tape-recorded the interview. The adjuster always records and transcribes interviews and attaches them to his report.

At trial, Dawn seeks to admit the insurance adjuster's report, which contains a transcribed copy of the interview. What objection should Massive Retail's attorney make? How should Dawn's attorney respond? How should the judge rule, and why?

Problem 23-5. Dilbert filed a claim with his automobile insurance company for damage to his vehicle that occurred in a parking lot. The insurance company refused to pay, alleging that Dilbert's policy had lapsed for nonpayment of insurance premiums for the 3 months prior to the accident. Dilbert said he did pay the premiums.

    a. At trial, Dilbert attempts to introduce his checkbook register to prove payment. The insurance company objects on hearsay grounds. How should the judge rule, and why?

    b. Later in the trial, the insurance company calls a clerk to testify that she searched the company's records and could find no evidence of payment the prior 3 months. Dilbert objects that this is inadmissible hearsay. How should the insurance company's attorney respond? How should the judge rule, and why?

Hearsay within Hearsay, Recorded Recollection and Business Records: Quick Hits

- When a hearsay source, such as a document, includes other out-of-court statements or assertions, each "level" of statements or assertions must (1) be admissible as non-hearsay, (2) satisfy a hearsay exclusion, or (3) be admissible as a hearsay exception in order to be admitted.

- When a witness is unable to remember or feigns forgetfulness of facts she once knew, Rule 803(5) provides for the admissibility of a memorandum or record made or adopted by the witness when the matter was still fresh in her mind.

- Business records are admissible as hearsay exceptions if they were made in the regular course of business by persons with a business duty to report information.

- The absence of information in a regularly kept business record is admissible of proof of the non-existence of a fact.

- Business records may be self-authenticating or authenticated by a foundation witness.

Chapter References

CHRISTOPHER B. MUELLER & LAIRD C. KIRKPATRICK, EVIDENCE §§ 8.43–8.48, 8.79 (4th ed. 2009).

GLEN WEISSENBERGER & JAMES J. DUANE, FEDERAL RULES OF EVIDENCE: RULES, LEGISLATIVE HISTORY, COMMENTARY AND AUTHORITY §§ 803.22–803.38, 805 (6th ed. 2009).

JACK B. WEINSTEIN & MARGARET A. BERGER, WEINSTEIN'S FEDERAL EVIDENCE §§ 803.07–803.09, 805 (Joseph M. McLaughlin ed., Matthew Bender 2d ed. 1997).

KENNETH S. BROUN, McCORMICK ON EVIDENCE §§ 279–94, 324.1 (6th ed. 2006).

STEVEN GOODE & OLIN GUY WELLBORN III, COURTROOM HANDBOOK ON FEDERAL EVIDENCE Ch. 5 (West 2010).

III. APPLICATION EXERCISES

Past Recollection Recorded

Uses of Past Recollection Recorded at Trial

Rule 803(5) permits an advocate to introduce the record of a witness's past recollection, provided that the witness has experienced a genuine or feigned loss of memory at trial that cannot be refreshed under Rule 612. With friendly witnesses, attorneys should be prepared for lapses in a witness's memory by identifying records that could be used to refresh recollection under Rule 612 or be introduced for their substance under Rule 803(5) if necessary. With hostile witnesses, attorneys should be prepared to punish mendacity in the form of feigned forgetfulness by using the witness's own recorded recollections against her.

The Exercise

Objective: To demonstrate proficiency in using Rule 803(5) with both friendly and hostile witnesses.

Factual Scenario: Return to the basic fact scenario in Problem 23-1: Wil Arthur, a newspaper columnist, has written a father's day column about the reunion of a father and son outside the city jail. The local police used information in the column to solve an auto theft and arrested a woman named Priscilla. Wil has been called as a witness at trial.

Advance Preparation: Prepare two examinations of Wil Arthur. The first is a prosecution direct examination of Wil in which Wil is a cooperative witness who suffers from amnesia in the aftermath of an automobile accident. Efforts to refresh his recollection under Rule 612 will fail in this examination because of genuine memory loss. The second is a prosecution direct examination of Wil in which Wil is a hostile, uncooperative witness whose forgetfulness appears to be feigned.

In-Class Exercise. Students will be prepared to play the role of prosecutor, defense counsel, witness and judge. In Round 1, the prosecution will conduct an examination of a genuinely forgetful, but cooperative, Wil, attempting to refresh his recollection under 612 and then attempting to admit his newspaper article after laying a foundation under Rule 803(5). Opposing counsel will make appropriate objections. In Round 2, the prosecution will conduct an examination of a hostile Wil whose forgetfulness is feigned and will attempt to admit the newspaper article under Rule 803(5). Opposing counsel will make appropriate objections.

Business Records

Introducing Business Records at Trial

As previously mentioned, business records play a prominent role in modern American litigation. Proponents must be prepared to admit business records using self-authentication certificates or records custodians. Opponents must be prepared to contest the admissibility of records when there are genuine issues regarding the trustworthiness of the records and to employ Rule 805 and Rule 802 to exclude portions of records that include hearsay that is not independently admissible.

When records are introduced using a self-authentication certificate, the certificate itself must comply with the requirements of Rule 803(6), Rule 902(11) or 902(12), and other applicable statutory law. The advocate must provide an opportunity for the opposing side to inspect the record far enough in advance of trial to challenge the record if necessary.

When records are introduced using a custodian, the advocate must lay a proper foundation for the record. The foundation consists of the following elements:

1. The witness is familiar with the process for creating and maintaining records within the business activity and can explain the basis for this familiarity.

2. The regular practice of the business activity was to make such a record.

3. The record was made at or near the time of the event recorded therein.

4. The record was made by, or from information transmitted by, a person with personal knowledge and a business duty to report.

The Exercise

Objective: To demonstrate proficiency in introducing business records into evidence at trial.

Factual Scenario: Students will be divided into groups as assigned by the instructor. Each group is responsible to create its own brief factual scenario based on an existing business record selected by the group. For example, the group could use the record of an automobile repair to create a dispute over payment or the quality of services rendered. The only limitations for the fact scenario are the collective imagination of the group members and the necessity to use an actual business record as the basis for the scenario.

Advance Preparation. Create a brief summary of your factual scenario and bring it to class. Prepare a direct examination of a fact witness in which the business record will be entered into evidence. Identify a records custodian from the business activity in your scenario. Create a self-authentication certificate that complies with Rules 803(6) and 902(11) or 902(12). In addition, prepare a direct examination of the records custodian that lays the appropriate foundation for the record. The records custodian and your fact witness cannot be the same person.

In-Class Exercise. Students within a group will play the attorney and witness roles. Other students will be chosen from class to play the role of opposing counsel and the judge. The group will explain its factual scenario to the class then call its fact witness. In Round 1, the record will be introduced using a self-authentication certificate. In Round 2, assume there is no self-authentication certificate and that a records custodian must be called to lay the foundation for the record. The opposing side will have the opportunity to object and conduct cross-examination prior to the judge ruling on the admissibility of the record.

Chapter 24

HEARSAY AND PUBLIC RECORDS: RULES 803(8) & 803(10)

Chapter Objectives:

- Introduce the hearsay exceptions for public records and the absence of entries in public records
- Analyze and discuss issues pertaining to the admissibility of public records
- Apply the concepts from this chapter in a courtroom application exercise

I. BACKGROUND AND EXPLANATORY MATERIAL

Introduction

Governments create and maintain an enormous variety of records pertaining to virtually all aspects of public and private existence in the modern world. In fact, it is difficult to imagine any form of government that does not generate, disseminate, rely on, and store records. The public, in turn, relies on government records to help facilitate personal business, commercial enterprise and interaction between citizens and government entities. Public records provide reliable proof of vital statistics, property boundaries, tax obligations, criminal and civil investigations, and a nearly limitless array of both public and private information, activities and decisions. In addition, public records help facilitate the transparency and accountability of government; conceivably, any determined citizen who knows where to look can find evidence of the government's internal workings, compliance with the law, use of public funds, and fulfillment of legal duties.

Given the vast scope and reach of activities performed by public agencies, it is not surprising that government records are frequently introduced in litigation. In fact, records of litigation in the courts also become public records themselves. Similar to business records, public records are hearsay. The information contained in these records is, however, considered valuable and reliable enough to admit the records into evidence. In addition, the absence of an entry in the public record where this type of information would be found can be offered as proof of the non-existence of a material fact.

There are two primary rules pertaining to public records. Rule 803(8), Public Records and Reports, is the foundational rule for public records. Rule 803(10), Absence of Public Record or Entry, is similar to Rule 803(7) in that it can be used to prove the nonoccurrence or nonexistence of a matter. The text of these two rules follows:

Through Dec. 1, 2011	After Dec. 1, 2011
Rule 803. Hearsay Exceptions; Availability of Declarant Immaterial The following are not excluded by the hearsay rule, even though the declarant is available as a witness:	**Rule 803. Exceptions to the Rule Against Hearsay — Regardless of Whether the Declarant Is Available as a Witness** The following are not excluded by the rule against hearsay, regardless of whether the declarant is available as a witness:

(8) Public records and reports. Records, reports, statements, or data compilations, in any form, of public offices or agencies, setting forth (A) the activities of the office or agency, or (B) matters observed pursuant to duty imposed by law as to which matters there was a duty to report, excluding, however, in criminal cases matters observed by police officers and other law enforcement personnel, or (C) in civil actions and proceedings and against the Government in criminal cases, factual findings resulting from an investigation made pursuant to authority granted by law, unless the sources of information or other circumstances indicate lack of trustworthiness.	*(8) Public Records*. A record or statement of a public office if:
	
	(A) it sets out:
	
	    (i) the office's activities;
	
	    (ii) a matter observed while under a legal duty to report, but not including, in a criminal case, a matter observed by law-enforcement personnel; or
	
	    (iii) in a civil case or against the government in a criminal case, factual findings from a legally authorized investigation; and

(10) Absence of public record or entry. To prove the absence of a record, report, statement, or data compilation, in any form, or the nonoccurrence or nonexistence of a matter of which a record, report, statement, or data compilation, in any form, was regularly made and preserved by a public office or agency, evidence in the form of a certification in accordance with rule 902, or testimony, that diligent search failed to disclose the record, report, statement, or data compilation, or entry.	(B) neither the source of information nor other circumstances indicate a lack of trustworthiness. *(10) Absence of a Public Record*. Testimony — or a certification under Rule 902 — that a diligent search failed to disclose a public record or statement if the testimony or certification is admitted to prove that: (A) the record or statement does not exist; or (B) a matter did not occur or exist, if a public office regularly kept a record or statement for a matter of that kind.

Basis

The law of evidence has long recognized hearsay exceptions for public records. Under the common law, written records and reports made by public officials could be admitted in evidence if they were based on first-hand knowledge of the facts and created by officials who had a duty to make them.[1] Prior to the enactment of the Federal Rules of Evidence, various types of public records were also admissible under a variety of different statutes.[2]

Public records are considered reliable for several reasons. The foundational presumption is that the declarant (the public official) will be motivated to create accurate records by the duties of his or position. This presumption is strengthened by the fact that most public records are open to inspection by members of the public; public inspection serves as a deterrent against malfeasance and also as a mechanism to correct any inaccuracies that might occur inadvertently.

A second reason is that the "business of government" would suffer without accurate records. For example, municipalities might be deprived of significant property tax revenues in the absence of accurate property valuation records. In this respect, public records are much like business records: they carry built-in institutional incentives for reliability.

A third reason is that, given the volume of transactions conducted by most public agencies, public officials could not possibly be expected to independently remember all the facts recorded in public records. From a purely pragmatic standpoint, government operations might be brought to a grinding halt if public officials and employees were required to testify in court about their first-hand knowledge of matters recorded in public records.

As with other types of written records, the multiple hearsay rule applies to public records. A public record might contain properly recorded hearsay statements from a person without an official duty to create records or observe and report matters. For example, a police officer's report might contain matters directly observed by the police officer while performing his duties, but also hearsay statements from eyewitnesses. Such statements must be independently evaluated for their admissibility under the hearsay rules.

Foundational Elements

Public Records

1. The record is a certified copy of a public record or report. Rule 902(1)-(4) provides for the self-authentication of public documents and records.

2. The record meets one of the three clauses of Rule 803(8):

> (A) It sets forth the activities of the office or agency. Clause A records simply need to be authenticated under Rule 902 to satisfy admissibility requirements.

---

[1] 2 McCormick on Evidence § 295.

[2] *See* Fed. R. Evid. 803(7) advisory committee's note; *see also* Glen Weissenberger & James J. Duane, Federal Rules of Evidence: Rules, Legislative History, Commentary and Authority § 803.39 (6th ed. 2009).

(B) It contains matters observed pursuant to duty imposed by laws as to which there was a duty to report. The foundation for Clause B records includes the following additional elements:

1. The government employee or agent must have firsthand knowledge of the event or condition described in the report.

2. The source of the information must be under a legal duty to report the information.

3. The public agency must have a legal obligation to prepare and maintain the record.

(C) It contains factual findings from an investigation conducted pursuant to legal authority.

Absence of Public Record or Entry

1. The same elements to establish the existence of an actual record in which there is no entry, or the type of record where the information or matter would be recorded if it existed.

2. Live testimony or a certificate that complies with Rule 902 that diligent search failed to disclose the record, report, statement, or data compilation, or entry.

Public Records in Application

Rule 803(8) divides public records into three categories: (A) the activities of the office or agency; (B) matters observed pursuant to duty imposed by law as to which there was a duty to report; and (C) factual findings made pursuant to authority granted by law. It should be noted from the outset that some records do not cleanly fall within a particular category and could, in fact, fit within two or even three of the categories. To quote the influential evidence scholars Christopher Mueller and Laird Kirkpatrick, "Often it makes no difference whether an item fits clause A rather than B or C, or fits two or even all three. But sometimes it does matter, since the three are subject to different use restrictions and foundation requirements."[3] This section discusses and explains each of the categories in turn. The analysis and discussion section presents hypothetical problems exploring the use restrictions and differences between the categories of public records defined by Rule 803(8).

Clause A: Activities of the Office or Agency

This is the most straightforward of the three clauses in Rule 803(8). Clause A provides for the admissibility of records pertaining to the "the activities of the office or agency." Clause A records include such things as: "accounting records of government agencies; dockets and journal entries of courts, legislative bodies and administrative tribunals; certificates of title, registry, death, and birth; records of

---

[3] Christopher B. Mueller and Laird C. Kirkpatrick, Evidence § 8.50 (4th ed. 2009).

licensing agencies; and records of deeds and conveyances."[4]

In many respects, this clause bears remarkable similarity to the business records exception: it includes records that, for the most part, pertain to the internal operations and mission of the public agency; the records are reliable because they were created routinely, in the regular course of an agency's business, and based on trustworthy information. There is little reason to question the accuracy or validity of these records because they constitute the core business of the agency. For example, court records such as dockets and journal entries pertain to the core functions of the court; they are an intrinsic and necessary part of the court's operations.

Clause B: Matters Observed Pursuant to Duty Imposed by Law

Clause B provides for the admissibility of records pertaining to "matters observed pursuant to duty imposed by law as to which matters there is a duty to report." The classic example of a Clause B record is a police report. The officer records personal observations pursuant to his or her legal duties as defined by law, and the agency keeps the report on file as part of its legal duties. Other Clause B records include "records of the United States agencies or armed forces, and records of state agencies, bureaus and administrative bodies."[5]

Even a cursory reading of Clause B reveals the possibility of overlap between Clause A and Clause B records. Indeed, many records could easily be admitted under either clause without controversy. But the two clauses do have different purposes, and they necessarily focus on different things. A useful way to distinguish between the two is to look at the focus of the record: Clause A records, as discussed above, pertain to the internal, core business of the agency and its purpose for existence; Clause B records also pertain to the business of the agency, but they are externally focused.[6] An example is weather records. Pursuant to duty imposed by law, officials of a weather agency take measurements of weather-related data and create records in accordance with legal requirements. Even though the business of the agency is to measure weather, it does not *internally produce or generate* weather; there must be an external focus in order to obtain the information in the agency's records. Contrast this to the operations of a licensing agency: the agency takes in certain information required for it to *internally generate* a license; the ultimate purpose of the agency is to grant and track licenses in its area of responsibility.

It is important to recognize that Clause B records encompass simple factual observations rather than conclusions or opinions. Evaluative records containing

---

[4] GLEN WEISSENBERGER & JAMES J. DUANE, FEDERAL RULES OF EVIDENCE: RULES, LEGISLATIVE HISTORY, COMMENTARY AND AUTHORITY § 803.42 (6th ed. 2009).

[5] GLEN WEISSENBERGER & JAMES J. DUANE, FEDERAL RULES OF EVIDENCE: RULES, LEGISLATIVE HISTORY, COMMENTARY AND AUTHORITY § 803.43 (6th ed. 2009).

[6] For a more thorough discussion of the internal/external distinctions between Clause A and Clause B, see generally GLEN WEISSENBERGER & JAMES J. DUANE, FEDERAL RULES OF EVIDENCE: RULES, LEGISLATIVE HISTORY, COMMENTARY AND AUTHORITY §§ 803.42–803.43 (6th ed. 2009).

conclusions and/or opinions are covered by Clause C of Rule 803(8). In addition, because the reliability of Clause B records is based on the official duty of a government employee or agent to report matters personally observed, statements made by others and included in a record that otherwise qualifies under Clause B cannot be admitted under Rule 803(8). Instead, pursuant to Rule 805, the multiple hearsay rule, these statements must be evaluated separately to see whether they are independently admissible under other exceptions to the hearsay rule.

Finally, there is an important caveat in Clause B that is rooted in the Confrontation Clause of the Sixth Amendment. In criminal cases, the rule excludes "matters observed by police officers and other law enforcement personnel." This is because in criminal matters, the law generally views police as having an adversarial relationship with criminal defendants. This adversarial relationship can color a law enforcement officer's observations. Confrontation is the best way to protect the rights of the criminal defendant. Thus, a law enforcement officer in a criminal case must testify from memory and subject to cross-examination, like any other witness, and the police report or other record is not independently admissible in evidence. This caveat does not apply "to reports found to be of routine and non-adversarial nature."[7]

The topic of confrontation and public records will be addressed in greater detail later in this chapter.

Clause C: Evaluative Records and Investigative Reports

The third clause of Rule 803(8) provides for the admissibility of records containing "factual findings resulting from an investigation made pursuant to authority granted by law." Records admitted under Clause C contain an interpretive or evaluative element not present in Clause B records. A Clause B record, strictly construed, is nothing more than a record of factual matters personally observed by a public official pursuant to a legally imposed duty. The interpretation of those facts is left to someone else. Clause C, in contrast, provides for the admissibility of records in which public officials apply their expertise to make findings, evaluate information and reach conclusions. For example, National Transportation Safety Board (NTSB) investigations into the causes of aircraft accidents include findings about the reasons for the aircraft crash. Those findings are the result of experienced investigators collecting facts, evaluating them, and reaching conclusions about what happened.

A public official's findings under Clause C can be based on evidence that might otherwise be inadmissible. Suppose, for instance, that during an aircraft accident investigation an NTSB investigator interviewed all the pilot's friends and learned that the pilot had a reputation for taking unnecessary risks. Those statements made by friends would be hearsay. And yet, coupled with the facts and other information available to the investigator, the statements could form the basis of the investigator's finding that pilot error contributed to the accident. Rule 805, the multiple hearsay rule, would, however, prevent those statements from being admitted into

---

[7] GLEN WEISSENBERGER & JAMES J. DUANE, FEDERAL RULES OF EVIDENCE: RULES, LEGISLATIVE HISTORY, COMMENTARY AND AUTHORITY § 803.45 (6th ed. 2009).

evidence along with the investigator's findings, unless, of course, the statements were somehow independently admissible in evidence.

The plain language of Rule 803(8) provides for the admission of "factual findings resulting from an investigation." For a number of years, there was considerable litigation and a split in the federal courts concerning the meaning of the phrase "factual findings" — and in particular, whether Clause C required the exclusion of opinions and evaluations. In 1988, the Supreme Court settled the issue, holding that the phrase "factual findings" in Rule 803(8)(C) includes both facts and opinions.[8] Thus, in the example of the NTSB investigator above, the investigator's opinions about the likely cause of the crash would be admissible alongside his factual findings. This makes sense, because it is not always easy to distinguish between a factual finding and an opinion; often, they are one and the same.

The public records covered by Clause C do not have the same built-in guarantees of accuracy and reliability as the other categories of records in Rule 803(8). There are several reasons for this. First, evaluative work carries with it greater subjectivity and opportunities for error than the largely administrative tasks that create Clause A and Clause B records. Second, mistakes, flawed investigative methodologies, inexperience, professional shortcomings or deep-seated biases of agencies or public officials can taint factual findings and investigation results. Third, many investigations depend on information provided by people who do not have an official duty to the agency. Fourth, the types of records covered by Clause C records fall on a reliability continuum depending on how they are created. On one end of the continuum are informal investigations with minimal procedural guarantees of reliability or trustworthiness. On the other end are reports generated by administrative bodies that have held thorough hearings with high procedural guarantees of reliability and trustworthiness.

Because not all findings and reports are alike in quality and evidentiary reliability, Clause C contains an important "escape clause" that prevents unreliable or untrustworthy reports from being entered into evidence. The opponent of the evidence bears the burden of showing that the record is untrustworthy. This can be done by showing inexperience or ineptitude on the part of the investigator, shortcomings in the investigation methodology, bias or partiality, and so forth.

Clause C records cannot be admitted against a criminal accused at trial, regardless of whether they were prepared by police or law enforcement personnel. This is more restrictive than Clause B, which only prohibits the introduction in criminal trials of Clause B records created by police or law enforcement personnel; other Clause B records are presumptively admissible in a criminal case against the accused, subject to the requirements of the Confrontation Clause (see discussion later in this chapter). Clause C does permit the admission of investigative findings in civil actions against either side, and against the government in criminal cases.

---

[8] *See* Beech Aircraft Corp. v. Rainey, 488 U.S. 153, 170 (1988).

Confrontation and Public Records

As we have repeatedly seen, one of the chief dangers of hearsay is that it can deprive the opposing party of the opportunity to confront the declarant; it is impossible to cross-examine someone who is not in the courtroom. The dangers are particularly grave in criminal cases, where the defendant faces the stigma of a criminal conviction and the loss of life or liberty. For this reason, the Supreme Court held in *Crawford v. Washington* that testimonial hearsay cannot be introduced against a criminal defendant unless the Confrontation Clause of the Sixth Amendment has been satisfied.

The overwhelming majority of business and public records are not testimonial, create no confrontation clause issues, and can be freely admitted against a criminal defendant at trial. In fact, the Supreme Court observed in *Crawford* that, under the common law, business records "by their nature were not testimonial."[9]

Many public records are similar to business records because of the routine nature of most government functions and the built-in incentives for reliability and trustworthiness associated with government record-keeping. Clause A records, for instance, are closely akin to business records of the government, being concerned with "the activities of the office or agency." It is highly unlikely that these records would be testimonial under any circumstances. Many Clause B records, "matters observed pursuant to duty imposed by law," are routine in nature, reliable, and not testimonial. Some Clause B records, however, become testimonial in nature because of the adversarial nature of the interaction between law enforcement officers and criminal defendants. Clause B recognizes this by excluding such records in criminal cases. The same holds true for Clause C records, which by their nature are almost all testimonial in nature; these records are never admissible against a defendant in a criminal case.

The issue of confrontation arises through the introduction of laboratory records in criminal cases. In the case of government laboratories, such as state crime laboratories, the reports generated are often Clause B public records under Rule 803(8); depending on circumstances, reports from private laboratories may qualify as business records under Rule 803(6). Regardless of how they are characterized, laboratory records play an important role in criminal trials. Moreover, the issues pertaining to their admissibility at trial are not necessarily clear-cut or simple, as the following excerpt from a law review article explains:

Paul C. Gianelli, *The Admissibility of Laboratory Reports in Criminal Trials: The Reliability of Scientific Proof*
49 Ohio St. L.J. 671 (1988)

The use of scientific evidence in criminal prosecutions has increased significantly. The number of crime laboratories has tripled in the last two decades. New scientific procedures are introduced in evidence every year. Neutron activation, analysis, atomic absorption, scanning electron microscopy, and trace metal detection are but a few of the techniques now used in criminal prosecutions. A

---

[9] Crawford v. Washington, 541 U.S. 36, 56 (2004).

survey of lawyers and judges revealed that "[t]hree quarters of the responders indicated about 1/3 of their cases utilized scientific evidence." More important, however, is the impact of this type of evidence. One study, which surveyed jury attitudes, observed:

> "About one quarter of the citizens who had served on juries which were presented with scientific evidence believed that had such evidence been absent, they would have changed their verdicts-from guilty to not guilty.' "[10]

Frequently, the most expedient way to introduce scientific evidence at trial is through the admission of a laboratory report. The results of drug analyses, fingerprint examinations, intoxication tests, rape victim examinations, and various other scientific techniques have been admitted in this fashion. Similarly, pathological findings have been introduced through autopsy reports. Some of these reports have been prepared by public agencies, such as police crime laboratories and medical examiner offices. Others have been prepared by private hospitals. In some cases, laboratory reports have been used to establish ultimate issues, such as the identity of a controlled substance in a drug prosecution.

The admissibility of scientific reports raises a number of evidentiary issues. Sometimes the report is used in conjunction with expert testimony, either to refresh recollection or as recorded recollection. In either case, the expert is present in court and subject to cross-examination on such matters as his qualifications, the procedures employed, and the meaning of any conclusions reached. When the report is used as a substitute for expert testimony, however, cross-examination is foreclosed and important hearsay and confrontation issues are raised.

Prior to the adoption of the Federal Rules of Evidence (Federal Rules) in 1975, most federal courts admitted laboratory reports under either the public or business records exceptions to the hearsay rule. State cases were in accord. In addition, many courts had rejected confrontation challenges. . . .

Although Rule 803(8) was intended to facilitate the use of public records, its application in criminal cases has spawned a number of problems. Initially, the classification of different kinds of public records can sometimes be troublesome. The rule recognizes three types of public records. . . . The distinctions between these subdivisions are not precise and thus there may be an "overlap." Because the limitations on admissibility differ depending on the type of public record involved, it is sometimes critical to determine which subdivision of the rule applies. Courts have considered both subdivision (B) and subdivision (C) when ruling on the admissibility of laboratory reports. . . .

Rule 803(8)(C) encompasses public records containing "factual findings resulting from an investigation made pursuant to authority granted by law." The federal drafters referred to such records as "evaluative reports." In a leading case, *United States v. Oates*,[11] the Second Circuit stated that it "seems indisputable to us that the chemist's official report and worksheet [identifying a substance as heroin] . . . can

---

[10] [n.8] Peterson, Ryan, Houlden & Mihajlovic, The Uses and Effects of Forensic Science in the Adjudication of Felony Cases, 321. Forensic Sci. 1730, 1748 (1987).

[11] [n.41] 560 F.2d 45 (2d Cir. 1977).

be characterized as [investigative] reports. . . ."[12] As the rule explicitly provides, investigative reports are not admissible in criminal cases when offered *against the accused*; they are, however, admissible if offered against the prosecution. According to the federal drafters, this result is required "in view of the almost certain collision with confrontation rights which would result from their use against the accused in a criminal case."[13]

If accepted, the *Oates* position would be dispositive: Congress presumably agreed with the confrontation analysis offered by the drafters, and laboratory reports, as investigative reports, are therefore inadmissible. . . .

As noted earlier, the prior federal cases generally had admitted laboratory reports. Although the court in believed that the prior cases were not dispositive, the issue remains debatable because laboratory reports were never mentioned in the legislative history.[14]

The conflict between *Oates* and the prior cases, however, may involve more than an issue of congressional intent. The *Oates* court obviously viewed the underlying chemical procedure as an "evaluative" process. In contrast, one of the leading pre-Federal Rules cases viewed a blood alcohol test as involving "an objective fact, not a mere expression of opinion."[15] This latter characterization suggests that rule 803(8)(C) may not apply; the rule governs only investigative or evaluative reports, not the simple recording of objective facts. Hence, an appreciation of the scientific procedure is as important as an understanding of the legal issues.

Courts have also considered the admissibility of laboratory reports under rule 803(8)(B) - reports of matters observed and recorded pursuant to a legal duty. For example, the court in Oates concluded that laboratory reports "might also be within the ambit" of this provision, a ruling that required the court to examine rule 803(8)(B)'s explicit exclusion of police records: "[I]n criminal cases matters observed by police officers and other law enforcement personnel" are inadmissible.

The police records exclusion did not appear in the rule as promulgated by the Supreme Court. It was added by amendment from the floor of the House of Representatives. . . .

In *Oates* the Second Circuit adopted a literal interpretation of the police records exclusion, under which all police reports are inadmissible. According to the court, prosecution laboratory reports fell within the exclusion. In contrast, other courts have adopted a more flexible approach, holding that the exclusion does not apply to all police records. For example, the Ninth Circuit has held that "Congress did not

---

[12] [n. 42] Id. at 67. See also Bradford Trust Co. v. Merrill Lynch, Pierce, Fenner & Smith, Inc., 805 F.2d 49, 54-55 (2d Cir. 1986) (fingerprint and handwriting reports admissible under rule 803(8)(C) in a civil case).

[13] [n.44] Fed. R. Evid. 803(8) advisory committee note.

[14] [n.52] *See* Alexander, *The Hearsay Exception for Public Records in Federal Criminal Trials*, 47 ALBANY L. REV. 699, 720 (1983) ("The problem with [the Oates] interpretation of rule 803(C) . . . is that prior to adoption of the Federal Rule, federal courts approved the admissibility of certain types of laboratory reports under the business records exception." (footnote omitted)).

[15] [n. 53] Kay v. United States, 255 F.2d 476, 481 (4th Cir. 1958), cert. denied, 358 U.S. 825 (1958).

intend to exclude [police] records of routine, nonadversarial matters. . . ."[16] The court focused on the Senate Committee Report's language concerning the "adversarial nature of the confrontation" between the police and the defendant "at the scene of the crime or the apprehension of the defendant." One court accepting this view has stated:

> In the case of documents recording routine, objective observations, made as part of the everyday function of the preparing official or agency, the factors likely to cloud the perception of an official engaged in the more traditional law enforcement functions of observation and investigation of crime are simply not present. Due to the lack of any motivation on the part of the recording official to do other than mechanically register an unambiguous factual matter. . . . such records are, like other public documents, inherently reliable.[17]

Under this approach courts have admitted police reports containing the routine recording of license plate and serial numbers, chain of custody documents, warrants of deportation, a marshall's return on service of an injunction, and breathalyzer calibration certificates.

If laboratory analyses are considered routine and objective, they are admissible under this approach. According to one court, a chemist "does no more than seek to establish an intrinsically neutral fact. . . ."[18] Another has stated that reports of chemical analyses "contain[ ] objective facts rather than expressions of opinion."[19]

Thus, one commentator has written:

> [A] routine report which merely identifies a substance or describes its objective characteristics, such as a report which states that a specimen is cocaine, or that a vaginal swab contains seminal fluid, or that a blood sample contains.15% alcohol, should qualify for admission under [rule 803(8)] if the tests upon which such a report is based are ministerial in nature, requiring the analyst to do little more than record the results of a mathematical computation or the reading of a dial.[20]

The characterization of laboratory procedures as routine and objective is not without problems. As noted by one court, a laboratory report identifying a substance as marijuana is "not concerned with routine observations of acts,

---

[16] [n. 68] United States v. Orozco, 590 F.2d 789, 793 (9th Cir.), *cert. denied*, 442 U.S. 920 (1979).

[17] [n. 70] United States v. Quezada, 754 F.2d 1190, 1194 (5th Cir. 1985) (citations omitted).

[18] [n. 78] United States v. Evans, 21 C.M.A. 579, 582, 45 C.M.R. 353, 356 (1972) (LSD analysis).

[19] [n. 79] Howard v. United States, 473 A.2d 835, 839 (D.C. App. 1984). *See also* Kay v. United States, 255 F.2d 476, 481 (4th Cir.) (Certificate of blood alcohol test results involves "an objective fact, not a mere expression of opinion . . ."), *cert. denied*, 358 U.S. 825 (1958).

[20] [n. 80] Alexander, supra note 52, at 727-28 (footnote omitted). See also S. SALTZBURG & K. REDDEN, FEDERAL RULES OF EVIDENCE MANUAL 837 (4th ed. 1986) ("But it is by no means clear that reports like those offered in [Oates], laboratory reports conducted according to scientific principles utilized in experiments conducted day after day the same way in controlled circumstances, were meant to be included under the heading 'Police Reports.' ").

conditions or events observed or recorded by presumably neutral public officials."[21] Rather, it involves "the examination and evaluation of crucial evidence against a defendant made after the commencement of a criminal prosecution and for use in that prosecution." Here again, the legal issue turns on an understanding of the scientific procedures involved-whether these procedures are "routine and objective" or "evaluative."

As Gianelli's article suggests, the admissibility of laboratory records in criminal cases can be a complex endeavor. Balancing the right of confrontation with the requirements of the public records and business records hearsay exceptions is no easy task. But as we will see in the next section, the Supreme Court has stepped in and clarified some of the issues pertaining to confrontation and laboratory records in criminal cases.

II.   CASES, DISCUSSION QUESTIONS AND PROBLEMS

MELENDEZ-DIAZ v. MASSACHUSETTS
Supreme Court of the United States
129 S. Ct. 2527 (2009)

Justice Scalia delivered the opinion of the Court.

The Massachusetts courts in this case admitted into evidence affidavits reporting the results of forensic analysis which showed that material seized by the police and connected to the defendant was cocaine. The question presented is whether those affidavits are "testimonial," rendering the affiants "witnesses" subject to the defendant's right of confrontation under the Sixth Amendment.

[Boston police officers arrested the defendant and another man after receiving a report of suspicious activity at a K-Mart. During the drive to the police station, the officers observed the men fidgeting in the back seat. A subsequent search revealed 19 small plastic bags containing a substance. The officers submitted this to the state laboratory required by law to conduct chemical analysis on police request.]

Melendez-Diaz was charged with distributing cocaine and with trafficking in cocaine in an amount between 14 and 28 grams. Ch. 94C, §§ 32A, 32E(b)(1). At trial, the prosecution placed into evidence the bags seized from [co-defendant] Wright and from the police cruiser. It also submitted three "certificates of analysis" showing the results of the forensic analysis performed on the seized substances. The certificates reported the weight of the seized bags and stated that the bags "[h]a[ve] been examined with the following results: The substance was found to contain: Cocaine." App. to Pet. for Cert. 24a, 26a, 28a. The certificates were sworn to before a notary public by analysts at the State Laboratory Institute of the Massachusetts Department of Public Health, as required under Massachusetts law. Mass. Gen. Laws, ch. 111, § 13.

---

[21] [n. 81] State v. Matulewicz, 198 N.J. Super. 474, 477, 487 A.2d 772, 773 (App. Div. 1985) (emphasis added).

Petitioner objected to the admission of the certificates, asserting that our Confrontation Clause decision in Crawford v. Washington, 541 U.S. 36, 124 S. Ct. 1354, 158 L. Ed. 2d 177 (2004), required the analysts to testify in person. The objection was overruled, and the certificates were admitted pursuant to state law as "prima facie evidence of the composition, quality, and the net weight of the narcotic . . . analyzed." Mass. Gen. Laws, ch. 111, § 13.

The jury found Melendez-Diaz guilty. He appealed, contending, among other things, that admission of the certificates violated his Sixth Amendment right to be confronted with the witnesses against him. . . .

In Crawford, after reviewing the Clause's historical underpinnings, we held that it guarantees a defendant's right to confront those "who 'bear testimony'" against him. 541 U.S., at 51, 124 S. Ct. 1354, 158 L. Ed. 2d 177. A witness's testimony against a defendant is thus inadmissible unless the witness appears at trial or, if the witness is unavailable, the defendant had a prior opportunity for cross-examination. Id., at 54, 124 S. Ct. 1354, 158 L. Ed. 2d 177.

Our opinion described the class of testimonial statements covered by the Confrontation Clause. . . .

There is little doubt that the documents at issue in this case fall within the "core class of testimonial statements" thus described. Our description of that category mentions affidavits twice. The documents at issue here, while denominated by Massachusetts law "certificates," are quite plainly affidavits: "declaration[s] of facts written down and sworn to by the declarant before an officer authorized to administer oaths." Black's Law Dictionary 62 (8th ed. 2004). They are incontrovertibly a "'solemn declaration or affirmation made for the purpose of establishing or proving some fact.'" Crawford, supra, at 51, 124 S. Ct. 1354, 158 L. Ed. 2d 177 (quoting 2 N. Webster, An American Dictionary of the English Language (1828)). The fact in question is that the substance found in the possession of Melendez-Diaz and his codefendants was, as the prosecution claimed, cocaine — the precise testimony the analysts would be expected to provide if called at trial. The "certificates" are functionally identical to live, in-court testimony, doing "precisely what a witness does on direct examination." Davis v. Washington, 547 U.S. 813, 830, 126 S. Ct. 2266, 165 L. Ed. 2d 224 (2006) (emphasis deleted).

Here, moreover, not only were the affidavits "'made under circumstances which would lead an objective witness reasonably to believe that the statement would be available for use at a later trial,'" Crawford, supra, at 52, 124 S. Ct. 1354, 158 L. Ed. 2d 177, but under Massachusetts law the sole purpose of the affidavits was to provide "prima facie evidence of the composition, quality, and the net weight" of the analyzed substance, Mass. Gen. Laws, ch. 111, § 13. We can safely assume that the analysts were aware of the affidavits' evidentiary purpose, since that purpose — as stated in the relevant state-law provision — was reprinted on the affidavits themselves. See App. to Pet. for Cert. 25a, 27a, 29a.

In short, under our decision in Crawford the analysts' affidavits were testimonial statements, and the analysts were "witnesses" for purposes of the Sixth Amendment. Absent a showing that the analysts were unavailable to testify at trial and that petitioner had a prior opportunity to cross-examine them, petitioner was entitled to " 'be confronted with' " the analysts at trial. Crawford, supra, at 54, 124 S. Ct. 1354, 158 L. Ed. 2d 177.1. . . .

B

. . . A second reason the dissent contends that the analysts are not "conventional witnesses" (and thus not subject to confrontation) is that they "observe[d] neither the crime nor any human action related to it." Post, at ____, 174 L. Ed. 2d, at 343. The dissent provides no authority for this particular limitation of the type of witnesses subject to confrontation. Nor is it conceivable that all witnesses who fit this description would be outside the scope of the Confrontation Clause. For example, is a police officer's investigative report describing the crime scene admissible absent an opportunity to examine the officer? The dissent's novel exception from coverage of the Confrontation Clause would exempt all expert witnesses — a hardly "unconventional" class of witnesses.

A third respect in which the dissent asserts that the analysts are not "conventional" witnesses and thus not subject to confrontation is that their statements were not provided in response to interrogation. Ibid. See also Brief for Respondent 29. As we have explained, "[t]he Framers were no more willing to exempt from cross-examination volunteered testimony or answers to open-ended questions than they were to exempt answers to detailed interrogation." Davis, supra, at 822-823, n 1, 126 S. Ct. 2266, 165 L. Ed. 2d 224. Respondent and the dissent cite no authority, and we are aware of none, holding that a person who volunteers his testimony is any less a " 'witness against' the defendant," Brief for Respondent 26, than one who is responding to interrogation. In any event, the analysts' affidavits in this case were presented in response to a police request. See Mass. Gen. Laws, ch. 111, §§ 12-13. If an affidavit submitted in response to a police officer's request to "write down what happened" suffices to trigger the Sixth Amendment's protection (as it apparently does, see Davis, 547 U.S., at 819-820, 126 S. Ct. 2266, 165 L. Ed. 2d 224; id., at 840, n 5, 126 S. Ct. 2266, 165 L. Ed. 2d 224 (Thomas, J., concurring in judgment in part and dissenting in part)), then the analysts' testimony should be subject to confrontation as well.

C

Respondent claims that there is a difference, for Confrontation Clause purposes, between testimony recounting historical events, which is "prone to distortion or manipulation," and the testimony at issue here, which is the "resul[t] of neutral, scientific testing." Brief for Respondent 29. Relatedly, respondent and the dissent argue that confrontation of forensic analysts would be of little value because "one would not reasonably expect a laboratory professional . . . to feel quite differently about the results of his scientific test by having to look at the defendant." Id., at 31 (internal quotation marks omitted); see post, at ____ - ____, 174 L. Ed. 2d, at 339. . . .

Respondent and the dissent may be right that there are other ways — and in some cases better ways — to challenge or verify the results of a forensic test.[22] But the Constitution guarantees one way: confrontation. We do not have license to suspend the Confrontation Clause when a preferable trial strategy is available.

Nor is it evident that what respondent calls "neutral scientific testing" is as neutral or as reliable as respondent suggests. Forensic evidence is not uniquely immune from the risk of manipulation. According to a recent study conducted under the auspices of the National Academy of Sciences, "[t]he majority of [laboratories producing forensic evidence] are administered by law enforcement agencies, such as police departments, where the laboratory administrator reports to the head of the agency." National Research Council of the National Academies, Strengthening Forensic Science in the United States: A Path Forward 6-1 (Prepublication Copy Feb. 2009) (hereinafter National Academy Report). And "[b]ecause forensic scientists often are driven in their work by a need to answer a particular question related to the issues of a particular case, they sometimes face pressure to sacrifice appropriate methodology for the sake of expediency." Id., at S-17. A forensic analyst responding to a request from a law enforcement official may feel pressure — or have an incentive — to alter the evidence in a manner favorable to the prosecution.

Confrontation is one means of assuring accurate forensic analysis. While it is true, as the dissent notes, that an honest analyst will not alter his testimony when forced to confront the defendant, post, at ___, 174 L. Ed. 2d, at 339, the same cannot be said of the fraudulent analyst. See Brief for National Innocence Network as Amicus Curiae 15-17 (discussing cases of documented "drylabbing" where forensic analysts report results of tests that were never performed); National Academy Report 1-8 to 1-10 (discussing documented cases of fraud and error involving the use of forensic evidence). Like the eyewitness who has fabricated his account to the police, the analyst who provides false results may, under oath in open court, reconsider his false testimony. See Coy v. Iowa, 487 U.S. 1012, 1019, 108 S. Ct. 2798, 101 L. Ed. 2d 857 (1988). And, of course, the prospect of confrontation will deter fraudulent analysis in the first place.

Confrontation is designed to weed out not only the fraudulent analyst, but the incompetent one as well. Serious deficiencies have been found in the forensic evidence used in criminal trials. One commentator asserts that "[t]he legal community now concedes, with varying degrees of urgency, that our system produces erroneous convictions based on discredited forensics." Metzger, Cheating the Constitution, 59 Vand. L. Rev. 475, 491 (2006). One study of cases in which exonerating evidence resulted in the overturning of criminal convictions concluded that invalid forensic testimony contributed to the convictions in 60% of the cases. . . .

Like expert witnesses generally, an analyst's lack of proper training or deficiency in judgment may be disclosed in cross-examination.

This case is illustrative. The affidavits submitted by the analysts contained only the bare-bones statement that "[t]he substance was found to contain: Cocaine." App. to

---

[22] [n.5] Though surely not always. Some forensic analyses, such as autopsies and breathalyzer tests, cannot be re-peated, and the specimens used for other analyses have often been lost or degraded.

Pet. for Cert. 24a, 26a, 28a. At the time of trial, petitioner did not know what tests the analysts performed, whether those tests were routine, and whether interpreting their results required the exercise of judgment or the use of skills that the analysts may not have possessed. While we still do not know the precise tests used by the analysts, we are told that the laboratories use "methodology recommended by the Scientific Working Group for the Analysis of Seized Drugs," App. to Brief for Petitioner 1a-2a. At least some of that methodology requires the exercise of judgment and presents a risk of error that might be explored on cross-examination. See 2 P. Giannelli & E. Imwinkelried, Scientific Evidence § 23.03[c], pp 532-533, ch. 23A, p 607 (4th ed. 2007) (identifying four "critical errors" that analysts may commit in interpreting the results of the commonly used gas chromatography/mass spectrometry analysis); Shellow, The Application of Daubert to the Identification of Drugs, 2 Shepard's Expert & Scientific Evidence Quarterly 593, 600 (1995) (noting that while spectrometers may be equipped with computerized matching systems, "forensic analysts in crime laboratories typically do not utilize this feature of the instrument, but rely exclusively on their subjective judgment").

The same is true of many of the other types of forensic evidence commonly used in criminal prosecutions. "[T]here is wide variability across forensic science disciplines with regard to techniques, methodologies, reliability, types and numbers of potential errors, research, general acceptability, and published material." National Academy Report S-5. See also id., at 5-9, 5-12, 5-17, 5-21 (discussing problems of subjectivity, bias, and unreliability of common forensic tests such as latent fingerprint analysis, pattern/impression analysis, and toolmark and firearms analysis). Contrary to respondent's and the dissent's suggestion, there is little reason to believe that confrontation will be useless in testing analysts' honesty, proficiency, and methodology — the features that are commonly the focus in the cross-examination of experts.

D

Respondent argues that the analysts' affidavits are admissible without confrontation because they are "akin to the types of official and business records admissible at common law." Brief for Respondent 35. But the affidavits do not qualify as traditional official or business records, and even if they did, their authors would be subject to confrontation nonetheless.

Documents kept in the regular course of business may ordinarily be admitted at trial despite their hearsay status. See Fed. Rule Evid. 803(6). But that is not the case if the regularly conducted business activity is the production of evidence for use at trial. Our decision in Palmer v. Hoffman, 318 U.S. 109, 63 S. Ct. 477, 87 L. Ed. 645 (1943), made that distinction clear. There we held that an accident report provided by an employee of a railroad company did not qualify as a business record because, although kept in the regular course of the railroad's operations, it was "calculated for use essentially in the court, not in the business." Id., at 114, 63 S. Ct. 477, 87 L. Ed. 6457 The analysts' certificates — like police reports generated by law enforcement officials — do not qualify as business or public records for precisely the same reason. See Rule 803(8) (defining public records as "excluding, however, in criminal cases matters observed by police officers and other law enforcement personnel"). . . .

The dissent identifies a single class of evidence which, though prepared for use at trial, was traditionally admissible: a clerk's certificate authenticating an official record — or a copy thereof — for use as evidence. See post, at ___, 174 L. Ed. 2d, at 344. But a clerk's authority in that regard was narrowly circumscribed. He was permitted "to certify to the correctness of a copy of a record kept in his office," but had "no authority to furnish, as evidence for the trial of a lawsuit, his interpretation of what the record contains or shows, or to certify to its substance or effect." State v. Wilson, 141 La. 404, 409, 75 So. 95, 97 (1917). . . . The dissent suggests that the fact that this exception was " 'narrowly circumscribed' " makes no difference. See post, at ___, 174 L. Ed. 2d, at 344. To the contrary, it makes all the difference in the world. It shows that even the line of cases establishing the one narrow exception the dissent has been able to identify simultaneously vindicates the general rule applicable to the present case. A clerk could by affidavit authenticate or provide a copy of an otherwise admissible record, but could not do what the analysts did here: create a record for the sole purpose of providing evidence against a defendant.

Far more probative here are those cases in which the prosecution sought to admit into evidence a clerk's certificate attesting to the fact that the clerk had searched for a particular relevant record and failed to find it. Like the testimony of the analysts in this case, the clerk's statement would serve as substantive evidence against the defendant whose guilt depended on the nonexistence of the record for which the clerk searched. Although the clerk's certificate would qualify as an official record under respondent's definition — it was prepared by a public officer in the regular course of his official duties — and although the clerk was certainly not a "conventional witness" under the dissent's approach, the clerk was nonetheless subject to confrontation. . . .[23]

Respondent also misunderstands the relationship between the business-and-official-records hearsay exceptions and the Confrontation Clause. As we stated in Crawford: "Most of the hearsay exceptions covered statements that by their nature were not testimonial — for example, business records or statements in furtherance of a conspiracy." 541 U.S., at 56, 124 S. Ct. 1354, 158 L. Ed. 2d 177. Business and public records are generally admissible absent confrontation not because they qualify under an exception to the hearsay rules, but because — having been created for the administration of an entity's affairs and not for the purpose of establishing or proving some fact at trial — they are not testimonial. Whether or not they qualify as business or official records, the analysts' statements here — prepared specifically for use at petitioner's trial — were testimony against

---

[23] [n.9] An earlier line of 19th century state-court cases also supports the notion that forensic analysts' certificates were not admitted into evidence as public or business records. See Commonwealth v. Waite, 93 Mass. 264, 266, 11 Allen 264 (1865); Shivers v. Newton, 45 N. J. L. 469, 476 (Sup. Ct. 1883); State v. Campbell, 64 N. H. 402, 403, 13 A. 585, 586 (1888). In all three cases, defendants — who were prosecuted for selling adulterated milk — objected to the admission of the state chemists' certificates of analysis. In all three cases, the objection was defeated because the chemist testified live at trial. That the prosecution came forward with live witnesses in all three cases suggests doubt as to the admissibility of the certificates without opportunity for cross-examination.

petitioner, and the analysts were subject to confrontation under the Sixth Amendment.

E

Respondent asserts that we should find no Confrontation Clause violation in this case because petitioner had the ability to subpoena the analysts. But that power — whether pursuant to state law or the Compulsory Process Clause — is no substitute for the right of confrontation. Unlike the Confrontation Clause, those provisions are of no use to the defendant when the witness is unavailable or simply refuses to appear. See, e.g., Davis, 547 U.S., at 820, 126 S. Ct. 2266, 165 L. Ed. 2d 224 ("[The witness] was subpoenaed, but she did not appear at . . . trial"). Converting the prosecution's duty under the Confrontation Clause into the defendant's privilege under state law or the Compulsory Process Clause shifts the consequences of adverse-witness no-shows from the State to the accused. More fundamentally, the Confrontation Clause imposes a burden on the prosecution to present its witnesses, not on the defendant to bring those adverse witnesses into court. Its value to the defendant is not replaced by a system in which the prosecution presents its evidence via ex parte affidavits and waits for the defendant to subpoena the affiants if he chooses.

F

Finally, respondent asks us to relax the requirements of the Confrontation Clause to accommodate the " 'necessities of trial and the adversary process.' " Brief for Respondent 59. It is not clear whence we would derive the authority to do so. The Confrontation Clause may make the prosecution of criminals more burdensome, but that is equally true of the right to trial by jury and the privilege against self-incrimination. The Confrontation Clause — like those other constitutional provisions — is binding, and we may not disregard it at our convenience. . . .

Perhaps the best indication that the sky will not fall after today's decision is that it has not done so already. Many States have already adopted the constitutional rule we announce today, while many others permit the defendant to assert (or forfeit by silence) his Confrontation Clause right after receiving notice of the prosecution's intent to use a forensic analyst's report, id., at 13-15 (cataloging such state laws). Despite these widespread practices, there is no evidence that the criminal justice system has ground to a halt in the States that, one way or another, empower a defendant to insist upon the analyst's appearance at trial. . . .

In their simplest form, notice-and-demand statutes require the prosecution to provide notice to the defendant of its intent to use an analyst's report as evidence at trial, after which the defendant is given a period of time in which he may object to the admission of the evidence absent the analyst's appearance live at trial. Contrary to the dissent's perception, these statutes shift no burden whatever. The defendant always has the burden of raising his Confrontation Clause objection; notice-and-demand statutes simply govern the time within which he must do so. States are free to adopt procedural rules governing objections. It is common to require a defendant to exercise his rights under the Compulsory Process Clause in advance of trial, announcing his intent to present certain witnesses. There is no conceivable reason why he cannot similarly be compelled to exercise his Confrontation Clause rights before trial. See Hinojos-Mendoza v. People, 169 P. 3d 662, 670 (Colo. 2007) (discussing and approving Colorado's notice-and-demand provision). Today's decision will not disrupt criminal prosecutions in the many large States whose practice is already in accord with the Confrontation Clause.

BEECH AIRCRAFT v. RAINEY
Supreme Court of the United States
488 U.S. 153 (1988)

[A Navy training aircraft crashed in Alabama in 1982 after making a sharp turn to avoid another training aircraft. The plaintiffs brought a product liability suit alleging a defective fuel control system. The defendants claimed that the crash occurred because of pilot error.]

At trial, the only seriously disputed question was whether pilot error or equipment malfunction had caused the crash. Both sides relied primarily on expert testimony. One piece of evidence presented by the defense was an investigative report prepared by Lieutenant Commander William Morgan on order of the training squadron's commanding officer and pursuant to authority granted in the Manual of the Judge Advocate General. This "JAG Report," completed during the six weeks following the accident, was organized into sections labeled "finding of fact," "opinions," and "recommendations," and was supported by some 60 attachments. . . .

The trial judge initially determined, at a pretrial conference, that the JAG Report was sufficiently trustworthy to be admissible, but that it "would be admissible only on its factual findings and would not be admissible insofar as any opinions or conclusions are concerned." The day before trial, however, the court reversed itself and ruled, over the plaintiffs' objection, that certain of the conclusions would be admitted. Accordingly, the court admitted most of the report's "opinions," including the first sentence of paragraph 5 about the impossibility of determining exactly what happened, and paragraph 7, which opined about failure to maintain proper interval as "[t]he most probable cause of the accident."

[After a two-week trial, the jury returned a verdict for the aircraft company. On appeal, a panel of the 11th Circuit reversed and remanded for a new trial, holding (as per precedent in the circuit) that Rule 803(8)(C) did not encompass evaluative conclusions or opinions. An en banc panel of the 11th Circuit reinstated the panel's judgment. The Supreme Court granted certiorari.] . . .

Controversy over what "public records and reports" are made not excludable by Rule 803(8)(C) has divided the federal courts from the beginning. In the present litigation, the Court of Appeals followed the "narrow" interpretation of Smith v. Ithaca Corp., supra, at 220-223, which held that the term "factual findings" did not encompass "opinions" or "conclusions." Courts of Appeals other than those of the Fifth and Eleventh Circuits, however, have generally adopted a broader interpretation. For example, the Court of Appeals for the Sixth Circuit, in Baker v. Elcona Homes Corp., 588 F. 2d 551, 557-558 (1978), cert. denied, 441 U.S. 933

(1979), held that "factual findings admissible under Rule 803(8)(C) may be those which are made by the preparer of the report from disputed evidence. . . ." The other Courts of Appeals that have squarely confronted the issue have also adopted the broader interpretation. . . .

Because the Federal Rules of Evidence are a legislative enactment, we turn to the "traditional tools of statutory construction," INS v. Cardoza-Fonseca, 480 U.S. 421, 446 (1987), in order to construe their provisions. We begin with the language of the Rule itself. Proponents of the narrow view have generally relied heavily on a perceived dichotomy between "fact" and "opinion" in arguing for the limited scope of the phrase "factual findings." Smith v. Ithaca Corp. contrasted the term "factual findings" in Rule 803(8)(C) with the language of Rule 803(6) (records of regularly conducted activity), which expressly refers to "opinions" and "diagnoses." "Factual findings," the court opined, must be something other than opinions. 612 F. 2d, at 221-222.

For several reasons, we do not agree. In the first place, it is not apparent that the term "factual findings" should be read to mean simply "facts" (as opposed to "opinions" or "conclusions"). A common definition of "finding of fact" is, for example, "[a] conclusion by way of reasonable inference from the evidence." Black's Law Dictionary 569 (5th ed. 1979). To say the least, the language of the Rule does not compel us to reject the interpretation that "factual findings" includes conclusions or opinions that flow from a factual investigation. Second, we note that, contrary to what is often assumed, the language of the Rule does not state that "factual findings" are admissible, but that "reports . . . setting forth . . . factual findings" (emphasis added) are admissible. On this reading, the language of the Rule does not create a distinction between "fact" and "opinion" contained in such reports.

Turning next to the legislative history of Rule 803(8)(C), we find no clear answer to the question of how the Rule's language should be interpreted. Indeed, in this litigation the legislative history may well be at the origin of the dispute. Rather than the more usual situation where a court must attempt to glean meaning from ambiguous comments of legislators who did not focus directly on the problem at hand, here the Committees in both Houses of Congress clearly recognized and expressed their opinions on the precise question at issue. Unfortunately, however, they took diametrically opposite positions. Moreover, the two Houses made no effort to reconcile their views, either through changes in the Rule's language or through a statement in the Report of the Conference Committee. . . .

Clearly this legislative history reveals a difference of view between the Senate and the House that affords no definitive guide to the congressional understanding. It seems clear however that the Senate understanding is more in accord with the wording of the Rule and with the comments of the Advisory Committee.

The Advisory Committee's comments are notable, first, in that they contain no mention of any dichotomy between statements of "fact" and "opinions" or "conclusions." What was on the Committee's mind was simply whether what it called "evaluative reports" should be admissible. Illustrating the previous division among the courts on this subject, the Committee cited numerous cases in which the admissibility of such reports had been both sustained and denied. It also took note of various federal statutes that made certain kinds of evaluative reports admissible in evidence. What is striking about all of these examples is that these were reports that stated conclusions. E. g., Moran v. Pittsburgh-Des Moines Steel Co., 183 F. 2d 467, 472-473 (CA3 1950) (report of Bureau of Mines concerning the cause of a gas tank explosion admissible); Franklin v. Skelly Oil Co., 141 F. 2d 568, 571-572 (CA10 1944) (report of state fire marshal on the cause of a gas explosion inadmissible); 42 U. S. C. § 269(b) (bill of health by appropriate official admissible as prima facie evidence of vessel's sanitary history and condition). The Committee's concern was clearly whether reports of this kind should be admissible. Nowhere in its comments is there the slightest indication that it even considered the solution of admitting only "factual" statements from such reports. Rather, the Committee referred throughout to "reports," without any such differentiation regarding the statements they contained. What the Committee referred to in the Rule's language as "reports . . . setting forth . . . factual findings" is surely nothing more or less than what in its commentary it called "evaluative reports." Its solution as to their admissibility is clearly stated in the final paragraph of its report on this Rule. That solution consists of two principles: First, "the rule . . . assumes admissibility in the first instance. . . ." Second, it provides "ample provision for escape if sufficient negative factors are present."

That "provision for escape" is contained in the final clause of the Rule: evaluative reports are admissible "unless the sources of information or other circumstances indicate lack of trust-worthiness." This trustworthiness inquiry — and not an arbitrary distinction between "fact" and "opinion" — was the Committee's primary safeguard against the admission of unreliable evidence, and it is important to note that it applies to all elements of the report. Thus, a trial judge has the discretion, and indeed the obligation, to exclude an entire report or portions thereof — whether narrow "factual" statements or broader "conclusions" — that she determines to be untrustworthy.[24] Moreover, safeguards built into other portions of the Federal Rules, such as those dealing with relevance and prejudice, provide the court with additional means of scrutinizing and, where appropriate, excluding evaluative reports or portions of them. And of course it goes without saying that the admission of a report containing "conclusions" is subject to the ultimate safeguard — the opponent's right to present evidence tending to contradict or diminish the weight of those conclusions.

In a case similar in many respects to these, the trial court applied the trustworthiness requirement to hold inadmissible a JAG Report on the causes of a Navy airplane accident; it found the report untrustworthy because it "was prepared by an inexperienced investigator in a highly complex field of investigation." Fraley v. Rockwell Int'l Corp., 470 F. Supp. 1264, 1267 (SD Ohio 1979). In the present litigation, the District Court found the JAG Report to be

---

[24] [n.11] The Advisory Committee proposed a nonexclusive list of four factors it thought would be helpful in passing on this question: (1) the timeliness of the investigation; (2) the investigator's skill or experience; (3) whether a hearing was held; and (4) possible bias when reports are prepared with a view to possible litigation (citing Palmer v. Hoffman, 318 U.S. 109 (1943)). Advisory Committee's Notes on Fed. Rule Evid. 803(8), 28 U. S. C. App., p. 725; see Note, The Trustworthiness of Government Evaluative Reports under Federal Rule of Evidence 803(8)(C), 96 Harv. L. Rev. 492 (1982).

trustworthy. App. 35. As no party has challenged that finding, we have no occasion to express an opinion on it.

Our conclusion that neither the language of the Rule nor the intent of its framers calls for a distinction between "fact" and "opinion" is strengthened by the analytical difficulty of drawing such a line. It has frequently been remarked that the distinction between statements of fact and opinion is, at best, one of degree. . . .

In the present action, the trial court had no difficulty in admitting as a factual finding the statement in the JAG Report that "[a]t the time of impact, the engine of 3E955 was operating but was operating at reduced power." Surely this "factual finding" could also be characterized as an opinion, which the investigator presumably arrived at on the basis of clues contained in the airplane wreckage. Rather than requiring that we draw some inevitably arbitrary line between the various shades of fact/opinion that invariably will be present in investigatory reports, we believe the Rule instructs us — as its plain language states — to admit "reports . . . setting forth . . . factual findings." The Rule's limitations and safeguards lie elsewhere: First, the requirement that reports contain factual findings bars the admission of statements not based on factual investigation. Second, the trustworthiness provision requires the court to make a determination as to whether the report, or any portion thereof, is sufficiently trustworthy to be admitted.

A broad approach to admissibility under Rule 803(8)(C), as we have outlined it, is also consistent with the Federal Rules' general approach of relaxing the traditional barriers to "opinion" testimony. Rules 702-705 permit experts to testify in the form of an opinion, and without any exclusion of opinions on "ultimate issues." And Rule 701 permits even a lay witness to testify in the form of opinions or inferences drawn from her observations when testimony in that form will be helpful to the trier of fact. We see no reason to strain to reach an interpretation of Rule 803(8)(C) that is contrary to the liberal thrust of the Federal Rules.[25]

We hold, therefore, that portions of investigatory reports otherwise admissible under Rule 803(8)(C) are not inadmissible merely because they state a conclusion or opinion. As long as the conclusion is based on a factual investigation and satisfies the Rule's trustworthiness requirement, it should be admissible along with other portions of the report. As the trial judge in this action determined that certain of the JAG Report's conclusions were trustworthy, he rightly allowed them to be admitted into evidence. We therefore reverse the judgment of the Court of Appeals in respect of the Rule 803(8)(C) issue.

---

[25] [n.12] The cited Rules refer, of course, to situations — unlike that at issue — where the opinion testimony is subject to cross-examination. But the determination that cross-examination was not indispensable in regard to official investigatory reports has already been made, and our point is merely that imposing a rigid distinction between fact and opinion would run against the Rules' tendency to deemphasize that dichotomy.

DISCUSSION QUESTIONS

1. *Melendez-Diaz* holds that certain laboratory reports are testimonial, requiring confrontation in order to be introduced into evidence. Compare the holding in *Melendez-Diaz* with the statement in Gianelli's article about the routine nature of many laboratory reports that merely identify substances or describe their objective characteristics, a task described as "ministerial" in nature. In the aftermath of *Melendez-Diaz*, are there still ministerial laboratory reports that can (or should) be admitted into evidence in criminal cases as public records or business records?

2. Suppose that several analysts worked on identifying evidence in a case and producing a laboratory report. Does the Confrontation Clause require the production of all of them in court for cross-examination? Why or why not? Where and how would you draw the line?

3. A notice-and-demand statute establishes a statutory deadline by which a criminal defendant must provide notice to the prosecution of its demand to exercise its confrontation rights. Do these statutes adequately protect the defendant's Confrontation Clause rights? What are some of the benefits of such statutes? What are their drawbacks? Do these statutes amount to burden shifting? Make the case for and against an argument of burden-shifting.

4. In *Beech Aircraft v. Rainey*, the Supreme Court settled a circuit split about the meaning of the term "factual findings" in Clause C of Rule 803(8). If a trial judge decides that opinions — such as the ones in the *Beech Aircraft* case — are trustworthy and permits the record to be introduced without cross-examination, does this impinge on the fact-finding role of the jury in the case? Why or why not? If a report is entered into evidence against a party, what recourse does that party have to ensure the jury is aware of the trustworthiness issues with the report?

PROBLEMS

Problem 24-1. Amy and Brandon run a daycare center that serves federally subsidized meals to children. For several years, the center has submitted an inflated count of meals served to the government.

During a state agency administrative hearing, Brandon tells investigators that no one at the center ever knowingly submitted an inflated count. He says they were merely using a formula that had been provided to them by the government for estimating meals served. The hearing officer included Brandon's testimony in the final report. At the time of the hearing, neither Amy nor Brandon had yet been charged with any crime, although later, both were.

At her criminal trial, Amy wants to introduce Brandon's testimony from his hearing under 803(8). Is the report admissible? Why or why not?

Problem 24-2. Larry was indicted for lying to a grand jury about a trip to Mexico last July 15. At trial, the government offered into evidence a computer printout from the Department of Homeland Security listing the license plate numbers of all vehicles that had crossed the border on July 15. Larry's license plate number was on the list. Under what rule should the prosecution seek to admit the list? How should the defense respond? How should the judge rule?

Problem 24-3. Dan Defendant was pulled over for driving erratically in Calamity City. The arresting officer noticed a strong odor of alcohol emanating from Dan, and he had Dan perform a field sobriety test. Dan failed the test and refused to take a Breathalyzer test. The officer obtained a warrant to seize blood from Dan and have it tested for blood-alcohol content. The blood was properly drawn and sent to the Calamity State Police Crime Lab. Alan Analyst ran the standard tests on the blood, using a gas chromatograph machine, and determined that Dan's blood alcohol content was .18, well above the legal limit for driving. The laboratory report contained the following information: (1) the arresting officer's name; (2) reason the suspect was stopped (the officer wrote, "driving erratically" in this block); (3) the date and time the blood was drawn; (4) signature blocks of the officer who observed the blood draw, the nurse who drew the blood, and the intake clerk at the Crime Lab. The report also contained a "Certificate of Analyst," signed by Alan Analyst. The certificate recorded Dan's blood alcohol level as 0.18 grams per hundred milliliters, and affirmed the following: (1) the seal of the sample was received intact and broken in the laboratory; (2) the statements in the analyst's block of the report are correct; and (3) that Alan had followed the proper procedures to retain the sample container and raw data. The certificate also contained the signature of Sue Supervisor, who certified that she had reviewed Alan's work, that Alan had followed established procedures in examining the sample, and that Alan was qualified to conduct the BAC test using a gas chromatograph.

At Dan's trial for aggravated DUI, the state announced that Alan was out on unpaid leave and would not be testifying at trial. The state offered to introduce the report standing alone under Rule 803(8). It proposed in the alternative to call Charles Chemist, another analyst at the lab, to testify about the procedures employed at the lab and to introduce the report as a business record under Rule 803(6). Charles Chemist and Alan Analyst do similar work but do not know each other and have never worked on the same project.

What arguments can the prosecution make in favor of admitting the report? How should the defense respond? How should the judge rule, and why?

Public Records: Quick Hits

- Public records and reports are considered trustworthy because of the motivation of public servants and government officials to perform their duties and the scrutiny to which public records are subjected.

- Rule 803(8) covers three types of public records: (A) those setting forth activities of the office or agency; (B) matters observed pursuant to duty imposed by law; (C) factual findings resulting from investigations.

- Because of confrontation clause issues, Clause B records created by the police and Clause C records are not admissible in evidence against criminal defendants.

- The absence of an entry in a public record where one would expect to find it is admissible of proof as non-existence of a fact.

- Many government records are self-authenticating.

Chapter References

CHRISTOPHER B. MUELLER & LAIRD C. KIRKPATRICK, EVIDENCE §§ 8.49–8.54 (4th ed. 2009).

GLEN WEISSENBERGER & JAMES J. DUANE, FEDERAL RULES OF EVIDENCE: RULES, LEGISLATIVE HISTORY, COMMENTARY AND AUTHORITY §§ 803.39–803.46, 803.51–803.52 (6th ed. 2009).

JACK B. WEINSTEIN & MARGARET A. BERGER, WEINSTEIN'S FEDERAL EVIDENCE §§ 803.10–803.12 (Joseph M. McLaughlin ed., Matthew Bender 2d ed. 1997).

KENNETH S. BROUN, MCCORMICK ON EVIDENCE §§ 295–300 (6th ed. 2006).

STEVEN GOODE & OLIN GUY WELLBORN III, COURTROOM HANDBOOK ON FEDERAL EVIDENCE Ch. 5 (West 2010).

III.   APPLICATION EXERCISE

Uses of Public Records at Trial

If admitted into evidence, a public record goes back into the jury room with the rest of the evidence that has been admitted at trial. Thus, even if the public official is present to testify at trial and be cross-examined, there is a powerful incentive to have the report admitted into evidence. The report will be available to the jury in written form and will therefore be available for review and use in the jury's deliberations, unlike live testimony, which is subject to the vagaries of juror memory during deliberations.

As discussed earlier in this chapter, sometimes it makes no difference whether a document is admissible under Rule 803(6) or any of the three clauses of Rule 803(8) — and sometimes it makes a profound difference. In dealing with public records at trial, counsel should be prepared to address all possible theories of admissibility, whether they are seeking to admit or exclude a public record.

The Exercise

Objective: To demonstrate understanding of the foundational elements and permissible uses of a record during a criminal trial.

Factual Scenario: The Calamity State Department of Human Services (DHS) brought a child-in-need of care petition to remove 10-year-old Doyle Donner from his home last year. The primary allegation was neglect. School officials contacted DHS and reported that Doyle was dirty, undernourished, and inadequately clothed for weather conditions. DHS sent a social worker, Les Landers, to investigate the situation. Landers' report was, to say the least, not flattering to Dale and Denise Donner, Doyle's parents.

Based on the report, DHS officials removed Doyle from the home and filed a petition in state court. Doyle was removed from the home by order of a judge. Not long after the removal, the State's Attorney filed felony Child Neglect charges against Doyle's parents. Denise Donner pled guilty, but Dale Donner insisted on a jury trial, alleging he had done nothing wrong. He is represented at trial by an attorney from the Public Defender Service.

Advance Preparation: Review the materials appended to the end of this exercise. Prepare direct and cross-examinations of Les Lander. Prepare arguments for and against the admissibility of the records in this case.

The report written by Les Landers is attached.

A brief written report of a physical examination of Doyle, accompanied by a self-authentication certificate from the doctor's office, is also attached.

In addition, the summarized transcript of Lander's testimony in support of the Child in Need of Care petition is attached.

In-Class Exercise: Students will play the roles of Les Lander, State's Attorney, Defense Attorney and Judge. The State's Attorney will call Les Lander as a witness and conduct a direct examination of Les. The attorney will attempt to introduce Les's report and the medical record into evidence using the appropriate rules of evidence. The defense attorney will make appropriate objections to the report. The judge will rule.

Documents for Exercise

DHS Child Neglect Investigation Official Report

Date: February 15, Last Year.

Executive Summary

On February 10, Last Year, the undersigned, Les Lander, LCSW, received an assignment from Donnie Brook, Supervisor of the Calamity City Field Office of the DHS, to investigate a report of child neglect from the Calamity City Elementary School. The allegation was that Doyle Donner was a neglected child and was dirty, malnourished and inadequately clothed. In the course of the investigation, the undersigned interviewed Wilma Einstein, the child's teacher; Dwight Shrift, the assistant principal; and Dale and Denise Donner, the child's parents. The undersigned also visited the Donner home.

Based on these interviews and home visit, the undersigned concludes that the report of child neglect is founded and that the child should be removed from the home and placed in care of the Calamity DHS.

Investigative Findings

1. On February 9, Last Year, Dwight Shrift, assistant principal of Calamity City Elementary School, called DHS to report a possible case of child neglect. Shrift stated that Doyle Donner, a 10-year-old child was "dirty, unkempt, ill-clothed, and malnourished." Shrift expressed concern that Doyle was being neglected by Dale and Denise Donner, the parents. The report was logged by Reba Record, a DHS intake clerk and examined by the undersigned prior to beginning the investigation.

2. On the afternoon of February 10, last year, the undersigned met with Shrift. Also present at the meeting was Wilma Einstein, Doyle's teacher. Both reported that Doyle consistently had poor hygiene and often smelled bad. They reported that on the 9th, Doyle came to school without a coat. Einstein said that Doyle was often hungry, especially at school parties, and seemed to "have a tapeworm." He once ate 6 Devil's Food cupcakes. Both reported that Doyle was thin and appeared "poorly."

3. Shrift said that in his past dealings with the parents, they were belligerent, unsupportive, and indifferent. He reported that Doyle had experienced a number of discipline-related problems at school and that the parents seemed inappropriately unconcerned about them.

4. On February 11, last year, the undersigned conducted a home visit of the Donner residence at 1235 North Main Street in Calamity City. The home is located in a rough part of town. The lawn is ill-kept, trash litters the yard, and the home itself is deteriorating from a lack of maintenance. The interior of the home smells strongly of cat urine. The undersigned observed animal fecal matter and garbage strewn throughout the house.

5. Both of the Donners were present. They are unemployed and disabled. Doyle is an only child. The parents are both obese. They were hostile and suspicious. Mrs. Donner accused me of trying to take away her baby. Mr. Donner expressed concern that they would receive lower AFDC payments if the child were taken. When asked about the hygiene conditions in the home, Mrs. Donner said it was a little cluttered, but she wasn't the best housekeeper in the world. Mr. Donner said that Doyle refused to bathe or wear a coat, and there was nothing anyone could do about that. When asked to produce Doyle's coat, he could not locate it and said Doyle had probably hidden it somewhere.

6. Mrs. Donner admitted to withholding food from Doyle as a punishment but could not remember the last time she had done it. Both parents said Doyle was naturally skinny, and Mr. Donner said he had once looked exactly like Doyle.

7. Mr. Donner called both Shrift and Einstein "morons," and indicated they were out to get him because he had threatened to call the police on Shrift.

8. The Donners refused to let me talk to Doyle without an attorney present.

9. Based on the reports of school officials, the condition of the home, and the attitude of the parents, it is my professional opinion that Doyle is a neglected child within the meaning of the Calamity Code § 45-678(1).

10. The undersigned recommends immediate removal of the child from the home.

/s/

Les Lander, LCSW

Physical Examination of Doyle Donner

On February 12, 2010, DHS officials presented Doyle Donner, a 10-year-old child, to this office for an examination. I examined the child.

[Assume this is a standard physical form, recording that Doyle is a 10-year-old child. He is 4'5" and 53 pounds. His height and weight are in the bottom 10% of children for his age. He is healthy, but malnourished. No signs of physical abuse are noted.]

Physician's note: When I asked Doyle why he was so skinny, he told me that "Mom and Dad get mad at me and won't let me eat anything." Doyle said this happens an average of 2-3 times per week and he is often locked in his room during these times.

/s/

Doctor Love, M.D.

Pediatrician

Certificate of Authentication

1. The undersigned certifies that the above record was made at or near the time of the occurrence of the matters set forth in the record by a person with knowledge of the matters contained in the record.

2. The record is kept and maintained as part of the regular course of activity Calamity Charity Hospital in Calamity City, Calamity.

/s/ and sealed

Robert Recorder

Records Clerk

Calamity Charity Hospital

Lander Transcript

This is a summarized transcript of the testimony of Les Lander, the LCSW from the Business and Public Records Application Exercise, in support of the child in need of care petition that removed Doyle from his parents' care. You may use this transcript for additional information to assist you in preparing for the application exercise.

Les Lander, LCSW, Calamity State DHS, was called and testified substantially as follows in the Matter of Doyle Donner.

Lander became involved in case after receiving assignment from Donnie Brook, supervisor. The agency received a report that Doyle was a neglected child. Report was taken by Reba Record, a clerk, and recorded on Form 2-1. According to the form, Doyle's teachers believed he was neglected because he was dirty, malnourished, and dressed inappropriately for weather conditions. The form no longer exists. Lander believes he lost the form when some papers blew out of his state vehicle during the investigation.

Lander then called the school to set up an appointment with Dwight Shrift and Wilma Einstein. Shrift was school principal. Einstein was Doyle's teacher. They met at the school on Feb. 10. In the interview, Shrift and Einstein told Lander that Doyle was dirty, often smelled bad and was always hungry. He once ate 6 king-size Devil's Food cupcakes at a school party. He always looked hungry and acted like he had a tapeworm. His personal hygiene was bad. He wore dirty clothes, had greasy hair, and smelled as if he had not bathed. He did not wear appropriate clothing for weather conditions, usually a light jacket or nothing at all. On Feb. 9, the day of the report, Doyle did not wear a coat to school. This caused concern because it was only 15 degrees on the 9th, there was freezing rain, and the child walked to school.

Following the interview, Lander decided to make a home visit and made an appointment to visit the next day, Feb. 11, at 3 pm. Lander kept the appointment.

The home was filthy. It smelled of cat urine. There were dog and cat feces on the floor all over the house. Dirty clothes everywhere. Dirty dishes in the sink. The smell of rotting food from the kitchen. Cigarettes and body odor. Upon walking in door, Lander said, under breath, "this is one of the dirtiest places I've ever seen in my life." Mrs. Donner overheard the statement and replied "I'm not the best housekeeper in the world. Sometimes it gets a little cluttered around here." Lander said that was the understatement of the year.

The parents were suspicious, upset and belligerent in attitude. Lander asked about the boy's hygiene, and they replied that Doyle didn't like to bathe, so they didn't push the point with him. Lander asked about the boy's appetite. His mother said he was always hungry, like he had a tapeworm. The father said Doyle reminded him of himself at that age.

Lander asked whether Doyle received adequate nutrition at home. The mother claimed to feed him three meals a day, except when he was in trouble. Lander asked for clarification and was told that if Doyle was disrespectful to his parents in any way, they would withhold meals from him. The parents were not sure how often this occurred but thought about once a week. They told Landers they thought this was an appropriate form of discipline. The father said, "It worked for me when I was his age, and it works for him."

Landers next discussed the issue of Doyle's inappropriate clothing. He told the parents that the school reported that Doyle was walked to school on a 15-degree day with icy rain. In response, Mr. Donner became extremely upset. His face turned red, and he started hyperventilating a little, and he said, "Shrift is a jackass. He's out to get me." Lander followed up and learned that earlier in the week, Mr. Donner had called Shrift to complain about a detention Doyle had received. During their conversation, Donner threatened to call the police on Shrift. Donner also threatened to call the police on Lander and report him for harassment.

Lander returned to the subject of the coat. The parents admitted Doyle had gone to school without a coat and said you just couldn't get him to wear a coat, so they let him go out without one if that's what he wanted to do. Lander asked to see the coat and the parents could not produce or find it. Mr. Donner said that Doyle had probably hidden it.

The next day, Lander took Doyle to see Dr. Love, a pediatrician at Calamity Charity Hospital. He sat in on the examination, as per standard protocol. He recalls Doyle telling the doctor that he was hungry all the time and his parents were always making him go to bed without supper. Dr. Love's opinion was that the boy was probably malnourished.

Chapter 25

HEARSAY EXCEPTIONS REQUIRING THE UNAVAILABILITY OF THE DECLARANT: RULE 804

> ## Chapter Objectives:
>
> - Introduce and explain the hearsay exceptions requiring unavailability under Rule 804
> - Analyze and discuss issues pertaining to unavailability and the admissibility of hearsay under Rule 804
> - Apply the concepts from this chapter in a courtroom application exercise

I. BACKGROUND AND EXPLANATORY MATERIAL

Introduction to Hearsay Exceptions Requiring Unavailability

Admissible hearsay under the Rules is broadly divided into two major categories: (1) Rule 803, hearsay where the availability of the declarant is immaterial; and (2) Rule 804, hearsay requiring a prior finding of unavailability. The reason for requiring unavailability is that the types of hearsay encompassed by Rule 804 are considered less trustworthy than hearsay under Rule 803. The Advisory Committee notes to Rule 804 explain the difference in treatment of hearsay under Rules 803 and 804:

> Rule 803 supra, is based upon the assumption that a hearsay statement falling within one of its exceptions possesses qualities which justify the conclusion that whether the declarant is available or unavailable is not a relevant factor in determining admissibility. The instant rule proceeds upon a different theory: hearsay which admittedly is not equal in quality to testimony of the declarant on the stand may nevertheless be admitted if the declarant is unavailable and if his statement meets a specified standard. The rule expresses preferences: testimony given on the stand in person is

preferred over hearsay, and hearsay, if of the specified quality, is preferred over complete loss of the evidence of the declarant.

Thus, evidence offered under Rule 804 falls into a hierarchy under which live testimony is preferred to hearsay, but hearsay is preferred to no testimony at all.

Each of the hearsay exceptions codified in Rule 804 is based on common law doctrines developed over the course of many years. Rule 804 provides for the admissibility of five types of hearsay statements: (1) former testimony; (2) dying declarations; (3) statements against interest (penal, pecuniary or proprietary); (4) statements of personal or family history; and (5) statements admissible because of a party's wrongdoing that results in the unavailability of a witness.

This chapter first addresses the concept of unavailability, then discusses the Rule 804 hearsay exceptions. Rule 804(b)(4), statements of personal or family history, is not covered in this text. Rule 804(b)(6), forfeiture by wrongdoing, is covered in the section on unavailability.

Unavailability

Through Dec. 1, 2011	After Dec. 1, 2011
Rule 804. Hearsay Exceptions; Declarant Unavailable	**Rule 804. Exceptions to the Rule Against Hearsay — When the Declarant Is Unavailable as a Witness**
(a) Definition of unavailability. "Unavailability as a witness" includes situations in which the declarant—	**(a) Criteria for Being Unavailable.** A declarant is considered to be unavailable as a witness if the declarant:
(1) is exempted by ruling of the court on the ground of privilege from testifying concerning the subject matter of the declarant's statement; or	(1) is exempted from testifying about the subject matter of the declarant's statement because the court rules that a privilege applies;
(2) persists in refusing to testify concerning the subject matter of the declarant's statement despite an order of the court to do so; or	(2) refuses to testify about the subject matter despite a court order to do so;
(3) testifies to a lack of memory of the subject matter of the declarant's statement; or	(3) testifies to not remembering the subject matter;
(4) is unable to be present or to testify at the hearing because of death or then existing physical or mental illness or infirmity; or	(4) cannot be present or testify at the trial or hearing because of death or a then-existing infirmity, physical illness, or mental illness; or
(5) is absent from the hearing and the proponent of a statement has been unable to procure the declarant's attendance (or in the case of a hearsay exception under subdivision (b)(2), (3), or (4), the declarant's attendance or testimony) by process or other reasonable means.	(5) is absent from the trial or hearing and the statement's proponent has not been able, by process or other reasonable means, to procure:
	(A) the declarant's attendance, in the case of a hearsay exception under Rule 804(b)(1) or (6); or
A declarant is not unavailable as a witness if exemption, refusal, claim of lack of memory, inability, or absence is due to the procurement or wrongdoing of the proponent of a statement for the purpose of preventing the witness from attending or testifying.	(B) the declarant's attendance or testimony, in the case of a hearsay exception under Rule 804(b)(2), (3), or (4).
	But this subdivision (a) does not apply if the statement's proponent procured or wrongfully caused the declarant's unavailability as a witness in order to prevent the declarant from attending or testifying.

The proponent of evidence under Rule 804 has the burden to demonstrate unavailability of the hearsay declarant by a preponderance of the evidence. The threshold finding of unavailability is critical to this rule because of the strong preference for live testimony and cross-examination at trial. The determination of unavailability is a judicial decision under Rule 104(a).

Death is the ultimate, irrefutable form of unavailability, but unavailability can also be caused by other factors including the exercise of a privilege, refusal to testify, forgetfulness, mental or physical illness, or absence because legal process cannot be used to secure the declarant's testimony. A party seeking a declaration of unavailability must have clean hands: Rule 804(a) specifically precludes the use of hearsay if the declarant's unavailability is "due to the procurement or wrongdoing of the proponent of a statement for the purpose of preventing the witness from attending or testifying."

As a corollary to this principle, Rule 804(b)(6) provides that an opponent of a hearsay statement forfeits the exclusion of evidence under the hearsay rule if the opponent "has engaged or acquiesced in wrongdoing that was intended to, and did, procure the unavailability of the declarant of the witness." In criminal cases involving forfeiture by wrongdoing, an accused forfeits not only his hearsay objections to evidence, but also any constitutional objections — such as confrontation — to the introduction of the evidence against him.

Making a claim of unavailability is not merely a *pro forma* exercise under the Rules. For example, in the case of unavailability due to the exercise of a privilege, an actual claim of privilege in court is generally required. This means that the witness who will be unavailable because of a privilege must show up in court and actually claim the privilege. It is not enough for the proponent of the evidence to aver or predict that the witness would claim the privilege. There are exceptions, of course: in some circumstances, such as a co-defendant's exercise of the constitutional privilege against self-incrimination, courts may not require an in-person claim of the privilege. A criminal defendant's exercise of the privilege against self-incrimination does not entitle the defendant to introduce his own prior statements under Rule 804.

In the case of refusal to testify, the witness will not be declared unavailable until after the judge has ordered the witness to testify and the witness has refused. A mere declaration from an attorney that a witness is unwilling to testify does not carry the same significance as an in-court order to testify, followed by the witness's refusal to do so.

When a party claims that a witness is unavailable because of illness or infirmity, the judge must consider both the duration and the severity of the illness and/or the nature of the infirmity before declaring the witness unavailable. In many instances, a short trial delay or re-ordering of the witnesses under Rule 611 (which recognizes the judge's power to exercise "reasonable control over the mode and order of interrogating witnesses") will be sufficient to solve a temporary problem with unavailability.

Physical absence from the proceedings is another reason to claim unavailability. In order to maintain a claim of unavailability, the proponent must not only enter the situation with clean hands, but must also demonstrate efforts to procure the attendance of the witness at trial. In criminal cases, the prosecution must show a good-faith effort to procure the attendance of witnesses. Of course, the Confrontation Clause must also be satisfied before testimonial hearsay from absent witnesses can be introduced at trial.

In civil cases, parties must demonstrate efforts to procure the attendance of witnesses by serving a subpoena and tendering appropriate fees under Federal

Rule of Civil Procedure 45 or an equivalent state rule. Where a witness is not amenable to process — for example, if the witness is located more than 100 miles from the trial location — the proponent still must show that it used reasonable means to procure the witness's presence. In some cases, witnesses might be willing to attend the trial voluntarily or be able to testify by means of electronic technology.

II.   ANALYSIS AND DISCUSSION

Former Testimony

Through Dec. 1, 2011	After Dec. 1, 2011
Rule 804. Hearsay Exceptions; Declarant Unavailable	**Rule 804. Exceptions to the Rule Against Hearsay — When the Declarant Is Unavailable as a Witness**
(b) Hearsay exceptions. The following are not excluded by the hearsay rule if the declarant is unavailable as a witness:	**(b) The Exceptions**. The following are not excluded by the rule against hearsay if the declarant is unavailable as a witness:
(1) Former testimony. Testimony given as a witness at another hearing of the same or a different proceeding, or in a deposition taken in compliance with law in the course of the same or another proceeding, if the party against whom the testimony is now offered, or, in a civil action or proceeding, a predecessor in interest, had an opportunity and similar motive to develop the testimony by direct, cross, or redirect examination.	*(1) Former Testimony*. Testimony that: (A) was given as a witness at a trial, hearing, or lawful deposition, whether given during the current proceeding or a different one; and (B) is now offered against a party who had — or, in a civil case, whose predecessor in interest had — an opportunity and similar motive to develop it by direct, cross-, or redirect examination.

Basis

The adversarial trial system favors the production and presence of live witnesses at trial whenever possible. With a live witness, the jury can view for itself a witness's demeanor, presentation, sincerity, narrative ability, and perhaps most importantly, performance in the face of cross-examination. The introduction of hearsay evidence at trial is disfavored because it deprives the jury of the opportunity to gauge the declarant's credibility first-hand in evaluating the testimony.

Former testimony differs from other hearsay exceptions under Rules 803 and 804 because it has already passed through many of the significant reliability portals provided by the adversarial trial system: it was given under oath, in a deposition or adversary proceeding, subject to cross-examination. Because of these factors, former testimony is considered much more reliable than other forms of hearsay; in fact, the great 20th century evidence scholar Dean John Wigmore held the view that former testimony should be considered as nonhearsay.[1] The Federal Rules of Evidence, however, define former testimony as hearsay and classify it under Rule 804 in order to emphasize the preference for live testimony at trial, as explained by the Supreme Court in a 1986 opinion:

> Unlike some other exceptions to the hearsay rules, or the exemption from the hearsay definition involved in this case, former testimony often is only a weaker substitute for live testimony. It seldom has independent evidentiary significance of its own, but is intended to replace live testimony. If the declarant is available and the same information can be presented to the trier of fact in the form of live testimony, with full cross-examination and the opportunity to view the demeanor of the declarant, there is little justification for relying on the weaker version. When two versions of the same evidence are available, longstanding principles of the law of hearsay, applicable as well to Confrontation Clause analysis, favor the better evidence. *See* Graham, *The Right of Confrontation and the Hearsay Rule: Sir Walter Raleigh Loses Another One*, 8 Crim. L. Bull. 99, 143 (1972). But if the declarant is unavailable, no "better" version of the evidence exists, and the former testimony may be admitted as a substitute for live testimony on the same point.[2]

It should be noted that either party can introduce former testimony at trial if the declarant is unavailable. The rule contains confrontation-based requirements that protect the interests of the party against whom the testimony is offered at trial. These requirements will be discussed in more detail later in this chapter.

Key Foundational Elements

The proponent of evidence under this section must establish the following:

a. The declarant is unavailable under Rule 804(a).

b. The former statement was made in an authorized deposition or in another proceeding.

c. The former statement was made under oath.

d. The party against whom the statement is offered, or a predecessor in interest, had a similar motive to develop the testimony.

The Rule in Application

Most of the foundational elements of this rule are easy to meet and uncontroversial. Demonstrating unavailability is a relatively simple process. Proving that the former testimony took place under oath in a deposition or in another proceeding presents little difficulty, particularly when the parties use an official transcript. In the vast majority of cases, official transcripts are used, although the rule does not require their use: a party can also call a witness with first-hand knowledge of the prior proceeding to testify concerning the substance of the former testimony.

---

[1] 5 Wigmore, Evidence in Trials at Common Law § 1370 (Chadbourne Rev. 1974).

[2] United States v. Inadi, 475 U.S. 387, 394–95 (1986).

A significant amount of litigation takes place with respect to the rule's requirement that "the party against whom the testimony is now offered, or, in a civil action or proceeding, a predecessor in interest, had an opportunity and similar motive to develop the testimony by direct, cross, or redirect examination." Courts have taken a variety of approaches when interpreting whether the party against whom the evidence is offered truly had an opportunity and similar motive to develop the prior testimony, depending on whether the court's main interest is ensuring accuracy of the former testimony or fairness to the party against whom the former testimony is offered.[3] The following excerpt from a law review article outlines the evolution of the rule from the common law to the Federal Rules of Evidence and explains the competing interpretive approaches — accuracy or fairness — to the rule.

Glen Weissenberger, *The Former Testimony Hearsay Exception: A Study in Rulemaking, Judicial Revisionism, and the Separation of Powers*
67 N.C. L. REV. 295, 306–311(1989)

The underlying fairness policy for admitting prior testimony was expressed in an early common-law rule which required absolute identity of the parties and issues in the former and the instant litigation. One English court explained the reason for delimiting the admissibility of former testimony as follows:

> The rule of the common law is, that no evidence shall be admitted but what is or might be under the examination of both parties; and it is agreeable also to common sense, that what is imperfect, and, if I may so say, but half an examination shall not be used in the same way as if it were complete.[4]

Under the original common-law rule, both parties to the former and subsequent suits were required to be the same, such that if the former testimony could not be received against one party, that party could not benefit by offering it against her adversary. The early inflexible rule became tempered in much the same fashion as the party admission exception. It was later refined to provide that former testimony could be admitted in a subsequent trial when the party against whom the former testimony was offered was the same party who had developed the original testimony. In essence, it appeared fair to estop such a party from objecting to evidence developed by that party, and the absolute identity and mutuality of parties requirement was abandoned.

Additionally, consistent with the development of the party admission exception, the former testimony exception evolved to qualify the testimony developed by a predecessor of a party when such predecessor was a litigant in the prior suit. This doctrine was based on concepts of fairness and estoppel borrowed from the party admissions exception. Forcing a party to accept another litigant's cross-examination seemed unfair unless there was only a nominal change in parties, as when the

---

[3] *See generally* Glen Weissenberger, *The Former Testimony Hearsay Exception: A Study in Rulemaking, Judicial Revisionism, and the Separation of Powers*, 67 N.C. L. REV. 299 (1989).

[4] [n. 65] Cazenove v. Vaughn, 105 Eng. Rep. 2, 3 (1813).

parties were connected by privity, meaning they were privies in blood, property, or law, and held the same rights and protected the same interests. It did not appear unfair to hold a party responsible for a previous litigant's examination or cross-examination of a witness when the party against whom the prior testimony was offered had succeeded to the position of the predecessor litigant conducting the examination or cross-examination in the prior action. Consequently, the rule requiring privity between a predecessor in prior litigation and the party against whom the prior testimony is offered is traceable to the party admissions exception and its connection to principles of real property law. . . .

Through such a legal relationship the successor stood in the place of the predecessor and succeeded to all of the benefits and liabilities of that interest, including prior claims and attendant trial conduct concerning the interest. Consequently, courts permitted not only the admission of the predecessor's own statements against the subsequent privy (an admission of a party's predecessor), but also the admission of testimony developed in a predecessor's litigation that pertained to the shared or transferred interest. In contrast, the testimony developed by a stranger not standing in privity with the party in the subsequent trial would not qualify; to admit such evidence would bind a person who was not accountable for the development of the prior testimony and, therefore, would be "against natural justice."[5]

Fairness to the individual litigant was fundamental to the common-law adversarial system. This value was repeatedly expressed through the party/privity requirements of procedural and evidentiary rules: imposing evidence on a party, when that evidence is not attributable to the party or his predecessor in privity, was commonly perceived to be unfair.

B. Recent Developments in Evidentiary Rules: The Trend Toward an Emphasis on Accuracy

Throughout the late nineteenth and twentieth centuries, the party/privity rules of the party admission exception and the former testimony exception drew increasing criticism as courts and commentators began to emphasize accuracy as the ultimate goal of evidentiary rules.

Concern for trustworthiness, as expressed by Professor Morgan, ultimately prevailed over the emphasis on fairness, and none of the recent evidence codifications (the Model Code of Evidence, the Uniform Rules of Evidence, or the Federal Rules of Evidence) accept privity alone as a basis for admitting out-of-court statements of predecessors of parties.

Similarly, the restrictive rule that prior testimony could only be admitted against the party who developed the testimony or his successor in privity was expanded because courts began to emphasize accuracy over fairness. The idea that binding a party to a stranger's cross-examination is unfair became subordinated to the need for accurate evidence. The rule became liberalized primarily as a result of Dean Wigmore's influence. . . . As a result of Wigmore's influence, courts began to accept

---

[5] [n. 76] Morgan, supra note 43; Morgan, *Admissions*, 12 Wash. L. Rev. 181 (1937). Indeed, he was right, but the privity doctrine was never designed to ensure fairness. Even under modern principles, the party admission exception is justified by estoppel notions and not accuracy. See Fed. R. Evid. 801(d)(2)(A) advisory committee's note.

a theory very similar to that of Morgan regarding party admissions, that is, "no magic" is reposed in a connection by blood, property, or law. Courts and commentators reasoned that because the primary issue in achieving accuracy is the similarity of interests which motivates examination or cross-examination, former testimony should be admissible not only against the original party who developed the testimony and his successors in privity, but against anyone with sufficiently similar interests. Once a commentator with the stature of Dean Wigmore redirected the analysis of the prior testimony exception, it was inevitable that it would become more liberalized.

If the issue is framed to ask whether any significant accuracy is sacrificed by abandoning the absolute mutuality and privity requirements, the search for more helpful and useful evidence would naturally encourage the elimination of these strictures. Without question, the strictures add little or nothing to ensuring accuracy. But mutuality and privity were requirements never designed to ensure accuracy. Rather, these requirements were imposed because it was recognized that former testimony possesses a potency and character lacking in other forms of admissible hearsay. As the Supreme Court has recently reaffirmed, prior testimony is a form of hearsay that seldom has independent evidentiary significance; its purpose is to replace live testimony when such testimony is unavailable. Operating as a substitute for live testimony, prior testimony has the virtual force of an in-court witness, and thus its receipt is justifiably restrained when unfairness would result.

With respect to difficulty of admission, former testimony under Rule 804(b) falls on a continuum, ranging from easy and obvious cases on one end to complex and difficult cases on the other. Several factors come into play when evaluating the admissibility of former testimony: identity of parties, similarity of motives to develop testimony, and prior opportunities to develop testimony.

(1) *Identity of Parties*

In a criminal case, the confrontation clause of the Sixth Amendment is the chief constraint limiting the admissibility of former testimony against a criminal defendant. The right of confrontation is personal to a criminal defendant. This means that the defendant himself must have had the opportunity to confront the declarant whose former testimony is being offered at the current trial. In practical terms, this limits the types of former testimony that can be introduced against a defendant in a criminal trial: depositions in the current case under Federal Rule of Criminal Procedure 15 or its equivalent;[6] testimony given during motions or in preliminary

---

[6] Rule 15. Depositions

(a) When Taken. (1) In General. A party may move that a prospective witness be deposed in order to preserve testimony for trial. The court may grant the motion because of exceptional circumstances and in the interest of justice. If the court orders the deposition to be taken, it may also require the deponent to produce at the deposition any designated material that is not privileged, including any book, paper, document, record, recording, or data. (2) Detained Material Witness. A witness who is detained under 18 U.S.C. § 3144 may request to be deposed by filing a written motion and giving notice to the parties. The court may then order that the deposition be taken and may discharge the witness after the witness has signed under oath the deposition transcript.

hearings; and testimony given in former trials against the same defendant of the same factual case. When the *defendant* seeks to introduce a declarant's former testimony against the government in a criminal case, the confrontation clause does not present an impediment to the introduction of the former testimony at trial.

Civil cases present a more challenging situation. The simple case is one in which there is an absolute identity of parties; in other words, the party against whom the former testimony is offered is the same party that had the opportunity to develop the former testimony by cross-examination or other means. But complications arise in civil litigation: additional parties are added to lawsuits, successors in interest take over, parties are dropped from lawsuits, the party that brought the original action dies, and so forth.[7] The common law's solution to these problems was to require strict privity or identity between parties, as described in the earlier excerpt from Weissenberger's article. Although the strict privity requirements of the common law have disappeared, the rule still recognizes

> that it is generally unfair to impose upon the party against whom the hearsay evidence is being offered responsibility for the manner in which the witness was previously handled by another party[, . . . unless] a party's

---

(b) Notice. (1) In General. A party seeking to take a deposition must give every other party reasonable written notice of the deposition's date and location. The notice must state the name and address of each deponent. If requested by a party receiving the notice, the court may, for good cause, change the deposition's date or location. (2) To the Custodial Officer. A party seeking to take the deposition must also notify the officer who has custody of the defendant of the scheduled date and location.

(c) Defendant's Presence. (1) Defendant in Custody. The officer who has custody of the defendant must produce the defendant at the deposition and keep the defendant in the witness's presence during the examination, unless the defendant: (A) waives in writing the right to be present; or (B) persists in disruptive conduct justifying exclusion after being warned by the court that disruptive conduct will result in the defendant's exclusion. (2) Defendant Not in Custody. A defendant who is not in custody has the right upon request to be present at the deposition, subject to any conditions imposed by the court. If the government tenders the defendant's expenses as provided in Rule 15(d) but the defendant still fails to appear, the defendant — absent good cause — waives both the right to appear and any objection to the taking and use of the deposition based on that right.

(d) Expenses. If the deposition was requested by the government, the court may — or if the defendant is unable to bear the deposition expenses, the court must — order the government to pay: (1) any reasonable travel and subsistence expenses of the defendant and the defendant's attorney to attend the deposition; and(2) the costs of the deposition transcript.

(e) Manner of Taking. Unless these rules or a court order provides otherwise, a deposition must be taken and filed in the same manner as a deposition in a civil action, except that: (1) A defendant may not be deposed without that defendant's consent. (2) The scope and manner of the deposition examination and cross-examination must be the same as would be allowed during trial. (3) The government must provide to the defendant or the defendant's attorney, for use at the deposition, any statement of the deponent in the government's possession to which the defendant would be entitled at trial.

(f) Use as Evidence. A party may use all or part of a deposition as provided by the Federal Rules of Evidence.

(g) Objections. A party objecting to deposition testimony or evidence must state the grounds for the objection during the deposition.

(h) Depositions by Agreement Permitted. The parties may by agreement take and use a deposition with the court's consent.

[7] For multiple examples of situations involving various types of predecessors in interest, see generally 2 McCORMICK ON EVIDENCE § 303, notes 5–8 and accompanying text (6th ed. 2006).

     predecessor in interest in a civil action or proceeding had an opportunity
     and similar motive to examine the witness.[8]

Accordingly, the rule requires the former testimony be developed either by the party against whom it is being offered or by a predecessor in interest. Rule 804(b)(1) does not, however, define "predecessor in interest."

     Courts have adopted several approaches in interpreting the term "predecessor in interest." The most common approach is to examine the interests and motives of the prior party and compare them with those of the party against whom the evidence is being offered in the current trial.[9] Another related, but discrete, approach is the "community of interest analysis," in which the courts examine whether there is a shared interest between the parties that would help to insure the adequacy of cross-examination."[10] A third approach, somewhat broader, focuses on whether the prior cross-examination "can fairly be held against the later party."[11] Using this approach, an objecting party can demonstrate the inadequacy of a prior cross-examination "by, for example, setting out the additional questions or lines of inquiry that he or she would have pursued."[12]

(2) *Similar Motive and Opportunity to Develop Testimony*

     The issue of motive and opportunity to develop prior testimony is less of a barrier to admitting former testimony than it might seem at first blush. The common law required, in addition to privity of parties, strict identity of issues. This combination created a significant barrier to the introduction of former testimony at a subsequent trial. Rule 804(b)(1), which requires only "an opportunity and similar motive" to develop the former testimony, is neither written nor interpreted so narrowly. In the words of Weissenberger and Duane, "Different causes of action, additional issues, or a shift in theory are of no substantive consequence under the Rule and should not defeat admissibility."[13] In practical terms, this means that there are a variety of ways to find that the party — or its predecessor in interest — had an adequate opportunity and motive to develop testimony at a prior proceeding. The main test is whether the prior proceeding and current proceeding involve the same factual issues.

     The clearest example of former testimony involves a rehearing of a fully-tried case. The parties and issues in a rehearing are likely to be almost exactly the same as at the former trial. For the most part, their interests — and motives for developing the testimony of witnesses — will be identical to what they were at the first trial. With the benefit of hindsight, the parties might wish to change tactics, ask

---

   [8] Report of Committee on the Judiciary, House of Representatives, 93d Cong., 1st Sess., Federal Rules of Evidence, No. 93-650, p. 15 (1973).

   [9] *See* Author's Comments to Rule 804(b)(1), STEVEN GOODE & OLIN GUY WELLBORN III, COURTROOM HANDBOOK ON FEDERAL EVIDENCE, at 490 (2010).

   [10] 2 McCORMICK ON EVIDENCE § 303 (6th ed. 2006).

   [11] 2 McCORMICK ON EVIDENCE § 303 (6th ed. 2006).

   [12] 2 McCORMICK ON EVIDENCE § 303 (6th ed. 2006).

   [13] GLEN WEISSENBERGER & JAMES J. DUANE, FEDERAL RULES OF EVIDENCE: RULES, LEGISLATIVE HISTORY, COMMENTARY AND AUTHORITY § 804.15 (6th ed. 2009).

additional questions of witnesses, and so forth, but the basic issues, motives and tactics will generally be identical, or nearly so.

Other proceedings are not quite so clear-cut in their identity of factual issues and commonality of the opposing party's motives to develop testimony. This is because the goals, strategies and tactics that a party uses during a specialized hearing are likely to be different in scope and purpose from those used at trial. Examples of other proceedings include grand jury testimony offered against the government, preliminary hearing testimony offered against the criminal defendant at trial, administrative hearing transcripts, or a civil deposition offered against the party that originally took the deposition. A party is likely to develop testimony in different ways depending on the type and purpose of the proceeding.

Consider, for instance, depositions. There are two commonly recognized types of depositions: the discovery deposition and the *de bene esse* deposition.[14] They differ in purpose: "The purpose of a discovery deposition is to discover information; the purpose of a *de bene esse* deposition is to preserve testimony for trial."[15] Because a discovery deposition is designed to elicit information, not to advance or solidify a trial position, the incentive to vigorously cross-examine a discovery deponent is low at best. And yet discovery depositions are often admitted as former testimony under Rule 804(b)(1), with courts using "[i]ncompleteness and the freer range of questions and answers for the purpose of discovery" as "factors that . . . bear on the weight of the testimony and not on its admissibility."[16]

Not only are there differences in the nature and goals of prior proceedings and the current trial, but the form of questioning used in the two proceedings might be remarkably different. Rule 804(b)(1) recognizes three methods for developing former testimony: direct examination, cross examination and re-direct examination. From an advocacy standpoint, these three types of questions have different goals and uses. For example, an advocate typically uses open-ended questions on direct examination with friendly witnesses, leading questions on cross-examination with hostile witnesses, and some combination of open and leading questions on redirect examination to rehabilitate a witness. These are not hard-and-fast rules, of course, because an advocate can vary questioning methods for any number of reasons: the formality of the proceedings, whether a judge is present, to help achieve tactical objectives or surprise, and so forth. Tactical interests and the form of questions are not dispositive in deciding whether there has been opportunity and similar motive to develop testimony.

The advisory committee notes to Rule 804(b)(1) explain some of the issues that arise when the prior proceedings or form of questions are different in nature than the current proceeding:

> Under the exception, the testimony may be offered (1) against the party *against* whom it was previously offered or (2) against the party *by* whom it was previously offered. In each instance the question resolves itself into

---

[14]   7 Moore's Federal Practice § 30.02 (3d ed. 1997).

[15]   7 Moore's Federal Practice § 30.02 (3d ed. 1997).

[16]   7 Moore's Federal Practice § 32.22 (3d ed. 1997).

whether fairness allows imposing, upon the party against whom now offered, the handling of the witness on the earlier occasion. (1) If the party against whom now offered is the one against whom the testimony was offered previously, no unfairness is apparent in requiring him to accept his own prior conduct of cross-examination or decision not to cross-examine. Only demeanor has been lost, and that is inherent in the situation. (2) If the party against whom now offered is the one by whom the testimony was offered previously, a satisfactory answer becomes somewhat more difficult. One possibility is to proceed somewhat along the line of an adoptive admission, i.e. by offering the testimony proponent in effect adopts it. However, this theory savors of discarded concepts of witnesses' belonging to a party, of litigants' ability to pick and choose witnesses, and of vouching for one's own witnesses. Cf. McCormick § 246, pp. 526-527; 4 Wigmore § 1075. A more direct and acceptable approach is simply to recognize direct and redirect examination of one's own witness as the equivalent of cross-examining an opponent's witness. Falknor, Former Testimony and the Uniform Rules: A Comment, 38 N.Y.U.L.Rev. 651, n. 1 (1963); McCormick § 231, p. 483. See also 5 Wigmore § 1389. Allowable techniques for dealing with hostile, doublecrossing, forgetful, and mentally deficient witnesses leave no substance to a claim that one could not adequately develop his own witness at the former hearing. An even less appealing argument is presented when failure to develop fully was the result of a deliberate choice.[17]

The key is not an exact identity of trial strategies and tactical interests, but rather a general identity of primary factual issues between the prior proceeding and the trial. According to *McCormick on Evidence*, "If the accepted requirements of an oath, adequate opportunity to cross-examine on substantially the same issue, and present unavailability of the witness are satisfied, then the character of the tribunal and the form of the proceedings are immaterial, and the former testimony should be received."[18]

Cases, Discussion Questions and Problems

UNITED STATES v. VARTANIAN
United States Court of Appeals, Sixth Circuit
245 F.3d 609 (6th Cir. 2001)

[The Stringers, an African-American family, decided to purchase a new family home in the Detroit suburb of Harper Woods. Their real estate agent was a man named Steven Weiss. Through Weiss, they made an offer that was accepted by the seller. On the day of the property inspection, the seller's next-door neighbors, the DeCraenes, approached the real estate agents to complain about how their lives would be ruined by having African-American neighbors. Although they were animated, the DeCraene's made no threats.]

---

[17] FED. R. EVID. 804(b)(1) advisory committee's note.

[18] 2 McCORMICK ON EVIDENCE § 305 (6th ed. 2006).

[Within minutes of the conversation between the next-door neighbors and the real estate agents] the defendant, who owned the property across the street from the seller, ran across the road and began ranting at the agents assembled there. He exclaimed that he would not have invested $10,000 in a swimming pool in his yard had he known African-Americans would move in across the street, and then backed Kathy Martin [the seller's real estate agent] up into her vehicle, all the while spewing invective. The defendant also told Kathy Martin that he and his neighbors would boycott the Martins' real estate agency, that he had a friend who was a police officer who could trace the agents from their vehicle's license plate number, and that he (Vartanian) would find the Martins, destroy their car, chop them into little pieces, and bury them in the backyard where nobody would ever find them. Mr. DeCraene corroborated the account given by the real estate agents and related that Vartanian "said that he could cut these people in pieces or some-thing."

Before the situation escalated further, the Martins and Weiss left the area, only to reassemble later that evening at the local police station to report the incident. The police official assigned to the case contacted Vartanian and arranged to interview him the following morning. At that time, the defendant attempted to cast his actions in an innocent light. Despite conceding that he had copied down the Martins' license plate number in order to have a friend on the Detroit police force "run a check" on the car, Vartanian denied threatening the agents. Instead, he claimed only that he had stated, "I'm going to buy a house near your house and rent it to blacks. See how your neighbors like it. They will probably cut you up into little pieces and bury you in the back yard."

Shortly after the defendant's altercation with the real estate agents, Weiss contacted the Stringers and requested a meeting with them without the Stringers' children present. At that meeting, he informed them of the threats uttered by Vartanian and volunteered to return the couple's earnest money if they chose to rescind their purchase offer. The Stringers nevertheless decided to go through with the purchase of the home, but they kept strict watch over their children so as to protect them from possible attacks or mischief from their neighbors.

Eventually, Weiss and the Stringers filed a civil suit against Vartanian, alleging violations of the housing provisions of Michigan's Elliott-Larsen Civil Rights Act, M.C.L.A. §§ 37.2501-2507. This litigation eventually resulted in a judgment and a substantial monetary award in favor of the plaintiffs. Simultaneously with the unfolding of the civil proceedings, the federal grand jury returned an indictment against the defendant, charging him with one count of using "force and threat of force . . . [to] intimidate [the real estate agents]" and, in a second count, with "intimidating and interfering with an African-American family with regard to their opportunity to . . . purchase" the house in Harper Woods by "force and threat of force" against the agents. [Later, a superseding indictment was filed in the case, upon which the case was actually tried.]

At the conclusion of the criminal trial, Vartanian was convicted by a jury on both counts. . . .

In challenging his convictions, Vartanian first alleges that the district court violated his Sixth Amendment right to confront the witnesses against him. In support of that claim, the defendant notes that the trial court allowed the prosecution to read into evidence testimony offered by a now-deceased witness who had testified at an earlier civil trial against Vartanian. The defendant asserts that even though he enjoyed the assistance of a civil defense attorney and of a criminal defense attorney at the respective trials, the lawyers did not have similar motives to develop direct, cross-examination, and redirect testimony at the two proceedings.

In pertinent part, the Sixth Amendment to the United States Constitution provides that "in all criminal prosecutions, the accused shall enjoy the right . . . to be confronted with the witnesses against him." Read literally, the constitutional mandate "would require, on objection, the exclusion of any statement made by a declarant not present at trial," including "virtually every hearsay exception, a result long rejected as unintended and too extreme." Ohio v. Roberts, 448 U.S. 56, 63, 100 S. Ct. 2531, 65 L. Ed. 2d 597 (1980). . . .

In challenging the admissibility at his criminal trial of testimony given by real estate agent Steven Weiss at an earlier civil trial, the defendant does not contest the fact that Weiss was unavailable to testify. Indeed, the parties agree that Weiss died between the conclusion of the civil proceedings and the beginning of the criminal trial. See Fed. R. Evid. 804(a)(4). Rather, Vartanian focuses his objection on his belief that the evidence admitted fails to fall within "a firmly rooted hearsay exception." In response, the government contends that Weiss's prior testimony was indeed admissible because it fell squarely within the recognized hearsay exception for former testimony. Pursuant to Federal Rule of Evidence 804(b)(1), if a declarant is unavailable as a witness, a court may accept:

> testimony given as a witness at another hearing of the same or a different proceeding, or in a deposition taken in compliance with law in the course of the same or another proceeding, if the party against whom the testimony is now offered, or, in a civil action or proceeding, a predecessor in interest, had an opportunity and similar motive to develop the testimony by direct, cross, or redirect examination.

(Emphasis added.)

Weiss's testimony in the civil litigation addressed allegations that the defendant communicated threats to the real estate agents intended to intimidate and thereby also interfered with the Stringers' rights to purchase free from intimidation. Similarly, the object of Vartanian's criminal trial was to determine whether the defendant voiced threats intended to intimidate and thereby interfere with the agents' sale and the Stringers' purchase of the home. Furthermore, the parties do not dispute that Vartanian's attorney during the civil proceedings had every opportunity to develop facts and theories in support of his client's legal position. Where the parties diverge in their legal analysis of the legitimacy of the district court's decision to admit Weiss's former testimony is in their understandings of the motives of the civil and criminal attorneys to develop such testimony.

Before this court, the defendant insists that allowing Weiss's civil trial testimony to be admitted in the criminal proceeding without the opportunity for cross-examination effectively nullified his right to attack the witness's account of the incident at issue, because Vartanian's civil attorney did not have the same motive or legal strategy as his criminal defense attorney. Specifically, the defendant contends that the plan at the civil trial was to establish that Vartanian was not liable to the Stringers and to Weiss for any threatening or intimidating comments because any objectionable statements were made not to them, but rather to Kathy and Mike Martin, who had not filed any civil claims against the defendant. By contrast, Vartanian contends that because one count of the criminal information lodged against him alleged threats and intimidation against the Martins and against Weiss, the concessions made and strategy employed in the civil trial actually helped prove the government's case against him in the criminal proceedings.

On a purely theoretical level, Vartanian's argument has some appeal. In its application to the facts of this case, however, the assertion is meritless. It is clear that the government read to the jury only portions of Weiss's direct testimony that recounted the agents' confrontation with Vartanian and Weiss's subsequent reactions, information that was properly admissible and non-objectionable at either trial. The portion of the cross-examination of agent Weiss at the civil trial that was read at the criminal proceeding, moreover, was brief and consisted entirely of Weiss's agreement that Vartanian never mentioned the Stringers directly during his tirade. Again, the motives of the civil action lawyer would necessarily be synonymous with those of the criminal defense attorney regarding the elicitation or possible challenge to such testimony.

For the reasons set out above, we AFFIRM the judgment of the district court.

DISCUSSION QUESTIONS

1. Think about the differences between a civil and criminal case. Even if the cases involve — as the Vartanian case did — the very same factual scenario, why would a cross-examination in a civil trial differ from the cross-examination of the same witness in a subsequent criminal trial? Are the values of the confrontation clause preserved when civil trial testimony is admitted against a defendant in a criminal case?

2. Courts tend to generously interpret the "opportunity and similar motive" language of Rule 804(b)(1), as opposed to the old common-law identity of parties and interests test. Considering what you know about both approaches, which do you think is superior, and why? Does the modern approach sacrifice fairness on the altar of accuracy?

3. How does understanding Rule 804(b)(1) affect the way an advocate should prepare, approach, and conduct the development of testimony in a proceeding that is based on the same factual situation as a case that might later go to trial?

PROBLEMS

Problem 25-1. Raskolnikov is a Russian citizen who has been living illegally in the State of Calamity in the United States. He was arrested by Calamity City Police for alleged involvement in a weapons-distribution ring. During his arrest, a police officer clubbed him in the head with a nightstick as another officer used a Taser on him. The officers claimed the force was necessary to subdue Raskolnikov, but he claimed the force was unnecessary. He filed a civil suit in the United States District Court for the District of Calamity, alleging that the officers violated his civil rights under 42 USC 1983 by using excessive force against him. Shortly after the suit was filed, Raskolnikov was deported to Russia for an immigration violation. He illegally re-entered the country not long afterwards. A few months later, attorneys for the Calamity City Police deposed Raskolnikov. Before trial, fearing arrest and imprisonment for being in the United States in violation of a standing deportation order, Raskolnikov returned to Russia. He was unwilling to return for trial, not wanting to risk imprisonment. He made no attempts to obtain a temporary visa to attend trial or to arrange for video testimony. At trial, his attorney attempts to introduce Raskolnikov's deposition as former testimony under Rule 804(b)(1).

What objections should the defendant (Calamity City Police) make to the introduction of the deposition as former testimony? How should the plaintiff reply? What ruling should the judge make, and why?

Problem 25-2. Rivera was a leader of the notorious street gang Calamity AK47. Along with some fellow gang members, he murdered Diaz by stabbing him and slitting his throat. Government agents arrested Rivera and he was held without bond pending trial. While he was incarcerated, agents interviewed his girlfriend Vicky in the presence of Watson, a court-appointed guardian ad litem. Vicky told agents that Rivera had admitted killing Diaz and said it was "just like killing a chicken for dinner." The gang found out about Vicky's cooperation with the government, and gang leaders ordered a hit on her. The day before the hit, a gang member visited Rivera in prison and told him of the planned hit. Rivera's response was, "Do what you got to do. I guess I'll just have to miss her forever." Vicky was subsequently murdered to prevent her from testifying at trial. Rivera played no role planning or carrying out the murder.

At Rivera's trial, the prosecution called Watson to testify about what Vicky told the agents concerning Rivera's role in the murder of Diaz. Rivera's attorney objected that the statements were inadmissible testimonial hearsay and violated Rivera's confrontation rights. How should the prosecution respond? How should the judge rule?

Statement Under Belief of Impending Death

Through Dec. 1, 2011	After Dec. 1, 2011
Rule 804. Hearsay Exceptions; Declarant Unavailable	**Rule 804. Exceptions to the Rule Against Hearsay — When the Declarant Is Unavailable as a Witness**
(b) Hearsay exceptions. The following are not excluded by the hearsay rule if the declarant is unavailable as a witness::	**(b) The Exceptions**. The following are not excluded by the rule against hearsay if the declarant is unavailable as a witness:
(2) Statement under belief of impending death. In a prosecution for homicide or in a civil action or proceeding, a statement made by a declarant while believing that the declarant's death was imminent, concerning the cause or circumstances of what the declarant believed to be impending death.	**(2) Statement Under the Belief of Imminent Death**. In a prosecution for homicide or in a civil case, a statement that the declarant, while believing the declarant's death to be imminent, made about its cause or circumstances.

Basis

Rule 804(b)(2) is based on the venerable common-law hearsay exception for dying declarations. The dying declaration rule predates the Constitution and the Bill of Rights and was specifically recognized by the Supreme Court in *Crawford v. Washington* as a possible exception to the prohibition against testimonial hearsay at trial in the absence of confrontation.[19] The common law exception applied only to criminal homicide, and it had three strict requirements: (1) the declarant had to be dead at the time of trial; (2) the statement had to relate to the cause of the death; and (3) the statement had to be made when the declarant subjectively knew that death was certain and inevitable. Under those circumstances, the statement was admissible at trial against the defendant.

Over the years, scholars and commentators recognized that the strict constraints of the dying declaration did not always make sense. For example, the common law permitted dying declarations in homicide cases but not civil wrongful death cases. In addition, on occasion an individual would survive what he believed to be his impending death with no memory of what had happened to him; the common law forbade use of the exception unless the declarant was actually dead. Nonetheless, the common law itself did not loosen the requirements to admit dying declarations.

The theory behind the common law's dying declaration hearsay exception was that a person about to meet his maker would not leave his earthly existence with a

---

[19] Crawford v. Washington, 541 U.S. 36, 56 n.6 (2004):

> The one deviation we have found involves dying declarations. The existence of that exception as a general rule of criminal hearsay law cannot be disputed. Although many dying declarations may not be testimonial, there is authority for admitting even those that clearly are. We need not decide in this case whether the Sixth Amendment incorporates an exception for testimonial dying declarations. If this exception must be accepted on historical grounds, it is sui generis.

(internal citations omitted).

lie on his lips; the fear of eternal punishment would ensure the reliability of the statement. In addition, there was a very practical reason for the exception — society's interest in ensuring that murderers would not escape punishment simply by virtue of killing the only witnesses to the crime.

The modern rule is predicated on similar notions of reliability and necessity. Although society is no longer as religiously oriented as it was during the common law era, death is still considered mysterious and powerful. Statements made under the belief of an impending death are viewed as reliable on the grounds that such a belief provides a psychological incentive to tell the truth; the dying declarant has no real reason to lie. It should be noted that critics of both the common law and modern rules have always felt that there are no special trustworthiness guarantees provided by the imminence of death; they maintain that a dying person is perfectly capable of telling vicious lies, and, moreover, might be experiencing serious issues with perception and communication abilities.[20] The necessity prong of the rule remains as strong as ever, inasmuch as such statements might well be the only evidence available of culpability for a death in either a criminal or civil case.

Foundational Elements

The proponent of the evidence must establish the following:

a. The declarant is unavailable under Rule 804(a). Note that unlike the common law, proof of the declarant's death is not required.

b. The statement was made when the declarant believed death was imminent.

c. The statement related to the cause or circumstances of what the declarant subjectively believed to be his impending death.

d. The statement was based on the declarant's first-hand knowledge of such causes or circumstances.

The Rule in Application

The modern rule is more flexible than the common law dying declaration. The drafters of the Federal Rules of Evidence expanded the scope of the dying declaration to include both criminal homicide cases and civil cases. They reduced the "substantial certainty" requirement to one of subjective *belief* that death was imminent. As with the common law exception, the statement must relate to the cause or circumstances of what the declarant believed to be his impending death.

The definition of "unavailability" is the same as the other Rule 804 exceptions. This means that statements can be offered into evidence even if the declarant is still alive at trial but is unavailable for any of the reasons listed in Rule 804(a), with the most likely reasons being lack of memory or inability to testify at the hearing because of illness or infirmity.

---

[20] *See generally* GLEN WEISSENBERGER & JAMES J. DUANE, FEDERAL RULES OF EVIDENCE: RULES, LEGISLATIVE HISTORY, COMMENTARY, AND AUTHORITY § 804.17, notes 106–109 and accompanying text (6th ed. 2009).

The proponent of a statement under Rule 804(b)(2) must frequently rely on circumstantial evidence to establish the declarant's subjective belief of death. This could include evidence of such things as "the apparent fatal quality of the wound, by the statements made to the declarant by doctors or others of the hopelessness of the condition, or by other circumstances"[21] that would help to establish the declarant's belief that death was at hand.

The rule does not require spontaneity; in other words, the dying declaration could be made in response to questions. If a declaration is spontaneously made, advocates should be aware that many of the circumstantial qualities that support the admissibility of a statement as a dying declaration could also provide a foundation for alternative theories of admissibility such as the present sense impression or the excited utterance.

Cases, Discussion Questions and Problems

UNITED STATES v. LAWRENCE
United States Court of Appeals, Third Circuit
349 F.3d 109 (3d Cir. 2003)

Lawrence was convicted of murder in the first degree . . . and use of a firearm during and in relation to a crime of violence. . . . [The convictions stemmed from the April 22, 2000 shooting of George "Josh" Hodge, Jr. at a bar in St. Thomas, Virgin Islands, by a man known to witnesses as Trini. Three witnesses later identified the defendant in a photo array as the shooter.]

Hodge spoke only briefly to a police officer who arrived on the scene. He told the officer that the shooter grabbed his gold Gucci chain and shot him. However, he gave no description, and said nothing else that was helpful to the ensuing investigation. When Hodge arrived at the hospital, doctors learned that he was paralyzed from the neck down and unable to speak due to his injuries and a subsequent tracheotomy. . . .

On May 20, 2000, . . . Police Officer Cordell Rhymer showed Hodge a photographic array assisted by a nurse. The nurses had developed a method of non-verbal communication with Hodge whereby he would blink and/or nod in response to questions. When Rhymer showed Hodge the photograph array, the nurse recorded on Hodge's chart that he blinked and nodded as if to select the fourth photograph. That was a picture of Dale "Ogami" Benjamin. Ogami was apparently on the beach when the shooting occurred. The defendant's photograph was not in the array. [Five days later, officers had Hodge view another photo array that contained the defendant's picture.] The officers asked Hodge if his assailant was pictured in the array, and they relied upon his non-verbal interactions to interpret his response. . . . [The government and the defendant each interpreted Hodge's non-verbal responses differently.]

Hodge finally lost his battle to stay alive on May 30, 2000 after showing early signs of pneumonia and failing to respond to treatment for multiple organ failure.

---

[21] 2 McCormick on Evidence § 310 (6th ed. 2006).

The government also filed a motion in limine to preclude the defendant from admitting testimony regarding Hodge's reference to "Ogami" when Hodge was shown the photographic array on May 20, and Hodge's identification of another person as the shooter in an array including Lawrence on May 25. The government argued that the "identifications" constituted hearsay, and that they were also so ambiguous as to be meaningless. Lawrence responded by insisting that the identifications constituted dying declarations that were an exception to the hearsay rule. He also argued that the identifications met the standard of materiality under the residual hearsay exception.

The court granted the government's motion and ruled that Lawrence could not elicit evidence of Hodge's reference to "Ogami." The court held that neither identification constituted a dying declaration because the evidence did not establish that Hodge believed he was dying at the time of the declarations. The court also ruled that the videotape recording of police presenting the photo array to Hodge on May 25 was too unreliable to be received into evidence. After viewing the recording during the hearing, the court reasoned that Hodge was uncommunicative and confused, and that any response he may have made to the photo array was too ambiguous to suggest that he was attempting to identify the shooter. The court also concluded that the May 20 identification in the presence of Officer Rhymer was not probative either because it was not clear whether Hodge was asked to identify his shooter or just identify persons who may have been on the scene and witnessed the shooting. Although Ogami was apparently present when Hodge was shot, there was no evidence to suggest he was the shooter except for the inference Lawrence tried to force from Hodge's in-conclusive reaction to the photo array. . . .

The Court's Exclusion of Hodge's Purported Identifications . . .

The May 25, 2000 Videotape

Lawrence argues that Hodge's response when shown the photo array on May 25 was admissible either as a dying declaration or under the residual hearsay exception. We disagree.

A declarant's statement identifying his/her assailant can be admitted as an exception to the hearsay rule if the declarant believes that he/she is facing imminent death. However, in order for this "dying declaration" to be admissible, the declarant "must have spoken with the consciousness of a swift and certain doom." Shepard v. United States, 290 U.S. 96, 100, 54 S. Ct. 22, 78 L. Ed. 196 (1933). Here, the district court concluded that Lawrence had not established that either of Hodge's "identifications" were made while Hodge believed death was imminent. The record supports that finding. Hodge's medical treatment was rigorous and undertaken with the expectation that he would survive. Hodge was never told by medical staff or police that he was going to die. Although Hodge had to realize that he had extremely serious injuries, doctors had been discussing the care he would need following his release from the hospital and the sub-sequent rehabilitation that everyone thought he would have to undergo. Moreover, when Hodge finally succumbed to his injuries on May 30, he had just recovered from major surgery and appeared on the way to recovery.

Moreover, he was shown the first array five days before he died. In addition, it is uncontested that not only did no one tell Hodge he was going to die because his death was not expected, the nursing staff purposely tried to manifest an up-beat attitude around him to help keep his spirits up. Thus, the court correctly concluded that the evidence simply did not allow the foundation necessary to admit Hodge's purported identification of "Ogami" as a dying declaration. . . .

DISCUSSION QUESTIONS

1. In this case, the district court excluded evidence of a purported identification of a person other than the defendant on strict adherence to the foundational requirements of Rule 804(b)(2). Should the rules be relaxed when they benefit a criminal defendant? Why or why not?

2. What would prevent the defendant from attempting to offer the decedent's alleged identification as "not hearsay" under Rule 801(d)(1)(C)?

PROBLEMS

Problem 25-3. On July 15 of last year, Vinny Victim was shot multiple times by a rival gang member in a public park. There were no other eyewitnesses to the event. When police arrived at the scene, they found Vinny bleeding to death from his wounds. They called paramedics, knowing the call would be futile; Vinny was doomed. A police officer looked at Vinny and said, "Who did this to you?" There was no response. The officer leaned down and said, "You aren't going to make it. Just tell us who did it and we'll go get them." Vinny spoke in a hoarse whisper, "It was Darryl Devious." Devious was a rival gang member who had stolen Vinny's girlfriend and shot his dog, in return for which Vinny had shot out the windows of Devious's house and hung his dog by the neck on a streetlight pole. The two men hated each other, and each had been heard to threaten the life of the other.

Vinny died shortly thereafter, before paramedics could arrive. Prior to trial, the defense filed a motion *in limine* to exclude Vinny's statement identifying Devious as the killer. The defense argued that, while the statement qualified as a dying declaration, it was testimonial because it was made in response to police questioning, therefore, admitting it in evidence would violate Devious's right of confrontation, an especially grave danger because of the antipathy between Devious and Vinny.

How should the prosecution respond to the defense motion? How should the judge rule?

Statements Against Interest

Through Dec. 1, 2011	After Dec. 1, 2011
Rule 804. Hearsay Exceptions; Declarant Unavailable	**Rule 804. Exceptions to the Rule Against Hearsay — When the Declarant Is Unavailable as a Witness**
(b) Hearsay exceptions. The following are not excluded by the hearsay rule if the declarant is unavailable as a witness::	**(b) The Exceptions**. The following are not excluded by the rule against hearsay if the declarant is unavailable as a witness:
(3) Statement against interest. A statement that:	**(3) Statement Against Interest**. A statement that:
(A) a reasonable person in the declarant's position would have made only if the person believed it to be true because, when made, it was so contrary to the declarant's proprietary or pecuniary interest or had so great a tendency to invalidate the declarant's claim against someone else or to expose the declarant to civil or criminal liability; and	(A) a reasonable person in the declarant's position would have made only if the person believed it to be true because, when made, it was so contrary to the declarant's proprietary or pecuniary interest or had so great a tendency to invalidate the declarant's claim against someone else or to expose the declarant to civil or criminal liability; and
(B) is supported by corroborating circumstances that clearly indicate its trustworthiness, if it is offered in a criminal case as one that tends to expose the declarant to criminal liability.	(B) is supported by corroborating circumstances that clearly indicate its trustworthiness, if it is offered in a criminal case as one that tends to expose the declarant to criminal liability.

Basis

The hearsay exception for statements against interest dates back to the common law. It is based on the theory that human beings do not make factual statements contrary to their own interests unless those statements are true. The common law rule was limited to statements against a person's pecuniary or proprietary interest. As codified in Rule 804(b)(3), the modern exception also includes statements that would expose the declarant to tort liability, as well as corroborated statements against the declarant's penal interests.

Foundational Elements

a. The declarant is unavailable to testify at trial.

b. The declarant has first-hand knowledge of the factual matters in the statement.

c. The nature of the statement is such that a reasonable person would not have made it unless believing it to be true.

d. At the time of utterance, the statement must be contrary to the declarant's pecuniary, proprietary, or penal interest.

e. If the statement is against the declarant's penal interest, it must be supported by corroborating circumstances that indicate its trustworthiness.[22]

The Rule in Application

(1) *Contrast Between Statements Against Interest and Admissions of a Party Opponent*

Students often confuse statements against interest under Rule 804(b)(3) with admissions of a party opponent under Rule 801(d)(2). It is critical to recognize and understand the differences between the two rules, particularly that admissions of a party opponent are more easily admissible at trial and should be used as a theory of admissibility in preference to statements against interest whenever possible and applicable. As a rough rule of thumb, use Rule 801(d)(2) as a theory of admissibility for *any* statements made by a party opponent, and use Rule 804(b)(3) for statements against interest made by witnesses and non-parties.

(1) Hearsay v. "Not Hearsay". First and foremost, statements against interest under Rule 804(b)(3) are considered hearsay. Like all hearsay statements, they are presumptively inadmissible under Rule 802 unless the proponent can demonstrate that they qualify for an exception to the rule. In contrast, admissions of a party opponent are exempted from the hearsay rule under Rule 801(d)(2), which means that if they are relevant, they are presumptively admissible.

(2) Availability of Declarant. Rule 804(b)(3) requires threshold proof of the declarant's unavailability. An admission of a party opponent under Rule 801(d)(2), in contrast, is admissible regardless of the availability of the party opponent at trial. As a practical matter, of course, the party opponent will almost always be available at trial.

(3) Requirement of First-Hand Knowledge. Statements admitted under Rule 804(b)(3) must be based on the first-hand knowledge of the declarant. Admissions of a party opponent, in contrast, have no such requirement.

(4) Nature and Basis of Statement. Statements admitted under Rule 804(b)(3) must be based on a factual matter that is against a recognized interest of the declarant at the time it was made. An objective test is applied to the statement to determine whether a reasonable person in the declarant's position would have made the statement, believing it to be true at the time of utterance. In contrast, there is no requirement that an admission of a party opponent be factually based, against interest or objectively reasonable. The mere fact that a party opponent made a statement is sufficient to qualify it for admission and exclude it from the hearsay rule under Rule 801(d)(2). While it is true that many party admissions under Rule 801(d)(2) are against interest, this is not a requirement for admissibility.

---

[22] *See* GLEN WEISSENBERGER & JAMES DUANE, FEDERAL RULES OF EVIDENCE: RULES, LEGISLATIVE HISTORY, COMMENTARY AND AUTHORITY § 804.20 n.132 and accompanying text (6th ed. 2009).

(2) *Statements Against Penal Interest*

The common law doctrine for statements against interest did not permit statements against the declarant's penal interest — in other words, statements that would tend to expose the declarant to criminal liability. As a matter of logic, such statements seem inherently reliable — common sense and experience tell us that most people would not make statements exposing themselves to potential criminal liability unless they were true. The common law, however, distrusted third-party confessions, as explained in the following Advisory Committee note:

> The refusal of the common law to concede the adequacy of a penal interest was no doubt indefensible in logic, but one senses in the decisions a distrust of evidence of confessions by third persons offered to exculpate the accused arising from suspicions of fabrication either of the fact of the making of the confession or in its contents, enhanced in either instance by the required unavailability of the declarant. Nevertheless, an increasing amount of decisional law recognizes exposure to punishment for crime as a sufficient stake. The requirement of corroboration is included in the rule in order to effect an accommodation between these competing considerations. When the statement is offered by the accused by way of exculpation, the resulting situation is not adapted to control by rulings as to the weight of the evidence and, hence the provision is cast in terms of a requirement preliminary to admissibility. Cf. Rule 406(a). The requirement of corroboration should be construed in such a manner as to effectuate its purpose of circumventing fabrication.[23]

Broadly speaking, there are two categories of statements against a declarant's penal interest: statements that exculpate the criminal defendant and incriminate the declarant, and statements that incriminate both the declarant and the criminal defendant. The statements can be made to the police, either spontaneously or during a custodial interrogation; or they can be made under non-testimonial circumstances to someone else, such as a friend, confidante or stranger. When made to the police, the statements must be evaluated not only under the rules of evidence, but also in the light of applicable constitutional criminal procedure precedents and standards.

The threshold requirement for either type of statement is unavailability. The declarant may be unavailable at trial for any of the reasons listed in Rule 804(a), but one of the most common reasons for unavailability is the declarant's exercise of his privilege against self-incrimination. Unless he receives a grant of immunity, a hearsay declarant who has made an out-of-court statement against his penal interest is unlikely to repeat the statement in testimony at someone else's trial, because the statements could later be used against him in his own trial as an admission of a party opponent. The only way to get those statements into evidence is to introduce them as hearsay under Rule 804(b)(3).

At trial, the defendant is likely to seek admission of the first category of statement to save his own skin, and the prosecution is likely to seek admission of the second to aid in convicting the defendant. For testimonial statements that (1)

---

[23] FED. R. EVID. 804(b)(3), advisory committee notes (internal citations deleted).

incriminate both the declarant and the defendant, and (2) are offered by the prosecution against the defendant at trial, the Confrontation Clause, as interpreted by the Supreme Court's in *Crawford v. Washington*, presents a major barrier to admission.

Regardless of whether the statement is exculpatory or inculpatory of the defendant, Rule 804(b)(3) requires that the statements be corroborated. Corroboration is necessary because the declarant, being unavailable to testify, will not be subject to cross-examination about the statement. The standard is "circumstances that clearly indicate its trustworthiness." Corroboration applies to the trustworthiness of the declarant's statement and not the trustworthiness of the witness who quotes the statement in court. Factors for corroboration are determined on a case-by-case basis and include the circumstances surrounding the making of the statement and the motives of the declarant.[24]

Cases, Discussion Questions and Problems

IN RE SEPTEMBER 11 LITIGATION
United States District Court for the Southern District of New York
621 F. Supp. 2d 131 (S.D.N.Y. 2009)

Three wrongful death cases and nineteen property damage cases arising from the terrorist-related crashes into the World Trade Center remain to be tried against the Aviation Defendants.[25]

The trial against the Aviation Defendants will focus on what they knew and should have known about terrorist threats to civil aviation, and on what they did and should have done to protect against such threats. . . .

The Aviation Defendants wish to argue at trial that the terrorists would have succeeded in their plans and caused the damage of which plaintiffs complain regardless of the Aviation Defendants' negligence. They seek to show that the terrorists had trained to evade airport and airplane security and to accomplish their planned hijackings despite proper security procedures.

For example, the Aviation Defendants seek to introduce evidence that the terrorists had planned to use as weapons only implements that were then permitted on airplanes, and that they had trained in hand-to-hand combat so that they could accomplish their mission if airport security stripped them even of those weapons. The Boeing Company wishes to argue that the terrorists were planning to take over the cockpit early in the flight, when the cockpit door typically was open. Boeing claims that its alleged negligence in constructing a cockpit door that is impenetrable when locked did not matter; for the terrorists had planned to advance when the door was open.

The Aviation Defendants should be allowed to develop this defense. If the terrorists

---

[24] 2 McCormick on Evidence § 319, notes 35–37 and accompanying text (6th ed. 2006).

[25] The "Aviation Defendants" include airlines and various other entities that the plaintiffs argued had a duty to prevent the seizure of aircraft and destruction of buildings and aircraft during the September 11 terrorist attacks.

would have been able to pass through airport security with their weapons, overcome security procedures aboard airplanes, overcome resistance of passengers and crew, and fly jumbo jets into buildings even if the Aviation Defendants had acted meticulously, plaintiffs may be unable to prove proximate causation, or at least a jury might so decide. . . .

The Aviation Defendants seek an admissibility ruling on a document containing statements attributed to, and describing the conduct of, Khalid Sheikh Mohammed. They argue that since the document, Mohammed's "substitute testimony," was admitted in the punishment phase of Zacarias Moussaoui's criminal trial, where a sentence of life or death was in issue, it should be admissible at the civil trial of the Aviation Defendants. The Aviation Defendants assert that Mohammed is unavailable, and that the statements are against his interest and are reliable. See Fed. R. Evid. 804(b)(3), 807.

Zacarias Moussaoui pleaded guilty to conspiracy to commit acts of terrorism, commit aircraft piracy, destroy aircrafts, use weapons of mass destruction, murder United States employees, and destroy property, as part of the September 11 attacks. See United States v. Zacarias Moussaoui, 01 Cr. 455 (LMB) (E.D. Va.) (plea accepted April 22, 2005) ("Moussaoui Trial"). . . .

At trial, the defense presented a statement attributed to Khalid Sheikh Mohammed, his "substitute testimony."[26] The document was based on the intelligence that the government gathered from Mohammed during his time spent in custody. As a prisoner in various locations, he was subjected to various conditions. At the time of the Moussaoui trial, Mohammed was being held in the United States Naval Base at Guantanamo Bay, Cuba. Mohammed's "substitute testimony" was a summary of his responses during his interrogations, written and compiled by his various interrogators. The district court admitted into evidence the "substitute testimony" as a stipulation by government and defense counsel, worded in the third person. 18 U.S.C. App'x § 6(c). Mohammed did not appear in court, and his statement was not sworn.

The "substitute testimony" is over fifty pages long, contains 114 numbered paragraphs, and is written in a neutral tone. The document describes the planning of the September 11 attacks, including planning for an additional "second wave" of attacks that did not materialize. It also identifies the hijackers and their accomplices and discloses how money was sent to them in the United States, how they learned to live and train as pilots here, and how they argued among themselves and with other Al Qaeda leaders. The Aviation Defendants seek to admit the "substitute testimony," in part, to support the argument that the terrorists' plot would have succeeded despite the Aviation Defendants' alleged negligence. . . .

A hearsay statement of a declarant who is unavailable to testify at trial may be

---

[26] [n.15] Mohammed was not available to attorneys either for the prosecution or the defense because he was in custody, following his capture in March 2003, and any deposition or testimony threatened to expose information that would jeopardize national security. Pursuant to 18 U.S.C. App'x § 6(c), a provision in the Classified Information Procedure Act, 18 U.S.C. App'x III, the district court admitted a summary of the relevant information elicited from Mohammed in a form approved by the intelligence agencies.

admissible if the statement "so far tended to subject the declarant to civil or criminal liability . . ., that a reasonable person in the declarant's position would not have made the statement unless believing it to be true." Fed. R. Evid. 804(b)(3). Mohammed is unavailable to testify, and likely to remain so, because of the strictness and secrecy that surrounds his detention. Fed. R. Evid. 804(a)(5). However, the other criteria of Rule 804(b)(3) are not satisfied.

First, Mohammed's "substitute testimony" is not, in form and most likely in substance, his "oral or written assertion." Fed. R. Evid. 801(a). The statement is at least two steps removed: a stipulation, extracted from various summaries and memoranda written and edited by his interrogators and their supervisors over an appreciable period of time. Moussaoui Trial Tr. 2418. Segregable portions of the "substitute testimony" might possibly qualify, but Mohammed's "substitute testimony," as a whole, is not his statement for the purposes of Rule 804(b)(3). . . .

Second, Mohammed's interrogators allegedly subjected him to pressures that may have caused him to exaggerate, or otherwise fabricate, his responses, aiming to satisfy his interrogators rather than to accurately recount events that had occurred. A court should examine the specific circumstances of the declarant, noting any motivations that may have influenced a reasonable person in the situation to make a statement against his interest. See, e.g., United States v. Lang, 589 F.2d 92, 97 (2d Cir. 1978) (remarking that declarant was in custody, of below average intelligence, facing a long sentence, and cognizant of the implications of cooperating with authorities). The issue raises the concern that a reasonable person in Mohammed's circumstances might have made the statements attributable to him, even if they were not entirely true. See United States v. Oliver, 626 F.2d 254, 260 (2d Cir. 1980). A reasonable person in Mohammed's place, intent on winning favor from his jailers or causing them to stop harsh interrogation methods, might well have been motivated to tell his jailers what he thought they would want to hear, regardless of its truth. If he had a substantial motive not to tell the truth when he made his statement, his statement is not admissible under Rule 804(b)(3). See United States v. Paulino, 445 F.3d 211, 220 (2d Cir. 2006) (excluding statement against criminal interest where declarant had motive to accept guilt to protect his son from culpability). Compare Lang, 589 F.2d at 97 ("We conclude that there was no motive here for [declarant] to lie. . . ."); with Oliver, 626 F.2d at 261 (finding that a reasonable person might have made untrue, self-inculpatory statements while in FBI custody, in order to mitigate a long prison sentence for himself and avoid criminal prosecution of his son).

Furthermore, Mohammed may not have acted as a reasonable person. The rule is premised on the notion that the declarant has acted reasonably — the declarant's rational compunctions are the foundation for his statement's presumed reliability. See Kenneth S. Broun, McCormick on Evidence § 319(g) (6th ed. 2006); 5 Weinstein's Federal Evidence § 804.06[4][c] (2d ed. 2005). Mohammed is a terrorist, willing to give his life, and assist others in giving theirs, so as to murder innocents. I will not base my ruling here on the presumption that he is a reasonable man.

Third, only self-inculpatory statements are admissible under Rule 804(b)(3). Williamson v. United States, 512 U.S. 594, 599-600, 114 S. Ct. 2431, 129 L. Ed. 2d

476 (1994) ("We see no reason why collateral statements, even ones that are neutral as to interest . . . should be treated any differently from other hearsay statements that are generally excluded."); United States v. Williams, 506 F.3d 151, 155 (2d Cir. 2007). Given the form of the "substitute testimony," it is not possible to determine which of Mohammed's statements were against his interest. No showing is made as to when each of the underlying statements were made, or what information Mohammed had been given at those times as to what crimes he was suspected of, what evidence against him the authorities possessed, what cooperation agreements were available to him, or any other such details that would shed light on whether each underlying statement was "sufficiently inculpatory" to render it reliable. Williamson, 512 U.S. at 606.

Because of these and other difficulties, the "substitute testimony" of Khalid Sheikh Mohammed, as a whole, is not admissible under Rules 804(b)(3), 402, and 403. . . .

DISCUSSION QUESTIONS

1. What does the *In re September 11 Litigation* case suggest about the possible uses of statements against interest at trial?

2. What are the constraints and limitations that apply to the admission of statements against interest at trial? Based on the facts as you have them, is there anything the plaintiffs could have done to cure the admissibility problems with the substitute testimony?

3. Suppose this was a criminal case rather than a civil case and that the defendant wanted to introduce the substitute testimony at trial as part of his defense. Suppose further that because of national security concerns, there is no possibility of obtaining this evidence in any form other than the substitute testimony document. Would the same result be reached? Why or why not?

PROBLEMS

Problem 25-4. Dirk Dagger, a prison inmate, is being prosecuted for stabbing Gary Guard at the penitentiary. There were no witnesses, and Gary never saw who did it. The primary evidence against Dirk was a threat he made to Gary a week earlier to "watch your back." A few weeks after the incident, Sam Snitch, another prison inmate, spoke to a police investigator and said, "Dirk and I planned the whole thing together, but I tried to talk him out of it. He wanted to go ahead anyway, and I said, sure, go for it. But then he got cold feet, and at the time of the stabbing, he and I were playing dice in our cellblock." Unfortunately for Snitch, he died under mysterious circumstances prior to trial. Analyze the admissibility of his statement under Rule 804.

Problem 25-5. On an icy day in Calamity City, Doyle's car hit a patch of black ice and skidded out of control, plowing into a car driven by Vonda. The accident caused considerable damage to Vonda's car and severe injuries to Vonda. Vonda remained lucid throughout the rescue process, and when a police officer interviewed him to find out what had happened, Vonda said, "There was nothing that guy could have done to prevent the accident. It was just bad luck, hitting that black ice. It could have happened to anyone. Could have happened to me." A few days later, Vonda died from injuries sustained during the accident. Her widower, Wilt, filed suit against Doyle for negligence. At trial, Doyle's attorney seeks to introduce Vonda's statement to the police officer as a statement against interest. Analyze the admissibility of Vonda's statement under Rule 804.

Problem 25-6. Mary Jones, a divorced mother of two young children, died in a car accident. Her husband, Julius, was in prison serving a lengthy sentence for bank robbery. Mary died intestate and without having named a guardian for her children in the event of her death. Following Mary's death, her parents, Mike and Marla Morton, filed an action in Calamity County Court for custody of the children. Julius's parents, Jack and Jill Jones, also filed a petition for custody of the children. The court consolidated the petitions and held a hearing to determine who would have custody of the children. Each side called witnesses to testify about its fitness to raise the children. The attorney for Jack and Jill Jones called several witnesses to testify that Mary had told them she had been sexually abused by Mike Morton, her father, for most of her life as a child. The attorney for the Mortons objected that the statements were hearsay. The Jones attorney replied that it was a statement against interest, because no one would tell a story like that to others unless it was true. The judge admitted the statements under Rule 804(b)(3) as statements against interest. On appeal, how should the appellate court rule, and why?

Hearsay Requiring Unavailability of Declarant: Quick Hits

- Hearsay declarants can be declared unavailable based on absence, serious illness, death, refusal to testify, inability to remember, exercise of a privilege, or because of the wrongdoing of a party.

- Rule 804 is a rule of preference in which live testimony is preferred, but hearsay is better than no testimony at all.

- Former testimony under 804(b)(1) is considered trustworthy because of the protections provided by the opportunity to develop witness testimony by cross-examination.

- Dying declarations under 804(b)(2) are considered trustworthy because of the assumption that a person would not lie about the cause of death when faced with imminent mortality.

- Statements against interest are admissible when such statements were contrary to the declarant's pecuniary, penal or proprietary interest at the time they were made.

- A party that has wrongfully procured the unavailability of a witness forfeits the right to complain about the witness's hearsay statements being used against him at trial.

Chapter References

Christopher B. Mueller & Laird C. Kirkpatrick, Evidence §§ 8.63–8.78 (4th ed. 2009).

Glen Weissenberger & James J. Duane, Federal Rules of Evidence: Rules, Legislative History, Commentary and Authority § 804 (6th ed. 2009).

Jack B. Weinstein & Margaret A. Berger, Weinstein's Federal Evidence § 804 (Joseph M. McLaughlin ed., Matthew Bender 2d ed. 1997).

Kenneth S. Broun, McCormick on Evidence §§ 253, 301–20 (6th ed. 2006).

Steven Goode & Olin Guy Wellborn III, Courtroom Handbook on Federal Evidence Ch. 5 (West 2010).

III.   APPLICATION EXERCISE

Former Testimony at Trial

One of the issues that arises in applying the former testimony exception of Rule 804(b)(1) is whether the party against whom the evidence is being offered had an opportunity and similar motive to develop the testimony by direct, cross or redirect examination. Some cases are easy. For example, suppose a criminal defendant successfully appeals his conviction and the appellate court orders a rehearing. Further suppose that the government's chief witness testified at the first trial and was thoroughly cross-examined by the defendant's attorney. If that witness is unavailable at the second trial for any of the reasons listed in Rule 804, it does no violence to the letter or spirit of the rule to introduce that former testimony against the defendant at the second trial.

Other cases are a bit more complex. Depending on the type of former proceeding, the issues raised, or the theory of the case, genuine questions may exist on the issue of whether the party (or predecessor in interest) had an opportunity and similar motive to develop the testimony at the former proceeding. An advocate seeking to keep out testimony from a prior proceeding must carefully analyze the direct and cross examination of the witness at the former proceeding, the language of Rule 804, the advisory committee notes, and interpretative case law.

After the advocate wins the battle to have former testimony introduced, it can be done in several ways: (1) by introducing into evidence an official copy of the transcript under Rule 803(8); (2) by a witness testifying from unaided memory about what was said; (3) by the testimony of a witness testifying from memory that was refreshed by viewing the transcript; (4) a witness who made notes or a memorandum of the former trial while it was fresh in her mind, could use the notes as past recollection recorded under Rule 803(5) if a sufficient foundation were laid. A common way to introduce former testimony at trial is to read the transcript of the former testimony into the record, with the attorney reading the questions aloud and someone sitting in the witness stand reading the answers.

Opponents of former testimony may raise substantive objections to it for the first time at the subsequent trial. Objections to the form of the questions that could have been raised at the first trial cannot be raised at the subsequent trial.

The Exercise

Factual Scenario: Darryl and Darla Defendant are a married couple who live a life of crime. They use and sell drugs, primarily methamphetamines, cocaine and stolen prescription drugs. They have spent most of their adult lives in a drug-induced fog.

On July 15 of last year, officials found the body of Vince Victim, a small-time drug dealer, in a field not far from the couple's home. Victim had been beaten and stabbed to death, then lit on fire. There was no forensic evidence on the corpse that could be used to identify a killer.

Acting on a tip from Stan Snitch, a local police informant, authorities visited the Defendants' home at 1315 Mockingbird Lane on July 16. They found copious amounts of Victim's blood and the signs of a struggle in the home. No weapons, however, could be found.

According to Stan Snitch, he and his friend Melvin Malum were invited guests at the Defendants' home, where the four of them got high by smoking a batch of stolen Cialis. While they were high, Victim came to the house with some cocaine he was trying to sell. Rather than purchase the cocaine, Darryl and Malum attacked Victim, beating him to death with hammers and wrenches. Darla then helped drag the body to Malum's pickup truck. Snitch, Malum and Darryl drove the body to the field, where Malum and Darryl poured gasoline on it and lit it on fire. Darla stayed home to clean up the blood and dispose of the murder weapons. Snitch admitted to being present but claimed to have no other involvement in the crime.

Both Darla and Darryl admitted that Victim had perished in their home at the hands of Malum and Snitch and that they had exercised poor judgment by not calling the authorities to report the crime. They claimed it was an understandable oversight, given that neither of them wanted to be arrested for violating their probation. After providing this information, each of them requested a lawyer and declined to talk to police.

All four individuals were charged with first-degree murder for the death of Vinny Victim. Stan Snitch cut a deal with the prosecution and agreed to plead guilty to misuse of a prescription drug in return for his truthful testimony against the other three. Malum was tried first and was convicted of first-degree murder based on Snitch's testimony and some admissions he made to police while being interrogated.

Darla and Darryl were both represented by Carla Callow, a recent law school graduate who had never tried a felony case before. The defense theory at trial was that Darla and Darryl were horrified bystanders to the murder, which was committed by Malum and Snitch, and that neither of them was guilty of anything more than failing to report the crime to police.

Callow did a horrible job at trial. She made promises in her opening statement that she did not keep. She failed to put on a defense, not calling a single defense witness, including either Darla or Darryl. She ignored strong evidence that Darla was the victim of domestic violence at the hands of Darryl, and failed to consider that Darla and Darryl might have divergent interests at trial. Snitch testified at the joint trial, and Callow conducted a tactically unsound cross-examination.

On appeal, the celebrated attorney Matlock Schroeder filed an ineffective assistance of counsel claim against Callow. He alleged that she had committed prejudicial misconduct by not advising Defendants about her conflict of interest, and that she had compounded her errors by badly trying the case and failing to present a defense. Schroeder's appeal was successful, and the appellate court set aside the conviction and ordered a retrial.

While the appeal was pending, Snitch died of a drug overdose after injecting a solution of nitroglycerin, methamphetamine and rat poison into his veins.

Darla and Darryl obtained different attorneys for the rehearing. Darryl's attorney intended to present a general denial defense, claiming that his client had nothing to do with the crime. Darla's attorney intended to present a defense that Darla — a victim of years of domestic abuse — stood helplessly by and watched while her husband, Snitch and Malum beat Victim to death. Conditioned by abuse not to question her husband, she failed to run away or report the incident.

Prior to trial, the prosecution filed notice of its intent to use Snitch's testimony at the first trial on retrial. Darla's attorney believed the testimony was admissible against Darryl, but not Darla. Darla's attorney moved *in limine* to exclude the use of Snitch's testimony at Darla's trial.

Pretrial Preparation. Prepare defense arguments to exclude this testimony, using the rule, advisory committee notes and interpretive case law. Prepare a prosecution response using the same categories of sources. The prosecution should be prepared to enter the former testimony into evidence using (1) the official transcript; and (2) the testimony of a paralegal who attended the first trial and can testify from refreshed recollection about what was said. Review the trial transcript of Stan Snitch.

The Exercise. Students will play the role of Darla's attorney, the prosecuting attorney, the judge, and a paralegal who can testify from refreshed recollection about the trial testimony.

A tabular version of the transcript is provided below.

Direct Examination.

Q		A	
1	Please state your name.		Stanley Snitch
2	[Other background info]		[background answers]
3	Do you know Darryl and Darla Defendant?		Yes
4	How?		We were neighbors, and we used to do drugs together.

Q		A	
5	What kinds of drugs?		Speed, blow, weed, prescription drugs. Anything we could get our hands on.
6	I'd like to turn your attention to July 15 of last year. Do you remember where you were that day?		Yes
7	Where?		At Defendants' home. 1315 Mockingbird Lane, here in Calamity.
8	Who else was there?		Well, Darla and Darryl was there. And Melvin Malum was there.
9	Who was Malum?		Another friend of ours. He did drugs with us.
10	Why was Malum there? **Objection: The witness can't read Malum's mind, your honor** **Response: The witness knows Malum was there to use drugs and can tell that to the jury** **Ruling: Overruled.**		To use drugs with us.
11	What drugs were you using that day?		We was smoking Cialis
12	Why Cialis?		Darryl or Darla, I can't remember which one, robbed this old guy that lived in a trailer next to the Elks Lodge. He had a big bottle of it.
13	How long were you smoking it?		Maybe four hours. We'd smoke some and pass out, then smoke some more.
14	When did Vince Victim come in?		Sometime in the afternoon. I don't know.
15	Why was he there?		He said he had some drugs to sell.
16	Did anyone buy them?		No.
17	Why?		Well, two reasons. One, we was all broke and couldn't pay. And two, Darryl and Malum killed the guy. Beat him to death.
18.	You must have been horrified by that.		I don't know about that, but it made me sick at my stomach and scared.

Q		A	
19	Let's talk more about the actual murder itself. Why did they do it?		To get drugs.
20	Did they get the drugs?		I don't know. I think so. But I don't know. Maybe Darla got them. I didn't get them.
21	Who struck the first blow?		They both kind of did it at the same time. Darryl had a hammer and Malum had a wrench.
22	Whose idea was it?		Don't know. They both kind of just did it.
23	Where was Darla at this time?		In the room
24	What was she doing?		Watching. With me. Except she was cheering them on, like she was at a fight. And she told Darryl to hurry up and kill the guys so she could get the drugs.
25	What did you do while this was going on?		Thought to myself, them guys are in a bunch of trouble. Then got a little scared they might do something to me, you know?
26	Did you say anything to them?		I think I said something like, "hey guys, this is too much. You should stop." Something like that.
27	And how did they reply? **Objection: Hearsay Response: No, it isn't. Ruling: Objection overruled.**		Darryl said, "You'll shut up if you know what's good for you. You could be next. Now go to the garage and get the gas can."
28	What did you do?		Went to the garage and got the gas can.
29	Then what happened?		When I come out of the garage, I seen Darla and Malum dragging the guy through the kitchen and into the garage. Then Darryl and Malum picked the guy up and put him in the pickup. Then Darla went in and got a sheet off the bed and put it on top of him.

Q		A	
30	How did you feel? **Objection: Who cares how he felt? This case isn't about how he felt.** **Ruling: Sustained.** **Response: May I be heard, your honor? The witness's abject fear of harm at the hands of Darla, Darryl and Malum affected his judgment. Please reconsider** **Ruling: Objection overruled.**		I was scared that Darla, Darryl and Malum might do something to me.
31	So what happened next?		Well, Darryl said, "I guess we got to take this guy to the field and burn him." And Malum said, "Yep. Dead men tell no tales." And then Malum said, "You're going with us.
32	And then what happened?		We drove off to the field and Darryl and Malum burned the guy.
33	What did you do?		Nothing. Just watched.
34	Do you have a deal with the prosecution today?		Yes.
35	What is it?		Tell the truth and I won't get charged with murder.
36	Did you have anything to do with the murder of Vince Victim?		No.
37	Who did it?		Darryl and Malum.
38	And what about Darla?		Well, she cheered them on, and then she helped clean up afterwards.
39	Finally, have you ever been convicted of a serious crime before?		Yes.
40	What?		Well, assault with a deadly weapon. But that was back in high school.
41	Have you stayed away from violence since then?		Yes, sir.
42	Would you ever lay a hand on anyone?		No, sir.
43	Why not?		It's wrong.

Q		A	
44	And again, who killed Victim?		Darryl and Malum. They beat him with a hammer and wrench, then stabbed him and burned him.

Cross Examination

	Q	A	
1	Just a few questions for you, Mr. Snitch. You had a deal with police?		Yes
2	And why did you cut the deal, were you trying to lie and save your hide by turning in other people?		No. Just trying to tell the truth. Just trying to do the right thing. I wish I'd said something right away and maybe stopped it, but I was so afraid, especially of Darryl. He has a temper.
3	If the only thing you got charged with is misusing a prescription drug, how is that fair to anyone?		Well, it's what I done. But I never killed no one. That was Darryl and Malum.
4	Wouldn't you agree with me that Darryl and Darla were in the back bedroom the whole time and didn't come out until after you and Malum had actually killed the victim?		No.
5	Why not?		Because that isn't what happened. I mean, they might have been in the bedroom sometime during the day, but when Victim come over to the house, we was all there in the living room, and that's when Darryl and Malum started hitting on him.
6	Are you sure your memory isn't affected by the great deal the government gave you?		Yes. I'm telling it just like I remember it. Which is the truth.

7	Now, you said you were afraid of Darryl. Considering that the two of you were best friends since grade school, isn't that kind of a lie?	No. Not really. He can be really mean. Once I seen him kill a dog that went on his lawn. He called it over, then broke its neck. Then he told me, "you ever piss on my lawn, I'll do the same to you." So, yeah, I was afraid. And I'd seen him hurt other people bad. He used to beat on Darla.
8	Isn't it possible that you and Malum did all this and are just trying to frame Darla and Darryl?	No.
9	But it could be possible, right?	Only if I was lying.
10	So if the jury doesn't believe you, then they could believe that Darla and Darryl didn't do this?	Well, Darla never done none of the killing. That was Darryl and Malum. She just sat around cheering everyone on, then she helped drag the body out to the truck. So I don't see how they could believe that Darryl didn't do it.
11	And you're saying you didn't do anything. Do you really expect the jury to believe that?	Yes.
12	Why?	Because it's the truth.
13	But if Darla and Darryl get convicted today, you won't go to jail, will you, and that means you have something to gain by lying to put them in jail, isn't that true, JUST ANSWER YES OR NO?	No. If I tell the truth, I won't get charged with what they done.
14	Are you aware that rumor on the street is that you had more to do with this than you're letting on? **Objection: Hearsay. Response: Your honor, I think I'm entitled to talk about what people are saying about this trial. Ruling: Sustained**	

15	Isn't it true that people are saying you had something to do with this? **Objection: Same objection, your honor.** **Response: Your honor, this is relevant and material to my case.** **Ruling: Sustained.**		
16	No further questions		

Chapter 26

HEARSAY FINALE: RULES 806 AND 807

Chapter Objectives:

- Introduce and explain the final two hearsay rules: Rule 806 (attacking and supporting credibility of declarants) and Rule 807 (residual hearsay)
- Analyze and discuss issues pertaining to the credibility of hearsay declarants and the introduction of residual hearsay at trial
- Apply the concepts from this chapter in a courtroom application exercise

I. BACKGROUND AND EXPLANATORY MATERIAL

The final two rules in the hearsay pantheon are not used nearly so often as the first five. Nevertheless, they are important and can make the difference between victory and defeat at trial. The purpose of this chapter is to introduce the two rules and ensure a basic level of familiarity with them.

Attacking and Supporting the Credibility of Hearsay Declarants

Through Dec. 1, 2011	After Dec. 1, 2011
Rule 806. Attacking and Supporting Credibility of Declarant	**Rule 806. Attacking and Supporting the Declarant's Credibility**
When a hearsay statement, or a statement defined in Rule 801(d)(2)(C), (D), or (E), has been admitted in evidence, the credibility of the declarant may be attacked, and if attacked may be supported, by any evidence which would be admissible for those purposes if declarant had testified as a witness. Evidence of a statement or conduct by the declarant at any time, inconsistent with the declarant's hearsay statement, is not subject to any requirement that the declarant may have been afforded an opportunity to deny or explain. If the party against whom a hearsay statement has been admitted calls the declarant as a witness, the party is entitled to examine the declarant on the statement as if under cross-examination.	When a hearsay statement — or a statement described in Rule 801(d)(2)(C), (D), or (E) — has been admitted in evidence, the declarant's credibility may be attacked, and then supported, by any evidence that would be admissible for those purposes if the declarant had testified as a witness. The court may admit evidence of the declarant's inconsistent statement or conduct, regardless of when it occurred or whether the declarant had an opportunity to explain or deny it. If the party against whom the statement was admitted calls the declarant as a witness, the party may examine the declarant on the statement as if on cross-examination.

Basis, Foundational Requirements and Applications at Trial

Rule 806 is based on the recognition that "[t]he declarant of a hearsay statement which is admitted in evidence is in effect a witness. His credibility should in fairness be subject to impeachment and support as though he had in fact testified."[1] The rule is designed to level the playing field at trial when an out-of-court statement is introduced as hearsay or as "not hearsay" under Rule 801(d)(2)(C),(D), or (E). Even though the opponent might be deprived of the opportunity to cross-examine the hearsay declarant in open court, the opponent can still introduce evidence pertaining to the declarant's credibility for the fact-finder to consider.

Recall that the rules of evidence provide several avenues for attacking (or supporting, after attack) the credibility of a witness. Under Rule 608, the character for untruthfulness of any witness may be attacked by reputation or opinion testimony; once attacked, the witness's character for truthfulness may be supported by the same kind of evidence. Rule 609 permits witnesses to be impeached by evidence of conviction of a qualifying crime. Rule 613 allows impeachment by proof of prior inconsistent statements. In addition, although not mentioned in the Federal Rules of Evidence, witnesses can be impeached by specific contradiction or by extrinsic proof of bias or motive to misrepresent.

---

[1]   FED. R. EVID. 806, advisory committee notes.

The foundational requirements for impeaching an absent hearsay declarant are the same as they would be if the declarant had testified at the trial in person, and reference should be made to the rules governing individual impeachment methods and doctrines. Rule 806 contains two changes to regular impeachment and examination procedures. First, with respect to extrinsic proof of inconsistent statements, the rule does away with Rule 613(b)'s requirement that the impeached witness be "afforded an opportunity to explain or deny the same and the opposite party is afforded an opportunity to interrogate the witness thereon." Second, the rule states that if the party against whom the hearsay is offered wishes to call the hearsay declarant to the stand to be impeached, the party is permitted to examine the declarant as if on cross-examination.

Cases, Discussion Questions and Problems

UNITED STATES v. GOLDWIRE
United States Court of Appeals, Armed Forces
55 M.J. 139 (C.A.A.F. 2001)[2]

[Appellant Goldwire, an Air Force servicemember, was charged with raping Airman K, a female servicemember, at a party. Everyone at the party became extremely intoxicated. Airman K fell asleep on a couch in the living room, and Goldwire fell asleep in a bedroom. Airman K testified that the next thing she remembered after falling asleep was waking up in the bedroom, nearly naked, with the appellant on top of her and raping her.]

Appellant did not testify at trial. Special Agent Donald I. Phillips was called by the Government and testified that following a rights advisement, appellant gave an oral statement in December, approximately five months after the incident with Airman K. In the statement, appellant admitted having sexual intercourse with Airman K. Appellant also stated that prior to having sex with him, Airman K had not said anything, and her eyes were closed. However, he claimed there were a couple of times when his penis came out of Airman K's vagina and she reinserted it.

During cross-examination of Agent Phillips, defense counsel established that a number of facts contained in appellant's statement were consistent with a consensual act of intercourse: Airman K was not so intoxicated that she could not participate in foreplay; Airman K rubbed the back of appellant's neck prior to sexual intercourse; twice she asked appellant to stop and he did stop; and appellant told Agent Phillips that when they completed having sexual intercourse, they talked.

Later, the military judge, after a timely objection by trial defense counsel, permitted appellant's first sergeant, Master Sergeant (MSgt) Gary E. Green, to offer his opinion of appellant's character for truthfulness. MSgt Green testified as follows:

---

[2] Note: the Military Rules of Evidence cited in this case are identical to their counterparts in the Federal Rules of Evidence.

Q.   *Sergeant Green, in your duties as first sergeant have you had contacts with the accused?*

A.   *Yes, I have.*

Q.   *And, based on those contacts with the accused, have you been able to form an opinion as to his character for truthfulness?*

A.   *Yes, I have.*

Q.   *What is that opinion?*

A.   *That he is not truthful. . . .*

Appellant contends that when trial defense counsel cross-examined Agent Phillips about appellant's oral statement, appellant was merely exercising his rights under the rule of completeness. As such, this did not put appellant's credibility in issue, and admission of MSgt Green's opinion regarding appellant's character for truthfulness was improper. Appellant also asserts that his statement to the investigator should not have been admitted as hearsay, but rather, should have been admitted as an admission by a party-opponent under Mil.R.Evid. 801(d)(2)(A), Manual for Courts-Martial, United States (2000 ed.). Consequently, his credibility was not subject to attack under Mil.R.Evid. 806. Moreover, he argues that the probative value of MSgt Green's opinion was far outweighed by the danger of unfair prejudice to the appellant. . . .

We review the decision by the military judge to admit the first sergeant's opinion evidence under the abuse of discretion standard. United States v. Johnson, 46 M.J. 8, 10 (1997).

This is a case where the defense counsel attempted to advocate his cause through the use of his client's out-of-court statement to an investigator. That statement contained both exculpatory and inculpatory facts. Trial defense counsel elicited appellant's exculpatory statements through his zealous cross-examination of a government witness, and in so doing, suggested to the factfinder that the exculpatory statements deserved more weight than appellant's inculpatory statements. Proper resolution of the granted issue requires us to discuss a number of interlocking rules of evidence and theories, to include Mil.R.Evid. 106, 304, 607, and 806, as well as the common law rule of completeness.

1. Rule of Completeness

Mil.R.Evid. 106, the rule of completeness, which is taken "without change" from the federal rule (Drafters' Analysis of Mil.R.Evid. 106, Manual, supra at A22-4), provides:

> When a writing or recorded statement or part thereof is introduced by a party, an adverse party may require that party at that time to introduce any other part or any other writing or recorded statement which ought in fairness to be considered contemporaneously with it.

The rule of completeness is a rule that governs the scope of evidence. It particularizes the type of evidence (written and oral), the relationship between when all or part of a written or oral statement may be introduced, and the operation of procedural rules.

Moreover, in *Beech Aircraft Corp. v. Rainey*, 488 U.S. 153, 172, 109 S. Ct. 439, 102 L. Ed. 2d 445 (1988), the Court indicated that Fed.R.Evid. 106 "partially codified" the common law completeness doctrine. Under the common law rule of completeness, "the opponent, against whom a part of an utterance has been put in, may in his turn complement it by putting in the remainder, in order to secure for the tribunal a complete understanding of the total tenor and effect of the utterance." Id. at 171, quoting 7 Wigmore, Evidence § 2113 at 653 (Chadbourn rev. 1978).

The rule of completeness must be examined in terms of the common law rule and the authority of the judge under Fed.R.Evid. 611(a). Under either the federal or military rules version, Rule 106 only applies to written or recorded statements. However, under the common-law version, and at the discretion of the judge under Rule 611(a), the rule is applicable to oral testimony as well. See, e.g., United States v. Alvarado, 882 F.2d 645, 650 n.5 (2d Cir. 1989).

Under Fed.R.Evid. 106 and its military counterpart, the opponent may demand that the proponent expand the scope of questioning and introduce the entire statement to avoid creating a misleading impression. If the defense in this case had required the prosecution to introduce the remainder of appellant's statement to Agent Phillips, that would not have prevented the application of Rule 806, as explained below.

Here, the defense did not require the prosecution to introduce a part of the statement during its direct examination. Rather than invoking Rule 106, the defense applied the common law completeness doctrine and waited for their own stage of presentation of proof. Since the prosecution had introduced part of the statement, the defense could introduce the remainder, since there was no question as to its relevance.

The defense argues that since they introduced the rest of the statement through their cross-examination of Agent Phillips, that precluded the Government from relying on Rule 806. But had the entire statement been introduced by the prosecution, Rule 607 would not have precluded them, as the proponent of the evidence, from impeaching their own witness. But as we indicated, the judge has discretion under Rule 6ll(a) and Rule 403 to exclude the evidence when its introduction may be unfair to a party, a waste of time, or confusing to the jury.

Thus, Rule 106 permits the defense to interrupt the prosecution's presentation of the case as to written and recorded statements. See, e.g., United States v. Branch, 91 F.3d 699 (5th Cir. 1996) (some circuits have held that Rule 106 does not apply to testimony concerning oral conversations).

It must be recognized that some states have broadened their counterpart to Fed.R.Evid. 106 by covering all statements, whether or not written or recorded. See Iowa R. Evid. 106; Oregon Evid. Code, Rule 106. We need not decide this issue on the common law rule because [Mil.R.Evid. 304(h)(2) permits the defense to complete an incomplete statement regardless of whether it was oral or in writing.].

2. Impeachment of Non-Testifying Declarant

Mil.R.Evid. 806 provides in part:

> When a hearsay statement, or a statement defined in Mil.R.Evid. 801(d)(2)(C), (D), or (E), has been admitted in evidence, the credibility of the declarant may be attacked, and if attacked may be supported, by any evidence which would be admissible for those purposes if [the] declarant had testified as a witness.

By its terms, Rule 806 applies to the introduction of "a hearsay statement, or a statement defined in Mil.R.Evid. 801(d)(2), (C), (D), or (E)."

The first part of the rule would encompass a "hearsay" admission by appellant. When considering adoption of Rule 806, the Senate Judiciary Committee "considered it unnecessary to include statements contained in rule 801(d)(2)(A) and (B) — the statement by the party-opponent himself or the statement of which he has manifested his adoption — because the credibility of the party opponent is always subject to an attack on his credibility [sic]." S.Rep. No. 93-1277 (1974), reprinted in 1974 U.S.C.C.A.N. 7051, 7069 n.28. This is not a case where the prosecution sought to introduce the accused's inconsistent statement under Mil.R.Evid. 801(d)(2)(A) or (B) for the purpose of impeaching the accused under Mil.R.Evid. 806. In these situations, the trial judge has the discretion under Rule 403 to balance equities and control the introduction of evidence. See United States v. Dent, 984 F.2d 1453, 1460 (7th Cir. 1993).

Although it was able to find no military cases that address this exact issue, the Court of Criminal Appeals resolved that it was not reasonable to conclude that attacks on the credibility of the speaker's statement are excluded merely because the statement is admitted as made by a party-opponent. 52 M.J. at 733. In so doing, the lower court relied on the rationale of the Senate Judiciary Committee, as well as the holdings of two federal Circuit Courts that previously confronted the very same issue. Id.; United States v. Shay, 57 F.3d 126, 132 (1st Cir. 1995); United States v. Velasco, 953 F.2d 1467, 1473 (7th Cir. 1992). We agree with both the Court of Criminal Appeals and the First and Seventh Circuits. When the defense affirmatively introduces the accused's statement in response to the prosecution's direct examination, the prosecution is not prohibited from impeaching the declarant under Mil.R.Evid. 806.

3. Character Evidence

. . . The first sergeant was acquainted with appellant through his role as first sergeant and as an investigator and could form an opinion of appellant's character through that exposure. In this case, before the judge allowed the witness to testify in front of the members, he limited the testimony and excluded the details that were used to establish an adequate foundation.

MSgt Green testified out of the hearing of the members that he was appellant's first sergeant at the 338th Training Squadron, Keesler Air Force Base. He addressed appellant's involvement with underage drinking at his off-post apartment. He saw appellant numerous times, both before and after the date of the offense, and was personally involved with appellant on at least two occasions, including disciplinary actions against appellant. As the first sergeant, he investigated the incidents involving appellant.

We hold that the prosecution established an adequate foundation for the first sergeant's opinion as to appellant's untruthfulness, and that the judge correctly precluded specific instances of misconduct to be introduced to support that opinion.

The decision of the United States Air Force Court of Criminal Appeals is affirmed.

DISCUSSION QUESTIONS

1. What impact do you think the character witness's testimony about the appellant's character had on the military jury? Was it magnified because the appellant did not actually give live testimony in the courtroom?

2. Assume that the judge's ruling about the character evidence was erroneous. Conduct a harmless-error analysis of the ruling.

3. What principles does this case teach about the interlocking nature of the rules of evidence and the responsibilities of counsel at trial?

PROBLEMS

Problem 26-1. One day, while parking his car in the parking lot of a grocery store, Walter witnessed an accident between a green pickup truck and a red sports car. The two vehicles collided with each other when they both tried to enter the same parking spot at the same time. Although no one was injured, both vehicles were totaled. Walter was genuinely shocked and startled by the accident; it was the first time he had ever seen an accident. When a police officer arrived a few minutes later, Walter immediately approached him and said, "Officer, it's the damnedest thing I ever saw! The green pickup truck was about halfway into his turn to get into that parking spot when the red car turned right in front of him trying to get into the same spot." The officer duly noted the information in his report.

The driver of the pickup truck sued the driver of the sports car for negligence. During the discovery phase of the trial, attorneys for the defendant hired a private investigator. The investigator learned that Walter frequently went to a local bar, where he often told the story of the accident. The investigator learned that Walter had told at least three versions of the story: version one assigned culpability to driver of the red car; version two assigned culpability to the driver of the green truck; and version three assigned culpability to the brightness of the sun on that day, which would have blinded the drivers of both cars and made it impossible for either of them to see the other. The investigator also learned that in the bartender's opinion, Walter was "a lying blowhard who would say anything to get attention." Neither side deposed Walter or put him on the witness list for trial.

At trial, the plaintiff called the police officer to testify about his investigation of the accident. The officer quoted Walter's statement to him in the parking lot, which was admitted into evidence without defense objection. On the defense case in chief, the defense intends to call the private investigator to testify about Walter's three versions of the event from the bar and the bartender to testify about Walter's character. Evaluate the admissibility of the defense evidence in this case.

Residual Hearsay

Through Dec. 1, 2011	After Dec. 1, 2011
Rule 807. Residual Exception	**Rule 807. Residual Exception**
A statement not specifically covered by Rule 803 or 804 but having equivalent circumstantial guarantees of trustworthiness, is not excluded by the hearsay rule, if the court determines that (A) the statement is offered as evidence of a material fact; (B) the statement is more probative on the point for which it is offered than any other evidence which the proponent can procure through reasonable efforts; and (C) the general purposes of these rules and the interests of justice will best be served by admission of the statement into evidence. However, a statement may not be admitted under this exception unless the proponent of it makes known to the adverse party sufficiently in advance of the trial or hearing to provide the adverse party with a fair opportunity to prepare to meet it, the proponent's intention to offer the statement and the particulars of it, including the name and address of the declarant.	**(a) In General**. Under the following circumstances, a hearsay statement is not excluded by the rule against hearsay even if the statement is not specifically covered by a hearsay exception in Rule 803 or 804: (1) the statement has equivalent circumstantial guarantees of trustworthiness; (2) it is offered as evidence of a material fact; (3) it is more probative on the point for which it is offered than any other evidence that the proponent can obtain through reasonable efforts; and (4) admitting it will best serve the purposes of these rules and the interests of justice. **(b) Notice**. The statement is admissible only if, before the trial or hearing, the proponent gives an adverse party reasonable notice of the intent to offer the statement and its particulars, including the declarant's name and address, so that the party has a fair opportunity to meet it.

Basis, Foundational Requirements and Applications at Trial

The drafters of the Federal Rules of Evidence created a comprehensive set of rules involving hearsay, but they recognized that the rules might not cover all conceivable hearsay situations:

> The preceding 23 exceptions of Rule 803 and the first five [four] exceptions of Rule 804(b), infra, are designed to take full advantage of the accumulated wisdom and experience of the past in dealing with hearsay. It would, however, be presumptuous to assume that all possible desirable exceptions to the hearsay rule have been catalogued and to pass the hearsay rule to oncoming generations as a closed system. [The residual hearsay exceptions] are accordingly included. They do not contemplate an unfettered

exercise of judicial discretion, but they do provide for treating new and presently unanticipated situations which demonstrate a trustworthiness within the spirit of the specifically stated exceptions. Within this framework, room is left for growth and development in the law of evidence in the hearsay area, consistently with the broad purposes expressed in Rule 802.[3]

The drafters originally created two companion residual hearsay rules and codified them as Rules 803(24) and 804(b)(5). In 1997, the rules were combined as Rule 807.

The purpose of the residual hearsay rule is to provide for the admission of trustworthy hearsay statements that would not otherwise fit into a recognized hearsay exception. It was never intended as an easy alternative route for admitting unreliable hearsay or statements that fail for good reason to meet the foundational requirements of a codified exception. On the other hand, if a reliable hearsay statement meets most of the foundational requirements of a codified exception — a "near miss" as it is often termed by cases and commentators — it could be an ideal candidate for admission as residual hearsay.

In order to ensure that residual hearsay is a relative rarity at trial, the drafters erected some substantial foundational and procedural barriers to its admission.

Residual hearsay cannot be admitted at trial unless it satisfies the following elements:

(1) The proponent has provided notice to the adverse party sufficiently in advance of the trial or hearing to enable a fair opportunity for the adverse party to prepare to meet it;

(2) The statement bears circumstantial guarantees of trustworthiness equivalent to those of the twenty-three exceptions under Rule 803 and/or the five exceptions of Rule 804;

(3) The statement is offered as proof of a material fact at trial;

(4) The statement is more probative on the point for which it is being offered than any other evidence that the proponent can procure through reasonable efforts;

(5) The statement's admission into evidence serves the general purposes of the Federal Rules of Evidence and the interests of justice.

(6) For testimonial statements in a criminal case, the defendant's confrontation rights have been satisfied.

These elements make it much more difficult to lay the foundation for residual hearsay than for any other codified hearsay exceptions; in effect, they establish a necessity requirement for residual hearsay at trial. The advocate must persuade the judge not only that the hearsay is trustworthy, but also that it is the best available evidence to help prove a material fact at trial.

The most challenging element to establish is that the statement has circumstantial guarantees of trustworthiness equivalent to the codified hearsay exceptions.

---

[3] FED. R. EVID. 803(24), advisory committee notes.

The methods of showing trustworthiness are as varied as the factual circumstances in the case. The influential treatise *McCormick on Evidence* identifies a number of trustworthiness factors from case law: the declarant's motivation to speak truthfully or untruthfully; spontaneity of the statement; whether the statement was elicited by leading questions; time lapse between event and statement; whether the declarant was subject to cross-examination at the time the statement was made; relationship between declarant and the person to whom the statement was made; whether declarant recanted or reaffirmed the statement; whether the statement was recorded or videotaped; and whether the declarant's first-hand knowledge is clearly demonstrated.[4]

Another common method of proving trustworthiness is to compare the characteristics of the proffered hearsay to the foundational requirements of an existing hearsay exception. For example, in *United States v. Medico*,[5] a bank robbery case, the trial judge admitted as residual hearsay a bank employee's testimony about statements made to him by unidentified bystanders about the make, model and license plate number of the getaway car approximately five minutes after the robbery was over. The judge did not admit the statements as present sense impressions because of an advisory committee note expressing disapproval of admitting statements under that exception when a bystander's identity is unknown.[6] The appellate court affirmed the admission, holding that the statements were very similar to present sense impressions under Rule 803(1) and also had other factual indicia of trustworthiness.[7]

Cases, Discussion Questions and Problems

DALLAS COUNTY v. COMMERCIAL UNION ASSURANCE CO.
United States Court of Appeals, Fifth Circuit
286 F.2d 388 (5th Cir. 1961)

This appeal presents a single question — the admissibility in evidence of a newspaper to show that the Dallas County Courthouse in Selma, Alabama, was damaged by fire in 1901. We hold that the newspaper was admissible, and affirm the judgment below.

[The clock tower of the Dallas County Courthouse in Selma, Alabama, collapsed on a Sunday morning, July 7, 1957. The debris revealed some charred timbers. An expert witness reported that the charring was evidence of a lightning strike, and several witnesses reported that a bolt of lightning had struck the courthouse on July 2, 1957. Dallas County was insured for loss to the courthouse caused by fire or lightning. The insurer's investigators and engineers claimed the courthouse was not struck by lightning but had collapsed because of structural weakness, faulty design, deterioration and overloading. They opined that the charred timbers were

---

[4] 2 McCORMICK ON EVIDENCE § 324, notes 12–23 and accompanying text (6th ed. 2006).

[5] 557 F.2d 309 (2d Cir. 1977).

[6] *Id.* at 315.

[7] *Id.*

the result of a fire that must have occurred many years earlier.] The insurers denied liability.

The County sued its insurers in the Circuit Court of Dallas County. [The cases were removed to federal court and consolidated.] The case went to the jury on one issue: did lightning cause the collapse of the clock tower?

The record contains ample evidence to support a jury verdict either way. The County produced witnesses who testified they saw lighting strike the clock tower; the insurers produced witnesses who testified an examination of the debris showed that lightning did not strike the clock tower. Some witnesses said the char was fresh and smelled smoky; other witnesses said [it] was obviously old and had no fresh smoky smell at all. Both sides presented a great mass of engineering testimony bearing on the design, construction, overload or lack of overload. All of this was for the jury to evaluate. The jury chose to believe the insurers' witnesses and brought in a verdict for the defendants.

During the trial the defendants introduced a copy of the Morning Times of Selma for June 9, 1901. This issue carried an unsigned article describing a fire that occurred at two in the morning of June 9, 1901, while the courthouse was still under construction. The article stated, in part: 'The unfinished dome of the County's new courthouse was in flames at the top, and * * * soon fell in. The fire was soon under control and the main building was saved. * * *' The insurers do not contend that the collapse of the tower resulted from unsound charred timbers used in the repair of the building after the fire; they offered the newspaper account to show there had been a fire long before 1957 that would account for charred timber in the clock tower.

As a predicate for introducing the newspaper in evidence, the defendants called to the stand the editor of the Selma Times-Journal who testified that his publishing company maintains archives of the published issues of the Times-Journal and of the Morning Times, its predecessor, and that the archives contain the issue of the Morning Times of Selma for June 9, 1901, offered in evidence. The plaintiff objected that the newspaper article was hearsay; that it was not a business record nor an ancient document, nor was it admissible under any recognized exception to the hearsay doctrine. The trial judge admitted the newspaper as part of the records of the Selma Times-Journal. The sole error Dallas County specifies on appeal is the admission of the newspaper in evidence.

In the Anglo-American adversary system of law, courts usually will not admit evidence unless its accuracy and trust-worthiness may be tested by cross-examination. Here, therefore, the plaintiff argues that the newspaper should not be admitted: 'You cannot cross-examine a newspaper.' Of course, a newspaper article is hearsay, and in almost all circumstances is inadmissible. However, the law governing hearsay is somewhat less than pellucid. And, as with most rules, the hearsay rule is not absolute; it is replete with exceptions. Witnesses die, documents are lost, deeds are destroyed, memories fade. All too often, primary evidence is not available and courts and lawyers must rely on secondary evidence. . . .

There are no cases clearly in point — at least none that we have found — in Alabama decisions, in the decisions of other states, or in the federal decisions. We decide this case, therefore, on general principles of relevancy and materiality. . . .

We turn now to a case, decided long before the Federal Rules were adopted, in which the court used an approach we consider appropriate for the solution of the problem before us. G. & C. Merriam Co. v. Syndicate Pub. Co., 2 Cir., 1913, 207 F. 515, 518, concerned a controversy between dictionary publishers over the use of the title 'Webster's Dictionary' when the defendant's dictionary allegedly was not based upon Webster's dictionary at all. The bone of contention was whether a statement in the preface to the dictionary was admissible as evidence of the facts it recited. Ogilvie, the compiler of the dictionary, stated in his preface that he used Webster's Dictionary as the basis for his own publication. The dictionary, with its preface, was published in 1850, sixty-three years before the trial of the case. Ogilvie's published statement was challenged as hearsay. Judge Learned Hand, then a district judge, unable, as we are here, to find a case in point, for authority relied solely on Wigmore on Evidence (then a recent publication), particularly on Wigmore's analysis that 'the requisites of an exception to the hearsay rule are necessity and circumstantial guaranty of trustworthiness'. Wigmore on Evidence, §§ 1421, 1422, 1690 (1st ed. 1913). Applying these criteria, Judge Hand held that the statement was admissible as an exception to the hearsay rule:

> 'Ogilvie's preface is of course an unsworn statement and as such only hearsay testimony, which may be admitted only as an exception to the general rule. The question is whether there is such an exception. I have been unable to find any express authority in point and must decide the question upon principle. In the first place, I think it fair to insist that to reject such a statement is to refuse evidence about the truth of which no reasonable person should have any doubt whatever, because it fulfills both the requisites of an exception to the hearsay rule, necessity and circumstantial guaranty of trustworthiness. Wigmore, §§ 1421, 1422, 1690, * * * Besides Ogilvie, everyone else is dead who ever knew anything about the matter and could intelligently tell us what the fact is. * * * As to the trustworthiness of the testimony, it has the guaranty of the occasion, at which there was no motive for fabrication.' 207 F. 515, 518.

The Court of Appeals adopted the district court's opinion in its entirety.

The first of the two requisites is necessity. As to necessity, Wigmore points out this requisite means that unless the hearsay statement is admitted, the facts it brings out may otherwise be lost, either because the person whose assertion is offered may be dead or unavailable, or because the assertion is of such a nature that one could not expect to obtain evidence of the same value from the same person or from other sources. Wigmore, § 1421 (3rd ed.). 'In effect, Wigmore says that, as the word necessity is here used, it is not to be interpreted as uniformly demanding a showing of total inaccessibility of firsthand evidence as a condition precedent to the acceptance of a particular piece of hearsay, but that necessity exists where otherwise great practical inconvenience would be experienced in making the desired proof. (Wigmore, 3rd Ed., Vol. V, sec. 1421; Vol. VI, sec. 1702). * * * If it were otherwise, the result would be that the exception created to the hearsay rule would thereby be mostly, if not completely, destroyed.' United States v. Alu-minum Co. of America, D.C.1940, 35 F.Supp. 820, 823.

The fire referred to in the newspaper account occurred fifty-eight years before the trial of this case. Any witness who saw that fire with sufficient understanding to observe it and describe it accurately, would have been older than a young child at the time of the fire. We may reasonably assume that at the time of the trial he was either dead or his faculties were dimmed by the passage of fifty-eight years. It would have been burdensome, but not impossible, for the defendant to have discovered the name of the author of the article (although it had no by-line) and, perhaps, to have found an eye-witness to the fire. But it is improbable — so it seems to us — that any witness could have been found whose recollection would have been accurate at the time of the trial of this case. And it seems impossible that the testimony of any witness would have been as accurate and as reliable as the statement of facts in the contemporary newspaper article.

The rationale behind the 'ancient documents' exception is applicable here: after a long lapse of time, ordinary evidence regarding signatures or handwriting is virtually unavailable, and it is therefore permissible to resort to circumstantial evidence. Thus, in Trustees of German Township, Montgomery County v. Farmers & Citizens Savings Bank Co., Ohio Com.Pl.1953, 113 N.E.2d 409, 412, affirmed Ohio App., 115 N.E.2d 690, the court admitted as ancient documents newspapers eighty years old containing notices of advertisements for bids relating to the town hall: 'Such exhibits, by reason of age, alone, and unquestioned authenticity, qualify as ancient documents.' The ancient documents rule applies to documents a generation or more in age. Here, the Selma Times-Journal article is almost two generations old. The principle of necessity, not requiring absolute impossibility or total inaccessibility of first-hand knowledge, is satisfied by the practicalities of the situation before us.

The second requisite for admission of hearsay evidence is trustworthiness. According to Wigmore, there are three sets of circumstances when hearsay is trustworthy enough to serve as a practicable substitute for the ordinary test of cross-examination: 'Where the circumstances are such that a sincere and accurate statement would naturally be uttered, and no plan of falsification be formed; where, even though a desire to falsify might present itself, other considerations, such as the danger of easy detection on the fear of punishment, would probably counteract its force; where the statement was made under such conditions of publicity that an error, if it had occurred, would probably have been detected and corrected.' 5 Wigmore, Evidence, § 1422 (3rd ed.) These circumstances fit the instant case.

There is no procedural canon against the exercise of common sense in deciding the admissibility of hearsay evidence. In 1901 Selma, Alabama, was a small town. Taking a common sense view of this case, it is inconceivable to us that a newspaper reporter in a small town would report there was a fire in the dome of the new courthouse — if there had been no fire. He is without motive to falsify, and a false report would have subjected the newspaper and him to embarrassment in the community. The usual dangers inherent in hearsay evidence, such as lack of memory, faulty narration, intent to influence the court proceedings, and plain lack of truthfulness are not present here. To our minds, the article published in the Selma Morning-Times on the day of the fire is more reliable, more trustworthy, more competent evidence than the testimony of a witness called to the stand fifty-eight years later.

We hold, that in matters of local interest, when the fact in question is of such a public nature it would be generally known throughout the community, and when the questioned fact occurred so long ago that the testimony of an eye-witness would probably be less trustworthy than a contemporary newspaper account, a federal court . . . may relax the exclusionary rules to the extent of admitting the newspaper article in evidence. We do not characterize this news-paper as a 'business record', nor as an 'ancient document', nor as any other readily identifiable and happily tagged species of hearsay exception. It is admissible because it is necessary and trustworthy, relevant and material, and its admission is within the trial judge's exercise of discretion in holding the hearing within reasonable bounds.

Judgment is affirmed.

DISCUSSION QUESTIONS

1. Compare this opinion with Rule 807. What similarities and differences are there between the common-law doctrine espoused in *Dallas County* and the rule that was eventually codified as Rule 807?

2. Could the hearsay code be simplified if all trustworthy hearsay was presumptively admissible? Would that be a desirable result? Why or why not?

3. What should be the proper balancing test for necessity and trustworthiness? Suppose that a residual hearsay statement was highly trustworthy but of moderate to marginal necessity — would the trustworthiness weigh in favor of admissibility? What if it was or moderate to marginal trustworthiness but highly necessary — even critical — to proving a material fact in a case?

PROBLEMS

Problem 26-2. Melissa is a 16-year-old child with cancer. During a hospital stay, a doctor told her she was about to die. Moments later, she tearfully told her mother that she had been involved in a sexual relationship with one of her teachers at the high school for most of the school year. She also told her mother that she had committed some petty crimes in the past year: shoplifting, underage drinking and curfew violations. The mother called the police, who interviewed Melissa and videotaped the interview. Her statement and interview formed the basis for an investigation against the teacher.

At the teacher's trial, Melissa, still alive, is available to testify. She cannot, however, remember anything about the statement to her mother, or the alleged sexual relationship with her teacher. There is no other evidence available of sexual abuse.

Can her statement and interview be used at trial?

Credibility of Hearsay Declarants and Residual Hearsay: Quick Hits

- When a hearsay declarant's testimony is introduced into evidence, the declarant becomes a witness in the proceedings.

- The credibility of a hearsay declarant may be attacked and/or supported using the methods that would be available had the declarant testified in person at the proceedings.

- Residual hearsay permits the introduction of trustworthy hearsay if it is necessary, the interests of justice would be served, and it is the best evidence available on the issue that the proponent could reasonably procure.

- Establishing the trustworthiness of residual hearsay can often be accomplished by analogizing it to existing, established hearsay exceptions.

Chapter References

CHRISTOPHER B. MUELLER & LAIRD C. KIRKPATRICK, EVIDENCE §§ 8.80–8.82 (4th ed. 2009).

GLEN WEISSENBERGER & JAMES J. DUANE, FEDERAL RULES OF EVIDENCE: RULES, LEGISLATIVE HISTORY, COMMENTARY AND AUTHORITY §§ 806–07 (6th ed. 2009).

JACK B. WEINSTEIN & MARGARET A. BERGER, WEINSTEIN'S FEDERAL EVIDENCE §§ 806–07 (Joseph M. McLaughlin ed., Matthew Bender 2d ed. 1997).

KENNETH S. BROUN, McCORMICK ON EVIDENCE §§ 321–27 (6th ed. 2006).

STEVEN GOODE & OLIN GUY WELLBORN III, COURTROOM HANDBOOK ON FEDERAL EVIDENCE Ch. 5 (West 2010).

III. APPLICATION EXERCISE

Preparing to Attack or Support the Credibility of a Hearsay Declarant

As we have seen throughout our study of hearsay, advocates frequently become aware of hearsay issues during the discovery and pretrial stages of a case. This is particularly true when the hearsay is a significant part of a party's case. For purposes of this discussion and this exercise, "hearsay declarant" also includes someone whose testimony is admitted under the hearsay exemptions of Rule 801(d)(2).

The opponent of hearsay evidence should always have a fallback position in case the hearsay is admitted over objection. Rule 806 can play an important role in helping to call into impeach the hearsay testimony of the declarant. If the identity of the declarant is known, the opponent can investigate the declarant and prepare an impeachment, just with any other witness. With modifications as contained in Rule 806, all of the impeachment methods available for a live witness may be used for a hearsay declarant's testimony. Likewise, the proponent of the evidence can anticipate attacks and prepare to support the credibility of the declarant.

The Exercise

Objective: To demonstrate proficiency in impeaching the testimony of a hearsay declarant.

Factual Scenario. Use **Problem 26-2,** above, as the basic factual scenario for this exercise. Assume that the judge has admitted the declarant's videotaped testimony into evidence as residual hearsay. Further assume that the declarant is lucid and available to testify, although she claims not to remember what she said in the hospital or that the abuse actually occurred.

Add the following additional facts:

1) The declarant, an honor student, had received a "D" in the teacher's class the previous semester. The teacher alleged that the declarant had plagiarized a paper and had given her a zero on it. The declarant was very angry about this.

2) Two high school students, Bob and Maggie, are available to testify about the declarant's character for truthfulness. Bob, who does not personally know the declarant but has heard about the plagiarizing episode as well as some gossip about the declarant, will testify that she has a reputation for untruthfulness. Maggie, the declarant's best friend, will testify that in her opinion, the declarant is a truthful person.

3) The declarant kept a daily diary from the time she was 13 up until the present day. Her diary records her first kiss, the first time she drove a car, her first class in high school, her first day of work, and many other milestones. It records her thoughts and feelings about her friends, teachers and boyfriends. The diary mentions nothing about a sexual relationship with the teacher. A defense investigator, Irving, has read the entire diary in preparation for trial.

Advance Preparation: Be able to explain at the beginning of the exercise why the judge permitted the admissibility of the declarant's videotaped statement as residual hearsay. Armed with the knowledge that the declarant's video testimony will be admitted into evidence, prepare a defense impeachment of the declarant using the available facts, Rule 806, and the impeachment rules and doctrines you studied earlier in the semester. Prepare prosecution responses to these impeachment efforts.

In-class Exercise: Students will play the following roles: judge, prosecuting attorney, defense attorney, Bob, Irving and Maggie. The declarant is also available for examination under Rule 806.

PART SEVEN
_____
OPINION TESTIMONY AND EXPERT WITNESSES

Chapter 27

RULE 701 AND LAY OPINION TESTIMONY

Chapter Objectives:

- Introduce and explain lay opinion testimony under Rule 701 and the differences between lay and expert opinions
- Analyze and discuss issues pertaining to lay opinion testimony
- Apply the concepts from this chapter in a courtroom application exercise

I. BACKGROUND AND EXPLANATORY MATERIAL

Introduction to Opinion Testimony

Earlier in this book, we discussed the law of witnesses and learned that Rule 602 requires witnesses to have personal knowledge of the facts in order to testify; these witnesses are known as "fact" or "percipient" witnesses. Under most circumstances, percipient witnesses are permitted to testify only about what they have seen, heard, or otherwise experienced with their senses. To borrow the famous words of Sergeant Joe Friday in *Dragnet*, witness testimony must convey "Just the facts, ma'am." Percipient witnesses are not permitted to draw conclusions, interpret events, speculate about what someone else might have been thinking, or otherwise deviate from the straight and narrow path of fact-based testimony.

When witnesses draw conclusions, speculate, or interpret facts, their testimony crosses the line from "just the facts" to opinion testimony. To be sure, the line between fact and opinion is often blurry: even the simplest factual observation involves processing input, interpreting information and reaching a conclusion; in essence, a statement of fact is nothing more than the witness's opinion of what the observed fact is. McCormick used an example that illustrates the thin line that separates fact from opinion:

> The difference between the statement, "He was driving on the left-hand side of the road" which would be classed as "fact" under the rule, and "He was driving carelessly" which would be called "opinion" is merely a

difference between a more concrete and specific form of descriptive statement and a less specific and concrete form.[1]

Nonetheless, the law of evidence recognizes a difference between statements of fact and opinion, favoring the former and generally discouraging the latter.

The reason for discouraging opinion testimony is based on the role of the fact-finder in the adversary trial system. Conclusions and decisions are reserved for the fact-finder, which must sort between partisan presentations by opposing parties to determine the truth. To the extent the fact-finder places excessive trust in a witness's opinion, the fact-finder abdicates its role at trial.

Although the use of opinion testimony at trial is limited, it is not entirely forbidden. Chapters Eight and Nine introduced the concept of opinion testimony in the context of character evidence. When character is at issue under Rules 404, 413-415 or Rule 608, witnesses can testify about their opinions concerning another person's character traits. Character opinion testimony is limited to broad, conclusory statements such as, "In my opinion, the defendant is peaceful," or "in my opinion, Witness A is not truthful." These opinions are essentially a shorthand summary of the factual interactions between the witness and the individual whose character is at issue.

The rules of evidence contemplate another kind of opinion testimony. Under limited circumstances, certain witnesses are permitted to share their inferences and interpretations of factual events with the fact-finder. Admissible opinions run the gamut from simple observations such as "the car was speeding," to complex conclusions such as "the physician failed to meet the standard of care in treating this patient."

Opinion testimony can be valuable to a fact-finder in an adversary trial system. If the fact-finder trusts the witness, it can rely on the witness's opinion in helping to decide the central issues in the case. For example, it is common practice in medical malpractice cases for each side to call expert witnesses to give opinions about whether the defendant met the standard of care in treating a patient. The specialized knowledge required to render such an opinion would be beyond the understanding of the typical citizen, and therefore, an accepted opinion could form a critical aspect of the fact-finder's decision.

The difference between using fact and opinion testimony at trial is like the difference between taking a train and a car to a destination. Generally speaking, train tracks are much more restrictive than roads; the train traveler is rail-bound until she reaches her destination; she cannot choose alternative routes or stops. Even though an automobile driver is bound by the rules of the road, she has more flexibility in choosing routes and places to stop along the way; she can take shortcuts and, in most cases, reach her destination more quickly than the train traveler. Similarly, a witness who can give an opinion at trial is able to testify more freely than other witnesses, although still required to follow the other rules of evidence.

---

[1] 1 McCormick § 12.

Opinion testimony is divided in two categories by the rules of evidence, lay opinion and expert opinion. This chapter provides a general introduction to both types of opinion testimony, with a focus on the differences between lay and expert opinion testimony.

Lay Opinion Testimony

Through Dec. 1, 2011	After Dec. 1, 2011
Rule 701. Opinion Testimony by Lay Witnesses	**Rule 701. Opinion Testimony by Lay Witnesses**
If the witness is not testifying as an expert, the witness' testimony in the form of opinions or inferences is limited to those opinions or inferences which are (a) rationally based on the perception of the witness, and (b) helpful to a clear understanding of the witness' testimony or the determination of a fact in issue, and (c) not based on scientific, technical, or other specialized knowledge within the scope of Rule 702.	If a witness is not testifying as an expert, testimony in the form of an opinion is limited to one that is: (a) rationally based on the witness's perception; (b) helpful to clearly understanding the witness's testimony or to determining a fact in issue; and (c) not based on scientific, technical, or other specialized knowledge within the scope of Rule 702.

By definition, a layman is someone "who is not a member of a profession or an expert on a particular subject."[2] Lay opinion testimony is testimony that does not depend upon a professional license or access to a specialized body of knowledge. It is opinion testimony based on the common experiences of ordinary human beings.

Under Rule 701, lay opinion testimony is nothing more than a different form of percipient testimony. Like other percipient witnesses, the lay witness is qualified to testify at trial based on direct sensory observations and experiences. Some observations, however, do not easily lend themselves to simple statements of fact. For example, age estimates are almost always a matter of opinion based on experience. It would be very difficult for a witness to explain all of the facts and experiences leading to a particular conclusion about another person's age, so the law permits the witness to render an estimate in the form of an opinion: "She looked like she was somewhere around her mid-twenties." The jurors can then compare the opinion to their own memories and experiences of seeing women in their mid-twenties, forming a mental image that captures the woman's approximate age. Thus, by tapping into the common experiences of ordinary people, lay opinion testimony can be helpful to a jury.

---

[2] Black's Law Dictionary (8th ed. 2004).

On opinions related to age, the Ninth Circuit Court of Appeals has explained the necessity and usefulness of lay opinion testimony in *United States v. Yazzie*,[3] a case in which the trial judge erroneously prohibited the defendant and his witnesses in a statutory rape case from giving their opinions concerning the age of the alleged victim:

> Our finding that the trial judge erred in not admitting the opinions of Yazzie's witnesses as to the minor's age is supported by all of the considerations that underlie Rule 701's authorization of the use of lay opinion testimony. First, it is difficult to distinguish a fifteen-and-a-half-year-old from a sixteen-year-old, and it is still more difficult to put into words why one believes that a person is one age and not the other. There is a certain intangible element involved in one's conclusions on such a question. We form an opinion of a person's age from "a combination of circumstances and appearances which cannot be adequately described and presented with the force and clearness as they appear[]" to us. Skeet, 665 F.2d at 985. Mannerisms and facial features are notoriously difficult to describe accurately, and one's reasons for concluding that a person is a particular age are both too complex and too indefinable to set out fully.
>
> In addition, a witness may not know, let alone be able to report precisely, what factors induced his or her conclusion. In such a case, the fact that the witness reached the conclusion is the important part of the testimony, not the largely undeterminable or inexplicable reasons that prompted the conclusion.
>
> Furthermore, age is a matter on which everyone has an opinion. Knowingly or unknowingly, we all form conclusions about people's ages every day. It is therefore particularly appropriate for a lay witness to express an opinion on the subject.[4]

Other matters that are appropriate for lay opinion testimony include opinions about another person's mood or emotional state; estimates of another person's height and/or weight; speed estimates for moving vehicles; whether a drier was in control of a vehicle; identification of another person; the meaning of code words used by co-conspirators, and the like.

The key factors for lay opinion testimony are established in Rule 701, which requires such opinions to be (1) rationally based on the perception of the witness; and (2) helpful to a clear understanding of the witness's testimony or an important fact at issue in the case. It is relatively easy to develop foundational facts to demonstrate that the opinion is based on the witness's perception. Deciding whether the opinion testimony is helpful is less clear-cut. The judge must determine when an opinion can help overcome the obstacles presented by trying to channel complex information into the narrow confines of direct sensory observation. In *United States v. Skeet*, the 9th Circuit provided a list of factors that are useful in determining when to admit lay opinion testimony:

---

[3] 976 F.2d 1252 (9th Cir. 1992).

[4] Id. at 1255–56.

[O]pinions of non-experts may be admitted where the facts could not otherwise be adequately presented or described to the jury in such a way as to enable the jury to form an opinion or reach an intelligent conclusion. If it is impossible or difficult to reproduce the data observed by the witnesses, or the facts are difficult of explanation, or complex, or are of a combination of circumstances and appearances which cannot be adequately described and presented with the force and clearness as they appeared to the witness, the witness may state his impressions and opinions based upon what he observed. It is a means of conveying to the jury what the witness has seen or heard.[5]

Lay opinion testimony, then, is helpful when it can help facilitate a common understanding based on universal experiences that are difficult to break down into their constituent facts.

In addition to monitoring the lines between fact and opinion, a judge must also ensure that advocates do not attempt to smuggle expert opinion testimony into the courtroom under the guise of lay opinion testimony. Rule 701 contains a third factor in evaluating lay opinion testimony: the opinion cannot be based on "scientific, technical, or other specialized knowledge within the scope of Rule 702." Opinions based on these factors require someone qualified as an expert witness under Rule 702 and its supporting case law.

Sound reasons exist for differentiating lay and opinion testimony. Because there are no special requirements associated with lay opinion testimony, there is no need to provide notice to opposing counsel and an opportunity to introduce a counter-opinion. In contrast, Rule 26 of the Federal Rules of Civil Procedure and Rule 16 of the Federal Rules of Criminal Procedures — as well as many state counterparts to these rules — require advance notice of expert opinion testimony. These notice requirements provide the opponent the opportunity to contest the expert's qualifications and the reliability of the methods or data used in rendering an opinion, as well as to hire an expert of its own choosing, if necessary.

Counsel must be alert to an opponent's efforts to extend lay opinion testimony into the realm of expert opinion testimony. One of the most common scenarios for this concerns the testimony of police officers. Most police officers testify at trial as fact witnesses, relating to the jury what they, like any other percipient witness, saw, heard or experienced when investigating a case. When advocates ask police officers to render opinions as to the meaning or interpretation of their observations, this may cross the line into expert testimony.

---

[5] United States v. Skeet, 665 F.2d 983, 985 (9th Cir. 1982).

II. CASES, DISCUSSION QUESTIONS AND PROBLEMS

UNITED STATES v. MIRANDA
United States Court of Appeals, Fifth Circuit
248 F.3d 434 (5th Cir. 2001)

A large-scale investigation by the Federal Bureau of Investigation ("FBI") and the Dallas Police Department into the distribution of cocaine and marijuana in the Dallas, Texas area led to a nineteen-count federal indictment against twenty-one individuals. The indictment alleged, in pertinent part, that from May 1996 until June 1997, Appellants (1) conspired to possess with the intent to distribute marijuana, cocaine, and cocaine base, in violation of 21 U.S.C. § 856; (2) distributed or possessed cocaine and cocaine base in violation of 21 U.S.C. § 841; and (3) used a telephone to facilitate the distribution of cocaine and cocaine base. Appellants, all related to one another by blood or marriage, sold drugs primarily out of crack houses or "trap" houses. They did a high volume of small quantity sales, typified by "dime rocks" of cocaine — $10 rocks with an estimated weight of.125 grams.

Appellants were jointly tried, along with Roberto Garcia, in July 1998. After a two-and-a-half-week trial, the jury returned a verdict acquitting Garcia and finding the remaining defendants (Appellants) guilty on all counts.

B. Evidentiary Rulings

Appellants challenge the district court's admission of evidence in two separate instances during trial. We review evidentiary rulings for abuse of discretion. See United States v. Parsee, 178 F.3d 374, 379 (5th Cir. 1999).

2. Testimony regarding the use of code words in recorded calls

FBI Special Agent Amado Vega-Irizarry ("Vega") testified at trial that he had been involved in the investigation of the conspiracy and in translating intercepted phone calls from Spanish to English. Vega identified various code words that callers had used and the English drug terms to which the words referred. On the third day of Vega's testimony, Hector Espinoza objected on the grounds that Vega was testifying as an expert. The district court overruled Hector Espinoza's objections, holding that Vega was not testifying as an expert, but stated that if he were, he nonetheless had "the necessary expertise to be able to give this testimony in light of his experience in the law enforcement area."

On appeal, Hector Espinoza maintains that the district court abused its discretion because Vega's testimony "crossed the line" from lay to expert opinion testimony, citing United States v. Griffith, 118 F.3d 318, 321 (5th Cir. 1997) (stating that "drug traffickers' jargon is a specialized body of knowledge, familiar only to those wise in the ways of the drug trade, and therefore a fit subject for expert testimony"), and that Vega was not qualified to testify as an expert on the subject of drug dealers' jargon or code words.

The government replies that Vega's testimony was admissible pursuant to Federal Rule of Evidence 701, which provides:

if the witness is not testifying as an expert, the witness' testimony in the form of opinions or inferences is limited to those opinions or inferences which are (a) rationally based on the perception of the witness and (b) helpful to a clear understanding of the witness' testimony or the determination of a fact in issue.

We agree. Vega's extensive participation in the investigation of this conspiracy, including surveillance, undercover purchases of drugs, debriefings of cooperating witnesses familiar with the drug negotiations of the defendants, and the monitoring and translating of intercepted telephone conversations, allowed him to form opinions concerning the meaning of certain code words used in this drug ring based on his personal perceptions. We therefore hold that Vega's testimony was admissible pursuant to Rule 701 and that the district court did not abuse its discretion in admitting his testimony.

UNITED STATES v. PEOPLES
United States Court of Appeals, Eighth Circuit
250 F.3d 630 (8th Cir. 2001)

Cornelius Peoples and Xavier Lightfoot were convicted of aiding and abetting the murder of a federal government witness in violation of 18 U.S.C. §§ 1512(a)(1)(A), 1512(a)(1)(C), 1512(a)(2), and 1111. The district court sentenced each of them to life imprisonment without the possibility of parole. Both defendants appeal their convictions. We reverse and remand for a new trial.

I.

In December of 1997, Lightfoot was arrested and charged with the robbery of a federally insured credit union in Omaha, Nebraska, based on information supplied by Jovan Ross, who shared a house with Lightfoot. Ross had met with state and federal law enforcement officers in early December of 1997. Federal Bureau of Investigation (FBI) agents executed a search warrant for the Ross-Lightfoot house on December 11, 1997, and recovered items taken from the Omaha credit union. Lightfoot was held at a private pretrial detention facility operated by the Corrections Corporation of America (CCA facility), where he remained at all times relevant to this case. Through the discovery process in the robbery case, Lightfoot learned of Ross's cooperation with law enforcement. Shortly before Lightfoot's trial was scheduled to begin, Ross was murdered.

The government's theory at trial was that Lightfoot and Peoples entered into a contract to pay unknown persons to kill Ross because he was providing information about Lightfoot's criminal activity to law enforcement. Although Ross had no substantial information implicating Peoples in criminal activity, the government argued that Peoples believed that his involvement would be discovered if Ross continued to cooperate with law enforcement. The government further argued that Peoples and others had robbed a jewelry store in St. Joseph, Missouri, to obtain funds to pay the killers. At trial, the government offered into evidence recordings of conversations between Lightfoot and Peoples that occurred while Lightfoot was incarcerated at the CCA facility.

On appeal, the defendants contend that the district court erred in . . . admitting certain testimony.

4. Police Officer's Lay Opinion Testimony

The defendants also challenge the admission of the lay opinion testimony of Lieutenant Timothy Cavanaugh of the Omaha Police Department. A district court's decision to admit or exclude lay opinion testimony is reviewed for abuse of discretion. Wactor v. Spartan Transp. Corp., 27 F.3d 347, 350 (8th Cir. 1994). Although the trial court has broad discretion to admit lay opinions, that discretion may be exercised only after the court finds "that the witness'[s] testimony is based upon his or her personal observation and recollection of concrete facts . . . ,and that those facts cannot be described in sufficient detail to adequately convey to the jury the substance of the testimony." Wactor, 27 F.3d at 350 (internal quotations omitted). Lieutenant Cavanaugh testified about his first-hand observations of one of the robberies. He also gave his opinion, formed in the course of his investigation of one of the robberies, regarding the relationship among the four robberies. Accordingly, we conclude that the district court did not abuse its discretion in admitting Lieutenant Cavanaugh's opinions that were drawn from his personal observations regarding the robberies. The court also properly admitted Lieutenant Cavanaugh's lay opinion regarding the similarities and possible relationship among the robberies.[6]

5. Special Agent Neal's Testimony

Special Agent Joan Neal, the FBI case agent in charge of the investigation of Ross's murder, testified in connection with the recorded telephone and visitation conversations between Peoples and Lightfoot. Drawing on her investigation, Agent Neal gave her opinion regarding the meaning of words and phrases used by the defendants during those conversations. Her testimony was not limited to coded, oblique language, but included plain English words and phrases. She did not personally observe the events and activities discussed in the recordings, nor did she hear or observe the conversations as they occurred. Agent Neal's testimony included her opinions about what the defendants were thinking during the conversations, phrased as contentions supporting her conclusion, repeated throughout her testimony, that the defendants were responsible for Ross's murder.

At various points during her testimony, Agent Neal asserted that Peoples went to Ross's house to murder Ross, that he had paid "the killers to do the job," that Peoples's various comments about being in need of money revolved around his debt to hit men, and that both defendants had sought confirmation of Ross's death. She asserted that during the course of her investigation she had uncovered hidden meanings for apparently neutral words; for example, she testified that when one of the defendants referred to buying a plane ticket for Ross, he in fact meant killing Ross. In short, as the recordings of the Peoples/Lightfoot conversations were played for the jury, Agent Neal was allowed to offer a narrative gloss that consisted

---

[6] [n.1] We offer no opinion whether Cavanaugh's opinions, to the extent that they were based on specialized knowledge resulting from his experience as a police officer, would be admissible under the revised version of Rule 701 that became effective on December 1, 2000. (Under revised Rule 701(c), lay opinion testimony may not be based on specialized knowledge within the scope of Rule 702.)

almost entirely of her personal opinions of what the conversations meant. During several hours of testimony alternating with recorded conversation, Agent Neal made the argument that the defendants had conspired to hire someone to kill Ross, had tendered substantial sums as a partial payment, and then had become anxious when Ross's death was not publicly reported. During direct examination, the prosecutor referred to Agent Neal's statements both as Agent Neal's contentions and as the contentions of the government.

The following excerpts are examples of Agent Neal's testimony. After a recording of Lightfoot requesting a loan was played, Agent Neal stated, "I contend [Lightfoot] is needing a loan to pay the hit man to actually murder Ross." Peoples made repeated references in the taped conversations to "lost and found situations." Agent Neal stated, "When he discusses lost and found, I believe he is talking about no one had found the body yet. It's just a lost situation until somebody finds the body." After the jury heard a recording of Peoples saying, "I done already gave my loot," Agent Neal stated, "I contend that he has already paid the killers to do the job." In response to conversations that related to the burglary of Ross's house, Agent Neal testified, "I believe [Peoples] was there to actually murder Ross at the time."

Both before and during trial, the defendants objected to the admission of Agent Neal's testimony. The government responded by arguing that Agent Neal's contentions constituted lay opinions admissible under Rule 701 of the Federal Rules of Evidence.[7] Stating that it was "possible though not certain" that Agent Neal's testimony was admissible under Rule 701, the district court ruled that her contentions were being admitted as "snippets of early argument from the witness stand" and not as evidence.

Federal Rule of Evidence 602 requires that a witness have personal knowledge of the matters about which she testifies, except in the case of expert opinions. Rule 701 adds that testimony in the form of lay opinions must be rationally based on the perception of the witness. When a law enforcement officer is not qualified as an expert by the court, her testimony is admissible as lay opinion only when the law enforcement officer is a participant in the conversation, has personal knowledge of the facts being related in the conversation, or observed the conversations as they occurred. See, e.g., United States v. Parsee, 178 F.3d 374, 379 (5th Cir. 1999) (witness was a participant in the conversation); United States v. Saulter, 60 F.3d 270, 276 (7th Cir. 1995) (witness had first hand knowledge of the facts being related); United States v. Awan, 966 F.2d 1415, 1430 (11th Cir. 1992) (undercover agent was a participant in the conversations and had personal knowledge of the facts being discussed). Lay opinion testimony is admissible only to help the jury or the court to understand the facts about which the witness is testifying and not to provide specialized explanations or interpretations that an untrained layman could

---

[7] [n.2] The government now argues that Agent Neal's testimony was admissible under Rule 702. At trial, however, the government conceded that Agent Neal was not offering expert testimony, and the district court made clear that it did not consider Agent Neal's contentions as constituting such testimony. Thus, we reject the government's belated argument that Rule 702 provides a basis for admitting Agent Neal's contentions.

not make if perceiving the same acts or events.[8] n3 See United States v. Cortez, 935 F.2d 135, 139-40 (8th Cir. 1991); United States v. Figueroa-Lopez, 125 F.3d 1241, 1244-45 (9th Cir. 1997).

Law enforcement officers are often qualified as experts to interpret intercepted conversations using slang, street language, and the jargon of the illegal drug trade. See, e.g., United States v. Delpit, 94 F.3d 1134, 1144 (8th Cir. 1996) (police officer gave expert testimony interpreting slang and drug codes in connection with recorded telephone calls); United States v. Plunk, 153 F.3d 1011, 1017 (9th Cir. 1998) (police officer gave experttestimony based on his specialized knowledge of narcotics code terminology); United States v. Earls, 42 F.3d 1321, 1324-25 (10th Cir. 1994) (expert testimony was proper to show that defendants were speaking in code). What is essentially expert testimony, however, may not be admitted under the guise of lay opinions. Such a substitution subverts the disclosure and discovery requirements of Federal Rules of Criminal Procedure 26 and 16 and the reliability requirements for expert testimony as set forth in Daubert v. Merrell Dow Pharmaceuticals, Inc., 509 U.S. 579 (1993) and Kumho Tire Co. v. Carmichael, 526 U.S. 137 (1999).

Agent Neal lacked first-hand knowledge of the matters about which she testified. Her opinions were based on her investigation after the fact, not on her perception of the facts. Accordingly, the district court erred in admitting Agent Neal's opinions about the recorded conversations. The court's instructions to the jury that Agent Neal's opinions constituted argument rather than evidence finds no warrant in the Federal Rules of Evidence and could not serve to render admissible that which was inadmissible testimony.

There remains the question whether the admission of Agent Neal's testimony constituted harmless error. We conclude that it did not. The erroneous admission of testimony is not harmless when there is a significant possibility that the testimony had a substantial impact on the jury. See Delpit, 94 F.3d at 1145.

In Delpit, we held that the admission of expert testimony interpreting wire-tapped telephone conversations was harmless despite the fact that the police expert's testimony "appeared on occasion to have gone beyond" its permissible scope because the expert's "occasional elaborations" were supported by other evidence. Id. Unlike Agent Neal, however, the police witness in the Delpit case was qualified as an expert in interpreting street slang and code words. Id. Moreover, the Delpit error resulted only in occasional impermissible interjections within a body of properly admissible testimony, id., whereas the error in this case infected the totality of Agent Neal's testimony. Nor can we describe Agent Neal's testimony as "grounded in other evidence," id., because it consisted largely of her assertions about the meaning of apparently clear statements, together with her addition of details and explanations absent from the recordings. Under the guise of offering lay opinion, Agent Neal was allowed to emboss apparently neutral conversations between the defendants with the imprimatur of the government's case. Rather than

---

[8] [n.3] Although not in effect at the time of trial, the 2000 revisions to Rules 701 and 702 emphasize this distinction between lay and expert opinion testimony. See Fed. R. Evid. 701 advisory committee's note to 2000 Amendments.

offering evidence of which she had personal knowledge, such as the details of her investigation, she was allowed repeatedly to assert that the defendants were discussing not everyday events, but a complicated murder plot.

We note that Larry Platt, a participant in some of the robberies, testified extensively against the defendants. His testimony, however, was not so damaging to them as to render Agent Neal's testimony harmless. Platt had no first-hand knowledge of Ross's murder, and he testified only to a series of conversations about "issuing a plane ticket" to Ross, conversations that he admits he never told anyone about until after he was charged in the robberies. Agent Neal's testimony contained conversations and details that were absent from Platt's testimony, particularly regarding the defendants' efforts to get money to pay hit men and to discover whether Ross's murder had been accomplished. The defendants also subjected Platt to rigorous cross-examination as an interested witness whose story had changed dramatically, and the jury may well have found his testimony inadequate to support a guilty verdict beyond a reasonable doubt had it not been buttressed by Agent Neal's supporting information and opinions.

Moreover, the jury may well have been inclined to give Agent Neal's conclusions undue weight because of her status as an FBI agent. Despite the fact that the court did not qualify her as an expert, Agent Neal was identified as a law enforcement officer, and we cannot rule out the possibility that the jurors may have been inclined to substitute her conclusions on the ultimate issue of the defendants' guilt for their own. In a word, Agent Neal's testimony so invaded the province of the jury that we cannot with confidence say that there was no significant possibility that it had substantial impact on the jury. Accordingly, we must set aside the convictions.

The judgments of conviction are reversed, and the case is remanded to the district

DISCUSSION QUESTIONS

1. What factors help determine whether a witness is giving lay or expert opinion testimony?

2. Is there an analytical difference in the Miranda and Peoples cases? If so, what is it? Why permit the officer in Miranda to interpret conversations but not the agent in Peoples? Which Circuit gets it right: the 5th or the 8th?

3. Both of these cases pre-date the 2001 amendment to FRE 701 that added the "scientific and technical knowledge" disqualifier to lay opinion testimony. Would Miranda have to be decided differently under the current version of Rule 701? Why or why not?

PROBLEMS

Problem 27-1. Darla is a 16-year-old child with developmental disabilities. Although her physical development is normal for a girl her age, she has the mental state and capacity of a 7-year-old girl. When her stepfather sexually abuses her, she reports the incident to her mother using language one might expect from a small child to describe the incident and her stepfather's physical characteristics.

She uses the same language at trial. The prosecution calls her mother to the stand to testify about when Darla reported the abuse to her. During the mother's testimony, the following exchange takes place:

Q: *Some of the language Darla used in describing the incident to you and also here in this courtroom seems inappropriate for a child of her age. Why is that?*

A: *She has a developmental disability.*

Q: *Can you explain to the jury what her "mental age" is, and how this affects her ability to experience and talk about things that happen to her?*

           Opposing counsel: Objection. This calls for expert opinion testimony, and this witness has not been qualified as an expert. Furthermore, we've been given no notice of expert testimony on this matter.

How should the judge rule on this objection, and why?

Quick Hits: Opinion Testimony

- Opinion testimony is a useful way for witnesses to discuss observations that would otherwise be difficult to communicate in the form of discrete factual statements

- Lay opinion testimony is another form of percipient witness testimony and must be based on the observations and ordinary life experience of the witness

- Expert opinion testimony involves the application of specialized knowledge or experience

- Rule 701 forbids the subterfuge introduction of expert opinion testimony under the label of lay opinion testimony

---

Chapter References

CHRISTOPHER B. MUELLER & LAIRD C. KIRKPATRICK, EVIDENCE §§ 7.1–7.4 (4th ed. 2009).

GLEN WEISSENBERGER & JAMES J. DUANE, FEDERAL RULES OF EVIDENCE: RULES, LEGISLATIVE HISTORY, COMMENTARY AND AUTHORITY § 701 (6th ed. 2009).

JACK B. WEINSTEIN & MARGARET A. BERGER, WEINSTEIN'S FEDERAL EVIDENCE § 701 (Joseph M. McLaughlin ed., Matthew Bender 2d ed. 1997).

KENNETH S. BROUN, MCCORMICK ON EVIDENCE §§ 10–12 (6th ed. 2006).

STEVEN GOODE & OLIN GUY WELLBORN III, COURTROOM HANDBOOK ON FEDERAL EVIDENCE Ch. 5 (West 2010).

III.   APPLICATION EXERCISE

Ensuring the Proper Use of Opinion Testimony at Trial

Because opinion testimony represents a departure from the norm of witnesses testifying about facts and direct observations, it is important to ensure that juries do not overvalue the use of opinion testimony at trial. The jury is charged with deciding the factual issues in the case. One way that judges and attorneys assist jurors in properly weighing and evaluating lay opinion testimony at trial is through the use of jury instructions. A well-drafted jury instruction defines lay opinion testimony, reminds the jury of the lay opinion testimony that was admitted at trial, and informs the jury of its role in deciding facts at trial — including its power to disregard any witness's factual observations or opinions. Samples of such instructions are available in the pattern jury instruction books that are used in most American courts. Pattern jury instructions are jurisdiction-specific and are available in law libraries, and in many instances, online.

The Exercise

1. *Objective.* To identify lay opinion testimony, make proper objections and responses to it, and draft an instruction ensuring the proper use of this testimony by the jury.

2. *Factual Scenario.* Return to the Doyle Donner case familiar to us from recent chapters. The tabular-form transcript below is the testimony of Principal Shrift at the felony child neglect trial of Doyle's father.

	Question	Response
1	Please introduce yourself to the jury.	I am Dwight Shrift.
2	What is your occupation?	I am the principal of the Shady Acres Elementary School here in Calamity City.
3	Are you familiar with a young man named Doyle Donner?	Yes, I am.
4	Let's talk about the Doyle Donner case. How did you get involved in the case?	One of my jobs as principal is to look after the well-being of the children in the school and make sure they are not victims of abuse or neglect. Doyle was a neglected child.
5	Why do you say he was a neglected child?	He was always dirty, unkempt, and hungry. He was skinny and looked starved, like one of those pictures of kids in *National Geographic*.

	Question	Response
6	What about his parents — how effective were they?	Well, he was neglected, so not very effective.
7	In your opinion, were the parents capable of taking care of Doyle?	They had some serious psychological issues; the mom seemed like she was probably schizophrenic and the dad had some sociopathic tendencies.
8	Let's turn your attention to February 8 of last year. Were you working that day?	Yes, I was.
9	Please describe the weather conditions.	It was really cold. There was a freezing rain and a pretty stiff wind. Horrible weather. It was probably the coldest day of the winter.
10	Did Doyle go to school that day?	Yes.
11	How did he get there?	He walked.
12	How do you know that?	I saw him approaching the school on foot from a block away.
13	What was he wearing?	A light windbreaker, a thin T-shirt, and jeans with holes in them.
14	Was his outfit appropriate for weather conditions?	No. Appropriate clothing would have included at least a heavy winter coat, gloves, and a hat. Ideally some warmer clothes underneath. He could have gotten frostbite. Maybe even hypothermia.
15	Did you talk to Doyle that day?	Yes, I did. When he arrived at the school.
16	What did you say?	I asked him where his coat was.
17	What was his reply?	He said he didn't have a coat.
18	What did you say to that?	I told him we could give him a coat. He said it wouldn't matter. His father would just hide it from him to punish him.
19	What was Doyle's condition when he arrived at school?	Early stages of hypothermia. He was cold. Teeth chattering. Red face. Blue lips. Nose running.
20	Let's discuss Doyle's father. Did you have occasion to interact with him?	Yes. And excuse my French, but the man is an abusive jackass. I think he's probably a sociopath.
21	Why do you say that?	Every time we talked, he would get angry, call me names, and threaten to sue me.
22	What makes you think he was a sociopath?	The man had zero empathy for other human beings. Especially Doyle. Also, he never took responsibility for Doyle's condition.

	Question	Response
23	Did you contact Doyle's father on this occasion?	Yes.
24	How did he react?	The usual. He got angry. He was very sarcastic and condescending to me.
25	What did you say to him?	I told him Doyle was dressed inappropriately for weather conditions.
26	What was his reply?	That it was none of my business.
27	What did you say next?	I told him I would be reporting him to the Department of Human Services.
28	What was his reaction to that?	He called me a dirty name and said, "Bring it on. I'll sue them and you."
29	What happened after that?	I hung up and called the DHS hotline.
30	Based on your experience as a principal, do you believe Doyle was a neglected child?	Yes, I do.
31	On a scale of 1 to 10, with 10 being the worst, how badly was he neglected?	Eleven.
32	Thank you. No further questions.	

3. *Advance Preparation.* Read the transcript of Principal Shrift's testimony. Decide where, if anywhere, opposing counsel should object to improper opinion testimony, and how the prosecution should respond. As assigned by your professor, go to the pattern jury instructions for your jurisdiction and write a draft limiting instruction that tells the jury how to properly use and consider lay opinion testimony.

4. *In-Class Exercise.* Students will play the following roles: judge, prosecuting attorney, defense attorney, and Dwight Shrift. Following the transcript above, the defense attorney will object to improper opinion testimony, the prosecutor will respond, and the judge will rule. The defense will present a proposed limiting instruction to the judge, who will make appropriate modifications and then read the instruction to the class.

Chapter 28

RULE 702: QUALIFICATIONS TO TESTIFY AS AN EXPERT

> **Chapter Objectives:**
>
> - Define and explain the role of an expert witness at trial and the qualifications required by Rule 702 to give expert opinion testimony at trial
> - Analyze and discuss issues pertaining to expert witness qualifications
> - Apply the concepts from this chapter in a courtroom application exercise

I. BACKGROUND AND EXPLANATORY MATERIAL

Introduction

In the discussion of lay opinion testimony under Rule 701 in the previous chapter, you have already been introduced to the concept of expert testimony under Rule 702. The difference between an expert witness and all other witnesses at trial is considerable. The expert is allowed to answer hypothetical questions, evaluate data that would otherwise be inadmissible in court, and even render opinions based on the testimony and demeanor of other witnesses in the courtroom. Rule 702 governs the use of expert testimony at trial.

Through Dec. 1, 2011	After Dec. 1, 2011
Rule 702. Testimony by Experts	**Rule 702. Testimony by Expert Witnesses**
If scientific, technical, or other specialized knowledge will assist the trier of fact to understand the evidence or to determine a fact in issue, a witness qualified as an expert by knowledge, skill, experience, training, or education, may testify thereto in the form of an opinion or otherwise, if (1) the testimony is based upon sufficient facts or data, (2) the testimony is the product of reliable principles and methods, and (3) the witness has applied the principles and methods reliably to the facts of the case.	If scientific, technical, or other specialized knowledge will assist the trier of fact to understand the evidence or to determine a fact in issue, a witness qualified as an expert by knowledge, skill, experience, training, or education, may testify thereto in the form of an opinion or otherwise, if (1) the testimony is based upon sufficient facts or data, (2) the testimony is the product of reliable principles and methods, and (3) the witness has applied the principles and methods reliably to the facts of the case.

There are two necessary foundational elements that must be satisfied in order to introduce expert opinion testimony at trial. First, the witness must be qualified as an expert based on knowledge, skill, training, experience, or education. Second, the expert's opinion must satisfy the reliability criteria of Rule 702 and the *Daubert* line of cases. This chapter addresses the witness's qualifications as an expert.

Qualifying a Witness as an Expert

The standards for qualifying a witness as an expert under Rule 702 are quite broad. The rule contemplates that a wide variety of people can serve as expert witnesses at trial, provided that they possess specialized knowledge outside the common understanding of ordinary people. This knowledge can be gained from work experience, educational experiences, research, study, or other training. The inclusive language of the rule suggests that its requirements should be generously interpreted. Thus, at trial, a vast array of witnesses can qualify as experts: automobile mechanics, surgeons, licensed tradesmen, business consultants, academics, and others.

Attorneys are required to lay a foundation that establishes an expert's qualifications. Typically, a foundation includes identifying the area of expertise and establishing the basis for the witness's specialized knowledge or experience. With experts who have considerable academic qualifications, laying the foundation informs the jury of the critical qualifying elements of the expert's *curriculum vitae.* For other experts, including technical experts or those whose training is based on skill or experience, a foundation should establish similar factors that let the judge and jury know why they should give credence to this witness's opinions in the courtroom.

Some jurisdictions require a ritualistic procedure in which the attorney asks the foundational questions, opposing counsel examines the witness in aid of objection (a process also known as "voir dire"), and the proponent formally tenders the witness as an expert. There is a trend, especially in federal courts, to strip away some of the formality associated with expert testimony and avoid labeling a witness as an expert in the courtroom. The justification for this is explained in the Advisory Committee notes to Rule 702:

> The amendment continues the practice of the original Rule in referring to a qualified witness as an "expert." This was done to provide continuity and to minimize change. The use of the term "expert" in the Rule does not, however, mean that a jury should actually be informed that a qualified witness is testifying as an "expert." Indeed, there is much to be said for a practice that prohibits the use of the term "expert" by both the parties and the court at trial. Such a practice "ensures that trial courts do not inadvertently put their stamp of authority" on a witness's opinion, and protects against the jury's being overwhelmed by the so-called 'experts.' [citations omitted]

Counsel should become familiar with prevailing practice in their jurisdiction on tendering witnesses.

II.   CASES, DISCUSSION QUESTIONS AND PROBLEMS

JONES v. LINCOLN ELECTRIC
United States Court of Appeals, Seventh Circuit
188 F.3d 709 (7th Cir. 1999)

KANNE, Circuit Judge.

[Plaintiff Terry Jones, a welder, sued various manufacturers of welding rods for neurological injuries he allegedly sustained as a result of exposure to manganese. Manganese is an element contained in steel welding rods to prevent cracking. In low concentrations, it is not harmful to the body; in fact, it is necessary. In high concentrations, it can be toxic. He claimed that the manufacturers should have warned him of the dangers associated with these fumes.]

Defendants denied that Jones's neurological condition was caused by his exposure to welding rod fumes, maintaining instead that Jones suffered from idiopathic Parkinson's disease-a disease unrelated to manganese overexposure. . . .

Although there are several different forms or types of Parkinsonism, the two types relevant to this case are idiopathic Parkinson's disease and manganese-induced Parkinsonism or "manganism." Although occasionally described at trial as a type of Parkinsonism, idiopathic Parkinson's disease is basically Parkinson's disease without a known cause. A person suffering from this disease will exhibit most, if not all, of the general Parkinsonian symptoms described above as the disease progresses. Manganism, by contrast, is a medical term used to describe a neurological disease similar to idiopathic Parkinson's disease that is caused by overexposure to manganese. The two are distinct medical conditions with manganism usually marked by the absence of some of the above-mentioned general symptoms and the presence of other "atypical" features normally not found in patients suffering from idiopathic Parkinson's disease. . . . Manganism . . . is quite rare with only a few documented cases in the United States. Jones believes that he suffers from manganism and that he developed this disease through his exposure to manganese contained in welding fumes given off by Defendants' welding rods. . . .

[Defendants offered testimony from Jones's own treating physicians as well as testimony from a defense expert in support of their theory that Jones suffered from idiopathic Parkinson's disease that was causally unrelated to any manganese exposure from their products.

The plaintiff called his own expert witness, Dr. Klawans, to testify that he was actually suffering from manganism and not idiopathic Parkinson's disease. On cross-examination, the expert admitted that with the exception of one symptom, everything he had found was consistent with the plaintiff suffering from idiopathic Parkinson's disease.]

Although the bulk of the trial focused on the issue of whether Jones actually suffered from manganism, the parties also contested whether manganese, in the form it takes in the mild steel welding fumes generated by Defendants' welding rods, could cause the type of neurological injuries claimed by Jones. Jones asserted that the welding fumes emitted by the burning of Defendants' welding rods caused him to develop manganism. In support of that theory, Jones offered the testimony of Dr. Klawans who testified that medical research showed that manganese contained in welding fumes could lead to the onset of manganism in welders and that it was his opinion that Jones developed manganism as a result of his exposure to the manganese generated by Defendants' welding rods.

Defendants offered contrary evidence suggesting Jones's manganese exposure from their welding rods was too insignificant to actually cause manganism. Dr. Thomas Eager, a professor of materials engineering and the head of the Department of Material Science and Engineering at the Massachusetts Institute of Technology, testified for the Defendants as an expert witness in metallurgy. Dr. Eager provided testimony at trial on a number of subjects, including the history and uses of welding, a description of how the welding process works and how welding fumes are generated, the chemical composition of welding fumes, proper ventilation during welding, and an estimate of how long a person who is welding is actually exposed to welding fumes. Dr. Eager has an extensive background in welding and testified that it was his expert opinion that Jones's manganese exposure from welding with Defendants' welding rods would have been less than the industry recommended maximum manganese exposure levels ("threshold limit values") given the work environments in which Jones worked, the type of welding he engaged in, the form of the manganese in the welding fumes, and the amount of time he actually spent welding.

On appeal, Jones argues that the district court improperly admitted portions of Dr. Eager's testimony, and as a result, he is entitled to a new trial. Specifically, Jones challenges the admission of Dr. Eager's testimony regarding (1) his role in research studying the effects of welding fumes on the lungs of animals and the results of that research ("Joint Research") and (2) an epidemiological study of welders at Caterpillar ("Caterpillar Study").

With respect to Dr. Eager's testimony regarding the Joint Research, Dr. Eager testified that the form of the manganese in the welding fumes is different in chemical composition than naturally occurring manganese. The manganese takes on this different form by combining with other elements given off by the melting of the mild steel and, according to Dr. Eager, this causes the manganese contained in welding fumes to have a different reactivity with the lungs than pure manganese. Defense counsel then asked Dr. Eager whether he believed this would have an impact on the body's ability to absorb the manganese. At this point, Jones objected on the basis that this line of questioning sought testimony from Dr. Eager that was outside his expertise as a metallurgist. The district court sustained the objection subject to defense counsel laying a proper foundation.

In an attempt to lay a foundation for this testimony, Dr. Eager testified, over several objections, that he conducted "joint research" studying the effect of welding fumes in the lungs of laboratory animals with Dr. Joseph Brain, a professor at the Harvard University School of Public Health, and Dr. Gael Ulrich, a professor of chemical engineering at the University of New Hampshire. Dr. Eager indicated that he worked with Dr. Brain for the last three to four years, that they had discussed their research activities with each other, and that they had published papers together and reached certain conclusions from their Joint Research. After this testimony was elicited, defense counsel asked Dr. Eager about the conclusions the Joint Research reached regarding the form of the manganese in the welding fumes and the ability of the body to absorb manganese in that form. Jones again objected, arguing that each of the professors brought their own expertise to the research and that Dr. Eager sought to testify about medical matters that were outside his expertise. Jones complained that the medical expert, Dr. Brain, was not present to discuss the conclusions reached regarding the body's ability to absorb manganese and the basis for those conclusions. The district court overruled Jones's objection, concluding that the professors discussed their joint research and, in essence, taught one another their particular areas of expertise. On that basis, the district court concluded that Dr. Eager was qualified to testify as to the conclusions reached by the Joint Research.

Dr. Eager then proceeded to testify that the Joint Research concluded that there was no difference between placing welding fumes or saline solution or non-toxic iron oxide into the animal's lungs. Defense counsel then asked Dr. Eager whether their research led to any conclusions regarding the toxicity of manganese in welding fumes. Jones again objected on the ground that the question called for testimony beyond Dr. Eager's expertise. After Dr. Eager explained that the conclusions were drawn by all three professors after discussing the various disciplines involved in reaching the conclusions, the district court allowed Dr. Eager to proceed and he testified that there was no measurable effect of welding fumes containing manganese on the lungs. . . .

At the close of Dr. Eager's testimony, which concluded the testimony for the day, Jones made an oral motion to strike Dr. Eager's testimony regarding the Joint Research on the ground it was outside his expertise. . . . [This was followed with a written motion to strike the next morning.] The district court denied that motion on the same basis it had denied the prior oral objections.

The jury returned a verdict in favor of Defendants on all counts alleged in the complaint. Jones then filed his first appeal, arguing that the district court erred in overruling his objections to the admission of Dr. Eager's testimony regarding both the Caterpillar Study and the Joint Research. . . .

II. Analysis

A. Jones Is Not Entitled To A New Trial On The Ground That The District Court Erred In Overruling His Objections To Certain Portions of Dr. Eager's Testimony

We first address Jones's arguments that the district court erred in overruling his objections to the portions of Dr. Eager's testimony regarding the Joint Research and the Caterpillar Study. In order to convince us that a new trial is warranted based on the admission of this testimony, Jones must satisfy three conditions. First, for those portions of the challenged testimony for which the district court ruled that Jones's objection was untimely and, therefore, waived, Jones must show that he objected in a timely and proper manner before the district court. Second, he must show that the district court abused its discretion in admitting the challenged testimony. Third, he must show that any error made by the district court in admitting the evidence was more than harmless error by showing that the exclusion of this evidence probably would have produced a different outcome in the case.

1. Dr. Eager's Testimony Regarding the Joint Research

Jones argues that the district court erred in permitting Dr. Eager to testify regarding the ability of the body to absorb manganese from welding fumes generated by mild steel welding rods, the toxicity of manganese contained in welding fumes, and the results of the Joint Research concerning the effect of manganese from welding fumes on lungs of animals, because Dr. Eager was not qualified under Federal Rule of Evidence 702 to offer an opinion on these matters. . . .

We review a district court's decision to admit expert testimony under an abuse of discretion standard. . . . [O]ur review of the district court's determination of an expert's qualifications to testify is necessarily deferential. However, in the present case, we are not wholly convinced that the district court exercised proper discretion in concluding that Dr. Eager was qualified to testify as to the challenged matters relating to the Joint Research.

Rule 702 of the Federal Rules of Evidence sets the standard governing the admissibility of expert testimony and that Rule provides:

> If scientific, technical, or other specialized knowledge will assist the trier of fact to understand the evidence or to determine a fact in issue, a witness qualified as an expert by knowledge, skill, experience, training, or education, may testify thereto in the form of an opinion or otherwise.

Fed.R.Evid. 702. Pursuant to Rule 702, a witness may offer an expert opinion only if he or she draws on some special "knowledge, skill, experience, training, or education" to formulate that opinion. Id. However, "the opinion must be an expert opinion (that is, an opinion informed by the witness' expertise) rather than simply an opinion broached by a purported expert." United States v. Benson, 941 F.2d 598, 604 (7th Cir.1991) "Whether a witness is qualified as an expert can only be determined by comparing the area in which the witness has superior knowledge, skill, experience, or education with the subject matter of the witness's testimony." Carroll v. Otis Elevator Co., 896 F.2d 210, 212 (7th Cir.1990).

The challenged testimony offered by Dr. Eager regarding the Joint Research concerns matters that are most aptly classified as medical or biological in nature given that Dr. Eager was asked to testify as to the toxicity of manganese in manganese fumes and the lung's ability to absorb manganese from those fumes. However, Dr. Eager's formal education and experience lie in the field of material science and metallurgy and he was offered as an expert in metallurgy at trial. He has a Bachelor of Science degree in Metallurgy and Material Science from MIT and a Doctorate in Metallurgy from the same institution. While Dr. Eager undoubtedly is a very intelligent individual, he is not a medical doctor nor is there any indication in the record that suggests that he has any experience in assessing the toxicology or other health effects of manganese on the body aside from his participation in the Joint Research with Dr. Brain. Indeed, Dr. Eager acknowledged on cross-examination that he was not a toxicologist and that toxicology and how certain substances are absorbed into the body were areas that were outside of his expertise. It stands to reason then that the underlying basis for the medical conclusions to which Dr. Eager testified was derived primarily, if not completely, from Dr. Brain's expertise and that these conclusions were rooted in medical knowledge and training which Dr. Eager did not have. As such, we believe that Dr. Eager lacked sufficient expertise to testify about the conclusions reached by the Joint Research, and, therefore, the district court should have barred him from testifying on these matters. See, e.g., United States v. Hirschberg, 988 F.2d 1509, 1514 (7th Cir.1993) ("Expert opinion is gained from a 'special skill, knowledge, or experience,' and is a reasoned decision drawn from the witness' expertise." (quoting United States v. Benson, 941 F.2d 598, 604 (7th Cir.1991))); United States v. Kladouris, 964 F.2d 658, 670 (7th Cir.1992) (affirming district court's ruling that a proffered witness's lack of training in chemistry prevented him from testifying as an expert on the significance of the presence of chemicals at the scene of the fire). Furthermore, to the extent that Dr. Eager was merely conveying Dr. Brain's conclusions with respect to the Joint Research, Dr. Brain, not Dr. Eager, would be the proper person to testify about those findings.

Moreover, while it is true that Rule 702 provides that a witness can be qualified as an expert without formal training or education by virtue of his or her experience, we do not believe that Dr. Eager's participation in the Joint Research is the kind of experience that Rule 702 contemplates as the basis for qualifying an expert to testify at trial-i.e., extensive hands-on experience over a meaningful period of time during which a person develops a working expertise in a certain area. See, e.g., United States v. Tipton, 964 F.2d 650, 654 (7th Cir.1992). Dr. Eager testified that he was not involved in the day-to-day research of the Joint Research and it appears that his knowledge regarding the matters upon which he testified was derived mostly from periodic discussions with Dr. Brain and others involved in the research. We seriously doubt that the discussions that occurred between Drs. Eager, Brain, and Ulrich were comprehensive enough either in scope or detail to allow Dr. Eager to develop the expertise required by Rule 702 with respect to this testimony.

[6][7][8] Nevertheless, even though the district court may have abused its discretion in admitting Dr. Eager's testimony on these matters, reversal is required, and a new trial is warranted under Rule 103(a), only if the error has affected "a substantial right of the party." See Fed.R.Evid. 103(a) ("Error may not be predicated upon a ruling which admits or excludes evidence unless a substantial right of the party is affected. . . ."); see also Fed.R.Civ.P. 61 ("No error in either the admission or the exclusion of evidence . . . is ground for granting a new trial . . . unless [the] refusal to take such action appears to the court inconsistent with substantial justice."). Accordingly, we will not reverse a jury verdict if an erroneous admission of expert testimony is harmless. See DeBiasio v. Illinois Cent. R.R., 52 F.3d 678, 685 (7th Cir.1995); see also Cook v. Hoppin, 783 F.2d 684, 691 (7th Cir.1986) ("The improper admission of evidence provides a basis for granting a new trial only if the error is prejudicial."). An error is considered to be harmless if it did not contribute to the verdict in a meaningful manner. See Chapman, 386 U.S. at 22-24, 87 S.Ct. 824; see also DeBiasio, 52 F.3d at 685 ("An erroneous evidentiary ruling is harmless and 'does not affect substantial rights unless there is a significant chance that it has affected the result of the trial.' " (quoting Walton v. United Consumers Club, Inc., 786 F.2d 303, 313 (7th Cir.1986))). After careful review of the record, we conclude that the exclusion of Dr. Eager's testimony relating to the Joint Research would most likely not have resulted in a jury verdict in Jones's favor; thus, any error in admitting Dr. Eager's testimony was harmless. We reach this conclusion for three reasons.

[First, the court found that the evidence at trial did not establish that Jones actually suffered from manganism; rather, the evidence established idiopathic Parkinson's disease.]

Second, given the fact that Dr. Eager is not a medical doctor or toxicologist, and that Jones highlighted this fact during cross-examination, the jury is likely to have heavily discounted his testimony concerning the conclusions reached by the Joint Research, especially when Defendants did not enter into evidence any substantiating documents underlying the Joint Research. As such, Jones clearly conveyed Dr. Eager's lack of qualification to testify on these matters to the jury. "[G]enerally, the jury is intelligent enough, aided by counsel, to ignore what is unhelpful in de-liberations." Benson, 941 F.2d at 605 (internal quotations and citation omitted).

Third, Jones introduced a number of studies and other documentary materials into evidence that suggested that manganese in welding fumes could lead to the onset of manganism and other health problems in welders. In addition, Jones's medical expert testified that, in his opinion, welding fumes containing manganese could cause manganism in welders by allowing manganese to enter into the lungs when the welder breathes in these fumes. Manganese may then be absorbed into the bloodstream and make its way into the brain where it may cause neurological damage. Thus, even if the jury accepted Dr. Eager's testimony as reliable, Jones introduced evidence to challenge those conclusions. In fact, we believe the jury likely placed little weight on Dr. Eager's testimony given that Defendants placed warnings on their products that breathing welding fumes could be hazardous to the welder's health.

For these reasons, we conclude that any error by the district court in allowing Dr. Eager to testify as to the conclusions reached by the Joint Research was harmless.

DISCUSSION QUESTIONS

1. How closely should the expert's specialized knowledge fit with the exact facts of the case?

2. According to the court, what would it take for Dr. Eager to be qualified as an expert on the effects of manganese fumes on the body? Would it have made a difference if Dr. Eager had participated in the day-to-day work of the Joint Research? Why or why not?

3. From the standpoint of efficiency and controlling costs, wouldn't it make sense to permit an expert to testify about matters pertaining not only to his assigned area of expertise, but also closely related matters about which the expert could provide some modicum of assistance to the jury?

PROBLEMS

Problem 28-1. Bertha is the alleged mastermind of a criminal gang that has committed a string of robberies and assaults in Calamity City. She is charged with conspiracy to commit robbery and robbery stemming from an incident in which several of her gang members used a gun to rob the OK Corral Convenience store on July 15. In addition to stealing checks and money from the store, the robbers took the clerk's genuine gold Rolex watch. When arrested, everyone "lawyered up" immediately and refused to give statements to police.

A few weeks after the robbery, Bertha was photographed at a party wearing a gold Rolex watch matching the description of the clerk's stolen watch. Police were unable to find the watch in a search of Bertha's apartment. The photograph is the only evidence potentially linking Bertha to the conspiracy and the robbery.

The prosecution proposes to call a local jeweler to testify that the Rolex in the picture is genuine and made of actual gold. This is to counter the defense's anticipated argument that the Rolex in the picture is a cheap imitation. The jeweler has been in business for over twenty years. He does not actually sell or repair Rolex watches but has seen them at trade shows. He does sell a considerable amount of gold jewelry and claims to be generally familiar with the appearance of genuine gold v. imitation gold in photographs.

Should the judge permit the jeweler to testify as an expert? Why or why not?

Problem 28-2. Plaintiff purchased an expensive, sea-going motorboat from Marine Enterprises. The boat was equipped with a specially modified Chevrolet engine. Marine enterprises had altered the fuel management system, customizing it for a marine environment. Plaintiff experienced several problems with the engine and eventually sued Marine Enterprises. At trial, Plaintiff called Ward Wrench, a licensed mechanical engineer with a degree in mechanical engineering and considerable experience with engines, including marine engines. Wrench lacked specific training or experience, however, with marine fuel management systems such as the one installed on the engine by Marine Enterprises. Wrench's proffered testimony was that the fuel management system was defective and caused the engine to stall and backfire. Defendants objected to Wrench's testimony, claiming that his training and experience did not relate to fuel management systems, and therefore he was not qualified as an expert. How should the judge rule in this case, and why?

Quick Hits: Expert Qualifications

- No witness can give expert opinion testimony without first being qualified as an expert under Rule 702

- Rule 702's expert qualification requirements are simple and easily met: a person can be qualified as an expert based on knowledge, skill, training, education or experience

- Some jurisdictions require a formal process for tendering a person as an expert witness

- The trend in federal courts is to qualify a witness as an expert with a formal tender

---

Chapter References

CHRISTOPHER B. MUELLER & LAIRD C. KIRKPATRICK, EVIDENCE §§ 7.5–7.7 (4th ed. 2009).

GLEN WEISSENBERGER & JAMES J. DUANE, FEDERAL RULES OF EVIDENCE: RULES, LEGISLATIVE HISTORY, COMMENTARY AND AUTHORITY § 702 (6th ed. 2009).

JACK B. WEINSTEIN & MARGARET A. BERGER, WEINSTEIN'S FEDERAL EVIDENCE § 702 (Joseph M. McLaughlin ed., Matthew Bender 2d ed. 1997).

KENNETH S. BROUN, MCCORMICK ON EVIDENCE §§ 10–18 (6th ed. 2006).

STEVEN GOODE & OLIN GUY WELLBORN III, COURTROOM HANDBOOK ON FEDERAL EVIDENCE Ch. 5 (West 2010).

III. APPLICATION EXERCISE

Laying a Foundation for an Expert's Qualifications

In order for a witness to give expert opinion testimony, the witness must first be qualified as an expert witness. The proponent of the testimony bears the burden to establish the witness's expertise. This is done by laying a foundation. The foundation must include the following:

1. The area of expertise (for instance, metallurgy or medicine)

2. The basis for the expert's expertise. Rule 702 permits an expert to testify based on knowledge, skill, training, experience or education. Thus, the advocate must ask sufficient questions for a judge to determine, as a matter of law under Rule 104, that the expert is indeed qualified to testify in that area.

3. In many jurisdictions, the proponent formally tenders the witness as an expert witness. Note that the advisory committee note recommends not formally tendering the witness and that in a number of federal jurisdictions, the practice of formal tendering is no longer followed.

4. The opposing party is given the opportunity to examine the witness regarding his or her qualifications. At the close of the examination, the opposing party may object to the expert's qualifications.

5. The proponent responds to any objections, and the judge rules.

The Exercise

1. *Objective.* To practice laying the foundation for and tendering an individual as an expert witness.

2. *Factual Scenario.* Using your own knowledge, training, education, skill or experience, identify an area in which you are an expert.

3. *Advance Preparation.* Prepare a hard-copy foundation script that would qualify you as an expert in that particular area. Bring the script to class.

4. *In-class Exercise.* Students will play the following roles: expert witness, proponent, opponent and judge. The instructor will select a student to be the expert witness. That student will provide a foundation script to the proponent, who will use it in class to qualify the witness as an expert. The opponent will examine the witness in aid of objection. The judge will rule.

Chapter 29

RULE 702: THE RELIABILITY OF EXPERT OPINIONS

Chapter Objectives:

- Introduce and explain the judge's gatekeeping role under Rule 702, *Daubert* and *Kumho Tire* in ensuring that expert testimony at trial is reliable
- Analyze and discuss issues pertaining to the reliability of scientific and technical evidence in trial
- Apply the concepts from this chapter in a courtroom application exercise

---

I. BACKGROUND AND EXPLANATORY MATERIAL

There are three major tests a proponent must satisfy before being permitted to introduce expert opinion testimony at trial: (1) the relevance (or helpfulness) of the opinion; (2) qualifications of the expert; and (3) reliability of the principles and methods used by the expert. The first two tests are easily satisfied. Determining whether "scientific, technical, or other specialized knowledge will assist the trier of fact to understand the evidence or to determine a fact in issue" is nothing more than a restated relevance standard, no more complicated than any other relevance analysis under the Rules. As to the second test, Rule 702 suggests that a broad spectrum of people, with varied backgrounds and experience levels, can qualify as experts under the rule. Indeed, as we have seen, courts tend to interpret generously Rule 702's requirements for qualifying a witness as an expert.

The third test — reliability — presents more complications than the other two. This is because Rule 702 and its seminal interpretative cases require a judge to make decisions about the reliability and validity of scientific theories, technical knowledge, and even experiential observations. These types of decisions are outside the traditional provenance of most judges, who are trained to analyze legal issues but not scientific or technical theories. The *Daubert* case, in section II *infra*, refers to the judge as a "gatekeeper," someone who must ensure evidentiary validity by determining scientific or theoretical reliability.

Rule 702 was amended in 2000 to codify the three major elements of the reliability analysis. The first element is that the testimony must be based on sufficient facts or data. The information the judge needs to make this decision is developed as part of the adversary trial process. The second element is that the testimony is the product of reliable principles and methods. The standards used to determine reliability are contained in the *Daubert* and *Kumho Tire* cases in section II. The information a judge needs to make this decision is also developed as part of the adversary trial process. Finally, the third element is that the witness has applied the principles reliably to the facts of the case.

Frequently — especially when the expert's opinion is based on novel or controversial theories — judges will hold a Rule 104 hearing, called a *Daubert* hearing, to determine whether the standards of Rule 702 have been met. The proponent of the expert bears the burden of proving that the expert is qualified, the opinion will be helpful, and the reliability standards of Rule 702 and *Daubert* have been satisfied.

II. CASES, QUESTIONS AND PROBLEMS

DAUBERT, ET AL. v. MERRELL DOW PHARMACEUTICALS, INC.

Supreme Court of the United States
509 U.S. 579 (1993)

[Petitioners, two minor children and their parents, alleged in their suit against respondent that the children's serious birth defects had been caused by the mothers' prenatal ingestion of Bendectin, a prescription drug marketed by respondent. The District Court granted respondent summary judgment based on a well-credentialed expert's affidavit concluding, upon reviewing the extensive published scientific literature on the subject, that maternal use of Bendectin has not been shown to be a risk factor for human birth defects. Although petitioners had responded with the testimony of eight other well-credentialed experts, who based their conclusion that Bendectin can cause birth defects on animal studies, chemical structure analyses, and the unpublished "reanalysis" of previously published human statistical studies, the court determined that this evidence did not meet the applicable "general acceptance" standard for the admission of expert testimony. The Court of Appeals agreed and affirmed, citing *Frye v. United States*, 293 F. 1013, 1014, 54 App. D.C. 46, 47, for the rule that expert opinion based on a scientific technique is inadmissible unless the technique is "generally accepted" as reliable in the relevant scientific community.]

In this case we are called upon to determine the standard for admitting expert scientific testimony in a federal trial.

We granted certiorari, 506 U.S. 914 (1992), in light of sharp divisions among the courts regarding the proper standard for the admission of expert testimony. [Citations omitted.]

II.

A

In the 70 years since its formulation in the *Frye* case, the "general acceptance" test has been the dominant standard for determining the admissibility of novel scientific evidence at trial. See E. Green & C. Nesson, Problems, Cases, and Materials on Evidence 649 (1983). Although under increasing attack of late, the rule continues to be followed by a majority of courts, including the Ninth Circuit.

The Frye test has its origin in a short and citation-free 1923 decision concerning the admissibility of evidence de-rived from a systolic blood pressure deception test, a crude precursor to the polygraph machine. In what has become a famous (perhaps infamous) passage, the then Court of Appeals for the District of Columbia described the device and its operation and declared:

> "Just when a scientific principle or discovery crosses the line between the experimental and demonstrable stages is difficult to define. Somewhere in this twilight zone the evidential force of the principle must be recognized, and while courts will go a long way in admitting expert testimony deduced from a well-recognized scientific principle or discovery, the thing from which the deduction is made must be sufficiently established to have gained general acceptance in the particular field in which it belongs." 54 App. D.C. at 47, 293 F. at 1014 (emphasis added).

Because the deception test had "not yet gained such standing and scientific recognition among physiological and psychological authorities as would justify the courts in admitting expert testimony deduced from the discovery, development, and experiments thus far made," evidence of its results was ruled inadmissible. Ibid.

The merits of the *Frye* test have been much debated, and scholarship on its proper scope and application is legion. Petitioners' primary attack, however, is not on the content but on the continuing authority of the rule. They contend that the *Frye* test was superseded by the adoption of the Federal Rules of Evidence. We agree.

We interpret the legislatively enacted Federal Rules of Evidence as we would any statute. Beech Aircraft Corp. v. Rainey, 488 U.S. 153 (1988). [The court reviews the relevance standards of Rules 401 and 402, stating that these rules are the baseline for admitting evidence under the Federal Rules.] The Rules' basic standard of relevance thus is a liberal one. . . .

Here there is a specific Rule that speaks to the contested issue. Rule 702, governing expert testimony, provides:

> "If scientific, technical, or other specialized knowledge will assist the trier of fact to understand the evidence or to determine a fact in issue, a witness qualified as an expert by knowledge, skill, experience, training, or educa-tion, may testify thereto in the form of an opinion or otherwise."

Nothing in the text of this Rule establishes "general acceptance" as an absolute prerequisite to admissibility. Nor does respondent present any clear indication that Rule 702 or the Rules as a whole were intended to incorporate a "general acceptance" standard. The drafting history makes no mention of *Frye*, and a rigid "general acceptance" requirement would be at odds with the "liberal thrust" of the Federal Rules and their "general approach of relaxing the traditional barriers to 'opinion' testimony." Beech Aircraft Corp. v. Rainey, 488 U.S. at 169 (citing Rules 701 to 705). See also Weinstein, Rule 702 of the Federal Rules of Evidence is Sound; It Should Not Be Amended, 138 F.R.D. 631 (1991) ("The Rules were designed to depend primarily upon lawyer-adversaries and sensible triers of fact to evaluate conflicts"). Given the Rules' permissive backdrop and their inclusion of a specific rule on expert testimony that does not mention "general acceptance," the assertion that the Rules somehow assimilated *Frye* is unconvincing. *Frye* made "general acceptance" the exclusive test for admitting expert scientific testimony. That austere standard, absent from, and incompatible with, the Federal Rules of Evidence, should not be applied in federal trials.

B

That the *Frye* test was displaced by the Rules of Evidence does not mean, however, that the Rules themselves place no limits on the admissibility of purportedly scientific evidence. Nor is the trial judge disabled from screening such evidence. To the contrary, under the Rules the trial judge must ensure that any and all scientific testimony or evidence admitted is not only relevant, but reliable.

The primary locus of this obligation is Rule 702, which clearly contemplates some degree of regulation of the subjects and theories about which an expert may testify. "If scientific, technical, or other specialized knowledge will assist the trier of fact to understand the evidence or to determine a fact in issue" an expert "may testify thereto." (Emphasis added.) The subject of an expert's testimony must be "scientific . . . knowledge."[1] The adjective "scientific" implies a grounding in the methods and procedures of science. Similarly, the word "knowledge" connotes more than subjective belief or unsupported speculation. The term "applies to any body of known facts or to any body of ideas inferred from such facts or accepted as truths on good grounds." Webster's Third New International Dictionary 1252 (1986). Of course, it would be unreasonable to conclude that the subject of scientific testimony must be "known" to a certainty; arguably, there are no certainties in science. [Citations omitted.] But, in order to qualify as "scientific knowledge," an inference or assertion must be derived by the scientific method. Proposed testimony must be supported by appropriate validation — i.e., "good grounds," based on what is known. In short, the requirement that an expert's testimony pertain to "scientific knowledge" establishes a standard of evidentiary reliability.[2]

Rule 702 further requires that the evidence or testimony "assist the trier of fact to understand the evidence or to determine a fact in issue." This condition goes primarily to relevance. "Expert testimony which does not relate to any issue in the

---

[1] [n.8] Rule 702 also applies to "technical, or other specialized knowledge." Our discussion is limited to the scientific context because that is the nature of the expertise offered here.

[2] [n.9] We note that scientists typically distinguish between "validity" (does the principle support what it purports to show?) and "reliability" (does application of the principle produce consistent results?). [Citations omitted.] In a case involving scientific evidence, evidentiary reliability will be based upon scientific validity.

case is not relevant and, ergo, non-helpful." 3 Weinstein & Berger P702[02], p. 702-18. See also United States v. Downing, 753 F.2d 1224, 1242 (CA3 1985) ("An additional consideration under Rule 702 — and another aspect of relevancy — is whether expert testimony proffered in the case is sufficiently tied to the facts of the case that it will aid the jury in resolving a factual dispute"). The consideration has been aptly described by Judge Becker as one of "fit." Ibid. "Fit" is not always obvious, and scientific validity for one purpose is not necessarily scientific validity for other, unrelated purposes. The study of the phases of the moon, for example, may provide valid scientific "knowledge" about whether a certain night was dark, and if darkness is a fact in issue, the knowledge will assist the trier of fact. However (absent creditable grounds supporting such a link), evidence that the moon was full on a certain night will not assist the trier of fact in determining whether an individual was unusually likely to have behaved irrationally on that night. Rule 702's "helpfulness" standard requires a valid scientific connection to the pertinent inquiry as a precondition to admissibility.

That these requirements are embodied in Rule 702 is not surprising. Unlike an ordinary witness, see Rule 701, an expert is permitted wide latitude to offer opinions, including those that are not based on firsthand knowledge or observation. See Rules 702 and 703. Presumably, this relaxation of the usual requirement of firsthand knowledge — a rule which represents "a 'most pervasive manifestation' of the common law insistence upon 'the most reliable sources of information,'" Advisory Committee's Notes on Fed. Rule Evid. 602, 28 U.S.C. App., p. 755 (citation omitted) — is premised on an assumption that the expert's opinion will have a reliable basis in the knowledge and experience of his discipline.

C

Faced with a proffer of expert scientific testimony, then, the trial judge must determine at the outset, pursuant to Rule 104(a), whether the expert is proposing to testify to (1) scientific knowledge that (2) will assist the trier of fact to understand or determine a fact in issue. This entails a preliminary assessment of whether the reasoning or methodology underlying the testimony is scientifically valid and of whether that reasoning or methodology properly can be applied to the facts in issue. We are confident that federal judges possess the capacity to undertake this review. Many factors will bear on the inquiry, and we do not presume to set out a definitive checklist or test. But some general observations are appropriate.

Ordinarily, a key question to be answered in determining whether a theory or technique is scientific knowledge that will assist the trier of fact will be whether it can be (and has been) tested. "Scientific methodology today is based on generating hypotheses and testing them to see if they can be falsified; indeed, this methodology is what distinguishes science from other fields of human inquiry." Green 645. See also C. Hempel, Philosophy of Natural Science 49 (1966) ("The statements constituting a scientific explanation must be capable of empirical test"); K. Popper, Conjectures and Refutations: The Growth of Scientific Knowledge 37 (5th ed. 1989) ("The criterion of the scientific status of a theory is its falsifiability, or refutability, or testability") (emphasis deleted).

Another pertinent consideration is whether the theory or technique has been subjected to peer review and publication. Publication (which is but one element of peer review) is not a sine qua non of admissibility; it does not necessarily correlate with reliability[.] [Citations omitted.] Some propositions, moreover, are too particular, too new, or of too limited interest to be published. But submission to the scrutiny of the scientific community is a component of "good science," in part because it increases the likelihood that substantive flaws in methodology will be detected. [Citations omitted.] The fact of publication (or lack thereof) in a peer reviewed journal thus will be a relevant, though not dispositive, consideration in assessing the scientific validity of a particular technique or methodology on which an opinion is premised.

Additionally, in the case of a particular scientific technique, the court ordinarily should consider the known or potential rate of error, see, e.g., United States v. Smith, 869 F.2d 348, 353-354 (CA7 1989) (surveying studies of the error rate of spectrographic voice identification technique), and the existence and maintenance of standards controlling the technique's operation, see United States v. Williams, 583 F.2d 1194, 1198 (CA2 1978) (noting professional organization's standard governing spectrographic analysis), cert. denied, 439 U.S. 1117 (1979).

Finally, "general acceptance" can yet have a bearing on the inquiry. A "reliability assessment does not require, although it does permit, explicit identification of a relevant scientific community and an express determination of a particular degree of acceptance within that community." United States v. Downing, 753 F.2d at 1238. See also 3 Weinstein & Berger P702[03], pp. 702-41 to 702-42. Widespread acceptance can be an important factor in ruling particular evidence admissible, and "a known technique which has been able to attract only minimal support within the community," Downing, 753 F.2d at 1238, may properly be viewed with skepticism.

The inquiry envisioned by Rule 702 is, we emphasize, a flexible one. Its overarching subject is the scientific validity — and thus the evidentiary relevance and reliability — of the principles that underlie a proposed submission. The focus, of course, must be solely on principles and methodology, not on the conclusions that they generate.

Throughout, a judge assessing a proffer of expert scientific testimony under Rule 702 should also be mindful of other applicable rules. Rule 703 provides that expert opinions based on otherwise inadmissible hearsay are to be admitted only if the facts or data are "of a type reasonably relied upon by experts in the particular field in forming opinions or inferences upon the subject." Rule 706 allows the court at its discretion to procure the assistance of an expert of its own choosing. Finally, Rule 403 permits the exclusion of relevant evidence "if its probative value is substantially outweighed by the danger of unfair prejudice, confusion of the issues, or misleading the jury. . . ." Judge Weinstein has explained: "Expert evidence can be both powerful and quite misleading because of the difficulty in evaluating it. Because of this risk, the judge in weighing possible prejudice against probative force under Rule 403 of the present rules exercises more control over experts than over lay witnesses." Weinstein, 138 F.R.D. at 632.

III

We conclude by briefly addressing what appear to be two underlying concerns of the parties and amici in this case. Respondent expresses apprehension that abandonment of "general acceptance" as the exclusive requirement for admission will result in a "free-for-all" in which befuddled juries are confounded by absurd and irrational pseudoscientific assertions. In this regard respondent seems to us to be overly pessimistic about the capabilities of the jury and of the adversary system generally. Vigorous cross-examination, presentation of contrary evidence, and careful instruction on the burden of proof are the traditional and appropriate means of attacking shaky but admissible evidence. See Rock v. Arkansas, 483 U.S. 44 (1987). [The court lists other safeguards including summary judgment and directed verdicts, to protect against the dangers of unreliable expert testimony.] These conventional devices, rather than wholesale exclusion under an uncompromising "general acceptance" test, are the appropriate safeguards where the basis of scientific testimony meets the standards of Rule 702.

Petitioners and, to a greater extent, their amici exhibit a different concern. They suggest that recognition of a screening role for the judge that allows for the exclusion of "invalid" evidence will sanction a stifling and repressive scientific orthodoxy and will be inimical to the search for truth. See, e.g., Brief for Ronald Bayer et al. as Amici Curiae. It is true that open debate is an essential part of both legal and scientific analyses. Yet there are important differences between the quest for truth in the courtroom and the quest for truth in the laboratory. Scientific conclusions are subject to perpetual revision. Law, on the other hand, must resolve disputes finally and quickly. The scientific project is advanced by broad and wide-ranging consideration of a multitude of hypotheses, for those that are incorrect will eventually be shown to be so, and that in itself is an advance. Conjectures that are probably wrong are of little use, however, in the project of reaching a quick, final, and binding legal judgment — often of great consequence — about a particular set of events in the past. We recognize that, in practice, a gatekeeping role for the judge, no matter how flexible, inevitably on occasion will prevent the jury from learning of authentic insights and innovations. That, nevertheless, is the balance that is struck by Rules of Evidence designed not for the exhaustive search for cosmic understanding but for the particularized resolution of legal disputes. . . ..

Accordingly, the judgment of the Court of Appeals is vacated, and the case is remanded for further proceedings consistent with this opinion.

KUMHO TIRE COMPANY v. CARMICHAEL
Supreme Court of the United States
526 U.S. 137 (1999)

I

On July 6, 1993, the right rear tire of a minivan driven by Patrick Carmichael blew out. In the accident that followed, one of the passengers died, and others were severely injured. In October 1993, the Carmichaels brought this diversity suit against the tire's maker and its distributor, whom we refer to collectively as Kumho Tire, claiming that the tire was defective. The plaintiffs rested their case in significant part upon deposition testimony provided by an expert in tire failure analysis, Dennis Carlson, Jr., who intended to testify in support of their conclusion.

[Carlson was an engineer who had developed his own methodology for determining whether tire failures were caused by design and manufacturing defects, or by poor maintenance, operator error or other factors.]

Kumho Tire moved the District Court to exclude Carlson's testimony on the ground that his methodology failed Rule 702's reliability requirement. The court agreed with Kumho that it should act as a *Daubert*-type reliability "gate-keeper," even though one might consider Carlson's testimony as "technical," rather than "scientific." See Carmichael v. Samyang Tires, Inc., 923 F. Supp. 1514, 1521-1522 (SD Ala. 1996). The court then examined Carlson's methodology in light of the reliability-related factors that *Daubert* mentioned, such as a theory's testability, whether it "has been a subject of peer review or publication," the "known or potential rate of error," and the "degree of acceptance . . . within the relevant scientific community." 923 F. Supp. at 1520 (citing *Daubert*, 509 U.S. 579 at 592-594). The District Court found that all those factors argued against the reliability of Carlson's methods, and it granted the motion to exclude the testimony (as well as the defendants' accompanying motion for summary judgment).

[The plaintiffs asked for reconsideration, and the District Court granted it. It applied the *Daubert* factors flexibly, but it reached the same conclusions as before: that Carlson's methodology was not reliable.]

It consequently affirmed its earlier order declaring Carlson's testimony inadmissable and granting the defendants' motion for summary judgment.

The Eleventh Circuit reversed. See Carmichael v. Samyang Tire, Inc., 131 F.3d 1433 (1997). It "reviewed . . . de novo" the "district court's legal decision to apply Daubert." 131 F.3d at 1435. It noted that "the Supreme Court in Daubert explicitly limited its holding to cover only the 'scientific context,'" adding that "a *Daubert* analysis" applies only where an expert relies "on the application of scientific principles," rather than "on skill- or experience-based observation." 131 F.3d at 1435-1436. It concluded that Carlson's testimony, which it viewed as relying on experience, "falls outside the scope of *Daubert*," that "the district court erred as a matter of law by applying *Daubert* in this case," and that the case must be remanded for further (non-*Daubert*-type) consideration under Rule 702. Id. at 1436.

Kumho Tire petitioned for certiorari, asking us to determine whether a trial court "may" consider *Daubert*'s specific "factors" when determining the "admissibility of an engineering expert's testimony." Pet. for Cert. i. We granted certiorari in light of uncertainty among the lower courts about whether, or how, *Daubert* applies to expert testimony that might be characterized as based not upon "scientific" knowledge, but rather upon "technical" or "other specialized" knowledge. Fed. Rule Evid. 702. [Citations omitted.]

II

A

In *Daubert*, this Court held that Federal Rule of Evidence 702 imposes a special obligation upon a trial judge to "ensure that any and all scientific testimony . . . is not only relevant, but reliable." 509 U.S. at 589. The initial question before us is whether this basic gatekeeping obligation applies only to "scientific" testimony or to all expert testimony. We, like the parties, believe that it applies to all expert testimony. See Brief for Petitioners 19; Brief for Respondents 17.

For one thing, Rule 702 itself says:

> "If scientific, technical, or other specialized knowledge will assist the trier of fact to understand the evidence or to determine a fact in issue, a witness qualified as an expert by knowledge, skill, experience, training, or education, may testify thereto in the form of an opinion or otherwise."

This language makes no relevant distinction between "scientific" knowledge and "technical" or "other specialized" knowledge. It makes clear that any such knowledge might become the subject of expert testimony. In *Daubert*, the Court specified that it is the Rule's word "knowledge," not the words (like "scientific") that modify that word, that "establishes a standard of evidentiary reliability." 509 U.S. at 589-590. Hence, as a matter of language, the Rule applies its reliability standard to all "scientific," "technical," or "other specialized" matters within its scope. We concede that the Court in *Daubert* referred only to "scientific" knowledge. But as the Court there said, it referred to "scientific" testimony "because that was the nature of the expertise" at issue. 509 U.S. at 590, n.8.

Neither is the evidentiary rationale that underlay the Court's basic *Daubert* "gatekeeping" determination limited to "scientific" knowledge. *Daubert* pointed out that Federal Rules 702 and 703 grant expert witnesses testimonial latitude unavailable to other witnesses on the "assumption that the expert's opinion will have a reliable basis in the knowledge and experience of his discipline." 509 U.S. at 592 (pointing out that experts may testify to opinions, including those that are not based on firsthand knowledge or observation). The Rules grant that latitude to all experts, not just to "scientific" ones.

Finally, it would prove difficult, if not impossible, for judges to administer evidentiary rules under which a gate-keeping obligation depended upon a distinction between "scientific" knowledge and "technical" or "other specialized" knowledge. There is no clear line that divides the one from the others. Disciplines such as engineering rest upon scientific knowledge. Pure scientific theory itself may depend for its development upon observation and properly engineered machinery. And conceptual efforts to distinguish the two are unlikely to produce clear legal lines capable of application in particular cases. [Citations omitted.]

Neither is there a convincing need to make such distinctions. Experts of all kinds tie observations to conclusions through the use of what Judge Learned Hand called "general truths derived from . . . specialized experience." Hand, Historical and Practical Considerations Regarding Expert Testimony, 15 Harv. L. Rev. 40, 54

(1901). And whether the specific expert testimony focuses upon specialized observations, the specialized translation of those observations into theory, a specialized theory itself, or the application of such a theory in a particular case, the expert's testimony often will rest "upon an experience confessedly foreign in kind to [the jury's] own." Ibid. The trial judge's effort to assure that the specialized testimony is reliable and relevant can help the jury evaluate that foreign experience, whether the testimony reflects scientific, technical, or other specialized knowledge.

We conclude that *Daubert's* general principles apply to the expert matters described in Rule 702. The Rule, in respect to all such matters, "establishes a standard of evidentiary reliability." 509 U.S. at 590. It "requires a valid . . . connection to the pertinent inquiry as a precondition to admissibility." 509 U.S. at 592. And where such testimony's factual basis, data, principles, methods, or their application are called sufficiently into question, see Part III, infra, the trial judge must determine whether the testimony has "a reliable basis in the knowledge and experience of [the relevant] discipline." 509 U.S. at 592.

B

The petitioners ask more specifically whether a trial judge determining the "admissibility of an engineering expert's testimony" may consider several more specific factors that *Daubert* said might "bear on" a judge's gate-keeping determination. These factors include:

— Whether a "theory or technique . . . can be (and has been) tested";

— Whether it "has been subjected to peer review and publication";

— Whether, in respect to a particular technique, there is a high "known or potential rate of error" and whether there are "standards controlling the technique's operation"; and

— Whether the theory or technique enjoys "general acceptance" within a "relevant scientific community." 509 U.S. at 592-594.

Emphasizing the word "may" in the question, we answer that question yes.

[The Court recognizes that there are many types of expertise, some of which are based on scientific foundations, and some of which are based on other foundations such as experience.] The conclusion, in our view, is that we can neither rule out, nor rule in, for all cases and for all time the applicability of the factors mentioned in *Daubert*, nor can we now do so for subsets of cases categorized by category of expert or by kind of evidence. Too much depends upon the particular circumstances of the particular case at issue. *Daubert* itself is not to the contrary. It made clear that its list of factors was meant to be helpful, not definitive. Indeed, those factors do not all necessarily apply even in every instance in which the reliability of scientific testimony is challenged. It might not be surprising in a particular case, for example, that a claim made by a scientific witness has never been the subject of peer review, for the particular application at issue may never previously have interested any scientist. Nor, on the other hand, does the presence of *Daubert's* general acceptance factor help show that an expert's testimony is reliable where the discipline itself lacks reliability, as, for example, do theories grounded in any so-called generally accepted principles of astrology or necromancy.

At the same time, and contrary to the Court of Appeals' view, some of *Daubert's* questions can help to evaluate the reliability even of experience-based testimony. In certain cases, it will be appropriate for the trial judge to ask, for example, how often an engineering expert's experience-based methodology has produced erroneous results, or whether such a method is generally accepted in the relevant engineering community. Likewise, it will at times be useful to ask even of a witness whose expertise is based purely on experience, say, a perfume tester able to distinguish among 140 odors at a sniff, whether his preparation is of a kind that others in the field would recognize as acceptable.

We must therefore disagree with the Eleventh Circuit's holding that a trial judge may ask questions of the sort *Daubert* mentioned only where an expert "relies on the application of scientific principles," but not where an expert relies "on skill- or experience-based observation." 131 F.3d at 1435.We do not believe that Rule 702 creates a schematism that segregates expertise by type while mapping certain kinds of questions to certain kinds of experts. Life and the legal cases that it generates are too complex to warrant so definitive a match.

To say this is not to deny the importance of *Daubert's* gatekeeping requirement. The objective of that requirement is to ensure the reliability and relevancy of expert testimony. It is to make certain that an expert, whether basing testimony upon professional studies or personal experience, employs in the courtroom the same level of intellectual rigor that characterizes the practice of an expert in the relevant field. Nor do we deny that, as stated in *Daubert*, the particular questions that it mentioned will often be appropriate for use in determining the reliability of challenged expert testimony. Rather, we conclude that the trial judge must have considerable leeway in deciding in a particular case how to go about determining whether particular expert testimony is reliable. That is to say, a trial court should consider the specific factors identified in *Daubert* where they are reasonable measures of the reliability of expert testimony. . . .

III

We further explain the way in which a trial judge "may" consider *Daubert's* factors by applying these considerations to the case at hand, a matter that has been briefed exhaustively by the parties and their 19 amici. The District Court did not doubt Carlson's qualifications, which included a masters degree in mechanical engineering, 10 years' work at Michelin America, Inc., and testimony as a tire failure consultant in other tort cases. Rather, it excluded the testimony because, despite those qualifications, it initially doubted, and then found unreliable, "the methodology employed by the expert in analyzing the data obtained in the visual inspection, and the scientific basis, if any, for such an analysis." Civ. Action No. 93-0860-CB-S (SD Ala., June 5, 1996), App. to Pet. for Cert. 6c. After examining the transcript in "some detail," 923 F. Supp. at 1518-519, n. 4, and after considering respondents' defense of Carlson's methodology, the District Court determined that Carlson's testimony was not reliable. It fell outside the range where experts might reasonably differ, and where the jury must decide among the conflicting views of different experts, even though the evidence is "shaky." *Daubert*, 509 U.S. at 596. In our view, the doubts that triggered the District Court's initial inquiry here were reasonable, as was the court's ultimate conclusion.

[The Court exhaustively reviews Carlson's specific methodology, which, for those who love tires, is fascinating and is available in the Court's unedited opinion.]

Respondents now argue to us, as they did to the District Court, that a method of tire failure analysis that employs a visual/tactile inspection is a reliable method, and they point both to its use by other experts and to Carlson's long experience working for Michelin as sufficient indication that that is so. But no one denies that an expert might draw a conclusion from a set of observations based on extensive and specialized experience. Nor does anyone deny that, as a general matter, tire abuse may often be identified by qualified experts through visual or tactile inspection of the tire. [Citation omitted.] As we said before, supra, at 14, the question before the trial court was specific, not general. The trial court had to decide whether this particular expert had sufficient specialized knowledge to assist the jurors "in deciding the particular issues in the case." 4 J. McLaughlin, Weinstein's Federal Evidence P702.05[1], p. 702-33 (2d ed. 1998) [other citations omitted].

The particular issue in this case concerned the use of Carlson's two-factor test and his related use of visual/tactile inspection to draw conclusions on the basis of what seemed small observational differences. We have found no indication in the record that other experts in the industry use Carlson's two-factor test or that tire experts such as Carlson normally make the very fine distinctions about, say, the symmetry of comparatively greater shoulder tread wear that were necessary, on Carlson's own theory, to support his conclusions. Nor, despite the prevalence of tire testing, does anyone refer to any articles or papers that validate Carlson's approach. [The Court cites a number of tire engineering papers, none of which, presumably, validate the approach.] . . . Of course, Carlson himself claimed that his method was accurate, but, as we pointed out in *Joiner*, "nothing in either *Daubert* or the Federal Rules of Evidence requires a district court to admit opinion evidence that is connected to existing data only by the ipse dixit of the expert." 522 U.S. at 146.

Respondents additionally argue that the District Court too rigidly applied *Daubert's* criteria. They read its opinion to hold that a failure to satisfy any one of those criteria automatically renders expert testimony inadmissible. [The original opinion might have been read this way, but not the opinion or decision on reconsideration.] [On reconsideration, the District Court] explicitly recognized that the relevant reliability inquiry "should be 'flexible,'" that its "'overarching subject [should be] . . . validity' and reliability," and that "*Daubert* was intended neither to be exhaustive nor to apply in every case." App. to Pet. for Cert. 4c (quoting Daubert, 509 U.S. at 594-595). And the court ultimately based its decision upon Carlson's failure to satisfy either *Daubert'* s factors or any other set of reasonable reliability criteria. In light of the record as developed by the parties, that conclusion was within the District Court's lawful discretion.

In sum, Rule 702 grants the district judge the discretionary authority, reviewable for its abuse, to determine reliability in light of the particular facts and circumstances of the particular case. The District Court did not abuse its discretionary authority in this case. Hence, the judgment of the Court of Appeals is Reversed.

DISCUSSION QUESTIONS

1. What was the *Frye* test that was in general use prior to the *Daubert* decision? Was *Frye* consistent with Rule 702? Why or why not?

2. The Court established a non-exclusive four-factor test for evaluating the reliability of expert opinions and testimony. What are these four factors — and what is the significance of each factor?

3. From a judge's perspective, does *Kumho Tire* make the process of evaluating non-scientific expert testimony easier or harder? Why?

4. If the *Daubert* factors prove inapplicable or unhelpful in evaluating a particular type non-scientific testimony, to what sources can a judge look to determine the reliability of the expert's theories and methods?

PROBLEMS

Problem 29-1. Thad Thinskin is the plaintiff in a defamation case against The Calamity City Crier, a leading newspaper in the State of Calamity. Thad is the chief financial officer for the Calamity City Unified School District. Lately, the district has faced hard financial times and has had to lay off several teachers and support personnel. The Crier published an essay alleging that Thad was "reckless and irresponsible" and specifically condemned Thad for several risky investments. According to the Crier, Thad's investment strategy was little better than shooting craps in an alleyway.

In its defense, the Crier alleges that Thad Thinskin in fact has the character traits of recklessness and irresponsibility. The Crier intends to call several witnesses, including Thad's ex-wife, to testify about his character. Pursuant to FRE 405, this testimony includes reputation, opinion, and instances of specific conduct.

Thad intends to call Electra Divine, a local phrenologist, to testify about his character as manifested in the morphology of the skull. Divine will testify that she examined his skull, mapped it, and determined that he has strong character traits for responsibility and carefulness. Divine has been a phrenologist for fifteen years. Her practice is located in a small shop in the avant-garde district of Calamity City, between a drug paraphernalia shop and a comic book trading center. She received her training from a mail-order course offered by the Pan-American Phrenological Society. Read the Wikipedia article on phrenology at http://en.wikipedia.org/wiki/Phrenology and identify the arguments for and against her testimony under Rule 702, Daubert and Kumho Tire.

Reliability of Expert Opinions: Quick Hits

- Prior to the adoption of the Federal Rules of Evidence, federal courts used the Frye general acceptability test. This test is still used in some state jurisdictions.

- Rule 702, Daubert, and Kumho Tire replaced Frye with a test in which scientific reliability is used as an indicator of evidentiary reliability for scientific, technical and other forms of expert opinion.

- Judges serve as gatekeeper to evaluate the reliability of an opinion.

- The four non-exclusive Daubert scientific reliability factors are: (1) whether the theory can or has been tested; (2) whether the theory has been subjected to peer review and publication; (3) the known or potential error rate of the theory; (4) the extent to which the theory has been accepted by others in the field.

Chapter References

CHRISTOPHER B. MUELLER & LAIRD C. KIRKPATRICK, EVIDENCE §§ 7.5–7.7 (4th ed. 2009).

GLEN WEISSENBERGER & JAMES J. DUANE, FEDERAL RULES OF EVIDENCE: RULES, LEGISLATIVE HISTORY, COMMENTARY AND AUTHORITY § 702 (6th ed. 2009).

JACK B. WEINSTEIN & MARGARET A. BERGER, WEINSTEIN'S FEDERAL EVIDENCE § 702 (Joseph M. McLaughlin ed., Matthew Bender 2d ed. 1997).

KENNETH S. BROUN, MCCORMICK ON EVIDENCE §§ 10–18 (6th ed. 2006).

STEVEN GOODE & OLIN GUY WELLBORN III, COURTROOM HANDBOOK ON FEDERAL EVIDENCE Ch. 5 (West 2010).

III.   APPLICATION EXERCISE

Daubert Hearings at Trial

In trials involving expert witness testimony, the parties are expected to use the adversarial trial system to assist the judge's gatekeeping function under Rule 702 and *Daubert.* One of the tools available for accomplishing this is a pretrial hearing under Rule 104(a) to determine (1) whether the expert is qualified, and (2) whether the expert's testimony meets the reliability standards of Rule702 and *Daubert.*

Depending on local court rules and practice, the party opposing the expert testimony frequently files a motion contesting the expert's qualifications and the reliability of the testimony. The proponent of the expert files a responsive motion, and the court holds a pretrial hearing to consider evidence and arguments in support of the motion. *Daubert* hearings can be relatively simple in scope, or, as in situations similar to the *Daubert* case itself, they can involve lengthy motions and briefs, extensive hearings, dueling experts, voluminous evidence and formal written opinions by judges.

The Exercise

Objective: To demonstrate proficiency in identifying, writing about, and arguing issues pertaining to the reliability of expert witness testimony.

Factual Scenario: Use problem 29-1 as the factual basis for this exercise. The plaintiff has served notice in accordance with the Calamity Rules of Civil Procedure of its intent to call Elektra Divine as an expert witness in phrenology. The plaintiff has also provided a copy of Ms. Divine's curriculum vitae (CV). The CV is consistent with the information in problem 26-1. In case analysis, the defense has decided not to attack Ms. Divine's qualifications as a phrenologist, but rather to attack the reliability of phrenology itself.

Advance Preparation: Part of the class, as assigned by the professor, will prepare a defense motion to exclude Ms. Divine's phrenological testimony as unreliable under *Daubert, Kumho Tire* and Rule 702. Support your motion with rules, case law and information about the scientific reliability and acceptability of phrenology. Another portion of the class will prepare a plaintiff's response to the motion. Although the plantiff will not have a copy of the defense motion to respond to, it should be a fairly simple matter for the plaintiff's attorneys to predict the defense arguments and rebut them. Support your response with rules, case law and information about the scientific reliability and acceptability of phrenology.

The Exercise: As assigned by the professor, students will play the following roles: judge, plaintiff's attorney, defense attorney. The judge will conduct a *Daubert* hearing on the issue of whether phrenology meets the reliability requirements of Rule 702, *Daubert* and *Kumho Tire*. The defense counsel will make arguments in support of the motion and may present documents or call witnesses in support of the motion, as permitted by Rule 104(a). The plaintiff's counsel will make arguments opposing the motion and may present documents, call witnesses, and/or cross-examine defense witnesses. The judge will make findings and verbally rule on the motions in class. The rest of the class will serve as a court of appeals.

Chapter 30

RULES 703-705: BASIS AND SCOPE OF EXPERT OPINION

Chapter Objectives:

- Introduce and explain the following: (1) the acceptable basis for expert opinions (Rule 703); (2) disclosure requirements for materials relied on by experts (Rule 705); (3) the acceptable scope of an expert's opinion (Rule 704)
- Analyze and discuss issues pertaining to the basis and scope of expert opinions
- Apply the concepts from this chapter in a courtroom application exercise

---

I.   BACKGROUND AND EXPLANATORY MATERIAL

Basis for Expert Opinion and Disclosure Requirements

Unlike percipient witnesses or lay opinion witnesses, expert witnesses are not limited to testifying about their direct sensory observations in a case. Instead, Rule 703 permits expert witnesses to base their opinions on a variety of sources and information, including some that would not be admissible in evidence. In forming their opinions, experts can conduct their own tests and investigations, answer hypothetical questions posed to them in the courtroom, observe and comment on the demeanor of other witnesses, read reports generated by others, or use any source of facts or data that would be considered reliable by other experts in their field. Rule 705 permits experts to testify about their opinions first having to disclose the underlying facts or bases.

Through Dec. 1, 2011	After Dec. 1, 2011
Rule 703. Bases of Opinion Testimony by Experts	**Rule 703. Bases of an Expert's Opinion Testimony**
The facts or data in the particular case upon which an expert bases an opinion or inference may be those perceived by or made known to the expert at or before the hearing. If of a type reasonably relied upon by experts in the particular field in forming opinions or inferences upon the subject, the facts or data need not be admissible in evidence in order for the opinion or inference to be admitted. Facts or data that are otherwise inadmissible shall not be disclosed to the jury by the proponent of the opinion or inference unless the court determines that their probative value in assisting the jury to evaluate the expert's opinion substantially outweighs their prejudicial effect.	An expert may base an opinion on facts or data in the case that the expert has been made aware of or personally observed. If experts in the particular field would reasonably rely on those kinds of facts or data in forming an opinion on the subject, they need not be admissible for the opinion to be admitted. But if the facts or data would otherwise be inadmissible, the proponent of the opinion may disclose them to the jury only if their probative value in helping the jury evaluate the opinion substantially outweighs their prejudicial effect.

Through Dec. 1, 2011	After Dec. 1, 2011
Rule 705. Disclosure of Facts or Data Underlying Expert Opinion	**Rule 705. Disclosing the Facts or Data Underlying an Expert's Opinion**
The expert may testify in terms of opinion or inference and give reasons therefor without first testifying to the underlying facts or data, unless the court requires otherwise. The expert may in any event be required to disclose the underlying facts or data on cross-examination.	Unless the court orders otherwise, an expert may state an opinion — and give the reasons for it — without first testifying to the underlying facts or data. But the expert may be required to disclose those facts or data on cross-examination.

There are dangers inherent in a rule that permits experts to base their opinions on inadmissible evidence. In the case of hearsay, for example, it is possible for an expert to base his opinion entirely on information that would not satisfy any recognized hearsay exclusion or exception. Furthermore, in order to assist the jury in evaluating the strengths or weaknesses of the expert's opinion, it might be necessary to discuss such evidence at trial on direct or cross-examination. Finally, if testimony is not structured properly, it is possible for an expert witness to effectively become a conduit through which the proponent can introduce otherwise inadmissible evidence to the jury, a practice known as "hearsay smuggling."

Rules 703 and 705 provide some barriers and protections against the improper disclosure of inadmissible evidence through expert witnesses. First, Rule 705 makes it clear that the expert can testify about his opinion without having to first reveal the underlying facts or data. For example, assume that an expert in a medical malpractice case relied on medical records prepared by other physicians, as well as deposition transcripts and sworn statements, in forming his opinion that the treating physician met the standard of care. Under Rule 705, the expert would be permitted to give his opinion without having to quote from the depositions or medical records.

Second, Rule 705 shifts the risk of disclosing inadmissible evidence to the opposing party. Even though the Rule does not require the expert to testify to the facts or data underlying his opinion, it states that "the expert may in any event be required to disclose the underlying facts or data on cross-examination." If the opponent believes it can gain an advantage by cross-examining the expert on the underlying facts and data, Rule 705 allows it. Thus, the risk of disclosing otherwise inadmissible evidence shifts to the opposing party under Rule 705.

Third, Rule 703 erects a barrier to a proponent disclosing otherwise inadmissible evidence through an expert witness. The rule alters the standard Rule 403 balancing test. Recall that Rule 403 is a rule of presumptive admissibility, under which evidence is excluded only if its probative value is substantially outweighed by one of the dangers listed in the rule. Rule 703 excludes otherwise inadmissible evidence introduced through an expert unless the probative value of the evidence substantially outweighs its substantial effect.

Scope of Expert Testimony: Ultimate Opinion Testimony

Through Dec. 1, 2011	After Dec. 1, 2011
Rule 704. Opinion on Ultimate Issue	**Rule 704. Opinion on Ultimate Issue**
(a) Except as provided in subdivision (b), testimony in the form of an opinion or inference otherwise admissible is not objectionable because it embraces an ultimate issue to be decided by the trier of fact.	**(a) In General — Not Automatically Objectionable**. An opinion is not objectionable just because it embraces an ultimate issue.
(b) No expert witness testifying with respect to the mental state or condition of a defendant in a criminal case may state an opinion or inference as to whether the defendant did or did not have the mental state or condition constituting an element of the crime charged or of a defense thereto. Such ultimate issues are matters for the trier of fact alone.	**(b) Exception**. In a criminal case, an expert witness must not state an opinion about whether the defendant did or did not have a mental state or condition that constitutes an element of the crime charged or of a defense. Those matters are for the trier of fact alone.

Rule 704 lays to rest the old common law rule that an expert could not testify about the ultimate issue in a case. Predicated on the jury's role as the finder of fact, the common law rule embodied a concern that an expert's opinion on the ultimate issue could invade the province of the jury. Attorneys practicing under the common law rules were forced to present elaborate hypothetical questions to expert witnesses in lieu of asking them about the ultimate issue in a case. The hypotheticals, of course, were remarkably similar to the actual cases, but the rule strictly forbade the expert from rendering opinions on the ultimate issue in the case at bar. For example, if the case was about a bridge collapse, an expert witness could be called to answer hypothetical questions about bridges and the effects of particular conditions on bridges of a specific design; but the expert could not answer questions about the bridge at issue in the case.

Provided that the opinion is couched in such a way that the final legal decision in a case rests with the jury, Rule 704 permits an expert to render opinions on the ultimate issue. Returning to the bridge case, a modern-day expert could answer questions about this bridge — its design, maintenance, the cause of the collapse, and so forth — but the jury would still have the ability to decide whether to believe the expert and, most importantly, whether the defendant was negligent and should be held liable.

As recognized in Rule 704(b), criminal cases present a twist to this formula. The mental state of the defendant — his mens rea — is frequently the ultimate issue in a criminal case. In a homicide case, for example, death and causation may not be contested — but the mens rea of the defendant could make the difference between first-degree murder and manslaughter. Rule 704(b), therefore, prohibits experts from giving opinions about the defendant's "mental state or condition constituting an element of the crime charged or of a defense thereto."

In criminal cases, expert witness testimony can be used to help establish causation, explain how a crime could have been committed, or help jurors understand victim behavior or other issues in the case. There is, however, a delicate balance that must be struck to avoid invading the province of the jury at trial. To avoid this, experts in criminal cases testify in terms of what is "consistent with" a particular condition or behavior. For example, sometimes experts in Rape Trauma Syndrome will testify at trial regarding the counterintuitive behavior of an alleged rape victim — such things as failing to fight the assailant, delaying a report, or even the alleged victim blaming herself for the assault. To give an expert opinion that the alleged victim had in fact been raped would invade the province of the jury; thus, a Rape Trauma Syndrome expert could testify that the alleged victim's behavior and symptoms were "consistent with" those of rape victims.

II.   CASES, DISCUSSION QUESTIONS AND PROBLEMS

HUTCHINSON v. GROSKIN
United States Court of Appeals, Second Circuit
927 F.2d 722 (2d Cir. 1991)

Plaintiff Bonnie J. Hutchinson appeals from the June 12, 1990 judgment of the District of Vermont, Albert W. Coffrin, Judge, entered in favor of defendant Stephen Groskin, M.D., after a five-day trial. [Plaintiff sought treatment from defendant for a suspicious mole on her abdomen in April 1985. Defendant told her to monitor it and return if it increased in size. In November, plaintiff visited defendant and reported that it had increased in size. The defendant did a biopsy and cauterized the mole.]

Defendant sent the tissue specimen to a pathologist. Two weeks later, plaintiff called defendant to learn the results. Defendant, who had had a telephone conversation with the pathologist but had not received the written pathology report, told plaintiff that "there was a ninety-five percent chance that things looked okay." Shortly thereafter, defendant received the pathology report, which indicated that plaintiff had superficial spreading melanoma. Defendant did not inform plaintiff about the written report.

In January 1986, plaintiff sought a second opinion from Dr. Roger Foster of Burlington, Vermont. Dr. Foster examined her, reviewed the pathology report and informed her for the first time that she had cancer. Within four days, Dr. Foster did a wide excision of the area where the mole had been.

In September 1987, Dr. Foster determined that plaintiff's cancer had spread to one of her right inguinal (groin) lymph nodes. Plaintiff underwent surgery for removal of all nodes in the region. She was hospitalized for a week. For one month following surgery, plaintiff had a device inserted in her leg to drain excess lymphatic fluids. Since its removal, she has worn a heavy elastic, full-length, support stocking and has had continual pain and swelling in her right leg and foot.

In March 1988, plaintiff, a citizen of New York, brought this negligence action in the District of Vermont, basing jurisdiction on diversity of citizenship. She alleges that defendant was negligent in not performing a biopsy at her first visit, in April, and later in failing to inform her that she had malignant melanoma. Additionally, she contends that defendant should have disclosed diagnostic and treatment alternatives and advised her of the risks involved with recently-developed and changing moles. Plaintiff claims that when the biopsy indicated that she had cancer, defendant should have made a wide excision of the area. According to plaintiff, defendant's negligence resulted in the cancer's spread to her lymph node and an increased risk of recurrence and death.

On appeal, plaintiff argues that several related evidentiary errors warrant reversal and a new trial, namely, that the district court erred in permitting defendant to use three letters in the redirect examination of defense expert David Bronson.

During Dr. Bronson's redirect examination, the following exchange occurred:

Q.   *[DEFENSE COUNSEL]: Showing you Defendant's A for identification, B for identification, and C for identification, would you identify each of those documents by date and author for the jury, please, Dr. Bronson?*

A.   *This is a letter dated June 5th from Roswell Park Memorial Institute from Dr. Karkousis [sic], who's the associate chief of surgical oncology and chief of the Soft Tissue Melanoma and Bone Service at Roswell Park. It's a letter to you.*

Q.   *Does he offer an opinion there as to [Hutchinson's] prognosis?*

A.   *Yes, he does.*

            [PLAINTIFF'S COUNSEL]: Excuse me. Note my objection, hearsay.

THE COURT: Well, he hasn't testified as to what the opinion is.

[PLAINTIFF'S COUNSEL]: He's starting to read from the report, I think, your Honor. That's why I'm objecting at this point.

THE COURT: Well, is that what you have in mind?

[DEFENSE COUNSEL]: It isn't, your Honor.

Q.   *Would you identify Defendant's B for identification, Dr. Bronson?*

A.   *Yes, this is a letter dated May 25th, 1990, to you, regarding Bonnie Hutchinson, whom Dr. Patterson had seen, from Dr. Bradford Patterson, director of cancer control, Dana Farber Cancer Institute.*

Q.   *What does that mean to be director of cancer control from Dana Farber Institute?*

A.   *I expect he leads a very broad program of managing cancer patients at that center.*

Q.   *Are you personally familiar with Dr. Patterson?*

A.   *Yes. He came and — his reputation is quite good. He came and actually spoke at our institution a year ago. Was an invited speaker.*

Q.   *What is his medical specialty, Doctor?*

A.   *He's a surgical oncologist.*

Q.   *And Defendant's C for identification? What is the date of that and who's it authored by?*

A.   *This is a letter dated August 8th, 19 — I'm sorry, August 11th, 1989, by Dr. Darrell S. Rigel, clinical assistant professor at New York University Medical Center.*

Q.   Is that the same Dr. Rigel that [plaintiff's counsel] was having you read from?

A.   *Yes, yes.*

Q.   *In that letter does Dr. Rigel offer an opinion as to Mrs. Barton's prognosis?*

A.   *Yes, he does.*

[PLAINTIFF'S COUNSEL]: Excuse me. Note my continuing objection, your Honor.

THE COURT: All right.

Q.   *With respect to your opinion as to [Hutchinson's] prognosis today, Dr. Bronson, what is it?*

A.   *My opinion is that she has a ninety percent chance of never seeing melanoma again.*

Q.   *Is your opinion based in any way on those documents we have just discussed?*

A.	*It's based upon my clinical experience, looking at the literature, looking at not only the textbook that talks about day one, but the fact that she's two years since her resection and has no other evidence of recurrence. That puts her in a much better prognostic category. The longer — the longer period of time you have without it returning, the better off you are.*
Q.	*Is your testimony as to [Hutchinson's] prognosis consistent with that of Doctors Patterson, Rigel and Karakousis?*
A.	*Yes, very much so.*

Such use of the letters was error, to which plaintiff properly objected. By asking Dr. Bronson to identify the documents, offer his own opinion regarding plaintiff's prognosis, and then state whether his opinion was consistent with those expressed in the documents, defense counsel used Dr. Bronson as a conduit for hearsay testimony. Defense counsel thereby introduced the purported opinions of Doctors Patterson, Rigel, and Karakousis, who were not disclosed as experts during discovery and whom plaintiff had no opportunity to examine. Moreover, in closing argument, counsel reminded the jury several times that Dr. Bronson's opinion was consistent with these other physicians'. Thus defense counsel's tactic simultaneously conveyed hearsay testimony to the jury and improperly bolstered Dr. Bronson's credibility.

We find similar error in the redirect examination of defense expert Johannes C. Nunnink. The following exchange took place between defense counsel and the witness:

Q.	*Now, today I showed you Defendant's A for identification. That's the letter of Dr. Karakousis, dated June 5, 1990?*
A.	*Yes.*
Q.	*And does he in that letter offer an opinion as to Mrs. Barton's prognosis?*
A.	*Yes, he does.*
Q.	*Is your opinion consistent with Dr. Karakousis's opinion?*
A.	*Yes, it is.*
	[PLAINTIFF'S COUNSEL]: I'm going to object, your honor.
	THE COURT: Well, he's already testified that it was.
	[PLAINTIFF'S COUNSEL]: I understand. And he knows this is improper. It's piggybacking of expert opinions. It's a hearsay letter.
	THE COURT: Well, we'll let the answer stand. The doctor's already testified to it.

On appeal, defendant argues that error cannot be predicated upon this ruling because the objection was not timely. Fed. R. Evid. 103(a)(1). We disagree. To be timely, an objection or motion to strike must be "made as soon as the ground of it is known, or reasonably should have been known to the objector." See United States v. Check, 582 F.2d 668, 676 (2d Cir. 1978) (quoting 21 C. Wright and K. Graham,

Federal Practice and Procedure § 5037, at 188 (1977)). Although, the objection should be made after the question has been asked but before an answer has been given, this rule is not inflexible.

Here, plaintiff's counsel objected just after Dr. Nunnink responded to the question. The court was well aware of the basis for the objection, as it had previously been made and overruled during Dr. Bronson's testimony. Even if plaintiff's counsel had not objected, the court should have barred the use of such evidence, as it was plain error. Fed. R. Evid. 103(d).

The court's rulings regarding the use of the letters permitted defense counsel to convey to the jury the purported opinions of three physicians who were not disclosed as experts during discovery, pursuant to Fed. R. Civ. P. 26(b)(4). Moreover, it is not clear that the documents were what they purported to be. If the documents were authentic, this evidence was hearsay; plaintiff could not cross-examine the physicians to challenge their qualifications and the bases of their opinions. Two of the three letter writers had never seen the plaintiff and must have based their opinions on records and information supplied by defense counsel. Further, neither witness testified that he relied on these specific documents in the formulation of his own opinion. Cf., O'Gee v. Dobbs Houses, Inc., 570 F.2d 1084 (2d Cir. 1978) (permitting expert witness to testify regarding reports of treating physicians on which he relied in formulating his opinion). To the contrary, they used the documents in an attempt to prove that other experts agreed with their opinions on the issue of plaintiff's prognosis.

The court had insufficient evidence from which to judge whether the jury should consider such opinions, which essentially were offered by defense counsel as expert testimony. Thus the court could not make and did not make the required ruling on the propriety of receiving such evidence.

Despite these infirmities, the three letters were treated as evidence on the issue of prognosis and enhanced the credibility of Drs. Bronson and Nunnink. The nature of these letters could not be developed by plaintiff's counsel without running the risk of emphasizing the inadmissible opinions of the three physicians.

The court's rulings in these two instances deprived the plaintiff of a fair trial; it affected a substantial right of the plaintiff and warrants reversal and a new trial.

DISCUSSION QUESTIONS

1. Dusting off an issue we discussed long ago, discuss the timeliness of the objection under Rule 103. Do you agree with the court that the objection was timely, or should opposing counsel — who had the benefit of discovery and prior case planning — have objected earlier?

2. What was the problem with the expert's testimony in this case?

3. How would you recommend drawing the line between hearsay smuggling and establishing enough foundational evidence for the jury to evaluate the expert's opinion?

UNITED STATES v. TRAUM
United States Court of Appeals, Armed Forces
60 M.J. 226 (C.A.A.F. 2004)

On the morning of December 21, 1998, base emergency medical personnel received a phone call from Appellant indicating that her eighteen-month old daughter Caitlyn was not breathing. During the call, Appellant suggested that the child might be having a seizure. Minutes later, medical personnel arrived at Appellant's quarters and began to treat the unresponsive child. The child was transported by ambulance to the hospital where efforts to revive her continued. Despite the efforts of hospital personnel, Caitlyn was pronounced dead shortly after arriving at the emergency room. Appellant was home alone with the child at the time the emergency call was made. . . .

[During a post-polygraph interview with an Air Force Office of Special Investigations agent], Appellant disclosed that she had killed Caitlyn by pushing the child's head into the couch and suffocating her. Appellant reduced this confession to writing and signed it. This written statement recounts that Appellant "gently pressed Cait's head into the couch" ostensibly to save Caitlyn from her father's abusive ways. Appellant included in her statement that she decided to take the child's life "around midnight on the 20 or 21st Dec. 98." When asked why she smothered the child as opposed to killing her in some other way, Appellant's written response was, "I didn't want her to hurt." . . .

[Appellant was unsuccessful at trial in attempting to suppress her post-polygraph confession.]

The Government's case on the merits was comprised of Appellant's confession, testimony from the emergency first responders, the medical examiner, a forensic pediatrician, and several witnesses who described Appellant's inappropriate grief response [among other things, she talked about how mean her daughter had been and how there would no longer be a need for Christmas presents].

Unsuccessful in its efforts to suppress the confession, the defense proceeded at trial on the theory that Appellant's statement of January 13 was the false product of the agents' efforts to induce Appellant into making a statement. The defense also suggested during its opening statement that the child may have died as a result of a seizure; a possibility the defense maintained could not be eliminated beyond a reasonable doubt by the Government. Finally, the defense attacked the credibility and competence of the Government's medical examiner.

This issue focuses upon the testimony of the Government's forensic pediatrician Dr. Cooper. Dr. Cooper was called by the Government to discuss child abuse in general and in the words of trial counsel, to help the members understand how "parents can kill their children." The defense moved in limine to preclude the witness from offering what it felt was inadmissible profile evidence and evidence of parental behavior that should otherwise be the subject of eye-witness rather than expert witness testimony. . . .

[The doctor explained her methodology.] Dr. Cooper went on to explain that this tripartite methodology - history, parental/custodial behavior, and examination - was relied on by "numerous specialists in the field." She then named some of these "specialists," including several forensic pediatricians whom Dr. Cooper described as "well-known" authorities in their field as well as certain law enforcement professionals.

Trial counsel then shifted the focus of Dr. Cooper's testimony to the area of single episodes of child abuse versus multiple episodes. Relying on a work by a Dr. James A. Monteleone entitled Child Maltreatment (2d ed. 1998), which Dr. Cooper considered an authoritative reference, she testified that "in eighty percent of fatal child abuse cases, that fatal event is the first time that that child has ever been abused." Next, relying on a report by the Advisory Board on Child Abuse and Neglect, Dr. Cooper testified that according to the report "the people most likely to kill children are their biological parents - overwhelmingly so." Citing to professional literature in her field, Dr. Cooper further testified that there are two different categories of predisposing factors to child abuse and neglect - one category pertaining to the child and one pertaining to the adult. Regarding the category relevant to the child, Dr. Cooper stated that "the leading cause of trauma death, now, in the United States, for children under the age of four, is child maltreatment." She then discussed the adult category that included such factors as the presence of substance abuse, the presence of biological parents as opposed to step-parents and babysitters, and whether the child was in a military family setting.

Finally, following Dr. Cooper's testimony pertaining to the methodology that considers history, behavior, and physical examination, trial counsel sought Dr. Cooper's ultimate opinion as to Caitlyn Traum's cause of death. Before doing so, however, trial counsel asked Dr. Cooper what evidence and documents she reviewed in forming her opinion. She stated that she reviewed Caitlyn's medical records, Caitlyn's sister's medical records, and the investigation reports that included Appellant's confession, the emergency medical responses, Family Advocacy records, and the autopsy reports. She then opined, "I feel that her cause of death is homicide or an inflicted fatal child abuse." Dr. Cooper added that she believed the child died as a result of inadequate oxygen consistent with asphyxiation and that Caitlyn "was asphyxiated through a suffocation method." [The doctor testified as to why she reached that conclusion.]

Following the testimony presented at the [pretrial hearing], defense counsel challenged Dr. Cooper's tripartite methodology. The defense focused on Dr. Cooper's use of the victim's history as well as her use of the behavior of the custodial parent. Defense counsel also argued that Dr. Cooper's consideration of Appellant's inconsistent history regarding Caitlyn's condition amounted to an expert's assessment of Appellant's credibility and was therefore impermissible.

Finally, the defense asserted that Dr. Cooper's reliance on Appellant's alleged inappropriate grief response was inadmissible character evidence because it portrayed Appellant as a bad parent. While defense counsel suggested that the doctor's opinion was based on only one aspect of Appellant's conduct, her grieving reaction, Dr. Cooper steadfastly insisted that this factor was merely one of a number of factors considered in the "whole assessment when you look at the history, behavior, physical examination and autopsy finding."

After taking Dr. Cooper's testimony at the [pretrial hearing], the military judge heard argument from both sides as to their view of the permissible parameters of Dr. Cooper's testimony before the members. The military judge then ruled that he would allow Dr. Cooper's testimony regarding child abuse in general, her testimony regarding single episode versus multiple episodes of child abuse, her statement that biological parents are the most likely to fatally abuse their children, and the factors relevant to history, behavior, and physical examinations relied upon by experts in diagnosing fatal child abuse. The military judge reasoned that this testimony would be allowed because "it is counterintuitive for a parent to kill their eighteen month old child, based on the facts that have come out so far."

The military judge also ruled that the expert would not be allowed to testify regarding the so-called adult category of predisposing factors of child abuse. The judge prohibited such testimony because he felt it got into profile evidence and ran "awfully close to the types of things that the courts have found to be error." He also ruled that the witness would not be allowed to testify about a typical grieving parent's reaction as contrasted against that of a non-grieving parent. The judge reached this decision because "the [Rule 403] [prejudice] aspect here outweighs the probative value for the members."

Finally, the judge determined that Dr. Cooper would not be permitted to render her opinion that the cause of death was inflicted fatal child abuse. However, he did rule that the witness could give her opinion that the cause of death was non-accidental asphyxiation. After further discussion, defense counsel indicated that he understood the military judge's ruling, but indicated his objection to the testimony still stood. Thereafter, the military judge concluded the [pretrial hearing].

2. Dr. Cooper's testimony before the members

During the trial before the members, trial counsel elicited testimony from Dr. Cooper consistent with the rulings by the military judge. In particular, she testified, "Overwhelmingly, the most likely person to kill a child is going to be his or her own biological parent." Dr. Cooper also testified that "if a child is less than four years of age, the most common cause of trauma death is going to be child maltreatment." The third statement given before the members was, "Eighty percent of children who die, die from a one-time event." After further testimony relevant to various seizure disorders, sudden infant death syndrome, means by which children accidentally suffocate, and other aspects of fatal child abuse, Dr. Cooper concluded her testimony with the following statement: "It is my medical opinion that the cause of death for Caitlyn Traum was asphyxiation of a non-accidental nature." There was no cross-examination from the defense.

B. Discussion

Appellant challenges Dr. Cooper's testimony on two grounds. First, Appellant asserts that three of Dr. Cooper's opinions that were presented to the members constituted profile evidence. In particular, the defense focused on these statements:

"if a child is less than four years of age, the most common cause of trauma death is going to be child maltreatment";

"Eighty percent of children who die, die from a one-time event"; and

"Overwhelmingly, the most likely person to kill a child is going to be his or her own biological parent."

Second, Appellant maintains that the military judge erred in admitting Dr. Cooper's testimony because it was based on Dr. Cooper's review of Appellant's behavior in the emergency room. We review Appellant's arguments in turn to determine whether the military judge abused his discretion in allowing all or part of Dr. Cooper's testimony. See United States v. Houser, 36 M.J. 392, 397 (C.M.A. 1993).

1. Profile Evidence

Before expert testimony may be admitted, the following factors must be established by the proponent of such testimony:

(A) the qualifications of the expert, Mil.R.Evid. 702; (B) the subject matter of the expert testimony, Mil.R.Evid. 702; (C) the basis for the expert testimony, Mil. R.Evid. 703; (D) the legal relevance of the evidence, Mil.R.Evid. 401 and 402; (E) the reliability of the evidence, United States v. Gipson, 24 M.J. 246 (CMA 1987), and Mil.R.Evid. 401; and (F) whether the 'probative value' of the testimony outweighs other considerations, Mil.R.Evid. 403. [Note: the cited Military Rules of Evidence are identical to the Federal Rules of Evidence.]

At trial, the military judge accepted Dr. Cooper as an expert in the field of forensic pediatrics without objection from defense counsel. Thus, Dr. Cooper's qualifications are not in issue on appeal.

Expert testimony is admissible when "scientific, technical, or other specialized knowledge will assist the trier of fact to understand the evidence or to determine a fact in issue[.]" M.R.E. 702. "The test is not whether the jury could reach some conclusion in the absence of the expert evidence, but whether the jury is qualified without such testimony 'to determine intelligently and to the best possible degree the particular issue without enlightenment from those having a specialized under-standing of the subject[.]' " Houser, 36 M.J. at 398.

In contrast, "generally, use of any characteristic 'profile' as evidence of guilt or innocence in criminal trials is improper." United States v. Banks, 36 M.J. 150, 161 (C.M.A. 1992). See Brunson v. State, 349 Ark. 300, 79 S.W.3d 304, 313 (Ark. 2002) (rejecting testimony that the defendant met eight of ten risk factors for batterers likely to kill); Commonwealth v. Day, 409 Mass. 719, 569 N.E.2d 397, 400 (Mass. 1991) (child battering profile inadmissible); State v. Clements, 244 Kan. 411, 770 P.2d 447, 454 (Kan. 1989) (finding evidence of psychology and treatability of a child sexual offender inadmissible); United States v. Garcia, 25 M.J. 159 (C.M.A. 1987) (summary disposition) (rejecting testimony that appellant's psychological profile was consistent with a person who sexually abused children); United States v. August, 21 M.J. 363 (C.M.A. 1986) (rejecting a profile of the "usual" sexual child abuser); Sanders v. State, 251 Ga. 70, 303 S.E.2d 13 (Ga. 1983) (state cannot introduce evidence of battering parent syndrome); State v. Loebach, 310 N.W.2d 58, 64 (Minn. 1981) (evidence placing the defendant within the profile of a battering parent inadmissible). Profile evidence is evidence that presents a "characteristic profile" of an offender, such as a pedophile or child abuser, and then places the accused's personal characteristics within that profile as proof of guilt.

The question in this case is whether Dr. Cooper's opinions constituted impermissible profile evidence or whether they were admissible opinions of specialized knowledge under M.R.E. 702. Child abuse is an area where specialized knowledge regarding pediatric forensics and child abuse may indeed be helpful to members. Children incur all sorts of injuries as they move through infancy to the toddler years and beyond. Thus, a panel might well benefit from an understanding of the methodology doctors use to determine the cause of an infant's injury. In the case of fatal child abuse, the value of such specialized knowledge is equally apparent. Such information helps members discern the critical elements of testimony and place that testimony within an analytic framework. This information may also help disabuse members of preconceptions that might cloud their ability to focus on the evidence presented as opposed to preconceptions about the nature of the offense at issue. In light of this predicate, we believe Dr. Cooper's first two statements fall within the rubric of specialized knowledge that is useful to the members in understanding the evidence and determining a fact in question. This testimony was given in the context of her general description of fatal child abuse. Further, these particular statements relate to the characteristics of the child victim in this case rather than Appellant. Comparable evidence has been admitted in cases involving rape trauma syndrome. See United States v. Reynolds, 29 M.J. 105, 111 (C.M.A. 1989). Similarly, evidence of battered child syndrome is often admitted to show that a particular injury "is not accidental or is not consistent with the explanation offered therefore but is instead the result of physical abuse by a person of mature strength." United States v. White, 23 M.J. 84, 87 (C.M.A. 1986).

As we explained in Banks, the ban on profile evidence exists because this process treads too closely to offering character evidence of an accused in order to prove that the accused acted in conformity with that evidence on a certain occasion and committed the criminal activity in question. This, of course, is prohibited under M.R.E. 404(a)(1). See Banks, 36 M.J. at 161. These two statements by Dr. Cooper do not implicate that concern because they relate to the characteristics of the child victim in this case rather than Appellant.

What we condemned in Banks was the Government's construction of a syllogism "(major premise, minor premise, and conclusion)" used in persuading the members that the appellant was a child abuser. 36 M.J. at 162 n.11. In that case, the Government, through its expert witness, presented the major premise that families with a profile of three particular identified risk factors presented an increased risk of child sexual abuse. The Government then established through further testimony the minor premise that Banks and his family fit this profile. Finally, the prosecution argued for the conclusion that since the minor premise established the major premise, the members could not help but decide that Banks was a child abuser. We discern no such tactic in the record of this case.

Testimony setting up a child battering profile must be distinguished from testimony focusing on the characteristics of a battered child. See Day, 569 N.E.2d at 400. See also Myrna S. Raeder, The Better Way: The Role of Batterers' Pro-files and Expert "Social Framework" Background in Cases Implicating Domestic Violence, 68 U.

Colo. L. Rev. 147, 160 (1997) (discussing the distinction between battered wife syndrome and evidence of a batterer profile). The former is irrelevant because it is not necessarily true that an accused is a batterer just because the individual fits a certain profile. However, the latter is often helpful in determining a fact in issue. This is especially true when deciding, as in the instant case, whether the child died from a seizure as posited by the defense or whether she was suffocated as alleged by the Government. We conclude Dr. Cooper's testimony was the latter.

Dr. Cooper's third statement, "Overwhelmingly, the most likely person to kill a child is going to be his or her own biological parent," is more troubling. Following Dr. Cooper's testimony and counsel's respective arguments at the [pretrial hearing], the military judge contextually culled out the testimony he considered profile in nature. Consequently, the military judge attempted to limit Dr. Cooper's testimony to child characteristics of abuse like the history of diagnosing child abuse, fatal versus nonfatal child abuse, and single episode versus multiple episodes of abuse. The judge barred Dr. Cooper from testifying regarding adult characteristics of child abusers, like substance abuse, living in a military environment, and the parent of an unplanned pregnancy.

Nevertheless, Dr. Cooper's statement regarding biological parents clearly reached both the characteristics of the victim as well as the characteristics of the typical offender. It is not enough to say that the Government did not expressly place the accused within the statistic presented, for the accused manifestly fit the statistical pattern presented without the Government connecting the dots. Moreover, while Dr. Cooper's testimony did not come in the form of numeric probability, members might have been left with the impression that if the testimony indicated Appellant's daughter died as a result of child abuse, the probability Appellant committed the offense was "overwhelming," regardless of what specific evidence was presented. In essence, the statement placed a statistical probability on the likelihood that Appellant committed the offense. Thus, we conclude that it was impermissible profile evidence.

However, any error in admitting this statement was harmless. First, the evidence was introduced after Appellant's confession had been admitted and presented to the members. Second, the critical question in this case was whether the victim died by accidental or intentional asphyxiation, not the identity of the perpetrator. Appellant did not contest being alone with the victim at the time of the child's injury.

2. Basis for the Expert's Opinion

Appellant also argues that Dr. Cooper should not have been allowed to give her ultimate opinion on the cause of Caitlyn's death because it was not based solely upon medical evidence, but also rested upon her subjective evaluation of Appellant's grieving conduct. In particular, during the Article 39(a) session, Dr. Cooper testified that when forming her opinions she considered the fact that Appellant gave differing accounts regarding Caitlyn's condition to the 911 operator, the paramedics when they arrived at her quarters, and to the hospital personnel when the child arrived at the emergency room.

Dr. Cooper also considered certain statements Appellant allegedly made to witnesses at the hospital as suggestive of an uncharacteristic and inappropriate grief response. For example, Appellant was alleged to have stated to one witness who was trying to console her at the hospital, "I'm just glad I saved the toy receipts." Traum, 2002 CCA LEXIS 153 at *4, No. ACM 34225. When this witness commented that the dead child had been a beautiful girl, Appellant stated, "She really was mean. She was mean to her sister and really active." 2002 CCA LEXIS 153 at *4. At root, Appellant argues these remarks were observations lay persons could observe and testify to without medical knowledge. Therefore, Dr. Cooper's testimony was not based on specialized medical knowledge, but ordinary lay observations already offered to the members by non-expert witnesses.

An expert's opinion may be based upon other sources such as "personal knowledge, assumed facts, documents supplied by other experts," or the testimony of witnesses at trial. Houser, 36 M.J. at 399; M.R.E. 703. Dr. Cooper's testimony indicates that her opinions were not based solely on Appellant's grieving reaction, but on a tripartite methodology generally accepted as authoritative in the forensic pediatric field. This methodology focuses on the history of events leading to a child's condition, the behavior of the custodial caretaker, and the physical examination reports including those from the autopsy. Further, the record supports a conclusion that this methodology is relied on by experts in the field of forensic pediatrics. M.R.E. 703 allows experts to rest their opinions on precisely this basis. Therefore, it is clear Dr. Cooper's testimony was rooted in more than lay observations regarding Appellant's conduct. Moreover, it was the eyewitnesses and not Dr. Cooper who testified to the members about Appellant's reactions in the emergency room.

3. Probative Value

However relevant and reliable an expert's testimony might be, such evidence "may be excluded if its probative value is substantially outweighed by the danger of unfair prejudice, confusion of the issues, or misleading the members[.]" M.R.E. 403. The record indicates that the military judge was acutely aware of the dangers of profile evidence. It is worth noting the military judge's comment at the time he made his ruling with regard to admission of Dr. Cooper's testimony. The judge clearly considered the expert's testimony balanced against "the facts that have come out so far." When Dr. Cooper testified during the trial, the members had already received Appellant's confession, the testimony of the medical examiner, and the testimony of various witnesses concerning statements Appellant made indicating either a lack of grief or at best, an inappropriate grief response. Further, the military judge culled out what he thought was impermissible profiling of Appellant and allowed opinions that were based on the professional literature of the field of expertise and on a methodology accepted by experts in that field. Finally, it is clear the military judge understood the constraint of M.R.E. 403 when he was determining what would or would not be allowed. Based on this record, we cannot say the military judge abused his discretion in weighing the probative value of the expert testimony against any prejudicial effect it might have presented.

DISCUSSION QUESTIONS

1. What did you learn from this opinion about the importance of a pre-trial Daubert hearing? What do you think would have happened on appeal if counsel and the judge had not developed the facts at the pretrial hearing as thoroughly as they did here?

2. What is the difference between victim and offender profile evidence? Why does it matter in a case?

3. What was objectionable about the expert's testimony at trial, and why? Did the court find reversible error? Why or why not?

4. Reading this opinion in light of Rule 703, how can counsel establish the basis for an expert's opinion and whether it is of a type reasonably relied on by experts in the field.

PROBLEMS

Problem 30-1. Return to the factual scenario from Problem 29-1 (Thad Thinskin suing the *Calamity Crier* for defamation.) In Thad Thinskin's case, the defendant Calamity Crier calls a behavioral expert of its own, Fran Freudkin, an expert in financial psychology. Assume that Freudkin is qualified to testify on the basis of knowledge, training, education and experience. Freudkin has published two articles: one the psychology of risk in One-Armed Bandit, a trade publication of the gambling industry; and the other on legal and ethical ways to exploit risk-taking investors in Compounding Fees, a collection of essays and training materials published by a leading brokerage firm. Neither article was peer-reviewed.

Freudkin used the following materials in forming her opinion: the Crier's editorial; interviews with Thinskin's ex-wife; and telephonic interviews with several people recommended by Thinskin's ex-wife. All sources vilified Thinskin. The interviewees recounted times that Thinskin had taken what they considered to be unnecessary financial risks and gave specific examples based on their personal experiences with him — everything from paying a lawyer to fight higher alimony payments, and then losing and having to make the payments anyway; betting on the losing team in the Super Bowl for 15 consecutive years; borrowing money at Cholesterol Hut, an all-you-can eat rib restaurant, and forgetting to pay it back; never buying clothing on sale; purchasing consumer goods and products without first reading Consumer Reports; and rolling over all his personal investments in Enron stock just two weeks before it crashed.

Freudkin intends to testify that in her expert opinion, Thinskin was addicted to risk, tended to act irresponsibly, and was addicted to "investment gambling" with others' money.

Evaluate her testimony under Rule 703 and 705. What foundational elements would you have to establish in order for her to testify under 703? If you were the opponent, what concerns would you have about the basis for her opinion? How would you attack the basis of her opinion? If you were the proponent, how could you structure her testimony to avoid introducing inadmissible evidence?

Basis and Scope of Expert Opinion: Quick Hits

- In forming an opinion, an expert can consider inadmissible evidence, hypothetical questions, and even direct observations of the courtroom testimony of others, provided that the facts or data are of the same type relied on by other experts in the field.

- Otherwise inadmissible facts or data cannot be disclosed to the jury unless the court decides their probative value in evaluating the expert's opinion substantially outweighs prejudicial effect.

- The opposing side may require the expert to disclose the underlying facts or data, even if otherwise inadmissible, on cross-examination.

- Experts are permitted to testify about the ultimate issue in a case but cannot invade the province of the jury.

- While victim profile evidence is permissible at trial, offender profile evidence is not.

Chapter References

CHRISTOPHER B. MUELLER & LAIRD C. KIRKPATRICK, EVIDENCE §§ 7.8–7.16 (4th ed. 2009).

GLEN WEISSENBERGER & JAMES J. DUANE, FEDERAL RULES OF EVIDENCE: RULES, LEGISLATIVE HISTORY, COMMENTARY AND AUTHORITY §§ 703–05 (6th ed. 2009).

JACK B. WEINSTEIN & MARGARET A. BERGER, WEINSTEIN'S FEDERAL EVIDENCE §§ 703–05 (Joseph M. McLaughlin ed., Matthew Bender 2d ed. 1997).

KENNETH S. BROUN, MCCORMICK ON EVIDENCE §§ 10–18 (6th ed. 2006).

STEVEN GOODE & OLIN GUY WELLBORN III, COURTROOM HANDBOOK ON FEDERAL EVIDENCE Ch. 5 (West 2010).

III. APPLICATION EXERCISE

Presenting and Opposing Expert Witnesses at Trial

Expert witnesses regularly testify in civil and criminal jury trials in the United States. Indeed, cases often become a battle of the experts, with each side calling dueling expert witnesses to present contrary testimony on the same subject. In many cases, the first shots are fired long before the actual trial itself in pretrial motions in limine to settle issues such as the expert's qualifications, the reliability of the testimony, the underlying basis of the expert's opinion or the acceptable scope of testimony at trial. In some cases, depending on the customs and practices of the jurisdiction, these issues have not been resolved in pretrial hearings and must be taken care of at trial.

After these issues have been resolved, the task of presenting the expert at trial still remains. The proponent wants to convince the jury that the expert is qualified, establish the basis, credibility and reliability of the expert's opinion, and persuasively employ the expert to teach the jury or help them to make a better decision about a material issue at trial. The opponent may have the opposite goals, or may in the alternative wish to co-opt the expert and use the expert to help advance the opponent's theory of the case.

Advocacy books are filled with advice and strategies about how to present experts or defend against them. Space and time limitations prevent us from discussing the relative merits or drawbacks of these various approaches. The rules of evidence, however, provide a basic structure to presenting or opposing an expert witness at trial.

Step One: Establish (or contest) the expert's qualifications.

Even if the judge has already ruled in a pretrial hearing that the expert is qualified, the proponent wants to ensure that the *jury* knows the expert is qualified. Rule 702 states that an expert is qualified based on knowledge, skill, experience, training, or education. To satisfy this step, the proponent must ask questions that establish the expert's qualifications in their particular field. At the end of this step, in most jurisdictions, the proponent formally tenders the witness to the court as an expert in the field. Some jurisdictions do not permit the formal process of tendering a witness as an expert; as the advisory committee notes to Rule 702 observe,

> The use of the term "expert" in the Rule does not, however, mean that a jury should actually be informed that a qualified witness is testifying as an "expert." Indeed, there is much to be said for a practice that prohibits the use of the term "expert" by both the parties and the court at trial. Such a practice "ensures that trial courts do not inadvertently put their stamp of authority" on a witness's opinion, and protects against the jury's being "overwhelmed by the so-called 'experts.' "[1]

In some jurisdictions, after the proponent has established the expert's qualifications on the record, the opponent is then permitted to examine the witness in aid of objection, or "voir dire" the witness on qualifications. The procedure for this is a brief cross-examination by the opponent, limited to the issue of qualifications. At the end of the cross-examination, the opponent can object that the expert is not qualified.

---

[1] FED. R. EVID. 702, advisory committee notes (internal citations omitted).

Step Two: Establish (or contest) the reliability of the expert's testimony.

Rule 702 permits an expert to testify if "(1) the testimony is based upon sufficient facts or data, (2) the testimony is the product of reliable principles and methods, and (3) the witness has applied the principles and methods reliably to the facts of the case." After the expert's qualifications have been established, the proponent establishes the reliability of the expert's opinion for the fact-finder. The proponent does this by building a direct examination on the framework of the three factors mentioned in Rule 702. For example, if the expert witness is an economist, a direct examination might be structured as follows: (1) an explanation of the basic principles of economics; (2) why the body of knowledge (economics) is reliable; (3) the facts and data the expert used in forming an opinion; (4) how the expert applied the theory to the facts and data; and (5) the conclusion the expert reached.

In attacking the reliability of an expert's testimony, the opponent should examine the three factors in Rule 702 to determine where the expert is most vulnerable. Returning to the economics expert, it might be difficult to mount a credible attack on the basic principles and reliability of economics. If, however, the expert relied on flawed data, or committed errors in evaluating the data, the opponent's cross examination should focus on those mistakes. The opponent may also want to call an expert of its own to contest the theories and conclusions of the other party's expert — thus leading to the proverbial "battle of the experts" that often occurs in jury trials.

Step 3: Use Rules 703–705 and 803(18) as needed in the first two steps.

When presenting or contesting expert testimony, the advocate should be prepared to use all the ammunition that the Rules offer. As discussed in the preceding chapter, Rules 703-705 can be used at trial to expand, limit or shape the expert's testimony at trial. For example, if the proponent of the expert wants to introduce otherwise inadmissible evidence through the expert under Rule 703, she should be prepared to persuade the judge that the probative value of such evidence substantially outweighs its prejudicial effect. On the other hand, if the opponent wants to demonstrate the weaknesses and flaws in the materials the expert relied on in formulating an opinion, Rule 705 permits the opponent to disclose these materials in cross-examination of the expert.

Rule 803(18), Learned Treatises, is a hearsay exception that helps a jury evaluate the reliability of the expert's theories. The rule states:

> To the extent called to the attention of an expert witness upon cross-examination or relied upon by the expert witness in direct examination, statements contained in published treatises, periodicals, or pamphlets on a subject of history, medicine, or other science or art, established as a reliable authority by the testimony or admission of the witness or by other expert testimony or by judicial notice. If admitted, the statements may be read into evidence but may not be received as exhibits.

The rule is most often used on cross-examination of an expert in order to help cast doubt on the theories or methodology employed by the expert. After establishing the authoritative and reliable nature of the treatise,

The Exercise

Objective: To demonstrate proficiency in the direct and cross-examination of an expert forensic scientist in a criminal case.

Factual Scenario: The basic factual scenario is as follows. Supplemental facts may be provided to you by your professor in preparation for the assignment.

On July 15, last year, the body of Cougar Meadows, a retired professional tennis player in his early '40's, was found in the freezer at the local Cool Stone Ice Cream Shoppe. The body was discovered by the manager, who arrived at Cool Stone a few minutes before the store opened at 11 a.m. Meadows had been assigned closing duties at the Cool Stone the night of July 14, and he was last seen alive by an employee at 11:15 pm, 15 minutes after Cool Stone closed. Meadows had told the employee, "I'll lock up. You go home." The employee, whose fiancée was waiting for her in the parking lot, and who had immediately gone to a bar for drinks with some friends, had an airtight alibi and was not a suspect.

Meadows's hands were bound behind his back and tied to a chair. His shirt was found nearby on the floor, apparently having been ripped off. The cause of death was an icepick wound to the temple and exposure from the cold temperatures in the freezer. The coroner estimated that Meadows had been deceased for about 8 hours. It appeared that prior to his death, he had been subjected to a form of psychosexual torture.

Multiple photos of the scene were taken, including photos of bite marks on the neck and left nipple of Meadows. Tests were also done for fingerprints as well as hair and fibers. The fingerprint tests were inconclusive, but a single strand of blond hair was found on the victim's body. Forensic scientists were never able to match the hair with anyone.

Upon investigation, local authorities found out that Meadows had been separated from his wife for several months. Needing money to pay support to his wife and children, he took a job as an assistant manager at Cool Stone in January of last year. Meadows subsequently developed a love interest with one of the employees, Heather Hunter. Everyone knew the two of them were having an affair.

Several employees told police investigators about an incident in late May between Meadows and Hunter during an employee meeting. The two of them got into a screaming argument that started when Meadows told Hunter he was attempting to work things out with his wife and had plans to return to his family. In front of everyone, Hunter flew into a rage and screamed, "What about your promise to divorce her and marry me? What about that?! I ought to kill you!"

Immediately after the meeting, the manager fired Hunter because of the threat she had made.

As a part of the investigation, a Forensic Odontologist, Carie Incisor, compared the dental records, X-Rays, and a mold of Hunter's teeth (which she voluntarily provided) to the photos of the bite marks found on Meadows' neck and nipple.

Further, one week after the murder, Dr. Incisor compared the mold of the teeth to the bite marks on the skin of Meadows by placing the mold upon the skin atop of the bite marks. Dr. Incisor noted that the bite mark on the neck included three teeth from the top set of teeth, and four from the bottom set of teeth. The bite mark on the nipple of the body was made with only two top teeth and two bottom teeth. Dr. Incisor was able to identify five unique teeth from the bite on the neck and four from the bite upon the nipple.

The prosecution has now charged Heather Hunter with first-degree murder. A major part of the prosecution's evidence is based upon the bite marks found on Meadows' body. Dr. Incisor is willing to testify in court that s/he is 100 percent certain, to the exclusion of all other possibilities, the bite marks on the body of Meadows were made by Heather Hunter.

Advance Preparation. As assigned by your professor, prepare a direct examination of Dr. Incisor for the prosecution or a cross-examination for the defense. In preparing the examinations, research forensic odontology in order to ask the necessary questions on direct or cross examination. Your professor may provide you with a list of sources to assist you in this endeavor.

The Exercise. In class, students will play the following roles: prosecutor, defense attorney, judge, and witness. Assume that Dr. Incisor has survived a pretrial *Daubert* motion. Dr. Incisor's CV is reproduced below for your convenience.

CURRICIULUM VITAE OF DR. CARIE INCISOR

I. PROFESSIONAL AFFILIATION AND CONTACT INFORMATION

Adjunct Professor of Oral Medicine
Calamity State University School of Dental Medicine
188 Bitemark Blvd.
Calamity City, Calamity
(666)123?4567
CarieIncisor@clsu.edu

Chief Forensic Odontologist
Office of the Calamity County Medical Examiner
Calamity County Hospital
Calamity City, Calamity
(666) 123-7654
CarieIncisor@calamityco.gov

II. EDUCATION

DDS, *Magna Cum Laude*

Calamity State University School of Dental Medicine

Calamity City, Calamity, May 1990

Bachelor of Science, Biology, *Magna Cum Laude*, University of Calamity, Calamity City, Calamity, May 1986

III. Professional Experience

July 2000 — Present. Adjunct Professor of Oral Medicine, Calamity State University School of Dental Medicine, Calamity City, Calamity. Currently teach orthodontic mechanotherapy, interdisciplinary orthodontics, ortho — - surgery, and biomechanics and early orthodontic treatment.

October 1997 — Present. Chief Forensic Odontologist, Office of the Calamity County Medical Examiner, Calamity County Hospital, Calamity City, Calamity. Assist investigative authorities and prosecutors in identification of human remains, disaster identification, and bitemarks.

May 1990 — October 1997. Forensic Odontologist, Office of the Calamity County Medical Examiner, Calamity County Hospital, Calamity City, Calamity. Assist chief forensic odontolgist and chief medical examiner in the identification of human remains and bitemarks.

IV. Research and Creative Activity

A. **Interests and Specialties**

Forensic Odontology, Ortho — surgery, Orthodontic Mechanotherapy.

B. **Papers and Presentations at Professional Meetings**

Workshop, Dental Identification and Multiple Fatality Incident Management, Calamity Civic Center, Calamity City, Calamity, August 2009

Article, *Are Bitemarks the Rosetta Stone of Criminal Forensics?*, 22 Journal of Forensic Science, Linguistics and Social Sciences 7–10 (2009)

Workshop, Expert Witness Testimony, Calamity State University School of Dental Medicine, Calamity City, Calamity, October 2008

Training Symposium for Calamity County Law Enforcement, Bite Mark Management, Calamity State University School of Dental Medicine, Calamity City, Calamity, September 2008

Training Symposium and Workshop, Forensic Pathology and Autopsy, Calamity State University School of Dental Medicine, Calamity City, Calamity, July 2008

V. Professional Service

A. **Membership in Professional Associations**

American Board of Forensic Odontology

American Academy of Forensic Sciences — Odontology Section

B. **Offices Held and Honors Awarded in Professional Associations**

Fellow, American Academy of Forensic Sciences — Odontology Section

Diplomat, American Board of Forensic Odontology

Chapter 31

PRIVILEGES

```
┌─────────────────────────────────────────────────────────────────┐
│                                                                   │
│  Chapter Objectives:                                              │
│                                                                   │
│  • Introduce and explain the concept of privileges and Rules 501-502 │
│  • Analyze and discuss issues pertaining to privileges            │
│  • Apply the concepts from this chapter in a courtroom application │
│    exercise                                                       │
│                                                                   │
└─────────────────────────────────────────────────────────────────┘
```

I. BACKGROUND AND EXPLANATORY MATERIAL

The Concept

An evidentiary privilege is the legal right of an individual to prohibit the introduction into evidence at trial of information covered by the privilege. Examples include the attorney-client privilege, spousal privilege, marital communications privilege, priest-penitent privilege, physician-patient privilege, national security privilege, and many other privileges recognized under the Constitution, state laws or the federal common law of evidence. Privileges exist to validate, protect and enhance social relationships and societal values that are external to the adversary trial process. Every privilege represents a cost-benefit analysis in which the benefit of supporting the value or relationship recognized by the privilege is deemed to outweigh the cost of depriving the fact-finder of valuable information. Simply put, evidentiary privileges trump the maxim that the public is entitled to every man's evidence at trial, a principle that usually compels the disclosure of even private information in favor of the public good.

Privileged information is frequently relevant, reliable and otherwise admissible under the rules; in some cases, it may be the best evidence that exists to prove a fact of consequence in a case. For example, a criminal defendant's detailed confession to his priest is likely to be accurate and reliable evidence of the defendant's guilt and would otherwise be admissible under Rule 801(d)(2). Nonetheless, in order to protect the integrity and confidential nature of the priest-penitent relationship and encourage people to unburden their souls to obtain absolution, our adversary justice system accepts the price to be paid by precluding the use of this evidence at trial.

For analytical purposes, privileges can be divided into two broad categories, based on the primary reason for the privilege's existence. The first category is privileges that are justified for utilitarian — what evidence scholars call "instrumental" — reasons. Utilitarian reasons include supporting and encouraging people to do socially valuable things such as seeking advice from lawyers, speaking honestly to therapists or doctors, repenting to clergy members, and the like. The second category is privileges that are based privacy concerns, such as ensuring confidential communications in a marriage, protecting the identity of informants in criminal cases or preserving national security secrets.

The rule pertaining to privileges "applies at all stages of all actions, cases, and proceedings." Fed. R. Evid. 1101(c). The privilege rules also apply in hearings conducted pursuant to FRE 104(a) to determine the preliminary admissibility of evidence.

Holding, Claiming, Waiving and Commenting on Privileges

The holder of a privilege is the person whose information the privilege is designed to protect. A holder may be, but is not always, a party to the litigation.

Privileges are personal to the holder and may not be waived by anyone else. Under an agency theory, however, privileges may be claimed by an attorney on behalf of the holder. For example, the holder of information under the attorney-client privilege is the client, not the attorney. Only the client can decide whether to waive privileged attorney-client information. At trial, however, an attorney can claim the privilege on behalf of a client, and this claim of privilege is presumptively valid. Another example is the national security privilege, which is ultimately held by the President of the United States. At trial, an attorney representing the United States can claim the privilege on behalf of the President, but cannot waive it on behalf of the President.

The holder of the privilege can prevent someone else from disclosing information, even if that person might otherwise want to disclose it. One example of this is the common law spousal communication privilege, which protects confidential communications made by one spouse to another during the marriage. The holder of this privilege is the spouse who made the communication. Thus, even if the witness spouse is willing to testify, the holder may exercise the privilege and prevent the witness spouse from testifying.

Waiver can occur two ways. The first is formal, voluntary waiver at trial, in which the holder informs the court of his intent to waive the privilege. The second is informal, voluntary waiver, in which the holder discloses the information to others without concern for its continued confidentiality. The significance of this type of waiver is that disclosure to one person is generally viewed as disclosure to all. For example, if a client disclosed personal and confidential information to her attorney, it would be privileged under the attorney-client relationship. If, however, she disclosed the same information to her best friend or another person with whom the law does not recognize a privilege, she has waived the privilege and cannot block the introduction of that evidence at trial.

When privileged information is involuntarily disclosed, intercepted, or disclosed without authorization, the holder of the privilege may still be able to claim the privilege at trial. This is done in order preserve the purposes underlying the law of privilege. The holder of a privilege should not be rendered impotent to prevent the use of privileged information at trial merely because of a forced or unauthorized disclosure.

Privilege law also protects the holder from having to endure adverse comments or inferences at trial pertaining to the exercise of a privilege. In criminal cases when the defendant exercises his privilege against self-incrimination under the Fifth Amendment, this protection is mandated by the Constitution. There is no constitutional mandate prohibiting adverse comments or inferences on the exercise of statutory or common law privileges, however, as Mueller and Kirkpatrick note, "[t]he direction of modern cases and statutes is toward extending these procedural protections to statutory and common law privileges as well."[1]

There are just two rules pertaining to privileges in the Federal Rules: Rule 501, the general rule on privileges; and Rule 502, which covers limitations on waiver for the attorney client and work product privileges. Because most students taking this course have already studied the attorney-client and work product privileges in civil procedure and/or legal ethics courses, this text will not cover Rule 502. The text of Rule 501 follows:

Through Dec. 1, 2011	After Dec. 1, 2011
Rule 501. General Rule	**Rule 501. Privilege in General**
Except as otherwise required by the Constitution of the United States or provided by Act of Congress or in rules prescribed by the Supreme Court pursuant to statutory authority, the privilege of a witness, person, government, State, or political subdivision thereof shall be governed by the principles of the common law as they may be interpreted by the courts of the United States in the light of reason and experience. However, in civil actions and proceedings, with respect to an element of a claim or defense as to which State law supplies the rule of decision, the privilege of a witness, person, government, State, or political subdivision thereof shall be determined in accordance with State law.	The common law — as interpreted by United States courts in the light of reason and experience — governs a claim of privilege unless any of the following provides otherwise: • the United States Constitution; • a federal statute; or • rules prescribed by the Supreme Court. But in a civil case, state law governs privilege regarding a claim or defense for which state law supplies the rule of decision.

Rule 501, the general rule on privileges, provides that in federal question cases and criminal cases in federal court, the law of privilege "shall be governed by the principles of the common law as they may be interpreted by the courts of the United States in the light of reason and experience." In cases where state law is the rule of

---

[1] Mueller & Kirkpatrick § 5.4.

decision, Rule 501 provides that privilege rules will be determined according to the applicable state laws; in this respect, Rule 501 codifies the principles of *Erie R. Co. v. Tompkins*.[2]

It might seem strange that federal privilege rules remained uncodified when the Federal Rules of Evidence were promulgated. In fact, the original draft of the Federal Rules contained thirteen rules pertaining to privileges. These rules would have applied to all trials in federal courts, even those in which state law provided the rule of decision. The proposed rules failed to include some privileges — such as the physician-patient, spousal communication and journalist privileges — that had widespread support. The rules also changed the scope of some government information privileges, which proved to be a political hot potato in the immediate aftermath of the Watergate scandal. In the end, the proposed privilege rules were so controversial that they had to be deleted in order to assure passage of the Federal Rules.

The thirteen proposed rules on privilege remain available to attorney as an influential guide to privilege law, but they are not binding on the courts. Instead, privilege law is unique among the modern rules of evidence because of its reliance for future development on the archaic forms of the common law.

The seminal Supreme Court case on privileges, *Jaffee v. Redmond*, illustrates the process of deciding whether a privilege exists under Federal common law.

JAFFEE v. REDMOND
Supreme Court of the United States
518 U.S. 1 (1996)

JUSTICE STEVENS delivered the opinion of the Court.

After a traumatic incident in which she shot and killed a man, a police officer received extensive counseling from a licensed clinical social worker. The question we address is whether statements the officer made to her therapist during the counseling sessions are protected from compelled disclosure in a federal civil action brought by the family of the deceased. Stated otherwise, the question is whether it is appropriate for federal courts to recognize a "psychotherapist privilege" under Rule 501 of the Federal Rules of Evidence.

I

Petitioner is the administrator of the estate of Ricky Allen. Respondents are Mary Lu Redmond, a former police officer, and the Village of Hoffman Estates, Illinois, her employer during the time that she served on the police force.

Petitioner commenced this action against respondents after Redmond shot and killed Allen while on patrol duty.

On June 27, 1991, Redmond was the first officer to respond to a "fight in progress"

---

[2] 304 U.S. 64 (1938).

call at an apartment complex. As she arrived at the scene, two of Allen's sisters ran toward her squad car, waving their arms and shouting that there had been a stabbing in one of the apartments. Redmond testified at trial that she relayed this information to her dispatcher and requested an ambulance. She then exited her car and walked toward the apartment building. Before Redmond reached the building, several men ran out, one waving a pipe. When the men ignored her order to get on the ground, Redmond drew her service revolver, Allen was brandishing a butcher knife and disregarded her repeated commands to drop the weapon. Redmond shot Allen when she believed he was about to stab the man he was chasing. Allen died at the scene. Redmond testified that before other officers arrived to provide support, "people came pouring out of the buildings," App. 134, and a threatening confrontation between her and the crowd ensued.

Petitioner filed suit in Federal District Court alleging that Redmond had violated Allen's constitutional rights by using excessive force during the encounter at the apartment complex. The complaint sought damages under Rev. Stat. § 1979, 42 U.S.C. § 1983 and the Illinois wrongful death statute, Ill. Comp. Stat., ch. 740, § 180/1 et seq. (1994). At trial, petitioner presented testimony from members of Allen's family that conflicted with Redmond's version of the incident in several important respects. They testified, for example, that Redmond drew her gun before exiting her squad car and that Allen was unarmed when he emerged from the apartment building.

During pretrial discovery petitioner learned that after the shooting Redmond had participated in about 50 counseling sessions with Karen Beyer, a clinical social worker licensed by the State of Illinois and employed at that time by the Village of Hoffman Estates. Petitioner sought access to Beyer's notes concerning the sessions for use in cross-examining Redmond. Respondents vigorously resisted the discovery. They asserted that the contents of the conversations between Beyer and Redmond were protected against involuntary disclosure by a psychotherapist-patient privilege. The district judge rejected this argument. Neither Beyer nor Redmond, however, complied with his order to disclose the contents of Beyer's notes. At depositions and on the witness stand both either refused to answer certain questions or professed an inability to recall details of their conversations.

In his instructions at the end of the trial, the judge advised the jury that the refusal to turn over Beyer's notes had no "legal justification" and that the jury could therefore presume that the contents of the notes would have been unfavorable to respondents. The jury awarded petitioner $45,000 on the federal claim and $500,000 on her state-law claim.

The Court of Appeals for the Seventh Circuit reversed and remanded for a new trial. Addressing the issue for the first time, the court concluded that "reason and experience," the touchstones for acceptance of a privilege under Rule 501 of the Federal Rules of Evidence, compelled recognition of a psychotherapist-patient privilege. 51 F.3d 1346, 1355 (1995). "Reason tells us that psychotherapists and patients share a unique relationship, in which the ability to communicate freely without the fear of public disclosure is the key to successful treatment." Id., at 1355-1356. As to experience, the court observed that all 50 States have adopted some form of the psychotherapist-patient privilege. Id., at 1356. The court attached particular significance to the fact that Illinois law expressly extends such a privilege to social workers like Karen Beyer. Id., at 1357. The court also noted that, with one exception, the federal decisions rejecting the privilege were more than five years old and that the "need and demand for counseling services has skyrocketed during the past several years." Id., at 1355-1356.

The Court of Appeals qualified its recognition of the privilege by stating that it would not apply if "in the interests of justice, the evidentiary need for the disclosure of the contents of a patient's counseling sessions outweighs that patient's privacy interests." Id., at 1357. Balancing those conflicting interests, the court observed, on the one hand, that the evidentiary need for the contents of the confidential conversations was diminished in this case because there were numerous eyewitnesses to the shooting, and, on the other hand, that Officer Redmond's privacy interests were substantial. n5 Id., at 1358. Based on this assessment, the court concluded that the trial court had erred by refusing to afford protection to the confidential communications between Redmond and Beyer.

> n5 "Her ability, through counseling, to work out the pain and anguish undoubtedly caused by Allen's death in all probability depended to a great deal upon her trust and confidence in her counselor Karen Beyer. Officer Redmond, and all those placed in her most unfortunate circumstances, are entitled to be protected in their desire to seek counseling after mortally wounding another human being in the line of duty. An individual who is troubled as the result of her participation in a violent and tragic event, such as this, displays a most commendable respect for human life and is a person well-suited 'to protect and to serve.' " 51 F.3d at 1358.

The United States courts of appeals do not uniformly agree that the federal courts should recognize a psychotherapist privilege under Rule 501. [Citations omitted.] Because of the conflict among the courts of appeals and the importance of the question, we granted certiorari. 516 U.S. (1995). We affirm.

II

Rule 501 of the Federal Rules of Evidence authorizes federal courts to define new privileges by interpreting "common law principles . . . in the light of reason and experience." The authors of the Rule borrowed this phrase from our opinion in Wolfe v. United States, 291 U.S. 7, 12 (1934), which in turn referred to the oft-repeated observation that "the common law is not immutable but flexible, and by its own principles adapts itself to varying conditions." Funk v. United States, 290 U.S. 371, 383, (1933). See also Hawkins v. United States, 358 U.S. 74, 79 (1958) (changes in privileges may be "dictated by 'reason and experience' "). The Senate Report accompanying the 1975 adoption of the Rules indicates that Rule 501 "should be understood as reflecting the view that the recognition of a privilege based on a confidential relationship . . . should be determined on a case-by-case basis." S. Rep. No. 93- 1277, p. 13 (1974). The Rule thus did not freeze the law governing the privileges of witnesses in federal trials at a particular point in our history, but rather directed federal courts to "continue the evolutionary development of testimonial privileges." Trammel v. United States, 445 U.S. 40, 47 (1980); see also University of Pennsylvania v. EEOC, 493 U.S. 182, 189 (1990).

The common-law principles underlying the recognition of testimonial privileges can be stated simply. " 'For more than three centuries it has now been recognized as a fundamental maxim that the public . . . has a right to every man's evidence. When we come to examine the various claims of exemption, we start with the primary assumption that there is a general duty to give what testimony one is capable of giving, and that any exemptions which may exist are distinctly exceptional, being so many derogations from a positive general rule.' " United States v. Bryan, 339 U.S. 323, 331 (1950) (quoting 8 J. Wigmore, Evidence § 2192, p. 64 (3d ed. 1940)). See also United States v. Nixon, 418 U.S. 683, 709 (1974). Exceptions from the general rule disfavoring testimonial privileges may be justified, however, by a " 'public good transcending the normally predominant principle of utilizing all rational means for ascertaining the truth.' " Trammel, 445 U.S. at 50, quoting Elkins v. United States, 364 U.S. 206, 234 (1960) (Frankfurter, J., dissenting).

Guided by these principles, the question we address today is whether a privilege protecting confidential communications between a psychotherapist and her patient "promotes sufficiently important interests to outweigh the need for probative evidence. . . ." 445 U.S. at 51. Both "reason and experience" persuade us that it does.

III

Like the spousal and attorney-client privileges, the psychotherapist-patient privilege is "rooted in the imperative need for confidence and trust." Trammel, 445 U.S. at 51. Treatment by a physician for physical ailments can often proceed successfully on the basis of a physical examination, objective information supplied by the patient, and the results of diagnostic tests. Effective psychotherapy, by contrast, depends upon an atmosphere of confidence and trust in which the patient is willing to make a frank and complete disclosure of facts, emotions, memories, and fears. Because of the sensitive nature of the problems for which individuals consult psychotherapists, disclosure of confidential communications made during counseling sessions may cause embarrassment or disgrace. For this reason, the mere possibility of disclosure may impede development of the confidential relationship necessary for successful treatment. As the Judicial Conference Advisory Committee observed in 1972 when it recommended that Congress recognize a psychotherapist privilege as part of the Proposed Federal Rules of Evidence, a psychiatrist's ability to help her patients

> "is completely dependent upon [the patients'] willingness and ability to talk freely. This makes it difficult if not impossible for [a psychiatrist] to function without being able to assure . . . patients of confidentiality and, indeed, privileged communication. Where there may be exceptions to this general rule . . . , there is wide agreement that confidentiality is a sine qua non for successful psychiatric treatment." Advisory Committee's Notes to Proposed Rules, 56 F.R.D. 183, 242 (1972) (quoting Group for Advancement of Psychiatry, Report No. 45, Confidentiality and Privileged Communication in the Practice of Psychiatry 92 (June 1960)).

By protecting confidential communications between a psychotherapist and her patient from involuntary disclosure, the proposed privilege thus serves important private interests.

Our cases make clear that an asserted privilege must also "serve public ends." Upjohn Co. v. United States, 449 U.S. 383, 389 (1981). Thus, the purpose of the attorney-client privilege is to "encourage full and frank communication between attorneys and their clients and thereby promote broader public interests in the observance of law and administration of justice." Ibid. And the spousal privilege, as modified in Trammel, is justified because it "furthers the important public interest in marital harmony," 445 U.S. at 53. See also United States v. Nixon, 418 U.S. at 705; Wolfle v. United States, 291 U.S. at 14. The psychotherapist privilege serves the public interest by facilitating the provision of appropriate treatment for individuals suffering the effects of a mental or emotional problem. The mental health of our citizenry, no less than its physical health, is a public good of transcendent importance.

In contrast to the significant public and private interests supporting recognition of the privilege, the likely evidentiary benefit that would result from the denial of the privilege is modest. If the privilege were rejected, confidential conversations between psychotherapists and their patients would surely be chilled, particularly when it is obvious that the circumstances that give rise to the need for treatment will probably result in litigation. Without a privilege, much of the desirable evidence to which litigants such as petitioner seek access — for example, admissions against interest by a party — is unlikely to come into being. This unspoken "evidence" will therefore serve no greater truth-seeking function than if it had been spoken and privileged.

That it is appropriate for the federal courts to recognize a psychotherapist privilege under Rule 501 is confirmed by the fact that all 50 States and the District of Columbia have enacted into law some form of psychotherapist privilege. We have previously observed that the policy decisions of the States bear on the question whether federal courts should recognize a new privilege or amend the coverage of an existing one. See Trammel, 445 U.S. at 48-50; United States v. Gillock, 445 U.S. 360, 368, n. 8 (1980). Because state legislatures are fully aware of the need to protect the integrity of the factfinding functions of their courts, the existence of a consensus among the States indicates that "reason and experience" support recognition of the privilege. In addition, given the importance of the patient's understanding that her communications with her therapist will not be publicly disclosed, any State's promise of confidentiality would have little value if the patient were aware that the privilege would not be honored in a federal court. Denial of the federal privilege therefore would frustrate the purposes of the state legislation that was enacted to foster these confidential communications.

It is of no consequence that recognition of the privilege in the vast majority of States is the product of legislative action rather than judicial decision. Although common-law rulings may once have been the primary source of new developments in federal privilege law, that is no longer the case. In Funk v. United States, 290 U.S. 371 (1933), we recognized that it is appropriate to treat a consistent body of policy determinations by state legislatures as reflecting both "reason" and "experience." Id., at 376-381. That rule is properly respectful of the States and at the same time reflects the fact that once a state legislature has enacted a privilege there is no longer an opportunity for common-law creation of the protection. The history of the psychotherapist privilege illustrates the latter point. In 1972 the members of the Judicial Conference Advisory Committee noted that the common law "had indicated a disposition to recognize a psychotherapist-patient privilege when legislatures began moving into the field." Proposed Rules, 56 F.R.D. at 242 (citation omitted). The present unanimous acceptance of the privilege shows that the state lawmakers moved quickly. That the privilege may have developed faster legislatively than it would have in the courts demonstrates only that the States rapidly recognized the wisdom of the rule as the field of psychotherapy developed.

The uniform judgment of the States is reinforced by the fact that a psychotherapist privilege was among the nine specific privileges recommended by the Advisory Committee in its proposed privilege rules. In United States v. Gillock, 445 U.S. 360, 367-368 (1980), our holding that Rule 501 did not include a state legislative privilege relied, in part, on the fact that no such privilege was included in the Advisory Committee's draft. The reasoning in Gillock thus supports the opposite conclusion in this case. In rejecting the proposed draft that had specifically identified each privilege rule and substituting the present more open-ended Rule 501, the Senate Judiciary Committee explicitly stated that its action "should not be understood as disapproving any recognition of a psychiatrist-patient . . . privilege contained in the [proposed] rules." S. Rep. No. 93-1277, at 13.

Because we agree with the judgment of the state legislatures and the Advisory Committee that a psychotherapist-patient privilege will serve a "public good transcending the normally predominant principle of utilizing all rational means for ascertaining truth," Trammel, 445 U.S. at 50, we hold that confidential communications between a licensed psychotherapist and her patients in the course of diagnosis or treatment are protected from compelled disclosure under Rule 501 of the Federal Rules of Evidence.

It is so ordered.

JUSTICE SCALIA, with whom THE CHIEF JUSTICE joins as to Part III, dissenting.

The Court has discussed at some length the benefit that will be purchased by creation of the evidentiary privilege in this case: the encouragement of psychoanalytic counseling. It has not mentioned the purchase price: occasional injustice. That is the cost of every rule which excludes reliable and probative evidence — or at least every one categorical enough to achieve its announced policy objective. In the case of some of these rules, such as the one excluding confessions that have not been properly "Mirandized," see Miranda v. Arizona, 384 U.S. 436 (1966), the victim of the injustice is always the impersonal State or the faceless "public at large." For the rule proposed here, the victim is more likely to be some individual who is prevented from proving a valid claim — or (worse still) prevented from establishing a valid defense. The latter is particularly unpalatable for those who love justice, because it causes the courts of law not merely to let stand a wrong, but to become themselves the instruments of wrong.

In the past, this Court has well understood that the particular value the courts are distinctively charged with preserving — justice — is severely harmed by contravention of "the fundamental principle that " 'the public . . . has a right to every man's evidence.' " " Trammel v. United States, 445 U.S. 40, 50 (1980) (citation omitted). Testimonial privileges, it has said, "are not lightly created nor expansively construed, for they are in derogation of the search for truth." United States v. Nixon, 418 U.S. 683, 710 (1974) (emphasis added). Adherence to that principle has caused us, in the Rule 501 cases we have considered to date, to reject new privileges, see University of Pennsylvania v. EEOC, 493 U.S. 182 (1990) (privilege against disclosure of academic peer review materials); United States v. Gillock, 445 U.S. 360 (1980) (privilege against disclosure of "legislative acts" by member of state legislature), and even to construe narrowly the scope of existing privileges, see, e.g., United States v. Zolin, 491 U.S. 554, 568-570 (1989) (permitting in camera review of documents alleged to come within crime-fraud exception to attorney-client privilege); Trammel, supra (holding that voluntary testimony by spouse is not covered by husband-wife privilege). The Court today ignores this traditional judicial preference for the truth, and ends up creating a privilege that is new, vast, and ill-defined. I respectfully dissent.

I

The case before us involves confidential communications made by a police officer to a state-licensed clinical social worker in the course of psychotherapeutic counseling. Before proceeding to a legal analysis of the case, I must observe that the Court makes its task deceptively simple by the manner in which it proceeds. It begins by characterizing the issue as "whether it is appropriate for federal courts to recognize a 'psychotherapist privilege,' " ante, at 1, and devotes almost all of its opinion to that question. Having answered that question (to its satisfaction) in the affirmative, it then devotes less than a page of text to answering in the affirmative the small remaining question whether "the federal privilege should also extend to confidential communications made to licensed social workers in the course of psychotherapy," ante, at 13.

Of course the prototypical evidentiary privilege analogous to the one asserted here — the lawyer-client privilege — is not identified by the broad area of advice-giving practiced by the person to whom the privileged communication is given, but rather by the professional status of that person. Hence, it seems a long step from a lawyer-client privilege to a tax advisor-client or accountant-client privilege. But if one recharacterizes it as a "legal advisor" privilege, the extension seems like the most natural thing in the world. That is the illusion the Court has produced here: It first frames an overly general question ("Should there be a psychotherapist privilege?") that can be answered in the negative only by excluding from protection office consultations with professional psychiatrists (i.e., doctors) and clinical psychologists. And then, having answered that in the affirmative, it comes to the only question that the facts of this case present ("Should there be a social worker-client privilege with regard to psychotherapeutic counseling?") with the answer seemingly a foregone conclusion. At that point, to conclude against the privilege one must subscribe to the difficult proposition, "Yes, there is a psychotherapist privilege, but not if the psychotherapist is a social worker."

Relegating the question actually posed by this case to an afterthought makes the impossible possible in a number of wonderful ways. For example, it enables the Court to treat the Proposed Federal Rules of Evidence developed in 1972 by the Judicial Conference Advisory Committee as strong support for its holding, whereas they in fact counsel clearly and directly against it. The Committee did indeed recommend a "psychotherapist privilege" of sorts; but more precisely, and more relevantly, it recommended a privilege for psychotherapy conducted by "a person authorized to practice medicine" or "a person licensed or certified as a psychologist," Proposed Rule of Evidence 504, 56 F.R.D. 183, 240 (1972), which is to say that it recommended against the privilege at issue here. That condemnation is obscured, and even converted into an endorsement, by pushing a "psychotherapist privilege" into the center ring. The Proposed Rule figures prominently in the Court's explanation of why that privilege deserves recognition, ante, at 12-13, and is ignored in the single page devoted to the sideshow which happens to be the issue presented for decision, ante, at 13-14.

This is the most egregious and readily explainable example of how the Court's misdirection of its analysis makes the difficult seem easy; others will become apparent when I give the social-worker question the fuller consideration it deserves. My initial point, however, is that the Court's very methodology — giving serious consideration only to the more general, and much easier, question — is in violation of our duty to proceed cautiously when erecting barriers between us and the truth.

II

To say that the Court devotes the bulk of its opinion to the much easier question of psychotherapist-patient privilege is not to say that its answer to that question is convincing. At bottom, the Court's decision to recognize such a privilege is based on its view that "successful [psychotherapeutic] treatment" serves "important private interests" (namely those of patients undergoing psychotherapy) as well as the "public good" of "the mental health of our citizenry." Ante, at 7-9. I have no quarrel with these premises. Effective psychotherapy undoubtedly is beneficial to individuals with mental problems, and surely serves some larger social interest in maintaining a mentally stable society. But merely mentioning these values does not answer the critical question: are they of such importance, and is the contribution of psychotherapy to them so distinctive, and is the application of normal evidentiary rules so destructive to psychotherapy, as to justify making our federal courts occasional instruments of injustice? On that central question I find the Court's analysis insufficiently convincing to satisfy the high standard we have set for rules that "are in derogation of the search for truth." Nixon, 418 U.S. at 710.

When is it, one must wonder, that the psychotherapist came to play such an indispensable role in the maintenance of the citizenry's mental health? For most of history, men and women have worked out their difficulties by talking to, inter alios, parents, siblings, best friends and bartenders — none of whom was awarded a privilege against testifying in court. Ask the average citizen: Would your mental health be more significantly impaired by preventing you from seeing a psychotherapist, or by preventing you from getting advice from your mom? I have little doubt what the answer would be. Yet there is no mother-child privilege.

How likely is it that a person will be deterred from seeking psychological counseling, or from being completely truthful in the course of such counseling, because of fear of later disclosure in litigation? And even more pertinent to today's decision, to what extent will the evidentiary privilege reduce that deterrent? The Court does not try to answer the first of these questions; and it cannot possibly have any notion of what the answer is to the second, since that depends entirely upon the scope of the privilege, which the Court amazingly finds it "neither necessary nor feasible to delineate," ante, at 16. If, for example, the psychotherapist can give the patient no more assurance than "A court will not be able to make me disclose what you tell me, unless you tell me about a harmful act," I doubt whether there would be much benefit from the privilege at all. That is not a fanciful example, at least with respect to extension of the psychotherapist privilege to social workers. See Del. Code Ann., Tit. 24, § 3913(2) (1987); Idaho Code § 54-3213(2) (1994).

Even where it is certain that absence of the psychotherapist privilege will inhibit disclosure of the information, it is not clear to me that that is an unacceptable state of affairs. Let us assume the very worst in the circumstances of the present case: that to be truthful about what was troubling her, the police officer who sought counseling would have to confess that she shot without reason, and wounded an innocent man. If (again to assume the worst) such an act constituted the crime of negligent wounding under Illinois law, the officer would of course have the absolute right not to admit that she shot without reason in criminal court. But I see no reason why she should be enabled both not to admit it in criminal court (as a good citizen should), and to get the benefits of psychotherapy by admitting it to a therapist who cannot tell anyone else. And even less reason why she should be enabled to deny her guilt in the criminal trial — or in a civil trial for negligence — while yet obtaining the benefits of psychotherapy by confessing guilt to a social worker who cannot testify. It seems to me entirely fair to say that if she wishes the benefits of telling the truth she must also accept the adverse consequences. To be sure, in most cases the statements to the psychotherapist will be only marginally relevant, and one of the purposes of the privilege (though not one relied upon by the Court) may be simply to spare patients needless intrusion upon their privacy, and to spare psychotherapists needless expenditure of their time in deposition and trial. But surely this can be achieved by means short of excluding even evidence that is of the most direct and conclusive effect.

The Court confidently asserts that not much truth-finding capacity would be destroyed by the privilege anyway, since "without a privilege, much of the desirable evidence to which litigants such as petitioner seek access . . . is unlikely to come into being." Ante, at 10. If that is so, how come psychotherapy got to be a thriving practice before the "psychotherapist privilege" was invented? Were the patients paying money to lie to their analysts all those years? Of course the evidence-generating effect of the privilege (if any) depends entirely upon its scope, which the Court steadfastly declines to consider. And even if one assumes that scope to be the broadest possible, is it really true that most, or even many, of those who seek psychological counseling have the worry of litigation in the back of their minds? I doubt that, and the Court provides no evidence to support it.

The Court suggests one last policy justification: since psychotherapist privilege statutes exist in all the States, the failure to recognize a privilege in federal courts "would frustrate the purposes of the state legislation that was enacted to foster these confidential communications." Ante, at 11. This is a novel argument indeed. A sort of inverse pre-emption: the truth-seeking functions of federal courts must be adjusted so as not to conflict with the policies of the States. This reasoning cannot be squared with Gillock, which declined to recognize an evidentiary privilege for Tennessee legislators in federal prosecutions, even though the Tennessee Constitution guaranteed it in state criminal proceedings. Gillock, 445 U.S. at 368. Moreover, since, as I shall discuss, state policies regarding the psychotherapist privilege vary considerably from State to State, no uniform federal policy can possibly honor most of them. If furtherance of state policies is the name of the game, rules of privilege in federal courts should vary from State to State, a la Erie.

The Court's failure to put forward a convincing justification of its own could perhaps be excused if it were relying upon the unanimous conclusion of state courts in the reasoned development of their common law. It cannot do that, since no State has such a privilege apart from legislation.[3] What it relies upon, instead, is "the fact that all 50 States and the District of Columbia have [1] enacted into law [2] some form of psychotherapist privilege." Ante, at 10 (emphasis added). Let us consider both the verb and its object: The fact [1] that all 50 States have enacted this privilege argues not for, but against, our adopting the privilege judicially. At best it suggests

---

[3] [n.1] The Court observes: "In 1972 the members of the Judicial Conference Advisory Committee noted that the common law 'had indicated a disposition to recognize a psychotherapist-patient privilege when legislatures began moving into the field.' Proposed Rules, 56 F.R.D. at 242 (citation omitted)." Ante, at 12. The sole support the Committee invoked was a student Note entitled Confidential Communications to a Psychotherapist: A New Testimonial Privilege, 47 Nw. U. L. Rev. 384 (1952). That source, in turn, cites (and discusses) a single case recognizing a common-law psychotherapist privilege: the unpublished opinion of a judge of the Circuit Court of Cook County, Illinois, Binder v. Ruvell, No. 52-C-2535 (June 24, 1952) — which, in turn, cites no other cases.

I doubt whether the Court's failure to provide more substantial support for its assertion stems from want of trying. Respondents and all of their amici pointed us to only four other state-court decisions supposedly adopting a common-law psychotherapist privilege. See Brief for the American Psychiatric Association et al. as Amici Curiae 8, n. 5; Brief for the American Psychoanalytic Association et al. as Amici Curiae 15-16; Brief for the American Psychological Association as Amicus Curiae 8. It is not surprising that the Court thinks it not worth the trouble to cite them: (1) In In re "B", 482 Pa. 471, 394 A.2d 419 (1978), the opinions of four of the seven Justices explicitly rejected a nonstatutory privilege; and the two Justices who did recognize one recognized, not a common-law privilege, but rather (mirabile dictu) a privilege "constitutionally based," "emanating from the penumbras of the various guarantees of the Bill of Rights, . . . as well as from the guarantees of the Constitution of this Commonwealth." Id., at 484, 394 A.2d at 425. (2) Allred v. State, 554 P.2d 411 (Alaska 1976), held that no privilege was available in the case before the court, so what it says about the existence of a common-law privilege is the purest dictum. (3) Falcon v. Alaska Pub. Offices Comm'n, 570 P.2d 469 (1977), a later Alaska Supreme Court case, proves the last statement. It rejected the claim by a physician that he did not have to disclose the names of his patients, even though some of the physician's practice consisted of psychotherapy; it made no mention of Allred's dictum that there was a common-law psychiatrist-patient privilege (though if that existed it would seem relevant), and cited Allred only for the proposition that there was no statutory privilege, id., at 473, n. 12. And finally, (4) State v. Evans, 104 Ariz. 434, 454 P.2d 976 (1969), created a limited privilege, applicable to court-ordered examinations to determine competency to stand trial, which tracked a privilege that had been legislatively created after the defendant's examination.

In light of this dearth of case support — from all the courts of 50 States, down to the county-court level — it seems to me the Court's assertion should be revised to read: "The common law had indicated scant disposition to recognize a psychotherapist-patient privilege when (or even after) legislatures began moving into the field."

that the matter has been found not to lend itself to judicial treatment — perhaps because the pros and cons of adopting the privilege, or of giving it one or another shape, are not that clear; or perhaps because the rapidly evolving uses of psychotherapy demand a flexibility that only legislation can provide. At worst it suggests that the privilege commends itself only to decisionmaking bodies in which reason is tempered, so to speak, by political pressure from organized interest groups (such as psychologists and social workers), and decisionmaking bodies that are not overwhelmingly concerned (as courts of law are and should be) with justice.

And the phrase [2] "some form of psychotherapist privilege" covers a multitude of difficulties. The Court concedes that there is "divergence among the States concerning the types of therapy relationships protected and the exceptions recognized." Ante, at 12, n. 13. To rest a newly announced federal common-law psychotherapist privilege, assertable from this day forward in all federal courts, upon "the States' unanimous judgment that some form of psychotherapist privilege is appropriate," ibid. (emphasis added), is rather like announcing a new, immediately applicable, federal common law of torts, based upon the States' "unanimous judgment" that some form of tort law is appropriate. In the one case as in the other, the state laws vary to such a degree that the parties and lower federal judges confronted by the new "common law" have barely a clue as to what its content might be. . . .

DISCUSSION QUESTIONS

1. In some respects, the Jaffee case brings us full circle to some of the discussions about the development of evidence law we had at the beginning of the semester. After reading both the majority and dissenting opinions, what do you think of the advantages and disadvantages of codifying rules of evidence compared to their development under the common law?

2. Was the psychotherapist-patient privilege truly developed by the reason and experience of the common law, as required by Rule 501? Or is Justice Scalia right that the statutory pronouncements of state legislatures play a different function and should not be used as evidence of what the common law is?

3. If privileges are to be narrowly construed, does it make sense for communications to social workers to be covered by the psychotherapist-patient privilege?

Privileges: Quick Hits

- A privilege is the legal right of an individual (the holder of the privilege) to withhold evidence from trial, even if the evidence is relevant, probative and otherwise admissible in evidence.

- Privileges are designed to support relationships and communications that society deems valuable enough to interfere with the jury's right to hear "every man's evidence" at trial.

- For the most part, privileges are not codified under the Federal Rules of Evidence. Privileges in federal court arise from three primary sources:

  - Federal common law

  - Statutes

  - State privilege law, in cases where state law provides the rule of decision.

- The holder of a privilege can waive it. Waiver can occur in two ways:

  - A formal waiver of the privilege

  - Conduct (such as communicating where third parties can hear) inconsistent with the confidential nature of the privileged relationship.

Chapter References

CHRISTOPHER B. MUELLER & LAIRD C. KIRKPATRICK, EVIDENCE §§ 5.1–5.35 (4th ed. 2009).

GLEN WEISSENBERGER & JAMES J. DUANE, FEDERAL RULES OF EVIDENCE: RULES, LEGISLATIVE HISTORY, COMMENTARY AND AUTHORITY §§ 501–02 (6th ed. 2009).

JACK B. WEINSTEIN & MARGARET A. BERGER, WEINSTEIN'S FEDERAL EVIDENCE §§ 501–02 (Joseph M. McLaughlin ed., Matthew Bender 2d ed. 1997).

KENNETH S. BROUN, McCORMICK ON EVIDENCE §§ 72–77, 87–97 (6th ed. 2006).

STEVEN GOODE & OLIN GUY WELLBORN III, COURTROOM HANDBOOK ON FEDERAL EVIDENCE Ch. 5 (West 2010).

II.   APPLICATION EXERCISE

Objective: To demonstrate proficiency in researching, preparing written materials, and teaching a state or federal privilege to other students.

Factual Scenario: This exercise is different from most in the book. Instead of a courtroom scenario, this is a small-group teaching exercise in which students will research and prepare materials on a rule of evidence, then present their materials to the rest of the class.

Advance Preparation. As assigned by the professor, students work in small groups to research and prepare teaching materials on a state or federal privilege. Each group is assigned one of the rules for research and presentation. The group will create a one-page handout for distribution to the class and will prepare a 15-minute presentation (including time for questions and answers) on the rule.

The handout must contain the following components:

a.   The underlying extrinsic policy expressed by the privilege.

b.   Who holds the privilege.

c.   How the privilege is claimed and waived.

d.   What exceptions, if any, exist for the privilege.

e.   A short case brief from the jurisdiction construing the privilege.

f.   A hypothetical problem that helps illustrate the privilege.

In-Class Exercise. During class, each group will present and teach its assigned rule to the rest of the class.

APPENDIX A

FEDERAL RULES OF EVIDENCE

ARTICLE I. GENERAL PROVISIONS[1] Rule 101. Scope	ARTICLE I. GENERAL PROVISIONS Rule 101. Scope; Definitions

These rules govern proceedings in the courts of the United States and before the United States bankruptcy judges and United States magistrate judges, to the extent and with the exceptions stated in rule 1101.	**(a)** **Scope.** These rules apply to proceedings in United States courts. The specific courts and proceedings to which the rules apply, along with exceptions, are set out in Rule 1101.
	
	(b) **Definitions.** In these rules:
	
	   (1) "civil case" means a civil action or proceeding;
	
	   (2) "criminal case" includes a criminal proceeding;
	
	   (3) "public office" includes a public agency;
	
	   (4) "record" includes a memorandum, report, or data compilation;
	
	   (5) a "rule prescribed by the Supreme Court" means a rule adopted by the Supreme Court under statutory authority; and
	
	   (6) a reference to any kind of written material or any other medium includes electronically stored information.

Committee Note

The language of Rule 101 has been amended, and definitions have been added, as part of the general restyling of the Evidence Rules to make them more easily understood and to make style and terminology consistent throughout the rules. These changes are intended to be stylistic only. There is no intent to change any result in any ruling on evidence admissibility.

The reference to electronically stored information is intended to track the language of Fed. R. Civ. P. 34.

The Style Project

The Evidence Rules are the fourth set of national procedural rules to be restyled. The restyled Rules of Appellate Procedure took effect in 1998. The restyled Rules of Criminal Procedure took effect in 2002. The restyled Rules of Civil Procedure took effect in 2007. The restyled Rules of Evidence apply the same general drafting guidelines and principles used in restyling the Appellate, Criminal, and Civil Rules.

---

[1] Rules in effect on December 1, 2010 (including amendments to Rule 804(b)(3) scheduled to take effect on that date).

1.   General Guidelines

Guidance in drafting, usage, and style was provided by Bryan Garner, *Guidelines for Drafting and Editing Court Rules,* Administrative Office of the United States Courts (1969) and Bryan Garner, *Dictionary of Modern Legal Usage* (2d ed. 1995). *See also* Joseph Kimble, *Guiding Principles for Restyling the Civil Rules,* in *Preliminary Draft of Proposed Style Revision of the Federal Rules of Civil Procedure,* at page x (Feb. 2005) (available at http://www.uscourts.gov/uscourts/RulesAndPolicies/rules/Prelim_draft_proposed_pt1.pdf); Joseph Kimble, *Lessons in Drafting from the New Federal Rules of Civil Procedure,* 12 Scribes J. Legal Writing 25 (2008-2009). For specific commentary on the Evidence restyling project, see Joseph Kimble, *Drafting Examples from the Proposed New Federal Rules of Evidence,* 88 Mich. B.J. 52 (Aug. 2009); 88 Mich. B.J. 46 (Sept. 2009); 88 Mich. B.J. 54 (Oct. 2009); 88 Mich. B.J. 50 (Nov. 2009).

2.   Formatting Changes

Many of the changes in the restyled Evidence Rules result from using format to achieve clearer presentations. The rules are broken down into constituent parts, using progressively indented subparagraphs with headings and substituting vertical for horizontal lists. "Hanging indents" are used throughout. These formatting changes make the structure of the rules graphic and make the restyled rules easier to read and understand even when the words are not changed. Rules 103, 404(b), 606(b), and 612 illustrate the benefits of formatting changes.

3.   Changes to Reduce Inconsistent, Ambiguous, Redundant, Repetitive, or Archaic Words

The restyled rules reduce the use of inconsistent terms that say the same thing in different ways. Because different words are presumed to have different meanings, such inconsistencies can result in confusion. The restyled rules reduce inconsistencies by using the same words to express the same meaning. For example, consistent expression is achieved by not switching between "accused" and "defendant" or between "party opponent" and "opposing party" or between the various formulations of civil and criminal action/case/proceeding.

The restyled rules minimize the use of inherently ambiguous words. For example, the word "shall" can mean "must," "may," or something else, depending on context. The potential for confusion is exacerbated by the fact the word "shall" is no longer generally used in spoken or clearly written English. The restyled rules replace "shall" with "must," "may," or "should," depending on which one the context and established interpretation make correct in each rule.

The restyled rules minimize the use of redundant "intensifiers." These are expressions that attempt to add emphasis, but instead state the obvious and create negative implications for other rules. The absence of intensifiers in the restyled rules does not change their substantive meaning. *See, e.g.,* Rule 104(c) (omitting "in all cases"); Rule 602 (omitting "but need not"); Rule 611(b) (omitting "in the exercise of discretion").

The restyled rules also remove words and concepts that are outdated or redundant.

4.   Rule Numbers

The restyled rules keep the same numbers to minimize the effect on research. Subdivisions have been rearranged within some rules to achieve greater clarity and simplicity.

5.   No Substantive Change

The Committee made special efforts to reject any purported style improvement that might result in a substantive change in the application of a rule. The Committee considered a change to be "substantive" if any of the following conditions were met:

> *a.*   Under the existing practice in any circuit, the change could lead to a different result on a question of admissibility (e.g., a change that requires a court to provide either a less or more stringent standard in evaluating the admissibility of particular evidence);

> *b.*   Under the existing practice in any circuit, it could lead to a change in the procedure by which an admissibility decision is made (e.g., a change in the time in which an objection must be made, or a change in whether a court must hold a hearing on an admissibility question);

> *c.*   The change would restructure a rule in a way that would alter the approach that courts and litigants have used to think about, and argue about, questions of admissibility (e.g., merging Rules 104(a) and 104(b) into a single subdivision); or

> *d.*   The amendment would change a "sacred phrase" — one that has become so familiar in practice that to alter it would be unduly disruptive to practice and expectations. Examples in the Evidence Rules include "unfair prejudice" and "truth of the matter asserted."

Rule 102. Purpose and Construction	**Rule 102. Purpose**
These rules shall be construed to secure fairness in administration, elimination of unjustifiable expense and delay, and promotion of growth and development of the law of evidence to the end that the truth may be ascertained and proceedings justly determined.	These rules should be construed so as to administer every proceeding fairly, eliminate unjustifiable expense and delay, and promote the development of evidence law, to the end of ascertaining the truth and securing a just determination.

Committee Note

The language of Rule 102 has been amended as part of the restyling of the Evidence Rules to make them more easily understood and to make style and terminology consistent throughout the rules. These changes are intended to be stylistic only. There is no intent to change any result in any ruling on evidence admissibility.

Rule 103. Rulings on Evidence	Rule 103. Rulings on Evidence
(a) Effect of erroneous ruling. Error may not be predicated upon a ruling which admits or excludes evidence unless a substantial right of the party is affected, and 　**(1) Objection.** In case the ruling is one admitting evidence, a timely objection or motion to strike appears of record, stating the specific ground of objection, if the specific ground was not apparent from the context; or 　**(2) Offer of proof.** In case the ruling is one excluding evidence, the substance of the evidence was made known to the court by offer or was apparent from the context within which questions were asked. Once the court makes a definitive ruling on the record admitting or excluding evidence, either at or before trial, a party need not renew an objection or offer of proof to preserve a claim of error for appeal.	**(a) Preserving a Claim of Error.** A party may claim error in a ruling to admit or exclude evidence only if the error affects a substantial right of the party and: 　**(1)** if the ruling admits evidence, a party, on the record: 　　**(A)** timely objects or moves to strike; and 　　**(B)** states the specific ground, unless it was apparent from the context; or 　**(2)** if the ruling excludes evidence, a party informs the court of its substance by an offer of proof, unless the substance was apparent from the context. **(b) Not Needing to Renew an Objection or Offer of Proof.** Once the court rules definitively on the record — either before or at trial — a party need not renew an objection or offer of proof to preserve a claim of error for appeal.
(b) Record of offer and ruling. The court may add any other or further statement which shows the character of the evidence, the form in which it was offered, the objection made, and the ruling thereon. It may direct the making of an offer in question and answer form.	**(c) Court's Statement About the Ruling; Directing an Offer of Proof.** The court may make any statement about the character or form of the evidence, the objection made, and the ruling. The court may direct that an offer of proof be made in question-and-answer form.
(c) Hearing of jury. In jury cases, proceedings shall be conducted, to the extent practicable, so as to prevent inadmissible evidence from being suggested to the jury by any means, such as making statements or offers of proof or asking questions in the hearing of the jury.	**(d) Preventing the Jury from Hearing Inadmissible Evidence.** To the extent practicable, the court must conduct a jury trial so that inadmissible evidence is not suggested to the jury by any means.
(d) Plain error. Nothing in this rule precludes taking notice of plain errors affecting substantial rights although they were not brought to the attention of the court.	**(e) Taking Notice of Plain Error.** A court may take notice of a plain error affecting a substantial right, even if the claim of error was not properly preserved.

Committee Note

The language of Rule 103 has been amended as part of the restyling of the Evidence Rules to make them more easily understood and to make style and terminology consistent throughout the rules. These changes are intended to be stylistic only. There is no intent to change any result in any ruling on evidence admissibility.

Rule 104. Preliminary Questions	Rule 104. Preliminary Questions
(a) Questions of admissibility generally. Preliminary questions concerning the qualification of a person to be a witness, the existence of a privilege, or the admissibility of evidence shall be determined by the court, subject to the provisions of subdivision (b). In making its determination it is not bound by the rules of evidence except those with respect to privileges.	(a) **In General.** The court must decide any preliminary question about whether a witness is qualified, a privilege exists, or evidence is admissible. In so deciding, the court is not bound by evidence rules, except those on privilege.
(b) Relevancy conditioned on fact. When the relevancy of evidence depends upon the fulfillment of a condition of fact, the court shall admit it upon, or subject to, the introduction of evidence sufficient to support a finding of the fulfillment of the condition.	(b) **Relevance That Depends on a Fact.** When the relevance of evidence depends on whether a fact exists, proof must be introduced sufficient to support a finding that the fact does exist. The court may admit the proposed evidence on the condition that the proof be introduced later.

(c) Hearing of jury. Hearings on the admissibility of confessions shall in all cases be conducted out of the hearing of the jury. Hearings on other preliminary matters shall be so conducted when the interests of justice require, or when an accused is a witness and so requests.	(c) **Conducting a Hearing So That the Jury Cannot Hear It.** The court must conduct any hearing on a preliminary question so that the jury cannot hear it if:
	
	  (1) the hearing involves the admissibility of a confession;
	
	  (2) a defendant in a criminal case is a witness and so requests; or
	
	  (3) justice so requires.

(d) Testimony by accused. The accused does not, by testifying upon a preliminary matter, become subject to cross-examination as to other issues in the case.	(d) **Cross-Examining a Defendant in a Criminal Case.** By testifying on a preliminary question, a defendant in a criminal case does not become subject to cross-examination on other issues in the case.
(e) Weight and credibility. This rule does not limit the right of a party to introduce before the jury evidence relevant to weight or credibility.	(e) **Evidence Relevant to Weight and Credibility.** This rule does not limit a party's right to introduce before the jury evidence that is relevant to the weight or credibility of other evidence.

Committee Note

The language of Rule 104 has been amended as part of the restyling of the Evidence Rules to make them more easily understood and to make style and terminology consistent throughout the rules. These changes are intended to be stylistic only. There is no intent to change any result in any ruling on evidence admissibility.

Rule 105. Limited Admissibility	Rule 105. Limiting Evidence That Is Not Admissible Against Other Parties or for Other Purposes
When evidence which is admissible as to one party or for one purpose but not admissible as to another party or for another purpose is admitted, the court, upon request, shall restrict the evidence to its proper scope and instruct the jury accordingly.	If the court admits evidence that is admissible against a party or for a purpose — but not against another party or for another purpose — the court, on timely request, must restrict the evidence to its proper scope and instruct the jury accordingly.

Committee Note

The language of Rule 105 has been amended as part of the restyling of the Evidence Rules to make them more easily understood and to make style and terminology consistent throughout the rules. These changes are intended to be stylistic only. There is no intent to change any result in any ruling on evidence admissibility.

Rule 106. Remainder of or Related Writings or Recorded Statements	Rule 106. Remainder of or Related Writings or Recorded Statements
When a writing or recorded statement or part thereof is introduced by a party, an adverse party may require the introduction at that time of any other part or any other writing or recorded statement which ought in fairness to be considered contemporaneously with it.	If a party introduces all or part of a writing or recorded statement, an adverse party may require the introduction, at that time, of any other part — or any other writing or recorded statement — that in fairness ought to be considered at the same time.

Committee Note

The language of Rule 106 has been amended as part of the restyling of the Evidence Rules to make them more easily understood and to make style and terminology consistent throughout the rules. These changes are intended to be stylistic only. There is no intent to change any result in any ruling on evidence admissibility.

ARTICLE II. JUDICIAL NOTICE Rule 201. Judicial Notice of Adjudicative Facts	ARTICLE II. JUDICIAL NOTICE Rule 201. Judicial Notice of Adjudicative Facts
(a) Scope of rule. This rule governs only judicial notice of adjudicative facts.	**(a)** **Scope.** This rule governs judicial notice of an adjudicative fact only, not a legislative fact.
(b) Kinds of facts. A judicially noticed fact must be one not subject to reasonable dispute in that it is either (1) generally known within the territorial jurisdiction of the trial court or (2) capable of accurate and ready determination by resort to sources whose accuracy cannot reasonably be questioned.	**(b)** **Kinds of Facts That May Be Judicially Noticed.** The court may judicially notice a fact that is not subject to reasonable dispute because it: **(1)** is generally known within the trial court's territorial jurisdiction; or **(2)** can be accurately and readily determined from sources whose accuracy cannot reasonably be questioned.
(c) When discretionary. A court may take judicial notice, whether requested or not. **(d) When mandatory.** A court shall take judicial notice if requested by a party and supplied with the necessary information.	**(c)** **Taking Notice.** The court: **(1)** may take judicial notice on its own; or **(2)** must take judicial notice if a party requests it and the court is supplied with the necessary information.
(e) Opportunity to be heard. A party is entitled upon timely request to an opportunity to be heard as to the propriety of taking judicial notice and the tenor of the matter noticed. In the absence of prior notification, the request may be made after judicial notice has been taken.	**(d)** **Timing.** The court may take judicial notice at any stage of the proceeding.
(f) Time of taking notice. Judicial notice may be taken at any stage of the proceeding.	**(e)** **Opportunity to Be Heard.** On timely request, a party is entitled to be heard on the propriety of taking judicial notice and the nature of the fact to be noticed. If the court takes judicial notice before notifying a party, the party, on request, is still entitled to be heard.
(g) Instructing jury. In a civil action or proceeding, the court shall instruct the jury to accept as conclusive any fact judicially noticed. In a criminal case, the court shall instruct the jury that it may, but is not required to, accept as conclusive any fact judicially noticed.	**(f)** **Instructing the Jury.** In a civil case, the court must instruct the jury to accept the noticed fact as conclusive. In a criminal case, the court must instruct the jury that it may or may not accept the noticed fact as conclusive.

Committee Note

The language of Rule 201 has been amended as part of the restyling of the Evidence Rules to make them more easily understood and to make style and terminology consistent throughout the rules. These changes are intended to be stylistic only. There is no intent to change any result in any ruling on evidence admissibility.

ARTICLE III. PRESUMPTIONS IN CIVIL ACTIONS AND PROCEEDINGS Rule 301. Presumptions in General in Civil Actions and Proceedings	ARTICLE III. PRESUMPTIONS IN CIVIL CASES Rule 301. Presumptions in Civil Cases Generally
In all civil actions and proceedings not otherwise provided for by Act of Congress or by these rules, a presumption imposes on the party against whom it is directed the burden of going forward with evidence to rebut or meet the presumption, but does not shift to such party the burden of proof in the sense of the risk of nonpersuasion, which remains throughout the trial upon the party on whom it was originally cast.	In a civil case, unless a federal statute or these rules provide otherwise, the party against whom a presumption is directed has the burden of producing evidence to rebut the presumption. But this rule does not shift the burden of persuasion, which remains on the party who had it originally.

Committee Note

The language of Rule 301 has been amended as part of the restyling of the Evidence Rules to make them more easily understood and to make style and terminology consistent throughout the rules. These changes are intended to be stylistic only. There is no intent to change any result in any ruling on evidence admissibility.

Rule 302. Applicability of State Law in Civil Actions and Proceedings	Rule 302. Applying State Law to Presumptions in Civil Cases
In civil actions and proceedings, the effect of a presumption respecting a fact which is an element of a claim or defense as to which State law supplies the rule of decision is determined in accordance with State law.	In a civil case, state law governs the effect of a presumption regarding a claim or defense for which state law supplies the rule of decision.

Committee Note

The language of Rule 302 has been amended as part of the restyling of the Evidence Rules to make them more easily understood and to make style and terminology consistent throughout the rules. These changes are intended to be stylistic only. There is no intent to change any result in any ruling on evidence admissibility.

ARTICLE IV. RELEVANCY AND ITS LIMITS **Rule 401. Definition of "Relevant Evidence"**	ARTICLE IV. RELEVANCE AND ITS LIMITS **Rule 401. Test for Relevant Evidence**
"Relevant evidence" means evidence having any tendency to make the existence of any fact that is of consequence to the determination of the action more probable or less probable than it would be without the evidence.	Evidence is relevant if: **(a)** it has any tendency to make a fact more or less probable than it would be without the evidence; and **(b)** the fact is of consequence in determining the action.

Committee Note

The language of Rule 401 has been amended as part of the restyling of the Evidence Rules to make them more easily understood and to make style and terminology consistent throughout the rules. These changes are intended to be stylistic only. There is no intent to change any result in any ruling on evidence admissibility.

Rule 402. Relevant Evidence Generally Admissible; Irrelevant Evidence Inadmissible	**Rule 402. General Admissibility of Relevant Evidence**
All relevant evidence is admissible, except as otherwise provided by the Constitution of the United States, by Act of Congress, by these rules, or by other rules prescribed by the Supreme Court pursuant to statutory authority. Evidence which is not relevant is not admissible.	Relevant evidence is admissible unless any of the following provides otherwise: • the United States Constitution; • a federal statute; • these rules; or • other rules prescribed by the Supreme Court. Irrelevant evidence is not admissible.

Committee Note

The language of Rule 402 has been amended as part of the restyling of the Evidence Rules to make them more easily understood and to make style and terminology consistent throughout the rules. These changes are intended to be stylistic only. There is no intent to change any result in any ruling on evidence admissibility.

Rule 403. Exclusion of Relevant Evidence on Grounds of Prejudice, Confusion, or Waste of Time	Rule 403. Excluding Relevant Evidence for Prejudice, Confusion, Waste of Time, or Other Reasons
Although relevant, evidence may be excluded if its probative value is substantially outweighed by the danger of unfair prejudice, confusion of the issues, or misleading the jury, or by considerations of undue delay, waste of time, or needless presentation of cumulative evidence.	The court may exclude relevant evidence if its probative value is substantially outweighed by a danger of one or more of the following: unfair prejudice, confusing the issues, misleading the jury, undue delay, wasting time, or needlessly presenting cumulative evidence.

Committee Note

The language of Rule 403 has been amended as part of the restyling of the Evidence Rules to make them more easily understood and to make style and terminology consistent throughout the rules. These changes are intended to be stylistic only. There is no intent to change any result in any ruling on evidence admissibility.

Rule 404. Character Evidence Not Admissible to Prove Conduct; Exceptions; Other Crimes	Rule 404. Character Evidence; Crimes or Other Acts

(a) **Character evidence generally.** Evidence of a person's character or a trait of character is not admissible for the purpose of proving action in conformity therewith on a particular occasion, except:
 	
(1) **Character of accused.** In a criminal case, evidence of a pertinent trait of character offered by an accused, or by the prosecution to rebut the same, or if evidence of a trait of character of the alleged victim of the crime is offered by an accused and admitted under Rule 404(a)(2), evidence of the same trait of character of the accused offered by the prosecution;
 	
(2) **Character of alleged victim.** In a criminal case, and subject to the limitations imposed by Rule 412, evidence of a pertinent trait of character of the alleged victim of the crime offered by an accused, or by the prosecution to rebut the same, or evidence of a character trait of peacefulness of the alleged victim offered by the prosecution in a homicide case to rebut evidence that the alleged victim was the first aggressor;
 	
(3) **Character of witness.** Evidence of the character of a witness, as provided in Rules 607, 608, and 609.
	(a) **Character Evidence.**
	
	(1) *Prohibited Uses.* Evidence of a person's character or character trait is not admissible to prove that on a particular occasion the person acted in accordance with the character or trait.
	
	(2) *Exceptions for a Defendant or Victim in a Criminal Case.* The following exceptions apply in a criminal case:
	
	  (A) a defendant may offer evidence of the defendant's pertinent trait, and if the evidence is admitted, the prosecutor may offer evidence to rebut it;
	
	  (B) subject to the limitations in Rule 412, a defendant may offer evidence of an alleged victim's pertinent trait, and if the evidence is admitted, the prosecutor may:
	
	    (i) offer evidence to rebut it; and
	
	    (ii) offer evidence of the defendant's same trait; and
	
	  (C) in a homicide case, the prosecutor may offer evidence of the alleged victim's trait of peacefulness to rebut evidence that the victim was the first aggressor.
	
	(3) *Exceptions for a Witness.* Evidence of a witness's character may be admitted under Rules 607, 608, and 609.

(b) Other crimes, wrongs, or acts. Evidence of other crimes, wrongs, or acts is not admissible to prove the character of a person in order to show action in conformity therewith. It may, however, be admissible for other purposes, such as proof of motive, opportunity, intent, preparation, plan, knowledge, identity, or absence of mistake or accident, provided that upon request by the accused, the prosecution in a criminal case shall provide reasonable notice in advance of trial, or during trial if the court excuses pretrial notice on good cause shown, of the general nature of any such evidence it intends to introduce at trial.	**(b) Crimes, Wrongs, or Other Acts.** **(1) *Prohibited Uses.*** Evidence of a crime, wrong, or other act is not admissible to prove a person's character in order to show that on a particular occasion the person acted in accordance with the character. **(2) *Permitted Uses; Notice in a Criminal Case.*** This evidence may be admissible for another purpose, such as proving motive, opportunity, intent, preparation, plan, knowledge, identity, absence of mistake, or lack of accident. On request by a defendant in a criminal case, the prosecutor must: **(A)** provide reasonable notice of the general nature of any such evidence that the prosecutor intends to offer at trial; and **(B)** do so before trial — or during trial if the court, for good cause, excuses lack of pretrial notice.

Committee Note

The language of Rule 404 has been amended as part of the restyling of the Evidence Rules to make them more easily understood and to make style and terminology consistent throughout the rules. These changes are intended to be stylistic only. There is no intent to change any result in any ruling on evidence admissibility.

Rule 405. Methods of Proving Character	**Rule 405. Methods of Proving Character**
(a) Reputation or opinion. In all cases in which evidence of character or a trait of character of a person is admissible, proof may be made by testimony as to reputation or by testimony in the form of an opinion. On cross-examination, inquiry is allowable into relevant specific instances of conduct.	**(a) By Reputation or Opinion.** When evidence of a person's character or character trait is admissible, it may be proved by testimony about the person's reputation or by testimony in the form of an opinion. On cross-examination of the character witness, the court may allow an inquiry into relevant specific instances of the person's conduct.
(b) Specific instances of conduct. In cases in which character or a trait of character of a person is an essential element of a charge, claim, or defense, proof may also be made of specific instances of that person's conduct.	**(b) By Specific Instances of Conduct.** When a person's character or character trait is an essential element of a charge, claim, or defense, the character or trait may also be proved by relevant specific instances of the person's conduct.

Committee Note

The language of Rule 405 has been amended as part of the restyling of the Evidence Rules to make them more easily understood and to make style and terminology consistent throughout the rules. These changes are intended to be stylistic only. There is no intent to change any result in any ruling on evidence admissibility.

Rule 406. Habit; Routine Practice	Rule 406. Habit; Routine Practice
Evidence of the habit of a person or of the routine practice of an organization, whether corroborated or not and regardless of the presence of eyewitnesses, is relevant to prove that the conduct of the person or organization on a particular occasion was in conformity with the habit or routine practice.	Evidence of a person's habit or an organization's routine practice may be admitted to prove that on a particular occasion the person or organization acted in accordance with the habit or routine practice. The court may admit this evidence regardless of whether it is corroborated or whether there was an eyewitness.

Committee Note

The language of Rule 406 has been amended as part of the restyling of the Evidence Rules to make them more easily understood and to make style and terminology consistent throughout the rules. These changes are intended to be stylistic only. There is no intent to change any result in any ruling on evidence admissibility.

Rule 407. Subsequent Remedial Measures	Rule 407. Subsequent Remedial Measures
When, after an injury or harm allegedly caused by an event, measures are taken that, if taken previously, would have made the injury or harm less likely to occur, evidence of the subsequent measures is not admissible to prove negligence, culpable conduct, a defect in a product, a defect in a product's design, or a need for a warning or instruction. This rule does not require the exclusion of evidence of subsequent measures when offered for another purpose, such as proving ownership, control, or feasibility of precautionary measures, if controverted, or impeachment.	When measures are taken that would have made an earlier injury or harm less likely to occur, evidence of the subsequent measures is not admissible to prove: • negligence; • culpable conduct; • a defect in a product or its design; or • a need for a warning or instruction. But the court may admit this evidence for another purpose, such as impeachment or — if disputed — proving ownership, control, or the feasibility of precautionary measures.

Committee Note

The language of Rule 407 has been amended as part of the general restyling of the Evidence Rules to make them more easily understood and to make style and terminology consistent throughout the rules. These changes are intended to be stylistic only. There is no intent to change any result in any ruling on evidence admissibility.

Rule 407 previously provided that evidence was not excluded if offered for a purpose not explicitly prohibited by the Rule. To improve the language of the Rule, it now provides that the court may admit evidence if offered for a permissible purpose. There is no intent to change the process for admitting evidence covered by the Rule. It remains the case that if offered for an impermissible purpose, it must be excluded, and if offered for a purpose not barred by the Rule, its admissibility remains governed by the general principles of Rules 402, 403, 801, etc.

Rule 408. Compromise and Offers to Compromise	Rule 408. Compromise Offers and Negotiations
(a) Prohibited uses. Evidence of the following is not admissible on behalf of any party, when offered to prove liability for, invalidity of, or amount of a claim that was disputed as to validity or amount, or to impeach through a prior inconsistent statement or contradiction: (1) furnishing or offering or promising to furnish—or accepting or offering or promising to accept—a valuable consideration in compromising or attempting to compromise the claim; and (2) conduct or statements made in compromise negotiations regarding the claim, except when offered in a criminal case and the negotiations related to a claim by a public office or agency in the exercise of regulatory, investigative, or enforcement authority.	(a) Prohibited Uses. Evidence of the following is not admissible — on behalf of any party — either to prove or disprove the validity or amount of a disputed claim or to impeach by a prior inconsistent statement or a contradiction: (1) furnishing, promising, or offering — or accepting, promising to accept, or offering to accept — a valuable consideration in compromising or attempting to compromise the claim; and (2) conduct or a statement made during compromise negotiations about the claim — except when offered in a criminal case and when the negotiations related to a claim by a public office in the exercise of its regulatory, investigative, or enforcement authority.
(b) Permitted uses. This rule does not require exclusion if the evidence is offered for purposes not prohibited by subdivision (a). Examples of permissible purposes include proving a witness's bias or prejudice; negating a contention of undue delay; and proving an effort to obstruct a criminal investigation or prosecution.	(b) Exceptions. The court may admit this evidence for another purpose, such as proving a witness's bias or prejudice, negating a contention of undue delay, or proving an effort to obstruct a criminal investigation or prosecution.

Committee Note

The language of Rule 408 has been amended as part of the general restyling of the Evidence Rules to make them more easily understood and to make style and terminology consistent throughout the rules. These changes are intended to be stylistic only. There is no intent to change any result in any ruling on evidence admissibility.

Rule 408 previously provided that evidence was not excluded if offered for a purpose not explicitly prohibited by the Rule. To improve the language of the Rule, it now provides that the court may admit evidence if offered for a permissible purpose. There is no intent to change the process for admitting evidence covered by the Rule. It remains the case that if offered for an impermissible purpose, it must be excluded, and if offered for a purpose not barred by the Rule, its admissibility remains governed by the general principles of Rules 402, 403, 801, etc.

The Committee deleted the reference to "liability" on the ground that the deletion makes the Rule flow better and easier to read, and because "liability" is covered by the broader term "validity." Courts have not made substantive decisions on the basis of any distinction between validity and liability. No change in current practice or in the coverage of the Rule is intended.

Rule 409. **Payment of Medical and Similar Expenses**	Rule 409. **Offers to Pay Medical and Similar Expenses**
Evidence of furnishing or offering or promising to pay medical, hospital, or similar expenses occasioned by an injury is not admissible to prove liability for the injury.	Evidence of furnishing, promising to pay, or offering to pay medical, hospital, or similar expenses resulting from an injury is not admissible to prove liability for the injury.

Committee Note

The language of Rule 409 has been amended as part of the restyling of the Evidence Rules to make them more easily understood and to make style and terminology consistent throughout the rules. These changes are intended to be stylistic only. There is no intent to change any result in any ruling on evidence admissibility.

Rule 410. **Inadmissibility of Pleas, Plea Discussions, and Related Statements**	Rule 410. **Pleas, Plea Discussions, and Related Statements**
Except as otherwise provided in this rule, evidence of the following is not, in any civil or criminal proceeding, admissible against the defendant who made the plea or was a participant in the plea discussions:	**(a)** **Prohibited Uses.** In a civil or criminal case, evidence of the following is not admissible against the defendant who made the plea or participated in the plea discussions:
(1) a plea of guilty which was later withdrawn;	(1) a guilty plea that was later withdrawn;
(2) a plea of nolo contendere;	(2) a nolo contendere plea;
(3) any statement made in the course of any proceedings under Rule 11 of the Federal Rules of Criminal Procedure or comparable state procedure regarding either of the foregoing pleas; or	(3) a statement made during a proceeding on either of those pleas under Federal Rule of Criminal Procedure 11 or a comparable state procedure; or
(4) any statement made in the course of plea discussions with an attorney for the prosecuting authority which do not result in a plea of guilty or which result in a plea of guilty later withdrawn.	(4) a statement made during plea discussions with an attorney for the prosecuting authority if the discussions did not result in a guilty plea or they resulted in a later-withdrawn guilty plea.
However, such a statement is admissible (i) in any proceeding wherein another statement made in the course of the same plea or plea discussions has been introduced and the statement ought in fairness be considered contemporaneously with it, or (ii) in a criminal proceeding for perjury or false statement if the statement was made by the defendant under oath, on the record and in the presence of counsel.	**(b)** **Exceptions.** The court may admit a statement described in Rule 410(a)(3) or (4):
	(1) in any proceeding in which another statement made during the same plea or plea discussions has been introduced, if in fairness the statements ought to be considered together; or
	(2) in a criminal proceeding for perjury or false statement, if the defendant made the statement under oath, on the record, and with counsel present.

Committee Note

The language of Rule 410 has been amended as part of the restyling of the Evidence Rules to make them more easily understood and to make style and terminology consistent throughout the rules. These changes are intended to be stylistic only. There is no intent to change any result in any ruling on evidence admissibility.

Rule 411. Liability Insurance	Rule 411. Liability Insurance
Evidence that a person was or was not insured against liability is not admissible upon the issue whether the person acted negligently or otherwise wrongfully. This rule does not require the exclusion of evidence of insurance against liability when offered for another purpose, such as proof of agency, ownership, or control, or bias or prejudice of a witness.	Evidence that a person was or was not insured against liability is not admissible to prove whether the person acted negligently or otherwise wrongfully. But the court may admit this evidence for another purpose, such as proving a witness's bias or prejudice or proving agency, ownership, or control.

Committee Note

The language of Rule 411 has been amended as part of the general restyling of the Evidence Rules to make them more easily understood and to make style and terminology consistent throughout the rules. These changes are intended to be stylistic only. There is no intent to change any result in any ruling on evidence admissibility.

Rule 411 previously provided that evidence was not excluded if offered for a purpose not explicitly prohibited by the Rule. To improve the language of the Rule, it now provides that the court may admit evidence if offered for a permissible purpose. There is no intent to change the process for admitting evidence covered by the Rule. It remains the case that if offered for an impermissible purpose, it must be excluded, and if offered for a purpose not barred by the Rule, its admissibility remains governed by the general principles of Rules 402, 403, 801, etc.

Rule 412. Sex Offense Cases; Relevance of Alleged Victim's Past Sexual Behavior or Alleged Sexual Predisposition	Rule 412. Sex-Offense Cases: The Victim's Sexual Behavior or Predisposition
(a) Evidence Generally Inadmissible. The following evidence is not admissible in any civil or criminal proceeding involving alleged sexual misconduct except as provided in subdivisions (b) and (c): (1) Evidence offered to prove that any alleged victim engaged in other sexual behavior. (2) Evidence offered to prove any alleged victim's sexual predisposition.	(a) **Prohibited Uses.** The following evidence is not admissible in a civil or criminal proceeding involving alleged sexual misconduct: (1) evidence offered to prove that a victim engaged in other sexual behavior; or (2) evidence offered to prove a victim's sexual predisposition.
(b) Exceptions. (1) In a criminal case, the following evidence is admissible, if otherwise admissible under these rules: (A) evidence of specific instances of sexual behavior by the alleged victim offered to prove that a person other than the accused was the source of semen, injury or other physical evidence; (B) evidence of specific instances of sexual behavior by the alleged victim with respect to the person accused of the sexual misconduct offered by the accused to prove consent or by the prosecution; and (C) evidence the exclusion of which would violate the constitutional rights of the defendant. (2) In a civil case, evidence offered to prove the sexual behavior or sexual predisposition of any alleged victim is admissible if it is otherwise admissible under these rules and its probative value substantially outweighs the danger of harm to any victim and of unfair prejudice to any party. Evidence of an alleged victim's reputation is admissible only if it has been placed in controversy by the alleged victim.	(b) **Exceptions.** (1) *Criminal Cases.* The court may admit the following evidence in a criminal case: (A) evidence of specific instances of a victim's sexual behavior, if offered to prove that someone other than the defendant was the source of semen, injury, or other physical evidence; (B) evidence of specific instances of a victim's sexual behavior with respect to the person accused of the sexual misconduct, if offered by the defendant to prove consent or if offered by the prosecutor; and (C) evidence whose exclusion would violate the defendant's constitutional rights. (2) *Civil Cases.* In a civil case, the court may admit evidence offered to prove a victim's sexual behavior or sexual predisposition if its probative value substantially outweighs the danger of harm to any victim and of unfair prejudice to any party. The court may admit evidence of a victim's reputation only if the victim has placed it in controversy.

(c) **Procedure To Determine Admissibility.**	(c) **Procedure to Determine Admissibility.**
(1) A party intending to offer evidence under subdivision (b) must—	(1) *Motion.* If a party intends to offer evidence under Rule 412(b), the party must:
(A) file a written motion at least 14 days before trial specifically describing the evidence and stating the purpose for which it is offered unless the court, for good cause requires a different time for filing or permits filing during trial; and	(A) file a motion that specifically describes the evidence and states the purpose for which it is to be offered;
(B) serve the motion on all parties and notify the alleged victim or, when appropriate, the alleged victim's guardian or representative.	(B) do so at least 14 days before trial unless the court, for good cause, sets a different time;
(2) Before admitting evidence under this rule the court must conduct a hearing in camera and afford the victim and parties a right to attend and be heard. The motion, related papers, and the record of the hearing must be sealed and remain under seal unless the court orders otherwise.	(C) serve the motion on all parties; and
	(D) notify the victim or, when appropriate, the victim's guardian or representative.
	(2) *Hearing.* Before admitting evidence under this rule, the court must conduct an in camera hearing and give the victim and parties a right to attend and be heard. Unless the court orders otherwise, the motion, related materials, and the record of the hearing must be and remain sealed.
	(d) **Definition of "Victim."** In this rule, "victim" includes an alleged victim.

Committee Note

The language of Rule 412 has been amended as part of the restyling of the Evidence Rules to make them more easily understood and to make style and terminology consistent throughout the rules. These changes are intended to be stylistic only. There is no intent to change any result in any ruling on evidence admissibility.

Rule 413. Evidence of Similar Crimes in Sexual Assault Cases	Rule 413. Similar Crimes in Sexual-Assault Cases
(a) In a criminal case in which the defendant is accused of an offense of sexual assault, evidence of the defendant's commission of another offense or offenses of sexual assault is admissible, and may be considered for its bearing on any matter to which it is relevant.	**(a)** **Permitted Uses.** In a criminal case in which a defendant is accused of a sexual assault, the court may admit evidence that the defendant committed any other sexual assault. The evidence may be considered on any matter to which it is relevant.
(b) In a case in which the Government intends to offer evidence under this rule, the attorney for the Government shall disclose the evidence to the defendant, including statements of witnesses or a summary of the substance of any testimony that is expected to be offered, at least fifteen days before the scheduled date of trial or at such later time as the court may allow for good cause.	**(b)** **Disclosure to the Defendant.** If the prosecutor intends to offer this evidence, the prosecutor must disclose it to the defendant, including witnesses' statements or a summary of the expected testimony. The prosecutor must do so at least 15 days before trial or at a later time that the court allows for good cause.
(c) This rule shall not be construed to limit the admission or consideration of evidence under any other rule.	**(c)** **Effect on Other Rules.** This rule does not limit the admission or consideration of evidence under any other rule.
(d) For purposes of this rule and Rule 415, "offense of sexual assault" means a crime under Federal law or the law of a State (as defined in section 513 of title 18, United States Code) that involved—	**(d)** **Definition of "Sexual Assault."** In this rule and Rule 415, "sexual assault" means a crime under federal law or under state law (as "state" is defined in 18 U.S.C. § 513) involving:
(1) any conduct proscribed by chapter 109A of title 18, United States Code;	**(1)** any conduct prohibited by 18 U.S.C. chapter 109A;
(2) contact, without consent, between any part of the defendant's body or an object and the genitals or anus of another person;	**(2)** contact, without consent, between any part of the defendant's body — or an object — and another person's genitals or anus;
(3) contact, without consent, between the genitals or anus of the defendant and any part of another person's body;	**(3)** contact, without consent, between the defendant's genitals or anus and any part of another person's body;
(4) deriving sexual pleasure or gratification from the infliction of death, bodily injury, or physical pain on another person; or	**(4)** deriving sexual pleasure or gratification from inflicting death, bodily injury, or physical pain on another person; or
(5) an attempt or conspiracy to engage in conduct described in paragraphs (1)–(4).	**(5)** an attempt or conspiracy to engage in conduct described in subparagraphs (1)–(4).

Committee Note

The language of Rule 413 has been amended as part of the restyling of the Evidence Rules to make them more easily understood and to make style and terminology consistent throughout the rules. These changes are intended to be stylistic only. There is no intent to change any result in any ruling on evidence admissibility.

Rule 414. Evidence of Similar Crimes in Child Molestation Cases	Rule 414. Similar Crimes in Child-Molestation Cases
(a) In a criminal case in which the defendant is accused of an offense of child molestation, evidence of the defendant's commission of another offense or offenses of child molestation is admissible, and may be considered for its bearing on any matter to which it is relevant.	**(a)** **Permitted Uses.** In a criminal case in which a defendant is accused of child molestation, the court may admit evidence that the defendant committed any other child molestation. The evidence may be considered on any matter to which it is relevant.
(b) In a case in which the Government intends to offer evidence under this rule, the attorney for the Government shall disclose the evidence to the defendant, including statements of witnesses or a summary of the substance of any testimony that is expected to be offered, at least fifteen days before the scheduled date of trial or at such later time as the court may allow for good cause.	**(b)** **Disclosure to the Defendant.** If the prosecutor intends to offer this evidence, the prosecutor must disclose it to the defendant, including witnesses' statements or a summary of the expected testimony. The prosecutor must do so at least 15 days before trial or at a later time that the court allows for good cause.
(c) This rule shall not be construed to limit the admission or consideration of evidence under any other rule.	**(c)** **Effect on Other Rules.** This rule does not limit the admission or consideration of evidence under any other rule.
(d) For purposes of this rule and Rule 415, "child" means a person below the age of fourteen, and "offense of child molestation" means a crime under Federal law or the law of a State (as defined in section 513 of title 18, United States Code) that involved— **(1)** any conduct proscribed by chapter 109A of title 18, United States Code, that was committed in relation to a child; **(2)** any conduct proscribed by chapter 110 of title 18, United States Code; **(3)** contact between any part of the defendant's body or an object and the genitals or anus of a child; **(4)** contact between the genitals or anus of the defendant and any part of the body of a child; **(5)** deriving sexual pleasure or gratification from the infliction of death, bodily injury, or physical pain on a child; or **(6)** an attempt or conspiracy to engage in conduct described in paragraphs (1)–(5).	**(d)** **Definition of "Child" and "Child Molestation."** In this rule and Rule 415: **(1)** "child" means a person below the age of 14; and **(2)** "child molestation" means a crime under federal law or under state law (as "state" is defined in 18 U.S.C. § 513) involving: **(A)** any conduct prohibited by 18 U.S.C. chapter 109A and committed with a child; **(B)** any conduct prohibited by 18 U.S.C. chapter 110; **(C)** contact between any part of the defendant's body — or an object — and a child's genitals or anus; **(D)** contact between the defendant's genitals or anus and any part of a child's body; **(E)** deriving sexual pleasure or gratification from inflicting death, bodily injury, or physical pain on a child; or **(F)** an attempt or conspiracy to engage in conduct described in subparagraphs (A)–(E)

Committee Note

The language of Rule 414 has been amended as part of the restyling of the Evidence Rules to make them more easily understood and to make style and terminology consistent throughout the rules. These changes are intended to be stylistic only. There is no intent to change any result in any ruling on evidence admissibility.

Rule 415. Evidence of Similar Acts in Civil Cases Concerning Sexual Assault or Child Molestation	Rule 415. Similar Acts in Civil Cases Involving Sexual Assault or Child Molestation
(a) In a civil case in which a claim for damages or other relief is predicated on a party's alleged commission of conduct constituting an offense of sexual assault or child molestation, evidence of that party's commission of another offense or offenses of sexual assault or child molestation is admissible and may be considered as provided in Rule 413 and Rule 414 of these rules.	(a) **Permitted Uses.** In a civil case involving a claim for relief based on a party's alleged sexual assault or child molestation, the court may admit evidence that the party committed any other sexual assault or child molestation. The evidence may be considered as provided in Rules 413 and 414.
(b) A party who intends to offer evidence under this Rule shall disclose the evidence to the party against whom it will be offered, including statements of witnesses or a summary of the substance of any testimony that is expected to be offered, at least fifteen days before the scheduled date of trial or at such later time as the court may allow for good cause.	(b) **Disclosure to the Opponent.** If a party intends to offer this evidence, the party must disclose it to the party against whom it will be offered, including witnesses' statements or a summary of the expected testimony. The party must do so at least 15 days before trial or at a later time that the court allows for good cause.
(c) This rule shall not be construed to limit the admission or consideration of evidence under any other rule.	(c) **Effect on Other Rules.** This rule does not limit the admission or consideration of evidence under any other rule.

Committee Note

The language of Rule 415 has been amended as part of the restyling of the Evidence Rules to make them more easily understood and to make style and terminology consistent throughout the rules. These changes are intended to be stylistic only. There is no intent to change any result in any ruling on evidence admissibility.

ARTICLE V. PRIVILEGES Rule 501. General Rule	ARTICLE V. PRIVILEGES Rule 501. Privilege in General
Except as otherwise required by the Constitution of the United States or provided by Act of Congress or in rules prescribed by the Supreme Court pursuant to statutory authority, the privilege of a witness, person, government, State, or political subdivision thereof shall be governed by the principles of the common law as they may be interpreted by the courts of the United States in the light of reason and experience. However, in civil actions and proceedings, with respect to an element of a claim or defense as to which State law supplies the rule of decision, the privilege of a witness, person, government, State, or political subdivision thereof shall be determined in accordance with State law.	The common law — as interpreted by United States courts in the light of reason and experience — governs a claim of privilege unless any of the following provides otherwise: • the United States Constitution; • a federal statute; or • rules prescribed by the Supreme Court. But in a civil case, state law governs privilege regarding a claim or defense for which state law supplies the rule of decision.

Committee Note

The language of Rule 501 has been amended as part of the restyling of the Evidence Rules to make them more easily understood and to make style and terminology consistent throughout the rules. These changes are intended to be stylistic only. There is no intent to change any result in any ruling on evidence admissibility.

Rule 502. Attorney-Client Privilege and Work Product; Limitations on Waiver	Rule 502. Attorney-Client Privilege and Work Product; Limitations on Waiver
The following provisions apply, in the circumstances set out, to disclosure of a communication or information covered by the attorney-client privilege or work-product protection.	The following provisions apply, in the circumstances set out, to disclosure of a communication or information covered by the attorney-client privilege or work-product protection.
(a) Disclosure made in a Federal proceeding or to a Federal office or agency; scope of a waiver. When the disclosure is made in a Federal proceeding or to a Federal office or agency and waives the attorney-client privilege or work-product protection, the waiver extends to an undisclosed communication or information in a Federal or State proceeding only if: (1) the waiver is intentional; (2) the disclosed and undisclosed communications or information concern the same subject matter; and (3) they ought in fairness to be considered together.	**(a)** **Disclosure Made in a Federal Proceeding or to a Federal Office or Agency; Scope of a Waiver.** When the disclosure is made in a federal proceeding or to a federal office or agency and waives the attorney-client privilege or work-product protection, the waiver extends to an undisclosed communication or information in a federal or state proceeding only if: (1) the waiver is intentional; (2) the disclosed and undisclosed communications or information concern the same subject matter; and (3) they ought in fairness to be considered together.

(b) Inadvertent disclosure. When made in a Federal proceeding or to a Federal office or agency, the disclosure does not operate as a waiver in a Federal or State proceeding if:

(1) the disclosure is inadvertent;

(2) the holder of the privilege or protection took reasonable steps to prevent disclosure; and

(3) the holder promptly took reasonable steps to rectify the error, including (if applicable) following Federal Rule of Civil Procedure 26(b)(5)(B).

(c) Disclosure made in a State proceeding. When the disclosure is made in a State proceeding and is not the subject of a State-court order concerning waiver, the disclosure does not operate as a waiver in a Federal proceeding if the disclosure:

(1) would not be a waiver under this rule if it had been made in a Federal proceeding; or

(2) is not a waiver under the law of the State where the disclosure occurred.

(d) Controlling effect of a court order. A Federal court may order that the privilege or protection is not waived by disclosure connected with the litigation pending before the court—in which event the disclosure is also not a waiver in any other Federal or State proceeding.

(e) Controlling effect of a party agreement. An agreement on the effect of disclosure in a Federal proceeding is binding only on the parties to the agreement, unless it is incorporated into a court order.

(f) Controlling effect of this rule. Notwithstanding Rules 101 and 1101, this rule applies to State proceedings and to Federal court-annexed and Federal court-mandated arbitration proceedings, in the circumstances set out in the rule. And notwithstanding Rule 501, this rule applies even if State law provides the rule of decision.

(b) **Inadvertent Disclosure.** When made in a federal proceeding or to a federal office or agency, the disclosure does not operate as a waiver in a federal or state proceeding if:

(1) the disclosure is inadvertent;

(2) the holder of the privilege or protection took reasonable steps to prevent disclosure; and

(3) the holder promptly took reasonable steps to rectify the error, including (if applicable) following Federal Rule of Civil Procedure 26(b)(5)(B).

(c) **Disclosure Made in a State Proceeding.** When the disclosure is made in a state proceeding and is not the subject of a state-court order concerning waiver, the disclosure does not operate as a waiver in a federal proceeding if the disclosure:

(1) would not be a waiver under this rule if it had been made in a federal proceeding; or

(2) is not a waiver under the law of the state where the disclosure occurred.

(d) **Controlling Effect of a Court Order.** A federal court may order that the privilege or protection is not waived by disclosure connected with the litigation pending before the court — in which event the disclosure is also not a waiver in any other federal or state proceeding.

(e) **Controlling Effect of a Party Agreement.** An agreement on the effect of disclosure in a federal proceeding is binding only on the parties to the agreement, unless it is incorporated into a court order.

(f) **Controlling Effect of this Rule.** Notwithstanding Rules 101 and 1101, this rule applies to state proceedings and to federal court-annexed and federal court-mandated arbitration proceedings, in the circumstances set out in the rule. And notwithstanding Rule 501, this rule applies even if state law provides the rule of decision.

(g) Definitions. In this rule: (1) ''attorney-client privilege'' means the protection that applicable law provides for confidential attorney-client communications; and (2) ''work-product protection'' means the protection that applicable law provides for tangible material (or its intangible equivalent) prepared in anticipation of litigation or for trial.	**(g) Definitions.** In this rule: (1) "attorney-client privilege" means the protection that applicable law provides for confidential attorney-client communications; and (2) "work-product protection" means the protection that applicable law provides for tangible material (or its intangible equivalent) prepared in anticipation of litigation or for trial.

Committee Note

Rule 502 has been amended by changing the initial letter of a few words from uppercase to lowercase as part of the restyling of the Evidence Rules to make style and terminology consistent throughout the rules. There is no intent to change any result in any ruling on evidence admissibility.

ARTICLE VI. WITNESSES **Rule 601. General Rule of Competency**	**ARTICLE VI. WITNESSES** **Rule 601. Competency to Testify in General**
Every person is competent to be a witness except as otherwise provided in these rules. However, in civil actions and proceedings, with respect to an element of a claim or defense as to which State law supplies the rule of decision, the competency of a witness shall be determined in accordance with State law.	Every person is competent to be a witness unless these rules provide otherwise. But in a civil case, state law governs the witness's competency regarding a claim or defense for which state law supplies the rule of decision.

Committee Note

The language of Rule 601 has been amended as part of the restyling of the Evidence Rules to make them more easily understood and to make style and terminology consistent throughout the rules. These changes are intended to be stylistic only. There is no intent to change any result in any ruling on evidence admissibility.

Rule 602. Lack of Personal Knowledge	Rule 602. Need for Personal Knowledge
A witness may not testify to a matter unless evidence is introduced sufficient to support a finding that the witness has personal knowledge of the matter. Evidence to prove personal knowledge may, but need not, consist of the witness' own testimony. This rule is subject to the provisions of rule 703, relating to opinion testimony by expert witnesses.	A witness may testify to a matter only if evidence is introduced sufficient to support a finding that the witness has personal knowledge of the matter. Evidence to prove personal knowledge may consist of the witness's own testimony. This rule does not apply to a witness's expert testimony under Rule 703.

Committee Note

The language of Rule 602 has been amended as part of the restyling of the Evidence Rules to make them more easily understood and to make style and terminology consistent throughout the rules. These changes are intended to be stylistic only. There is no intent to change any result in any ruling on evidence admissibility.

Rule 603. Oath or Affirmation	Rule 603. Oath or Affirmation to Testify Truthfully
Before testifying, every witness shall be required to declare that the witness will testify truthfully, by oath or affirmation administered in a form calculated to awaken the witness' conscience and impress the witness' mind with the duty to do so.	Before testifying, a witness must give an oath or affirmation to testify truthfully. It must be in a form designed to impress that duty on the witness's conscience.

Committee Note

The language of Rule 603 has been amended as part of the restyling of the Evidence Rules to make them more easily understood and to make style and terminology consistent throughout the rules. These changes are intended to be stylistic only. There is no intent to change any result in any ruling on evidence admissibility.

Rule 604. Interpreters	Rule 604. Interpreter
An interpreter is subject to the provisions of these rules relating to qualification as an expert and the administration of an oath or affirmation to make a true translation.	An interpreter must be qualified and must give an oath or affirmation to make a true translation.

Committee Note

The language of Rule 604 has been amended as part of the restyling of the Evidence Rules to make them more easily understood and to make style and terminology consistent throughout the rules. These changes are intended to be stylistic only. There is no intent to change any result in any ruling on evidence admissibility.

Rule 605. Competency of Judge as Witness	Rule 605. Judge's Competency as a Witness
The judge presiding at the trial may not testify in that trial as a witness. No objection need be made in order to preserve the point.	The presiding judge may not testify as a witness at the trial. A party need not object to preserve the issue.

Committee Note

The language of Rule 605 has been amended as part of the restyling of the Evidence Rules to make them more easily understood and to make style and terminology consistent throughout the rules. These changes are intended to be stylistic only. There is no intent to change any result in any ruling on evidence admissibility.

Rule 606. Competency of Juror as Witness	Rule 606. Juror's Competency as a Witness
(a) **At the trial.** A member of the jury may not testify as a witness before that jury in the trial of the case in which the juror is sitting. If the juror is called so to testify, the opposing party shall be afforded an opportunity to object out of the presence of the jury.	**(a)** **At the Trial.** A juror may not testify as a witness before the other jurors at the trial. If a juror is called to testify, the court must give a party an opportunity to object outside the jury's presence.
(b) **Inquiry into validity of verdict or indictment.** Upon an inquiry into the validity of a verdict or indictment, a juror may not testify as to any matter or statement occurring during the course of the jury's deliberations or to the effect of anything upon that or any other juror's mind or emotions as influencing the juror to assent to or dissent from the verdict or indictment or concerning the juror's mental processes in connection therewith. But a juror may testify about (1) whether extraneous prejudicial information was improperly brought to the jury's attention, (2) whether any outside influence was improperly brought to bear upon any juror, or (3) whether there was a mistake in entering the verdict onto the verdict form. A juror's affidavit or evidence of any statement by the juror may not be received on a matter about which the juror would be precluded from testifying.	**(b)** **During an Inquiry into the Validity of a Verdict or Indictment.** **(1)** *Prohibited Testimony or Other Evidence.* During an inquiry into the validity of a verdict or indictment, a juror may not testify about any statement made or incident that occurred during the jury's deliberations; the effect of anything on that juror's or another juror's vote; or any juror's mental processes concerning the verdict or indictment. The court may not receive a juror's affidavit or evidence of a juror's statement on these matters. **(2)** *Exceptions.* A juror may testify about whether: **(A)** extraneous prejudicial information was improperly brought to the jury's attention; **(B)** an outside influence was improperly brought to bear on any juror; or **(C)** a mistake was made in entering the verdict on the verdict form.

Committee Note

The language of Rule 606 has been amended as part of the restyling of the Evidence Rules to make them more easily understood and to make style and terminology consistent throughout the rules. These changes are intended to be stylistic only. There is no intent to change any result in any ruling on evidence admissibility.

Rule 607. Who May Impeach	Rule 607. Who May Impeach a Witness
The credibility of a witness may be attacked by any party, including the party calling the witness.	Any party, including the party that called the witness, may attack the witness's credibility.

Committee Note

The language of Rule 607 has been amended as part of the restyling of the Evidence Rules to make them more easily understood and to make style and terminology consistent throughout the rules. These changes are intended to be stylistic only. There is no intent to change any result in any ruling on evidence admissibility.

Rule 608. Evidence of Character and Conduct of Witness	Rule 608. A Witness's Character for Truthfulness or Untruthfulness
(a) Opinion and reputation evidence of character. The credibility of a witness may be attacked or supported by evidence in the form of opinion or reputation, but subject to these limitations: (1) the evidence may refer only to character for truthfulness or untruthfulness, and (2) evidence of truthful character is admissible only after the character of the witness for truthfulness has been attacked by opinion or reputation evidence or otherwise.	**(a)** **Reputation or Opinion Evidence.** A witness's credibility may be attacked or supported by testimony about the witness's reputation for having a character for truthfulness or untruthfulness, or by testimony in the form of an opinion about that character. But evidence of truthful character is admissible only after the witness's character for truthfulness has been attacked.
(b) Specific instances of conduct. Specific instances of the conduct of a witness, for the purpose of attacking or supporting the witness' character for truthfulness, other than conviction of crime as provided in rule 609, may not be proved by extrinsic evidence. They may, however, in the discretion of the court, if probative of truthfulness or untruthfulness, be inquired into on cross-examination of the witness (1) concerning the witness' character for truthfulness or untruthfulness, or (2) concerning the character for truthfulness or untruthfulness of another witness as to which character the witness being cross-examined has testified. The giving of testimony, whether by an accused or by any other witness, does not operate as a waiver of the accused's or the witness' privilege against self-incrimination when examined with respect to matters that relate only to character for truthfulness.	**(b)** **Specific Instances of Conduct.** Except for a criminal conviction under Rule 609, extrinsic evidence is not admissible to prove specific instances of a witness's conduct in order to attack or support the witness's character for truthfulness. But the court may, on cross-examination, allow them to be inquired into if they are probative of the character for truthfulness or untruthfulness of: **(1)** the witness; or **(2)** another witness whose character the witness being cross-examined has testified about. By testifying on another matter, a witness does not waive any privilege against self-incrimination for testimony that relates only to the witness's character for truthfulness.

Committee Note

The language of Rule 608 has been amended as part of the general restyling of the Evidence Rules to make them more easily understood and to make style and terminology consistent throughout the rules. These changes are intended to be stylistic only. There is no intent to change any result in any ruling on evidence admissibility.

The Committee is aware that the Rule's limitation of bad-act impeachment to "cross-examination" is trumped by Rule 607, which allows a party to impeach witnesses on direct examination. Courts have not relied on the term "on cross-examination" to limit impeachment that would otherwise be permissible under Rules 607 and 608. The Committee therefore concluded that no change to the language of the Rule was necessary in the context of a restyling project.

Rule 609. Impeachment by Evidence of Conviction of Crime	**Rule 609. Impeachment by Evidence of a Criminal Conviction**
(a) **General rule.** For the purpose of attacking the character for truthfulness of a witness, (1) evidence that a witness other than an accused has been convicted of a crime shall be admitted, subject to Rule 403, if the crime was punishable by death or imprisonment in excess of one year under the law under which the witness was convicted, and evidence that an accused has been convicted of such a crime shall be admitted if the court determines that the probative value of admitting this evidence outweighs its prejudicial effect to the accused; and (2) evidence that any witness has been convicted of a crime shall be admitted regardless of the punishment, if it readily can be determined that establishing the elements of the crime required proof or admission of an act of dishonesty or false statement by the witness.	(a) **In General.** The following rules apply to attacking a witness's character for truthfulness by evidence of a criminal conviction: (1) for a crime that, in the convicting jurisdiction, was punishable by death or by imprisonment for more than one year, the evidence: (A) must be admitted, subject to Rule 403, in a civil case or in a criminal case in which the witness is not a defendant; and (B) must be admitted in a criminal case in which the witness is a defendant, if the probative value of the evidence outweighs its prejudicial effect to that defendant; and (2) for any crime regardless of the punishment, the evidence must be admitted if the court can readily determine that establishing the elements of the crime required proving — or the witness's admitting — a dishonest act or false statement.
(b) **Time limit.** Evidence of a conviction under this rule is not admissible if a period of more than ten years has elapsed since the date of the conviction or of the release of the witness from the confinement imposed for that conviction, whichever is the later date, unless the court determines, in the interests of justice, that the probative value of the conviction supported by specific facts and circumstances substantially outweighs its prejudicial effect. However, evidence of a conviction more than 10 years old as calculated herein, is not admissible unless the proponent gives to the adverse party sufficient advance written notice of intent to use such evidence to provide the adverse party with a fair opportunity to contest the use of such evidence.	(b) **Limit on Using the Evidence After 10 Years.** This subdivision (b) applies if more than 10 years have passed since the witness's conviction or release from confinement for it, whichever is later. Evidence of the conviction is admissible only if: (1) its probative value, supported by specific facts and circumstances, substantially outweighs its prejudicial effect; and (2) the proponent gives an adverse party reasonable written notice of the intent to use it so that the party has a fair opportunity to contest its use.

(c) Effect of pardon, annulment, or certificate of rehabilitation. Evidence of a conviction is not admissible under this rule if (1) the conviction has been the subject of a pardon, annulment, certificate of rehabilitation, or other equivalent procedure based on a finding of the rehabilitation of the person convicted, and that person has not been convicted of a subsequent crime that was punishable by death or imprisonment in excess of one year, or (2) the conviction has been the subject of a pardon, annulment, or other equivalent procedure based on a finding of innocence.	(c) **Effect of a Pardon, Annulment, or Certificate of Rehabilitation.** Evidence of a conviction is not admissible if: (1) the conviction has been the subject of a pardon, annulment, certificate of rehabilitation, or other equivalent procedure based on a finding that the person has been rehabilitated, and the person has not been convicted of a later crime punishable by death or by imprisonment for more than one year; or (2) the conviction has been the subject of a pardon, annulment, or other equivalent procedure based on a finding of innocence.
(d) Juvenile adjudications. Evidence of juvenile adjudications is generally not admissible under this rule. The court may, however, in a criminal case allow evidence of a juvenile adjudication of a witness other than the accused if conviction of the offense would be admissible to attack the credibility of an adult and the court is satisfied that admission in evidence is necessary for a fair determination of the issue of guilt or innocence.	(d) **Juvenile Adjudications.** Evidence of a juvenile adjudication is admissible under this rule only if: (1) it is offered in a criminal case; (2) the adjudication was of a witness other than the defendant; (3) an adult's conviction for that offense would be admissible to attack the adult's credibility; and (4) admitting the evidence is necessary to fairly determine guilt or innocence.
(e) Pendency of appeal. The pendency of an appeal therefrom does not render evidence of a conviction inadmissible. Evidence of the pendency of an appeal is admissible.	(e) **Pendency of an Appeal.** A conviction that satisfies this rule is admissible even if an appeal is pending. Evidence of the pendency is also admissible.

Committee Note

The language of Rule 609 has been amended as part of the restyling of the Evidence Rules to make them more easily understood and to make style and terminology consistent throughout the rules. These changes are intended to be stylistic only. There is no intent to change any result in any ruling on evidence admissibility.

Rule 610. Religious Beliefs or Opinions	Rule 610. Religious Beliefs or Opinions
Evidence of the beliefs or opinions of a witness on matters of religion is not admissible for the purpose of showing that by reason of their nature the witness' credibility is impaired or enhanced.	Evidence of a witness's religious beliefs or opinions is not admissible to attack or support the witness's credibility.

Committee Note

The language of Rule 610 has been amended as part of the restyling of the Evidence Rules to make them more easily understood and to make style and terminology consistent throughout the rules. These changes are intended to be stylistic only. There is no intent to change any result in any ruling on evidence admissibility.

Rule 611. Mode and Order of Interrogation and Presentation	Rule 611. Mode and Order of Examining Witnesses and Presenting Evidence
(a) **Control by court.** The court shall exercise reasonable control over the mode and order of interrogating witnesses and presenting evidence so as to (1) make the interrogation and presentation effective for the ascertainment of the truth, (2) avoid needless consumption of time, and (3) protect witnesses from harassment or undue embarrassment.	(a) **Control by the Court; Purposes.** The court should exercise reasonable control over the mode and order of examining witnesses and presenting evidence so as to: (1) make those procedures effective for determining the truth; (2) avoid wasting time; and (3) protect witnesses from harassment or undue embarrassment.
(b) **Scope of cross-examination.** Cross-examination should be limited to the subject matter of the direct examination and matters affecting the credibility of the witness. The court may, in the exercise of discretion, permit inquiry into additional matters as if on direct examination.	(b) **Scope of Cross-Examination.** Cross-examination should not go beyond the subject matter of the direct examination and matters affecting the witness's credibility. The court may allow inquiry into additional matters as if on direct examination.
(c) **Leading questions.** Leading questions should not be used on the direct examination of a witness except as may be necessary to develop the witness' testimony. Ordinarily leading questions should be permitted on cross-examination. When a party calls a hostile witness, an adverse party, or a witness identified with an adverse party, interrogation may be by leading questions.	(c) **Leading Questions.** Leading questions should not be used on direct examination except as necessary to develop the witness's testimony. Ordinarily, the court should allow leading questions: (1) on cross-examination; and (2) when a party calls a hostile witness, an adverse party, or a witness identified with an adverse party.

Committee Note

The language of Rule 611 has been amended as part of the restyling of the Evidence Rules to make them more easily understood and to make style and terminology consistent throughout the rules. These changes are intended to be stylistic only. There is no intent to change any result in any ruling on evidence admissibility.

Rule 612. Writing Used To Refresh Memory	Rule 612. Writing Used to Refresh a Witness's Memory
Except as otherwise provided in criminal proceedings by section 3500 of title 18, United States Code, if a witness uses a writing to refresh memory for the purpose of testifying, either— (1) while testifying, or (2) before testifying, if the court in its discretion determines it is necessary in the interests of justice, an adverse party is entitled to have the writing produced at the hearing, to inspect it, to cross-examine the witness thereon, and to introduce in evidence those portions which relate to the testimony of the witness. If it is claimed that the writing contains matters not related to the subject matter of the testimony the court shall examine the writing in camera, excise any portions not so related, and order delivery of the remainder to the party entitled thereto. Any portion withheld over objections shall be preserved and made available to the appellate court in the event of an appeal. If a writing is not produced or delivered pursuant to order under this rule, the court shall make any order justice requires, except that in criminal cases when the prosecution elects not to comply, the order shall be one striking the testimony or, if the court in its discretion determines that the interests of justice so require, declaring a mistrial.	**(a)** **Scope.** This rule gives an adverse party certain options when a witness uses a writing to refresh memory: **(1)** while testifying; or **(2)** before testifying, if the court decides that justice requires the party to have those options. **(b)** **Adverse Party's Options; Deleting Unrelated Matter.** Unless 18 U.S.C. § 3500 provides otherwise in a criminal case, an adverse party is entitled to have the writing produced at the hearing, to inspect it, to cross-examine the witness about it, and to introduce in evidence any portion that relates to the witness's testimony. If the producing party claims that the writing includes unrelated matter, the court must examine the writing in camera, delete any unrelated portion, and order that the rest be delivered to the adverse party. Any portion deleted over objection must be preserved for the record. **(c)** **Failure to Produce or Deliver the Writing.** If a writing is not produced or is not delivered as ordered, the court may issue any appropriate order. But if the prosecution does not comply in a criminal case, the court must strike the witness's testimony or — if justice so requires — declare a mistrial.

Committee Note

The language of Rule 612 has been amended as part of the restyling of the Evidence Rules to make them more easily understood and to make style and terminology consistent throughout the rules. These changes are intended to be stylistic only. There is no intent to change any result in any ruling on evidence admissibility.

Rule 613. Prior Statements of Witnesses	Rule 613. Witness's Prior Statement
(a) Examining witness concerning prior statement. In examining a witness concerning a prior statement made by the witness, whether written or not, the statement need not be shown nor its contents disclosed to the witness at that time, but on request the same shall be shown or disclosed to opposing counsel.	**(a) Showing or Disclosing the Statement During Examination.** When examining a witness about the witness's prior statement, a party need not show it or disclose its contents to the witness. But the party must, on request, show it or disclose its contents to an adverse party's attorney.
(b) Extrinsic evidence of prior inconsistent statement of witness. Extrinsic evidence of a prior inconsistent statement by a witness is not admissible unless the witness is afforded an opportunity to explain or deny the same and the opposite party is afforded an opportunity to interrogate the witness thereon, or the interests of justice otherwise require. This provision does not apply to admissions of a party-opponent as defined in rule 801(d)(2).	**(b) Extrinsic Evidence of a Prior Inconsistent Statement.** Extrinsic evidence of a witness's prior inconsistent statement is admissible only if the witness is given an opportunity to explain or deny the statement and an adverse party is given an opportunity to examine the witness about it, or if justice so requires. This subdivision (b) does not apply to an opposing party's statement under Rule 801(d)(2).

Committee Note

The language of Rule 613 has been amended as part of the restyling of the Evidence Rules to make them more easily understood and to make style and terminology consistent throughout the rules. These changes are intended to be stylistic only. There is no intent to change any result in any ruling on evidence admissibility.

Rule 614. Calling and Interrogation of Witnesses by Court	Rule 614. Court's Calling or Examining a Witness
(a) Calling by court. The court may, on its own motion or at the suggestion of a party, call witnesses, and all parties are entitled to cross-examine witnesses thus called.	**(a) Calling.** The court may call a witness on its own or at a party's request. Each party is entitled to cross-examine the witness.
(b) Interrogation by court. The court may interrogate witnesses, whether called by itself or by a party.	**(b) Examining.** The court may examine a witness regardless of who calls the witness.
(c) Objections. Objections to the calling of witnesses by the court or to interrogation by it may be made at the time or at the next available opportunity when the jury is not present.	**(c) Objections.** A party may object to the court's calling or examining a witness either at that time or at the next opportunity when the jury is not present.

Committee Note

The language of Rule 614 has been amended as part of the restyling of the Evidence Rules to make them more easily understood and to make style and terminology consistent throughout the rules.

These changes are intended to be stylistic only. There is no intent to change any result in any ruling on evidence admissibility.

Rule 615. Exclusion of Witnesses	Rule 615. Excluding Witnesses
At the request of a party the court shall order witnesses excluded so that they cannot hear the testimony of other witnesses, and it may make the order of its own motion. This rule does not authorize exclusion of (1) a party who is a natural person, or (2) an officer or employee of a party which is not a natural person designated as its representative by its attorney, or (3) a person whose presence is shown by a party to be essential to the presentation of the party's cause, or (4) a person authorized by statute to be present.	At a party's request, the court must order witnesses excluded so that they cannot hear other witnesses' testimony. Or the court may do so on its own. But this rule does not authorize excluding: **(a)** a party who is a natural person; **(b)** an officer or employee of a party that is not a natural person, after being designated as the party's representative by its attorney; **(c)** a person whose presence a party shows to be essential to presenting the party's claim or defense; or **(d)** a person authorized by statute to be present.

Committee Note

The language of Rule 615 has been amended as part of the restyling of the Evidence Rules to make them more easily understood and to make style and terminology consistent throughout the rules. These changes are intended to be stylistic only. There is no intent to change any result in any ruling on evidence admissibility.

ARTICLE VII. OPINIONS AND EXPERT TESTIMONY Rule 701. Opinion Testimony by Lay Witnesses	ARTICLE VII. OPINIONS AND EXPERT TESTIMONY Rule 701. Opinion Testimony by Lay Witnesses
If the witness is not testifying as an expert, the witness' testimony in the form of opinions or inferences is limited to those opinions or inferences which are (a) rationally based on the perception of the witness, and (b) helpful to a clear understanding of the witness' testimony or the determination of a fact in issue, and (c) not based on scientific, technical, or other specialized knowledge within the scope of Rule 702.	If a witness is not testifying as an expert, testimony in the form of an opinion is limited to one that is: **(a)** rationally based on the witness's perception; **(b)** helpful to clearly understanding the witness's testimony or to determining a fact in issue; and **(c)** not based on scientific, technical, or other specialized knowledge within the scope of Rule 702.

Committee Note

The language of Rule 701 has been amended as part of the general restyling of the Evidence Rules to make them more easily understood and to make style and terminology consistent throughout the rules. These changes are intended to be stylistic only. There is no intent to change any result in any ruling on evidence admissibility.

The Committee deleted all reference to an "inference" on the grounds that the deletion made the Rule flow better and easier to read, and because any "inference" is covered by the broader term "opinion." Courts have not made substantive decisions on the basis of any distinction between an opinion and an inference. No change in current practice is intended.

Rule 702. Testimony by Experts	Rule 702. Testimony by Expert Witnesses
If scientific, technical, or other specialized knowledge will assist the trier of fact to understand the evidence or to determine a fact in issue, a witness qualified as an expert by knowledge, skill, experience, training, or education, may testify thereto in the form of an opinion or otherwise, if (1) the testimony is based upon sufficient facts or data, (2) the testimony is the product of reliable principles and methods, and (3) the witness has applied the principles and methods reliably to the facts of the case.	A witness who is qualified as an expert by knowledge, skill, experience, training, or education may testify in the form of an opinion or otherwise if: (a) the expert's scientific, technical, or other specialized knowledge will help the trier of fact to understand the evidence or to determine a fact in issue; (b) the testimony is based on sufficient facts or data; (c) the testimony is the product of reliable principles and methods; and (d) the expert has reliably applied the principles and methods to the facts of the case.

Committee Note

The language of Rule 702 has been amended as part of the restyling of the Evidence Rules to make them more easily understood and to make style and terminology consistent throughout the rules. These changes are intended to be stylistic only. There is no intent to change any result in any ruling on evidence admissibility.

Rule 703. Bases of Opinion Testimony by Experts	Rule 703. Bases of an Expert's Opinion Testimony
The facts or data in the particular case upon which an expert bases an opinion or inference may be those perceived by or made known to the expert at or before the hearing. If of a type reasonably relied upon by experts in the particular field in forming opinions or inferences upon the subject, the facts or data need not be admissible in evidence in order for the opinion or inference to be admitted. Facts or data that are otherwise inadmissible shall not be disclosed to the jury by the proponent of the opinion or inference unless the court determines that their probative value in assisting the jury to evaluate the expert's opinion substantially outweighs their prejudicial effect.	An expert may base an opinion on facts or data in the case that the expert has been made aware of or personally observed. If experts in the particular field would reasonably rely on those kinds of facts or data in forming an opinion on the subject, they need not be admissible for the opinion to be admitted. But if the facts or data would otherwise be inadmissible, the proponent of the opinion may disclose them to the jury only if their probative value in helping the jury evaluate the opinion substantially outweighs their prejudicial effect.

Committee Note

The language of Rule 703 has been amended as part of the general restyling of the Evidence Rules to make them more easily understood and to make style and terminology consistent throughout the rules. These changes are intended to be stylistic only. There is no intent to change any result in any ruling on evidence admissibility.

The Committee deleted all reference to an "inference" on the grounds that the deletion made the Rule flow better and easier to read, and because any "inference" is covered by the broader term "opinion." Courts have not made substantive decisions on the basis of any distinction between an opinion and an inference. No change in current practice is intended.

Rule 704. Opinion on Ultimate Issue	Rule 704. Opinion on an Ultimate Issue
(a) Except as provided in subdivision (b), testimony in the form of an opinion or inference otherwise admissible is not objectionable because it embraces an ultimate issue to be decided by the trier of fact.	**(a)** **In General — Not Automatically Objectionable.** An opinion is not objectionable just because it embraces an ultimate issue.
(b) No expert witness testifying with respect to the mental state or condition of a defendant in a criminal case may state an opinion or inference as to whether the defendant did or did not have the mental state or condition constituting an element of the crime charged or of a defense thereto. Such ultimate issues are matters for the trier of fact alone.	**(b)** **Exception.** In a criminal case, an expert witness must not state an opinion about whether the defendant did or did not have a mental state or condition that constitutes an element of the crime charged or of a defense. Those matters are for the trier of fact alone.

Committee Note

The language of Rule 704 has been amended as part of the general restyling of the Evidence Rules to make them more easily understood and to make style and terminology consistent throughout the rules. These changes are intended to be stylistic only. There is no intent to change any result in any ruling on evidence admissibility.

The Committee deleted all reference to an "inference" on the grounds that the deletion made the Rule flow better and easier to read, and because any "inference" is covered by the broader term "opinion." Courts have not made substantive decisions on the basis of any distinction between an opinion and an inference. No change in current practice is intended.

Rule 705. Disclosure of Facts or Data Underlying Expert Opinion	Rule 705. Disclosing the Facts or Data Underlying an Expert's Opinion
The expert may testify in terms of opinion or inference and give reasons therefor without first testifying to the underlying facts or data, unless the court requires otherwise. The expert may in any event be required to disclose the underlying facts or data on cross-examination.	Unless the court orders otherwise, an expert may state an opinion — and give the reasons for it — without first testifying to the underlying facts or data. But the expert may be required to disclose those facts or data on cross-examination.

Committee Note

The language of Rule 705 has been amended as part of the general restyling of the Evidence Rules to make them more easily understood and to make style and terminology consistent throughout the rules. These changes are intended to be stylistic only. There is no intent to change any result in any ruling on evidence admissibility.

The Committee deleted all reference to an "inference" on the grounds that the deletion made the Rule flow better and easier to read, and because any "inference" is covered by the broader term "opinion." Courts have not made substantive decisions on the basis of any distinction between an opinion and an inference. No change in current practice is intended.

Rule 706. Court Appointed Experts	Rule 706. Court-Appointed Expert Witnesses

(a) Appointment. The court may on its own motion or on the motion of any party enter an order to show cause why expert witnesses should not be appointed, and may request the parties to submit nominations. The court may appoint any expert witnesses agreed upon by the parties, and may appoint expert witnesses of its own selection. An expert witness shall not be appointed by the court unless the witness consents to act. A witness so appointed shall be informed of the witness' duties by the court in writing, a copy of which shall be filed with the clerk, or at a conference in which the parties shall have opportunity to participate. A witness so appointed shall advise the parties of the witness' findings, if any; the witness' deposition may be taken by any party; and the witness may be called to testify by the court or any party. The witness shall be subject to cross-examination by each party, including a party calling the witness.	**(a)** **Appointment Process.** On a party's motion or on its own, the court may order the parties to show cause why expert witnesses should not be appointed and may ask the parties to submit nominations. The court may appoint any expert that the parties agree on and any of its own choosing. But the court may only appoint someone who consents to act.
	
	(b) **Expert's Role.** The court must inform the expert of the expert's duties. The court may do so in writing and have a copy filed with the clerk or may do so orally at a conference in which the parties have an opportunity to participate. The expert:
	
	    (1) must advise the parties of any findings the expert makes;
	
	    (2) may be deposed by any party;
	
	    (3) may be called to testify by the court or any party; and
	
	    (4) may be cross-examined by any party, including the party that called the expert.

(b) Compensation. Expert witnesses so appointed are entitled to reasonable compensation in whatever sum the court may allow. The compensation thus fixed is payable from funds which may be provided by law in criminal cases and civil actions and proceedings involving just compensation under the fifth amendment. In other civil actions and proceedings the compensation shall be paid by the parties in such proportion and at such time as the court directs, and thereafter charged in like manner as other costs.	**(c)** **Compensation.** The expert is entitled to a reasonable compensation, as set by the court. The compensation is payable as follows:
	
	    (1) in a criminal case or in a civil case involving just compensation under the Fifth Amendment, from any funds that are provided by law; and
	
	    (2) in any other civil case, by the parties in the proportion and at the time that the court directs — and the compensation is then charged like other costs.

(c) Disclosure of appointment. In the exercise of its discretion, the court may authorize disclosure to the jury of the fact that the court appointed the expert witness.	**(d)** **Disclosing the Appointment to the Jury.** The court may authorize disclosure to the jury that the court appointed the expert.
(d) Parties' experts of own selection. Nothing in this rule limits the parties in calling expert witnesses of their own selection.	**(e)** **Parties' Choice of Their Own Experts.** This rule does not limit a party in calling its own experts.

Committee Note

The language of Rule 706 has been amended as part of the restyling of the Evidence Rules to make them more easily understood and to make style and terminology consistent throughout the rules. These changes are intended to be stylistic only. There is no intent to change any result in any ruling on evidence admissibility.

ARTICLE VIII. HEARSAY Rule 801. Definitions	ARTICLE VIII. HEARSAY Rule 801. Definitions That Apply to This Article; Exclusions from Hearsay
The following definitions apply under this article: **(a) Statement.** A ''statement'' is (1) an oral or written assertion or (2) nonverbal conduct of a person, if it is intended by the person as an assertion.	**(a)** **Statement.** "Statement" means a person's oral assertion, written assertion, or nonverbal conduct, if the person intended it as an assertion.
(b) Declarant. A ''declarant'' is a person who makes a statement.	**(b)** **Declarant.** "Declarant" means the person who made the statement.
(c) Hearsay. ''Hearsay'' is a statement, other than one made by the declarant while testifying at the trial or hearing, offered in evidence to prove the truth of the matter asserted.	**(c)** **Hearsay.** "Hearsay" means a statement that: **(1)** the declarant does not make while testifying at the current trial or hearing; and **(2)** a party offers in evidence to prove the truth of the matter asserted in the statement.

(d) Statements which are not hearsay. A statement is not hearsay if—	**(d)** **Statements That Are Not Hearsay.** A statement that meets the following conditions is not hearsay:
(1) Prior statement by witness. The declarant testifies at the trial or hearing and is subject to cross-examination concerning the statement, and the statement is (A) inconsistent with the declarant's testimony, and was given under oath subject to the penalty of perjury at a trial, hearing, or other proceeding, or in a deposition, or (B) consistent with the declarant's testimony and is offered to rebut an express or implied charge against the declarant of recent fabrication or improper influence or motive, or (C) one of identification of a person made after perceiving the person; or	**(1)** *A Declarant-Witness's Prior Statement.* The declarant testifies and is subject to cross-examination about a prior statement, and the statement: **(A)** is inconsistent with the declarant's testimony and was given under penalty of perjury at a trial, hearing, or other proceeding or in a deposition; **(B)** is consistent with the declarant's testimony and is offered to rebut an express or implied charge that the declarant recently fabricated it or acted from a recent improper influence or motive in so testifying; or **(C)** identifies a person as someone the declarant perceived earlier.
(2) Admission by party-opponent. The statement is offered against a party and is (A) the party's own statement, in either an individual or a representative capacity or (B) a statement of which the party has manifested an adoption or belief in its truth, or (C) a statement by a person authorized by the party to make a statement concerning the subject, or (D) a statement by the party's agent or servant concerning a matter within the scope of the agency or employment, made during the existence of the relationship, or (E) a statement by a coconspirator of a party during the course and in furtherance of the conspiracy. The contents of the statement shall be considered but are not alone sufficient to establish the declarant's authority under subdivision (C), the agency or employment relationship and scope thereof under subdivision (D), or the existence of the conspiracy and the participation therein of the declarant and the party against whom the statement is offered under subdivision (E).	**(2)** *An Opposing Party's Statement.* The statement is offered against an opposing party and: **(A)** was made by the party in an individual or representative capacity; **(B)** is one the party manifested that it adopted or believed to be true; **(C)** was made by a person whom the party authorized to make a statement on the subject; **(D)** was made by the party's agent or employee on a matter within the scope of that relationship and while it existed; or **(E)** was made by the party's coconspirator during and in furtherance of the conspiracy. The statement must be considered but does not by itself establish the declarant's authority under (C); the existence or scope of the relationship under (D); or the existence of the conspiracy or participation in it under (E).

Committee Note

The language of Rule 801 has been amended as part of the general restyling of the Evidence Rules to make them more easily understood and to make style and terminology consistent throughout the rules. These changes are intended to be stylistic only. There is no intent to change any result in any ruling on evidence admissibility.

Statements falling under the hearsay exclusion provided by Rule 801(d)(2) are no longer referred to as "admissions" in the title to the subdivision. The term "admissions" is confusing because not all statements covered by the exclusion are admissions in the colloquial sense — a statement can be within the exclusion even if it "admitted" nothing and was not against the party's interest when made. The term "admissions" also raises confusion in comparison with the Rule 804(b)(3) exception for declarations against interest. No change in application of the exclusion is intended.

Rule 802. Hearsay Rule	Rule 802. The Rule Against Hearsay
Hearsay is not admissible except as provided by these rules or by other rules prescribed by the Supreme Court pursuant to statutory authority or by Act of Congress.	Hearsay is not admissible unless any of the following provides otherwise: • a federal statute; • these rules; or • other rules prescribed by the Supreme Court.

Committee Note

The language of Rule 802 has been amended as part of the restyling of the Evidence Rules to make them more easily understood and to make style and terminology consistent throughout the rules. These changes are intended to be stylistic only. There is no intent to change any result in any ruling on evidence admissibility.

Rule 803. Hearsay Exceptions; Availability of Declarant Immaterial	Rule 803. Exceptions to the Rule Against Hearsay — Regardless of Whether the Declarant Is Available as a Witness
The following are not excluded by the hearsay rule, even though the declarant is available as a witness: **(1) Present sense impression.** A statement describing or explaining an event or condition made while the declarant was perceiving the event or condition, or immediately thereafter.	The following are not excluded by the rule against hearsay, regardless of whether the declarant is available as a witness: **(1)** *Present Sense Impression.* A statement describing or explaining an event or condition, made while or immediately after the declarant perceived it.
(2) Excited utterance. A statement relating to a startling event or condition made while the declarant was under the stress of excitement caused by the event or condition.	**(2)** *Excited Utterance.* A statement relating to a startling event or condition, made while the declarant was under the stress of excitement that it caused.
(3) Then existing mental, emotional, or physical condition. A statement of the declarant's then existing state of mind, emotion, sensation, or physical condition (such as intent, plan, motive, design, mental feeling, pain, and bodily health), but not including a statement of memory or belief to prove the fact remembered or believed unless it relates to the execution, revocation, identification, or terms of declarant's will.	**(3)** *Then-Existing Mental, Emotional, or Physical Condition.* A statement of the declarant's then-existing state of mind (such as motive, intent, or plan) or emotional, sensory, or physical condition (such as mental feeling, pain, or bodily health), but not including a statement of memory or belief to prove the fact remembered or believed unless it relates to the validity or terms of the declarant's will.
(4) Statements for purposes of medical diagnosis or treatment. Statements made for purposes of medical diagnosis or treatment and describing medical history, or past or present symptoms, pain, or sensations, or the inception or general character of the cause or external source thereof insofar as reasonably pertinent to diagnosis or treatment.	**(4)** *Statement Made for Medical Diagnosis or Treatment.* A statement that: **(A)** is made for — and is reasonably pertinent to — medical diagnosis or treatment; and **(B)** describes medical history; past or present symptoms or sensations; their inception; or their general cause.

(5) Recorded recollection. A memorandum or record concerning a matter about which a witness once had knowledge but now has insufficient recollection to enable the witness to testify fully and accurately, shown to have been made or adopted by the witness when the matter was fresh in the witness' memory and to reflect that knowledge correctly. If admitted, the memorandum or record may be read into evidence but may not itself be received as an exhibit unless offered by an adverse party.

(5)   *Recorded Recollection.* A record that:

    (A)   is on a matter the witness once knew about but now cannot recall well enough to testify fully and accurately;

    (B)   was made or adopted by the witness when the matter was fresh in the witness's memory; and

    (C)   accurately reflects the witness's knowledge.

If admitted, the record may be read into evidence but may be received as an exhibit only if offered by an adverse party.

(6) Records of regularly conducted activity. A memorandum, report, record, or data compilation, in any form, of acts, events, conditions, opinions, or diagnoses, made at or near the time by, or from information transmitted by, a person with knowledge, if kept in the course of a regularly conducted business activity, and if it was the regular practice of that business activity to make the memorandum, report, record or data compilation, all as shown by the testimony of the custodian or other qualified witness, or by certification that complies with Rule 902(11), Rule 902(12), or a statute permitting certification, unless the source of information or the method or circumstances of preparation indicate lack of trustworthiness. The term "business" as used in this paragraph includes business, institution, association, profession, occupation, and calling of every kind, whether or not conducted for profit.

(6)   *Records of a Regularly Conducted Activity.* A record of an act, event, condition, opinion, or diagnosis if:

    (A)   the record was made at or near the time by — or from information transmitted by — someone with knowledge;

    (B)   the record was kept in the course of a regularly conducted activity of a business, organization, occupation, or calling, whether or not for profit;

    (C)   making the record was a regular practice of that activity;

    (D)   all these conditions are shown by the testimony of the custodian or another qualified witness, or by a certification that complies with Rule 902(11) or (12) or with a statute permitting certification; and

    (E)   neither the source of information nor the method or circumstances of preparation indicate a lack of trustworthiness.

(7) Absence of entry in records kept in accordance with the provisions of paragraph (6). Evidence that a matter is not included in the memoranda reports, records, or data compilations, in any form, kept in accordance with the provisions of paragraph (6), to prove the nonoccurrence or nonexistence of the matter, if the matter was of a kind of which a memorandum, report, record, or data compilation was regularly made and preserved, unless the sources of information or other circumstances indicate lack of trustworthiness.	(7) *Absence of a Record of a Regularly Conducted Activity.* Evidence that a matter is not included in a record described in paragraph (6) if: (A) the evidence is admitted to prove that the matter did not occur or exist; (B) a record was regularly kept for a matter of that kind; and (C) neither the possible source of the information nor other circumstances indicate a lack of trustworthiness.

(8) Public records and reports. Records, reports, statements, or data compilations, in any form, of public offices or agencies, setting forth (A) the activities of the office or agency, or (B) matters observed pursuant to duty imposed by law as to which matters there was a duty to report, excluding, however, in criminal cases matters observed by police officers and other law enforcement personnel, or (C) in civil actions and proceedings and against the Government in criminal cases, factual findings resulting from an investigation made pursuant to authority granted by law, unless the sources of information or other circumstances indicate lack of trustworthiness.	(8) *Public Records.* A record or statement of a public office if:
	
	(A) it sets out:
	
	    (i) the office's activities;
	
	    (ii) a matter observed while under a legal duty to report, but not including, in a criminal case, a matter observed by law-enforcement personnel; or
	
	    (iii) in a civil case or against the government in a criminal case, factual findings from a legally authorized investigation; and
	
	(B) neither the source of information nor other circumstances indicate a lack of trustworthiness.

(9) Records of vital statistics. Records or data compilations, in any form, of births, fetal deaths, deaths, or marriages, if the report thereof was made to a public office pursuant to requirements of law.	(9) *Public Records of Vital Statistics.* A record of a birth, death, or marriage, if reported to a public office in accordance with a legal duty.

(10) Absence of public record or entry. To prove the absence of a record, report, statement, or data compilation, in any form, or the nonoccurrence or nonexistence of a matter of which a record, report, statement, or data compilation, in any form, was regularly made and preserved by a public office or agency, evidence in the form of a certification in accordance with rule 902, or testimony, that diligent search failed to disclose the record, report, statement, or data compilation, or entry.	**(10)** *Absence of a Public Record.* Testimony — or a certification under Rule 902 — that a diligent search failed to disclose a public record or statement if the testimony or certification is admitted to prove that: **(A)** the record or statement does not exist; or **(B)** a matter did not occur or exist, if a public office regularly kept a record or statement for a matter of that kind.
(11) Records of religious organizations. Statements of births, marriages, divorces, deaths, legitimacy, ancestry, relationship by blood or marriage, or other similar facts of personal or family history, contained in a regularly kept record of a religious organization.	**(11)** *Records of Religious Organizations Concerning Personal or Family History.* A statement of birth, legitimacy, ancestry, marriage, divorce, death, relationship by blood or marriage, or similar facts of personal or family history, contained in a regularly kept record of a religious organization.
(12) Marriage, baptismal, and similar certificates. Statements of fact contained in a certificate that the maker performed a marriage or other ceremony or administered a sacrament, made by a clergyman, public official, or other person authorized by the rules or practices of a religious organization or by law to perform the act certified, and purporting to have been issued at the time of the act or within a reasonable time thereafter.	**(12)** *Certificates of Marriage, Baptism, and Similar Ceremonies.* A statement of fact contained in a certificate: **(A)** made by a person who is authorized by a religious organization or by law to perform the act certified; **(B)** attesting that the person performed a marriage or similar ceremony or administered a sacrament; and **(C)** purporting to have been issued at the time of the act or within a reasonable time after it.
(13) Family records. Statements of fact concerning personal or family history contained in family Bibles, genealogies, charts, engravings on rings, inscriptions on family portraits, engravings on urns, crypts, or tombstones, or the like.	**(13)** *Family Records.* A statement of fact about personal or family history contained in a family record, such as a Bible, genealogy, chart, engraving on a ring, inscription on a portrait, or engraving on an urn or burial marker.

(14) Records of documents affecting an interest in property. The record of a document purporting to establish or affect an interest in property, as proof of the content of the original recorded document and its execution and delivery by each person by whom it purports to have been executed, if the record is a record of a public office and an applicable statute authorizes the recording of documents of that kind in that office.	**(14) Records of Documents That Affect an Interest in Property.** The record of a document that purports to establish or affect an interest in property if: **(A)** the record is admitted to prove the content of the original recorded document, along with its signing and its delivery by each person who purports to have signed it; **(B)** the record is kept in a public office; and **(C)** a statute authorizes recording documents of that kind in that office.
(15) Statements in documents affecting an interest in property. A statement contained in a document purporting to establish or affect an interest in property if the matter stated was relevant to the purpose of the document, unless dealings with the property since the document was made have been inconsistent with the truth of the statement or the purport of the document.	**(15) Statements in Documents That Affect an Interest in Property.** A statement contained in a document that purports to establish or affect an interest in property if the matter stated was relevant to the document's purpose — unless later dealings with the property are inconsistent with the truth of the statement or the purport of the document.
(16) Statements in ancient documents. Statements in a document in existence twenty years or more the authenticity of which is established.	**(16) Statements in Ancient Documents.** A statement in a document that is at least 20 years old and whose authenticity is established.
(17) Market reports, commercial publications. Market quotations, tabulations, lists, directories, or other published compilations, generally used and relied upon by the public or by persons in particular occupations.	**(17) Market Reports and Similar Commercial Publications.** Market quotations, lists, directories, or other compilations that are generally relied on by the public or by persons in particular occupations.

(18) Learned treatises. To the extent called to the attention of an expert witness upon cross-examination or relied upon by the expert witness in direct examination, statements contained in published treatises, periodicals, or pamphlets on a subject of history, medicine, or other science or art, established as a reliable authority by the testimony or admission of the witness or by other expert testimony or by judicial notice. If admitted, the statements may be read into evidence but may not be received as exhibits.	**(18) *Statements in Learned Treatises, Periodicals, or Pamphlets.*** A statement contained in a treatise, periodical, or pamphlet if: **(A)** the statement is called to the attention of an expert witness on cross-examination or relied on by the expert on direct examination; and **(B)** the publication is established as a reliable authority by the expert's admission or testimony, by another expert's testimony, or by judicial notice. If admitted, the statement may be read into evidence but not received as an exhibit.
(19) Reputation concerning personal or family history. Reputation among members of a person's family by blood, adoption, or marriage, or among a person's associates, or in the community, concerning a person's birth, adoption, marriage, divorce, death, legitimacy, relationship by blood, adoption, or marriage, ancestry, or other similar fact of personal or family history.	**(19) *Reputation Concerning Personal or Family History.*** A reputation among a person's family by blood, adoption, or marriage — or among a person's associates or in the community — concerning the person's birth, adoption, legitimacy, ancestry, marriage, divorce, death, relationship by blood, adoption, or marriage, or similar facts of personal or family history.
(20) Reputation concerning boundaries or general history. Reputation in a community, arising before the controversy, as to boundaries of or customs affecting lands in the community, and reputation as to events of general history important to the community or State or nation in which located.	**(20) *Reputation Concerning Boundaries or General History.*** A reputation in a community — arising before the controversy — concerning boundaries of land in the community or customs that affect the land, or concerning general historical events important to that community, state, or nation.
(21) Reputation as to character. Reputation of a person's character among associates or in the community.	**(21) *Reputation Concerning Character.*** A reputation among a person's associates or in the community concerning the person's character.

(22) Judgment of previous conviction. Evidence of a final judgment, entered after a trial or upon a plea of guilty (but not upon a plea of nolo contendere), adjudging a person guilty of a crime punishable by death or imprisonment in excess of one year, to prove any fact essential to sustain the judgment, but not including, when offered by the Government in a criminal prosecution for purposes other than impeachment, judgments against persons other than the accused. The pendency of an appeal may be shown but does not affect admissibility.	**(22)** *Judgment of a Previous Conviction.* Evidence of a final judgment of conviction if: **(A)** the judgment was entered after a trial or guilty plea, but not a nolo contendere plea; **(B)** the conviction was for a crime punishable by death or by imprisonment for more than a year; **(C)** the evidence is admitted to prove any fact essential to the judgment; and **(D)** when offered by the prosecutor in a criminal case for a purpose other than impeachment, the judgment was against the defendant. The pendency of an appeal may be shown but does not affect admissibility.
(23) Judgment as to personal, family, or general history, or boundaries. Judgments as proof of matters of personal, family or general history, or boundaries, essential to the judgment, if the same would be provable by evidence of reputation.	**(23)** *Judgments Involving Personal, Family, or General History, or a Boundary.* A judgment that is admitted to prove a matter of personal, family, or general history, or boundaries, if the matter: **(A)** was essential to the judgment; and **(B)** could be proved by evidence of reputation.
(24) [Other exceptions.] [Transferred to Rule 807]	**(24)** *[Other Exceptions.]* [Transferred to Rule 807.]

Committee Note

The language of Rule 803 has been amended as part of the restyling of the Evidence Rules to make them more easily understood and to make style and terminology consistent throughout the rules. These changes are intended to be stylistic only. There is no intent to change any result in any ruling on evidence admissibility.

Rule 804. Hearsay Exceptions; Declarant Unavailable	Rule 804. Exceptions to the Rule Against Hearsay — When the Declarant Is Unavailable as a Witness
(a) **Definition of unavailability.** "Unavailability as a witness" includes situations in which the declarant—	(a) **Criteria for Being Unavailable.** A declarant is considered to be unavailable as a witness if the declarant:
(1) is exempted by ruling of the court on the ground of privilege from testifying concerning the subject matter of the declarant's statement; or	(1) is exempted from testifying about the subject matter of the declarant's statement because the court rules that a privilege applies;
(2) persists in refusing to testify concerning the subject matter of the declarant's statement despite an order of the court to do so; or	(2) refuses to testify about the subject matter despite a court order to do so;
(3) testifies to a lack of memory of the subject matter of the declarant's statement; or	(3) testifies to not remembering the subject matter;
(4) is unable to be present or to testify at the hearing because of death or then existing physical or mental illness or infirmity; or	(4) cannot be present or testify at the trial or hearing because of death or a then-existing infirmity, physical illness, or mental illness; or
(5) is absent from the hearing and the proponent of a statement has been unable to procure the declarant's attendance (or in the case of a hearsay exception under subdivision (b)(2), (3), or (4), the declarant's attendance or testimony) by process or other reasonable means.	(5) is absent from the trial or hearing and the statement's proponent has not been able, by process or other reasonable means, to procure:
A declarant is not unavailable as a witness if exemption, refusal, claim of lack of memory, inability, or absence is due to the procurement or wrongdoing of the proponent of a statement for the purpose of preventing the witness from attending or testifying.	(A) the declarant's attendance, in the case of a hearsay exception under Rule 804(b)(1) or (6); or
	(B) the declarant's attendance or testimony, in the case of a hearsay exception under Rule 804(b)(2), (3), or (4).
	But this subdivision (a) does not apply if the statement's proponent procured or wrongfully caused the declarant's unavailability as a witness in order to prevent the declarant from attending or testifying.

(b) Hearsay exceptions. The following are not excluded by the hearsay rule if the declarant is unavailable as a witness:	**(b)** **The Exceptions.** The following are not excluded by the rule against hearsay if the declarant is unavailable as a witness:
(1) Former testimony. Testimony given as a witness at another hearing of the same or a different proceeding, or in a deposition taken in compliance with law in the course of the same or another proceeding, if the party against whom the testimony is now offered, or, in a civil action or proceeding, a predecessor in interest, had an opportunity and similar motive to develop the testimony by direct, cross, or redirect examination.	**(1)** *Former Testimony.* Testimony that: **(A)** was given as a witness at a trial, hearing, or lawful deposition, whether given during the current proceeding or a different one; and **(B)** is now offered against a party who had — or, in a civil case, whose predecessor in interest had — an opportunity and similar motive to develop it by direct, cross-, or redirect examination.
(2) Statement under belief of impending death. In a prosecution for homicide or in a civil action or proceeding, a statement made by a declarant while believing that the declarant's death was imminent, concerning the cause or circumstances of what the declarant believed to be impending death.	**(2)** *Statement Under the Belief of Imminent Death.* In a prosecution for homicide or in a civil case, a statement that the declarant, while believing the declarant's death to be imminent, made about its cause or circumstances.
(3) Statement against interest. A statement that: **(A)** a reasonable person in the declarant's position would have made only if the person believed it to be true because, when made, it was so contrary to the declarant's proprietary or pecuniary interest or had so great a tendency to invalidate the declarant's claim against someone else or to expose the declarant to civil or criminal liability; and **(B)** is supported by corroborating circumstances that clearly indicate its trustworthiness, if it is offered in a criminal case as one that tends to expose the declarant to criminal liability.	**(3)** *Statement Against Interest.* A statement that: **(A)** a reasonable person in the declarant's position would have made only if the person believed it to be true because, when made, it was so contrary to the declarant's proprietary or pecuniary interest or had so great a tendency to invalidate the declarant's claim against someone else or to expose the declarant to civil or criminal liability; and **(B)** is supported by corroborating circumstances that clearly indicate its trustworthiness, if it is offered in a criminal case as one that tends to expose the declarant to criminal liability.

(4) Statement of personal or family history. (A) A statement concerning the declarant's own birth, adoption, marriage, divorce, legitimacy, relationship by blood, adoption, or marriage, ancestry, or other similar fact of personal or family history, even though declarant had no means of acquiring personal knowledge of the matter stated; or (B) a statement concerning the foregoing matters, and death also, of another person, if the declarant was related to the other by blood, adoption, or marriage or was so intimately associated with the other's family as to be likely to have accurate information concerning the matter declared.	**(4)** *Statement of Personal or Family History.* A statement about: **(A)** the declarant's own birth, adoption, legitimacy, ancestry, marriage, divorce, relationship by blood, adoption, or marriage, or similar facts of personal or family history, even though the declarant had no way of acquiring personal knowledge about that fact; or **(B)** another person concerning any of these facts, as well as death, if the declarant was related to the person by blood, adoption, or marriage or was so intimately associated with the person's family that the declarant's information is likely to be accurate.
(5) [Other exceptions.] [Transferred to Rule 807]	**(5)** *[Other Exceptions.]* [Transferred to Rule 807.]
(6) Forfeiture by wrongdoing. A statement offered against a party that has engaged or acquiesced in wrongdoing that was intended to, and did, procure the unavailability of the declarant as a witness.	**(6)** *Statement Offered Against a Party That Wrongfully Caused the Declarant's Unavailability.* A statement offered against a party that wrongfully caused — or acquiesced in wrongfully causing — the declarant's unavailability as a witness, and did so intending that result.

Committee Note

The language of Rule 804 has been amended as part of the general restyling of the Evidence Rules to make them more easily understood and to make style and terminology consistent throughout the rules. These changes are intended to be stylistic only. There is no intent to change any result in any ruling on evidence admissibility.

No style changes were made to Rule 804(b)(3), because it was already restyled in conjunction with a substantive amendment, effective December 1, 2010.

Rule 805. Hearsay Within Hearsay	Rule 805. Hearsay Within Hearsay
Hearsay included within hearsay is not excluded under the hearsay rule if each part of the combined statements conforms with an exception to the hearsay rule provided in these rules.	Hearsay within hearsay is not excluded by the rule against hearsay if each part of the combined statements conforms with an exception to the rule.

Committee Note

The language of Rule 805 has been amended as part of the restyling of the Evidence Rules to make them more easily understood and to make style and terminology consistent throughout the rules. These changes are intended to be stylistic only. There is no intent to change any result in any ruling on evidence admissibility.

Rule 806. Attacking and Supporting Credibility of Declarant	Rule 806. Attacking and Supporting the Declarant's Credibility
When a hearsay statement, or a statement defined in Rule 801(d)(2)(C), (D), or (E), has been admitted in evidence, the credibility of the declarant may be attacked, and if attacked may be supported, by any evidence which would be admissible for those purposes if declarant had testified as a witness. Evidence of a statement or conduct by the declarant at any time, inconsistent with the declarant's hearsay statement, is not subject to any requirement that the declarant may have been afforded an opportunity to deny or explain. If the party against whom a hearsay statement has been admitted calls the declarant as a witness, the party is entitled to examine the declarant on the statement as if under cross-examination.	When a hearsay statement — or a statement described in Rule 801(d)(2)(C), (D), or (E) — has been admitted in evidence, the declarant's credibility may be attacked, and then supported, by any evidence that would be admissible for those purposes if the declarant had testified as a witness. The court may admit evidence of the declarant's inconsistent statement or conduct, regardless of when it occurred or whether the declarant had an opportunity to explain or deny it. If the party against whom the statement was admitted calls the declarant as a witness, the party may examine the declarant on the statement as if on cross-examination.

Committee Note

The language of Rule 806 has been amended as part of the restyling of the Evidence Rules to make them more easily understood and to make style and terminology consistent throughout the rules. These changes are intended to be stylistic only. There is no intent to change any result in any ruling on evidence admissibility.

Rule 807. Residual Exception	Rule 807. Residual Exception
A statement not specifically covered by Rule 803 or 804 but having equivalent circumstantial guarantees of trustworthiness, is not excluded by the hearsay rule, if the court determines that (A) the statement is offered as evidence of a material fact; (B) the statement is more probative on the point for which it is offered than any other evidence which the proponent can procure through reasonable efforts; and (C) the general purposes of these rules and the interests of justice will best be served by admission of the statement into evidence. However, a statement may not be admitted under this exception unless the proponent of it makes known to the adverse party sufficiently in advance of the trial or hearing to provide the adverse party with a fair opportunity to prepare to meet it, the proponent's intention to offer the statement and the particulars of it, including the name and address of the declarant.	**(a)** **In General.** Under the following circumstances, a hearsay statement is not excluded by the rule against hearsay even if the statement is not specifically covered by a hearsay exception in Rule 803 or 804: **(1)** the statement has equivalent circumstantial guarantees of trustworthiness; **(2)** it is offered as evidence of a material fact; **(3)** it is more probative on the point for which it is offered than any other evidence that the proponent can obtain through reasonable efforts; and **(4)** admitting it will best serve the purposes of these rules and the interests of justice. **(b)** **Notice.** The statement is admissible only if, before the trial or hearing, the proponent gives an adverse party reasonable notice of the intent to offer the statement and its particulars, including the declarant's name and address, so that the party has a fair opportunity to meet it.

Committee Note

The language of Rule 807 has been amended as part of the restyling of the Evidence Rules to make them more easily understood and to make style and terminology consistent throughout the rules. These changes are intended to be stylistic only. There is no intent to change any result in any ruling on evidence admissibility.

ARTICLE IX. AUTHENTICATION AND IDENTIFICATION Rule 901. Requirement of Authentication or Identification	ARTICLE IX. AUTHENTICATION AND IDENTIFICATION Rule 901. Authenticating or Identifying Evidence
(a) General provision. The requirement of authentication or identification as a condition precedent to admissibility is satisfied by evidence sufficient to support a finding that the matter in question is what its proponent claims.	**(a)** **In General.** To satisfy the requirement of authenticating or identifying an item of evidence, the proponent must produce evidence sufficient to support a finding that the item is what the proponent claims it is.
(b) Illustrations. By way of illustration only, and not by way of limitation, the following are examples of authentication or identification conforming with the requirements of this rule:	**(b)** **Examples.** The following are examples only — not a complete list — of evidence that satisfies the requirement:
(1) Testimony of witness with knowledge. Testimony that a matter is what it is claimed to be.	**(1)** *Testimony of a Witness with Knowledge.* Testimony that an item is what it is claimed to be.
(2) Nonexpert opinion on handwriting. Nonexpert opinion as to the genuineness of handwriting, based upon familiarity not acquired for purposes of the litigation.	**(2)** *Nonexpert Opinion About Handwriting.* A nonexpert's opinion that handwriting is genuine, based on a familiarity with it that was not acquired for the current litigation.
(3) Comparison by trier or expert witness. Comparison by the trier of fact or by expert witnesses with specimens which have been authenticated.	**(3)** *Comparison by an Expert Witness or the Trier of Fact.* A comparison with an authenticated specimen by an expert witness or the trier of fact.
(4) Distinctive characteristics and the like. Appearance, contents, substance, internal patterns, or other distinctive characteristics, taken in conjunction with circumstances.	**(4)** *Distinctive Characteristics and the Like.* The appearance, contents, substance, internal patterns, or other distinctive characteristics of the item, taken together with all the circumstances.
(5) Voice identification. Identification of a voice, whether heard firsthand or through mechanical or electronic transmission or recording, by opinion based upon hearing the voice at any time under circumstances connecting it with the alleged speaker.	**(5)** *Opinion About a Voice.* An opinion identifying a person's voice — whether heard firsthand or through mechanical or electronic transmission or recording — based on hearing the voice at any time under circumstances that connect it with the alleged speaker.

(6) Telephone conversations. Telephone conversations, by evidence that a call was made to the number assigned at the time by the telephone company to a particular person or business, if (A) in the case of a person, circumstances, including self-identification, show the person answering to be the one called, or (B) in the case of a business, the call was made to a place of business and the conversation related to business reasonably transacted over the telephone.	**(6)** *Evidence About a Telephone Conversation.* For a telephone conversation, evidence that a call was made to the number assigned at the time to: **(A)** a particular person, if circumstances, including self-identification, show that the person answering was the one called; or **(B)** a particular business, if the call was made to a business and the call related to business reasonably transacted over the telephone.
(7) Public records or reports. Evidence that a writing authorized by law to be recorded or filed and in fact recorded or filed in a public office, or a purported public record, report, statement, or data compilation, in any form, is from the public office where items of this nature are kept.	**(7)** *Evidence About Public Records.* Evidence that: **(A)** a document was recorded or filed in a public office as authorized by law; or **(B)** a purported public record or statement is from the office where items of this kind are kept.
(8) Ancient documents or data compilation. Evidence that a document or data compilation, in any form, (A) is in such condition as to create no suspicion concerning its authenticity, (B) was in a place where it, if authentic, would likely be, and (C) has been in existence 20 years or more at the time it is offered.	**(8)** *Evidence About Ancient Documents or Data Compilations.* For a document or data compilation, evidence that it: **(A)** is in a condition that creates no suspicion about its authenticity; **(B)** was in a place where, if authentic, it would likely be; and **(C)** is at least 20 years old when offered.
(9) Process or system. Evidence describing a process or system used to produce a result and showing that the process or system produces an accurate result.	**(9)** *Evidence About a Process or System.* Evidence describing a process or system and showing that it produces an accurate result.
(10) Methods provided by statute or rule. Any method of authentication or identification provided by Act of Congress or by other rules prescribed by the Supreme Court pursuant to statutory authority.	**(10)** *Methods Provided by a Statute or Rule.* Any method of authentication or identification allowed by a federal statute or a rule prescribed by the Supreme Court.

Committee Note

The language of Rule 901 has been amended as part of the restyling of the Evidence Rules to make them more easily understood and to make style and terminology consistent throughout the rules. These changes are intended to be stylistic only. There is no intent to change any result in any ruling on evidence admissibility.

Rule 902. Self-authentication	Rule 902. Evidence That Is Self-Authenticating

Extrinsic evidence of authenticity as a condition precedent to admissibility is not required with respect to the following:
 	
(1) Domestic public documents under seal. A document bearing a seal purporting to be that of the United States, or of any State, district, Commonwealth, territory, or insular possession thereof, or the Panama Canal Zone, or the Trust Territory of the Pacific Islands, or of a political subdivision, department, officer, or agency thereof, and a signature purporting to be an attestation or execution.
	The following items of evidence are self-authenticating; they require no extrinsic evidence of authenticity in order to be admitted:
	
	(1) *Domestic Public Documents That Are Sealed and Signed.* A document that bears:
	
	   (A) a seal purporting to be that of the United States; any state, district, commonwealth, territory, or insular possession of the United States; the former Panama Canal Zone; the Trust Territory of the Pacific Islands; a political subdivision of any of these entities; or a department, agency, or officer of any entity named above; and
	
	   (B) a signature purporting to be an execution or attestation.

(2) Domestic public documents not under seal. A document purporting to bear the signature in the official capacity of an officer or employee of any entity included in paragraph (1) hereof, having no seal, if a public officer having a seal and having official duties in the district or political subdivision of the officer or employee certifies under seal that the signer has the official capacity and that the signature is genuine.	(2) *Domestic Public Documents That Are Not Sealed but Are Signed and Certified.* A document that bears no seal if:
	
	   (A) it bears the signature of an officer or employee of an entity named in Rule 902(1)(A); and
	
	   (B) another public officer who has a seal and official duties within that same entity certifies under seal — or its equivalent — that the signer has the official capacity and that the signature is genuine.

(3) Foreign public documents. A document purporting to be executed or attested in an official capacity by a person authorized by the laws of a foreign country to make the execution or attestation, and accompanied by a final certification as to the genuineness of the signature and official position (A) of the executing or attesting person, or (B) of any foreign official whose certificate of genuineness of signature and official position relates to the execution or attestation or is in a chain of certificates of genuineness of signature and official position relating to the execution or attestation. A final certification may be made by a secretary of an embassy or legation, consul general, consul, vice consul, or consular agent of the United States, or a diplomatic or consular official of the foreign country assigned or accredited to the United States. If reasonable opportunity has been given to all parties to investigate the authenticity and accuracy of official documents, the court may, for good cause shown, order that they be treated as presumptively authentic without final certification or permit them to be evidenced by an attested summary with or without final certification.

(3) *Foreign Public Documents.* A document that purports to be signed or attested by a person who is authorized by a foreign country's law to do so. The document must be accompanied by a final certification that certifies the genuineness of the signature and official position of the signer or attester — or of any foreign official whose certificate of genuineness relates to the signature or attestation or is in a chain of certificates of genuineness relating to the signature or attestation. The certification may be made by a secretary of a United States embassy or legation; by a consul general, vice consul, or consular agent of the United States; or by a diplomatic or consular official of the foreign country assigned or accredited to the United States. If all parties have been given a reasonable opportunity to investigate the document's authenticity and accuracy, the court may, for good cause, either:

(A) order that it be treated as presumptively authentic without final certification; or

(B) allow it to be evidenced by an attested summary with or without final certification.

(4) Certified copies of public records. A copy of an official record or report or entry therein, or of a document authorized by law to be recorded or filed and actually recorded or filed in a public office, including data compilations in any form, certified as correct by the custodian or other person authorized to make the certification, by certificate complying with paragraph (1), (2), or (3) of this rule or complying with any Act of Congress or rule prescribed by the Supreme Court pursuant to statutory authority.

(4) *Certified Copies of Public Records.* A copy of an official record — or a copy of a document that was recorded or filed in a public office as authorized by law — if the copy is certified as correct by:

(A) the custodian or another person authorized to make the certification; or

(B) a certificate that complies with Rule 902(1), (2), or (3), a federal statute, or a rule prescribed by the Supreme Court.

(5) Official publications. Books, pamphlets, or other publications purporting to be issued by public authority.

(5) *Official Publications.* A book, pamphlet, or other publication purporting to be issued by a public authority.

(6) Newspapers and periodicals. Printed materials purporting to be newspapers or periodicals.

(6) *Newspapers and Periodicals.* Printed material purporting to be a newspaper or periodical.

(7) Trade inscriptions and the like. Inscriptions, signs, tags, or labels purporting to have been affixed in the course of business and indicating ownership, control, or origin.	(7) *Trade Inscriptions and the Like.* An inscription, sign, tag, or label purporting to have been affixed in the course of business and indicating origin, ownership, or control.
(8) Acknowledged documents. Documents accompanied by a certificate of acknowledgment executed in the manner provided by law by a notary public or other officer authorized by law to take acknowledgments.	(8) *Acknowledged Documents.* A document accompanied by a certificate of acknowledgment that is lawfully executed by a notary public or another officer who is authorized to take acknowledgments.
(9) Commercial paper and related documents. Commercial paper, signatures thereon, and documents relating thereto to the extent provided by general commercial law.	(9) *Commercial Paper and Related Documents.* Commercial paper, a signature on it, and related documents, to the extent allowed by general commercial law.
(10) Presumptions under Acts of Congress. Any signature, document, or other matter declared by Act of Congress to be presumptively or prima facie genuine or authentic.	(10) *Presumptions Under a Federal Statute.* A signature, document, or anything else that a federal statute declares to be presumptively or prima facie genuine or authentic.
(11) Certified domestic records of regularly conducted activity. The original or a duplicate of a domestic record of regularly conducted activity that would be admissible under Rule 803(6) if accompanied by a written declaration of its custodian or other qualified person, in a manner complying with any Act of Congress or rule prescribed by the Supreme Court pursuant to statutory authority, certifying that the record— **(A)** was made at or near the time of the occurrence of the matters set forth by, or from information transmitted by, a person with knowledge of those matters; **(B)** was kept in the course of the regularly conducted activity; and **(C)** was made by the regularly conducted activity as a regular practice. A party intending to offer a record into evidence under this paragraph must provide written notice of that intention to all adverse parties, and must make the record and declaration available for inspection sufficiently in advance of their offer into evidence to provide an adverse party with a fair opportunity to challenge them.	(11) *Certified Domestic Records of a Regularly Conducted Activity.* The original or a copy of a domestic record that meets the requirements of Rule 803(6)(A)-(C), as shown by a certification of the custodian or another qualified person that complies with a federal statute or a rule prescribed by the Supreme Court. Before the trial or hearing, the proponent must give an adverse party reasonable written notice of the intent to offer the record — and must make the record and certification available for inspection — so that the party has a fair opportunity to challenge them.

(12) Certified foreign records of regularly conducted activity. In a civil case, the original or a duplicate of a foreign record of regularly conducted activity that would be admissible under Rule 803(6) if accompanied by a written declaration by its custodian or other qualified person certifying that the record—

(A) was made at or near the time of the occurrence of the matters set forth by, or from information transmitted by, a person with knowledge of those matters;

(B) was kept in the course of the regularly conducted activity; and

(C) was made by the regularly conducted activity as a regular practice.

The declaration must be signed in a manner that, if falsely made, would subject the maker to criminal penalty under the laws of the country where the declaration is signed. A party intending to offer a record into evidence under this paragraph must provide written notice of that intention to all adverse parties, and must make the record and declaration available for inspection sufficiently in advance of their offer into evidence to provide an adverse party with a fair opportunity to challenge them.

(12) *Certified Foreign Records of a Regularly Conducted Activity.* In a civil case, the original or a copy of a foreign record that meets the requirements of Rule 902(11), modified as follows: the certification, rather than complying with a federal statute or Supreme Court rule, must be signed in a manner that, if falsely made, would subject the maker to a criminal penalty in the country where the certification is signed. The proponent must also meet the notice requirements of Rule 902(11).

Committee Note

The language of Rule 902 has been amended as part of the restyling of the Evidence Rules to make them more easily understood and to make style and terminology consistent throughout the rules. These changes are intended to be stylistic only. There is no intent to change any result in any ruling on evidence admissibility.

Rule 903. Subscribing Witness' Testimony Unnecessary	Rule 903. Subscribing Witness's Testimony
The testimony of a subscribing witness is not necessary to authenticate a writing unless required by the laws of the jurisdiction whose laws govern the validity of the writing.	A subscribing witness's testimony is necessary to authenticate a writing only if required by the law of the jurisdiction that governs its validity.

Committee Note

The language of Rule 903 has been amended as part of the restyling of the Evidence Rules to make them more easily understood and to make style and terminology consistent throughout the rules. These changes are intended to be stylistic only. There is no intent to change any result in any ruling on evidence admissibility.

ARTICLE X. CONTENTS OF WRITINGS, RECORDINGS, AND PHOTOGRAPHS Rule 1001. Definitions	ARTICLE X. CONTENTS OF WRITINGS, RECORDINGS, AND PHOTOGRAPHS Rule 1001. Definitions That Apply to This Article
For purposes of this article the following definitions are applicable: (1) **Writings and recordings.** "Writings" and "recordings" consist of letters, words, or numbers, or their equivalent, set down by handwriting, typewriting, printing, photostating, photographing, magnetic impulse, mechanical or electronic recording, or other form of data compilation. (2) **Photographs.** "Photographs" include still photographs, X-ray films, video tapes, and motion pictures. (3) **Original.** An "original" of a writing or recording is the writing or recording itself or any counterpart intended to have the same effect by a person executing or issuing it. An "original" of a photograph includes the negative or any print therefrom. If data are stored in a computer or similar device, any printout or other output readable by sight, shown to reflect the data accurately, is an "original". (4) **Duplicate.** A "duplicate" is a counterpart produced by the same impression as the original, or from the same matrix, or by means of photography, including enlargements and miniatures, or by mechanical or electronic re-recording, or by chemical reproduction, or by other equivalent techniques which accurately reproduces the original.	In this article: (a) A "writing" consists of letters, words, numbers, or their equivalent set down in any form. (b) A "recording" consists of letters, words, numbers, or their equivalent recorded in any manner. (c) A "photograph" means a photographic image or its equivalent stored in any form. (d) An "original" of a writing or recording means the writing or recording itself or any counterpart intended to have the same effect by the person who executed or issued it. For electronically stored information, "original" means any printout — or other output readable by sight — if it accurately reflects the information. An "original" of a photograph includes the negative or a print from it. (e) A "duplicate" means a counterpart produced by a mechanical, photographic, chemical, electronic, or other equivalent process or technique that accurately reproduces the original.

Committee Note

The language of Rule 1001 has been amended as part of the restyling of the Evidence Rules to make them more easily understood and to make style and terminology consistent throughout the rules. These changes are intended to be stylistic only. There is no intent to change any result in any ruling on evidence admissibility.

Rule 1002. Requirement of Original	Rule 1002. Requirement of the Original
To prove the content of a writing, recording, or photograph, the original writing, recording, or photograph is required, except as otherwise provided in these rules or by Act of Congress.	An original writing, recording, or photograph is required in order to prove its content unless these rules or a federal statute provides otherwise.

Committee Note

The language of Rule 1002 has been amended as part of the restyling of the Evidence Rules to make them more easily understood and to make style and terminology consistent throughout the rules. These changes are intended to be stylistic only. There is no intent to change any result in any ruling on evidence admissibility.

Rule 1003. Admissibility of Duplicates	Rule 1003. Admissibility of Duplicates
A duplicate is admissible to the same extent as an original unless (1) a genuine question is raised as to the authenticity of the original or (2) in the circumstances it would be unfair to admit the duplicate in lieu of the original.	A duplicate is admissible to the same extent as the original unless a genuine question is raised about the original's authenticity or the circumstances make it unfair to admit the duplicate.

Committee Note

The language of Rule 1003 has been amended as part of the restyling of the Evidence Rules to make them more easily understood and to make style and terminology consistent throughout the rules. These changes are intended to be stylistic only. There is no intent to change any result in any ruling on evidence admissibility.

Rule 1004. Admissibility of Other Evidence of Contents	Rule 1004. Admissibility of Other Evidence of Content
The original is not required, and other evidence of the contents of a writing, recording, or photograph is admissible if—	An original is not required and other evidence of the content of a writing, recording, or photograph is admissible if:
(1) Originals lost or destroyed. All originals are lost or have been destroyed, unless the proponent lost or destroyed them in bad faith; or	(a) all the originals are lost or destroyed, and not by the proponent acting in bad faith;
(2) Original not obtainable. No original can be obtained by any available judicial process or procedure; or	(b) an original cannot be obtained by any available judicial process;
(3) Original in possession of opponent. At a time when an original was under the control of the party against whom offered, that party was put on notice, by the pleadings or otherwise, that the contents would be a subject of proof at the hearing, and that party does not produce the original at the hearing; or	(c) the party against whom the original would be offered had control of the original; was at that time put on notice, by pleadings or otherwise, that the original would be a subject of proof at the trial or hearing; and fails to produce it at the trial or hearing; or
(4) Collateral matters. The writing, recording, or photograph is not closely related to a controlling issue.	(d) the writing, recording, or photograph is not closely related to a controlling issue.

Committee Note

The language of Rule 1004 has been amended as part of the restyling of the Evidence Rules to make them more easily understood and to make style and terminology consistent throughout the rules. These changes are intended to be stylistic only. There is no intent to change any result in any ruling on evidence admissibility.

Rule 1005. Public Records	Rule 1005. Copies of Public Records to Prove Content
The contents of an official record, or of a document authorized to be recorded or filed and actually recorded or filed, including data compilations in any form, if otherwise admissible, may be proved by copy, certified as correct in accordance with rule 902 or testified to be correct by a witness who has compared it with the original. If a copy which complies with the foregoing cannot be obtained by the exercise of reasonable diligence, then other evidence of the contents may be given.	The proponent may use a copy to prove the content of an official record — or of a document that was recorded or filed in a public office as authorized by law — if these conditions are met: the record or document is otherwise admissible; and the copy is certified as correct in accordance with Rule 902(4) or is testified to be correct by a witness who has compared it with the original. If no such copy can be obtained by reasonable diligence, then the proponent may use other evidence to prove the content.

Committee Note

The language of Rule 1005 has been amended as part of the restyling of the Evidence Rules to make them more easily understood and to make style and terminology consistent throughout the rules. These changes are intended to be stylistic only. There is no intent to change any result in any ruling on evidence admissibility.

Rule 1006. Summaries	Rule 1006. Summaries to Prove Content
The contents of voluminous writings, recordings, or photographs which cannot conveniently be examined in court may be presented in the form of a chart, summary, or calculation. The originals, or duplicates, shall be made available for examination or copying, or both, by other parties at reasonable time and place. The court may order that they be produced in court.	The proponent may use a summary, chart, or calculation to prove the content of voluminous writings, recordings, or photographs that cannot be conveniently examined in court. The proponent must make the originals or duplicates available for examination or copying, or both, by other parties at a reasonable time and place. And the court may order the proponent to produce them in court.

Committee Note

The language of Rule 1006 has been amended as part of the restyling of the Evidence Rules to make them more easily understood and to make style and terminology consistent throughout the rules. These changes are intended to be stylistic only. There is no intent to change any result in any ruling on evidence admissibility.

Rule 1007. Testimony or Written Admission of Party	Rule 1007. Testimony or Statement of a Party to Prove Content
Contents of writings, recordings, or photographs may be proved by the testimony or deposition of the party against whom offered or by that party's written admission, without accounting for the nonproduction of the original.	The proponent may prove the content of a writing, recording, or photograph by the testimony, deposition, or written statement of the party against whom the evidence is offered. The proponent need not account for the original.

Committee Note

The language of Rule 1007 has been amended as part of the restyling of the Evidence Rules to make them more easily understood and to make style and terminology consistent throughout the rules. These changes are intended to be stylistic only. There is no intent to change any result in any ruling on evidence admissibility.

Rule 1008. Functions of Court and Jury	Rule 1008. Functions of the Court and Jury
When the admissibility of other evidence of contents of writings, recordings, or photographs under these rules depends upon the fulfillment of a condition of fact, the question whether the condition has been fulfilled is ordinarily for the court to determine in accordance with the provisions of rule 104. However, when an issue is raised (a) whether the asserted writing ever existed, or (b) whether another writing, recording, or photograph produced at the trial is the original, or (c) whether other evidence of contents correctly reflects the contents, the issue is for the trier of fact to determine as in the case of other issues of fact.	Ordinarily, the court determines whether the proponent has fulfilled the factual conditions for admitting other evidence of the content of a writing, recording, or photograph under Rule 1004 or 1005. But in a jury trial, the jury determines — in accordance with Rule 104(b) — any issue about whether: (a) an asserted writing, recording, or photograph ever existed; (b) another one produced at the trial or hearing is the original; or (c) other evidence of content accurately reflects the content.

Committee Note

The language of Rule 1008 has been amended as part of the restyling of the Evidence Rules to make them more easily understood and to make style and terminology consistent throughout the rules. These changes are intended to be stylistic only. There is no intent to change any result in any ruling on evidence admissibility.

ARTICLE XI. MISCELLANEOUS RULES

Rule 1101. Applicability of Rules

(a) Courts and judges. These rules apply to the United States district courts, the District Court of Guam, the District Court of the Virgin Islands, the District Court for the Northern Mariana Islands, the United States courts of appeals, the United States Claims Court, and to United States bankruptcy judges and United States magistrate judges, in the actions, cases, and proceedings and to the extent hereinafter set forth. The terms "judge" and "court" in these rules include United States bankruptcy judges and United States magistrate judges.

(b) Proceedings generally. These rules apply generally to civil actions and proceedings, including admiralty and maritime cases, to criminal cases and proceedings, to contempt proceedings except those in which the court may act summarily, and to proceedings and cases under title 11, United States Code.

(c) Rule of privilege. The rule with respect to privileges applies at all stages of all actions, cases, and proceedings.

(d) Rules inapplicable. The rules (other than with respect to privileges) do not apply in the following situations:

(1) Preliminary questions of fact. The determination of questions of fact preliminary to admissibility of evidence when the issue is to be determined by the court under rule 104.

(2) Grand jury. Proceedings before grand juries.

(3) Miscellaneous proceedings. Proceedings for extradition or rendition; preliminary examinations in criminal cases; sentencing, or granting or revoking probation; issuance of warrants for arrest, criminal summonses, and search warrants; and proceedings with respect to release on bail or otherwise.

ARTICLE XI. MISCELLANEOUS RULES

Rule 1101. Applicability of the Rules

(a) **To Courts and Judges.** These rules apply to proceedings before:

- United States district courts;
- United States bankruptcy and magistrate judges;
- United States courts of appeals;
- the United States Court of Federal Claims; and
- the district courts of Guam, the Virgin Islands, and the Northern Mariana Islands.

(b) **To Cases and Proceedings.** These rules apply in:

- civil cases and proceedings, including bankruptcy, admiralty, and maritime cases;
- criminal cases and proceedings; and
- contempt proceedings, except those in which the court may act summarily.

(c) **Rules on Privilege.** The rules on privilege apply to all stages of a case or proceeding.

(d) **Exceptions.** These rules — except for those on privilege — do not apply to the following:

(1) the court's determination, under Rule 104(a), on a preliminary question of fact governing admissibility;

(2) grand-jury proceedings; and

(3) miscellaneous proceedings such as:

- extradition or rendition;
- issuing an arrest warrant, criminal summons, or search warrant;
- a preliminary examination in a criminal case;
- sentencing;
- granting or revoking probation or supervised release; and
- considering whether to release on bail or otherwise.

(e) Rules applicable in part. In the following proceedings these rules apply to the extent that matters of evidence are not provided for in the statutes which govern procedure therein or in other rules prescribed by the Supreme Court pursuant to statutory authority: the trial of misdemeanors and other petty offenses before United States magistrate judges; review of agency actions when the facts are subject to trial de novo under section 706(2)(F) of title 5, United States Code; review of orders of the Secretary of Agriculture under section 2 of the Act entitled "An Act to authorize association of producers of agricultural products" approved February 18, 1922 (7 U.S.C. 292), and under sections 6 and 7(c) of the Perishable Agricultural Commodities Act, 1930 (7 U.S.C. 499f, 499g(c)); naturalization and revocation of naturalization under sections 310–318 of the Immigration and Nationality Act (8 U.S.C. 1421–1429); prize proceedings in admiralty under sections 7651–7681 of title 10, United States Code; review of orders of the Secretary of the Interior under section 2 of the Act entitled "An Act authorizing associations of producers of aquatic products" approved June 25, 1934 (15 U.S.C. 522); review of orders of petroleum control boards under section 5 of the Act entitled "An Act to regulate interstate and foreign commerce in petroleum and its products by prohibiting the shipment in such commerce of petroleum and its products produced in violation of State law, and for other purposes", approved February 22, 1935 (15 U.S.C. 715d); actions for fines, penalties, or forfeitures under part V of title IV of the Tariff Act of 1930 (19 U.S.C. 1581–1624), or under the Anti-Smuggling Act (19 U.S.C. 1701–1711); criminal libel for condemnation, exclusion of imports, or other proceedings under the Federal Food, Drug, and Cosmetic Act (21 U.S.C. 301–392); disputes between seamen under sections 4079, 4080, and 4081 of the Revised Statutes (22 U.S.C. 256–258); habeas corpus under sections 2241–2254 of title 28, United States Code; motions to vacate, set aside or correct sentence under section 2255 of title 28, United States Code; actions for penalties for refusal to transport destitute seamen under section 4578 of the Revised Statutes (46 U.S.C. 679); actions against the United States under the Act entitled "An Act authorizing suits against the United States in admiralty for damage caused by and salvage service rendered to public vessels belonging to the United States, and for other purposes", approved March 3, 1925 (46 U.S.C. 781–790), as implemented by section 7730 of title 10, United States Code.

(e) Other Statutes and Rules. A federal statute or a rule prescribed by the Supreme Court may provide for admitting or excluding evidence independently from these rules.

Committee Note

The language of Rule 1101 has been amended as part of the restyling of the Evidence Rules to make them more easily understood and to make style and terminology consistent throughout the rules. These changes are intended to be stylistic only. There is no intent to change any result in any ruling on evidence admissibility.

Rule 1102. Amendments	Rule 1102. Amendments
Amendments to the Federal Rules of Evidence may be made as provided in section 2072 of title 28 of the United States Code.	These rules may be amended as provided in 28 U.S.C. § 2072.

Committee Note

The language of Rule 1102 has been amended as part of the restyling of the Evidence Rules to make them more easily understood and to make style and terminology consistent throughout the rules. These changes are intended to be stylistic only. There is no intent to change any result in any ruling on evidence admissibility.

Rule 1103. Title	Rule 1103. Title
These rules may be known and cited as the Federal Rules of Evidence.	These rules may be cited as the Federal Rules of Evidence.

Committee Note

The language of Rule 1103 has been amended as part of the restyling of the Evidence Rules to make them more easily understood and to make style and terminology consistent throughout the rules. These changes are intended to be stylistic only. There is no intent to change any result in any ruling on evidence admissibility.

TABLE OF CASES

[References are to pages]

[References are to pages]

[References are to pages]

[References are to pages]

INDEX

[References are to pages.]

[References are to pages.]

[References are to pages.]

[References are to pages.]

HEARSAY—Cont.
Recorded recollection (See PAST RECOLLECTION RECORDED)
Residual hearsay
    Application . . . 534
    Basis . . . 534
    Case law . . . 536
    Foundational elements . . . 534

HEARSAY EXCEPTIONS
Generally . . . 393
Application . . . 416
Belief of impending death, statement under
    Application . . . 505
    Basis . . . 504
    Case law . . . 506
    Foundational elements . . . 505
Crawford problem and . . . 394
Cross examination . . . 523
Death, belief of (See subhead: Belief of impending death, statement under)
Direct examination . . . 519
Emotional condition (See subhead: Then-existing mental, emotional or physical condition)
Excited utterance (See EXCITED UTTERANCE)
Former testimony (See FORMER TESTIMONY EXCEPTIONS)
Interest, statements against
    Application . . . 510
    Basis . . . 509
    Case law . . . 512
    Foundational elements . . . 509
Medical diagnosis or treatment (See MEDICAL DIAGNOSIS OR TREATMENT)
Mental condition (See subhead: Then-existing mental, emotional or physical condition)
Physical condition (See subhead: Then-existing mental, emotional or physical condition)
Present sense impression (See PRESENT SENSE IMPRESSION)
Then-existing mental, emotional or physical condition
    Application . . . 407
    Basis . . . 406
    Foundational elements . . . 407
Unavailability, requirement of
    Generally . . . 487; 489
    Belief of impending death (See subhead: Belief of impending death, statement under)
    Cross examination . . . 523
    Death, belief of (See subhead: Belief of impending death, statement under)
    Direct examination . . . 519
    Former testimony (See FORMER TESTIMONY EXCEPTIONS)
    Interest (See subhead: Interest, statements against)

I

IDENTIFICATION
Voice identification . . . 297
Writings by opinion, of . . . 295

IMPEACHMENT
Generally . . . 245; 246
Application . . . 265
Bias impeachment . . . 255
Case law . . . 257
Character-based impeachment . . . 249
Contradiction, by . . . 256
Defective capacity . . . 256
Motivational impeachment . . . 255
Prior convictions
    Generally . . . 251
    Analytical template . . . 253
    Proving convictions . . . 255
Prior inconsistent statements, by (See PRIOR INCONSISTENT STATEMENTS)

INTRINSIC UNCHARGED ACTS
Generally . . . 174

J

JUDGES
Generally . . . 219
Adversarial system, in . . . 12
Best Evidence Rule . . . 324
Discretion . . . 97
Presumed incompetency of . . . 219

JUDICIAL NOTICE
Facts at trial by . . . 50

JURORS AND JURIES
Generally . . . 220
Adversarial system, in . . . 17
Best Evidence Rule . . . 324
Presumed incompetency of . . . 219

L

LAY OPINION TESTIMONY
Generally . . . 545; 547
Application . . . 557
Case law . . . 550

LEGAL ADMISSIBILITY
Preliminary hearings . . . 39

M

MEDICAL DIAGNOSIS OR TREATMENT
Application . . . 413
Basis . . . 412
Case law . . . 413
Foundational elements . . . 412

MENTAL CONDITION (See HEARSAY EXCEPTIONS, subhead: Then-existing mental, emotional or physical condition)

MOTIVATIONAL IMPEACHMENT
Generally . . . 255

[References are to pages.]

[References are to pages.]